READING IN THE
ELEMENTARY SCHOOL

Fourth Edition

ALLYN and BACON, Inc.
Boston, London, Sydney, Toronto

READING IN THE ELEMENTARY SCHOOL

George D. Spache
Professor Emeritus
University of Florida

Evelyn B. Spache
Spache Educational
Consultants

Copyright © 1977 by Allyn and Bacon, Inc.
470 Atlantic Avenue, Boston, Massachusetts 02210.

Copyright © 1973, 1969, 1964 by Allyn and Bacon, Inc.

Library of Congress Cataloging in Publication Data

Spache, George Daniel, 1909–
  Reading in the elementary school.

  Includes bibliographies and index.
  1. Reading (Elementary). I. Spache, Evelyn B.,
joint author. II. Title.
LB1573.S792 1977   372.4'1   76-57662

ISBN 0-205-05784-5

Printing number and year (last digits):
10 9 8 7 6   85 84 83 82 81 80

Contents

Preface to the Fourth Edition   ix
Preface to the First Edition   xi

PART ONE   *FOUNDATIONS OF READING*   1

1 • WAYS OF DEFINING THE READING PROCESS   *2*

Reading as Skill Development **4**;   Reading as a Visual Act **7**;   Reading as a Perceptual Act **11**;   Reading and Language **18**;   Reading as a Reflection of Cultural Background **19**;   Reading as a Psycholinguistic Process **24**;   Reading as Information Processing **27**;   Reading as Associational Learning **30**;   *Discussion Questions 36;   References 36*

PART TWO   *READING PRACTICES CURRENTLY IN USE*   39

2 • USING THE BASAL READER APPROACH   *40*

Use of Basal Readers **43**;   Limitations of the Basal Reader Approach **55**;   Improving the Basal Program **68**;   The Basal Versus Other Approaches **70**;   *Discussion Questions 74;   References 74*

3 • USING THE INDIVIDUALIZED APPROACH   *76*

Objectives and Assumptions **78**;   Principles and Problems of Individualized Reading **85**;   The Research **90**;   Operant Conditioning and Systems Approaches **92**;   *Discussion Questions 99;   References 100;   Supplementary Reading 101*

4 • USING THE LINGUISTIC APPROACHES   *102*

Schools Within Schools **104**;   Limitations of the Linguistic Approaches **108**;   The Research **115**;   Comments **117**;   *Discussion Questions 118; `References 118;   Supplementary Reading 120*

5 • USING THE LANGUAGE EXPERIENCE APPROACH   *122*

Objectives and Assumptions **125**;   Methods and Materials **126**;   Other Concepts of the Approach **129**;   Current Applications **131**;   Limitations of the Language Experience Approach **133**;   The Research **135**;   *Discussion Questions 138;   References 139;   Supplementary Reading 140*

PART THREE   THE PROGRAM OF THE FUTURE   **141**

6 · **READINESS AND READING FOR YOUNG CHILDREN**   *142*

At the Preschool Level **144;** In the Kindergarten **147;** Research on Readiness **148;** When Is a Child Ready to Read? **166;** *Summary 178; Discussion Questions 178; References 178; Supplementary Reading 180*

7 · **READINESS TRAINING**   *182*

Is Readiness Training Profitable? **185;** Training in Visual Perception **187;** Training in Auditory Discrimination **211;** Language Training **216;** Reading Concepts **220;** *Discussion Questions 222; References 222; Resources for the Teacher 224*

8 · **THE COMBINED PROGRAM FOR PRIMARY GRADES**   *226*

Readiness for Reading **228;** Beginning Reading **229;** The Method **235;** Oral Reading in the Primary Program **244;** The Primary Program with Gifted Pupils **256;** The Primary Program with Average Pupils **258;** The Primary Program with Slow Learners **264;** The Primary Program with the Disadvantaged Child **265;** *Discussion Questions 269; References 269; Professional References for the Teacher of the Disadvantaged 270; Oral Language Development 271; Other Professional References 272; Other Special Materials (for the Disadvantaged) 273*

9 · **THE COMBINED PROGRAM FOR INTERMEDIATE GRADES**   *274*

Basic Skills for Content Reading **278;** Plan for a Content Area Unit **295;** Reading in Science and Social Science **298;** Reading in Mathematics **301;** Reading in Literature **303;** *Discussions Questions 307; References 308; Resources for the Teacher 309*

10 · **STEPS TOWARD INDIVIDUALIZED READING**   *314*

Organizational Steps **316;** How to Start Individualizing **319;** Grouping by Learning Aptitudes **326;** Scheduling **327;** Record Keeping **328;** Using the Conference for Evaluation **332;** Taking Inventory in the Conference **337;** The Diagnostic Conference **340;** *A Footnote on Individualizing 352; Discussion Questions 353; References 354; Resources for Implementing Individualization 356*

11 · **WORD RECOGNITION TECHNIQUES AND SKILLS**   *360*

How We Now Teach Phonics **366;** How We Ought To Teach Phonics **380;** Alternative Approaches to Phonics **387;** Other Approaches to Phonics **391;** How We Teach Structural Analysis **392;** How We Teach Contextual Analysis **402;** *Discussion Questions 406; References 407; Resources for the Teacher 409; Instructional Materials 409; Programmed Materials 410; Selected Audiovisual Materials 410*

12 · **BUILDING SIGHT AND MEANING VOCABULARY**   *412*

Influences upon Reading Vocabulary Growth **415;** How Pupils Learn Words **416;** Learning Sight Vocabulary **418;** Learning Meaning Vocabulary **423;** *Discussion Questions 433; References 433; Resources for the Teacher 434; Meaning Vocabulary Development Materials 435*

13 · DEVELOPING COMPREHENSION AND CRITICAL READING SKILLS *438*

Comprehension as Skill Development **440**; Comprehension as a Decoding Process **440**; Comprehension as a Thinking Process **441**; Comprehension as Defined by Tests **443**; Defining Critical Reading **446**; Factors Influencing Comprehension and Critical Reading **447**; Developing Comprehension and Critical Thinking **451**; Strategies for Cognitive Growth **452**; Teachers' Questions and Children's Reading **455**; How To Use Questioning and To Stimulate Comprehension **457**; *Discussion Questions 460; References 460; Supplementary Reading 461*

14 · APPROACHES TO CLASSROOM MANAGEMENT *462*

Homogeneous versus Heterogeneous Groups **465**; Interclass Grouping **467**; Nongraded or Ungraded Primary **468**; Pupil Teams and Pupil Tutors **469**; Team Teaching, Cluster Grouping, and the Open Classroom **470**; Parents and Paraprofessionals **471**; *Discussion Questions 473; References 473; Supplementary Reading 474*

Index 477

Preface to the Fourth Edition

Even in the less than five years since the third edition of this book, certain dramatic trends have markedly affected reading instruction. There has been, for example, a renaissance of interest in the language experience approach, leading to its use for beginning readers of all ages and for those readers who have language or remedial problems. To us, who have long advocated this technique, its expanding role and the supporting research are highly gratifying.

The use of learning stations as arranged by teachers or in commercial kits has spread widely in this interval. Similarly, systems or management approaches, behavioral objectives, and criterion-referenced tests seem to be sweeping the country. This trend concerns those who espouse the humanistic view of learning, which emphasizes the reactions of the learner and his ability to integrate and apply his reading abilities for his own enjoyment and edification.

Even basal readers are changing in their arrangements—from graded readers assigned to a certain grade to levels of books representing stages in development. They are also changing in the sexist content and ethnic discrimination that characterized them earlier. The role of language development, bilingualism, and dialectism in reading progress is now fully recognized, and provisions are being made in these basic tools of instruction to promote language development as a corollary of reading growth. Individualizing has become the catchword of practically all approaches to instruction, including those stereotyped programs that lead all children through the same steps to skill development, through the same exercises and the same medium.

The move to earlier and stronger phonic programs in the primary grades, now called "decoding," has gone beyond a trend to become an almost universal practice in our beginning reading programs. The use of pupil and adult tutors is increasing, because of favorable research findings; at the same time, the fad of open classrooms is diminishing, because of a lack of supportive evidence.

We have expanded the treatment of these and other new developments in the fourth edition to keep our readers abreast of the times in this growing field.

Preface to the First Edition

This book offers what we believe is a different approach to the training of elementary teachers in methods of teaching reading. It is different in the sense that unlike many reading textbooks it does not simply present leading theories and methods and urge the teacher to formulate her own special combination of techniques. Without extensive classroom experience, the average teacher finds it difficult to make the judgments and choices of techniques and approaches which will work effectively for her. Rather than exposing the teacher to a medley of confusing and contradictory ideas, we will analyze the leading theories, note their advantages and limitations as we see them, and then point out a specific combined approach.

This approach, drawing upon the proved strengths of older methods, will try to avoid their obvious shortcomings and failures. This eclectic method will enable the teacher to abbreviate the trial-and-error process of finding the most effective procedures for individualizing instruction to pupils' reading needs. It is true, of course, that some teachers will adapt our suggestions more readily than will others. However, through this approach some will achieve the flexibility, the insights, and the efficiency which are the foundations of successful reading instruction. We sincerely hope that these will be the outcomes for all who accept our approach.

This book was inspired by the shocking revelations of Mary C. Austin et al.'s study of tomorrow's teachers of reading.* Only seven of our states require a course in the teaching of reading for certification of elementary teachers. As a result, instruction in reading methods is most often embedded in a block course, or in one in the language arts. In 60 percent of these broad courses, the actual time devoted to reading methods ranges from $4\frac{1}{2}$ to $11\frac{1}{4}$ clock hours; 30 percent of these courses give reading even less time. This is hardly sufficient time to read, much less to digest and discuss, one of the leading textbooks unless, of course, the teacher has been trained in one of the new dynamic reading teachniques which claim to teach her to read such a book in two or three minutes.

Nowhere in Austin et al.'s summaries of the contents of the training in reading methods or student learning experiences is there mention of emphasis upon the

* Mary C. Austin et al., *The Torch Lighters: Tomorrow's Teachers of Reading* (Cambridge, Mass.: Harvard University Press, 1961).

diagnosis of pupil needs by means of observation or clinical tools. It is to fulfill this gap in particular that this book is offered, since in our opinion diagnostic skill is the heart of the reading program. At the base of every reading failure there is the contributing factor of the teacher's inability to recognize the pupil's peculiar needs and handicaps and to adapt procedures accordingly. Therefore, our approach centers around training in effective use of the teacher — pupil conference for observing significant reading behaviors, and planning appropriate developmental and corrective steps in the classroom. It will not cure or prevent all reading failures or supplant the need for remedial clinics. But this approach will help the elementary school teacher in her diagnostic efforts.

To facilitate playing the diagnostic role, we have offered detailed suggestions for the conduct of the individual conference. We consider the diagnostic conference to be the most important skill that the teacher may bring to reading instruction. Second in importance is her knowledge of the proved values of basic approaches to reading. Thus this book attempts to build diagnostic and teaching skills upon a foundation of selected, proven methodological techniques.

PART
I

FOUNDATIONS OF
READING

1
Ways of Defining the Reading Process

PREVIEW

Reading is obviously a multifaceted process, a process that, like a chameleon, changes its nature from one developmental stage to the next. At one stage, the major performances may be visual discrimination among forms and words, and the learning of sufficient common words to enable the reader to begin the true act of reading. Later, the process may shift to one involving a number of thinking processes—recalling, interpreting, judging, evaluating. During both of these stages, the reader's success is conditioned by such factors as his language development, his readiness for the school's objectives as determined by his home background, and the accuracy of his perceptual behaviors in both visual and auditory discrimination.

To some teachers, reading is simply a matter of drilling at different times on vocabulary, word attack skills, and a multitude of comprehension skills. Somehow or other, the reader is eventually supposed to combine all these into a smooth, fluent processing of ideas in print. Other teachers recognize that skill drill may not result in an integrated process, and that hidden factors such as visual skills, perceptual discrimination, or lack of practice in a thinking activity such as interpreting may make reading a disjointed, fumbling effort. Only as we achieve this broad concept of the complex act we call reading can we be certain that our classroom practices are realistic and effective.

Although it is often avoided in books about reading, one of the major problems in reading instruction is a definition of reading. Without a clear-cut concept of the nature of the reading act and the reading process it is almost impossible to plan the goals of instruction. Without knowing what the process is, we cannot evaluate the reading behaviors of the pupils we train. Nor can we distinguish an individual who is truly adept in reading from one whose skills are only superficially adequate. Without thorough knowledge of the process, we are prone to accept many reading tests uncritically and use their results naively, making faulty judgments regarding pupil progress, appropriate teaching materials, and proper teaching method. Because of our ignorance, we stress only the simplest and most obvious reading skills, conceiving these to be atomistic essentials, and ignore completely the changing relationships among these at different stages of development. Goals, methods, skills, and evaluation are all dependent upon our definition of the reading process.

A process that we stress throughout the student's entire school career obviously cannot be a simple act. Reading changes from what is primarily considered word recognition, through development of sight and meaning vocabulary and several methods of word attack, through different types and degrees of comprehension, to a mature act involving most of the higher mental processes. Because of its complexity and the many stages of development, it is apparent that one simple definition will not suffice. For these reasons, we will describe or define reading in a variety of ways.

READING AS SKILL DEVELOPMENT

Paraphrasing Gray's description (16)* of reading in terms of skill development we might define reading in these words. The reader directs his attention to the printed page with his mind intent on meaning. He reacts to each word with a group of mental associations regarding the word form, its meaning, and its sound. With the aid of these associations, he discriminates this word from all others, also using clues of general configuration, distinctive characteristics of the shape, some of the letters or syllables, and the implications of the sense or pattern of the sentence. Thus the process begins with word recognition.

As the meanings of successive words become clear, they are fused into thoughts or ideas. This implies that the reader holds in mind the meanings of the first words of the sentence as he reads those that follow. Similarly, the more

* Italic numbers in parentheses refer to the References at the chapter endings.

mature reader retains the ideas of successive sentences, modifying gradually the total impression (main idea) as he reads through a paragraph or longer passage. Gray suggests that the reader achieves a literal meaning of the reading matter by attending to and anticipating meanings, relating ideas as they appear, and recognizing the author's organization of ideas. The reader evaluates the importance of the ideas offered, perhaps visualizing the events described, and adjusts his rate of reading to the difficulty of the material.

The reader may, in Gray's description, go beyond literal meanings in reacting to ideas implied but not stated by the author, and in identifying the author's purpose, mood, and attitude toward the reader. He may react to the occasion for the writing—the time and place setting, the writer's rhetorical devices, and the author's choice of words.

Some of the ideas gained from the reading material may be fused or blended with the reader's previous experiences, if they are not contradicted by these experiences and thus rejected. The new concepts may correct earlier ideas or be used to formulate even newer, broader concepts. Thus the experiences gained from reading must, according to Gray, become part of the reader's associations to be used in future reading and thinking activities. All this, from one viewpoint, is the reading process.

William D. Sheldon (35) describes the reading process in terms of stages, somewhat as follows. The first stage is a transitional period which begins with listening and concept building, and proceeds through picture reading. Stage two is characterized by experience charts, picture story reading, and the gradual introduction to reading of words in preprimers. The third stage promotes wide development of sight vocabulary, supported by training in auditory discrimination. A fourth stage introduces more careful discrimination by initial consonants, word endings, and the other phonic and structural details, as sight vocabulary continues to grow. The fifth stage in the primary period is, in Sheldon's words, a plateau during which the fundamental vocabulary is strengthened. The sixth stage introduces the intermediate-grade child to reading tasks in the content fields, to technical vocabularies and technical concepts. A seventh stage develops flexibility in reading—the adjustment of rate and degree of comprehension to varying purposes. The maturing reader also begins to show the rudiments of critical reading involving judgmental, comparative, and inferential thinking, as well as creative ability to use reading as a tool for solving personal and group problems. Here, again, we have a view of the reading process as it evolves through various skills and stages.

These definitions of reading in terms of skill development sometimes fail to convey the complete picture. The enumeration of stages and skills gives the impression that these are built upon each other or occur in some sort of sequence. However, such an overview is not realistic. Except for a few technical details which are introduced at certain stages in the process, practically all the skills enumerated are being taught to the child almost simultaneously. For example, although the first few months of reading instruction may appear to be concentrated on learning a few necessary words, other types of training are being offered. A background of experience to bring many associations and meanings to these beginning words is being built. Clues given by the pictures, the sentence pattern, and simple endings are pointed out to the child, and he is urged to use these to aid himself. The new ideas and concepts brought by the story are constantly compared and fused with the child's own experiences. Even at these primitive reading levels, the child is helped to do critical and creative reading. For example, he may be helped to tell his emotional reactions to the story content, to judge whether the story appealed to his sense of humor, sympathy, or realism. He may dramatize the story to portray his understanding of its action, the feelings of the characters, or the purpose of the author. As soon as he can, the child is helped to use the ideas and vocabulary he is learning for creative purposes—in his own writing, speech, storytelling, reporting to the group, and similar activities. Thus word recognition, word meanings, some method of word attack, retention and reaction to new ideas, critical and creative responses are interwoven simultaneously in the good reading program from the very first day. Learning to read is a complex process for which no one method or device is sufficient.

In our opinion the concept of reading as a skill development process is a very limited interpretation of what is really a very complex process. Overacceptance of this concept is widespread and often leads to stereotyped drill with isolated reading behavior or skills. Many teachers utilize their own or commercial materials for repeated practice such as in "reading for main ideas" or "reading for details" or a group of four or five such labeled skills. There are two assumptions present in such practice, namely, that each skill represents a distinct way of thinking that is trainable, and that all these behaviors are eventually blended together into intelligent reading after sufficient practice.

However, the reader hardly ever consciously reads for main ideas or any of the types of facts teachers label. Only when he has been given specific prereading instructions, or is aware of the type of fact he is supposed to secure, does the process tend to be channeled. Most of the time he just reads—processing the ideas he meets the best he can, combining them with his own, and later tries to sort out and answer the facts demanded. In other words, repeated practice in answering a certain type of question does not necessarily fix that skill in the reader's mind as a particular kind of reading he can do later upon demand. Reading is not a bundle of separate thinking skills.

What we are trying to say is that from the very beginning it makes sense to us to vary the types of questions, both before and after reading, to lead the reader to think his way through printed matter. Certain types of questions may be emphasized from time to time, as in more stress upon details in scientific, mathematical, and such materials. But too much emphasis upon one type of question will only tend to handicap the reader in his future reading, which, of course, usually demands a variety of reactions from him. Certain experiments show that continued practice of one type of comprehension tends to prevent the reader from securing a variety of ideas and facts as he normally would. Thus the practice actually results in less depth of comprehension than is desirable. Only limited practice in securing any one type of fact seems justifiable. Reading is not a group of separate skills to be practiced in isolation and later blended together into the total act. It is rather a total act from the beginning, limited, of course, by the reader's reasoning capacities, his experiences, and his reading abilities.

This reaction to reading as a skill development process immediately raises questions of what our definition of comprehension is, and if we do not follow the skills-drill approach, what sort of training in comprehension should be offered. Our ideas on this subject will certainly need extended discussion, and that is offered in a later chapter.

READING AS A VISUAL ACT

We may approach the definition of reading from an entirely different angle—as an almost purely visual act. This definition may seem to be a technical one that the classroom teacher need not understand completely. The average teacher may feel that this facet of the reading process is not within his special area of competence—he is not a vision specialist, nor is he directly responsible for visual training or the correction of visual defects. These opinions are not completely valid. Reading is, first of all, a visual act and it cannot ever be taught soundly if the functions of the eyes are not understood. Proper coordination of the eyes, the true eye span possible, the obstacles to successful reading in faulty movement patterns and various common visual defects must be understood by the classroom teacher if she is to be successful.

Children's vision is tested more often by teachers than by any other adults they meet, vision specialists included. In this vision testing, teachers accept the responsibility for finding those children who may have academic difficulties because of visual defects. In accepting this responsibility, teachers owe it to themselves and to their pupils to understand the relations between vision and reading in order to do a better job of testing vision and teaching reading. In later chapters, particularly those on readiness, we have tried to offer specific steps that teachers may follow to improve their effectiveness in both these areas. But even before these, teachers must understand reading as a visual act.

The reading process may be described in visual terms somewhat as follows. As the individual reads, his eyes hop or glide from one stop to the next from left to right. He does not read in a smooth sweep along the line but only when the eyes are at rest in each fixation. During the sweeps or swings from one fixation to the next the reader sees nothing clearly, for his eyes are temporarily out of focus. Each fixation during which reading actually occurs lasts from about one-third of a second in young children to about one-fourth of a second at the college level. In all probability most of the thinking that occurs during reading is done during this fractional part of a second, for a number of studies show that the duration of the fixation often lengthens if the reading material is very difficult. The fixations are the heart of the visual reading act, for they occupy about 90 percent of the time for reading, while interfixation and return sweeps account for the rest.

If the reader fails to recognize what he sees in a fixation, or to understand the idea offered, he tends to make a regression. That is, he makes another fixation at approximately the same place or he swings backward to the left to read again. He may regress several times until the word is recognized or the idea comprehended before resuming the normal left-to-right series of fixations. Then near the end of each line he makes one big return sweep to a fixation close to the beginning of the next line.

These facts are important to the classroom teacher because they explain the emphases in the reading program on controlled vocabulary, length of line, building of experiences with word meanings, and control of the difficulty of concepts. To help children acquire a normal visual act in reading, the reading program must be planned to promote this pattern. An excessive proportion of unknown words, inadequate experiences with the multiple meanings of words, and reading matter which is too complex for the child's experiences all promote a faulty reading pattern and lack of progress in reading. Every teacher of reading recognizes the need for control of these factors, but few realize the ultimate reasons for them.

Some self-proclaimed reading experts would have us begin reading with almost any random book or, worse yet, by an alphabetic or spelling approach. "Start him with the Bible or the Constitution of the United States," they say. "What better material could he hope to read?" "Teach him the letters or the sounds first." "Stop babying our children with a controlled vocabulary." "Let them stretch their minds with something hard and challenging," they urge us. Picture mentally, if you will, what would happen to the normal pattern of eye movements if we followed this advice. Children might learn to read by these approaches, as many did in earlier periods in American reading instruction. But what sort of speed, fluency, or forward movement would be promoted by these methods? When would the reader ever outgrow the process of deciphering or spelling letter by letter and achieve a normal pattern? When would he really learn to "read" in the appropriate pattern of eye movements we are describing here?

Almost from their beginning efforts, children vary in their speed of reading. Some read painfully slowly, word by word, for what seems to be a long part of their primary years. Other children read rapidly and smoothly, making it obvious that to them "Reading is really just talking written down." Because of these variations, reading teachers often try to urge children to read more fluently and naturally—in phrases or groups of words. Once again such practices display ignorance of the visual components of the reading act.

The normal beginning reader makes an average of two fixations per word or, in other words, sees or recognizes less than one whole word at each fixation. This statistic was determined by photographing the reading of over a thousand first graders by The Reading Eye, a camera made especially for this purpose (38). In this country-wide testing, each child read a selection of approximately 100 words. During the reading the average child made 224 fixations, about 2 fixations per word, or an eye span of .45 of a word. This average span of recognition increases very slowly to 1.11, or slightly more than one word per fixation, for normal college students reading at an average speed of 280 words per minute. The average number of words seen at each fixation does not reach one whole word until the eleventh grade.

Using a different technique of determining recognition span, that of reading through a small aperture, McConkie and Rayner (24) demonstrated that the length of a word can be distinguished for as far as 13 to 14 letters from the point of fixation. Actual shape of a word or letter was perceived no farther than 10 to 12 characters into the periphery. Identification of words was limited to a span encompassing 4 to 6 characters to the right of the fixation point. It is true, of course, that more can be read at a distance from a flash card or the chalkboard than at reading distance, as these two studies imply. As many as three or four words can be recognized in one brief exposure at distance. But, obviously, this span does not operate in reading a book.

Apparently, trying to teach children to recognize several words at each fixation by flash cards, pressure blackboard drills, or even mechanical training devices is a sheer waste of time. It is particularly pointless to try to speed up the child's reactions when he is reading aloud at sight without having read the selection silently first. Children can be taught to phrase *mentally,* to try to read in a natural speech cadence, but this is not accomplished by the methods, commonly employed. Natural reading, or reading which sounds like normal speech, can only be achieved with very simple, natural material, or selections previously practiced or read silently. Furthermore, natural reading cannot be obtained until the child realizes fully that reading is really a kind of talking with the words that are printed on the page. Dramatizations using the book as the script, reading silently first and then trying to repeat aloud the words as one would in normal speech may also help.

A second significant implication of the reader's true eye span is the degree of visual skill demanded. The young reader focuses, relaxes, focuses, relaxes almost 200 times per 100 running words. The eyes must converge to a focus in perfect alignment over and over again, or word recognition is inaccurate and reading becomes faulty. When we realize the frequency and minuteness of the visual adjustments needed for the reading act we may appreciate our responsibility for development of the highest degree of visual skill in our pupils.

Let us finish this description of reading as a visual act with a few more facts about the visual behaviors of the reader. Gilbert's eye-movement studies (11) led him to conclude that pupils do not naturally mature or improve in the pattern of eye movements simply because they have been exposed to a good reading program. Many who show apparently normal performances on ordinary measures of comprehension and rate employ ineffectual or even harmful visual patterns. They may, for example, consistently make excessive regressions, or have abnormal duration-of-fixation pauses or a very high number of fixations and a very small recognition span. Sometimes there are clues to this faulty development in the pupils' oral reading or in their very slow rate in silent or oral reading.

However, some pupils compensate for a narrow recognition span and many fixations by a shorter-than-normal duration of fixation, and their gross rate of reading does not reveal their lack of a normal visual pattern. This compensatory adjustment may be accompanied by a high degree of tension, excessive energy demands with consequent rapid fatigue and dislike for sustained reading— common symptoms among poor readers. Moreover, these readers who unconsciously have the habit of too short and too many fixations are likely to have comprehension difficulties. They do not allow time for the brain to process each idea and thus fail to comprehend. Furthermore, because the durations of the fixations are so brief, successive word images on the retina of the eye may overlap, making perception and comprehension very difficult. All this occurs, of course, without the conscious knowledge of the reader.

Many pupils tend to develop a pattern of reading which is relatively consistent, almost a habitual pattern. They do not necessarily alter this pattern in response to the difficulty of the material or to the purpose for which they are supposed to be reading. The visual pattern may be most ineffectual and interfere markedly with reading rate and comprehension, but the pupil unconsciously clings to the habits he has evolved. Some pupils habitually regress at certain points of every line. Others show an inaccurate return sweep, with visual fumbling at the beginning of each line. Poor directional attack may be shown by an excessive number of regressions in comparison with the total of fixations, or by excessive repetitions and a frequent tendency to lose the place. These disturbances in the visual pattern may or may not be manifest in the child's oral reading, but they will dramatically affect his comprehension and rate. Normally both eyes perform similarly in the reading act. But when coordination and good motility are lacking, the movements of one eye may be less pronounced than, or even different from, those of the other eye. One eye may not make the same sweeps between fixations as the other; it may overshoot on the return sweep, or the eyes may fail to converge at the beginning of each line. What do these facts mean to the classroom teacher?

These functional difficulties in the pattern of eye movements are reflected in such reading performances as losses of place, omissions, excessive repetitions, and slow rate. Defects in coordination or motility, directional attack, and form perception interfere with the development of a desirable pattern of eye movements, as we have illustrated. These problems can be approached by the classroom teacher in the way suggested in the chapters on readiness training. This visual training is not intended solely for beginning readers. The use of the eye camera reveals that many pupils of primary and intermediate levels manifest reading errors that reflect faulty or inadequate training in the visual components of the reading act. We are *not* saying that training in eye movements is the basic method for improving reading or overcoming reading difficulties. These problems may arise, as we have indicated, from inappropriate levels of reading materials, poor choice of method, and pressure to induce children to read in whole phrases. But in many cases the child's poor reading is simply and directly a result of faulty visual habits which can be recognized and attacked by the classroom teacher.

Before leaving this subject we must mention the most dramatic outcomes in American reading instruction that arose from the early scientific studies of the visual facets of the reading act. Until early in this century the primary emphasis in all our schools was upon oral reading. Skill in silent reading was of secondary importance. But the early eye-movement studies demonstrated very clearly that the average individual could read anywhere from one and one-half times to twice as fast silently as he could orally. Moreover, as other studies accumulated it became apparent that silent reading often yielded better comprehension (5). As these facts were widely accepted by leading reading authorities, a complete reversal in the goals of reading instruction occurred. Classroom practices soon followed the new viewpoint and assumed the present pattern, in which silent reading is the major instructional goal—at least above the primary grades. Thus the study of reading as a visual act once caused a revolution in reading methods. Thorough understanding of this aspect of the reading process by classroom teachers should continue to guide their daily procedures.

Occasionally our stress upon the visual elements of the reading act is reacted to as a completely mechanistic interpretation of the process. Because of our visual emphasis, some readers believe that we ignore the comprehension or thinking aspects in favor of simply getting the child's eyes functioning properly for word recognition. More careful reading, particularly of this edition, should help to correct this impression. Our true intention in this section is to provide sufficient background for the teacher to be acutely aware of this basic aspect of the reading process. By such understanding, we hope she will make attempts to relate her instructional practices, both with machines and otherwise, to the facts about visual behavior in reading. The teacher should be concerned, we believe, about the maturity of the visual functioning of her pupils, while trying to introduce them to a process which assumes highly developed visual skills.

We repeat that we are *not* proposing that learning to read is furthered by the simple training of eye movements, and certainly not in vain efforts to increase visual span. There are devices such as the *Controlled Reader,* the *Tach-X*, and a few others which do help establish desirable patterns of visual behavior in reading because they are specifically designed to simulate the natural reading act. But even these do not teach pupils to read, to think with symbols, or to react to ideas, which are the heart of reading. They simply aid children in achieving the visual skills which they must develop on the continuum toward true reading. We shall offer detailed suggestions later in this book of the ways and means the classroom teachers may utilize to accomplish this goal.

READING AS A PERCEPTUAL ACT

Perception may be defined, in psychological terms, as the preparation for a response, or as the processes which intervene between presentation of a stimulus and the ultimate response to it. In reading, this sequence includes the stimulus of the printed word, the processes of recognizing this word and attributing meaning to it, based on the reader's previous experiences. Thus, in its simplest form, reading may be considered a series of word perceptions.*

The process by which the child of five or six learns to read may be likened to the ways in which the child of one or two learns to perceive the world around him. In her excellent book, *The Psychology of Perception*, Magdalen Vernon has traced the development of the perception of objects in space. We will try to draw the analogy between these stages of perception, as described in Vernon's words, and the development of perception in the act of reading (41).

What does this definition of reading as a perceptual act mean to the classroom teacher? Explored thoroughly, there are a number of implications here for our approach to the teaching of reading. First, perception of the same stimulus differs greatly from one individual to the next. The sight of a mountain has vastly different meanings for a painter, a geologist, a mountain climber, and a man who returns to it as his birthplace. Printed words may have different meanings and connotations for each reader. For example, what is your first reaction to the word "fast"? Do you respond with the meaning "quick," or "attached to," or "strong, not yielding," or "dissipated," or "to abstain from food," or some other association? To be a fluent reader, the pupil must have a number of associations to each word so that he may select from among these the proper meaning for each context.

Perception in Infancy†	Perception in Reading
"...about the end of the first year that he begins to realize that objects have an identity and a permanent existence...that this identity remains the same although they are are shifted about in space" (pp. 18–19).	Words stand for objects, i.e., the label on the chair or table tells what it is. Although the tables and chairs may differ in size, shape and position, the label remains constant.
"...the same object may look different when it is seen from different aspects and at different distances ...a large number of visual patterns which belong to the same object" (p. 19).	All these patterns are really the same word: MOTHER mother *mother*

* This is a general definition of perception. The reader should be aware that perception may also be defined in terms of the sense modality involved, as visual perception, auditory perception, and so on.

†Reprinted from *The Psychology of Perception* by permission of the author, M. D. Vernon, and the publisher, Penguin Books Ltd., Harmondsworth, Middlesex, England, 1962.

"... a toy which at a distance looks very small is the same as one which near to looks big" (p. 20).

"A further difficulty for the young child is that he tends to perceive situations as a whole" (p. 21).

"If a thing is hidden in one place and he finds it there, and then later hidden in another, he may go back to the first place to look for it; the reappearance of the object is associated with his movements in finding it, rather than with the actual position of the object" (p. 19).

"... children asked to group sets of meaningless drawings, called one set 'prickly' and another set 'mean.' Thus these emotional characteristics seem in some cases to look to the child more striking than do the shape characteristics, which appear more obvious to us" (p. 27).

These are really the same word:

mother
mother
mother
mother

The separate words of the familiar sentence, "We went home" are not readily recognized when viewed in isolation or in new arrangements, as "Then home we went" or "We went to our home." The base word *talk* may be read for any of its derived forms, as *talks, talked, talking.*

When rereading to correct miscalling of a word, the child's pattern of search may be inconsistent. He may begin the sentence again, or read the entire line again, or just reread several words, or read the word in reverse or transpose several words in rereading. He may even lose his place on the line and pick up with the line above or below.

Some words have pleasant connotations which speed up their learning, as *Christmas, mother, elephant.* Others that seem threatening may cause blocking and apparent forgetfulness.

Second, the perceptual processes by which a word is recognized differ from one individual to another according to such factors as age, training, reading skill, and accuracy and maturity of visual discrimination. At one extreme we see preschool children, who don't know one letter or word from another, recognize or read the labels on products frequently advertised on television (and demand the purchase of these products when in the supermarket) (*18*). At the other extreme, the perceptual processes of the mature reader may involve a half-dozen such clues as common syllables, context or sense of the sentence, roots or base words and their affixes, as well as the general configuration. In the comprehensive reading program, maturation of perception must be promoted continuously by training in word recognition skills of gradually increasing complexity and variety, and by activities and experiences intended to broaden and deepen the pupil's reading vocabulary. The teacher must never lose sight of the perceptual nature of reading or he will fail to emphasize it sufficiently. This perceptual process must be refined and its base in experience with words broadened, perhaps in the ways we will suggest in later chapters.

There is nothing vague about the perceptual process in reading, for it has been the subject of research studies for more than fifty years (40). Among the types of perception employed to recognize words, the following have been clearly identified:

1. Recognition solely by setting or context, as reading a sign by its shape, is one perceptive process. A middle-aged, almost illiterate client of the writers' drove a car frequently, although she could not distinguish any of the words on road signs. We discovered that she discriminated by their shapes, colors, X-bars, and other features—a common perception among nonreaders.

2. Primary school children, or older persons beginning to learn to read, often perceive a word by some distinctive detail plus, of course, the general shape of the word. Some children readily discriminate *dog* from *boy* by the "curly tail" in the *g* of dog.

3. The general shape or configuration given by the ascending and descending letters is a significant part of the perceptual process for almost all readers. The distinctive shapes of words such as *little* or *elephant* or *Christmas* promote very rapid learning of these words or quick perception among many young readers. In contrast, words such as *their, then* or *these, those* are difficult to discriminate by this particular perceptual process. Thus these words tend to persist as sources of confusion among readers who depend heavily upon perception by general shape or configuration.

4. The visual recognition of the sound of the first few letters of a word, plus its general shape and the context, is another type of perception. Many teachers and parents have observed that when a pupil hesitates over a word, giving him the sound of the first letter or the initial blend will trigger almost immediate perception of the complete word.

5. A few children trained in an ultraphonic approach to words may perceive a word by sounding it letter by letter. However, unless held to this laborious method, most readers discard a letter-by-letter analysis in favor of other perceptual approaches.

6. As early as 1908 Edmund B. Huey (20) demonstrated the significance of the first half of a word for perception. His studies showed that this portion was much more helpful than the latter half of the words. Undoubtedly, the sense of the sentence, or the context, reinforces perception by the beginning of words. If you will slide a 3- by 5-inch card slowly along the first line of the next paragraph, stopping it to reveal only the first half of each word, you will recognize the potency of this type of perception.

7. Further studies by Huey also indicated the importance of the top halves of the letters in facilitating perception. In his early textbook, he contrasted several pages composed only of the top halves or the bottom halves of the printed words. Most readers find the reading of the upper portions much easier. If you

will cover the bottom half of the letters in the first line of the next paragraph, and reverse this in another line, you may make this comparison.

8. The general shape or configuration of a word is determined in part by the pattern of lines and circles within the word. The image which strikes the retina is probably more of a grid of dark lines and light spaces than a simple outline of the word as created by the ascending and descending letters. In a sense, the image registered on the retina resembles a photographic negative of the word. One of the writers' daughters demonstrated this perceptual process while in the primary grades in much simpler terms than we have described it here. The writer noted that when she encountered the word *look* she read it correctly, despite the fact that it had not occurred previously in her reading experiences. When questioned she explained quite simply, "Don't you see the two eyes (*oo*) there looking at you?"

9. In describing various forms of the perceptual process, we have noted several times that the sentence structure or pattern, or concept, is often an important element. There is undoubtedly an anticipation of sentence structure, or of the appearance of certain words, in order for the sentence to make sense. This anticipation is based upon the reader's many reading and auditory experiences with similar sentences, and with familiar language patterns. A very simple example of perception based on contextual clues is found in the last word of these two sentences. Can you supply the word?

"*This is a ball.*
It is a boy's _____."

10. Both beginning and mature readers employ a form of perception based on recognition of a base word and its endings. Almost any child who can read *walk* will probably recognize *walks, walked,* and *walking* in a context that leads him to expect such a word.

11. Compound words, composed of words already familiar to the reader, are quickly perceived, as in *milkman, houseboy.* Similarly, common syllables form convenient units to facilitate perception as in *con-fig-ur-a-tion.*

12. For some mature readers, word roots and their affixes promote word perception. If the reader is familiar with a root such as *aqua,* he may more readily recognize such related words as *aqueous, aquamarine,* and *aquatic.* Most readers recognize the effect of such prefixes as *in, im, en,* or *un* when these are affixed to a familiar word, as in *impossible, untruthful,* and *inaudible.* Similarly, the suffixes *er, or, tion, ance,* and the like, speed quicker perception of such words as *translator, manager, construction,* and *appearance.*

Training in these structural elements of words is ordinarily offered late in the reading program. However, it can be continued with profit almost indefinitely for each content field, and even professional courses introduce the reader to new, significant word parts.

Perceptual difficulties produce a wide variety of problem readers as these early descriptions show (27):

1. The nonreader—reads little or virtually none at all except under compulsion, although he can read if necessary.

2. The decipherer—can read easy material, but can only decipher partial meaning from selections usually assigned to his grade.
3. The slow but understanding reader—comprehends well but proceeds far too slowly.
4. The slow and superficial reader—recognizes words accurately although rather slowly. He does not grasp the meanings of words when combined into sentences and paragraphs.
5. The purposeless reader—apparently reads with normal ease and momentary understanding, but because of lack of purpose fails to apply or to profit perceptibly from what is read.
6. The literal-meaning reader—can read satisfactorily except when he encounters symbolic or figurative language.
7. The reader with single-track habits—has a style of reading so inflexible that he approaches every reading situation in the same manner, regardless of the type of material or the reason he is reading it.
8. The reader with narrow-gauge interest—can and does read on some one topic or in a particular field, but will read little or nothing else except by compulsion and reads with unsatisfactory comprehension except in the chosen area.
9. The semisilent reader—pronounces each word to himself so that his silent reading is merely inaudible oral reading.
10. The ineffective oral reader—stumbles over the pronunciation of words of which he knows the meaning, or perhaps reads without expression.
11. The rapid, superficial reader—recognizes words quickly, and so hurries along, giving little attention to meaning.
12. The bookworm—usually an efficient reader but, regardless of skill, spends too much time in reading—to the detriment of health, vision, social adjustment, and needed experiences with the world of reality.

Our descriptions of various forms of word perception in the reading process have, we hope, emphasized several implications. Perception, or word recognition as it is more generally called, is not a single, simple process. It takes many forms, only a few of which are spontaneous or original to the reader. Most forms of perception must be thoroughly taught as the reader matures and is ready for them. The reader may discard certain primitive types of perception such as the use of distinctive details or simple configurations. But these must be supplanted by instruction in more effective perceptual skills. Thus the well-planned reading program continues to emphasize training in perception and word recognition throughout the entire school career.

The last few years have witnessed a tremendous surge of interest in the perceptual aspects of reading. Tests of visual perception, as well as a variety of perceptual training materials, have been offered by a number of authors. Some of these authors, as in the Frostig battery, have offered little proof of the validity of their instruments. To them it seems sufficient to put together several tests of spatial relationship, matching of forms, hand–eye coordination, pattern reproduction, discrimination between figure and ground, and the like. Logically, these instruments might have some relationship to the discrimination involved in reading, and hence the tests are offered as prognostic and diagnostic measures for use in the beginning stages of reading. But little evidence is offered regarding which tests are significantly predictive, and therefore, which types of training might be really effective.

The mere fact that the total score on such a battery bears some relationship to early reading success is not sufficient justification for the use of parallel training materials based on each of the subtests. Instructional time is too valuable to be squandered on exercises of questionable merit, however logical they may appear. It would be a simple matter to determine just what tests are truly diagnostic, and whether exercises specifically keyed to each test result are efficiently corrective of perceptual deficits. But this research is still lacking in most of the commercial materials. Other independent research has indicated, as we might suspect, that portions of these hastily constructed batteries have little or no relationship to reading success. Hence parallel training materials are questionable.

The recent developments in the area of visual perception include several other rather loose practices. It has become fashionable to label retarded or poor readers as "perceptually disturbed." This label becomes a ready explanation of the reading retardation, relieves both children and their parents of anxieties about their own mental capacities, and relieves teachers of their guilt feelings in being unable to explain the child's failure. The corrective steps take a wide variety of forms, such as outdoor, large-muscle exercises involving balance boards and other types of physical education apparatus; small-muscle activities with pegs, puzzles, blocks; seatwork materials for copying designs, matching forms, tracing, drawing from dot to dot, and the like. While these activities certainly do promote either large- or small-muscle coordination—which are not, incidentally, closely interrelated or synonymous—and better hand–eye coordination, there is little evidence of the precise values of each for reading success.

With the tests currently available, we just do not know how to diagnose specific perceptual deficits, nor precisely what corrective training efforts to employ. We do not even know the composition of what is loosely termed visual perception, for only two factors of reproducing forms and matching forms have been identified. There may be other factors present, but the research necessary to identify and validate them has not yet been done. A study conducted by one of the authors did seem to indicate that a variety of blackboard exercises for directionality and hand–eye coordination in conjunction with paper and pencil seatwork in matching and reproducing forms were valuable. When this training was substituted for reading instruction for periods from two to six months, according to pupils' needs as indicated by pretesting on the *Thurstone Tests of Pattern Copying* and *Matching Forms,* initially low scorers showed marked success in first-grade reading. Despite an average of four months less reading instruction, children in the experimental classes equaled the control classes, who followed the usual basal reading program in reading achievement. Moreover, children of low socioeconomic status, or in the lowest quarter of the population in intelligence, excelled their basal control groups in reading, implying that those with the greatest need for such training were most benefited by it. One obvious implication of this study, in our opinion, is that when valid facets of perception are measured and corrective steps taken, children are helped to greater success. But many other studies are needed—to identify other components of visual perception, to determine their significance for reading, and to devise and prove the values of related corrective steps both for beginning readers and retarded readers. When all this research has been completed, we may be able to form a concise operational definition of visual perception as it relates to reading* and to deal constructively with each element of the process.

READING AND LANGUAGE

Recent literature in the field of reading strongly emphasizes the significance of language background and the development of reading success. One group of authors stresses that minority groups who speak in a dialect other than standard English are deficient in language development. They claim that their studies show these pupils to be lacking in range, level, and diversity of vocabulary; in the use of syntactic variations; and in such elements as clauses, infinitives, verbals, and linking verbs. When measured by the usual tests, their auditory discrimination is poor; final consonants such as *t, d, g,* and *k* are weak or missing; final *th* becomes a *v*; and unvoiced final *th* becomes an *f*. As a result of these language deficits, these authors say, the child's cognitive ability, his skill in thinking with words, is underdeveloped. All these differences are a serious handicap to reading success, and must be corrected, perhaps even before reading instruction begins (9,30).

This concept that the bilingual or dialect-speaking child must be taught to use standard English if he is to succeed academically is not a new development. The belief has been accepted since before the beginning of the twentieth century in dealing with immigrants to our country. Then, as now, the language problem was attacked by teaching pupils to speak the dialect of the middle-class school. The nature of the training has changed somewhat, to an emphasis upon auditory discrimination, use of proper syntactical endings and other conventions, and to practice with varying sentence patterns. But the goal of eradicating dialect and making the subject proficient in standard English has remained the same, and the acceptance of this as a primary goal is still very widespread in the American school system.

In direct contrast, experts today from a number of disciplines completely reject the deficit theory that dialect users are in need of corrective language training or special attention in auditory discrimination, cognitive abilities, or even vocabulary development. They point out that black dialect, which is at the center of the present controversy, is a systematic, complete form of language that enables its user to deal with any mental process (14). The variations in oral enunciation of certain sounds does not interfere with obtaining meaning in reading. The sup-

---

* When we speak of visual perception we refer here only to that aspect known as visual discrimination of symbols. We must omit discussion at this time of many other facets of visual perception, such as physiological, mechanical, visual, attitudinal, and postural influences.

posed lack of vocabulary in speech does not prove that these pupils cannot understand ordinary language in reading or listening. The dialect user's different syntax in speech does not prevent him from reading or listening to standard English, for he readily translates that dialect into his own (43). Training programs directly intended to correct dialect do not effect reading progress (23), nor does instruction in sentence patterns or techniques of teaching language borrowed from the methodology of foreign language instruction (17).

The linguistically different child's primary problem is the attitude of the middle-class standard-English-speaking teacher. The teacher's judgments of the student's oral reading are depressed by his "errors"; the evaluation of his thinking ability is lowered by his lack of fluency in expressing his thoughts; and the teacher's reactions to his cooperativeness are negative because of his apparent resistance to adopting the teacher's model of English. It does not occur to the teacher that these corrective efforts are perceived as a rejection of the child, his family, and his cultural background that will only be met with negativism and hostility, or passivity and withdrawal. As San-su Lin has expressed the situation, "To attack this dialect, whether directly or by implication, is to attack his loyalty to his group, his identity, his worth" (22, p. 753).

All of this is not to say that some aspects of language development do not directly affect reading progress. Retarded speech development does appear to create problems in early reading stages, as studies both in this country and England show (42). The evidence regarding articulatory disorders such as baby talk, substitutions, and lack of certain letter sounds is less consistent. Gaines (10) has shown that when these speech behaviors are judged by trained examiners, they are much less apt to appear a handicap to reading than when viewed subjectively by classroom teachers. Speech diagnosticians recognize that some of the defects reflect developmental stages that maturation will often eventually eliminate, whereas teachers are prone to consider them as reading errors to be corrected.

It is also true that cultural aspects of language, such as idioms, word meanings, word usage, and the presence of such variations as pidgin English in the home, are obstacles to reading progress for certain ethnic groups (28,44). But these problems are readily overcome by appropriate materials and instruction within the classroom reading program if they are approached as contrasting or different modes of expression rather than as language deficiencies.

We have tried to summarize a great mass of publications on the interaction of language and reading. Just what may or should be done for pupils who differ in dialect or native language will be discussed fully later as we consider the stages of the reading program.

READING AS A REFLECTION OF CULTURAL BACKGROUND

The reading process is undoubtedly based on sociological roots. Reading differs in its purposes, breadth, and quality among societies as well as among social classes within societies. Social factors such as education, cultural interests, income level, family stability, and vocational adjustment all affect the child's purposes and uses of the reading process. These factors determine the quantity and quality of reading materials available as well as the reading habits of the family and community—thus, in turn, influencing the reading behaviors of the child.

If we judge the statistics on book, newspaper, and magazine circulation in the United States, we receive a superficial impression that reading is a highly popular pursuit in our country. Approximately 12,000 new books and new editions of old titles are published annually in this country. Of these, over 2000 are titles for children. Over 7500 magazines are published yearly, with a total circulation close to 175 million. Almost 1800 daily newspapers are printed in English, with a combined circulation of about 55 million readers. New media, such as the paperback, have grown tremendously in recent years, with total publication figures well into the millions. These figures suggest that there is wide distribution and use of reading materials in our population.

Despite these impressive circulation statistics, there are a number of studies which show that reading is still not a widespread leisure-time activity. Three-fourths of the flood of paperbacks is purchased by about 10 percent of the population. Active readers, such as those who can truthfully claim to have read a book in the past month, seldom amount to more than 25 to 30 percent of any segment of the population. Between 60 and 70 percent regularly read one or several magazines, and 85 to 90 percent read a newspaper more or less regularly. Those who read to an appreciable degree are largely concentrated in the age group from twenty-one to twenty-nine and in the professional and skilled-worker categories. Those in the upper income and higher education groups form the bulk of the active readers in almost every comparison (1).

Approximately one in every four adults is registered with the public library, but only about 10 percent use the library as often as once a month. In other words, about three-fourths of the great bulk of reading is done by less than 5 percent of the adult population (1). Statistics on the reading of school children are not much more encouraging. Interest in reading, as recounted in many studies, gradually decreases from an initially strong position as children mature. After the freshman year of high school, interest in reading drops quite markedly, and this trend continues through the early college years. It has been estimated that use of the public library diminishes sharply in post–high school life, for some studies show that 90 percent of high school graduates let their library cards lapse soon after leaving school. College students, it is estimated, use about one book per month in free reading. But over half of this circulation from the college library is accounted for by about 20 percent of the students. Studies of the reading tastes of college students, both during and after college, show them to be far below their potential reading levels (2). It would thus appear that, despite availability of a wide variety of reading materials, serious reading is confined to a very small cross section of the adult and child population.

Economics and educational opportunities influence the extent of reading throughout the world. Of the approximately 500,000 books published in the world in 1969, the 13 percent of the world population in Europe had access to 45 percent of all the books. Asia, with 56 percent of the population, had only 20 percent; Africa, with 10 percent of the population, received only 2 percent; while North America, with 9 percent of the population, had 14 percent of the world's books. Four African countries have less than one copy of a daily newspaper *for every 1000 people* compared with one copy for every 2 persons in Sweden, 320 copies per 1000 in Russia, 331 per 1000 in West Germany, and 305 per 1000 in the United States (46).

It has been suggested that our concern about worldwide literacy is pointless, for television will eventually replace the need for reading. But for the economically deprived, this millenium is hardly likely. Of the 1 million TV sets in Africa, for example, 79 percent are concentrated in the three relatively affluent countries of Algeria, Morocco, and Egypt. Thus we see the dependence of literacy upon the national and personal economy.

Perhaps the most ambitious attempt to identify the characteristics of economically poor children who tend to fail in reading in our country is the large-scale study of Metfessel and Seng (26). Over 3000 rural and urban poor children of five different ethnic groups were studied to identify the profile of the low achiever. Five major areas of traits were studied: learning style, value framework and self-concept, cognitive structure, modes of behavior, and home environment. The learning style of poor achievers was visual and kinesthetic rather than responsive to oral or written stimuli, and hindered by poor attention span to multiple stimuli, and perseverance in a single task. Inductive approaches were responded to more readily than deductive. Moreover, these children are at a disadvantage in timed learning or testing situations because of lack of self-confidence and negative self-concept. Poor children seldom receive approval for success, and consequently expect to fail to achieve. They are accustomed to home discipline by physical force and often fail to respond to the school's discipline through reason or loss of privileges.

Cognitively, these economically deprived children are uneven in development and in fundamental knowledge for lack of parental stimulation, family activities, or games. Language development is retarded in the sense of awareness of the concept that all objects or events or people have labels. Even more significant in their development, however, are the models of behavior to which poor children are exposed. Their parents do not use a language model appropriate to the middle-class school nor do they value intellectual development. The parents generally work at levels not requiring much education and convey to their children a low evaluation of school learning for vocational goals. The attitude is that the needs of the family are more important than school-attendance laws. School is conceived of as a magic environment that teaches the child the basics of reading, writing, and arithmetic without requiring any parental approval or involvement.

Of course, not all poor children fail in school or in reading. Those who do succeed tend, as we would expect, to be opposite in their attributes to the low achiever. The greatest contrasts are in the area of values, self-concept, and behavior models. Successful pupils from the poverty culture tend to relate well to both peers and adults. They and their friends receive strong approval which enables them to learn to defer gratification and to expect success. Since they are conscious of the parental acceptance, they relate well to the values of their parents and teachers; in other words, they readily identify with the middle-class standards of the school. These achieving poor children become involved in school work, and like their parents, see it as valuable to their future, as challenging and rewarding.

In his contrasting study of learners and nonlearners, Irving D. Harris also emphasizes the influence of social class upon learning problems (19). He finds a direct relationship between lower-class origin and low-average intelligence scores, repetition of grades, low familial values on education, and less intellectual stimulation. Other socioeconomic characteristics which he believes contribute to academic and reading failures are employment of the mother outside the home, large families, and father's occupation and education. Like a number of other writers in this field. Harris stresses the inherent conflict between the mores of the lower-class child and the middle-class values of the school and of teachers as a source of what appear to be learning problems.

Barton and Wilder (3) consider socioeconomic class to be the most important single factor in reading progress in school. Their national survey of elementary school teachers permitted the classification of classrooms according to parental income and occupation. The data of the study indicated that reading retardation below expected grade norms rises steadily through the first six grades for working-class children, markedly so for the children of the lower-skilled, lower-paid working class. By the fourth grade about half of the classrooms of lower-class children show a degree of retardation as much as one year below grade level. The converse of this is also present in the Barton–Wilder study. Upper-class children tend to become advanced in reading from the first grade and to maintain this academic advantage. Some other observers of these trends would point out that they are reinforced by the differences among schools in upper- and lower-class communities in the training and skill of teachers, the supply of instructional materials, and, of course, teacher expectations.

We are not trying to imply here that reading failures are concentrated in any one social class or stratum of society. Rather, it is apparent that because the public school clings to what are basically upper-middle-class ideals, the proportion of failures is probably greater among those children whose social backgrounds do not fit them to meet these standards. As Keshian's study (21) shows, reading success is found frequently in high, medium, and low socioeconomic groups. He also points out, however, that the families of good readers fostered success by such practices as reading regularly to their young children and placing high values on reading. These families also tended to remain intact and produce children who were basically well adjusted socially and emotionally.

As Wallace Ramsey shows in his survey of 53 school systems in Kentucky, reading achievement is also closely related to the economic situation of the school district. Systems in the highest quarter of achievement had significantly greater local and total revenue per child. As a result, they paid higher teacher salaries, used supplementary and informal materials and activities twice as much, and had slightly larger classroom and school libraries. The more careful selection of teachers made possible resulted in a staff with significantly more college credits and fewer years of teaching experience. These more successful schools spent more class time per day (eighty versus sixty-five minutes) in reading activities and used more innovations (such as interclass grouping and individualized reading) four times as often as the lowest quarter of the school systems (29).

Allison Davis also emphasizes the class nature of school life, when he says (8, pp. 97–98):

> The present curricula are stereotyped and arbitrary selections from a narrow area of middle-class culture. Academic culture is one of the most conservative and ritualized aspects of human culture. Its formalization, its lack of functional connection with the daily problems of life, has given a bloodless, fossilized character to the classroom which all of us recognize.

And again he asks (8, p. 89):

> Does the public school select a range of mental problems and skills which is so narrow that the school fails to develop much of the mental potential of lower-class pupils?

Some school systems recognize the depth of this problem of overcoming the handicaps of the socioeconomically deprived child. Among the programs tried are special summer schools of ten weeks each in two successive primary years, or almost-all-year schooling. Others are attempting intensive study of the child and his family and provision of a richer background of experiences during the primary period with the support and help of the parents. This enlistment of parental aspirations is more significant in pupil academic success than socioeconomic status and cultural background of the family.

A recent report from New Zealand emphasizes the great importance of parental values. In a comparison of white, Maori, and Samoan children aged five to seven, Clay (7) found that although they were better in language tests at every level than the Samoan children who had recently immigrated to the country, the Maoris had twice as many in the low-progress groups. After only eighteen months of schooling (and learning English), the Samoan children were much more successful academically. Clay attributes the difference to the strong family unit; the high regard for education, teachers, Sunday school teachers, and ministers; and the firm child-rearing practices of the Samoan culture. The children readily became bilingual, unlike the Maori, who do not know their own language; and they take to reading and writing easily because of the almost daily Bible reading and correspondence with relatives "at home" in Western Samoa.

Concern for the successful education of children who are economically or language-deprived has increased tremendously in the past few years. In hundreds of federal and local projects, materials and means of aiding such children to succeed better in school are being explored. Typical of these is the downward extension of school services into the preschool years, as in Operation Head Start, which has shown the values of early attempts to stimulate language development and increase experiential backgrounds. Some researchers seem to think that the best program lies in simply beginning formal schoolwork earlier and offering lessons in reading, arithmetic, and spelling in a tightly scheduled program. Others point out that the earlier research in nursery education indicates that close scheduling at these ages creates resistance to authority and denies the individuality of child interest and development. Furthermore, the preschool specialists point out there is no evidence to show that the basic need of language-deprived children is met by formal schoolwork. Such children, they say, need most experiences with objects, people, and places to acquire the concepts and thinking which are expressed in language.

Other projects for these children have attempted to prepare special instructional materials, particularly in reading, which would reflect the living conditions and mores of groups other than the upper middle class. Thus by presenting a picture of life closer to reality as culturally deprived children know it, it is hoped that greater interest and success in reading will be stimulated. One serious question regarding the nature of the language to be employed plagues the producers of such reading materials. Should materials for a language-deprived child who speaks only nonstandard English be presented in the language he uses in order to facilitate easier reading? Or, in the hopes of improving the quality of his usage, should materials be phrased only in standard English? Although it might seem more logical to offer stories in the child's own version of English, the variety of dialects seems to make such an effort impractical. It just would not be feasible to mass-produce books in a dozen or more versions. Besides, the argument is offered that such children must eventually learn to understand standard English if they are to communicate effectively. And there is evidence that our language-deprived children do eventually learn to manage this more acceptable version of our language. In fact, some observers point out that by junior high school age, children have learned not only to use acceptable English in the classroom but also to communicate with their parents in their original dialect and with their peers in a jargon peculiar to present-day adolescents.

READING AS A PSYCHOLINGUISTIC PROCESS

In the past decade a fresh view of the reading process has been offered by psycholinguists, or those who approach the study of language from psychological grounds. To these specialists, reading is "a psycholinguistic guessing game" (12) involving a series of tentative decisions based on the reader's use of available language cues. In other words, the reader uses the graphic cues of letters, the semantic cues of word meanings, and the syntactic cues of word order to obtain the message of the selection. Reading is often likened to a communication process, a direct interpretation of the printed symbol into the reader's thought processes. In this sense, the act of reading is not a word recognition act or a translation of words, but a fluent, almost instantaneous combining of words into complete thoughts. The whole process begins with the young child's first reactions to the symbols about him—on the TV screen, cereal boxes, street and store signs, to his father's newspaper headlines, to the drawings in his picture books, and the like. Young children also react in this interpretative process to other types of symbols, such as the shapes of road signs, the geometric shapes among toys such as parquetry blocks, puzzles, cutouts, building blocks.

Thus the child reads or interprets many types of lettered and other symbols long before he begins to read in the usual sense. These early experiences with symbolic shapes and forms, in fact, are essential for the development of the visual discrimination, recognition, and interpretation behaviors of the reading act. We shall emphasize the primacy of this growth continuum in a later chapter, offering our suggestions regarding readiness training.

Although the beginning reader does read literally word by word, averaging no more than about one word per fixation until past the tenth grade, as we have pointed out, reading does not involve word-by-word thinking. Rather, even the young reader who tends to name or call words consecutively reacts to them collectively in terms of his familiarity with the structure and word order of the language. Partly because he has so often heard sentences with various patterns, he anticipates similar patterns in reading. In a sense, he expects sentences he reads to fall into the familiar auditory patterns, and to make sense linguistically. This anticipation explains the high frequency of errors (as well as the unobserved successes) of omission and of substitution in an effort to produce a sentence which is meaningful, at least to the reader.

In fact, as speed and fluency in silent reading increase, this dependence upon context becomes more and more evident. It is probably the mature reader's basic aid to analysis of new or difficult words and phrases. This thinking, along with the flow of ideas from the printed symbols, may also result in many substitutions and omissions in the oral reading act, a behavior which is disconcerting to the undiscerning teacher.

However, if we comprehend the nature of the reading act in its visual or mechanical sense, we realize the inevitability of these developments of dependence upon context and, consequently, toward the reader's combining his own vocabulary and concepts with those printed. As clarified in an earlier section of this chapter, the sole means of achieving rapid, fluent reading is not by increasing visual span but by speeding up fixations. This simply means reducing the time of processing words. In effect, every good reader must learn to react with gradually increasing speed of interpretation, which is equivalent to saying that he must learn to anticipate the flow of ideas presented more and more rapidly, if he is to read at his own thinking speed. The errors thus introduced into his reading are obviously an inescapable part of the increasing speed of flow of ideas and the strong tendency to read into the material. What we are trying to say is that one does not simply read the printed word, he reacts to what it says, bringing to bear all his language-thinking experiences.

Robert B. Ruddell calls reading "a complex psycholinguistic behavior which consists of decoding written language units, processing the resulting language counterparts through structural and semantic dimensions, and interpreting the deep structure data relative to an individual's established objectives" (32). This definition adds two concepts in stressing the importance of decoding in word recognition and the fact that the reader extracts from the printed matter those ideas which match his previous experiences and his purpose in reading.

While he recognizes decoding as part of the process, Goodman (15) subordinates it to a minor role. To him, decoding is simply intended to move the reader from the printed language to its meaning. Decoding is not primarily useful for aiding the reader to say the word, to hear the word, or to recognize it. The learning of sound–symbol correspondences is not decoding in Goodman's concept, for no written language is a one-to-one representation of the oral language. The correspondence is between patterns of letters and patterns of sounds. Teaching children to move from the graphic to the oral code is recoding, not decoding, and a process that short-circuits the obtaining of meaning, in this psycholinguist's view of the reading process. While some letter–sound relationships may be useful in the very early stages of learning to read, the child should be moved soon to reacting to the whole sentence, and to the meaning given to an unknown word by the context.

This view of reading has stimulated a number of research studies relevant to teaching methods. Goodman, for example, has demonstrated that most of children's oral reading errors can be attributed to the attempt to make linguistic sense (13). Therefore, prompting and correcting oral reading errors may interfere with the normal self-corrective efforts of the child by placing emphasis upon word recognition rather than obtaining meaning. Other studies support this argument in demonstrating that readers can recognize in context many of the words they cannot read in isolation. Similarly, trying to eliminate regressions or repetitions in oral reading, when these reflect self-corrective responses, is most unsound. Drill on isolated words out of meaningful contextual settings is pointless and inimical to the true goal of reading for meaning.

These suggestions for the teaching of reading do not pretend to constitute a method, for there is no psycholinguistic method (37). What these specialists hope to accomplish is to move our teaching and testing techniques toward a broader understanding of the reading process. They are not suggesting, as some other linguists do, that children would benefit from instruction in linguistics or sentence patterns. The rules for these areas could not be verbalized to children. Rather, readers need great experience with language, an opportunity to generate hypotheses about its structure, to test and modify these according to the unspoken rules about language that children generate. None of these can be expressed in behavioral objectives and programmed into children.

Psycholinguists are telling us that comprehension is a process by which the reader progresses from the printed display of words to the deeper structure or meaningful interpretation of the material, utilizing his past experiences and his knowledge of language. Three cueing systems underlie the reading process: first,

PART I   Foundations of Reading

the graphophonic system, using cues within words, such as letter—sound relationships, word parts or phonograms, phonics, and word shape or configuration. Second, the syntactic cueing, which uses inflectional endings, grammatical relationships, and word order and punctuation. Finally, there is the semantic system, which employs what has commonly been called the context. The values of these systems to the reader vary with his ability, for the highly proficient pupil uses a minimum of graphophonic cues to predict the syntactic structure and similarly increases his dependence upon semantic cues to support his expectations of what is to come on the printed page. The more control the learner has of oral language and the broader his experiences, the less visual information he needs from the text (45).

We will further emphasize the implications of psycholinguistic research in later chapters as it relates to the testing of oral reading, the learning of sight and meaning vocabulary, and the language problems of beginning readers. Also, in the later discussion of the so-called "linguistic" approach to teaching reading, we will contrast the views of the psycholinguists with those who produce what are called linguistic reading materials.

READING AS INFORMATION PROCESSING

Many contemporary psychologists, linguists, and reading specialists are currently emphasizing the reading process as information processing. We have attempted to combine these ideas as offered by experts from the different disciplines (6, 18, 25, 36). Their viewpoints do differ somewhat in their emphases upon the importance of the child's language experiences, in terminology for information processing, and in other details. But we will try to merge these into a single interpretation of the reading process based on what we now know about the way the brain handles this situation.

Reading is conceived of as visual scanning directed by the child's general information store (or long-term memory, as it is called) and the information derived from the material being read (which is temporarily stored in short-term memory). According to this concept of reading, new material is assimilated into past experiences of related nature (passing from short-term to long-term memory store). The exact details of the new information may be lost, but basic concepts are retained. This result is evidenced by the fact that we are unable to retain the exact words of a long statement (without considerable rehearsal) but can usually paraphrase and summarize the ideas encountered in listening to or reading that statement.

Long-term memory operates by clustering, chunking, or organizing the material in some fashion. When this material is called upon for recall, the clues in the stimulus (the meaning, salient physical features, associations, contextual or temporal information present in the stimulus to recall) are guides to searching the long-term storage areas of the brain.

In reading (visual scanning), words are identified by a search of the associative word stores of high-frequency and low-frequency words. If a search of both of these storage areas is unsuccessful, the reader engages in more visual scanning. Input is in terms of pairs or groups of letters, then words, then phrases and larger units, according to some writers in this field. Letter and word identification and meaning are secured by testing a sufficient number of the distinctive features. This does not mean that reading occurs letter by letter, for it requires fewer distinctive features to discriminate a letter within a word than the isolated letter, and words can be recognized without identifying any of the letters, in many instances.

The beginning reader is handicapped by an empty letter store and no store of the visual patterns of either high-frequency or low-frequency words. Thus he has difficulty identifying either letters or words directly and, some say, must map the word on to its sound pattern (which he often has already in storage) by using decoding or phonics as a means of mediation (handling the word recognition). Obviously, he must succeed in word identification in order to obtain some semblance of meaning, but these mediating behaviors tend to overload his visual information processing and memory systems; in other words, sometimes there are just too many new words for which he has no store of visual patterns to be able to read. To succeed in learning to read, he must soon learn to utilize the redundancies in the language of individual letters, patterns of letters (syllables), and sequences of words, or arrangements of words which impose semantic and syntactic constraints. In simpler words, he must learn the influence of word placement or word function in relation to the adjoining words upon the kind of word he is trying to read as well as upon its meaning.

To illustrate, "I stopped at the corner to read a sign which said Bus S_____. You can supply the missing word because of (1) the inherent meaningful message of the sentence, (2) the reproduction of the familiar visual pattern of a common sign, and (3) the additional clue of the first letter. Because of these clues (assuming you live in a country that has a bus system) you read the missing word as *Stop.* And because of the initial letter, you eliminated the possibility of *Change,* and the fact that the sign was on a corner eliminated *Station.* Or didn't it? The information processing you went through in using the message of the sentence, the constraint imposed by the phrase "at the corner," the further constraint of the initial letter, etc., were not conscious: they were never verbalized in words mentally or aloud, but they were part of the process of word recognition, just as they are for readers of all ages. Until the child acquires a store of visual patterns which permit quick identification of the parts or whole words, he is heavily dependent upon sheer visual information, the graphic clues of the letters to their sounds. Thus for a long period of time for some children reading is slow, laborious, and attended with little comprehension.

G.H. Bower (4) has summed it up well in saying: "No word is an island unto itself. It rather occupies the intersection of a vast number of classifying features." Would that some of this concept might penetrate the minds of teachers who "teach" vocabulary by rote memory, flash cards, machines, and other presentations carefully isolated from meaning!

Information processing specialists have, of course, ideas about the teaching of reading. John Merritt of Durham University in England (25) implores teachers:

- Try to match the child's language and the language of the book, thus strengthening the possibilities of his intelligent use of context (semantic and syntactic constraints). Children can comprehend reading materials phrased in familiar sentence patterns (similar to those they use in speech and writing) much more readily.
- To accomplish this parallelism, use the children's stories and those of other children as much as possible. In effect, use the language experience approach, Merritt recommends.
- To enable the child to deal with materials of more complex nature, give him practice with varying sentence patterns—i.e., different ways of saying something. To vary this practice, use the cloze procedure of deleting every fifth or tenth word and ask him to supply a sensible word. Compare children's word selections and discuss the reasons for their choices. Thus we may strengthen their abilities to use the semantic, syntactic, and graphic clues to word recognition and meaning.

Other experts point out the following implications of this concept of the reading process:

- Information transfer (from short-term to long-term memory storage) depends upon the learner's strategies for encoding, his cognitive readiness or capacity for coping and integrating; semantically or associatively meaningful materials and familiar items are retained better than single letters, nonsense groups, or letter strings, or other meaningless materials. Advance organizers (prereading questions) emphasizing major concepts, principles, or relationships to be found in the reading are helpful to some pupils. Some need to prepare their own advance organizers, however.
- Imagery is more easily evoked in older children (ages four to nine) and profit from visual representation intended to evoke imagery comes later; simultaneous storage of imagery is more profitable if accompanied by verbal representation, for older children. In other words, verbal—symbolic presentation (talking plus reading) is better for sequential or related information.
- Items to be learned (words, signs, forms) should be presented as concretely as possible, probably in pairs in which a relationship can be recognized. Arranging such items in some sort of hierarchy also provides a retrieval scheme (a clue to searching long-term memory)—for example, size, part–whole, synonyms, opposites, colors, action, common relationships (cars–people; pronouns for names; *cows* eat *hay*). Practice in shifting from one category to another, as recognizing that a father may also be a brother, a son, a cousin, or an uncle, is very desirable. Giving a set to look for certain attributes in a series (an advance organizer before presentation) facilitates scanning of the series.

There is not a great deal that is brand new in this interpretation of reading as an information processing behavior other than perhaps a number of technical terms. A real contribution to the teaching of reading is present, however, in the integration of scientific information from a wide variety of sources and the organizing of these data into a coherent concept of reading which does further our understanding of how children read and how we might better help them.

Many would be tempted to see here a simple analogy between a reader attempting to find a meaning for a word or phrase and a computer searching its memory bank for a fact we have commanded it to find. In some respects this analogy is correct (although human brains can do some things computers cannot and vice versa), and it has led some experts to believe that reading can be taught by a computer which has been programmed to anticipate and deal with most of the child's expected responses. As we point out later in our discussion of computer-assisted instruction, the analogy between the actions of a computer and those of a beginning reader is false in many respects. Learning to read does not occur simply as an isolated information processing act free from the dramatic effects of the child's emotions, attitudes, personality, motivation, attention, and cultural and language backgrounds. Information processing theory will bring us new insights into the learning process, but it does not yet deal with the human interrelationships present in the teacher–pupil interaction, which some of us believe are of paramount significance for the child's success.

READING AS ASSOCIATIONAL LEARNING

S. Jay Samuels of the University of Minnesota and a number of other educational psychologists have contributed markedly to our understanding of reading as an associational learning process. Deriving their insights from many studies of paired associate learning or experiments in learning to associate pairs of words, symbols, or the like, this group has brought together a body of observations of significance for the teacher of reading. Their theory, of course, does not encompass all facets of the reading process but rather is pertinent largely to word recognition, as Samuels points out (34).

Samuels emphasizes that reading is not a single-stage process of simply looking at a word and pronouncing it. First, there are the properties of the stimulus of letters and words. The child must discriminate among these stimuli and gradually acquire responses. These associations must be reinforced by a number of means we shall discuss later. There is also involved a mediational stage, that is, interpreting words and meanings by recognition of the syntactic relationships of the context, by categorizing, classifying, or reacting to them in various verbal ways.

Perception of symbols is also dependent upon the preperceptual field, the set to match symbols and words and meanings, as well as the reader's short-term and long-term memory storage banks. The reading process also involves attention, distinctive feature learning, visual-recognition memory, mediation, and hookup, as well as auditory discrimination and auditory memory. When we combine all these components, it is apparent why associational learning specialists consider reading a multistage, complex act. Let us clarify this view of reading by exploring each of the components these experts attribute to the reading process.

Attention.   Attention is essential for learning and is manifested by changes in the galvanic skin response, heart rate, brain rhythm, pupillary dilation, and blood volume. The position of the head and of the eyes provides a clue among most pupils. In a sense, the whole body of the child is mobilized to the present task, if he is really attending.

Since the teacher is not in a position to keep records of the physiological changes in pupils that indicate their degree of attention, we must look elsewhere for pertinent suggestions for the teacher from the field of associational learning. These experts confirm that distractions to attention make tasks more difficult and that those pupils low in academic achievement appear more distractible than others. Older children, contrary to the general opinion, are as distractible as some much younger, in the presence of some disturbing stimuli. Most teachers are familiar with these facts and try to control attention and prevent distractions by a number of well-known practices.

A basic problem in attention is the fact that the student may not know where to focus attention, particularly during his early learning experiences. He does not know whether or how to concentrate on letters, words, the meaning, the sounds of the letters, or what. When he discovers the relevant dimension that matches the word with his store of memories, even the mental retardate can show normal curves of learning. Because of these observations, Samuels and his coworkers question the early presentation of only whole words because their studies show that the transfer to new words (beginning with the same first or last letter or whatever cue the child was using) is poor, even among highly discriminable words normally recognized by their distinctive shape, length, and so on. These studies reemphasize the child's need for several realistic cues to word recognition early in the whole process to focus his attention.

Another example of the need for better clues to word recognition is present in the experiments with the use of color in learning words. Color appears to be a help in learning new words, but the aid is soon lost because all future reading must be in black and white. Other studies indicate that when color in the letters or the backgrounds is used in learning words, the pupils may well learn the colors but fail to learn the associated words. This type of data can be interpreted as confirming the child's difficulty in knowing what to attend to. Despite the importance of directing children's attention, Samuels points out that we have no studies yet of attention versus distractibility among first graders and the relationship to subsequent reading achievement, although almost every experienced primary teacher has an opinion on this subject.

Visual Discrimination.   To the associational learning specialists, visual discrimination implies learning the distinctive features of visual stimuli. They show that much discrimination training, such as that in the Frostig program, does not promote the kinds of discrimination involved in letters and words. Moreover, the relationship between geometric form discrimination and reading is questionable to them, for in their studies it seems relevant only for the extreme cases, high or low in discrimination.

Distinctive feature training (as in matching given stimuli to a sample) utilizing memory has been shown to give better letter–name learning results than similar training which does not require memory. Other studies also support the need to emphasize discrimination from memory, rather than simple matching, as we often see it in workbooks. Teaching like letters, such as *b–d*, in distinctive feature programs is more effective when these are presented separately and successively rather than at the same time. For unlike letters, such as *s–h*, simultaneous presentation appears efficient. Letters with alternative sounds, as *city–cow*, are best taught concurrently—not consecutively or at widely separated times as they are commonly scheduled in many reading programs.

Some studies have shown that cross modality training from blocks with raised letters to printed words, or from touch to vision, produces good transfer. Simultaneous discrimination with both touch and vision has also helped some pupils but appears to be most effective when memory is required. As a result of these latter studies, Samuels suggests touch training prior to visual training, as well as touch training on distinctive features to overcome poor readers' mistakes. Simultaneous training with touch and vision tends to lead only to distinctive feature learning, whereas successive training using these two media tends to help the reader formulate schema (draw conclusions about similarities and differences and combine both impressions into a clue) and learn distinctive features. The learning of letter names is facilitated and failure sizably reduced by training on the distinctive features of letters (by touch and then by vision) prior to introducing an association between the letter name and its symbol, unlike some current programs.

Some of these facts about learning the distinctive features of letters which will later serve as clues to word recognition, such as the value of touch or kinesthetic activities, have long been recognized by reading specialists. The procedure has often, however, been reserved for remedial work with poor readers. If we interpret him correctly, Samuels is recommending this type of training for most beginners, when they appear to profit from it. His suggestions regarding like and unlike letters, those with alternative sounds, and the use of touch–vision successively rather than simultaneously, as well as the practice of both these presentations prior to introducing names for the letter symbols, do offer some fresh insights on the beginning program.

Visual and Auditory Memory.   There is much attention to visual and auditory memory in many of today's "perceptual training" programs. But as we shall see, the terms are not synonymous with the concepts offered by educational psychologists. In their parlance there are three types of basic memory: the visual information store, in which images last for about a second; short-term memory, which lasts about fifteen seconds; and long-term memory, which persists over extended periods of time. An image flashed on the retina fades within a second, to be replaced by another image (the next letters or words or whatever). If this fading were not present, or, in other words, if our fixation pauses were not as brief as they are (about one-third to one-fifth of a second), a second image would compete with or superimpose itself on the first, with resulting confusion in perception.

The image in the visual information store usually passes to short-term memory. Because reading is basically a language act, and the reader tends to articulate the words he is reading,* the visual information is encoded verbally and placed in short-term memory as an auditory image and perhaps then later stored in long-term memory through some mediating generalization. There is, to be sure, evidence of visually stored images among infants prior to speech, in animals, and in aphasics who have temporarily lost speech. But mistakes in reading often reflect misarticulation, auditory confusion, and verbal substitutions, thus supporting the belief in the storage of visual images in reading as auditory memories. These types of errors reflect the decay of memories stored in the short-term bank. In this line of thinking, both auditory and visual memory do seem to be related to poor reading, in the sense that such pupils first have trouble identifying the distinctive features of letters and words and then appear to fail to encode (process) these clues with an accurate verbalization.

We are offered facts here which agree completely with our knowledge of the role of eye movements in the act of reading. We are also led to believe that because the reader, any reader, tends to verbalize or say the words he is reading, the words or concepts that he is processing are stored as auditory memories. Again, we see the evidence that successful comprehension in reading demands mediation (comparing, classifying) in the act of reading; otherwise, visual images cannot move from the momentary visual information store to short-term memory and on to long-term memory. Similarly, since auditory stimuli likewise decay steadily in less than fifteen seconds, some method of manipulating these signals must be utilized to induce them to pass from short-term to long-term memory.

We believe that associational learning experts, like information processing specialists, are telling us over and over that learning the distinctive features of letters and words (word recognition) is not a rote memory process accomplished by sheer repetition. It must be attended with meaningful associations and cognitive strategies or schema for generalizing about these symbols. Letters and words, we might say, are not learned as isolated items but in terms of their similarities and differences, their feel plus their visual images, and the organized meanings that children learn spontaneously or are led to recognize about these characteristics.

There would seem to be some support here for use of the following strategies in teaching letters:

1. Emphasizing physical similarities and differences by imitating shapes by bodily posture.

---

* Obvious articulation or subvocalization is almost always present in the reading act, almost as though it were an essential, contrary to the ideas of those who think to increase speed of reading by eliminating subvocalization. In proof, see Ake W. Edfeldt, *Silent Speech and Silent Reading* (Chicago: University of Chicago Press, 1960).

2. Writing the letters.
3. Tracing over letters in raised blocks or sandpaper forms or sand before stressing visual matching or comparison.
4. Encouraging or suggesting verbalizations about the similarities or differences, as tall versus short, fat versus thin, round versus straight.
5. Verbalizing the writing strokes.
6. Drawing simple analogies between the shapes of letters and common objects (e.g., *b* looks like a bat and ball).

Many of these mediating strategies are familiar to primary teachers. But our point here is that although different strategies work better for different children (and perhaps best if they are spontaneously offered), they are an essential aid to the storing of the visual images of letters and words as auditory (verbal) memories in the long-term memory bank.

Auditory Discrimination.   Samuels appears to be doubtful of the significance of auditory discrimination for beginning reading. As a number of studies show, the tests are of varying validity and often questionable reliability, particularly for nonstandard English speakers. In one study, in which children were tested on three successive days, the worst performance was on the first day. (Did the children have to learn what to attend to, before the test could really function?) Repeated testing is thus a must for young school children for any real degree of reliability.

Some auditory discrimination tests are criticized for being really tests of intelligence and the child's ability to follow directions. The most common type, using discrimination of word pairs differing in a single initial or final sound, appears too difficult for many primary children unless the test is repeated several times, as we have already shown.

Among nonstandard English speakers, the use of a test demanding discriminations lacking in many dialects again tends to give false results for these groups. Robinson's small-scale study (*31*) implies much lower reliability among disadvantaged children for what is considered one of the better measures involving word-pair discriminations. As a result of these observations, and in view of much evidence seemingly contradictory to an emphasis on a meaningful linkage among dialect, auditory discrimination, and reading, many language specialists reject any causal interaction. As Samuels expresses this disbelief, the reading difficulties of dialectal groups could more readily be attributed to deficiencies in attention, language development, and cognitive development. The weight of evidence is against poor auditory discrimination as a cause of poor reading among dialect speakers according to such linguists as Venezky (*39*). Linguists offer the additional supportive argument that such children can make the distinctions from context in listening or reading, even those they cannot evidence in the common test. Moreover, these users of nonstandard English can understand both their own dialect and that of the middle-class teacher, and as they mature they can answer her in her own dialect if they choose.

We are also of the opinion that dialect and what appears to be poor auditory discrimination are not major contributors to reading failure. Upon occasion and for some pupils there is some justification for attempting to improve auditory discrimination. Since this would usually take place during the readiness period, we will reserve our further discussion until we treat that subject.

Although the technical terms may bother some of our readers, this interpretation of reading as an associational process is actually defining reading in much the same way as the psycholinguists, the language specialists, or those experts that emphasize the visual or perceptual aspects. Perhaps we can integrate these concepts of reading into a single description.

Reading involves:

The Word Is   a very brief visual image recognized by distinctive features, such as:

        letter groups or common phonograms

        translation of some letters into sounds

        the initial or final letter or two

        a letter or two plus the configuration and the reader's anticipation as determined by the context

matched with an auditory memory and its associated ideas

accompanied by a meaning that is determined by:

        the reader's familiarity with or anticipation of syntax and word order

        his previous reading and life experiences stored as auditory memories in his long-term memory bank

The Sentence   is interpreted as a rough approximation of the overall meanings of the words

conveys a message which is not the sum of the words but the reader's own interpretation or understanding

The Paragraph   is a series of messages processed by the reader through inductive or deductive reasoning, in which the relationships among the messages (cause–effect, contrast, comparison, etc.) are recognized by the reader

results in a final overall impression (main idea, conclusion, inference, etc.) or a message that is matched with and modified by the previous learnings of the reader, which may or may not agree with the writer's intentions

To put these same concepts in the negative sense:

The Word Is Not   recognized by the sheer act of saying it aloud or subvocally

recognized because of repeated experiences simply in seeing and saying it

recognized solely as a visual image that is familiar

recognized letter by letter or phoneme by phoneme

The Sentence   does not require recognition of all the words to obtain the message

	is not the sum of all the meanings of all the words
	is not mentally classified as to type of structure (active, passive, negative, etc.)
	is not interpreted in terms of its exact phrasing or surface structure
The Paragraph	is not the sum of the facts presented
	is not comprehended exactly as presented

We have presented yet another group of scientifically based ideas about the nature of reading. This large body of studies has many implications for teaching children to read. We shall attempt to explore these implications thoroughly and to point out the teaching practices they seem to support as they are relevant to subsequent chapters of this book.

DISCUSSION QUESTIONS

1. What faulty classroom practices reflect a narrow or single concept of the nature of the reading process?

2. What are some of the dangers in an oversimplified understanding of the reading process?

3. About when does reading begin to become largely a thinking rather than a word recognition act?

4. What are the limitations in treating reading instruction as simply successive training in one skill after another?

5. What evidence is there which contradicts the concept of reading as the translation of successive letters into sounds and then into words?

6. Why did American schools gradually shift from an almost exclusive emphasis upon oral reading to a balance between oral and silent?

7. Does the present American reading program actually achieve a good balance between oral and silent reading? A good balance between skill development and thinking? Defend your answers.

8. Why do most spelling and oral reading errors seem to be concentrated in the middles of words? What does this observation imply in terms of word recognition?

9. What types of thinking are not usually demanded by teachers' questions? How then does reading ever become a well-rounded thinking behavior?

10. What would be the characteristics of a reading program that integrated these various views of the reading process?

REFERENCES

1. Asheim, Lester, "What Do Adults Read?" in *Adult Reading,* Nelson B. Henry, ed., Fifty-fifth Yearbook of the National Society for the Study of Education. Chicago: University of Chicago Press, 1956, 5–28.

2. Asheim, Lester, "A Survey of Recent Research," in *Reading for Life,* Jacob M. Price, ed. Ann Arbor, Mich.: University of Michigan Press, 1959, 3–26.

3. Barton, Allen H., and Wilder, David E., *Research and Practice in the Teaching of Reading: A Progress Report,* Study A–388. Bureau of Applied Research, Columbia University, New York, 1963.

4. Bower, G. H., "Organizational Factors in Memory," *Cognitive Psychology,* 1 (1970), 18–46.

5. Buswell, Guy T., "The Process of Reading,"

Reading Teacher, 13 (December 1959), 108–114.

6. Calfee, R., Chapman, R., and Venezky, R., "How a Child Needs To Think To Learn To Read," *Cognition in Learning and Memory,* I. L. Gregg, ed. New York: John Wiley & Sons, Inc., 1971.

7. Clay, Marie M., "Early Childhood and Cultural Diversity in New Zealand," *Reading Teacher,* 29 (January 1976), 333–342.

8. Davis, Allison, *Social-Class Influences upon Learning.* Cambridge, Mass.: Harvard University Press, 1961.

9. Deutsch, M., "The Role of Social Class in Language Development and Cognition," *American Journal of Orthopsychiatry,* 35 (1965), 78–88.

10. Gaines, Francis P., "Interrelations of Speech and Reading Disabilities," *Elementary School Journal,* 41 (April 1941), 605–613.

11. Gilbert, Luther C., "Functional Motor Efficiency of the Eyes and Its Relation to Reading," *University of California Publication in Education,* 11 (1953), 159–232.

12. Goodman, Kenneth S., "The Linguistics of Reading," *Elementary School Journal,* 64 (April 1964), 355–361.

13. Goodman, Kenneth S., "A Linguistic Study of Cues and Miscues in Reading," *Elementary English,* 42 (October 1965), 639–643.

14. Goodman, Kenneth S., "Dialect Rejection and Reading: A Response," *Reading Research Quarterly,* 5 (Summer 1970), 600–603.

15. Goodman, Kenneth S., "Decoding—From Code to What?" *Journal of Reading,* 14 (April 1971), 455–462, 498.

16. Gray, William S., "The Major Aspects of Reading," in *Sequential Development of Reading Abilities,* Helen M. Robinson, ed., Supplementary Educational Monographs, No. 90. Chicago: University of Chicago Press, 1960, 8–24.

17. Gunderson, Doris V., compiler, *Language and Reading: An Interdisciplinary Approach.* Washington, D.C.: Center for Applied Linguistics, 1970.

18. Haber, Ralph, ed., *Information Processing Approaches to Visual Perception.* New York: Holt, Rinehart and Winston, Inc., 1969.

19. Harris, Irving D., *Emotional Blocks to Learning.* New York: Free Press, 1961.

20. Huey, Edmund B., *The Psychology and Pedagogy of Reading.* New York: Macmillan Publishing Co., Inc., 1908.

21. Keshian, Jerry G., "How Many Children Are Successful Readers?" *Elementary English,* 38 (October 1961), 408–410.

22. Lin, San-su C., "Disadvantaged Student or Disadvantaged Teacher?" *English Journal,* 56 (May 1967), 751–756.

23. MacKinnon, A. R., "Insistent Tasks in Language Learning," *Toronto Education Quarterly,* 1 (Winter 1961–1962), 8–12.

24. McConkie, George W., and Rayner, Keith, "An On-Line Computer Technique for Studying Reading: Identifying the Perceptual Span," in *Diversity in Mature Reading: Theory and Research, I,* Phil L. Nacke, ed. Twenty-second Yearbook National Reading Conference, 1973, 119–130.

25. Merritt, John, "The Intermediate Skills," in *Reading Skills, Theory and Practice,* Keith Gardner, ed. Proceedings of the Sixth Annual Study Conference of the United Kingdom Reading Association, Nottingham, 1969, 42–63.

26. Metfessel, Newton S., and Seng, Mark W., "Correlates with the School Success and Failure of Economically Disadvantaged Children," in *Reading for the Disadvantaged,* Thomas D. Horn, ed. New York: Harcourt Brace Jovanovich, 1970, 75–96.

27. National Education Association, "Reading Instruction in Secondary Schools," *Research Bulletin,* 20 (January 1942), 14–16.

28. Philion, William L. E., and Galloway, Charles G., "Indian Children and the Reading Program," *Journal of Reading,* 12 (April 1969), 553–560.

29. Ramsey, Wallace, "Which School System Gets the Best Results in Reading?" *Journal of Reading Behavior,* 1 (Summer 1969), 74–80.

30. Reissman, Frank, *Helping the Disadvantaged Pupil To Learn More Easily.* Englewood Cliffs, N.J.: Prentice-Hall, Inc., 1966.

31. Robinson, H. Alan, "Reliability of Measures Related to Reading Success of Average, Disadvantaged and Advantaged Children," *Reading Teacher,* 20 (December 1966), 203–208.

32. Ruddell, Robert B., *Innovations in Reading-Language Instruction.* Englewood Cliffs, N.J.: Prentice-Hall, Inc., 1974.

33. Rystrom, Richard, "Linguistics and the Teaching of Reading," *Journal of Reading Behavior,* 4 (Winter 1971–1972), 34–39.

34. Samuels, S. Jay, "The Psychology of Language,"

Review of Educational Research, 37 (April 1967), 109–119.

35. Sheldon, William D., "Children's Experiences in Reading," in *Children and the Language Arts,* Vergil E. Herrick and Leland B. Jacobs, eds. Englewood Cliffs, N.J.: Prentice-Hall, Inc., 1955, 172–191.

36. Singer, Harry, and Ruddell, Robert B., eds., *Theoretical Models and Processes of Reading.* Newark, Del.: International Reading Association, 1970.

37. Smith, Frank, and Goodman, Kenneth S., "On the Psycholinguistic Method of Teaching Reading," *Elementary School Journal,* 71 (January 1971), 177–181.

38. Taylor, Stanford E., *Eye-Movement Photography with the Reading Eye.* Huntington, N.Y.: Educational Developmental Laboratories, 1958.

39. Venezky, R., *Nonstandard Language and Reading.* Madison, Wis.: Wisconsin Research and Development Center for Cognitive Learning, 1970.

40. Vernon, M. D., "The Perceptual Process in Reading," *Reading Teacher,* 13 (October 1959), 2–8.

41. Vernon, M. D., *The Psychology of Perception.* Baltimore, Md.: Penguin Books, 1962.

42. Warrington, Elizabeth K., "The Incidence of Verbal Disability Associated with Retardation in Reading," *Neuropsychologia,* 5 (1967), 175–179.

43. Weber, Rose-Marie, "Some Reservations on the Significance of Dialect in the Acquisition of Reading," in *Reading Goals for the Disadvantaged,* J. Allen Figurel, ed. Newark, Del.: International Reading Association, 1970, 124–131.

44. Werner, E. E., Simonian, K., and Smith, R. D., "Reading Achievement, Language Functioning and Perceptual Motor Development of 10 and 11 Year-olds," *Perceptual and Motor Skills,* 25 (1967), 409–420.

45. Wheat, Thomas E., and Edmond, Rose Mary, "An Analysis of the Concept of Comprehension," paper presented at the National Reading Conference, St. Petersburg, Fla., December 1975.

46. "World Education and Communication Seen Through Statistics," *Unesco Chronicle,* 18 (February 1972), 74–76.

PART
II

READING PRACTICES
CURRENTLY IN USE

2
Using the Basal
Reader Approach

PREVIEW

Perhaps because of its almost universal use in America, the basal reading program is the target of much criticism and abuse. Every self-appointed expert who appears on the educational horizon with his unique concept of the reading process feels obliged to attack this established approach in order to find some foundation for his own ideas. Some of these criticisms are undoubtedly justified, for at the hands of many teachers the program has become a stereotyped and discouraging experience for some pupils. Few teachers are conscious of the inherent limitations in submitting all pupils to basically the same group of reading experiences, varying perhaps only the pace of presentation. Even fewer teachers realize that the methods of learning emphasized in the program are not equally effective for all pupils, and that, in fact, their nature predestines some children to failure. How many basal teachers attribute pupil failure to their own disinclination to adapt their methods to differing pupil aptitudes? How many basal teachers attempt to discover through what medium—visual, auditory, kinesthetic, or multisensory—a failing pupil might learn more readily?

At the same time, there can be little doubt that if used intelligently, the basal program is relatively effective for a large proportion of pupils. Its highly complex structure represents the end product of more than one hundred years of experimentation, trial and error, and gradual improvement in materials and techniques of instruction. But since the basal program is not yet perfect nor any more effective than its users permit it to be, we believe that an objective, critical evaluation is needed.

The first series of what might be called basal readers appeared in America in 1790 under the authorship of Noah Webster. Prior to this time schools tended to use the same book at all grades, such as *The New England Primer* and similar books. Soon other authors followed Webster's example, but it was not until 1840 that the idea of graded readers was developed in the McGuffey series. This author controlled the difficulty of his books, he believed, by the length of words in stories. The opening book used only two- or three-letter words and longer words were gradually introduced in later books. Supplementary readers were introduced about fifty years later, in 1890, and they took the form of alphabetic or phonic systems, sentence or story methods, or literary readers. Little of the content of these early books had any relationship to children's life experiences. More often the books contained moralistic, religious, patriotic, or oratorical materials obviously intended to inculcate the proper values of life in the children.

Until about 1910 practically all classroom reading was oral, despite the criticisms of such observers as Horace Greeley that children were being trained to read without any real comprehension. But the discovery that silent reading rate and comprehension were definitely superior to that obtained in oral reading produced a dramatic change in teaching procedures. This new emphasis on silent reading necessitated such a different type of training for teachers that some sort of guide had to be devised for them. Thus, by necessity, teachers' manuals to accompany the readers were written to help teachers to present this new mode of learning. The emphasis on silent reading and, therefore, on independent activities demanded some means of assessing and directing children in seatwork. As a result, workbook exercises, first as single games and later in bound form, were invented. The woodcuts and reproduction of famous paintings common to the early readers were gradually replaced about 1890 by colored illustrations more closely related to the content.

Today the coordinated series of textbook, workbooks, and manuals known as a basal reading series undoubtedly forms the core of the American reading program. A survey of 1300 teachers sampled throughout the country indicates that 95 to 98 percent of primary teachers and at least 80 percent of intermediate-grade teachers use basal readers every school day. For example, a New England survey in six states indicates that the manual for a basal series is used as the basis of the reading program in 95 percent of the classrooms. About 20 percent also use a guide developed within the school system as their basis.*

In fact, the basal reader is the only instructional material in perhaps more than half of American classrooms (9). Nor is the extent of their use peculiar to American schools, for surveys in England indicate that 82 percent of the schools

*New England Educational Assessment Project, *Reading Instruction in New England's Public Schools,* ERIC/CRIER ED 032 996, 1969.

use a single basal, while the remainder use two or more such programs, as well as teacher-made materials. A group of instructional aids which receives such almost-universal acceptance certainly deserves our most serious consideration and evaluation.

USE OF BASAL READERS

Until about 1965, vocabulary control took the form of carrying forward or repeating practically every word presented in any reader in all subsequent books of the series; severely limiting the total number of new words or the rate of introduction of new words per page or per running words; and ensuring a high repetition of the basal vocabulary both in the readers and the accompanying workbooks, as well as in any parallel materials which were an integral part of the series. This vocabulary control showed a constant trend toward greater repetition and smaller vocabularies at every level for the preceding thirty years. For example, the primers published before 1928 presented an average vocabulary load of 369 words. By 1930–1931, the average primer had only 304 different words; and by 1936–1937, the number had dropped to 247. In a 1941 article by one of the authors it was noted that the range had decreased to 225–335 (34). By 1965, estimates ranged from 113 to 173 words. Thus the emphasis upon vocabulary control reduced the vocabulary burden in primary readers by 30 to 50 percent in three decades. Since that time, however, the trend has been reversed in most of the leading series, and a somewhat larger vocabulary is now being offered. For example, a 1974 report based on four prominent series published between 1960 and 1970 reported that the first-grade vocabulary ranged from 305 to 675 words.*

It is undoubtedly true that the use of an excessive number of unknown or difficult words will prevent the young learner from acquiring any fluency in reading. It will also interfere with the development of the normal pattern of progressive eye movements which is the visual component of the reading act, as we have pointed out. But, on the other hand, what was the justification for this constant reduction of the vocabulary of primary readers? No one really knows precisely how often words must be repeated for the average learner or how simple the material must actually be in order to ensure ease of learning for most children. No one knows whether basals are now simple enough or whether we had already passed this point in our efforts at vocabulary control, or whether the vocabulary should be increased.

It is probably true that slow learners need more repetition to ensure learning than do average learners, who, in turn, may need more repetitions than do rapid learners. Moreover, some early studies show that first graders who are introduced to a small, common vocabulary make better reading progress than do

*Leo V. Rodenborn and Earlene Washburn, "Some Implications of the New Basal Readers," *Elementary English*, 51 (September 1974), 885–888.

groups introduced to larger vocabularies. A small, controlled vocabulary tends to promote true reading in the sense that it is accompanied by meaning or reasoning, as opposed to a word-calling act. Very large, uncontrolled vocabularies tend to force children toward continual word analysis and word-by-word reading. These are a few of the sound justifications offered for the vocabulary control in basal readers.

Yet other studies we will discuss later raise some doubts about the use of highly repetitive materials. Is it the sheer repetition of a limited number of words which ensures success in reading above the first grade, or is this goal as readily accomplished by a variety of reading materials which includes a total vocabulary of reasonable size? Are the important beginning words of the primary grades learned best because they are repeated in the basal and supplementary basals, or are they learned because of the many associations built around them by a variety of visual, auditory, and language experiences? Is vocabulary control of great importance only at beginning stages and of decreasing significance at later primary- and intermediate-grade levels? Is vocabulary control closely related to the learning rates of children rather than essential for most children? Perhaps it is significant to note that the latest editions of some basal reading series are reversing this trend by increasing the breadth of the basal vocabulary.

Some of the same arguments used to justify teaching reading in the kindergarten are influencing the authors of the more recent basal series. They believe that children of today are more verbal; more widely experienced because of the mobility of the family, both in terms of residence and recreational travel; and have larger vocabularies due in part to televiewing experiences, and hence are capable of profiting from more broadly designed reading materials. As a result, newer series are lessening their vocabulary control dramatically. While aware of the limited learning capacities of young children, most authors are avoiding the carefully constructed, word-by-word count and substituting more original stories or those drawn from published children's literature. Control of the reading difficulty is ensured by readability formula analysis which enables monitoring of the breadth of vocabulary and the complexity of sentence structure.

There are at least three reasons which contradict the claim that a limited vocabulary is essential for the verbatim learning which is suposed to be the foundation of all future reading. First, certain studies show that average pupils who have advanced as far as the primer level spontaneously learn many words other than the basal vocabulary. Furthermore, the language facility and readiness of most pupils, as shown in their own speech vocabularies, are far in advance of the concept level of basal readers. It may be safely assumed that this spontaneous learning continues, and may even accelerate, throughout the child's school career. Second, except for a few hundred service words that recur frequently in practically all reading materials (mostly prepositions, conjunctions, verbs, and adverbs), there is hardly any such entity as an essential core or basal vocabulary.*

*As Groff points out (18), these service words, which are probably the only essential terms in any basal vocabulary, are readily available in any of a half-dozen recent word counts.

Numerous studies of the vocabularies of various basal series show very little overlap. For example, a recent survey by Selma E. Herr, cited by James M. Reid, found only 600 words used in all of the twelve series studied, out of a total of approximately 12,000 words. Furthermore, only 206 of the 12,000 words were introduced at the same grade level in more than one basal series. Apparently, each basal series has its own essential or core vocabulary that appears in no other series. How fundamental is a basal vocabulary which is not even required to read common supplementary basals?

Two research studies by Arthur I. Gates (*12,13*) point up a third reason against extreme vocabulary control. In his first study, some three hundred third-grade pupils, who were being taught by a basal reading method, were tested on their knowledge of the third- and fourth-grade vocabularies of their basal series. Gates discovered that on the average the pupils knew as many fourth-grade as third-grade words. Over half the pupils recognized practically all the third- and fourth-grade vocabularies. Even the poorest pupils recognized 90 percent as many fourth-grade words as they did third-grade. A second study by Gates (*12*) repeated this type of evaluation in two classes of average second graders. About 60 percent of the pupils knew 90 percent or more of the basal vocabulary to which they would be introduced in the first *four grades.* Seventy-five percent of the pupils knew at least 80 percent of this new vocabulary. Even the poorest 10 percent of the pupils had learned about half of the total vocabulary before they were supposed to. Can we now believe that in order to learn to read successfully, most pupils must be exposed to only a very small vocabulary in a piecemeal or spoon-feeding fashion?

This emphasis upon vocabulary control or the learning of words by sheer repetition is, in our opinion, faulty in several respects. First, the actual need for repetitions probably varies from child to child. We grant that a degree of overlearning (overrepetition?) may be sound, but must all children overlearn to much the same degree? Second, it is obvious that words are not learned simply because of the number of repetitions. Certain errors of usage in words persist all through the pupils' school career, as *their* for *there, two* for *too* for *to,* and the like. Words are not necessarily learned by repetition, for these are examples of words introduced in primary grades which are still used erroneously by college students. We will discuss the true nature of vocabulary growth at length later. Perhaps it will suffice here simply to point out that, contrary to the vocabulary control theory of basal readers, words are learned only by the building of a depth of varied associations with their meanings, pronunciation, usage, and the like—not mainly by repetition in simple contexts.

To keep the learning task reasonable, in terms of vocabulary and concept loads, recent series offer "levels" of books and other materials in graduated steps. In a series now in production, for example, there will be six levels in the kindergarten–first grade program. Three levels will offer readiness-reading training through the media of picture books, spirit masters, skill development workbooks, cassettes, and filmstrips. Following these introductory steps, three levels of similar aids plus readers will be used in the first grade. In the second, third, and subsequent grades, a collection of two levels per grade will be offered and enriched with a reading development kit and a language enrichment kit. These kits will function in lieu of supplementary readers in offering reading selections, skill development training, language development, listening training, and enrichment activities through printed matter, audiovisual aids, and games.

Among the justifications offered for these dramatic changes in the basic instructional tool are the elimination of rigidly graded and labeled materials and the consequent lockstep progress fostered by that arrangement; the provision for smaller, more frequent, less obvious steps in development; the provision for a multimedia, diversified body of instructional aids, each extending to a number of levels to permit individualized progress. In effect, these programs are rejecting the former dependence upon repetition of words to ensure learning to read and accepting instead the psycholinguistic emphasis upon obtaining meaning in reading, and enriching children's experiences and language facility through a wide variety of approaches.

These newer developments in basals have not yet effected all the changes in method and use of materials that their authors intend, since many school systems cling to the use of the older, graded series and, of course, because of the lag in educational practice behind current knowledge and theory. For this reason, in describing classroom procedures we are depending upon surveys and reports (8) that do not reflect the most modern arrangements. We shall describe, in general, what teachers are seen doing in the classroom and later comment upon the limitations of these practices which the newer series hope to eradicate.

The Method in First Grade

Following the use of a readiness test, a group intelligence test, a week or two of teacher observation, or some combination of these means of evaluation, the children are divided into groups according to the teacher's estimate of their probable progress. One group, considered relatively unready for reading instruction, will receive perhaps one to five weeks of prereading training. For a second group the readiness training may be abbreviated to just several weeks, and the mature groups may begin reading instruction after only a few days. Although some 83 percent of first-grade teachers believe that some children would benefit from substituting a full-year readiness program for formal instruction, administrative and parental pressures seldom permit this (9). Initial reading experiences may take the form of an experience story—a group composition of a "story" describing an experience of the group—within or outside the classroom. Phrases or sentences are offered by various pupils and coordinated by the teacher, who then writes them in manuscript on a large chart or the blackboard. The choice of words and the sentence structure are manipulated by the teacher to ensure simplicity and comprehension by all members of the group. Words, phrases, sentences, and the entire story are read several times by various members of the group, during the construction of the chart. The story may be used again on a number of occasions for individual or group reading.

Teachers vary, of course, in their initial approaches to beginning reading. Some may prefer to begin with the first preprimer in preference to experience charts, while others employ both types of materials in successive reading lessons. As the Columbia University survey shows (8), about 48 percent of first-grade teachers use the experience story approach once every two days or oftener, while another 33 percent claim to use charts many times during the year. These figures imply frequent use of the chart method by more than 80 percent of first-grade teachers. In addition to these more or less basic beginning steps, the average teacher will frequently incorporate some children's magazines or newspapers, will ensure daily use of the basal workbooks and teacher-prepared exercises, and, from time to time, may employ a film or filmstrip for the purpose of enriching the content of the basal program.

On the other hand, the average first-grade teacher does *not* usually employ any device for promoting the development of a normal eye-movement pattern, even for the group of immature pupils. She is not likely to use the films or filmstrips made available by the publisher of the basal series employed, despite their obvious relationships and values for reinforcement or motivation. The New England survey indicates that currently much emphasis is placed on phonics by 94 percent of teachers. At least three of every four teachers supplement the basal with phonics practice materials, and half of the teachers introduce materials of their own design.

According to Ralph C. Staiger's survey figures (37), about half of the first-grade teachers will stay quite closely to the materials of a single basal series, treating other basal books and general children's books as the basic sources of supplementary reading.

Two-thirds of primary teachers spend less than one hour per week on library activities and only an hour or two in independent reading or enrichment activities, despite classroom libraries of one to five books per child in over half the rooms, and nearby public libraries in a similar proportion.

We have already noted the deemphasis upon general configuration or details of the word outline at this level. The first-grade teacher may avoid these obvious clues to word recognition for fear of being accused of using a whole-word or look-and-guess method, a current criticism of our public school reading methods. On the other hand, most first-grade teachers do stress such word recognition techniques as context and picture clues, sounding out words from letters or letter combinations, and noting similar sounds in words and relating these to their representative letters.

The time devoted to reading instruction is usually two hours in the morning and another hour in the afternoon in first grade. In about a third of the classrooms, this time allotment is reduced to an hour in morning sessions and another hour in the afternoon.

The Method in Second and Third Grades

In the average second-or third-grade classroom, pupils are grouped presumably to permit greater recognition of individual differences, but actually, some would say, for convenience of the teacher. Despite the range of reading levels, which commonly extends over four or five grade levels, the almost universal practice is to form three reading groups: the *Bluebirds,* the *Redbirds,* and the *Buzzards,* or as one teacher frankly labeled this low group, the *Impossibles.* The low reading group usually includes about eight to nine pupils, while eleven to thirteen are placed in the middle and the high reading groups. All of these groups tend to remain approximately the same size throughout the school year *(19).* The groups allegedly are formed on the basis of reading ability, the three divisions probably corresponding to the teacher's belief that her pupils vary a total of three grades in reading levels despite the evidence in the information available to her. The results of standardized reading tests, the teacher's informal tests by having pupils read from various levels of materials, and perhaps the results of intelligence tests and last year's teacher's records, plus her own observations during the first week or so form the bases of the groupings which we find in about 90 percent of the second-and third-grade classrooms. Less than 5 percent of these primary teachers make any attempt to group children according to such recommended bases as social factors, interests, or need for specific training in important skills.

In many classrooms, each reading group may use a basal reader of a particular reading level. The low, middle, and high reading groups in a third-grade class, for example, may use second-, third-, and fourth-grade readers, respectively. The assumption is often made that this single level of instructional materials will suffice for each group. In reality, there is a distinct range of reading abilities in each group, particularly in the low and high reading groups. Bond and Tinker suggest that in the typical third-grade classroom the low group ranges from 1.4 to 2.7, while the high group varies from 3.3 to 5.0.* If there are real differences in difficulty between first- and second-grade readers, then certainly a second-grade selection is inappropriate for many of the low group. Similarly, a fourth-grade reader will fail to challenge a number of the high reading group. Thus unless the teacher recognizes the range of reading levels of the pupils in each group that she has formed, she may well only partially achieve the goal of providing for individual differences.

The fact that the reading groups seem intended to simplify the task of the teacher is evident in the limited number of groups, despite the actual range of reading abilities, and in the tendency to retain the size and personnel of these groups throughout the school year. Groff's survey of grouping practices *(19)* shows that in a thirteen-week period only about one-third of pupils are shifted from their original reading group placement. Practically all of these shifts occur in the first two to four weeks, indicating that they are due to quick revisions of the

---

* Guy L. Bond and Miles A. Tinker, *Reading Difficulties—Their Diagnosis and Correction* (New York: Macmillan Publishing Co., Inc., 1960).

teacher's initial judgment rather than to any developmental changes in pupil progress.

During the daily one or two reading periods, the teacher works separately with each reading group, often in a circle reading situation. While the teacher is engaged with one group in this fashion, the other groups pursue a variety of activities. Most frequently these activities are related to the portion of the reader already reviewed by the teacher, such as completing the workbook exercises, writing an experience chart, or rereading the story. These activities are almost always subsequent to their circle reading situation. Children are almost never allowed to read ahead in the daily lessons. Pupils incapable of such independent study activities may be told to complete a relevant drawing, engage in a picture word game, study their number work, or perform other such distantly related tasks. If we may judge from the usual classroom, the other groups' activities are not always closely related to their reading progress.

Perhaps the best picture of the basal reader approach may be conveyed by some description of the average, everyday reading activities which may be seen in classrooms using this method. Actual observation of the basal reader lesson is probably a more realistic way of recognizing all that is involved. But since we cannot take the reader to such a classroom, we must adopt the second-best course. We have attempted to describe a typical basal reading lesson in a primary classroom by paraphrasing the procedures outlined in a number of teachers' manuals.

Most reading units are outlined in four or five major steps in the manuals. The first of these involves introduction to the new vocabulary and concepts of the unit or story. The purpose and nature of this step varies greatly in certain recent series, as the reader will discover. Following this introduction, most series go to the guided silent reading, based upon purposes for reading evolved by both teacher and pupils. A few series then suggest oral reading as a follow-up to the silent reading purposes. Recent series tend to play down the use of oral reading to this extent, preferring a guided thinking in silent reading emphasis. A third major step is the stress upon skill-building exercises which all series employ. The emphasis varies, of course, from one grade level to the next, but this step is an important segment of every plan. The final step includes supplementary activities for enrichment and motivational purposes.

Typical Basal Primary Reading Lesson

Introduction of Vocabulary (Establishing Background, Preparation for Reading)

The new words of the story or unit are presented by—
1. Using the word cards supplied by the publisher or writing them on the blackboard in a list or in sentences; having children read or point out words, phrases, sentences.

2. Reacting to their meanings by questions, prereading discussion of the story or children's related experiences; that is, weave new words into contextual settings.
3. Pointing out their phonic, structural, or configuration characteristics, in keeping with the pupils' status in such skills, that is, by taking into account number of syllables, presence of phonic rule, the base word or root, and the affixes, differences in shapes, etc.
4. Reviewing briefly the familiar word recognition techniques or system of steps the pupils may employ with any unknown words they will meet in the story, that is, by distinguishing between long and short vowel sounds, recognizing a base word in a derived form, etc.
5. Establishing some experiential background when beginning a new unit or topic, by a related film, filmstrip, the pictures or selections read to or by the children. Into the discussions of these, weave the ideas, words, and concepts to be read in the unit.
6. Reviewing old vocabulary by word cards, blackboard presentation, as in steps 1 and 3.

Silent Reading (Guided Reading, Guiding Interpretation, Developing Pupil Purposes)

1. Create prereading practice in—
   (a) Locating information—finding title and page in table of contents; finding names of principal characters, or locale of story from title; for example, "Where does the title say this story took place?"
   (b) Drawing inferences—about the nature of the story from the title; identifying facts about the setting, time, characters, dress, living conditions, habitat, etc., from inspection of the introductory picture.
   (c) Setting a purpose for the reading—by raising simple questions about action, characters, sequence, etc., which will be answered by the reading of the first portion of the story; same for succeeding portions. Examples—"What is the name of the boy mentioned in the first paragraph? Who is he? Have you heard of him before?" or "Read the second paragraph and be ready to tell how to go from Bobby's home to his grandfather's farm."
      Vary the type of prereading questions to emphasize different skills, as gathering information, making judgments, finding a specific detail, summarizing a main idea, verifying an inference, seeing cause–effect relationships, visualizing action, and anticipating outcomes.
2. Read each portion of the story; wait for class discussion of the answers to the prereading question; listen to the next leading question; then read on.
3. If children request assistance in dealing with any words in the story, help them to apply their own word attack skills, rather than *simply telling them.* Urge them to use the context to derive a logical word, or the initial consonant sound or other phonic elements they already know, or a picture clue, or a structural clue.

Oral Reading (Purposeful Rereading, Guiding Interpretation)

1. Verification of facts—"Find and read the paragraph that proves Bobby's home was not far from his grandfather's farm."
2. Locating specific details—"Find and read each paragraph that tells the things Bobby saw on the way to his grandfather's farm."

3. Vocabulary review—"Whoever can read this new word (pointing to list on blackboard) may read page 86 for us."
4. Oral expression—"Do you think Happy Town is a pretty town? Find the sentences that tell how pretty it is."
5. Relating sequences—"Find and read the part of the story that tells what happened to Bobby at the top of the hill."
6. Dramatization—have children choose parts and read or dramatize the conversation between these characters.
7. Encouragement of expression and intonation—have pupils select and read appropriately various types of sentences: demands, requests, questions, exclamations, and poetry.
8. Preparation to read a story to the class—prepare a group of children for presentation by stressing the need to "talk like real people, show how you feel by your voice, read in complete sentences rather than line by line."
9. Use of oral reading to answer any of the prereading questions proposed earlier in the lesson.

Skill Building **(Word Recognition Techniques, Vocabulary Enrichment and Extension, Extending Competence, Related Comprehension and Vocabulary Building)**

1. Use new words of unit or previous story, review known phonic and structural elements. Use blackboard, word, or letter cards for presentation.
2. Teach new phonic or structural elements, such as the long sound of *e,* as these occur in the new vocabulary, by blackboard exercises.
3. Use related pages in the workbook or activity book to practice or supplement the skills stressed in the daily lesson.
4. Give training in careful reading of pictures (picture clues) by asking a variety of questions about pictures in text and groups of pictures collected by teacher or pupils.
5. Try to build word associations to new vocabulary, and a variety of meanings for each, by discussion, blackboard exercises, and the like.
6. Give practice in using synonyms, homonyms, descriptive phrases (similes and metaphors) as related to new vocabulary. Use teacher's sentences or those drawn from the text as sources of practice at blackboard or desk.

Supplementary Activities **(Enrichment Activities, Culminating Activities, Extending Interests)**

1. Read selections related to the content of the current unit or story in parallel readers of the same series, other basal readers, trade books, literary readers correlated with the basal.
2. Use the sequentially arranged learning activities in a kit supplied by the publisher or made by the teacher.
3. Administer progress or end-of-unit test in the activity book or workbook. Or, use such criterion-referenced tests as supplied by the publisher. Evaluate child's oral reading errors in individual oral reading test. Check progress in sight vocabulary, word attack, and comprehension skills by other tests.
4. Use informal dramatization of a story, choral speaking, rhymes, jingles, and poetry

to help develop normal expression in reading and to overcome the tendency to word-by-word naming or word calling.

5. Use recordings, films, filmstrips, and other related materials as listed in the manual to enrich the child's background for each unit or story.
6. Expand the meanings of a story or unit, as one on pets, by an experience story composed by the group, "How To Take Care of a Pet," or by individual children, "My Pet"; drawing or cutting out pictures to accompany these stories; constructing clay or papier mâché models of their pets; making a class booklet on caring for a classroom pet; making a mural or frieze on our pets; arranging pictures and news articles on a bulletin board; inviting a zoo attendant or pet store manager to talk to the class; taking a trip to a nearby pet shop; making hand puppets to present a dramatization of a conversation between two pets; assembling a series of children's pictures to be displayed on a TV or movie scroll; making model animals of paper, yarn, pipe cleaners, and spools.

In contrast to the first-grade reading program, a number of new trends or emphases appear in the other primary grades (9). Emphasis on reading skills is extended to the reading matter encountered in the areas of social science, science, and English by the average teacher. The use of experience stories, teacher-prepared worksheets, and supplementary basal readers is no longer usual in the average classroom. Use of the school or public library for recreational or supplementary reading becomes definitely more frequent. Emphasis upon phonics increases markedly, as shown by the frequent use of a special phonics workbook in almost 40 percent of the classrooms, and by increasing mention of stress upon letter sounds, phonic analysis of words, and phonic rules. Other practices found in marked frequency at these levels are the request to the children to write original stories based on experience or imagination, the study of synonyms and antonyms, and a questionable effort to induce children to look for small words within longer ones as an aid to recognition. Unfortunately, when common words seem to appear within other words, they seldom retain their original pronunciation. For example, the word *in* is no longer that word in such larger words as *ringing, line, ninety,* and *define.* In fact, one research study indicates that short, simple words more often than not vary from their usual pronunciation when combined in larger words.

Comments

The real degree of success of this primary reading program is a matter of acrid debate among various authorities (36). Estimates of the proportion of children failing to achieve sufficient reading skill to be able to meet the demands of the intermediate grades are around 15 to 25 percent (39). Whether it is possible under any circumstances for all children in any grade to be taught in such a manner that they would universally meet the standards of the next grade level is, of course, highly questionable. But a great many critics of current reading instruction feel that, first, too great a proportion of children are unprepared for each successive year; second, many pupils, particularly those of greater intelligence, should be offered a richer, more challenging program; and, third, the primary program does not adequately prepare children to use their reading skills effectively in the content-field reading characteristic of the intermediate grades.

Many other criticisms really reflect the inadequate training and insecurity of some teachers rather than inherent faults in the primary basal program. Among these are use of the basals not as the core but as the whole of the reading program, overdependence upon the workbooks for the teaching of skills, excessive oral reading without any real purposes, and a perfectionistic attitude toward the learning of the basal vocabulary (34). There is undoubtedly much to be done to improve both the basal program and teacher's application of it, as we shall point out.

The fact that a primary reading program centered around a basal series need not be stereotyped is shown in observation of a wide variety of such programs. Among these are:

1. Using the basal books from the very beginning.
2. Using the basic text after initial instruction in teacher-made materials. The basal serves to test the development of skills and for practice in relatively easy material.
3. Using the basals in exact consecutive order.
4. Using the basals through the primer and then turning to a variety of preprimers from other basal series. Repeating this use of an easier level basal material for extended reading at the conclusion of the first, or second, or third reader. There is little difference in final reading achievements, according to some studies, when broad supplementary reading is introduced at any of these levels.
5. Centering reading around experience units or interest units with readings selected from a variety of basals and trade books.
6. Continuing extensive use of experience stories throughout the primary period, as supplemental to the basals.
7. Using basals for the low reading group and, perhaps, for the average but substituting individualized, self-selected reading in the high reading group.

The Method in Intermediate Grades

Like the primary teacher, the intermediate-grade teacher frequently supplements the program with magazines and newspapers, uses the school or public library with her pupils, employs films or filmstrips a number of times for enrichment purposes, but does not utilize visual aids of these types that are specifically correlated with the basal series. She gives much less attention to training in word recognition through phonic, context, or picture clues, emphasizing rather the structural analysis of words by syllabication and word parts such as roots and affixes. The average intermediate-grade teacher devotes less time to direct instruction in reading, averaging 6 to 10 hours per week or less, with a larger proportion of this instruction being given to reading in science, social science, and English textbooks. She makes less use of the basal workbooks, although about 60 percent of these classrooms employ this tool every day or two. Teacher-planned exercise materials are used frequently in only about one-third of the classrooms, but special workbooks for phonics training are discontinued in most (in about 70 percent) (9). There are apparently conflicting opinions regarding the ways in which the reading program should be expanded in these grades. In about half of the classrooms children are introduced to a book club while at the same time the frequent use of trade books as part of the program increases slightly. This may reflect a tendency to regard recreational reading as an independent type of child activity rather than an integral part of the instructional program. For, actually, the average teacher allows less than an hour per week for library activities and a similar amount for independent reading or enrichment activities.

Dictionaries become a common aid to vocabulary building, and the intermediate-grade child is also introduced to a variety of other reference books, such as encyclopedias, almanacs, and yearbooks. Instruction in reading and study techniques such as outlining, summarizing, preparing book reports, and skimming is begun on a very simple level in the average classroom. However, little attention is given to improving such skills as recognizing bias or propaganda, reading or learning poetry, or choral reading. Oral reading from the basals or trade books decreases a great deal, although it is still frequently used in about half of the intermediate-grade classrooms (9). Locational skills receive much attention, while only about half of the teachers give some attention to organizational skills, critical readings, or the use of graphic materials such as maps, charts, and graphs.

The three-reading group plan strongly persists in these grades despite the fact that the common range of reading abilities is often as great as eight grades or more. The bases for grouping by reading ability continue to be some combination of standardized, criterion-referenced, or informal reading tests, observation, previous reading records, and, sometimes, the result of a group intelligence test. Perhaps at these levels, experimentation with various forms of grouping for reading instruction is more widespread than in the earlier years. Both teachers and administrators may feel freer to modify the program because of the greater maturity of the pupils and their subsequent ability to work more independently for longer periods of time. Thus we find various grouping plans which attempt to solve the problems of class size and individual differences in homogeneous grouping of whole classes by reading ability or intelligence or both. Another effort involves intraclass grouping in which children of similar reading level are drawn from several classes of the same grade level or from several grade levels. These children receive their instruction in one large group and, usually, from some teacher other than their own.

Comments

Despite the absurd claims of some critics of the modern reading program, and the limiting effects of the vocabulary control in basal readers, the average child does grow considerably in breadth and depth of sight and meaning vocabularies. Each intermediate-grade basal introduces the child to another 1200 to 1500 words beyond the primary reading vocabulary, which numbers approximately 2500 words.

Supporters of the basal reading program, and they are a majority among prominent reading authorities, agree on the following advantages of the basal reading program. We may have some mental reservations about some of these claims, for in the hands of uncreative or uninspired teachers their values may be lost. But these are undoubtedly the outstanding features of the program, at least in the intentions of the authors.

The basal reading series offers:

1. Systematic guidance in the development of recognition, comprehension, and vocabulary skills by carefully planned sequential learning. Modern educational psychology tells us that such a system is superior to trial and error or to incidental learning, or, probably, to a program planned by the teacher.
2. Materials based upon common child experiences and the well-known interests of children. Thus it provides for a common core of experiences for the entire group.
3. A program that is greatly superior to any that a modern teacher, in view of the breadth of her professional preparation or, rather, the lack of breadth in the area of reading methodology, could possibly create.
4. Techniques and materials for determining the readiness of the child to learn to read or to proceed from step to step by easy stages.
5. A basic or core vocabulary that is essential to any beginning or subsequent reading.
6. Materials that are carefully scaled in difficulty, sequentially arranged to promote learning, and more or less controlled in vocabulary. Thus the program ensures enjoyable and successful growth of the child's reading abilities. No other available body of reading materials possesses these characteristics.
7. Materials that follow the best knowledge in such aspects as typography, format, and physical readability.
8. A well-rounded selection of reading experiences. It includes both recreational and work-type reading, poetry and prose, factual and fictional matter, and informational and entertaining materials that extend the child's ideas and knowledge in many fields.

LIMITATIONS OF THE BASAL READER APPROACH

Readiness Program

In Chapter 6 we raise a number of questions about the validity of the readiness program usually outlined in the basal series. We note the inadequacy of most so-called "readiness tests"—their lack of diagnostic information, their weakness in predicting reading success, their failure to evaluate the really significant readiness factors, and their overdependence upon intelligence and preschool learning as predictive elements. We accuse the basal readiness program of recommending superficial and misleading methods of visual screening and of ignoring the implications of recent research on the importance of visual perception. In addition, the basal readiness program has not succeeded in clarifying the direct association between auditory training and word recognition.

This misconception of the basic theory underlying reading readiness promotes a number of other faulty classroom procedures. As Heilman (*21*, p. 17) notes, "Teachers rarely withhold basal reading materials from the least ready for more than a few weeks after the rest of the class has started to use them." Thus the entire purpose of readiness activities to prepare children for the act of reading and to facilitate the transition from a nonreading stage to beginning reading is defeated. For many teachers, readiness is simply a kind of workbook activity which happens to be employed prior to formal reading.

Even when teachers do comprehend the intrinsic purpose of readiness training, there is some doubt about the validity of the training materials currently offered. The experiments of Blakely and Shadle (*7*) and Ploghoft (*30*) agree in implying an inferior validity for common readiness workbooks. Goins' study (*15*) of the significance of visual perception led her to a similar conclusion. Other experiments that we have described on the types of visual perception training materials show no clear superiority for those in readiness workbooks. Even if we accept Allen's interpretation (*1*) of the values of various current workbook exercises, we note that these have only moderate relationships to success in beginning reading. We have gone beyond the point of accepting the readiness materials common to basal series simply because they seem to give some help to some children. A reorganization of these materials in terms of the optometric and psychological research information now available appears to be demanded, perhaps in the manner offered in Chapters 6 and 7.

Content of the Basals

Let us interject the comments of Otto Klineberg, a distinguished social psychologist, who has analyzed the content of such readers. Taken at random from his article, here are examples of the concepts of American society, of other peoples, and of the world as it is, as offered in current readers*:

> The American people are almost exclusively white or Caucasian. . . . North European in origin and appearance . . . almost exclusively, blondes . . . quite well-to-do.

> . . . South Europeans are organ grinders, peddlers, and fruit and vegetable vendors. . . . Either there are no Negroes, or they must not be mentioned.

* Otto Klineberg, "Life Is Fun in a Smiling, Fair-Skinned World," *Saturday Review,* 46 (February 16, 1963), 75–77, 87.

. . . a snowman laughs, animals talk to one another . . . trains converse, and so do airplanes and helicopters, cars and taxis. . . .

In fact, life in general is fun. . . . all is peaceful and happy . . . frustrations are rare and usually overcome quite easily. . . .

When, Klineberg asks, is the child helped to overcome these ethnocentric, animistic, anthropomorphic, social class barriers to true intellectual development? When is he to be exposed to curiosity-stimulating informational materials, or to making those distinctions which are "in harmony with the truth" of the world as it is?

Other observers point out that basal readers distort the reality of life not by invidious comparisons between cultures but by the almost complete omission of any culture except the upper-middle-class white group. Ethnic groups, except for the American Indian, are usually ignored; all adults are attractive, pleasant, well dressed, and kind. All children are clean, happy, kind, friendly, and honest, and more than adequately supplied with the world's goods. Nothing really unpleasant ever happens in the lives of the basal characters, and all are immediately rewarded for their obvious goodness. Do we really wish to encourage children to believe that life is like this? That everyone is generous, kind, and noble; that goodness is followed by extrinsic reward; that no problems in human relationships ever raise their unpleasant heads?

It is perhaps only human that any venture as widely accepted as the use of basal readers would be criticized by many who have not profited thereby. Moreover, much of the criticism of these books probably can be attributed to those who are simply chronic complainers against the status quo. On the other hand, there is an increasing volume of complaint from a wide variety of sources, even from within the ranks of those who have used or written basal reading materials. It is time that we listen to, and evaluate, this criticism.

The reader will note that many of these comments are directed against the manner in which basal readers are used rather than against the basal approach itself. There are some weaknesses in current basal programs to be sure. But most authors of basals have not made the grandiose assumptions of which they are accused. Perhaps their major mistakes were in preparing so highly organized a body of materials that partially trained teachers using the system were incapable of recognizing its weaknesses as well as it strengths.

A primary focus in the criticism of basal readers is upon their content. The remarks of James M. Reid, formerly school editor for Harcourt Brace Jovanovich, made as a result of observations in classrooms and interviews with more than one hundred persons concerned with this problem are sharply pertinent*:

A good many people wince over the lack of style in the writing of basal readers. Lack of a good writing style in itself kills interest. A good style helps to sweep a learner along. "So many of the stories are ridiculous," the pupils themselves say. And there is too much busy work in most of the basal readers. Even casual inspec-

---

* James M. Reid, "Report on Elementary Reading," p. 12. Quoted by permission of the author and Harcourt, Brace & World, Inc.

tion of the readers reveals that they attempt to be all things to all pupils and rarely touch the hot spots of interest. Perhaps basal readers cannot be made exciting and interesting because of the many restrictions of vocabulary control, repetitions and fear of offending any group—responsibilities they have taken on themselves. But one wonders.

It seems fair to say, however, that today's school readers are too much watered down and do not offer enough challenge to today's good pupils. At the very minimum, the basic reading series have sacrificed too much literary quality to the "necessities" of word control. As the poet Housman wrote, "Terence, this is stupid stuff."

Perhaps these are sharp words, but they are echoed around the country. By a noted child development specialist and author (25):

The penalty the child pays for becoming Six is to be fed a two-year-old diet.

By a large number of college teachers of reading*:

Further changes in basal readers would include an overall upgrading of content so that the material would more nearly coincide with a child's speaking and listening vocabulary at the various stages of his development. In addition, it was pointed out that basal readers in the future should include more material designed to capitalize on boys' interests in the primary grades (p. 66).

From Jack A. Holmes, analyst of the substrata factors underlying reading ability†:

The basal program is weakest in reinforcing the child's range of information. The series merely repeats the homely concepts of vocabulary already known to the child. The series never stretches the child's mind, never prepares him for the wide range of information he must know to read, to learn or to deal with the conceptualizations needed for power of reading. The child needs a wider vocabulary in his early reading, as well as more, deeper and wider concepts.

And, finally, from a noted reading consultant and researcher‡:

A growing body of professional opinion points out that we are in danger of producing skillful readers of basal reading series to the detriment of our larger aim. We may be handicapped, in other words, by the very virtues of these series—their carefully controlled vocabulary, their systematic attention to word attack skills

---

* Mary C. Austin et al., *The Torch Lighters: Tomorrow's Teachers of Reading* (Cambridge, Mass.: Harvard University Press, 1961). Quoted by permission of the author and publisher.

† Jack Holmes in "Symposium: Viewpoints on Comprehension," *Eleventh Yearbook National Reading Conference,* Texas Christain University, Fort Worth, Tex., December 7, 1961. Quoted by permission of the author.

‡ Agatha Townsend, "What Research Says to the Reading Teacher," *Reading Teacher,* 15 (May 1962), 459-462. Quoted by permission of the author and the editor, Russell G. Stauffer.

developed through familiar words, their provision for spaced practice through basic reader, workbooks, and teacher's manual (p. 459).

Over the years, there have been many other criticisms of the content of the average basal reading series from various sources. Among the faults decried are:

1. The distortion of reality of life not by invidious comparisons between cultures and classes but by the almost complete omission of any culture other than that of the upper-middle-class white group. The family is always presented as cheerful, prosperous, cohesive, harmonious, and as a complete unit. Father and mother have separate types of work (if, indeed, women at work are represented at all) and recreation. In fact, no recreational pursuits for women are represented since all are supposed to be very busy mothers, housekeepers, or teachers. Relations among children are friendly, subdued, and cooperative, with no racial interaction or conflict (17).

2. If present at all, blacks do not interact with whites; are engaged in unskilled labor or as servants; look more like suntanned whites than blacks; seldom occupy a major role in a story, and are often set apart from the milieu of the main characters by using dialect to represent their speech (4,28). The American Indian is only occasionally present, and then as a historical fact from past history rather than a living race. If portrayed in today's settings, the Indian male's activities completely parallel those of his white brothers, unless, of course, he is stereotyped as a chief or medicine man. The Indian woman is conspiciously absent. In fact, there are more animals than nonwhites in some basal series (29).

3. The world of work is unrealistically reflected in a number of respects. Professional and managerial occupations are markedly overrepresented; women are seldom portrayed in a variety of career roles; Asian Americans are depicted in careers typical of centuries ago or as they might function in countries other than the United States; career roles for other minority groups are stereotyped and extremely limited in number (8).

4. The relative roles of males and females, boys and girls are greatly distorted. Males are main characters three times as often as women and are occupied outside the home four times as often as women, when actually women form more than 40 percent of the working population. Boys are the main characters 70 to 75 percent of the time and are represented as such in more than two-thirds of the illustrations (16,38). Six times as many occupations are mentioned for males as for women. Father is the family leader; mother, the housekeeper and shopper. In one analysis, in only one of 734 stories was the mother the breadwinner (11).

It should be noted that most of this criticism of sexism in basal readers is based on surveys of books published prior to the 1970s.* The authors and publishers of several recent series have certainly been affected by this barrage of critical comments and many are attempting to make appropriate changes in this aspect of the content. It remains to be seen, however, how much real change will appear in the basals of the late 1970s and the 1980s.

* Anne Stevens Fishman, "A Criticism of Sexism in Elementary Readers," *Reading Teacher, 29* (February 1976), 443–445.

5. The content of the stories in basals is in great contrast to studies of children's actual reading interests. Children prefer stories about pranks, peer interaction, animals, make-believe, nature, and science. Boys prefer boy-activity stories; girls show no sex preferences and would read both boy- and girl-centered tales. The major diet offered by the average basal is child and child–adult interactions, "good children," the activities of six- to seven-year-olds without older brothers and sisters, and too much personal adventure and historical adventure, all of which are low in children's own choices of books (25,31).

6. Basal readers are commonly lavishly illustrated with expensive four-color pictures. The use of color actually adds little or nothing to recall of information over black and white, nor does it have any interaction with race or economic status. But it does contribute substantially to the cost of the book (27). Pictures do help in initial learning, if they are also present in posttesting. But when pictures are omitted from the test, a group taught without pictures was superior. Pictures used in initial word recognition training should be dispensed with as soon as possible, particularly for poorer readers (32). In terms of comprehension, illustrations highly relevant to the text are helpful when reading materials well within the child's reading level but not in difficult material. In the final analysis, the value of illustrations depends heavily upon the manner in which they are used to support the concepts underlying the vocabulary of the story by the pupils under teacher guidance (32).

The content of the basal reader has been criticized not only for these faults but also for its failure to provide an adequate foundation for the reading tasks of the content fields. Training in the reading of such materials as maps, charts, diagrams, and arithmetic problems is lacking in most basal series. Library skills—the proper use of reference materials, encyclopedias, almanacs, and the like—are hardly touched upon. Such organizing skills as summarizing, notetaking, and outlining are taught at so simple a level that they fail to function in the pupil's postelementary school life. The whole art of studying textbooks of various types and kinds with their varying demands for different rates of reading and degrees and types of comprehension is almost ignored. Similarly, because of the lack of training in samples of science, social science, natural history, and mathematical materials the pupil is not helped to differentiate the kinds of thinking demanded, the varying purposes inherent in these materials, and to make the constant readjustments needed.

Some basal authors would probably answer these criticisms by pointing out that their series do not intend to supply training in applied reading in the content fields. They argue that this type of preparatory training is not a fundamental goal of the basal program but should be accomplished during classroom use of the content textbooks. The basal program, its authors say, cannot be expected to supply complete training in all aspects of the reading program—namely, in content field skills and in recreational reading. Its task is to supply the impetus for the development of what are called basic reading skills. This is perhaps a reasonable defense but, in our opinion, it has one weakness. What skills are more basic for future academic success than training in content field reading?

The nature of the content of basals is not peculiar to America, however, for surveys of foreign beginning books give much the same picture. One analysis (23) of the readers of seventeen countries found that their greatest emphasis was upon family life; happy child–child and child–family relationships; and love, joy, and respect for parents. The patriotic theme, so strongly stressed during the crisis of World War II, has disappeared in most European readers, except in the Soviet Union. A few emphasize their cultural heritage through legends, folk tales, and similar content, or through religious themes.

The Basal Workbook

The actual contribution of workbooks to reading achievement is more apparent in the minds of their authors and classroom teachers than it is in the relevant research studies. Two articles report a study in Los Angeles in thirty-six classes in eighteen schools comparing reading scores under instruction with workbooks versus those with teacher-made materials (6,10). The basal workbook produced better vocabulary and comprehension scores in the second and third grades, on the average, and better comprehension in the fourth grade. In fifth and sixth grades there were no differences in reading skills with or without workbooks. In the first grade, as other studies also indicate (7,30), the nonworkbook classes were superior in both reading skills. When we read these studies carefully, however, we discover that most of the teachers did not like to prepare their own materials, including those who had to for the purposes of the experiment.

There is obviously truth on both sides of this question, for the crux of the matter is the way in which workbooks are used rather than the way they are constructed. For example, intelligent use would include varying amounts of teacher–pupil planning for the exercises and their evaluation. The true values cannot be achieved by routine, page-by-page use by all pupils. Rather, by using a variety of workbooks, disassembled and rearranged according to the skills stressed in a teacher-planned box, labeled for ready use by pupils, the ultimate values of such materials for diagnosis, enrichment, or reinforcement may be secured.

Teachers' comments and experts' opinions regarding workbooks have been sampled in a number of studies, including those we have mentioned above. Figure 2–1 (p. 62) summarizes the strengths and weaknesses of these tools, as seen by their users and critics.

Methods in the Basal System

In many schools, teachers employing the basal approach develop two undesirable practices—rigid structuring of three reading groups and excessive use of oral reading. These patterns are not necessarily suggested in the teachers' manual nor are they inherent in the basal approach. But somehow or other a large proportion of teachers gravitate toward these habits.

Strengths	Weaknesses
1. Stress sequential learning, help develop skills.	1. Are boringly factual.
2. Help to overcome effects of child absence.	2. Are limited in variety of materials (little science, geography, or human relations).
3. Aid in diagnosing difficulties.	3. Reflective thinking is sacrificed to unimportant objective responses (circles, lines, etc.).
4. Help test achievement.	
5. Offer opportunity for self-competition.	
6. Provide record of progress.	4. Emphasize mechanics; word recognition more often than comprehension.
7. Are more easily checked or graded.	
8. Save teacher time for preparation.	5. Often too hard for lower third of class, yet lacking in challenge for superior pupils.
9. Are prepared by skilled persons.	
10. Provide for extensive, effective drill.	6. Require much teacher time for checking, follow-up, and supervision.
11. Permit pupil check on own progress.	
12. Provide follow-up activities related to content of text.	7. May monopolize classroom time and leave none for creative activities.
13. Reinforce learning through repetition of vocabulary.	8. Not conducive to independent work habits.
	9. Poor in training of locational and organizing skills.
	10. Often lacking in clarity of directions and in adequate explanation of purpose.
	11. Tend to breed dependence on teacher.
	12. Offer monotonous, piecemeal approach.
	13. Disregard individual needs in attempting to provide material suitable to all.
	14. Develop skills in isolation from the reading act, yet assume transfer.
	15. Induce teachers to use in stereotyped, consecutive order.

FIGURE 2–1. *Evaluation of the Basal Reader Workbook*

Grouping.   There is nothing unsound in the practice of grouping children for instruction. On the contrary, grouping is economical of the teacher's planning and teaching time, fosters an *esprit* or group spirit among pupils, enables the teacher to work more intimately with a part of the class, and thus helps her to meet pupils' instructional needs. But in many classrooms there seems to be present a belief in the magic of number 3—three reading levels among the pupils, three reading groups, three levels of basal readers.

As we pointed out earlier, the average classroom above the first grade is very apt to show a greater range of reading levels than three grades. In fact, the higher the grade level, the greater the range of reading levels is apt to be. While the content of a second-grade basal reader may be reasonably suitable for a slow third-grade reading group, its structure and skill development may not be feasible for all the members of such a group. The slow reading group probably includes some pupils who read appropriately in high first-grade materials, as well as others who can perform adequately in beginning or high second-grade materials. If this range of ability is present, no one level of basal reader will suffice for all members of the group. First- and second-grade basal readers differ significantly in the rate of introduction of new words; the total number of different words; their demands for skill in phonic, structural, and contextual analysis; the complexity of the sentence patterns; the variety of alternative meanings of common words; and their assumptions about the children's experiential backgrounds. The pupils reading at the first-grade level and those at the second-grade level differ in these traits. We would conclude that the use of three reading groups using three levels of readers is not a satisfactory solution to the range of reading differences, particularly in the primary grades.

A survey of the reading practices in six New England states indicates that over two-thirds of teachers group within the classroom on the basis of general instructional level, not individual needs. The placement of the pupil is determined by his needs for specific skills in only 22 percent of the classes. Individualized instruction is utilized in only a minute proportion of classrooms. Grouping is commonly based, in order of frequency of use, on the previous book completed, skills tests, basal reader tests, and informal reading inventories. More than 70 percent of teachers in the New England area used one or several of these criteria in forming reading groups. This practice is in sharp contrast to the expressed belief of the same teachers that informal inventories and skills tests were the more reliable instruments for the purpose.

The social effects of this magical use of "3's" have other subtle effects upon pupil–teacher relationships and pupil self-concept. Teacher practices in grouping some 600 children were analyzed in terms of the pupils that the teachers preferred to teach (*26*). It became quite apparent that they preferred working with the better students, both boys and girls, in the top reading group. Poorer readers ranked lower in teacher preference, and thus tended to receive the least positive, inspiring lessons, despite their greater needs. Certainly, also, these pupils soon become aware of the teacher's attitude, and their feelings of rejection and inadequacy are reinforced.

Perhaps the most significant social implication of the failure of the three-reading-group plan is its inadequacy for the training of superior or gifted children, our future leaders. A. Sterl Artley, co-author of a leading basal series, deplores the tendency to underestimate the gifted pupil's capabilities and his needs for opportunities to do research reading, to develop reading maturity, and to find stimulating, challenging situations in reading (3). A study by Harvey L. Saxton (33) adds strength to this criticism. His investigation suggests that most superior readers do not need basals to achieve desired reading skills, although some certainly need directed, planned training to achieve their full potentials. Other articles reinforce this criticism of basals by pointing out the special reading problems of gifted children that are not met by the three-reading-group plan.

In our opinion, the entire concept of grouping children by reading levels is often based upon a false premise—that the results of an informal or standardized reading test reflect an accurate, overall picture of the child's reading abilities. Even at the primary reading levels, where differentiation of various reading skills is less, the average formal or informal reading test may yield only a superficial classification of pupils. The reading test usually completely ignores such highly significant determinants of pupil progress as the rate at which the child can learn new vocabulary; the effectiveness of his structural, phonic, and contextual word analysis skills; the breadth of his sight vocabulary; the depth and efficiency of his comprehension; and the quality of his comprehension when he is reading at different rates of speed. The reading test upon which grouping is based almost never yields such essential information as the extent of the child's dependence upon sheer memory for acquiring sight vocabulary, as contrasted with his use of other perceptual or analytic clues; the depth of his meaning vocabulary and his needs in experiential background as a foundation for multiplicity of meanings; the types of reading materials which appeal strongly to him; his efficiency in using reading as a tool to satisfy academic demands or personal and social needs. Furthermore, reading tests do not predict individual variations in the learning process such as spurts, plateaus, periods of acceleration, consolidation, or regression, which ultimately determine the nature of the pupil's progress. Nor do they usually yield information regarding the reasons for any of a number of reading difficulties.

The most disconcerting truth about commercial reading tests, in general, is that they do not reflect the actual level of the reading materials that the pupil can handle most effectively. This level or, more accurately, these levels of efficiency are determined by the constellation of the very reading skills that most tests fail to consider, as we have just pointed out. Perhaps the words of the psychologist Grace Arthur (2, p. vii) may be appropriate to this critical evaluation of grouping practices in the basal system:

> Group instruction presupposes similar intellectual needs among the members of the group to be taught. In order to profit from the instruction, all the members of the group must be ready to start at about the same point, be interested in the same type of material, and be able to learn by means of the same general methods.

Does the three-reading-group plan meet Arthur's criteria for group instruction or, indeed, any of the criteria we have suggested? Or it might be more truthful to say, as Heilman does (*21*, pp. 74–75):

> The curriculum of the school rests on the premise that children in a given classroom read at or near a particular level. Once the curriculum and graded reading materials have been determined, the tendency is to try to fit the learner to the materials. It is much easier to cling to an original false premise than it is to revise the curriculum and the grade level system to fit the facts of learner variability.

Some observers feel that while the teacher is engaged with a particular group, much time is wasted in the unsupervised groups. This apparent loss of efficiency may be due to the lack of maturity, or of training of the pupils in self-direction, or because of the omission of clear-cut directions by the teacher. Many teachers and pupils seem to believe that the oral reading done in the circle group is not only an essential procedure, but also the only true reading experience of the day. Perhaps this assumption explains the average teacher's lack of real concern about the learning value of the activities in which other groups engage (as shown by her rather casual planning of these supplementary activities).

The busywork of the unsupervised groups is seldom planned in detail by the joint action of the teacher and individual students or groups. The child's concepts of what he is trying to do, or exactly what he is supposed to be learning, are often quite vague. Most often he is not expected to maintain any records of his progress in a skill or of his independent reading. Nor is he given any means of self-evaluation of such progress. As some critics say, it appears that the teacher's only concern during this rather extended period of time is that the other groups keep themselves busy and quiet.

These descriptive generalizations regarding the ways in which group instruction functions in the daily basal reading lesson reflect, of course, the authors' interpretation of their firsthand observations in many classrooms. Certainly some teachers plan their groups' work more efficiently than this. On the other hand, others do not even pretend to differentiate their classes into groups. We have seen schools in a number of states where the use of a single reader for the entire class was not an isolated practice but common in every classroom in the system.

As we have admitted earlier, many of the criticisms of the basal reading program are really leveled at teacher practice more than at the series of books itself. At the same time, it must be recognized that some of these faulty practices are in a sense promoted by the nature of the system, and sometimes more directly by the authors. The very title of a basal reading series carries the implication that the material is almost absolutely essential for practically all children. Second, no series has ever attempted to provide for the actual range of reading levels within the average classroom, despite the fact that even authors of basals recognize this range. Some authors perpetuate the illusion that this range can be dealt with by using a three- or four-grade span of their readers, thus supporting the three-group practice. Although the manuals often speak of independent reading, and may even list some appropriate books, are these ever recommended as possible substitutes for the basal? How often is a teacher advised in the manuals to skip a portion of the reader with an advanced or rapidly learning group? Where is the suggestion that some of the children in almost any classroom need not read faithfully through a basal series story by story?

Oral Reading. Oral reading, in the basal reader program, has developed a number of most undesirable aspects which are supported and abetted by the very nature of the basal series. We know of no manual for a basal series which suggests these practices but believe they are a logical outcome of the overemphasis upon the importance of the basic vocabulary. One of these faulty practices is the round-robin or circle reading seen in most of today's classrooms. A reading group assembles in a semicircle around the teacher and the children take turns reading aloud to the group. All the children use the same book and attempt to follow silently as each pupil has his oral reading turn. About the only real purpose for this practice is to permit the teacher to observe the accuracy with which each pupil reads the words of the text. At worst, this practice violates the known fact that both oral reading and comprehension are superior when silent reading of a selection precedes oral. The relevant research indicates that this circle reading is probably one of the most effective devices yet discovered for practicing poor reading. What litterally happens in this almost universal technique is that the listeners are forced to attempt to follow and imitate the halting reading of the leader. As a result, as Gilbert (*14*) has shown, the children's reading performances are worse when reading in the circle than they would normally be. All the legitimate purposes of oral reading, which we will discuss in a subsequent chapter, are violated in the round-robin act. Other critics of this practice point out that this faulty oral reading does not contribute to reading development, contrary to most teachers' assumptions. Oral reading, as commonly practiced in the basal program, is really a word-calling rather than a thought-getting process. In fact, its excessive use may well retard the development of good silent reading habits, which are the real goal of all reading instruction. Despite these pointed criticisms, this type of oral reading continues to be practiced, perhaps because it makes so little demand upon teacher planning.

Oral reading may have values in the reading program if it is conceived of as a communication skill—a way of delivering information or entertainment to listeners. If this view prevails, each act of oral reading must be planned for a specific purpose: sharing materials, proving a point, clarifying an idea, presenting a play or a poem, or for some other purpose. In this view, the listener must be prepared for the oral reading so that he may realize its purpose, and the reader must be rehearsed so that he may be maximally effective. Constructive listening purposes will be clarified to the audience, discussion by them will be encouraged, and if information is the desired result, the questions will be addressed to the listeners, not to the reader. Within this framework of its function as a communication skill, oral reading is an essential part of the program.

Word Attack Skills.   Areas of sharp debate regarding the basal reading system have been its success and methods in teaching effective word attack skills. The system has been criticized for failing to teach phonic skills, for promoting sheer guessing as the sole method of word recognition, for overdependence upon a visual or sight-word method, and for teaching practices which actually rob children of the opportunity of using the word attack skills that they have been taught or that they have developed spontaneously.

As we have pointed out elsewhere, the bases for some of these criticisms are not only ill-founded and, in some cases, absurd, but they may also arise from personal rather than objective reasons. On the other hand, there are serious flaws in the basal program of word attack skills. Betts (5) says:

> Today there are too many first-grade classrooms in which the so-called "word method" of teaching *beginning* reading is used. When this so-called method is stripped of its "pedaguese," including the term sight words, it is merely a tell-the-child-the-word procedure. And telling isn't teaching! The word method, therefore, is a nothing-for-nothing proposition, emphasizing rote learning.

Betts is referring here to the common practice of delaying functional phonics during a large part of the first year until the child has learned a group of fifty to one hundred sight words. He does not point out that this practice is based on the indications of several early research studies which purported to show that training in phonics was ineffectual with children below a mental age of seven. The methods of teaching phonics have changed materially since that research and as a result its implications have become inappropriate today. Many recent phonics experiments, to which we will refer later in detail, show that functional, useful phonics can be taught during the entire first grade, or even during kindergarten. As a result, most of the recent basals offer a more functional phonic program in the first grade. Only one series, however, has extended it into the kindergarten.

Overdependence of both teacher and pupil upon the sight-word method of recognizing words only by their general configurations is promoted by another practice often seen in the average reading program. The presenting of the new vocabulary before the child reads the basal material is a practice recommended in many basal series. In our opinion, this procedure deprives children of most opportunities for the exercise of their word attack skills, even though structural and phonic elements in these words are emphasized in this prereading presentation. Thus the habit of a most primitive word recognition technique may be promoted by some of the common elements of the daily reading lesson, as well as by the tell-the-child-the-word habit that Betts decries. In contrast, MacKinnon (24) demonstrated that when primary school children were permitted complete independence of the teacher, they developed a high degree of word attack skill. In his experiment children in one group were never told a new word before they attempted the reading material, nor were they prompted by the teacher during the reading. Rather, they were constantly urged to attempt to recognize the word by their own efforts at structural, contextual, or phonic analysis. The result was that the children evolved a remarkable degree of independence and spontaneous word attack skill.

As shown by the statistics of most reading clinics, a large proportion of the children evidencing difficulties in reading are characterized by extremely weak word attack skills. They are almost completely ineffectual in phonic, contextual, or structural analysis of unknown words. Just how effective other pupils, who do not come to the attention of reading clinics, are in this respect no one really knows. As Dolch* says,

> First, we must admit that our group reading system is a rather dismal failure when it comes to teaching sounding. Sounding is supposed to be taught in the primary grades. But we find in the middle grades that half cannot sound, and so we have a sounding program in the middle grades. Still we find in high school that a fourth or a fifth of the children cannot sound. . . . The fact seems to be that having a small group of children sitting in front of the teacher (the rest at the seats), going through the prescribed steps given by the manual, does not successfully teach sounding to all.

From more than two decades of experience in a college-level reading clinic, we can reinforce Dolch's complaint by pointing out that the problem of ineffectual word attack skills is also great at that level.

As we shall point out later in our treatment of this topic of word attack skills, the basal system does appear to offer sequential training in word attack. But this program is sometimes introduced too late, divorced from its functional application to the act of reading, poorly related to the relevant research, dictated by the vagaries of the basal author's beliefs, and finally, taught by teachers who are woefully weak in their understanding and personal practice of good word attack skills. Certainly some new approach to these problems inherent in the basal approach seems indicated.

IMPROVING THE BASAL PROGRAM

In a second Carnegie study† Mary C. Austin and Coleman Morrison studied reading programs by questionaire in over 1000 school systems. Later these authors and their staff visited approximately 1800 classrooms in fifty-one communities throughout the United States. Some of their forty-five recommendations for the improvement of current reading programs appear to agree with our observations regarding the limitations of the basal program. They suggest:

* E. W. Dolch, "Individualized Reading vs. Group Reading I," *Elementary English,* 38 (December 1961), 566–575. Quoted by permission of National Council of Teachers of English.
† Mary C. Austin and Coleman Morrison, *The First R* (New York: Macmillan Publishing Co., Inc., 1963).

1. That schools should reassess current readiness programs by research efforts to determine the values of these programs for reading success.
2. That greater emphasis must be placed on promoting comprehension rather than word calling in the reading act.
3. That the oral reading circle be largely replaced by more functional oral reading practices.
4. That teachers be trained in more intelligent use of basal readers.
5. That the contents of basals should be carefully studied for the purpose of determining any need for their change.
6. That teachers should be led to realize that basal manuals are to be regarded as guides or aids rather than prescriptions.
7. That current uses of workbooks must be examined to determine whether they can be employed more constructively or should be abandoned.
8. That flexible grouping determined by the nature and activities of the program be substituted for the three-group practice.

As we have noted earlier, authors and publishers of basal books have responded to criticisms by major modifications in their most recent editions. Among some of the changes are increases in the vocabulary taught at each level; greater diversity of story material; deemphasis upon stereotyped middle-class settings and characters; greater emphasis upon earlier and stronger phonics programs; and provision for separate basal readers, games, and other materials at each grade level for children of high, average, or low achievement levels.

More science materials have been added even at primary-grade levels; stories with definitely masculine appeal are being featured; settings include apartment houses, trailers, and a variety of family backgrounds in addition to the little white house with the white fence around it; a greater use is being made of stories drawn from good children's literature and professional writers for children are lending their skills to the basal reading program. Other modifications are the new aids, such as ditto masters, filmstrips, recordings and cassettes, programmed supplementary materials, and packages or kits of supplementary reading materials rather than just lists, and a greater emphasis upon writing in the workbooks.

To offset the ethnic and upper-middle-class bias, readers are beginning to offer materials on many ethnic and racial groups, in urban as well as suburban settings. The most striking of these is the *Skyline Series* (Webster) with its emphasis upon stories of child relationships in a multiethnic setting. Scott, Foresman offers a multiethnic series and the *Bank Street Readers* (Macmillan) is a third such series. The *Great Cities Reading Improvement Program* (Follett) represents a very gradual development of materials highly suited to urban children of mixed backgrounds and races.

In choosing selections for the readers, the best of the minority literature by black, Indian, Mexican-American, and other such authors is also being introduced. Stories of urban, ghetto life as it really is are beginning to appear in our books. There is some evidence that use of this multiethnic material can help reduce the racial prejudice so common in our society (*22*). Children's attitudes toward other races do tend to improve as they gain information about the similarities and differences among groups. However, one author objects strenuously, and with merit, to our depicting the sordid life experiences of ghetto children as a perpetuation of the middle-class stereotyped concept of other children. Another investigator found that slum children preferred the usual family–pets–friends theme of basals to those in urban, multiethnic settings. Other analyses of the available multiethnic readers indicate that they fail both in illustrations and story line to convey the picture of a racially mixed, community-centered society, but are still overemphasizing young children in a family-centered theme (29). There are certainly still problems to be solved in these attempts to have our readers truly representative of the whole of American society.

Finally, by examining the current crop of basals we see a real recognition of the need for more mature, less repetitive language usage. No longer are primary children judged incapable of reading (even though they speak in such terms) such structures as complex sentences, contractions, direct quotations, and the like. The manuals accompanying some basal series recognize this trend and aid the teacher in providing a wide variety of experiences with sentence patterns and structures in keeping with the child's own language development.

In the later discussion of the primary and intermediate reading programs, we will offer specific suggestions for overcoming the inherent limitations of the basal, and the current practices in grouping and oral reading in pointing out possible improvements in classroom practices.

THE BASAL VERSUS OTHER APPROACHES

In the summer of 1964, an invitation was offered by the Office of Education, Cooperative Research Branch, for the submission of proposed studies of the effectiveness of various instructional approaches in the first grade. Twenty-seven such studies were finally approved and completed during the school year 1964–1965.* Many of these studies were comparisons among such methods as the basal program, I.T.A., the language experience, the linguistic and phonic systems. Fuller details of certain of the studies and their outcomes are presented in a later chapter.

However, it is pertinent to review briefly the results of the studies in which the basal method was one of the techniques employed. Fifteen of the first-grade projects used the basal and some other approach as experimental treatments. In all, five instructional systems were compared with the basal in typical populations, and we should consider these results.

The significance of the conclusions based on these studies may be judged

---

* Russell G. Stauffer, ed., *The First Grade Reading Studies; Findings of Individual Investigations* (Newark, Del.: International Reading Association, 1967).

by the quality of the research plans and the size of the populations involved. The entire plan for parallel research in tests—background data on pupils, schools, and teachers; evaluation of outcomes; control of pupil and teacher selection; and the other relevant variables plan—was evolved in a series of meetings of the project directors with the Coordinating Center at the University of Minnesota. Furthermore, to improve the values of the individual studies, it was agreed that method comparisons would involve at least twenty experimental and twenty control classes, about 1000 pupils in each study.

Combining the results of fifteen of the first-grade studies* permits large-scale comparisons of five variations in reading methods.

Basal Versus I.T.A.

1. No significant differences in test of comprehension.
2. I.T.A. produces superior word recognition as measured by three separate tests.
3. Evidence regarding spelling ability was inconclusive, the basals being superior in three studies, the I.T.A. in one.
4. No differences in accuracy or rate of oral reading.

Basal Versus Basal Plus Phonics

1. In general, basal plus phonics resulted in significantly greater reading achievement, both in comprehension and word recognition.
2. No differences in rate or accuracy of oral reading.
3. The actual differences were hardly educationally significant, averaging one to two months of achievement in favor of the basal plus phonics.

Basal Versus Language Experience

1. Relatively few significant differences between the effectiveness of these two approaches.
2. Pupils taught by the language experience method tended to test superior in word reading and comprehension, but the differences varied considerably from one project to another.
3. Results were similarly better for the language experience in vocabulary, but again varied inconsistently.

* Guy L. Bond and Robert Dykstra, "The Cooperative Research Program in First-Grade Reading Instruction," *Reading Research Quarterly,* 2 (Summer 1967), 1–142.

Basal Versus Linguistic Systems

1. On the whole, there were no major differences between these treatments.
2. Linguistic groups tended to be superior in word recognition.
3. Basal groups tended to be superior in speed and accuracy of reading.
4. No differences in comprehension were apparent.

Basal Versus Lippincott

1. Lippincott groups tended to be superior in word reading, comprehension, spelling, and phonic skills.
2. In only one of the three studies were these differences educationally significant. In the other two studies, most of the differences were as slight as one month achievement or less.
3. No differences in rate or accuracy of oral reading.

The general conclusion that may be drawn from this general review of the first-grade reading studies is that no one method seems consistently superior to any other method. Some methods do yield higher test scores in certain skills, as the basal plus phonics or the Lippincott, but the differences are hardly educationally significant. There may be other differences among these methods with respect to their effect upon boys or girls, on breadth of reading, on pupils of varying mental ability, and on attitudes toward reading that may be just as significant as the test scores. We will consider these other details in a later chapter.

Subsequently, the reports of the second year of some of these studies have been released. Ten studies were concerned with normal pupil populations now in the second grade of school, who were studied in the original first-grade studies. Some of the same types of comparison between methods can be made from the results of these follow-up studies:

Basal Versus I.T.A.

1. I.T.A. superior in word recognition skills and spelling.
2. No significant differences in comprehension, rate or accuracy of oral reading, usage, and English mechanics.

Basal Versus Language Experience

1. No real differences in spelling, word study skills, comprehension, or word recognition.

2. Some tendency for language experience pupils to write longer stories with more varied vocabulary.

Basal Versus Linguistic Systems

1. In some projects, linguistic pupils were superior in word recognition, but, in other projects, there were no such differences.
2. No differences in comprehension.
3. Basal pupils generally scored higher in phonic skills.

Basal Versus Lippincott

1. Lippincott tended to produce greater achievement in reading, spelling, and general language ability.
2. Most of these differences were not educationally significant, for they were very slight.

If we were to believe, as some language specialists say, that the pupil's major task is to develop graphemic symbols into sounds, and by so decoding words he will understand their meaning, then the various teaching systems emphasizing sound–symbol relationships seem quite effective. The I.T.A. Lippincott, and linguistic programs do appear to produce generally greater skill in word recognition (although they do not necessarily produce better phonic skills). But this superiority in word recognition does not produce greater comprehension or wider reading experience or greater liking for reading—all of which are presumably primary goals of any good reading program. Nor do these systems consistently effect any superiority in the mechanics, fluency, or depth of children's writing and speaking abilities. It still remains to be seen whether a teaching system which emphasizes letter sounds as one of its major goals can do no more than produce fluent word callers. Can such systems really produce fluent, comprehending readers, as well as the basal system does? Can they provide the breadth of reading and writing experience that the basal or language experience approaches offer? Finally, we see that these letter–sound systems are often more effective than the basal with the brighter pupils and sometimes less effective with below-average pupils. Perhaps their proper future role in the reading program is as an adjunct to certain current practices, rather than as an approach offered for the instruction of all or even most pupils.

DISCUSSION QUESTIONS

1. What recent changes have you noted in basal readers? How would you explain these changes?

2. Discuss the question: Must beginning teachers use the basal reader approach because of their inexperience?

3. What defenses or criticisms do you have to offer of the basal reader based on your own experience?

4. What improvements in basals and basal reading instruction are essential if they are to deal with individual differences realistically?

5. Discuss grouping practices in the average basal reading program and suggest improvements.

6. Have you any idea for what types of pupils, under what circumstances, basal readers might be the best possible program?

7. Analyze the teacher's guide for any basal reader available to you.

(a) What provisions do you find for individual differences according to reading levels?

(b) What resources are offered to aid in the teaching of the skills, other than the workbook?

(c) What suggestions are given to aid the applications of reading skills in independent work?

(d) What are the steps of the typical reading lesson? Can you defend this arrangement?

8. Analyze the workbook accompanying a basal reader.

(a) For variety and depth of questioning used. (Compare with Guilford's and Holmes's analyses of reading process in Chapter 1.)

(b) For provision for individual differences in pupil need for skill training.

(c) For relevance of the workbook exercises to the content of the reader.

(d) For its values in diagnosing pupil needs.

REFERENCES

1. Allen, Ruth J., et al., "The Relationships of Readiness Factors to January First-Grade Reading Achievement." Master's group thesis, Boston University, 1959.

2. Arthur, Grace, *Tutoring as Therapy.* New York: Commonwealth Fund, 1946.

3. Artley, A. Sterl, "Some Musts Ahead in Teaching Reading," *Reading for Today's Children,* Thirty-fourth Yearbook. Washington, D.C.: Department of Elementary School Principals, National Education Association, 1955.

4. Baxter, Katherine B., "Combatting the Influence of Black Stereotypes in Children's Books," *Reading Teacher,* 27 (March 1974), 540–544.

5. Betts, Emmett A., "How Well Are We Teaching Reading?" *Elementary English,* 38 (October 1961), 377–381.

6. Black, Millard H., and Whitehouse, La Von Harper, "Reinforcing Reading Skills Through Workbooks," *Reading Teacher,* 15 (September 1961), 19–24.

7. Blakely, W. Paul, and Shadle, Erma M., "A Study of Two Readiness-for-Reading Programs in Kindergarten," *Elementary English,* 38 (November 1961), 502–505.

8. Britton, Gwyneth E., "Danger: State Adopted Texts May Be Hazardous to Our Future," *Reading Teacher,* 29 (October 1975), 52–58.

9. Bureau of Applied Social Research, "Reading Instruction in the United States." Preliminary report, Columbia University, 1961.

10. Doctor, Robert L., "Reading Workbooks: Boon or Busy Work?" *Elementary English,* 39 (March 1962), 224–228.

11. Frasher, Ramona, and Walker, Annabelle, "Sex Roles in Early Reading Textbooks," *Reading Teacher,* 25 (May 1972), 741–749.

12. Gates, Arthur I., "Vocabulary Control in Basal Reading Material," *Reading Teacher,* 15 (November 1961), 81–85.

13. Gates, Arthur I., "The Word Recognition Ability and the Reading Vocabulary of Second- and Third-Grade Children," *Reading Teacher,* 15 (May 1962), 443–448.

14. Gilbert, Luther C., "The Effect on Silent Reading of Attempting to Follow Oral Reading," *Elementary School Journal,* 40 (April 1940), 614–621.

15. Goins, Jean T., *Visual Perceptual Abilities and Early Reading Progress,* Supplementary Education

Monographs, No. 87. Chicago: University of Chicago Press, 1958.

16. Graebner, Dianne Bennett, "A Decade of Sexism in Readers," *Reading Teacher,* 26 (October 1972), 52–58.

17. Grenda, Edward R., "The Image of Canadian Society in Grades 1 and 2 Reading Textbooks Used in British Columbia Elementary Schools," *Elementary School Journal,* 69 (December 1968), 143–150.

18. Groff, Patrick J., "The Problem of Vocabulary Load in Individualized Reading," *Reading Teacher,* 14 (January 1961), 188–190.

19. Groff, Patrick J., "A Survey of Basal Reading Grouping Practices," *Reading Teacher,* 15 (January 1962), 232–238.

20. Habecker, James E., "How Can We Improve Basic Readers?" *Elementary English,* 36 (December 1959), 560–563.

21. Heilman, Arthur W., *Principles and Practices of Teaching Reading.* Columbus, Ohio: Charles E. Merrill Publishing Company, 1967.

22. Litcher, J. H., and Johnson, D. W., "Changes in Attitudes Toward Negroes of White Elementary Students After Use of Multiethnic Readers," *Journal of Educational Psychology,* 60 (1969), 148–152.

23. Lyon, Rozeene E. A., "Comparative Analysis of Foreign Beginning Readers To Identify Values Emphasized in the Content," *Reading Quarterly* (Kansas State College), 3 (August 1970), 25—28.

24. MacKinnon, A. R., *How Do Children Learn To Read?* Toronto: The Copp Clark Pub. Co. Ltd., 1959.

25. Meisel, Stephen, and Glass, Gerald G., "Voluntary Reading Interests and the Interest Content of Basal Readers," *Reading Teacher,* 23 (April 1970), 655–659.

26. Miller, Harry B., and Hering, Steve, "Teacher's Ratings—Which Reading Group Is Number One?" *Reading Teacher,* 28 (January 1974), 389–391.

27. Morgan, Robert L., "The Effects of Color in Textbook Illustrations on the Recall and Retention of Information by Students of Varying Socio-economic Status," *Technical Paper No. 10.* Center for Occupational Education, North Carolina State University.

28. O'Donnell, Holly, "Cultural Bias: A Many-Headed Monster," *Elementary English,* 51 (February 1974), 181–189.

29. Parker, Lenore D., and Campbell, Ellen K., "A Look at Illustrations in Multi-racial First Grade Readers," *Elementary English,* 48 (January 1971), 67–74.

30. Ploghoft, Milton H., "Do Reading Readiness Workbooks Promote Readiness?" *Elementary English,* 36 (October 1959), 424–426.

31. Rose, Cynthia, Zimet, Sara G., and Blom, Gaston E., "Content Counts: Children Have Preferences in Reading Textbook Stories," *Elementary English,* 49 (January 1972), 14–19.

32. Samuels, S. Jay, "Effects of Pictures on Learning to Read, Comprehension and Attitudes," *Review of Educational Research,* 40 (June 1970), 397–407.

33. Saxton, Harvey L., *An Investigation of the Value in Basal Reading Materials for Superior Readers,* Publication No. 23. Storrs, Conn.: University of Connecticut, 1957.

34. Spache, George D., "New Trends in Primary Grade Readers," *Elementary School Journal,* 42 (December 1941), 283–290.

35. Spache, George D., "Using Tests in a Small School System," *Educational and Psychological Measurement,* 6 (September 1946), 99–110.

36. Spache, George D., *Toward Better Reading.* Champaign, Ill.: Garrard Publishing Company, 1963, Chap. II.

37. Staiger, Ralph C., "How Are Basal Readers Used?" *Elementary English,* 35 (January 1958), 46–49.

38. Stefflre, Buford, "Run, Mama, Run: Women Workers in Elementary Readers," *Vocational Guidance Quarterly,* 18 (December 1969), 99–102.

39. Traxler, Arthur E., "Research in Reading in the United States," *Journal of Educational Research,* 42 (March 1949), 496.

3
Using the Individualized Approach

PREVIEW

For the first time in American reading instruction an approach to teaching reading emphasizes the development of the individual pupil rather than the importance of the materials, their sequence, and their absolute essentiality. Such a departure from long-established methods might be expected to meet with resistance and negative attitudes. The critics ask: How can a teacher possibly plan and direct a completely different program for each pupil? How many teachers know enough about reading to depart from use of the teachers' guides of the basal system? Where will the teacher find the time to offer individual instruction to each child (not to mention the obvious uneconomical use of time implied in such a practice)?

As we have tried to portray, these questions are based in part upon false concepts of the individualized approach, its organizational procedures, and its use of grouping. Hardly any teachers completely individualize all aspects of reading instruction. Most teachers move gradually toward this approach, using manuals and checklists to supplement their knowledge of the details of the reading program. Small-group, large-group, whole-class, and individualized activities all appear in the program. Progressing from large to small groups and then to individualized teaching, and back again to group work as the situation demands, the teacher learns to meet individual differences among her pupils.

The realization that learners show individual differences that affect or modify the teacher's approach was probably a very early learning experience of the world's first teacher. Differences among pupils have been a constant source of concern for educators in all ages and civilizations. In this country, for example, this concern was shown in the title of the *Twenty-fourth Yearbook* of the National Society for the Study of Education, "Adapting the Schools to Individual Differences" (*37*). In the yearbook, many experiments and trials of individualized instruction were described as they were operating in such school systems as Winnetka, Illinois; Madison, Wisconsin; Detroit; Los Angeles; and San Francisco. However, these experiments in meeting pupil differences varied somewhat from the current emphasis upon individualized reading. For the most part, they were oriented to subject matter assignments that were short, simple, and sequential, and adapted to permitting the child to progress at his own rate of learning.

In contrast, individualized reading is concerned with the overall development of the child's reading skills and interests. This approach traces its origin not so much to the general theory of individual differences and the earlier experiments we have mentioned, but to a series of principles of child development—seeking, self-selection, and self-pacing. These principles are attributed by the leaders of the individualized reading movement to the research and observations of the child development specialist, Willard C. Olson, who first suggested their relevance to the teaching of reading.

However, as Alexander Frazier has noted (*14*), several other influences, in addition to those we have suggested, have played a significant role in creating a possible foundation for an individualized approach to reading. Among these forces has been an increasing recognition of the importance of firsthand experiences in developing the child's background for obtaining meaning from reading. Supplementary reading of all types has gradually been accepted as an integral part of the total reading program. School libraries, particularly in elementary schools, have increased materially in numbers and in adequacy in recent years. The supply of trade books which can actually be read by children with primary or limited reading ability has increased tremendously in the past decade. Finally, Frazier points out the obvious impetus toward an individualized approach created by contemporary educational concern with the impact of reading upon the learner's personal and social interests, values, and needs. In all probability all these factors have helped crystallize and support the individualized reading approach.

OBJECTIVES AND ASSUMPTIONS

Like any other reading method, the objective of the individualized school is to promote the fullest development of the pupil's skills, capacities, and interests. The assumptions on which these goals are based differ, however, from those of any other school of thought. Olson's study of the variability in child growth patterns led him to suggest three major principles—seeking, self-selection, and self-pacing. It was his impression that each child carries within him the seeds of a drive for maturation and a pattern of development. Skills, habits, and attitudes, consequently, are not to be imposed from without but are acquired at the child's natural pace and in accordance with his readiness. According to this philosophy, the child, motivated by internal needs, will attempt to read those materials suited to his needs and interests, and will progress in level and skills as his growth pattern and readiness for new learnings permit. By individualizing the teacher's approach to reading instruction, some means of dealing with these problems may be found: the range of individual differences, the creation of permanent reading interests and tastes, and the avoidance of the harmful effects of interpupil competition and rigid academic standards.

The Method

For the sake of convenience we shall divide the description of the individualized approach into the topics of organizing procedures, the individual conference, skills practice, independent activities, and record keeping.

Organizing an individualized reading program requires perhaps more detailed teacher planning than some other approaches. First there is the problem of securing a wide variety of reading materials, including magazines, newspapers, pamphlets, trade books, and basals, drawn from a number of reading levels. The actual number of books and other materials needed by an average class of thirty pupils, assuming that all would engage in individualized reading, is quite large. Some writers have observed that as many as five hundred titles were used in a fifth-grade class, and over one hundred at the second-grade level. Individual pupils are reported to have read from five to one hundred books during a semester under this plan. Estimates of the number needed in the classroom at any one time range from two to ten books per child, of which perhaps a quarter should be multiple copies of the same books. Some teachers make a real effort to determine the readability levels of the materials and to familiarize themselves thoroughly with their contents. One teacher, for example, prepared specific summaries and exercises for each book, including a short description, a list of difficult words, and questions on comprehension. Other teachers have spent the entire summer in this type of previewing, grading, and identifying books by a colored label, and preparing comprehension checks in preparing for a third-grade program.

The collected reading materials must be planned to appeal to a wide variety of common pupil interests ranging over a number of grade levels of difficulty and to include information, reference, and recreational materials. Preparation of a large selection of spirit masters or mimeographed exercises in word recognition skills, word attack techniques, word meaning, vocabulary building, and other skills is often made at this time. Some teachers may substitute exercises drawn from a number of workbooks for their own devices but, in any event, a wide variety of these tools at different reading levels is most desirable. In addition to these basic materials, we suggest the need for preparation of work centers and other equipment such as bulletin boards, picture file, science center, puppet theater, painting and clay center, the library corner or reading center, a worktable or center where a supply of exercises or worksheets is stored, a workshop or make-it table, a writer's table, and a supply of audiovisual aids such as records, films, and filmstrips.

Some of the problems inherent in organizing for individualized reading depend on the way to initiate the program, the influence of class size, preparation of pupils (and their parents) for the new approach, pupil maturity in habits of independent work individually and in small groups, in-service training and supervisory needs of teachers inexperienced with this method, selection of pupils for this method, and suitability of the approach for pupils of varying mental abilities. Administrative problems include judgment of the teacher's readiness and flexibility, her degree of personal organization and planning skill, her overall efficiency and rapport with children, her need for further in-service training and supervision, and the strength of her authoritarian leanings. There are no easy answers to these organizational and administrative questions, for very little of expository or research material on these is available. We simply do not know the maximum class size for which this approach is still feasible, whether it is wiser to begin with the fast reading group and later extend the procedure to other pupils, whether this approach is best for high-, medium-, or low-ability groups or equally effective with all, or what the characteristics of those teachers best suited to the method are, although partial answers to some of these questions are offered in the chapter list of resources for the teacher.

In striking contrast to the common belief that individualizing becomes too difficult for the teacher with a class of thirty or more pupils, some teachers' experiences with so large a group have been very positive. With a large class, it becomes necessary to conduct four or five or perhaps more reading groups, but there just is not enough instructional time for that many daily reading lessons. Besides, the preparation time for these lessons becomes excessive. The individualized program with its elements of whole class, large- and small-group instruction, individual conferences, and record keeping is more readily fitted into the available instructional time and less demanding of formal preparation time, some teachers tell us.

The *individual conference* as a substitute for group instruction in basal reading materials is probably the unique element in this approach. Occasionally, a small group of children may read the same basal or trade book under direct teacher supervision, but the reading circle of the basal method is taboo according to most protagonists of the individualized school. Instead of reading in the circle the child usually reads orally a portion he has selected from the book he is reading. During the oral reading, the teacher observes the child's reading errors and other behaviors, and checks his comprehension by improvised questions or questions prepared beforehand. She also discusses the book with the child and may suggest another to be read next (although the extent to which this guidance is extended is a question of sharp debate among different sects of the individualized reading school). The teacher makes plans with the child for future small-group work on the skills in which he appears to be weak, or gives him definite assignments in a workbook or worksheet intended to provide skill training, or suggests follow-up activities related to the content of his reader. The teacher may also suggest ways in which the pupil may share his enjoyment or learning with other members of the class.

Some teachers make use of the conference to observe both oral and silent reading skills of the child, to check on his understanding of word meanings as well as sight vocabulary, to discuss ways of selecting future reading materials, and to look over the child's reading records. The conference may be extended to a small group of children, who gather around the teacher and read silently while awaiting their turn for the conference. In some classes children volunteer for the conference or sign up on a schedule sheet as they feel the need for teacher help or wish to share the book they are reading with her. A few teachers hold conferences throughout the school day upon request from pupils, but most hold only as many as can be scheduled during that part of the regular reading period when the teacher is not otherwise engaged. The length of time given to each individual conference varies from as short as two or three minutes to as long as ten minutes (10). Two to four conferences a week for each pupil are recommended, if the teacher can accomplish it. Class size, proportion of the reading period devoted to small-group work, teaching of the whole class, sharing periods, follow-up activities, and other elements of the program obviously limit the possible number and the length of the individual conferences. Individual pupil needs for support and guidance also determine to some degree the number of conferences given weekly. Some children need almost daily brief conferences, while once or twice a week may suffice for others. The maturity of the child as well as his ability to work independently of teacher supervision, either alone or in small groups, must influence the teacher's judgment of his needs for conferences.

Skills practice for small groups, usually with teacher direction, arises directly from the observations made during the individual conference. Some teachers who have described their experiences with individualized reading are quite vague about the details of the materials or content of the small-group skills practice. Other leaders of the individualized reading school are, however, more emphatic in demanding skills training. Young (38) notes the words that the children misread during the conference. After a number of conferences she employs the list of words as a basis for instruction of the whole class in word attack techniques. One teacher used basal readers two days a week as the basis of her training in skills, but substituted a variety of follow-up activities for the basal workbooks. Darrow and Howes (10) recommend that the teacher prepare a detailed plan for skills training based on such available sources as courses of study, workbooks, basal manuals, and textbooks on reading. Some teachers offer the entire class a short lesson in skills at the close of the reading period, but most teachers, according to their reports, are more likely to offer this instruction during the individual conference or to a small group called together for that specific purpose (35).

In some cases, skills training is based almost entirely upon basal workbooks, but more commonly, teachers use the worksheets they have devised plus a wide variety of individual group follow-up activities, such as we will describe later. In a few classrooms skills training under teacher direction may be as infrequent as once a month, while most teachers emphasize skills daily either in a special lesson for a group or the entire class, or in conjunction with spelling lessons, language periods, or during social studies, science, and literature lessons.

In many individualized programs it is apparent that the pupils assume a larger part of the responsibility for their own skills development. They are frequently expected to work independently, with a helper, or in a team, on assignments in workbooks or worksheets, follow-up activities, or committee work. They may also work preparing reading materials for the teacher–pupil conference or the sharing period, demonstrating reading skills in content field books, and carrying on various types of group projects and self-expressive activities.

Many of these activities in self-improvement in reading skills are conducted with what appears to the casual observer to be a minimum of teacher supervision, although, of course, they are initiated and monitored by the teacher.

To develop vocabulary, for example, the child is often expected to keep a list of the unknown words he encounters, to study these independently or with the aid of a child helper, and to be ready to demonstrate his understanding of them in the teacher–pupil conference. From the list, a "word bank" box (words on cards) for varied practice in learning new words is kept in the pupil's desk. In any event, the pupil's independence and self-direction are important elements in his eventual skill development.

We have alluded to a number of the *independent activities* which seem to be an integral part of the individualized approach. For some these are a way of applying reading skills and relating them to language development in its many facets. One teacher achieves an interrelationship among the independent reading materials and language arts by stimulating the children to write letters to the authors, book reviews, a class newspaper and a magazine, poetry or free verse, and by planning a Book Week show. In addition to the skills practice we have mentioned, Darrow and Howes (*10*) speak of the following independent activities as preparation for sharing reading: reading a notice on a bulletin board, making posters and book jackets, dramatizing part of the story, and practicing for the oral reading of a portion in an audience situation. Project work involving the construction of models, dioramas, murals, or play properties is often related to the independent reading. Self-expressive activities which may be an outgrowth of reading include displays of hobbies and collections, science experiments, poetry or stories, committee research work to prepare reports, oral reporting to the class, and artwork in paint, clay, or crayon.

As is true in the area of skills practice, pupils are expected to display a significant measure of independence, motivation, and persistence in these follow-up activities. Groups of children must learn to function together effectively— as helpers, teams, or committees—in following their special interests, in preparing projects, and in sharing the ideas gained from their independent reading, often with a minimum of teacher direction and supervision.

Perhaps, before discussing other facets of the individualized program, it is appropriate here to introduce an actual description of the daily activities in one classroom. This diary may serve to show how one teacher integrated the individual conference, skills practice, and independent activities (10).*

Monday: All children read individually. Worked with Mary, Tom . . . on comprehension—had group read and discuss selection from _____ . Held reading conferences with Joe, Sara, June. . . .

Tuesday: Worked with Susan, John . . . on double vowel sounds. Helped small-group planning of St. Valentine's Day with their play to share with class. Other children worked on independent activities or read individually. Had reading conferences with _____ .

Wednesday: Taught proper names to children using Book 2. Helped Carl prepare a story to read to class. Worked with small group on dictionary skills. Several children worked on creative activities; others read individually.

Thursday: Had children read to each other in small groups while I circulated; each child kept record of unfamiliar words. Had Tom, Larry, and Ella read orally to class.

Friday: Worked with group of eight children on word recognition—asked them to make a list of *R* words. Other children read or worked on independent activities. Had class evaluate the week's reading.

Monday: Had short class phonetics drill. Individual reading conferences with six children—others read silently at seat. Worked with a group of four on word games. Had all children tell what they read over weekend. Made class summary sheet of time spent on reading.

Tuesday: Had twelve children read silently at my desk while others engaged in independent activities. Asked three children to read orally in class. Worked on comprehension with Becky, Larry, _____ .

Wednesday: Circulated while children read independently at their seats. Had children bring news items for our reading bulletin board—small group arranged the display.

The informality of the individualized reading classroom, the freedom of pupils to select their own reading materials, and the amount of time given to activities independent of teacher direction make careful *record keeping* essential to a successful individualized program. Pupil records may take a variety of forms and include:

1. A daily log of reading accomplishments, plans, and projects.
2. A file of cards giving such facts as the date, title of book read, plans for sharing, and results of this plan.

* From *Approaches to Individualized Reading* by Helen Fisher Darrow and Virgil M. Howes. Copyright © 1960. By permission of Appleton-Century-Crofts, Educational Division, Meredith Corporation.

3. A list of the new or unknown words met in reading, giving the title of book, page, and context for each word.
4. A brief summary of the book, giving its type, title, author, pupil's reactions or recommendations, and a brief description.
5. A small chart listing types of books. Pupil indicates the variety of his reading by inserting titles of books he has read.

A sample of a summary record written by a sixth grader is:

Wibberly, Leonard, *DEADMAN'S CAVE*   *Pages: 234**

This is an exciting adventure story about a runaway servant, Tom Lincoln, and his experiences with pirates. The story takes place toward the end of the 1600s and is mostly a sea story. The book is written in first person and is in dialect. The print is large and wide-set.

Source: Boulder Public Library

Ronnie Eaton   February

Some teachers also keep additional records of the pupils' independent activities, written work, projects, and participation in sharing. This record can serve to indicate both the teacher's suggestions given during the conference and the actual outcomes of the child's follow-up.

Comments

Our description of the individualized reading program scarcely does justice to the tremendous enthusiasm with which some teachers seem to meet this method. Most of the teachers' self-reports in the recent literature are enthusiastic. Among the outcomes such teachers seem to see are the following:

1. Great increase in the volume of children's reading.
2. Growth in skill in sharing the pleasure of reading, interests, and tastes.
3. Marked increase in the range of reading test scores, particularly at the upper end.
4. Increase in feelings of security and self-sufficiency due to the absence of pupil competition and comparison.
5. Growth in independence, planning ability, and persistence in follow-up.
6. Real enjoyment and interest in reading and in self-improvement.
7. Constant encouragement and support derived from the repeated experience of success.
8. Marked progress in the breadth and variety of reading in informational, reference, and recreational materials.
9. Opportunity to progress in reading in accordance with child's own pace and interests, to be informed of own progress, and to play a significant role in determining this development.
10. Marked increase in level of social studies and science achievement due to wide reading in related areas, observed by some teachers.

*Reprinted by permission of the National Council of Teachers of English.

At the conclusion of their large-scale questionnaire and observation study, as reported in *The First R* (New York: Macmillan Publishing Co., Inc., 1963), Mary C. Austin and Coleman Morrison made these recommendations regarding the individualized concept:

1. That all pupils be permitted to cross grade lines with all reading materials, including basals, in order that intelligent adjustments would be made in terms of children's progress.
2. That certain aspects of the individualized approach, such as self-selection of reading materials, individual conferences, and written records of pupil progress, be used as integral parts of all elementary school reading programs.

PRINCIPLES AND PROBLEMS OF INDIVIDUALIZED READING

As Frazier (*14*) has suggested, the significance of the principle of *self-selection* is much overemphasized in the literature of individualized programs. The principle assumes an almost endless variety of books from which to choose and a minor role of both the group and the teacher in influencing the selection of reading materials. The principle of individualized reading does not imply that the teacher abandon her guidance or supervisory function toward children's reading. Frazier (*14*, p. 60) points out that teachers must continue to help the reader "find satisfying experiences in keeping with his interests, purposes, and ability, all at the same time." We would add that the teacher continues to play a significant role in stimulating and shaping these interests and purposes, and in helping the child realistically evaluate his abilities. Like so many of the terms characteristic of the school, *individualized, self-selection,* and *seeking* are misnomers, for in actual practice they do not mean what they seem to mean. The approach does not completely individualize instruction, for grouping remains present in many contexts; basal reading is often still present in the program. Self-selection does not mean that children have complete freedom or independence of choice, nor does seeking mean that all have an instinctual drive to read more and more.

In the individualized program, children are not constantly taught in a one-to-one setting with the teacher. While she does spend more time with individual children than in other approaches to reading, much of her instruction in skills will be done in small groups. These groups will be formed for a specific purpose, will perhaps use the same book or skill development material for a time, and then, when their needs have been met, will disband. Thus, from time to time a child may be a member of a group for word analysis training, or because of a special interest, or to plan the sharing of reading with the rest of the class, to plan a play or a puppet show, to practice choral reading or role playing, or for any of a dozen reasons. Like other teachers, individualized practitioners are aware that the teaching of a group is more economical of their time, and that working in a group which shares a common purpose produces better learning than does solitary work or instruction.

Organizational Problems

In a recent article, Jerry L. Abbott, an elementary school principal, enumerated fifteen reasons why individualized reading will not work. His article was written with tongue in cheek, for he soon points out that none of his reasons are really barriers to successful individualization. Actually, they are simply inherent problems such as class size, book supply, teacher competencies, cost, record keeping, and the like. These problems are numerous in individualized reading, perhaps even more than in other approaches, because this method depends so heavily upon the organizing ability of the teacher (24). Many teachers who try this approach discover that they are unable to schedule their time efficiently for sufficient conferences with pupils—conferences that are long enough and really private or free from interruptions. Other teachers feel the need for more planning time, perhaps as much as one free period before each reading period, to prepare materials, complete records, and plan for individual pupils. In many classrooms the question of logistics—or an adequate supply of reading materials, exercises, and seatwork activities, workbooks, and other tools—is a problem. Where does the teacher find the time to preview all these books, to familiarize herself with their significant meanings, to prepare adequate checks upon pupil comprehension, to identify and label these according to their difficulty of vocabulary and sentence structure? Even the most simple but objective methods of determining grade levels of books, such as the readability formulas, take from twenty to sixty minutes per book, depending upon the size of the book. Or, as some writers seem to imply, are we to believe that this approach does not necessitate teacher familiarity with the contents of the books that the children will read, that it is not essential that she know the approximate grade level of each book?

The teacher obviously must have some scheme for scheduling herself and her pupils. This may take the form of posted sheets on which children sign up for conferences, and a checklist of the children's names, the dates of their conferences, and the outcomes. Time for conferences must be part of the teacher's daily schedule. She must certainly become familiar with the books of the classroom library and try to keep up with those obtained at intervals from the school or public library. This does not imply that she must have read all the books, or even prepared specific comprehension questions on each, or listed the new vocabulary (a pointless task in view of the diversified reading experiences of the pupils).

An inherent difficulty in utilizing the individualized approach is that of the high level of teacher effectiveness and skill demanded. There are no manuals to dictate each day's lessons, or to tell the teacher what skill-reinforcing materials to use, or what story a group should read next. Each individualized reading practitioner must know a good deal about the way children usually develop in the reading process, know how to detect deviations or gaps in this development, and know how and what to prescribe for these needs as they are revealed during conferences or group work. The teacher is likely to need experienced help and supervision during the early stages of development of this approach. Appropriate in-service training through grade conferences, teacher–supervisor meetings, and exchange of ideas with fellow staff members is as essential here as it would be in approaching any other new way of teaching reading.

The teacher herself faces several administrative problems in effective management of the class. The pupils often need training and direction in assuming the responsibility for their independent work. They must be able to act in a self-directing, responsible manner. They must understand the program, their own reading abilities and difficulties, and be able to organize their own efforts accordingly. If the pupils are unable to function efficiently without constant teacher supervision, the teacher must take the time and make the effort to teach them how to work independently. Most teachers have found that a gradual introduction to individualized reading, with considerable supervision at first of pupils during independent work, makes the program more feasible. Another successful variation of these beginning steps is to start with a small number of pupils, perhaps those of better reading ability, and then gradually extend the program to other pupils.

Some teachers encounter frustrating difficulties in introducing this approach in a traditional school system. Principals and other teachers who have long been accustomed to the regimentation often characteristic of the use of a basal reader often look askance at the whole idea of individualizing. They are apt to be very skeptical that pupils will develop the necessary skills without using a basal. Judging from their own shortcomings, they refuse to believe that such a degree of individualizing in instruction and materials is even possible. Often teachers may recognize the inherent criticism of their stereotyped approaches and resent the implications (without admitting the comparison, of course). If the teacher attempting individualized reading is young or new to the system, the task is sometimes made even more difficult by the attitudes of her colleagues.

Obviously, it requires a good deal of self-confidence to initiate the individualized approach under such conditions. The teacher must first convince the supervisor or principal that the method is not a hair-brained notion but a widely accepted classroom practice that produces pupils as competent in reading as any other method. It would be wise to offer some of the resource materials listed in this chapter, such as the Veatch text or even this book, to permit the administrator to become familiar with the concept. If administrative approval and support can be thus obtained, the situation will be much less complicated. As for fellow teachers, there is not a need to attempt to convince them of the merits of this approach. Let the test results and the actual reading progress of the pupils be the evidence of the soundness of the method.

Another personal problem of the teacher employing the individualized approach is the demand upon her personality and interpersonal skill. She is constantly attempting to work closely and intimately with different children. She must continuously adjust herself to the pupils' needs for support, encouragement, correction, guidance, constructive criticism, and directions for the use of materials. She must combine some of the attributes of therapist, teacher, librarian, parent, counselor, and reading specialist. Needless to say, not all teachers can fulfill these demands.

The ultimate success of an individualized program is, of course, influenced by the adequacy of the solutions to the organizational and administrative problems. But of even greater significance is the teacher's skill in *record keeping* and the *individual conference*. The whole program depends upon the cornerstone of teacher diagnostic skill in the conference in identifying children's needs in the areas of reading skills and selection of materials, and in evaluation of the pupils' progress.

Individual Conference

We have already noted that McKillop has observed that many individualized reading teachers have not solved the problem of finding sufficient time for the number of conferences they feel are really needed. These teachers feel that the conferences are not only too infrequent but also too brief and superficial. The majority of Sartain's second-grade teachers (*28*) had similar feelings of frustration after a three-month trial of the approach. These teachers frankly admitted that their diagnostic skills were inadequate in enabling them to note and understand pupil needs for skill training. Several writers speak out strongly against dependence upon the individual conference as a reliable means of evaluation of pupils' skill development and instructional needs. Both of these writers consider the conference as usually practiced in the individualized program as an opportunistic, catch-as-catch-can method of assessing pupil needs and planning for his instruction. Perhaps there is good reason for these negative reactions to the merits of the conference, unless it is carefully planned and the teacher is adequately trained.

All the information that a teacher might want to accumulate about each child certainly cannot be obtained in casual two-minute conferences. There must be different purposes for conferences and different types of conferences, as we shall illustrate later in this book. Some conferences may serve for diagnosis, others as progress checks, and others as motivational contacts with the pupil. Some conferences will be brief, while other conferences may be much longer. Some conferences will be with an individual child, as for diagnosis or progress checking, while others may involve several pupils, as for instruction, sharing, planning, or motivation.

One of our students wrote a term paper describing her experiences in learning the individualized approach. Among her comments are statements such as these:

> First and most important to the success of my program is that I realize my record keeping is not detailed enough. . . . I have found I need to take better inventories of each child's overall reading development. I also need to do more recording during the diagnostic conference time. I see now that I need to follow the suggestion in our text, *Reading in the Elementary School,* for recording oral errors and interpreting these errors.

Another big problem has been that I do not know the reading level of many of the books in my room library. . . . Actually I have been able to get along very well without this information, but I know it would be easier for me if I could quickly pick out a book for a specific child.

I found that I was putting too many books out at one time for the children to select. Now I choose about twenty-five books and put them on our library table and change them often.

When we first started using the reading record some of the children were so delighted with putting the names of the books in the notebook that they read all the picture books and easy books to get a long list of books recorded. I did not say anything about this to the children and the novelty wore off!

This student, Mary Beth Erb, goes on in her paper to describe her learning experiences in adjusting to the individualized approach. Like most practitioners, she discovered that skill in organizing her instructional time, scheduling conferences of different types, and helping children to learn to work independently of constant direction were among her major tasks. She also learned that individualized reading does not quite function in the manner implied by some of the authorities who speak for it. Conferences are not as frequent or as brief as some imply; each child does not actually always have a completely individualized program, for much activity occurs in small groups; and when the teacher discards the planned skill training of the basal program, she must formulate her own checklists of skills and related diagnostic measures.

Skills Training

Numerous studies show that many teachers are not very knowledgeable in the area of word analysis skills (31). If a teacher is to approach individualized reading, she must familiarize herself with the facts about phonics, phonic principles, and contextual and structural analysis, with the aid of some recent review of the literature, as we have provided in a later chapter. She should also help herself to learn more about his area with the aid of a detailed guide, such as Heilman's (18), or a self-teaching device, such as that offered by Marion A. Hull (20). Teachers attempting individualized reading cannot wait to learn something about word analysis from use of the teacher's manual, as so many teachers do. They cannot depend on being told what to teach when, as in the usual manual, for individualized instruction does not necessarily progress in the structured pattern of basals.

In this area of skills training, it is apparent that many teachers would experience marked difficulty in shifting from a basal to an individualized approach. These are teachers who have simply followed basal manuals because of their own lack of professional knowledge or of creativity in teaching. If, as the research studies show, professional education may not have supplied adequate knowledge of skills and their principles, such as phonics, syllabication, and word recognition techniques, a teacher may not be ready to begin a program of individualized diagnosis and small-group instruction without further study in this area.

In this area of skills development Frazier (*14*) raises a number of questions: How much training in word analysis do our children really need at primary, intermediate, and other levels? Just how much sight vocabulary is needed to enable children to begin to read on their own? Is it possible that many of these skills will develop spontaneously as a result of broadening reading experience? Can vocabulary be extended more rapidly when children use a variety of materials? Should not some of the performances thought of as reading skills be taught as study or learning skills in content texts and lessons?

These are indeed decisions to be made by the teacher who attempts individualization. Rather than taking each child through a preplanned skill development sequence (commonly known as a workbook), the teacher will be devising a tailormade developmental sequence for individuals and groups. Some children will need a great deal of help in this or that skill, while others may develop these spontaneously. Still others will be successful in reading by using some of these skills but not all of the skills. Individualization demands a true recognition of individual differences in learning rate, learning modalities, and the child's actual functioning in the act of reading.

THE RESEARCH

Objective observers of the outcomes of the individualized approach are still somewhat cautious in extending wholehearted approval. Irene W. Vite (*35*) has reviewed seven carefully controlled comparisons of the individualized approach versus ability grouping. Four of the control studies show significant test results favoring individualized reading, but three yielded conclusive results in favor of ability grouping. Reading test scores are quite inadequate in measuring many of the outcomes of a reading method, for most of the results of individualized reading that we have noted above cannot be evaluated in this fashion. Yet test results are highly valued by most educators as fundamental, objective methods of comparison, and their equivocal nature in these studies leaves many administrators in doubt.

Safford (*27*) compared reading gains with both local and national norms in seven classes using individualized reading. All the experimental classes made less than the expected gains, and there were no significant advantages for average or superior readers. Johnson (*22*) conducted a twenty-eight-class, three-year study which favored individualized reading at the end of the first and third grades in several measures of reading. Two of the Cooperative First-Grade Studies (*7*) obtained no significant differences at the end of the first grade (*23*). However, use of an attitude scale measuring the pupils' feelings about reading in these studies showed a very positive advantage for individualized reading.

After a two-year study, Cyrog (*9*) reports that there were still some pupils reading a year or more below their expected levels, although the great majority of pupils equaled or exceeded their mental age in reading achievement. Greenman and Kapilian's results (15) indicate a better-than-average gain in test scores but show that the greatest gains were present among the best pupils and some poor readers failed to show significant gains. Several other experiments in the primary grades showed that many children accustomed to a basal program made less than normal progress when shifted to the individualized one. Sartain's results (28) indicate a marked spurt in progress during the first few months of either basal or individualized method in comparable classes, thus perhaps demonstrating the marked significance of teacher enthusiasm or experimental conditions upon pupil reading achievement. His final results did not indicate any real difference in achievement for average or superior pupils under either method. Poor readers, in fact, made greater growth in word recognition in a basal program.

A distinct problem in interpreting the mass of studies claiming to test the values of individualized reading is the extreme variation from one study to the next in the experimenter's definition and implementation of this approach. For example, in another of the Cooperative First-Grade Studies (32), Doris U. Spencer used a group commercial phonics program, teams of pupils working together, individual conferences, and group instruction in language arts. With this "individualized reading" program, she obtained results that were superior to those found in the use of a basal reading series. Another report considered individualized reading to be the distribution of worksheets to be placed in the child's folder (although no free time to work on these was scheduled), plus providing cardboard carrels for small-group work. Still another experimenter used the same reader in an individual conference program versus a small-group plan (using the same reader). Perhaps these variations are the reason why reviews of the research (17) indicate that outcomes differ from one experiment in individualized reading to the next. Certainly there will and should be variations among the ways in which teachers implement the concept of individualized reading. This approach depends heavily on the personal organization, planning ability, and classroom management skills of the teacher. And teachers differ in these characteristics. But we must be careful not to be misled by those who think that any program which moves away in the smallest degree from constant teacher pacing through a reader is therefore an "individualized" program. We must also beware of entrepreneurs who try to capitalize on the term, and offer us programmed materials or sequential worksheets, or whatever, to be done in solitary seat work—all the activities to be done by all the pupils, in the same sequence, and employing only a single learning modality—in the name of individualized reading. There are, of course, a number of sound book collections, skill development kits, and other aids of use in an individualized program. We will explore these later in a chapter devoted to ways of implementing such a program.

Some protagonists for the individualized approach argue for its adoption because of certain conclusions that might be drawn from the comparative studies. They suggest that since test scores do not clearly show inferior results for the individualized program, it is justified on the basis of its other accomplishments in the areas of enjoyment, interest, breadth of reading, independence, and the like. Opponents are likely to point out that, despite its claims, individualized reading does not completely solve the range of differences in the classroom, does not produce increased rate of progress for all types of pupils at all levels of mental abilities, and that the program makes extraordinary demands upon teacher preparation and skill. These opposing viewpoints do not exhaust the arguments pro and con, but they suffice to show the distinct cleavage of opinion regarding this particular approach to the teaching of reading.

Advocates of individualized reading emphasize a number of subtle advantages in this approach. They point out, for example, that the self-selection feature avoids teacher pacing, with its leveling and retarding effects upon pupil progress. Motivation is thought to be greater in this program, for the child tends to realize his own goals of interest and information, rather than teacher goals which may be artificial. Self-selected reading provides a wide vocabulary in material on the child's level, thus stimulating marked growth in concepts, ideas, and facts, as well as words. Skill training is planned for each pupil or small group when it is appropriate rather than being offered in a set sequence to all pupils, regardless of their needs. Competition among children is diminished, greater socialization is promoted, and more pupil–teacher interaction on a one-to-one basis is present. Even though it may not be possible to show that the individualized program necessarily accelerates children in reading levels or test scores, these mental hygiene advantages remain highly significant.

Individualized reading, to be sure, has certain ideas and practices which might be incorporated into the total reading program, as we shall illustrate later. Adoption of these practices will make definite demands for better teacher training and practice—in diagnosis of pupil needs, in preparation and evaluation of a wide variety of teaching materials, and in detailed planning. But these demands can be met, and the values of these individualized practices realized, by interested teachers.

OPERANT CONDITIONING AND SYSTEMS APPROACHES

To this point we have been describing what might be considered the classical version of individualized instruction. In the past two decades, a series of very different approaches have appeared which, according to their protagonists, represent a more scientific attempt to individualize pupil learning. Basically these methods, programmed instruction, teaching machines, programs involving computers, management systems, and learning modules are developments from theories of operant conditioning. This concept of learning, derived largely from animal psychology, requires a detailed analysis of the desired performance of the learner, and the preparation and testing of activities arranged in very small, often-repetitive steps involving positive action of the student. These learning steps are reinforced usually almost immediately after the act by knowledge of the correct answer or by verbal or material rewards.

Materials and Methods

Programmed workbooks and teaching machines were the first application of operant conditioning to classroom instructional procedures in the 1950s. The machine would hold the printed program, expose one frame (task) at a time while the student responded, then permit the student to advance to the next frame, which also contained the answer to the preceding item. The pupil could not reverse the process to correct or change his response or attempt to copy the answer rather than supplying it. The frames were usually pretested and revised until the probability of student error was very small. Thus step by step he practiced a skill or learned facts or concepts and progressed at his own pace toward the desired behavior.

School systems, for a time, were flooded with a variety of programs, usable with or without machines, for teaching almost every area of academic study. Aside from the philosophical objections that we will discuss later, the cost of the teaching machines and even of the separate programmed workbooks slowed their adoption. Some teachers rejected the approach because they feared that their role was about to be taken over by the mechanized system of learning. Some feared that the learning retrogressed after the completion or even during the program (*12*). However, programs and machines are currently still in use in reading instruction in many classrooms at all educational levels.

A second stage in the application of operant-conditioning theory appeared in the use of *computers as an instructional device.* In computer-assisted instruction, as it is called, the child sits at a terminal resembling a typewriter; activates it to present a frame or a task; responds perhaps by a set of multiple-choice keys; is corrected sometimes by an auditory comment from the machine; is repracticed, as needed, or directed to the teacher if he makes repeated errors. The program is in a sense somewhat different for each child in that he may begin in a different place, may receive varying amounts of retraining, and may proceed at his own learning rate. Another version, computer-based instruction, is more closely related to the teacher's plans in that the child is sent to the terminal usually only to reinforce or repractice what the teacher has already presented (*11*). To illustrate the diversity of computer–assisted instruction, Majer (*25*) mentions those used in Washington, D.C., for deaf children; for the rural poor in Kentucky's Appalachia region; for retarded readers in New York City and Philadelphia; and one using student-directed or language experience materials for illiterate prison inmates as well as for normal schoolchildren.

A third development in the expanding of operant conditioning has been the recent and rapid proliferation of *management systems.*

In general, systems approaches have these characteristics:

1. The behavior desired is defined by a "behavioral objective" which describes exactly what the learner is to be able to do at the conclusion of the related training.
2. Hundreds of behavioral objectives are written to outline the many subskills that the program will cover; sometimes as many as 300 to 400 for the first six grades of school.
3. For each behavioral objective, activities are provided or recommended to practice each subskill. Usually a pretest is offered to determine the child's readiness for the skill or whether he has already acquired it. After completion of a period of practice, a posttest assesses his performance of the behavioral objective.
4. Pre- and posttests are called criterion-referenced tests, implying that they are not standardized instruments but rather graded according to a minimum standard set by the authors, perhaps such as 80 percent correct. If the child meets this criterion, he may proceed to the next portion; if not, some programs suggest or offer other sources of additional practice. Others offer no materials or teaching strategies to overcome the pupil's failure but simply direct him to go to the next step.

Learning modules are a logical outgrowth of this type of instruction but differ in the breadth of activities included. Perhaps after a diagnostic test or simply receiving a teacher assignment, the student begins the activities in a prepared outline. He may read certain materials, view films or filmstrips, carry out specific actions as directed, participate in small-group work, do a number of worksheets, and take a criterion-referenced posttest. The teacher may be involved in helping the pupil secure materials, organize and schedule them, maintain a record of progress, and evaluate his own work.

The resemblance of these learning modules to the learning units of Winnetka, for example, in the early part of this century is quite apparent. Both include a planned sequential development of skills and concepts, a wide variety of pupil activities, more or less self-directed, culminating in a self-evaluation and a test. One difference was the use of a formal diagnostic test before the unit and a comprehensive test at the end in the earlier versions, while today's modules employ only criterion-referenced tests. The end of unit tests in the earlier learning programs also often functioned as diagnostic tests for the next segment, thus emphasizing the sequential and interrelated aspects of the skills taught. The current learning modules are in use at all levels, including teacher training, in contrast to the almost exclusive application at elementary levels of the earlier Winnetka, Dalton, and other unit plans.

It will be desirable to examine examples of these programs, but perhaps a very brief description of several will convey a more complete picture (*4,26*).

Criterion-Referenced Reading (Random House, Inc.) offers about five Progress tests for each of 380 Outcomes Skills, extending from the kindergarten through the sixth grade. Each test is criterion-referenced, with a standard of about 80 percent performance expected. After successfully completing the Progress tests, the child's success with a subskill is assessed in the Outcomes measure, after which he may proceed to the next step. Parallel practice materials from the publisher are listed for the teacher. The worksheets and tests are bound in groups like common workbooks. Children and teacher maintain a record of the progress.

Croft Inservice Reading Program (Croft Educational Services) opens with an eight-session training program for teachers. Initially children are tested through the successive levels until their performances drop to a 50 percent level or lower. At this point, the child begins to work the five tests for readiness, seventeen phonic skills, and ten structural analysis skills and is expected to achieve a perfect score in each to show mastery, except for the readiness level, where 80 percent is acceptable. A parallel program for comprehension involves eighteen skills in oral language readiness, written language readiness, and pattern readiness, which is subdivided into four categories: classification, sequence, comparison, and causation. Four tests in literal reading, interpretive reading, analytic reading, and critical reading are also offered, in which a pupil is expected to achieve an 84 percent or higher criterion score for mastering each of these skills. Each skill test is available in a hand-scored spirit-master format in two versions. A large wall chart enables the teacher to record every pupil's progress in every skill in the word attack or the comprehension program. A teacher's guide offering models for the one or two recommended teacher presentations of each skill, plus a few suggestions and activities, is available.

Fountain Valley Teacher Support System (Richard L. Zweig Associates) stresses 367 skills and objectives for the first six grades. Seventy-seven self-scoring tests for which the directions are recorded on cassettes assess pupil mastery. After test administration, the individual pupil's needs are automatically indicated on the back of the test and then recorded in the child's file folder. Pupils are to be grouped for instruction with the aid of a large list of basal and supplementary materials keyed to the skill sequence of the program.

Prescriptive Reading Inventory (CTB/McGraw-Hill) offers seven groups of ninety skills and objectives identified by an analysis of basal reader programs. The categories include sound–symbol correspondence, visual discrimination, phonics, structural analysis, translation, literal, interpretive and critical comprehension, and study skills. Color-coded test booklets at four levels for the first six grades, each spanning a grade or two, are to be computer-scored by the publisher. Student profiles are then returned, indicating each child's needs to aid the teacher in grouping for instruction. Program Reference Guides list textbooks and other materials related to each specific objective. Those requiring teacher supervision are distinguished from materials that can be attempted independently. Extensive field testing of the tests was carried out to determine the suitability of the items and the objectives for the various grade levels.

Read On (Random House, Inc.) is a boxed kit of tests, cassettes, and scoring keys for sixty reading skills in auditory and visual discrimination, word attack, and comprehension. The tests are reproduced from spirit masters, administered by recorded directions, and scored by cardboard masks. A 90 percent performance is expected to show acquisition of each skill. The test results are recorded on a wall chart as the child progresses through the steps. Materials paralleling the objectives, each drawn from a specific source as a basal reader system, are bound in booklets to be purchased separately from the basic testing kit.

Wisconsin Design for Reading Skill Development (Interpretive Scoring Systems) contains six components as word attack, study skills, comprehension, self-directed reading, interpretive reading, and creative reading. Groups of skills and objectives have been identified for each component, as forty-five in the word attack element, and arranged in four to seven grade levels, ranging from kindergarten to sixth grade. Machine- or hand-scored tests of each skill on which pupils are expected to score 80 percent or higher, plus informal testing procedures outlined in an accompanying guide, are offered for assessment. Thirty-nine file folders for the teacher contain commercially available materials available for instruction as well as teacher ideas on successful teaching techniques in presenting word attack skills. The comprehension and other components of the total program are similarly arranged with tests, resource folders, and teacher suggestions.

Advantages of Operant Conditioning Approaches

Majer (25) offers a number of strong arguments for the adoption of computer-assisted instruction. Numerous programs he cites show that reading can be taught in this fashion, but there are almost no comparisons with other methods in any of the details of pupil achievement. As we might expect, students tend to respond enthusiastically and to be intrigued by the whole idea. In fact, in one study the pupils definitely preferred the computer to a teacher as a mode of instruction. Other advantages suggested are the ability of the computer to individualize instruction on a one-to-one basis about as well as a teacher can; to relieve the teacher of testing duties, record keeping, the analysis of diagnostic data, preparation of reports to parents, and many other clerical responsibilities.

Programmed instruction and management systems provide systematized sequential materials for skill development based on an analysis of the entire spectrum of reading behaviors. Learning is efficiently managed, constantly reinforced, evaluated at each step, and self-pacing. Lacks in teacher preparation or knowledge are compensated for by the completeness of the program. Teachers learn more about the intricate subskills of the reading process than in using any other approaches to instruction. Many pupils who do not respond favorably to teacher–pupil interactions or who have not progressed well under traditional instruction respond better to the impersonal, independent study aspect of these systems. Some types of these programs offer or recommend alternative sequences of steps, called branching or parallel practice materials, which are selected and used according to the success of the learner at key points in the sequence. The nature of the program makes the most efficient use of pupil and teacher time by providing specific tasks keyed to frequent testing, by giving guidelines for the teacher, and by replacing global diagnostic evaluations with detailed assessments.

Although both behavioristic and humanistic approaches to education are concerned with the issues of learning to read, there is strong disagreement on the appropriate techniques. The behavioristic tradition is built on animal study and laboratory-controlled experiments, which, in the opinion of the humanists, ignore the social sources of human motivation and desire. Humanists want to understand the human needs that are served by learning to read, and they see the learning process as significant for the fulfillment of intrinsic personal needs. In contrast, the operant-conditioning theory is concerned with human needs, if at all, only after it has identified what is to be learned and how the learner must be shaped toward that goal (8). The idea of manipulating and shaping humans and their behavior for scientific purposes is abhorrent to the humanist.

More specific criticisms offered by many sources point out the following (*19,21,36*):

1. Systems approaches, computers, and programmed instruction individualize instruction only in rate of learning. In fact, all students follow virtually the same program, using the same modalities, learning the same skills, in the same sequence. Apparently all pupils are to come out equal in knowledge, understanding, and abilities (*36*).
2. The "assembly-line" arrangement of the instructional plan stresses content, not process, in a tightly arranged structure. There is no room for incidental learning; and spontaneity, creativity, and innovation are almost excluded (5). Skill in trivial, measurable traits is overemphasized at the expense of interests in reading, the goal of liking for reading, or the willingness to read. Sustained reading for pleasure or the child's own goals are almost never promoted in these plans (5).
3. Programmed management or computer-based systems must fractionate the reading process into tiny bits and pieces to fit their step-by-step approach. Yet there is very little evidence that supports the reality of all these separate skills as significant elements in the reading act. There is also serious question whether these skills can be arranged in some sort of hierarchy or sequence (other than that of difficulty) that actually promotes more successful reading. In proof of this, there is no close agreement in the sequences, or even the inclusion of many "skills" in various systems. The whole idea appears to be a pedagogical convenience to "simplify the accounting problems and make the gathering of evaluative data cheap and easy" (*29,21*).
4. Despite the claims of a psycholinguistic basis in some systems (*2,3*), the content and the overstress on minute skills violates the emphasis of leaders of that discipline that reading is a facet of language development, interacting with other·language media, and that it is a meaning-oriented act, not simply a decoding process (*29*). The divorce of learning-to-read activities from extended oral and written language activities and of phonics training from the reading act also contravene the thinking of modern psycholinguists and many other reading authorities.

Because of the redundancy of language and the strength of contextual cues, the reader does not make use of all the graphophonetic information in the text. Rather he should use the semantic and syntactic cues for meanings, psycholinguists remind us.

The systems, computer, and programmed approaches treat reading almost as though it were exclusively reacting to graphic stimuli, not an interpretive act which blends the author's and the reader's concepts into messages.

5. Hoetker warns strongly against those systems that present solutions, implying that all children will learn to read by their plan, without having first recognized the problems of learning style, modality preference, motivation, need for repetition, and the other bases of individual differences (19). We might add to this caution the observation that there is no research to indicate that any approach to reading ever tried, particularly those that offer the same basic plan for all children, has been successful with 100 percent of its students. It is meretricious to imply that only children fail, not teachers or the system.

6. Many of the systems approaches appear to be designed as assessment techniques and to leave the instructional efforts to the teacher. But because of their complexity, and the volume of scoring and paperwork both for teachers and pupils, they tend to monopolize the available instructional time and, in effect, to become the reading program. In a trial in the schools of Florida monitored by the senior author, teachers found themselves struggling to keep up with the distribution of worksheets, tests, test scoring, and recording, which left them almost no time for actual lesson presentation.

7. There is the basic presumption that the skills emphasized in these approaches are necessary for reading comprehension for most, if not all children. Yet when Bolchazy (6) tested a number of eighth graders, above-average readers, in five of the word attack skills stressed in the Wisconsin Design for Reading Skill Development, over 60 percent of the pupils failed the criterion for the tests in final long vowel in a syllable and the use of accents. Obviously good readers do not have to know these phonic and accent conventions to achieve good comprehension. Conversely, the fact that the pupils passed the three other word attack tests does not prove them essential to reading. For all we know, the other skills or rules, although known, may not be functional in reading at this level. The fact that they were stressed because of their inclusion in basal reading programs, can be taught to children at certain grade levels, and the pupil performances tested with a high degree of reliability, as the authors of this system claim, are no proof of their essentiality or their actual functioning in the reading act. In a later chapter, other studies are cited to show that subskills are much less closely related among poor readers and that primary phonic skills are no longer closely related to comprehension by intermediate grades.

The criterion-referenced tests that are an integral part of the systems we have described above are challenged in a number of aspects. First, the authors assume the validity of the instruments without offering any data relating subject performances to any real measure of reading. Similarly, the reliability of the tests or the permanence of the supposed learning is ignored by most systems. We are asked to believe that the skills exist because the authors say they do and that they must be learned in the planned sequence for progress in reading. Yet in the field study project in Florida in which we were involved, teachers frequently complained that according to the test results they were being required to teach certain primary skills to pupils already functioning adequately at the intermediate grade levels.

Even if we agree that any one skill is probably essential, how can the necessary degree of mastery be decided before the test is even tried out? Or, before any relationship of the skill to reading has been demonstrated (21)? Assuming that a child does pass a test, on main ideas, should the teacher cease all further training and go on to the next skill as some systems would lead her to do? Because a child passes a certain skill test as of a certain date, does this imply that follow-up with skill maintenance is unnecessary and that the child's learning is permanent? The concept of prescriptive instruction based on pretesting appeals to logic, but some studies show that in some groups it is no more effective for vocabulary or comprehension growth than a basal reader approach (33). Should not the authors of these systems produce the data to tell us for what types of children, or at what grade levels, these plans can promote successful reading by teaching what skills?

Some of these objections stem, of course, from the fact that these systematic methods are likely to upset the status quo of the basal reader world. It is perhaps characteristic of our educational system that new ideas are presented overenthusiastically as panaceas for our problems, contested bitterly by those who have a stake in existing practices, and then gradually find their place among other methods. There is evidence that programmed, computer-assisted, or management system methods can serve as useful adjuncts to a basal system (13). Even the authors of these new methods have begun to recognize that this is probably the most effective role for their products (2). Used judiciously, they have demonstrated progress in promoting such skills as word naming and word recognition at primary levels and vocabulary or word meanings at higher levels. The evidence of their values for developing comprehension, any other language ability, skill in using syntactic or semantic cues to meaning, interests, or liking for reading is still quite weak.

DISCUSSION QUESTIONS

1. When a teacher or school is committed to the use of a basal reader, how may a greater degree of individualization be introduced?

2. Are all teachers capable of moving gradually toward individualization? If not, why not?

3. How do the demands upon teaching skills differ in the individualized approach, when compared to the basal program?

4. Is it feasible to use basal readers in the individualized program? If so, how might they be used, and to what degree?

5. What types of pupils are likely to benefit most from individualization? Can most pupils learn to function in this framework under appropriate teacher direction?

6. Is an individualized reading program possible only for the experienced teacher? Justify your opinion.

7. How might the handicap of an inadequate classroom or school library be overcome by the teacher who wishes to individualize?

8. What factors in many school systems militate against adoption of the individualized approach by a teacher? How can these be overcome?

9. What are your reactions to the author's evaluation of the operant-conditioning approach to teaching reading?

10. What possible roles can you see for this "individualized" system?

REFERENCES

1. Aaron, Ira E., "What Teachers and Prospective Teachers Know About Phonic Generalizations," *Journal of Educational Research,* 53 (May 1960), 323–330.

2. Atkinson, Richard C., and Fletcher, John D., "Teaching Children To Read with a Computer," *Reading Teacher,* 25 (January 1972), 319–327.

3. Atkinson, Richard C., and Hansen, Duncan N., "Computer-Assisted Instruction in Initial Reading: The Stanford Project," *Reading Research Quarterly,* 2 (Fall 1966), 5–26.

4. Baker, Frank B., "Computer-Based Instructional Management Systems: A First Look," *Review of Educational Research,* 41 (February 1971), 51–70.

5. Blackford, Jean S., "A Teacher Views Criterion-Referenced Tests," *Today's Education,* 64 (March–April 1975), 36.

6. Bolchazy, Marie Carducci, "How Necessary Are Certain Skills for Reading Comprehension?" Paper presented at the National Reading Conference, St. Petersburg, Fla., December 1975.

7. Bond, Guy L., and Dykstra, Robert, "The Cooperative Research Program in First-Grade Reading Instruction," *Reading Research Quarterly,* 2 (Summer 1967), 5–142.

8. Caldwell, Jay S., and Shnayer, Sidney W., "The Truth About Readiness," *School Library Journal,* 16 (May 1970), 39–40.

9. Cyrog, Frances, "The Principal and His Staff Move Forward in Developing New Ways of Thinking About Reading," *California Journal of Elementary Education,* 27 (February 1959), 178–187.

10. Darrow, Helen Fisher, and Howes, Virgil M., *Approaches to Individualized Reading.* New York: Appleton-Century-Crofts, 1960.

11. Deep, Donald, "The Computer Can Help Individualize Instruction," *Elementary School Journal,* 70 (April 1970), 351–358.

12. Educational Records Bureau, *Final Evaluation of Project Read in New York City Schools.* Greenwich, Conn.: The Bureau, 1971.

13. Ellson, W. G., et al., "Programmed Tutoring: A Teaching Aid and a Research Tool," *Reading Research Quarterly,* 1 (Fall 1965), 77–127.

14. Frazier, Alexander, "The Individualized Reading Program," *Controversial Issues in Reading and Promising Solutions,* Supplementary Educational Monographs, No. 91. Chicago: University of Chicago Press, 1961, 57–74.

15. Greenman, Ruth, and Kapilian, Sharon, "Individual Reading in the Third and Fourth Grades," *Elementary English,* 35 (April 1959), 234–237.

16. Groff, Patrick J., "Materials for Individualized Reading," *Elementary English,* 38 (January 1961), 1–7.

17. Groff, Patrick J., "Comparisons of Individualized and Ability Grouping Approaches to Reading Achievement," *Elementary English,* 40 (March 1963), 258–264, 276.

18. Heilman, Arthur W., *Phonics in Proper Perspective.* Columbus, Ohio: Charles E. Merrill Publishing Company, 1968.

19. Hoetker, James, Fichtenau, Robert, and Farr, Helen L. K., *Systems, Systems Approaches and the Teacher.* Urbana, Ill.: National Council of Teachers of English, 1972.

20. Hull, Marion A., *Phonics for the Teaching of Reading.* Columbus, Ohio: Charles E. Merrill Publishing Company, 1969.

21. Johnson, Dale D., and Pearson, P. David, "Skills Management Systems: A Critique," *Reading Teacher,* 28 (May 1975), 757–764.

22. Johnson, R. H., "Individualized and Basal Primary Reading Programs," *Elementary English,* 42 (December 1965), 902–904.

23. Macdonald, J. B., Harris, T. L., and Mann, J. S.,

"Individual Versus Group Instruction in First Grade Reading," *Reading Teacher,* 19 (May 1966), 643–647.

24. McKillop, Anne, "Special Problems Encountered in Individualized Reading Instruction," *Individualizing Reading Instruction.* Proceedings 39th Annual Education Conference, University of Delaware, 6, 1957, 68–76.

25. Majer, Kenneth, "Computer Assisted Instruction and Reading," in "Reading Process and Pedagogy," William E. Blanton and J. Jaap Tuinman, eds., *Bulletin of the School of Education, Indiana University,* 48 (September 1972), 77–98.

26. Rude, Robert T., "Objective-Based Reading Systems: An Evaluation," *Reading Teacher,* 28 (November 1974), 169–175.

27. Safford, Alton L., "Evaluation of an Individualized Reading Program," *Reading Teacher,* 13 (April 1960), 266–270.

28. Sartain, Harry W., "The Roseville Experiment with Individualized Reading," *Reading Teacher,* 13 (April 1960), 277–281.

29. Spache, George D., "A Reaction to 'Computer-Assisted Instruction in Initial Reading: The Stanford Project,'" *Reading Research Quarterly,* 3 (Fall 1967), 101–110.

30. Spache, George D., *Good Reading for Poor Readers.* Champaign, Ill.: Garrard Publishing Company, 1974.

31. Spache, George D., and Baggett, Mary E., "What Do Teachers Know About Phonics and Syllabication?" *Reading Teacher,* 19 (November 1965), 96–99.

32. Spencer, Doris U., "Individualized vs. a Basal Reader Program in Rural Communities, Grades One and Two," *Reading Teacher,* 21 (October 1967), 11–17.

33. Thiel, Norma A., *An Analysis of the Effectiveness of the Teaching of Reading by Individual Prescription,* ERIC/CRIER, ED 061 690, 1972.

34. Veatch, Jeanette, *Reading in the Elementary School.* New York: Ronald Press, 1966.

35. Vite, Irene W., "Individualized Reading—The Scoreboard on Control Studies," *Education,* 81 (January 1961), 285–290.

36. Weintraub, Samuel, "Programmed Reading Materials," in *Recent Developments in Reading,* H. Alan Robinson, ed., Supplementary Educational Monographs, No. 95. Chicago: University of Chicago Press, 1965, 64–69.

37. Whipple, Guy M., ed., "Adapting the Schools to Individual Differences," *Twenty-fourth Yearbook,* National Society for the Study of Education, Part II. Chicago: University of Chicago Press, 1923.

38. Young, Elizabeth, "Individualized Reading," *Baltimore Bulletin of Education,* 35 (May–June 1958), 29–32.

SUPPLEMENTARY READING

Atwood, Beth S., *Building Independent Learning Skills.* Palo Alto, Calif.: Education Today Co., 1974.

Barnes, Ellen, Eyman, Bill, and Engolz, Maddy Bragar, *Teach and Reach.* Syracuse, N.Y.: Human Policy Press, 1974.

Darrow, Helen Fisher, and Van Allen, Roach, *Independent Activities for Creative Learning.* New York: Teachers College Press, 1961.

Harris, Larry A., and Smith, Carl B., *Individualizing Reading Instruction: A Reader.* New York: Holt, Rinehart and Winston, Inc., 1972.

La Pray, Margaret, *Teaching Children To Become Independent Readers.* Washington, D.C.: Center for Applied Research in Education, 1972.

Learning Centers: Children on Their Own. Washington, D.C.: Association for Childhood Education, 1970.

Musgrave, Ray, *Individualized Instruction: Teaching Strategies Focusing on the Learner.* Boston: Allyn and Bacon, Inc., 1975.

Reid, Virginia, *Individualizing Your Reading Program.* New York: Resources for Learning, 1970.

Smith, James A., *Creative Teaching of the Language Arts.* Boston: Allyn and Bacon, Inc., 1973.

Veatch, Jeanette, *Reading in the Elementary School.* New York: Ronald Press, 1966.

Weisgerber, Robert A., ed., *Developmental Efforts in Individualized Learning.* Itasca, Ill.: Peacock Publishers, 1971.

4
Using the Linguistic Approaches

PREVIEW

"The linguist is carrying on his proper function when he advances linguistic generalizations that he believes apply to the teaching of reading. He is also performing a fitting and useful function when he criticizes the teaching of reading from his linguistic vantage point. But he is not on firm ground when he produces reading programs that are based solely on linguistic criteria."* This quotation from Kenneth S. Goodman sums up our judgment of the present relationship of linguistics to reading instruction.

Reading is certainly a use of language, and reading specialists need to have a broad background in the scientific facts of language. But some of the popularizing linguists who have rushed into print with contradictory reading programs have done the field of reading a disservice. By propounding conflicting and naive theories of the reading process, by producing programs that often are not discernibly different from approaches discarded many years ago, by refusing to accept that much of current reading instruction is based on psychological and physiological principles unfamiliar to them, many linguists have failed in their role of advisers to the reading specialist. If linguistics is to make a contribution, it will probably be in the study of language development of children, how language conveys meaning, and the relationships between language and reading development.

*Kenneth S. Goodman, "The Linguistics of Reading," *Elementary School Journal,* 64 (April 1964), 355–361.

Since the early 1960s, a group of language scientists, popularly known as linguists, have been proposing a variety of approaches to reading instruction that differ markedly from other methods. This group of materials offering a linguistic theory is proving to be somewhat confusing to the average classroom teacher. Without identifying their particular sphere of interest in linguistics, the authors offer quite conflicting explanations of the inadequacies of present teaching methods and how they might be improved by the adoption of their linguistic principles.

One linguist may attack the whole word or sight method (*2,3*), another concentrates on criticizing popular methods of phonics instruction (*23,24*), and a third finds fault with both these criticisms as well as any present procedures (*12*). Each critic offers a different substitute method of beginning instruction, and yet all these substitutes are called the linguistic approach.

SCHOOLS WITHIN SCHOOLS

The confusion lies in the fact that there are at least three kinds of linguists talking about reading instruction, each from within his own frame of reference in language research. These are the phonologists, the structuralists, and the psycholinguists.

The Phonologists' Definition of Reading

The phonologists concern themselves with the analysis of the sounds of spoken (and written) language. Leonard Bloomfield is credited by most of his fellow linguists with the identification of the various phonemes which are the basic sounds of our language. As early as 1942 Bloomfield (*2*) attempted to outline the implications of his research for reading instruction. Later, in 1961, Bloomfield offered instructional materials based on his phoneme–grapheme studies (*3*). Bloomfield (*3*) and Soffietti (*43*) recommend that reading be taught as a process of translating phonemes (basic sounds) into words. Working first with groups of letters, the child gradually learns words and later proceeds to larger units of sentence structure. Or, in the words of Goldberg and Rasmussen's article (*12*, p. 24):

> The main task in learning to read appears then to be able to produce the sounds of language when one sees the written marks which conventionally represent these sounds. . . . Even though one might insist that the derivation of meaning is a

necessary element in the reading process, we feel that a separation of the skill of associating sound with symbol from the aim of deriving meaning is important for the reason that the presentation of the subject of reading is made much less complicated by concentrating on the skill rather than the promotion of understanding.

In effect, their concept of the act of reading is a translation of the sounds for which letters stand, first into spoken sounds, then into words, and possibly later into sentences. Whether the process deals with meaningful units seems unimportant, or at least subordinate, to the translating into sounds. At first glance this seems like an ultraphonic approach, but the phonologists deny the similarity, as we shall see.

Fries enlarges this definition of the reading process, as he sees it, in such statements as: "Letters must be recognized as they appear in sequences. The order of the letters in the directional sequence of left to right acts as a fundamental marker for the discrimination of lexical units" (11). Fries points out, however, that he is not referring to the recognition of individual letters as they stand alone. To promote this type of learning, Fries insists that the words must appear in regularly arranged spelling patterns and repetitive sentences, but never with any pictures that might lead the child to react to clues other than the sequence of letters.

The Structuralists' Definition of Reading

A second school of linguists, sometimes called grammarians or structural linguists, has investigated the structure of language. They point out the essential elements of language that result in the communication of ideas, such as word order or word position, word function; word groups that modify, expand, or change simple expressions; and the signals of intonation, as pitch, stress, and pause. Other areas of structural linguistic research include the identification and frequency of types of sentences (simple statements, demands, requests, questions) and grammatical inflections or word changes to indicate tense and number. It is quite apparent that this approach to language would result in a quite different group of implications for reading instruction than would the work of the phonologists. As yet there are no teaching materials offered for reading instruction exemplifying the ideas of the structuralists.

According to Warfel and Lloyd (49), the reading process is a recognition of the structural principles of word order. A few hundred structure words link words into groups that must be read as such. Lefevre and others (23,24) stress recognition of larger speech patterns (simple statements, requests), or structural elements (noun groups, verb groups, phrases, clauses), or function words (articles, auxiliary verbs, prepositions), and grammatical inflections as the basic teaching material. Eye movements in reading must therefore be related to structural elements of sentences rather than to words. In another article, Warfel (48) enlarges upon this definition by stressing the fact that good reading requires an accompaniment of vocal sounds, at least during the primary stages. Only after wide oral reading experience is silent reading, as we commonly understand it, feasible or desirable.

Thus it appears that in the beginning, the child is to read by relating large units and patterns of speech to their graphic or symbolic representatives, the printed words. Children would be taught to react to signals such as capitals and periods; to the order and grouping of words; to the importance of such modifiers as articles, adverbs, and the like; and to the grammatical inflections of number, tense, and possession. Children would be alerted to the normal sentence order of subjects, verbs, and "completer" (direct object, object complement, or the like). Children would learn also to read the great variety of variations upon this normal sentence order possible through the use of function words *(the, into, when)* to signal additional elements. Just how this approach is to be implemented we will attempt to point out later.

Lefevre, a leading exponent of this particular linguistic approach to reading, has criticized the present authors for offering what he considers the most naive statement of the "simplistic word-perception theory" of reading. Lefevre believes rather that the sentence, not word perception, is the unit of meaning (25). He would have us teach reading by much listening to stories and by attention to sentence order, word order, and most important of all, intonation of sentences. Presumably, after such training the child would begin by reading whole sentences.

Psycholinguists

A third school of linguists concerns itself with psycholinguistics, which might be defined as the psychology of language. At present a number of their studies are relevant to reading, such as the meaning of children's oral reading errors (6,13,51), the relationship between decoding (translating letters into sounds) and encoding, the interpretation of the printed word (21,50), the influence of context upon comprehension (31,52), and other facets of the relationships of language to reading instruction.

Psycholinguistic concepts of the reading process were discussed in the opening chapter and are referred to later in reference to diagnosing oral reading and in teaching word recognition. The discussion below of "linguistic" teaching materials and their accompanying concepts are not characteristic of the thinking of that school of linguists.

The Materials

There are currently a number of materials which appear or claim to follow linguistic principles. Among these is the text *Let's Read,* prepared by Bloomfield (3) and published after his death by C. L. Barnhart, the famous lexicologist. The Bloomfield–Barnhart text follows these authors' version of a linguistic approach to teaching reading by presenting first a carefully controlled vocabulary of isolated words. Each list of words stresses a particular group of sounds of high consistency in the manner in which it is spelled. Thus a number of words containing the *an* spelling is presented, followed by another group containing the *at* spelling, etc. For the most part, each group of words with a common phoneme is composed of real or nonsense monosyllables. A second group of words varies only in vowel pattern (*mad-mid, hot-hut*). The progression continues from three- to four-letter words, from regulars to irregulars, and finally to polysyllabic words. Later lessons introduce the reading of unrelated sentences and brief stories in which words illustrating a certain sound are inserted. This is the approach endorsed by Hall (*16*), Fries (*11*), and a number of linguists who share Bloomfield's theoretical beliefs.

Other linguistically oriented series include *The Linguistic Readers* by Henry Lee Smith, Jr., Clara G. Stratemeyer, et al. (Benziger Corp.); *The Merrill Linguistic Readers* by C. C. Fries et al. (Charles E. Merrill); *The Basic Reading Series* by Lynn Goldberg and Donald Rasmussen (Science Research Associates); Frances Adkins Halls' *Sounds and Letters Series* (Linguistic); the *Miami Linguistic Readers* (D. C. Heath); and Catherine Stern's *The Structural Reading Series* (L. W. Singer).

Although all these readers are supposed to follow the tenets of linguistic science, there are interesting differences among them. Fries insists on no pictures; most of the other series are profusely illustrated. Fries insists on presentation of words in sentences; Barnhart offers nothing but lists of words for almost half of his text. Fries depends upon the use of only regularly spelled words; Goldberg and Rasmussen introduce both regular and irregular words. Smith and Stratemeyer utilize story and poetry content from the beginning, while Barnhart and Fries deemphasize the importance of meaningful content by using nonsense words and sentences. If all these readers are supposed to be based on the same fundamental principles of linguistics, the contradictory practices are puzzling, to say the least.

Certain other reading materials are sometimes referred to as representative of the linguistic theory, but in actuality differ materially from each other in content and rationale. The *Royal Road Readers* by J. C. Daniels and H. Diack (Chatto & Windus, London) are an example of such pseudolinguistic materials. They differ fundamentally in employing a contextual setting—a story thread—to introduce their vocabulary. The sentence patterns used in this material are not closely controlled or varied systematically, as the structuralist school suggests they should be. Second, although a majority of the words used in any story or booklet present a particular group of sounds, many other words, and hence sounds, are also introduced as needed to tell the story. It is probably more accurate to designate the *Royal Road Readers* as a type of phonics system, as the authors do, rather than a true linguistic approach.

A second group of materials loosely labeled as linguistic in orientation is the Richards–Gibson *First Steps to Reading* (Washington Square Press). These booklets control very carefully the introduction of letters and attempt also to offer a very simple group of sentence patterns. Furthermore, the vocabulary is highly concrete and profusely illustrated by simple drawings and stick figures.

The authors and A. R. MacKinnon (*28*), who made an intensive study of the values of this material, apparently share Bloomfield's belief that reading occurs letter by letter and that the letter controls they utilized simplified this process. MacKinnon's study did show that under certain grouping conditions the

Richards–Gibson materials produced significant reading growth. But he, like the authors, ignored the fact that the control of letters did not extend to the control of letter sounds, for many of the letters used varied widely in the sounds they represented in various words. Thus the material violates one of the basic principles of linguistic theory—consistency in the presentation of basic phonemes (sounds).

LIMITATIONS OF THE LINGUISTIC APPROACHES

The phonologists offer the following as linguistic principles which should be incorporated into or determine the nature of reading instruction.

1. Speech is the primary language function, and writing and reading are secondary or derived from oral language. Hence any child with normal speech is ready to begin reading.
2. Learning the names of the letters of the alphabet is of primary value in beginning reading (2,3).
3. Words offered for beginning texts must include only those regularly consistent in the grapheme–phoneme correspondence. Simple regular words and nonsense syllables are most appropriate.
4. Interpretation of the meaning of printed words is quite secondary to the process of sound–symbol recognition (11).
5. Words of similar pattern (called spelling patterns) should be introduced simultaneously so that the child will be led to emphasize the sound–symbol relationship rather than other possible clues to recognition.
6. Pictures tend to give clues to word recognition and hence should be omitted (2,3).
7. As presently taught, phonics should be eliminated because it teaches children (a) to sound words when they already know the sounds of their language; (b) that each letter has a sound (but letters do not make sounds—they stand for sounds); (c) that a letter makes a sound (people make the sound); (d) that there are silent letters (it is impossible for a letter to make a sound or a silence); (e) children are taught how to pronounce words when they should be reading them (39).
8. Word recognition occurs by the successive decoding of graphemes, not by recognition of word form, word length, or configuration, context clues, or the like (3,4,11).
9. It is a fallacy of the whole-word method to confuse reading and understanding. One may learn to read without being able to understand or comprehend (3,4,11,23).

In contrast, the structuralists offer these ideas, which are also supposed to be linguistic principles relevant to reading instruction.

1. Comprehension is based on auditory memories, and hence the reader's ability to hear the written word in its normal spoken inflection and to respond to the stress, tone, pitch, and junctures of the sentences as he reads silently.

2. Language patterns of the text should be as varied and complex as those present in the child's spoken language (*44*).
3. A conscious learning of syntax or sentence patterns is a significant aid to comprehension (*33*).
4. Early emphasis upon recognition or reading of structural units might help solve some of the problems of eye span (*33*).

Let us examine critically these linguistic principles offered by the various schools of language science.

The Phonological Approach

Reading Versus Speech.   The idea that reading is the mirror of speech is rejected by many reading and linguistic writers (*29,46,50*). They point out that the intonation patterns and tempo of spoken language, the pauses between ideas, and the meaningful silences, gestures, and grimaces of conversation are all lacking in the printed page. Other differences are the fewer phonetically different sounds in speaking (words and phrases are often run together), as well as the repetitive but structurally incomplete nature of spoken language. Book English just does not resemble the spoken word, any more than the written composition of children or adults mirrors their own speech.

Moreover, as Weaver (*50*) points out, reading is not a one-to-one translation of graphic symbols to verbal signs to mental interpretation, as some linguists seem to think. Decoding or translating graphemes into phonemes requires only recognition, not recall or interpretation. Encoding or interpreting reading has a higher information load, for the reader must incorporate the ideas he reads with his recall of previous ideas stored in his mind. Oral language, as in reading aloud, actually interferes with mental interpretation, and as a result oral reading produces weak comprehension.

Although we strive to make children believe that reading is talking written down by utilizing language experience charts and the like, unfortunately they are not parallel mental processes and the possession of normal language does not ensure success with reading.

The Alphabet.   Some believe that we read by the recognition of letters or even by spelling words mentally (*2,3,11*) rather than by the recognition of whole words. Thus they would begin with the names of the letters, some assuming that this learning even reveals the sounds of the letters. Alphabetic methods are ancient in the history of reading instruction and have never proved to be effective. It is true that the shapes, heights, and position of letters do contribute to word recognition, but they do this by providing a clue to the Gestalt, the overall pattern of the word. No reader in any alphabetic language recognizes words letter by letter, or by spelling. No reader is really conscious of the letters in a word, unless he fails utterly to recognize it. If we were conscious of the order of letters in words, how would we explain the tendency for errors in reading and spelling to cluster in the middles? Why does a reader read groups of words presented in a tenth of a second tachistoscopically, but only recognize strings of five to six letters?

If reading is a direct decoding of the letters of a word into sounds, how did the early Egyptians read their nonphonetic alphabet? How did the Phoenician manage to read an alphabet with no vowels? Many others reject the identification of words by the letters present (42) in pointing out that word identification is too fast for letter-by-letter recognition; words cannot be identified if letters are presented one at a time; the reaction time for a word is scarcely longer than that for a single letter, and, finally, words can be identified when the component letters are not individually discriminable.

Regular Versus Irregular Words.   The primary vocabulary should be carefully controlled in the regularity of the sounds the words contain, according to Bloomfield (2,3). He would include both real and nonsense words, provided they are regular. But nonsense words are not an aid to reading, for as Goldberg and Rasmussen found, such units are meaningless and unlearnable despite their phonemic consistency (12).

Our language is hardly phonetic, except in consonant sounds, and it is misleading to represent it in CVC (consonant–vowel–consonant) monosyllables. In Clymer's data (7), CVC introduces a short vowel sound in primary reading only 62 percent of the time. Other favorite units of the linguists, CVCe (silent *e*) is consistent 63 percent of the time, and CVVC (with a long and a silent vowel) is true only 45 percent of the time. The sounds of the vowels, as Venezky's analysis shows (46), are determined by the order of letters and by phonological habits, and the variations are great. Moreover, polysyllabic words are seldom combinations of these monosyllables, except in true compound words.

There is an element of logic in the phonetic consistency of the Bloomfield–Barnhart and Fries teaching materials. Grouping words according to the sounds composing them seems a sensible way of promoting the growth of phonic generalizations and skill in word attack. But like many of the other linguistic principles, this concept is not a new discovery. Note the marked similarity between the materials offered by Bloomfield–Barnhart and those from the *Gradual Primer* of 1853.

Bloomfield—Barnhart (3, p. 63)	*The Gradual Primer**
cap gap lap map nap rap sap tap	Pen led Let Bell
pap yap Hap	men bed pet tell
a cap a gap a lap	ten red yet well

* After David B. Tower, *The Gradual Primer* (Boston: Sanborn, Carter, Bazin and Co., 1853), as cited by Nila B. Smith, *American Reading Instruction* (New York: Silver Burdette Company, 1934), 110–111.

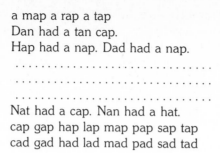

```
a map a rap a tap                    I met ten men.
Dan had a tan cap.                   I have a bad pen.
Hap had a nap. Dad had a nap.        Let men set a net.

. . . . . . . . . . . . . . . . . . . . . . . . . . . . .
. . . . . . . . . . . . . . . . . . . . . . . . . . . . .
. . . . . . . . . . . . . . . . . . . . . . . . . . . . .

Nat had a cap. Nan had a hat.
cap gap hap lap map pap sap tap
cad gad had lad mad pad sad tad
```

Even in 1853 the fallacy of teaching the entire alphabet before beginning reading, as Bloomfield–Barnhart materials do, was recognized. Letters and words illustrating their sounds were introduced gradually in a realistic recognition of pupil limitations in learning capacities, an area in which linguists appear to be inexperienced.

This pseudo-logical approach to beginning reading was finally discarded in America after exhaustive investigation proved it ineffective for modern reading goals. The artificial vocabulary divorced from its inherent meaningfulness and the overemphasis upon letter sounds produces overly cautious, slow, and uncomprehending readers. American children of the past eventually learned to read by this method, and many European children are still taught in this fashion. But, unfortunately for the linguists' goals, the phonic method is most effective in preventing the development of a sentence sense or a habit of responding to the structural elements of language. Probably more than any other method, the highly phonic system promotes the tendency to unintelligent word-by-word reading without the consequent recognition of the total significance of the context.

Spelling Patterns. The phonologists prefer to use a reading vocabulary of monosyllables spelled in a particular pattern, such as *rat, hat, fat.* Such a list is what the educational psychologists call a minimal contrast arrangement and it has been the subject of many studies. Levin and Watson (*26*) demonstrated that these lists are easier to learn than those in which sound–symbol correspondence varies, as *come, go, hot.* But the learning of other words later was less successful with minimal contrasts. Rothkopf (*34*), Hartley (*17*), and others have also shown that the learning of vocabulary is better when initial materials offer maximal contrasts.

There is, of course, the very relevant question of how and what kinds of words children learn most readily. To mention only a single study, Bickley (*1*) showed again that in a list of words of equal frequency and commonality, pupils learned best those organized in terms of their own meaningful associations, not those grouped by class, by logical order, or by spelling patterns. Frequency counts by a computer lead the linguists to teach such items as *dd, gg, ft* (left), *lf* (half), *ndk* (handkerchief), *nd* (handsome), *pb* (raspberry), and *di* (soldier) as significant clues to word recognition. The logic of this mathematical derivation of instructional units escapes most reading authorities, such as the present writers.

Decoding Versus Meaning.   To emphasize decoding as the heart of the reading process is consistent, we suppose, with the phonologists' preoccupation with reading by letters. We have already pointed out the fallacy in attempting to define reading as simply decoding letter sounds. Such a concept of the reading process leaves us without any understanding or explanation of comprehension.

One additional study may serve to make our point. Kolers (*21*) asked adult bilingual speakers to read mixed passages in their two languages. They tended to mispronounce and wrongly accent words of their native language, translated some words into the other language, and changed syntactic arrangements as they read. Obviously a lot more goes on in reading than just translating graphemes into phonemes, as Goodman says (*14*).

No Pictures.   It is true that there is some question whether the pictures used in readers make a contribution to comprehension. But, on the other hand, pictures related to words, as nouns and verbs, do help in word recognition, as MacKinnon and others (*20,28*) have shown. The decision to ban pictures in beginning reading is completely arbitrary, not based on any linguistic principles.

No Phonics.   The type of phonics training in distorted letter-by-letter sounding decried by linguists is also deplored by most basal authors and reading experts. For this, and any other current phonics approach, linguists would substitute learning sound–symbol relationships in a series of words varying only in the initial consonant. Long vowels are usually presented later in the questionable *CVCe* unit, and vowel combinations in the *CVVC* pattern. Thus, by repetition of words of certain patterns children presumably learn the grapheme–phoneme correspondence.*

Most linguistic series do not teach the generalizations about these sounds that basals do; they stress initial consonant substitution as the only phonic skill, omitting such others as blending syllables, the effect of the accent, and the multiple spellings possible for vowel sounds. Some teach consonant blends or trigraphs; others do not. Prefixes and suffixes are apt to be taught as letter combinations rather than as elements modifying the meaning of the root word.

Some psycholinguists consider this phonological approach limited in its failure to integrate the facts from psychology, sociology, and even some linguistic fields as semantics (meanings of words), structural linguistics, and morphemics (combinations of sounds).

Word Recognition Clues.   To accept the premise of those linguists who claim that word recognition occurs only by decoding, we would have to ignore all research on word recognition of the past half-century. Even the recent psycholinguistic studies of children's word recognition errors refute this argument. Analysis of children's errors over an entire year indicates that something like 90 percent of the substitutions are related to the contextual or syntactic nature of the material (*51*).

*See Robert Emans, "Linguists and Phonics," *Reading Teacher,* 26 (February 1973), 477–482.

Children tend to substitute words that make sense semantically and syntactically, as a noun for a noun, a verb for a verb. Goodman (*13*) has also shown that the average pupil corrected most of his errors in reading a list of words (two-thirds in first grade, three-fourths in second, and four-fifths in third grade) when reading the same words in context. Children do try to make use of the semantic and contextual information in sentences when reading.

Reading and Meaning.   Although some deny it, it is apparent that the authors of some linguistic readers do not believe that reading is a meaning-getting process, as evidenced by their presentation of words in lists; of nonsense as well as true words; the emphasis upon decoding words of similar patterns, whether or not the words are common in children's backgrounds; their deemphasis of readiness for reading; their omission of follow-up language activities to add depth of meaning; the overemphasis upon oral reading; the tendency to equate fluency in oral reading with comprehension; and, in some series, the use of materials never longer than a programmed frame or at best a sentence or two.

The Structural Approach

Auditory Memory.   No reading specialist questions whether reading is part of the language process and is strongly related to auditory memories of spoken words. Teachers of reading show their understanding of this relationship daily in using the spoken words of children as a source of reading materials in experience charts, stories, and records. Teachers strive to help children read aloud with normal intonations so that the reading will resemble familiar speech and the child will realize the inherent parallelism (*45*).

However, because of classroom experience with both normal and deaf children, teachers do not believe that success in reading is completely dependent upon auditory memory for speech. They teach deaf children to read who have no auditory memories as a source of constant reference. They see that even beginning readers can read silently, without having to hear every word in order to read it, as the linguists seem to feel they must. Auditory memories are helpful for beginning readers in the act of word recognition or word attack, but they are not absolutely essential.

This school of linguists tells us that children must learn to read by attending to the structural elements of sentences, to signals, modifiers, and inflections. No experienced reading teacher would refute this principle, for she knows that comprehension depends upon the correct interpretation of these structural components of language (*22*). She knows that inability to deal with complex combinations of structures interferes markedly with the child's reasoning while reading. But no linguist has yet explained or illustrated how this is to be implemented. How can a child learn to read large sentence elements or complete sentences without a sight vocabulary? The teaching of word recognition is strongly decried by some linguists, for it is destructive of sentence sense and the recognition of the greater significance of the complete element or sentence, they say. Are we then to return to the rote sentence method of the last century, which failed because it neglected to recognize the word as the basic unit of reading? This school of linguists has failed to read the message of our earlier failures and to learn that no reader can progress in his development without an ever-growing stock of sight words and skill in attacking new words. Reading is first a word recognition task and only secondly a process of interpretation of word combinations.

Language Patterns.   By comparing the sentence patterns in children's speech with those in their readers, Strickland (*44*) has declared that the readers should present sentence patterns as varied and complex as any of those used by children. Her definition of a sentence is an utterance that ends only when the speaker shows by silence or falling intonation that he has finished (or has run out of breath). With this unique definition of a sentence, Strickland, of course, found that children speak longer sentences than those in readers. She concludes that the simpler sentence structure of readers handicaps the children's language development.

It is true that many basal readers employ very short, simple, and repetitive sentences (and so do some of the linguistic readers). But this situation has changed markedly in recent editions. However, it does not follow that a child is ready to process sentences in reading as long or complex as those he sometimes speaks. The two processes differ, as we have pointed out, in terms of information load and retrieval of ideas. Besides, early reading is complicated by the constant task of word recognition, which interferes with comprehension—a problem completely absent in the child's own speech, and present only occasionally in listening to others.

Syntax.   Structuralists contend that a knowledge of syntactic patterns would improve reading comprehension at all levels. When we remember that children do use syntactic clues as an aid to word recognition, as shown earlier, this contention seems logical. However, experiments in teaching linguistic structure as a means of improving comprehension have been complete failures, according to O'Donnell (*32*) and Devine (*10*). As Sauer's study indicates (*37*), children vary in ability to handle sentence patterns at different rates, and a gradual gradation in sentence patterns in readers would meet children's developing skills more effectively.

Weaver (*50*) denies that structure of the sentence is the vehicle controlling word choice. Word choice is controlled by the message of the sentence, he contends. Moreover, children's short-term memory is not good enough to deal with sentences in a verbatim fashion (any more than adults can). Rather, the reader reacts to the message received, plus his previously stored ideas, not only to the syntactic structure of the sentence, in obtaining comprehension.

Structural Units and Eye Span.   The emphasis on reading by structural units rather than by words is, of course, based on the linguist's naive interpretation of the reading process. He believes that we read by groups of words—by structural components such as phrases, clauses, noun groups, and verb groups. Or, at least if we don't read in this fashion, we certainly should. We must stretch our eye span to encompass whole elements or sentences. The linguists are obviously unaware of the human visual limitations in the act of near-point reading, which make it impossible for us to see clearly letters much more than a half-inch from the point of fixation. As Hall (16) does, some linguists ignore the studies on eye movements or the psychology of reading and consequently urge us to do the impossible in the act of reading. It is undoubtedly true that the meaning of a sentence is greater than the significance of the separate words composing it. But this sentence must be read practically word by word and processed mentally before its total meaning is apparent.

Even punctuation does not have a significant influence upon comprehension when reading orally or silently, for its absence in the material read by college sophomores affected only rate of reading in Johnson's report (19). Eye-movement studies indicate that the pauses of the reader do not correspond either to the structure or the punctuation of the sentence. Ancient Greek contained no interword spaces or punctuation, and no indication of the boundaries of words or sentences, yet some of the world's masterpieces were written and read in this style.

THE RESEARCH

DeLawter (9) compared second graders who had been taught by a linguistic decoding approach (the Miami and the Merrill readers) with those using a basal system (the Chandler Language Experience readers). After two years of instruction, the meaning-oriented children tended toward oral miscues which were real words, while the linguistically trained pupils produced mostly nonword miscues. DeLawter concludes that the linguistic approach tends to produce a high percentage of mispronunciations or nonwords, errors that show graphic similarity to the printed word but are semantically inappropriate much of the time. Self-corrections by these pupils were made largely on the basis of graphic cues (letter sounds), not contextual or semantic cues. As the psycholinguists would say, these pupils had been trained to respond mainly to the graphophonemic cues, the least significant of the cues in printed matter for obtaining meaning.

Ruddell (35,36) compared basal, basal plus language structure, a programmed linguistic series, and the programmed plus language structure. The results varied at the end of the first and at the end of the second, but in summary it appeared that there were hardly any real differences between the effectiveness of the four approaches. The linguistic programmed series was improved by the language structure training, but the basal program was not. On the whole, the linguistic programs tended to show greater skill in word recognition than the basal.

One study compared basal and linguistic programs plus dialect training among four classes of rural, black children. It found no advantages under either reading method for the dialect training, and no differences in reading performances with either approach. Using the Fries readers versus a basal, Schneyer (*38*) reported the basal groups superior in paragraph meaning, spelling, and phonic skills in the total comparison. In comprehension, the basal produced superior results for average pupils only, and superior phonic skills for high-ability pupils only. In oral reading, basal pupils were superior in both rate and accuracy. The advantages of better writing mechanics, spelling, and total number of words in a writing sample among first-grade linguistic pupils disappeared in the second grade.

In a follow-up study at third grade with the same pupils, Schneyer (*38*) found the only significant difference to be in favor of basal pupils in phonic skills. In writing, linguistic pupils used more running words and they were superior in rate but not in accuracy in oral reading.

William D. Sheldon et al. (*40,41*) also continued their first-grade comparative study through the third grade. They contrasted a basal versus a modified linguistic (Stern's *Structural Reading*) versus a true linguistic (Bloomfield's *Let's Read*). At the end of the first grade, basal pupils were superior in rate and accuracy of oral reading only. In second grade, the two linguistic systems resulted in better word meaning, spelling, and oral comprehension. No differences in any reading skills appeared at the end of the third grade, and, as Sheldon pointed out, regardless of the system used, some pupils from each group were still disabled in reading.

Wyatt (*54*) compared three linguistic systems, *Royal Road Readers,* the *Linguistic Readers* (Benziger Corp.), and the *Lippincott Basic Readers,* with a multibasal program. At the end of the first grade, the linguistic systems gave superior results in word recognition only, and this difference was true just for girls.

J. Cayce Morrison (*30*) contrasted structural patterns versus vocabulary training versus both among Puerto Rican pupils in New York City. All three approaches produced gains in writing and speaking, but none affected reading scores. In fact, the structural patterns and the vocabulary plus structural groups showed losses in reading.

Davis (*8*) used modified Bloomfield materials as a supplement to a basal versus a basal. For a small number of first graders, the dual system produced better scores in word recognition only. Davis concluded that the linguistic materials did not retard reading development, but neither did they make much of a contribution.

Other studies of this type are reported by Wardhaugh (*47*), with quite similar results. Although all the results are not consistent, it does appear that linguistic systems tend to produce better word recognition only. In contrast, the same systems tend to produce inferior oral reading in both rate and accuracy than do common basal systems. The emphasis upon sound–symbol correspondence produces inconsistent results in current phonics tests and no differences in the ability to read regular or irregular words. The emphasis upon structural language knowledge does not produce any measurable improvement in comprehension. And despite the almost violent objections of the phonologists to current phonics teaching, their systems produce just about the same results—better word recognition.

At the moment we can see clearly several possible contributions of linguistics to reading. After the research has been done, perhaps we will discover the proper learning sequence and the most effective method of presentation of the basic sounds of our language. We hope, as Constance M. McCullough (27) has suggested, the linguists may help us in teaching the relativity of language—the variants in sounds because of adjoining letters and the influence of context upon word and sentence meanings. Perhaps they too will recognize the logic of teaching sounds, words, and forms together that are grossly different, for this is obviously the most effective approach. We may hope that linguists will cease trying to superimpose adult logic upon children's learning, for as Constance McCullough says, "We don't sound the whole sentence before we utilize clues to structure, sense some possible clues to meaning and relationship, formulate hunches about the total meaning, and see possible applications of this meaning to past and future ideas" (27, p. 189).

Since children's ability to deal with inflected words, as plurals, past tense, etc., seems to be related to reading, at least by the second grade (5), linguists might help us explore appropriate ways of conveying this information to children. Since both reading and language specialists believe that language development of the child is significant for reading success, perhaps they will enter into joint research to discover why certain studies seem to deny this relationship (4,53). Are the measures of language we are using inappropriate or is this really a tenable assumption? Reading specialists need information from linguists regarding the significance of dialect and context clues, Doris Gunderson says (15). She also questions why linguists do not try to help with studies of how language is learned, in relating this development to learning theory, in finding principles of learning language, in determining the interaction of learning style, racial and ethnic backgrounds, and language development. Some reading experts, such as Arthur W. Heilman, are pessimistic about such future possibilities, as expressed in his statement, "While every linguist is entitled to hypothesize as to how reading should be taught, there is nothing in the body of linguistic science which relates to the issue of *how children learn to read*" (18, p. 104).

Bill Martin, Jr., author of the delightful *Sounds of Language Series* (Holt, Rinehart and Winston), has said all this about linguistics much more entertainingly*:

> Even the new linguistic materials that gave us so much hope that children would have a chance to respond to the dependable and variable parts of language patterns are scarcely more than re-done phonics programs. They, too, seem to be trapped by their focus on individual words. The repetitive reading of similarly constructed syllables such as *ham, gam, bam, sam, pam, ram* and *dam* may trigger

* Reprinted from "Literature, Linguistics and Reading" by Bill Martin, Jr., *Florida Reading Quarterly,* 1 (March 1965), 9–22. By permission of the author and the editors of the *Quarterly.*

visual recognition of structure, but it leads no further than phonic programs which give children a meager and unwarranted picture of our language.

This does not deny the potential contribution of structural linguistics to children's reading materials once someone finds a way to translate linguistic insights into wholesome language patterns. But sentences such as "Nat has a fat bat" have been floating around in our readers since readers began and the fact that they are now paraded under the label of linguistics does not camouflage their weakness.

DISCUSSION QUESTIONS

1. Compare a basal reading series and a linguistic reading series using the guide outlined in the discussion questions at the end of Chapter 2.

2. How do linguistic concepts of the reading process differ from those believed by the authors of basals? Or those offered by other reading experts? (See Chapter 1 for various definitions of reading.)

3. Discuss your understanding of the parallelism between speech and reading, and the ease with which children may make the transition.

4. What is your reaction to the tendency by some linguists to equate the act of reading with spelling by controlling the reading vocabulary according to spelling patterns of words? In such an approach, how do you think those words which do not follow common spelling patterns would be taught? How does such an approach deal with the influence of word meaning upon learning?

REFERENCES

1. Bickley, A. C., "Categorization Constraints on Beginning Readers," *National Reading Conference Yearbook,* 1972.

2. Bloomfield, Leonard, "Linguistics and Reading," *Elementary English,* 19 (April 1942), 125–130, 183–186.

3. Bloomfield, Leonard, and Barnhart, C. L., *Let's Read.* Detroit: Wayne State University Press, 1961.

4. Bougere, Marguerite Bondy, "Selected Factors in Oral Language Related to First Grade Reading Achievement," *Reading Research Quarterly,* 5 (Fall 1969), 31–58.

5. Brittain, Mary M., "Inflectional Performance and Early Reading Achievement," *Reading Research Quarterly,* 6 (Fall 1970), 34–48.

6. Clay, Marie M., "Emergent Reading Behavior." Doctoral dissertation, University of Auckland, Auckland, New Zealand, 1966.

7. Clymer, Theodore, "The Utility of Phonic Generalizations in the Primary Grades," *Reading Teacher,* 16 (January 1963), 252–258.

8. Davis, David C., "Phonemic Structural Approach to Initial Reading Instruction," *Elementary English,* 41 (March 1964), 218–223.

9. DeLawter, Jayne A., "The Relationship of Beginning Reading Instruction and Miscue Patterns," in *Help for the Reading Teacher: New Directions in Research,* Wm. D. Page, ed. National Conference on Research in English, 1975, 42–51.

10. Devine, T. G., "Linguistic Research and the Teaching of Reading," *Journal of Reading,* 9 (March 1966), 272–277.

11. Fries, Charles C., *Linguistics and Reading.* New York: Holt, Rinehart and Winston, Inc., 1963.

12. Goldberg, Lynn, and Rasmussen, Donald, "Linguistics in Reading," in *Explorations in Reading,* Albert J. Mazurkiewicz, ed. Lehigh University Conference Proceedings, 2 (June 1962), 22–27.

13. Goodman, Kenneth S., "A Linguistic Study of Cues and Miscues in Reading," *Elementary English,* 42 (October 1965), 639–643.

14. Goodman, Kenneth S., "Decoding—From Code

to What?" *Journal of Reading,* 14 (April 1971), 455–462, 498.

15. Gunderson, Doris, "Are Linguistic Programs Different?" in *Some Persistent Questions on Beginning Reading,* Robert C. Aukerman, ed. Newark, Del.: International Reading Association, 1972.

16. Hall, Robert A., *Sounds and Spelling in English.* Philadelphia: Chilton Book Company, 1961.

17. Hartley, Ruth Norene, "Effect of List Types and Cues in the Learning of Word Lists," *Reading Research Quarterly,* 6 (Fall 1970), 97–112.

18. Heilman, Arthur W., "Research Findings Concerning Phonics in Beginning Reading," in *A Decade of Innovations: Approaches to Beginning Reading,* Elaine C. Vilscek, ed. Proceedings International Reading Association, 12, Part 3, 1968, 100–106.

19. Johnson, David C., "The Effect of Reading and Punctuation Variations upon Reading Comprehension," in *Reading: The Right to Participate.* 20th Yearbook National Reading Conference, 1971, 304–311.

20. King, Ethel M., and Muehl, S., "Different Sensory Cues as Aids in Beginning Reading," *Reading Teacher,* 19 (December 1965), 163–168.

21. Kolers, Paul A., "Reading Is Only Incidentally Visual," in *Psycholinguistics and the Teaching of Reading,* Kenneth S. Goodman and James T. Fleming, eds. Newark, Del.: International Reading Association, 1969, 8–16.

22. Langman, Muriel Potter, "What Other Magazines Say About Reading," *Reading Teacher,* 15 (March 1962), 379–384.

23. Lefevre, Carl A., "Language Patterns and Their Graphic Counterparts: A Linguistic View of Reading," in *Changing Concepts of Reading Instruction,* Proceedings International Reading Association, 6, 1961, 245–249.

24. Lefevre, Carl A. "Reading Instruction Related to Primary Language Learnings: A Linguistic View," *Journal of Developmental Reading,* 4 (Spring 1961), 147–158.

25. Lefevre, Carl A., "The Simplistic Standard Word-Perception Theory of Reading," *Elementary English,* 45 (March 1968), 349–353, 355.

26. Levin, Harry, and Watson, J., *The Learning of Variable Grapheme to Phoneme Correspondence: Variations in the Initial Consonant Position.* Cornell University Cooperative Research Project, No. 639, 1963.

27. McCullough, Constance M., "Applying Structural Linguistics in Beginning Reading: Vital Principles in Need of Application," in *A Decade of Innovations: Approaches to Beginning Reading,* Elaine C. Vilscek, ed. Proceedings International Reading Association, 12, Part 3, 1968, 180–191.

28. MacKinnon, A. R., *How Do Children Learn To Read?* Toronto: The Copp Clark Publishing Co. Ltd., 1959.

29. Marquardt, Wm. F., "Language Interference in Reading," *Reading Teacher,* 18 (December 1964), 214–218.

30. Morrison, J. Cayce, *The Puerto Rican Study.* New York: Board of Education, City of New York, 1958.

31. Nurss, J. R., "Oral Reading Errors and Reading Comprehension," *Reading Teacher,* 22 (March 1969), 523–527.

32. O'Donnell, Roy C., "The Relationship Between Awareness of Structural Relationships in English and Ability in Reading Comprehension." Doctoral dissertation, George Peabody College for Teachers, Nashville, Tenn., 1961.

33. Pival, J. G., "Stress, Pitch and Juncture: Tools in the Diagnosis and Treatment of Reading Ills," *Elementary English,* 55 (May 1968), 458–463.

34. Rothkopf, E. Z., "Stimulus Similarity and Sequence of Stimulus Presentation in Paired-Associate Learning," *Journal of Experimental Psychology,* 56 (1958), 114–122.

35. Ruddell, Robert B., "Reading Instruction in First Grade with Varying Emphasis upon the Regularity of Grapheme–Phoneme Correspondences and the Relation of Language Structure to Meaning," *Reading Teacher,* 19 (May 1966), 653–660.

36. Ruddell, Robert B., "Reading Instruction in First Grade with Varying Emphasis on the Regularity of Grapheme–Phoneme Correspondences and the Relation of Language Structure to Meaning—Extended into Second Grade," *Reading Teacher,* 20 (May 1967), 730–739.

37. Sauer, Lois E., "Fourth Grade Children's Knowledge of Grammatical Structure," *Elementary English,* 47 (October 1970), 807–813.

38. Schneyer, J. Wesley, "Reading Achievement of First Grade Children Taught by a Linguistic Approach and a Basal Reader Approach—Extended into Third Grade," *Reading Teacher,* 22 (January 1969), 315–319.

39. Seymour, Dorothy Z., "The Difference Between Linguistics and Phonics," *Reading Teacher,* 23 (November 1969), 99–102, 111.

40. Sheldon, William D., Nichols, Nancy J., and Lashinger, Donald R., "Effect of First Grade Instruction

Using Basal Readers, Modified Linguistic Materials and Linguistic Readers—Extended into Second Grade," *Reading Teacher,* 20 (May 1967), 720–725.

41. Sheldon, William D., Stinson, Frange, and Peebles, James D., "Comparison of Three Methods of Reading: A Continuation Study in the Third Grade," *Reading Teacher,* 22 (March 1969), 539–546.

42. Smith, Frank, and Holmes, Deborah Lott, "The Independence of Letter, Word and Meaning Identification in Reading," *Reading Research Quarterly,* 6 (Spring 1971), 394–415.

43. Soffietti, James P., "Why Children Fail To Read: A Linguistic Analysis," *Harvard Educational Review,* 25 (Spring 1955), 63–84.

44. Strickland, Ruth G., "The Language of Elementary School Children: Its Relationship to the Language of Reading Textbooks and the Quality of Reading of Selected Children," *Bulletin of the School of Education,* Indiana University, 38 (July 1962), 1–131.

45. Veatch, Jeanette, "Linguistic Instruction in the Teaching of Reading: Kill or Cure?" *Elementary English,* 39 (March 1962), 231–233, 243.

46. Venezky, R. L., "English Orthography: Its Graphical Structure and Its Relation to Sound," *Reading Research Quarterly,* 2 (Spring 1967), 75–105.

47. Wardhaugh, Ronald, "Is the Linguistic Approach an Improvement in Reading Instruction?" in *Current Issues in Reading,* Nila Banton Smith, ed. Proceedings International Reading Association, 13, Part 2, 1969, 254–267.

48. Warfel, Harry R., "A Bag with Holes," *Journal of Developmental Reading,* 3 (Autumn 1959), 43–50.

49. Warfel, Harry R., and Lloyd, Donald J., "The Structural Approach to Reading," *School and Society,* 85 (June 8, 1957), 199–201.

50. Weaver, Wendell, W., "Linguistic Assumptions and Reading Instruction," in *The Psychology of Reading Behavior,* Eighteenth Yearbook, National Reading Conference, 1969, 107–112.

51. Weber, Rose-Marie, "A Linguistic Analysis of First-Grade Reading Errors," *Reading Research Quarterly,* 5 (Spring 1970), 427–451.

52. Werner, Heinz, and Kaplan, Edith, "Development of Word Meaning Through Verbal Context: An Experimental Study," *Journal of Psychology,* 29 (April 1950), 251–257.

53. Winter, Clotilda, "Interrelationships Among Language Variables in Children of First and Second Grade," *Elementary English,* 34 (February 1957), 108–113.

54. Wyatt, Nita M., *Reading Achievements of First Grade Boys vs. First Grade Girls Using Two Approaches: A Linguistic Approach and a Basal Reader Approach with Boys and Girls Grouped Separately.* Project 2735, University of Kansas, 1966.

SUPPLEMENTARY READING

Aukerman, Robert C., *Some Persistent Questions on Beginning Reading.* Newark, Del.: International Reading Association, 1972.

Fries, Charles C., *Linguistics and Reading.* New York: Holt, Rinehart and Winston, Inc., 1963.

Goodman, Kenneth S., ed., *The Psycholinguistic Nature of the Reading Process.* Detroit: Wayne State University Press, 1968.

Goodman, Kenneth S., and Fleming, James T., eds., *Psycholinguistics and the Teaching of Reading.* Newark, Del.: International Reading Association, 1969.

Gunderson, Doris V., compiler, *Language and Reading: An Interdisciplinary Approach.* Washington, D.C.: Center for Applied Linguistics, 1970.

Henry, Nelson B., ed., *Linguistics in School Programs,* Sixty-ninth Yearbook, National Society for the Study of Education, Part II. Chicago: University of Chicago Press, 1970.

Lefevre, Carl A., *Linguistics and the Teaching of Reading.* New York: McGraw-Hill Book Company, 1964.

Ruddell, Robert B., *Innovations in Reading-Language Instruction.* Englewood Cliffs, N.J.: Prentice-Hall, Inc., 1974.

Savage, John F., *Linguistics for Teachers: Selected Readings.* Chicago: Science Research Associates, 1973.

Smith, Frank, *Understanding Reading: A Psycholinguistic Analysis of Reading and Learning To Read.* New York: Holt, Rinehart and Winston, Inc., 1971.

Smith, Nila B., ed., *Current Issues in Reading.* Proceedings International Reading Association, 13, Part 2, 1969.

Vilscek, Elaine C., ed., *A Decade of Innovations: Approaches to Beginning Reading.* Proceedings International Reading Association, 12, Part 3, 1968.

5
Using the Language Experience Approach

PREVIEW

More than any other approach to the teaching of reading, the language experience approach conceives of learning to read as part of the process of language development. It alone recognizes the close relationship among reading, speaking, writing, and listening. It alone realizes that progress in reading is determined by the extent of the child's experiences in all these language media, prior to and during his early school years. Proponents of this approach clearly see that a child cannot be expected to deal with ideas or language in reading that are much farther advanced than those he can speak or write.

Within such a philosophical framework, books become a resource tool rather than a basic device to teach children to read (or, as they really function, a device to help children memorize printed words). Books and readers help supply the vicarious experiences, the depth of meanings for the words which the child needs to express his ideas in oral and written work. Many other classroom and extra-classroom activities, plus teacher instruction and demonstration, further this development of concepts that will be translated into words. Learning to read then, in the language experience method, is interpreted as development in thinking and in expression of language.

In this approach to reading, the level of language at which the beginner functions is not highly significant. He may be language-deprived, or facile in the use of words. His progress becomes an individual matter with each child gradually developing a broader and deeper skill with words and moving toward more complex language patterns which help convey his thoughts.

In many institutions preparing students for elementary teaching, the training in reading methods is incorporated into a broad course on the language arts. Or even worse, it is a minor part of a general methods course which supposedly covers most elementary school subject matter. In such courses, the relative emphasis upon reading methods and techniques may be quite slight, for reading may be considered just one of the language skills or just another school subject. Unless the integration and interaction of the language skills are stressed, we see these elementary education majors later in their classrooms giving equal emphasis and separate instructional periods to speaking, listening, reading, writing, and spelling, as though these were independent areas of learning.

The language experience approach is unique among all other approaches in its rejection of this dichotomizing of language development into separate and unrelated learnings. It declares that speaking, listening, writing, and reading are interrelated and interdependent. It recognizes that the child learns to read out of his present and past experiences with language, not only by perusing the pages of a book. Only the language experience method begins where the child is in terms of his ability to think with words and stimulates simultaneously his language development in all media of expression and reception, in the hope of leading toward the ultimate goal of ability to read the writings of others.

Language experience maximizes the correspondence between the printed word and the child's language, since it is often his own language that he is reading. Moreover, the parallels between his speech and the reading matter provide for optimum success, as recent studies of the importance of using familiar oral sentence patterns in reading matter show.

Because of the current widespread attention to the language experience technique and the recent appearance of some commercial instructional materials, many teachers are under the impression that the practice is quite new and probably was invented by those authors. Actually, as Hildreth has shown in her historical review (*16*), it was used in several experimental schools before 1900, and discussed at considerable length in a yearbook on new materials of instruction in 1920. The term "language experience" was used first in 1934, by which time most of the basic practices of the method had been evolved. For example, the significant relationships of learning to read to writing, oral fluency, and the development of other language abilities was recognized. The use of children's own stories was considered a real reading experience at a pre-book stage, not simply readiness training or preparation for the vocabulary of basal readers. A wide variety of charts and stories was used for many learning activities as well as being the medium for the teaching of phonic and other skills. The values of the approach were wildly recognized, for Hildreth mentions its use in England, France, Central and South America, Turkey, and New Zealand prior to 1960.

The language experience approach attempts to bring reading and other communication skills together in the instructional program (4). No sharp distinction is made between the reading program and other language activities (9). In other words, the plan for reading instruction is based not on some series of books but upon the oral and written expression and identified needs of the children. The basic motivation is approached through the child's realization that his oral language, based on his thoughts and experiences as well as the ideas of others, can be written and thus read. This self-realization may be expressed, as the Allens have phrased it (2):

What I can think about, I can talk about.
What I can say, I can write.
What I can write, I can read.
I can read what I write and what other people can write for me to read.

The assumption present here is, of course, that reading is a by-product of the child's thinking and oral expression. Progress in reading is therefore directly dependent upon the child's growth in experiences which are translated into oral language and his own written expression. Our present knowledge of the significance of the young child's experiential background, his language development, and his understanding of spoken language for reading progress would seem to support these assumptions.

MaryAnne Hall offers what she terms a linguistic rationale for language experience as follows (11):

1. The beginning reader must be taught to view reading as a communication process.
2. The beginning reader is a user of language.
3. The beginning reader should understand the reading process as one of consciously relating print to oral language.
4. The beginning reader should incorporate the learning of writing with the learning of reading.
5. The beginning reader should learn to read with materials written in his language patterns.
6. The beginning reader should learn to read meaningful language.
7. The beginning reader should learn to read orally with smooth, fluent expression.

Hardly any reading expert would disagree with the general implications of Hall's statements, although many would question their exact meanings. In support of the use of writing as an aid to reading, Gertrude Hildreth (15) emphasizes the wide use of this procedure in other countries. She also believes that the simultaneous training promotes reading growth by aiding memory of letter forms, directing attention to structural elements and other details of words, helping to form the habit of left-to-right direction in dealing with words, and providing an overt activity for restless pupils. Other advantages to the program according to Hildreth, which we would certainly recognize as present in this approach to reading, are its tendency to strengthen association between word forms and meanings and to promote familiarity with sentence patterns.

METHODS AND MATERIALS

From the first day of school each child is encouraged to share his ideas and experiences with others through his oral expression and the pictures he creates. As the child paints, works with clay, conducts science experiments, looks at books, the teacher helps him to summarize his ideas and discoveries. He dictates and the teacher writes the ideas on his drawing or elsewhere. The charts which result are then shared with others as the child reads (tells) his recorded stories. During the writing of the chart the teacher discusses word choice, sentence structure, and the sounds of letters and words. But he does not censor or elaborate the story other than by preparing it in the proper experience chart manner.

As Russell G. Stauffer has pointed out, the language experience approach makes a strong contribution to beginning reading. He suggests that after several weeks of experience with group-composed charts, small groups be formed within the class. These groups are organized on the bases of language facility, social maturity, and the children's interests and compatibility. By the grouping, the teacher will have more opportunity for stimulating small-group or individually dictated stories. A rotating schedule for teacher-group conferences should be arranged, and as each group meets, individual charts on group stories dictated to the teacher. Since the stories should be quite brief, perhaps only two or three sentences at this stage, these activities are not as time-consuming as they might seem (29). The small groups also provide more opportunity for frequent exchange or presentation of children's own stories to other children. Small-group reading, learning to read one's own story independently, preparing illustrations for a story, practicing with individual word cards, using picture dictionaries or other related resource books for additional ideas or words are activities promoted even at this early reading stage.

Soon each child manifests the desire to write his own stories and he is immediately encouraged and helped to do so. This breakthrough from oral to written expression marks the beginning of the child's efforts to produce written material and the beginning of his instruction in reading and writing. Devices such as lists of service words, picture dictionaries, labels on classroom objects, lists of interest or topical words, and other children's charts help pupils rapidly extend their writing (and reading) vocabularies. Each child's charts are illustrated and bound into his book. Other books are created by collections of science, social science, and other content materials contributed by various pupils. Each child's charts and books, as well as the communal books, are shared freely and contribute to the writing and reading growth of the other children.

In the beginning months, the children's stories about their drawings or easel paintings take such forms as these, when written by the teacher:

> *This here is an alligator.*
> *He eats fish and golf balls.*

Later, the children may begin to label their own drawings:

> *See me Tommy.*
> *See Mary fish.*

The children are encouraged to read and write with the aid of model sentences. These are examples:

> *Something I like is _____.*
> *I don't like _____.*
> *I ran to the _____.*
> *Here is a big _____.*
> *I can help _____.*

Some groups prepare a class newspaper placed on a bulletin board just outside the room for passersby to read, as:

> *Fire!*
>
> *Did you see the fire?*
> *It was at the A & P store.*
> *It was a big fire.*
> *Joan's daddy works there.*
> *He didn't get hurt.*

Rhyme and other phonic characteristics of words are emphasized by encouraging children to illustrate and write about such word groups:

> *tail–mail*   *red–bed*
> *kite–bite*   *A goat in a coat.*
> *fun–done*   *The bean is green.*

Model sentences which emphasize initial consonants and context as clues to word meaning are to be completed by the children:

> *I caught a big f_____ on my line.*
> *Do you want s_____ for your lunch?*
> *Boots is a black-and-white c_____.*

These experiences lead rapidly toward increased development of written expression, resulting in such efforts, halfway through the first grade, as:

A HALLOWEEN MASK

Mother went to the store to buy a pumpkin. She saw all kinds of pumpkins. Some were big and some were little. She bought a little pumpkin and made a pumpkin pie. I made a halloween mask out of the shell.

Once upon a time I jumped into a pool and I drowned. I had to come up for breath. I came up and I got out of the pool. I went home and went to bed. I ate some fish.

Once upon a time there were two little boys. One was Cliff and one was Scott. They threw pie all over the school. They were bad.

Two little girls wanted to go trick or treating. The larger girls and boys went with them. They were frightened by a large flower. They all held hands and ran. Most of the children lost their trick or treatings. They all ran home.

A year later in the second grade some children are producing stories such as these (in their original spelling):

HOW WE GOT OUR CANERY

In first grade Mrs. Bankhead's room we wanted a canery, so we went to Woolworth on a bus. The other first grade went too. We all got us a bird and we were very happy, but it was funny. She never sang. We called her tweety.

Once Mrs. Zabcik said that who ever broght a note to school first would get to take the bird home for the summer. And I got to take the bird home. When I got the bird home it wouldent moov. The first day we washed it. It splashed and it got me all wet. The birds body was yellow and there was a little white spot on his head. Her name was Tweety. The summer was almost over and Tweety died.

Are you my mother. One day a mother bird felt a little tap from her egg. She sead I will go and get some food for my Baby. So she set off. Then pop out came a Baby Bird. It sead where is my mother he sead. He sead do I have a mother oh yes I do or I would not be here.

Various simple readers, trade books, science books, and so forth, are available to the class. These are constantly used as resource materials for ideas, for vocabulary, for enrichment, for spelling, and for other purposes. Each child, to a degree, learns a personal writing–reading vocabulary suitable to his needs for self-expression. No artificial controls are placed on the vocabulary any child employs. The service words which are significant for almost all reading and writing are given special attention by the teacher in charts available to all.

Phonics instruction is developed on a "say it"–"see it" basis, in which the child gradually learns how to represent by letters the sounds he wishes to record on paper. If generalizations or rules appear, they do because of spontaneous generalization by the pupils, not by deductive teaching. Phonic elements may be emphasized by the teacher in working with an individual or a small group, but the emphasis is purely on translating sounds of oral language into written form.

Emphasis is not placed upon separate periods for instruction in phonics or spelling. Rather these skills are based on the vocabulary used in the children's own stories. The sequence of instruction in phonics is similar to that of many basal programs, but the instruction is usually in small groups and related to the words and spelling in a particular composition of the children. Phonics, structural analysis, contextual analysis, and vocabulary are introduced as children appear to need them in writing and reading their own and the other children's materials. There may be assigned or suggested reading but, again, this is related to the purposes and needs of the children in producing their material. Dictionaries, charts of words grouped by common phonic elements or themes or spelling, and other sources of words are offered freely. Recreational or free reading in class and at home is encouraged by the provision of a wide variety of books and children's booklets.

In the language experience approach, evaluation of pupil progress is not based primarily on standardized or informal reading tests, for these would sample only one facet of the language development being stimulated. Rather, pupil growth in ability to express ideas in oral and written form and to comprehend the writings of peers and to react actively to these is constantly observed. Growth in clarity and depth of thinking, in sentence sense, mechanics, and spelling is revealed in the child's own productions.

A group of stories written by a child may be bound in an attractive folder decorated by the author and taken home to display his reading ability to his parents. Many teachers duplicate a collection of their pupil's stories and send this home with appropriate explanation and comments. Children are also encouraged to read from these booklets in class and at home, as well as to compose additional stories, book reports, and the like at home.

OTHER CONCEPTS OF THE APPROACH

Russell G. Stauffer has reacted to our reviews of the language experience method in other writings by reminding us that there are, as we might expect, a number of versions of the technique. Perhaps because of these variations, the research results of his and other trials we will cite later differ in their outcomes. Hence we should certainly point out some of the different concepts of this system.

Working with black children of low-socioeconomic background, Margaret Irish (17) has evolved an introduction to the method which is particularly relevant to these children. She chose a local black college basketball player who had achieved national recognition, as well as a $1 million contract upon entering the professional ranks. She supplied the children with photographs, drawings of his hands and feet, taped interviews, biographical and personal history information, and the like. A school day was designated in his honor and the food he liked was served. Stories were composed by individuals or groups first about their hero, later on other sports figures, themselves, book characters, etc. Thus she led the children from an intensely interesting figure with whom they readily identified to other more personal themes. In other ethnic groups, Irish has employed a different hero, suited to the nature of the children involved.

A number of other writers, including Goodman (7) and Shuy (28), have emphasized the desirability of the language experience approach for disadvantaged pupils. As Shuy suggests, using the child's own language avoids the types of sentences which give trouble to these children and minimizes the child's errors in omitting inflections and word endings and his problems with other aspects of standard English grammar.

Platt (26) has her own version of this technique for use with disadvantaged children. She labels the objects the child draws. Later she puts each child's drawings together into simple books, using the child's own words as the basis for simple stories that she writes in relation to each of the drawings. After a total vocabulary of 230 or so words has thus been learned, she moves the children into the basal first reader. We wonder why, if the method is satisfactory for the very beginning stages, Platt finds it necessary to drop it and move toward a structured system (which is often not really suitable for such pupils in its content).

Another version which has received wide attention is that termed "Organic Teaching," devised by Sylvia Ashton-Warner in her teaching Maori children in New Zealand. She recognizes four movements or periods in the child's development. The first is called the Output Period. Each day of this period, in a one-to-one session with the teacher, the child selects one word to be learned, out of the discussion of his personal feelings. He receives help in tracing and noting the distinctive features of the word as it is printed by the teacher on a small card. The next morning all the words of the children are placed in a pile, from which each must pick his Key Words. Those he does not remember are discarded as unrepresentative of his own inner feelings. During the daily Intake Period, new words are gathered from the activities in the classroom and at home, and added to the pile of Key Words (36).

Later stages of Ashton-Warner's system include the use of small chalkboards instead of paper, and instruction in letter formation to aid children in writing their Key Words (which are gradually expanded into phrases on new cards, presumably to introduce the essential function words). Small books are composed by the teacher from each child's word and phrase cards. Finally, small books are written by the children and these gradually progress to collections of the children's stories.

The use of a Key Word method of teaching word recognition, which probably follows at least in part Ashton-Warner's ideas, has been the subject of several evaluations. Packer (25) used this idea in four cities and discovered that the vocabulary learned by most of the children had little similarity to basal word lists. This must have been disappointing to him if, like Platt and others, he expected the Key Word approach to prepare children for a basal reader.

Roach Van Allen directed one of the earliest large-scale studies of language experience in a three-year trial in San Diego (1). On the whole, the results of this experiment indicated support for the system as a basic way of teaching beginning reading. On the basis of this experience, Allen and his wife prepared teachers' manuals and pupil activity books (2) presenting their version of the technique. The manual is an extensive presentation of the rationale and a guide to skill development and the use of the pupil books. These latter offer space for the child's drawings and writing centered around a theme presented by poetry, stories, discussion, and other teacher or class activities. Each theme is followed for two to five days with a variety of language and firsthand experiences. Some observers would question the structured, whole-class aspects of the Allen materials, while others might approve of the detailed assistance in skill development given the teacher who is new to this system, as well as the fact that the themes go beyond everyday events and children's experiences to include science, nature study, and other informational areas. Like other writers, the Allens recognize the need for personalized attention through individual conferences, thus moving gradually toward an individualized reading program.

Mary A. Cain (3) describes practices in British primary schools that emphasize the contribution of writing to learning to read. Materials for reading, both child-produced and commercial, are in prolific supply. If you cannot read it yourself, another child or an adult will read it to you. The books by the children are first planned by the author, then reviewed by the teacher, who helps add sources of information or point out gaps in the plan. After the first draft, the child reviews and corrects it for mechanics, spelling, and the like, often with some guidance from the teacher. Handwriting is also important in the rewriting of the initial version. Structural organization is not emphasized to the detriment of the pupil's expression; content and accurate, good-looking copies are stressed as more important at this time. Word cards drawn from the children's picture captions or stories are used for review and for beginning phonic training. Individual reactions to even a group experience are fostered, and children's books on every aspect of the event are promoted. Individual conferences are held to read with each child two or three times a week, to note the books he has read and suggest others, and to assess the skills the child needs to practice. Cain attributes much of the mature literacy of these five- to eleven-year-olds to this stimulating environment and teaching approach.

CURRENT APPLICATIONS

Since language experience stresses total language development at the child's rate of progress, it has been very appealing to those who deal with children with special problems. We find reports of its use with mentally retarded (38), with teenagers in need of remedial work (37), and with economically disadvantaged children. The present authors served as consultants to a project utilizing the language experience systems in content fields with junior high school students who were economically and academically disadvantaged. Five middle schools of Tampa, Florida, under the guidance of Erwin Franco, presented the content of science, social science, English, and mathematics through this medium. The procedure was to assemble all the information about each day's theme from textual materials, demonstrations, visual aids, and the informational backgrounds of the pupils in an organized manner on the chalkboard. These notes were then duplicated, as phrased by the pupils, and read and discussed the following day. Tests at the end of the first year of the project showed significantly greater gains in reading, language usage, study skills, and social science than these pupils had shown in previous years. Decreases in school dropouts and absences were also noted. Other applications of language experience are present in many classrooms which, in imitation of the British primary school, are called "open classrooms" (24). The personalized and spontaneous aspects of language experience seem particularly appealing to these new school arrangements.

In a review of the literature on the language experience approach with socioeconomically deprived and linguistically different persons, Hall (12) cites more than a half dozen additional research studies. These ranged from the readiness level, first grade and seventh grade, to job training programs for functionally illiterate adults. When control groups were used, there were no differences in word recognition, comprehension, and other reading skills between the language experience groups and those elementary pupils taught by various basal systems. Superior readiness, creative writing, and oral language abilities seemed to develop from this method in various studies. Literacy and communication skills were dramatically improved for the adults.

In a clinical situation, the senior author has employed language experience as the basic instructional approach in several very difficult cases. These severely brain-damaged (aphasic) patients were led by this method to recover their academic and vocational skills to the point where they were able to resume their schooling or work. One was a 14-year-old who has been able to complete high school in a private school setting with tutoring aid; a second case was an automobile mechanic who is now back at his job despite continuing partial paralysis and Jacksonian epilepsy stemming from the scar tissue of his brain tumor operation. The third case was a physician stricken by an embolism. He regained his reading skills by the approach and is now functioning as a medical technician. In less than a year, with concurrent speech and physical therapy, these cases were helped to recover their language abilities, particularly their reading skill, to almost their original educational levels.

In other reports, Miller and Johnson (22) emphasize the practicality of language experience for Navajo children on a reservation where cultural differences and lack of a written language make ordinary instructional materials utterly inappropriate. Curry (5) used this approach to teach blind children to read Braille, the system which demands learning different combinations of raised dots for letters, whole words, parts of words, abbreviations, and contractions. Learning the code became less a matter of rote memory for these handicapped children. Other advantages were the inherent verbal reality because the stories were the children's own, and the degree of independence in composing stories so essential to such restricted pupils.

In the second edition of his excellent book, Ronald Morris (23) strongly supports the language experience approach because of its "context support," as he terms it. Because he has just dictated or written the story, many of the cues present in oral language (and usually missing in written matter) are present for the child. Thus the reader does not depend so much on word recognition for obtaining the message. Raven I. McDavid, Jr., the linguist (21), stresses the importance of presenting reading materials, at any stage in the student's career, that employ language habits similar to those that the student has acquired in speaking, particularly for those for whom standard English is an alien idiom.

These statements and the variety of applications described certainly broaden the picture of language experience solely as a tool for primary reading development. Apparently, it is effective at any age as a means of acquiring initial language and reading skills, in difficult situations involving cultural or language differences, as a remedial technique in which the student cannot fail to read successfully, and even in teaching content matter to those who are academically retarded.

LIMITATIONS OF THE LANGUAGE EXPERIENCE APPROACH

Despite its many other applications, language experience is thought of as basically a way of introducing beginning reading. It has broadened beyond its original concept of a brief preliminary experience intended to convince children that reading is really talking written down, as it was used early in this century. It has grown beyond the limited use implied in the Key Word approach described above to be recognized as a total system for teaching reading. Although it may have motivational or remedial applications with older pupils, it remains largely a way of teaching beginning reading at the hands of many teachers.

It is argued that, if the language experience were continued much beyond the primary years as the basic instructional procedure, there is the possibility that it would retard the full development of reading ability. The child's reading and writing experiences would be too limited to permit him to deal with the more difficult materials of the content fields. Unless a transition to reading textbooks is somehow made, the child's learning would be limited to the informational backgrounds of his peers, and no planned sequence of introduction of factual learnings would be possible. There are those who doubt that use of language experience for the entire primary period would prepare pupils for textbook interpretation, or introduce them to adequate content matter. These critics ignore the fact that the program makes wide use of sources of reading other than the child's own productions. In fact, as the studies we will cite later show, children trained in this technique often show above-average learning in science, social science, and other content areas.

It is true that a child's vocabularies in speaking, writing, reading, and listening are dissimilar in breadth, depth, and fluency. At primary ages, the listening is normally the greatest, the speech vocabulary next, and reading and writing very small. These differences in facility with words in various media vary as the child matures, with listening excelling that in reading until about the sixth grade, when the trend is reversed. Meanwhile, his reading vocabulary grows apace, while his speaking and writing store of words grows quite slowly. Perhaps more than any other approach to reading, language experience capitalizes on the differential between listening and reading vocabularies and facilitates transfer of words (and ideas) from listening and speech into writing and reading. Some of the evidence of superior breadth and diversity of vocabulary in the writing of children trained by language experience cited later supports this viewpoint.

Another frequent question raised about language experience concerns its inherent lack of structured guides for the teacher and its problems of organization. As in individualized reading, the teacher does not have daily lesson plans outlined for him, nor does he deal with instructional materials in which, presumably, there are planned sequences of activities for skill development. His time is divided among individual, small-group, and whole-class activities. His criteria for evaluating children's progress are largely his own observations rather than the progress that is assumed in the child's completion of successive stories in a reader or pages in a workbook. Casual observers of language experience in action receive the impression hat the learning of skills is largely incidental. There appears to be little anxiety about the nature of the words children learn and use in their stories. These observers ask: "Where are the checklists of skills to guide the teacher? In what sequence are interdependent skills taught?" "Where is the basic word list?"

In the earlier editions of this book, we, too, raised these questions about language experience. But because we believed in the approach and tried to train a large number of teachers in its use, we have found some answers to these doubts. Although we have reservations about their structuring of learning on a whole-class basis, the Allens' manuals (2) are a great help to teachers new to the technique who need a source of ideas, literary materials, and the like. The books of Maryanne Hall (10), Russell G. Stauffer (30), and Vicinus et al. (33) offer many pertinent suggestions. The versions of language experience offered by these three authors differ, but they do assist the teacher in record keeping, evaluation, planning for skill development, and the other essentials of a reading program.

There are other problems in the language experience method mentioned by Stauffer (29). There is the tendency for some teachers to use the experience charts in the same stereotyped fashion in which they use basal readers. They go over and over the chart time after time, obviously expecting that the repetition will fix the words in the children's brains. They may constantly correct the spontaneous expressions of children in grammar, usage, and punctuation. They may not permit individual words which may fit the story, but are not "basic" words, to be used, in the belief that these words are not important or essential to the child's learning to read. They treat the charts as a temporary activity to be dropped as soon as the children can be introduced to book reading. These teachers fail to recognize the wide variety of charts which could function in the classroom, limiting them instead only to contemporary incidents or to colorless descriptions of class activities. All of these are, of course, criticisms of the manner in which the language experience approach may be employed rather than of the technique itself.

Like individualized reading, language experience is not an easy way to teach reading. It demands flexibility in classroom management, a recognition of individual differences in language development, personalized record keeping, and teacher skill in diagnosis and evaluation. Children must be helped to acquire the ability to work independently and cooperatively in small groups in this method, too.

THE RESEARCH

An example of the widespread interest in language experience is its inclusion in six of the large-scale First-Grade Reading Studies. To contrast the results in these comparisons with the basal program, we have prepared charts of the outcomes in the first-grade and the follow-up second-grade experiments.

In Table 5–1, *LE* signifies a superior result for the language experience method; *basal*, for the basal reading program. A blank space indicates no significant difference between the two methods. Kendrick and Bennett (*19*) separated their results for high socioeconomic (*HSE*) and low socioeconomic (*LSE*), as well as for boys (*B*) and girls (*G*).

TABLE 5–1. Language Experience Versus Traditional Method in First Grade

	Stauffer and Hammond (31)	Hahn (8)	McCanne (20)	Harris and Serwer (14)	Vilscek et al. (35)	HSE B	HSE G	LSE B	LSE G
Word meaning	LE	LE	Basal		LE				
Paragraph meaning	LE		Basal	Basal	LE	Basal		Basal	
Vocabulary		LE	Basal		LE				
Spelling	LE (girls)								
Word study (phonics)					LE				
Arithmetic	Basal						LE		
Oral—rate	LE								
Oral—accuracy									
Gates Word List	LE				LE				
Fry Word List	LE								
Karlsen Word List	LE				LE				
Attitudes			Basal	Basal	LE			LE	
Writing mechanics Spelling	LE								
Number of running words	LE		LE			LE	LE	LE	LE

The Kendrick and Bennett (19) columns are grouped under HSE (B, G) and LSE (B, G).

In Stauffer and Hammond's study, the language experience pupils excelled in nine of the ten areas in which significant differences were found. He would probably attribute this to the use of his Directed Reading–Thinking Activities, in which the children were introduced to the basal reader after a vocabulary of about 150 words had been acquired. However, without this type of training in the use of a basal, the results of Vilscek and colleagues are just about as positively in favor of language experience. The economically disadvantaged pupils in McCanne's study (Spanish-speaking or bilingual) and Harris's black, inner-city pupils did not respond favorably to this system, although Harris's experimental pupils scored higher than many comparable classes in the same schools, both types of classes being below national norms.

In the follow-up second-grade studies, with the same pupils, the results are presented in Table 5–2. Again, the results of Stauffer and Hammond, Hahn, Vilscek et al., and Kendrick and Bennett are in favor of the language experience

TABLE 5–2. Language Experience Versus Traditional Method in Second Grade

| | Stauffer and Hammond (31) | Hahn (8) | Vilscek et al. (35) | Kendrick and Bennett (19) | | | |
| | | | | HSE | | LSE | |
				B	G	B	G
Word meaning	LE	LE			Basal		
Paragraph meaning	LE	LE		Basal	Basal		
Spelling		LE	LE				
Word study		LE					
Vocabulary							
Arithmetic computation	Basal (boys)				Basal		
Arithmetic concepts			LE				LE
Science		LE	LE			LE	LE
Social studies concepts		LE	LE			LE	LE
Language usage		LE					
Oral—rate							
Oral—accuracy							
Gates Word List		LE					
Fry Word List		LE					
Karlsen Word List		LE					
Attitudes					Basal		
Writing mechanics	LE	Basal		Basal			
Number of running words	LE	LE					LE
Number of different words	LE						LE
Spelling	LE						LE
Number of books read		LE			Basal		

approach. In the case of this last study, language experience seems less effective among pupils from high socioeconomic groups and more effective among low socioeconomic. Harris's trial with inner-city blacks, in contrast, yielded no significant differences at all, which is the reason for its omission from the chart.

Some of the results favoring basal students in the first-grade Kendrick–Bennett study, as total words in speaking, were reversed in the second grade, favoring the language experience at that time. Other advantages of the basal, as the number of different words in speaking, persisted into the second grade. In writing, the advantage of the language experience in number of running words persisted into the second grade only for boys in the low-socioeconomic group.

Stauffer and Hammond (31,32) employed several unique measures in their experiments, such as originality of content, consistency in story sequence, and total polysyllabic words, and found language experience pupils consistently superior in these writing qualities, as we might expect.

Several of these studies continued their methods comparisons into the third grade. At that time Stauffer and Hammond (32) found language experience pupils superior in paragraph meaning (girls only), spelling, science, social studies concepts, oral rate and accuracy, and in two oral word lists, in writing mechanics, number of running words, and number of different words. Basal boys continued to show superiority in arithmetic computation, however.

After three years, Harris and Morrison (13) continued to report no significant differences in any test scores. As side effects of their experiment, however, they noted that after their trial with language experience, the teachers were more permissive and creative and less rigid, and they now tended to continue with language experience as an adjunct to their basal method.

In addition to these first- to third-grade cooperative studies, there are a few research reports from other sources. Cramer (4) explored the effects of language experience upon spelling and writing. He discovered that the pupils learned to spell both irregular and regular words equally well, and better than did basal pupils. They were also significantly better in the number of running words and different words in their compositions.

Keith (18) used a 200-day language experience program, taught in both Spanish and English, with a group of bilingual children. The themes in their stories were centered around the Spanish-American-Anglo heritage of the New Mexico area. She found that the language experience children excelled the basal in word discrimination and were also superior in this ability to a control group given a special oral language program in English. There were no differences among the groups in word knowledge or paragraph reading at the end of the first grade. Unfortunately, Keith did not evaluate the effect of bilingual instruction or the emphasis upon the cultural heritage of the children in his use of language experience. Hence her study cannot be considered as evidence in favor of the language experience per se.

In summarizing these one- to three-year studies, there do appear to be certain advantages for language experience. These results are not identical in all the experiments since the implementation of the idea varied from study to study. It is apparent, however, that in terms of various reading, phonic, and spelling skills, the evidence in favor of language experience grows stronger after the first grade. Moreover, the approach does seem to make a contribution to the length and breadth of vocabulary in children's compositions and to their spelling in these creative efforts. In the development of informational background, as in science, social science, and the like, language experience again makes a significant impression, as shown in the second-grade reports of Hahn, Vilscek et al., and Kendrick and Bennett, and again in the three-year report of Stauffer and Hammond.

There would seem to be ample support for such statements about language experience as these:

1. It must be recognized as an independent, effective method of teaching reading during primary levels of development.
2. It is not just an adjunct to or a preliminary stage to other methods, although it may be so used.
3. It is as effective in stimulating skill development among middle-class children as the basal approach.
4. Among low-socioeconomic or bilingual children, the supporting evidence is weak in the first grade, but grows to equal, at least, the basal method after two years of such instruction for these atypical pupils.
5. In measures of quantity, quality, and diversity of vocabulary in writing, the language experience appears to be superior, even in the first grade.
6. By the second grade, children trained by the language experience approach begin to evidence broader backgrounds in science and social science, and better spelling than basal pupils.
7. Teachers who have been trained in the language experience method tend to modify their classroom climate toward less authoritarian relationships. And even though test results in their populations may be inconclusive, these teachers tend to realize the advantages they apparently see in this approach by continuing to use it, even if they return to the use of the basal.
8. Successful applications of the technique have been made in a variety of situations ranging from early elementary grades to adults. These include initial language and reading development, clinical cases, remedial training, teaching content subjects, and in meeting the problems of those with cultural or language differences.

DISCUSSIONS QUESTIONS

1. How does the authors' concept of the language experience approach differ from the Key Word method? From other versions of the approach?

2. What do you consider to be the greatest strengths of the language experience approach? The greatest weaknesses?

3. Is it possible that this method will prove advantageous in remedial work with severely retarded readers? Why? How?

4. Can you offer any suggestions which might improve the effectiveness of language experience with pupils who present problems of language development

such as bilingual, inner-city, migrant, or American Indian pupils?

5. Why do you suppose the results varied so much from one large-scale study to the next? Is it possible that the language experience approach is still in the process of being defined?

6. What possibilities do you see for use of the language experience idea of having children prepare some of their own reading and study materials, in grades above the primary levels?

7. Present a topic to a small group of your pupils and arrange for them to prepare jointly a summary of their ideas or reactions. Bring this to class and be prepared to show how you might use the material for group development of a reading or study skill.

8. Compare the Allen manuals with a basal manual for the same grade level. Be prepared to present your analysis to your college class.

REFERENCES

1. Allen, Roach Van, *Report of the Reading Study Project,* Monograph No. 1. San Diego: Department of Education, San Diego County, 1961.

2. Allen, Roach Van, and Allen, Claryce, *Language Experiences in Reading: Teacher's Resource Book.* Chicago: Encyclopedia Britannica Press, 1966.

3. Cain, Mary A., "The Literate Children of British Primary Schools," *Elementary English,* 52 (January 1975), 84–87.

4. Cramer, Ronald L., "An Investigation of First-Grade Spelling Achievement," *Elementary English,* 47 (February 1970), 230–240.

5. Curry, Rebecca Gavurin, "Using LEA To Teach Blind Children to Read," *Reading Teacher,* 29 (December 1975), 272–279.

6. Department of Education, San Diego County, *Analysis of Pupil Data: San Diego County Reading Study Project.* Monograph No. 5. San Diego: Department of Education.

7. Goodman, Kenneth S., "Dialect Barriers to Reading Comprehension," *Elementary English,* 42 (December 1965), 852–860.

8. Hahn, Harry T., "Three Approaches to Beginning Reading Instruction—ITA, Language Experience and Basic Readers—Extended into Second Grade," *Reading Teacher,* 20 (May 1967), 711–715.

9. Halcomb, James F., "Reading: The Language Experience Approach," *Challenge and Experiment in Reading,* Proceedings International Reading Association, 7, 1962, 72–74.

10. Hall, Maryanne, *Teaching Reading as a Language Experience.* Columbus, Ohio: Charles E. Merrill Publishing Company, 1970.

11. Hall, Maryanne, "Linguistically Speaking: Why Language Experience?" *Reading Teacher,* 25 (January 1972), 328–331.

12. Hall, Maryanne, *The Language Experience Approach for the Culturally Disadvantaged.* Newark, Del.: ERIC/CRIER and International Reading Association, 1972.

13. Harris, Albert J., and Morrison, Coleman, "The Craft Project: A Final Report," *Reading Teacher,* 22 (January 1969), 335–340.

14. Harris, Albert J., and Serwer, Blanche L., "Comparing Reading Approaches in First Grade Teaching with Disadvantaged Children," *Reading Teacher,* 19 (May 1966), 698–703.

15. Hildreth, Gertrude H., "Early Writing as an Aid to Reading," *Elementary English,* 40 (January 1963), 15–20.

16. Hildreth, Gertrude H., "Experience-Related Reading for School Beginners," *Elementary English,* 42 (March 1965), 280–284, 289.

17. Irish, Margaret, "Role Playing for Reluctant Readers," *Florida Reading Quarterly,* 7 (January 1971), 20–22.

18. Keith, Mary T., "Sustained Primary Program for Bilingual Children," in *Reading Goals for the Disadvantaged,* J. Allen Figurel, ed. Newark, Del.: International Reading Association, 1970, 262–277.

19. Kendrick, William M., and Bennett, Clayton L., "A Comparative Study of Two First Grade Language Arts Programs—Extended into Second Grade," *Reading Teacher,* 20 (May 1967), 747–755.

20. McCanne, R., "Approaches to First Grade English Reading Instruction for Children from Spanish-Speaking

Homes," *Reading Teacher,* 19 (May 1966), 670–675.

21. McDavid, Raven I., Jr., "Dialectology and the Teaching of Reading," *Reading Teacher,* 18 (December 1964), 206–213.

22. Miller, D. D., and Johnson, Gail, "What We've Learned About Teaching Reading to Navajo Indians," *Reading Teacher,* 27 (March 1974), 550–554.

23. Morris, Ronald, *Success and Failure in Learning To Read,* 2nd ed. Baltimore, Md.: Penguin Books, 1973.

24. Moss, Joy F., "Growth in Reading in an Integrated Day Classroom," *Elementary School Journal,* 72 (March 1972), 304–320.

25. Packer, Athol B., "Ashton-Warner's Key Vocabulary for the Disadvantaged," *Reading Teacher,* 23 (March 1970), 559–564.

26. Platt, Penny, "Teaching Beginning Reading to Disadvantaged Children from Pictures Children Draw," in *Reading Goals for the Disadvantaged,* J. Allen Figurel, ed. Newark, Del.: International Reading Association, 1970, 84–90.

27. Serwer, Blanche L., "Linguistic Support for a Method of Teaching Reading to Black Children," *Reading Research Quarterly,* 4 (Summer 1969), 449–467.

28. Shuy, Roger W., "Some Considerations for Developing Beginning Reading Materials for Ghetto Children," *Journal of Reading Behavior,* 1 (Spring 1969), 33–44.

29. Stauffer, Russell G., "The Language Experience Approach," in *First Grade Reading Programs,* James F. Kerfoot, ed. Perspectives in Reading, No. 5. Newark, Del.: International Reading Association, 1965.

30. Stauffer, Russell G., *The Language-Experience Approach to the Teaching of Reading.* New York: Harper & Row, Inc., 1970.

31. Stauffer, Russell G., and Hammond, W. Dorsey, "The Effectiveness of Language Arts and Basic Reader Approaches to First Grade Reading Instruction—Extended into Second Grade," *Reading Teacher,* 20 (May 1967), 740–746.

32. Stauffer, Russell G., and Hammond, W. Dorsey, "The Effectiveness of Language Arts and Basic Reader Approaches to First Grade Reading Instruction—Extended into Third Grade," *Reading Research Quarterly,* 4 (Summer 1969), 468–499.

33. Vicinus, Charles H., Brunson, F. Ward, and Anderson, Adele M., *The Individualized Reader.* Alexandria, Va.: The Encabulator Corp., 1971.

34. Vilscek, Elaine, Cleland, Donald, and Bilka, Loisanne, "Coordinating and Integrating Language Arts Instruction," *Reading Teacher,* 21 (October 1967), 3–10.

35. Vilscek, Elaine, Morgan, Lorraine, and Cleland, Donald, "Coordinating and Integrating Language Arts Instruction in the First Grade," *Reading Teacher,* 20 (October 1966), 31–37.

36. Wassermann, Selma, "Aspen Mornings with Sylvia Ashton-Warner," *Childhood Education,* 48 (April 1972), 348–353.

37. Yerkes, Marie, "We're Helping Johnnie Read," *National Retired Teachers Association Journal,* 23 (January–February 1972), 27–28.

38. Young, Virgil M., and Young, Katherine A., "Special Education Children as the Authors of Books," *Reading Teacher,* 22 (November 1968), 122–125.

SUPPLEMENTARY READING

Ashton-Warner, Sylvia, *Spinster.* New York: Simon & Schuster, Inc., 1958.

Ashton-Warner, Sylvia, *Teacher.* New York: Simon & Schuster, Inc., 1963.

Darrow, Helen Fisher, and Van Allen, R., *Independent Activities for Creative Learning.* New York: Teachers College Press, 1961.

Hall, Maryanne, *Teaching Reading as a Language Experience.* Columbus, Ohio: Charles E. Merrill Publishing Company, 1970.

Hall, Maryanne, *The Language Experience Approach for the Culturally Disadvantaged.* Newark, Del.: ERIC/ CRIER and International Reading Association, 1972.

Lee, Doris M., and Van Allen, R., *Learning To Read Through Experience.* New York: Appleton-Century-Crofts, 1963.

Spache, Evelyn B., *Reading Activities for Child Involvement.* Boston: Allyn & Bacon, Inc., 1976.

Stauffer, Russell G., *The Language Experience Approach to the Teaching of Reading.* New York: Harper & Row, Inc., 1970.

Vicinus, Charles H., Brunson, F. Ward, and Anderson, Adele M., *The Individualized Reader.* Alexandria, Va.: The Encabulator Corp., 1971.

PART
III

THE PROGRAM OF
THE FUTURE

6
Readiness and Reading for Young Children

PREVIEW

Widely different definitions of readiness persist in current textbooks, as well as in instructional materials. These concepts and practices range from a trusting belief in the ultimate effects of simple maturation or the passage of time to highly developed programs based on diagnosis of pupil needs. However, at the moment a great variety of instructional materials and devices are appearing on the market. Many of these purport to provide perceptual training, to improve visual and auditory skills, or to promote hand, eye, and body coordination. Wide experimentation is occurring in efforts to enhance significant factors in early reading success, such as intelligence, language development, and teacher–pupil relationships. At the same time, school systems are beginning to experiment with a number of organizational patterns, such as preschool groups, prekindergarten classes, and transitional kindergartens or first grades extending such an experience for another year, and even nursery school classes.

It is apparent that these developments imply a growing concern for the success of the beginning reader. These experimental school arrangements and teaching materials are all intended to provide developmental training that will foster early adjustment to the school's demands. As this trend progresses, it moves us toward that day when preschool children and school entrants will really be carefully evaluated. They will receive training keyed to their needs and of sufficient duration to facilitate early school progress.

During the past few years, practices in reading instruction in America have shown a truly innovative trend—that of beginning reading during the nursery or pre-school years. The arguments offered for this downward extension of the school system are varied. Some point out that today's children are more mature and have greater vocabularies and wider experiences than the last generation or two. Because of their superior development, it is argued that children should be introduced to schoolwork earlier. Other writers have expressed their opinion that if school training began earlier, children could be accelerated through their entire school career. One or two experts offer the weak rationalization that since it has not been shown that early schooling actually harms children, it should be initiated.

AT THE PRESCHOOL LEVEL

Observers of such preschool programs as the nationwide Head Start note the growth in vocabulary and in cognitive or thinking skills of the children given special attention in some of the centers. This stimulation presumably helps many children from lower socioeconomic groups to deal with the school's highly verbal de-mands. The fact that some Head Start programs have been successful in these areas is now used as another support for early schooling. Trials with a "talking typewriter" and with a highly scheduled formal school day for preschoolers have shown certain types of success. Some of the young children have learned to read and write a few words and to do simple arithmetic. They also showed some gain on a reading readiness test after the training, indicating, perhaps, that they were better prepared for school entrance.

As is typical in American industry, as soon as the trend toward early schooling became obvious, many manufacturers and even some reading specialists offered a variety of materials and programs for young children. Among these are collections of large flash cards to be attached to objects in the home or to the family members; books on how to teach a baby to read; and readers, workbooks, games, and puzzles—usually emphasizing the learning of the al-phabet (10,29)—specifically designed for this early instruction. Federal and local projects were designed to train parents in tutoring their children or to employ parents as aides to teachers so that they might learn to reinforce the school's program by parallel coaching at home (35).

Some school systems have built new facilities for four- and five-year-olds; others have begun to require children to attend school during the summer prior to their formal school enrollment. A few schools have experimented with a twelve-month arrangement or with enrichment programs during the summer vacation. Special oral language programs often based on the practices used with adults in teaching English as a second language have been used prior to or early in the school years in many places. Several school systems have extended the kindergarten program to as long as three years by admitting the younger children to a prekindergarten program, followed by a transitional kindergarten and a traditional kindergarten of a year each.

The evidence regarding the effectiveness of such programs as Head Start, Title I, and Upward Bound, as well as individual efforts initiated by various school systems, is very ambiguous (28). The Head Start program for preschool children did not concern itself with what is needed to produce good readers in families in which the children typically do not learn to read well. Rather, it attempted to see how much good could be done in a predetermined time with a specific amount of money per child. The emphasis was upon medical, dental, nutritional, emotional, and cognitive improvement. Naturally the children profited from this massive treatment, and gains in the areas stressed in some cases were quite spectacular at the end of a year. But these gains in cognitive growth, alertness, general health, and the like were not sustained in the next four years, unless the program was constantly reinforced. Groups of untreated children, once they were exposed to a stimulating school experience, readily overtook the Head Start pupils. Perhaps the only significant outcome of these preschool and early school programs was the slowing down of the usual downward trend of intelligence and academic performances commonly present among socioeconomically handicapped children. To a sociologist, these ultimate outcomes would seem to have justified such programs, but, from their viewpoint, educators, in general, were disappointed in the lack of results more specifically related to early reading.

All these activities and programs tend to lead us to believe that early school instruction is being established on a wide and firm basis. But few of those promoting this new development have asked the question of what research really tells us about its values. There are at least three sources of information regarding the merits of early schooling. Comparative studies of British and American children's school progress provide one source. These studies indicate that although British children begin formal school a year earlier, they are no farther advanced in the curricula and content they can deal with in comparisons three or four years later with American pupils. A second clue to the outcome of formal programs for young children is given in the research studies of various child welfare research centers, such as that at the University of Iowa. Their reports show that routinized or structured programs for preschool children stimulate aggressive behavior among the children and negative feelings against the teacher. Highly directed training of preschool children does not appear to transfer to greater school achievement as well as imitative, incidental social learning in an atmosphere of warmth, acceptance, and encouragement. Moreover, the routinized day for preschoolers ignores their differences in attention span, their needs for bodily activity and freedom of movement, their inability to share the attention of an adult with their peers, as well as their needs for self-identification.

The two groups of studies just mentioned would certainly lead us to question the claims for early schooling. But the research of Dolores Durkin (6) on children who were reading well before entering school is directly relevant to this new trend. Durkin found forty-nine children in a total population of over 5000 school entrants whose performance on a formal reading test proved their reading ability. By interviews with their parents, she established that the children were of two types: those who had been tutored by their parents and those who had learned to read spontaneously and independently, often as a result of playing school with their older brothers and sisters. As one such child interviewed by the present writer said, "My sister brings her book home and tells me the words. The next day I know them. That's all!"

These forty-nine early readers were, on the average, quite superior in intelligence, very curious, and interested in words and letters. Follow-up studies of this group were made over a six-year period, while a second group of 156 early readers was studied over a three-year span. The longitudinal test results showed that, on the average, these children continued to be markedly accelerated in reading at the third and the sixth grades. However, those children tutored by their parents *did not maintain* the initial degree of acceleration. In the sixth grade their reading test scores were not as far accelerated as their generally superior intelligence would warrant.

Perhaps we should consider the implications of Durkin's studies before rushing into early formal schooling. It is apparent that only a very small proportion, perhaps less than 1 percent, of preschoolers, even with superior intelligence, readily learn to read before first grade. It is true that the proportion might be greater in a planned tutoring program, but since we do not know how many failed to learn to read despite their parents' efforts, we cannot be certain that the proportion would increase. What happened in this select group of interested, bright youngsters cannot readily be generalized to most preschoolers, either. While early progress in reading is accelerated, direct instruction apparently lacks permanent effects upon reading skill, interests, and attitudes. Certainly, if we can identify them, some of the bright children of four and five should be offered an opportunity to learn to read. But from Durkin's results it appears that this should be an informal program directed largely by the child's growing interest in words and letters rather than by parent or teacher scheduling.

Several studies have followed these implications of Durkin's research in offering unstructured, informal reading activities to those children who were interested in such a program. About half of the children, mainly those of better-than-average intelligence, learned to read. The other half, who were of average ability, did not. Those who learned to read early exceeded the others in testing at the end of the second and third grades, both groups being markedly above national norms, however. Even a control group of kindergarten children exceeded those who had failed to learn to read, by the third grade (54). In effect, Marjorie H. Sutton's results tell us that some children, whether average or above, even when exposed to a self-paced informal reading program in kindergarten, do not learn to read either then or in later primary grades, as well as other groups matched in ability. Thus the individual differences among young children continue to argue against early schooling for some—whether it is informal or formal in nature.

Other observers of early reading programs have noted that boys who are taught reading tend to develop less acceptable classroom behaviors than girls, or than boys and girls in a nontutored group. Jean E. Robertson of Alberta, Canada, offers several other cautions about early school programs (40). Since a number of speech sounds are not usually completely developed even by the age of eight, and because of the lesser auditory discrimination among boys, she doubts the advisability of the common programs emphasizing decoding or phonics. Robertson also emphasizes the difficulties of young children in dealing with successive sounds in words (that is, in auditory sequencing, synthesis, or blending) as another argument against the formal phonics programs so widely offered for this type of program.

Undoubtedly, more children are receiving some kind of early school experience today than even ten years ago. One recent survey indicates that the proportion of children attending preprimary programs has increased from 25 to 40 percent in this short space of time. Early childhood education is definitely becoming more widely accepted by both parents and school administrators. In our opinion the most defensible type of program would resemble one conducted in Carlsbad, New Mexico (9). Economically disadvantaged children of five were served by teachers and teacher aides, medical, dental, nursing, and psychiatric practitioners, guidance counselors, and speech consultants. Each child received a thorough physical examination and treatment for his needs. Throughout the year, careful observations were made of each child's progress in the physical and mental tasks five-year-olds should be able to handle. Activities were planned according to needs and deficiencies for the total group, as well as for individuals and small groups. Poems, stories, drama, crayons, clay, games and rhythmic actions, books, and pictures were used. The case history of the child, his progress, and his performances as judged by a preschool inventory test were prepared for the first-grade teacher. Because of its emphasis upon language skills, the informal nature of the program, the absence of formal school skills, and the individualization of corrective treatments and experiences, this project exemplifies what we could consider the only defensible approach to early schooling.

IN THE KINDERGARTEN

It was almost inevitable that the concern with early childhood education would have an impact upon kindergarten practices. Surveys of the current beliefs and practices of about 700 kindergarten teachers do indeed confirm this effect. One-third of such teachers expressed the belief that their pupils are ready to read. Even more now occasionally teach prereading and reading skills, such as letter names, writing letters, sounds of letters, likenesses and differences between words. From 29 to 40 percent of the teachers begin this instruction, but only 16 percent actually teach children to read words (24). According to another survey (56), 31 percent regularly teach reading using a readiness workbook, language experience charts, a classroom library, and dittoed worksheets, yet only 2 to 5 percent report using preprimers or primers. Only 19 percent of the kindergarten teachers refuse to teach any of these skills. A third survey of 354 kindergarten teachers in Virginia (45) indicated that 40 percent were in favor of teaching reading but only 25 percent saw a need for a planned readiness program prior to the introduction to reading. Among those who offered reading instruction, use of the language experience approach was most frequent, phonics programs second, and basal readers third.

In contrast to this approach, 62 percent of a sample of teachers in six New England states* used published readiness materials with *all* their pupils in addition to informal readiness activities. Most of these teachers expressed the belief that, whether they can already read or not, all children need the formal readiness program. Even the amount of time for the program, one to four weeks, was the same for average, below-average, and above-average pupils in these schools. Apparently, a readiness workbook is an absolute essential in the minds of some teachers. Certainly, these surveys show that the present-day kindergarten is moving in the direction of instruction in what we formerly thought of as readiness or beginning reading skills.

What are the results of kindergarten reading instruction? We already knew that ordinary kindergarten programs, when differentiated in terms of the child's needs, promoted higher scores on reading tests during the primary grades. The Sutton studies mentioned earlier and a number of others confirm the same result when readiness and beginning reading skills are presented in the kindergarten (12,22). What then, if anything, does adding readiness and reading training to the kindergarten program do for pupils? To our knowledge, it has not yet been shown that earlier emphasis upon reading in the kindergarten produces higher primary reading scores, more permanent acceleration, or better attitudes toward reading and school than a well-planned program without this emphasis. Perhaps this explains why only about one out of three kindergarten teachers is willing to move toward new types of readiness or reading training.

RESEARCH ON READINESS

Age at School Entrance

Despite the hope of many school administrators that raising the entrance age will reduce the number of early reading failures, there is practically no research support for this practice. Prescott's study (38) of over 14,000 beginning first-grade pupils showed no significant differences in readiness between "overage" pupils of seven years and two months and above, and "underage" pupils of five years and eight months and below. Many other earlier reports confirm the fact that the

---

* New England Educational Assessment Project, *Reading Instruction in New England's Public Schools,* ERIC/CRIER ED 032 996.

nature of the program offered and its flexibility and provision for individual differences are what determine the percentage of reading failures. Chronological age alone has very little significance in determining children's readiness for reading or subsequent success in reading achievement.

For example, for the past thirty years the public schools of Brookline, Massachusetts, have been admitting to kindergarten children with the minimum chronological age of four years and nine months.* During the first fifteen years of this admission policy children as young as four were admitted on trial. In 1948 a study of the success of the underage children showed that average marks and achievement test results, except in the kindergarten, were higher than those of other children in every grade in the schools. The margin of superior academic success actually increased as these underage children progressed through the eight grades of elementary school.

Because these children were admitted only after physical and psychological examinations, they were probably of superior mental ability. However, their success demonstrates that age is not a highly significant factor in school success. When special instructional efforts are made, and children are screened for physical and mental readiness, the Brookline results show that many children as young as four years and three months when admitted to kindergarten make good school progress.

In reviewing international practices in primary reading, Malmquist (27) again points out that the optimum age for beginning reading has not yet been determined by research, for it is relevant to a number of other factors. Some research he cites indicates that the earlier children go to school, the more negative their attitudes toward school become. Because of these findings, most European schools are continuing their current practices regarding the age of admission and rejecting early instruction in reading.

In American schools, however, age at school entrance continues to be practically the only criterion of readiness for school, perhaps for political or economic reasons. In a survey of six New England states, 88 percent of admissions to kindergarten are based on the single criterion of chronological age. Only 8 percent of the schools employed other criteria, such as intelligence tests, evaluation of the child's social maturity, or teacher judgment.

Sex

Several large-scale studies comparing the readiness of boys and girls confirm the widespread impression of the superiority of girls. Prescott's investigation (38), for example, concurs in this finding even when the groups were matched for chronological age. Despite the general greater readiness of girls, few schools, if any, differentiate early reading instruction on this basis.

---

* James R. Hobson, "Scholastic Standing and Activity Participation of Underage High School Pupils Originally Admitted to Kindergarten on the Basis of Physical and Psychological Examinations," Presidential Address, Division 16, American Psychological Association, September 1956.

It probably would not be feasible or necessary to offer a different type of instruction to the sexes or, as some might suggest, to have them enter school at different ages. The great mass of boys and girls entering school show a similar, average readiness. But at the lower extreme there is a real need for exploration of the specific needs of the boys who are unready for reading instruction.

Some authors interpret the differential success of boys and girls in American schools as reflecting some natural hereditary differences in physiological development. Girls are credited with a more rapid rate of physical maturation, and this is interpreted as the reason for their more frequent successes in reading and other types of school work. But the failure ratio is reversed in certain other countries, such as Germany. This observation denies the importance of any sex-linked hereditary factor in school success. It implies that the explanation for the difference in failure rate must be sought elsewhere. We believe it may more accurately be attributed to such factors as the attitudes of women teachers toward boy pupils, the socially conforming attitudes of American girls, and the proportion of male teachers in primary schools (as compared with Germany). What is thought to be a sex difference may well be simply a reflection of the pupil–teacher relationships and the climate of the classroom.

Dale D. Johnson (*18*) confirmed this interpretation by comparing the sexes in eighteen aspects of achievement in Canada, United States, England, and Nigeria. The differences favored girls in the United States and Canada, which have a majority of female teachers; and favored boys in England and Nigeria, where the sex ratio of teachers is less predominantly female. Boys and girls in these countries achieved exactly as the bulk of their teachers thought they would in the comparison of the sexes. Recent studies definitely support these inferences in pointing out that boys receive more negative comments and fewer opportunities to read in mixed classes. Furthermore, some studies indicate that when boys are separated into groups for reading instruction, their reading achievement is greater.

Physical Development

Measures of physical characteristics such as height and weight show some relationship to readiness in certain studies (*33*). Height, in particular, reflects nutrition and general health, which, in turn, reflect parental knowledge of hygiene and principles of physical health. Thus in a general sense, children whose parents provide appropriate diet and adequate medical care tend to enjoy greater success in school. However, the relationships between these factors and reading are not great enough for anything like individual predictions.

Vision

Although reading is first and foremost a visual act, and literally hundreds of studies show the importance of certain visual skills for successful reading, most readiness programs ignore these facts completely. The visual skills of the young child are, in our opinion, one of the most significant factors in his early reading success. But in most schools the child's vision is tested, if at all, by a Snellen chart, which measures nothing but his visual acuity or keenness of vision. This test is given at a 20-foot distance, thus determining visual acuity at this point—a measure which is comparatively unrelated to his vision at the reading distance. In fact, the Snellen test only reveals the nearsighted child, who, as the research shows, is *most likely to succeed in reading*. Because of the stage of their visual development, most young children are farsighted and can readily pass the distance test. Yet they may be suffering any of a half-dozen undetected visual defects that affect their near-point vision and limit their success in reading (47).

Studies conducted in California, in an attempt to devise a better vision screening program that would be feasible in schools, revealed the shocking inadequacy of the Snellen test (37). A careful examination of the results of testing with the Snellen alone showed that 60 percent of the first-grade children needing professional vision care would be entirely overlooked if the usual standard of 20/30 were used. When the standard of 20/40 was used, as some authorities recommend for this grade, 70 percent of the visually defective children were missed. These results are not peculiar to California, for a study in the New Haven schools (55) indicated that the Snellen test detected less than half of the elementary children who needed visual care. It is particularly interesting to note that, probably because of the tendency to farsightedness at this age, all the New Haven kindergarten children were found normal by the Snellen test when actually 46 percent were found defective in vision by more careful testing. This indictment of the Snellen test might be summarized in the words of one of the authors of the Orinda study in California, who pointed out that, in all, more than one-half of all children with real vision problems will pass this so-called test of vision (37).

Complete testing of vision is obviously a professional task and cannot be attempted by the teacher. But under the leadership of teachers and administrators who are concerned about vision screening, many schools are introducing significantly better methods (17,55). In most such communities these efforts are actively supported by the local Lions Clubs, local optometrists, and occasionally by interested medical specialists. Some nurses and physicians seem to fear that the teacher who is interested in better vision tests is attempting to usurp their medical functions. But dissemination of the facts about the Snellen test to parents, which can be accomplished by distributing informational literature obtainable from the American Optometric Association and other sources, often helps obtain favorable action.

It is obvious that schools must use better vision screening programs than the Snellen test if they are to find the 20 to 40 percent of children whose visual difficulties may hinder reading success (41). Most schools concerned about this problem have, like those in New Haven, formed committees composed of interested parents, local ophthalmologists and optometrists, school doctors and nurses, and teachers. When they approach the problem with an open mind, they can arrange simple screening programs to be administered by school nurses assisted by parents to find those pupils who need professional vision care. While these screening programs can be simple enough for a parent or teacher to administer, they should certainly include the skills of binocular acuity at near-point, binocular coordination, accommodation, and convergence. Many studies show these skills to be essential to successful reading (*42*).

Visual Perception

Visual discrimination or perception is derived from or based upon physical handling of objects. In other words, the child tends to explore objects in space—to learn shapes and spatial relationships first with his hands (and mouth), later with his eyes. During the preschool ages when vision is developing, the child learns to explore, recognize, and discriminate objects or forms by tactile and visual approaches, with a gradually greater dependence upon visual clues (*13*).

Those children who have had little experience with objects or forms at near-point have difficulty with the ultimate visual discriminations among words necessary for reading. We describe these difficulties in various ways: (1) he lacks visual discrimination or perception; (2) he lacks hand–eye coordination; (3) he lacks orientation to left and right (reversals, inversions, letter confusions); (4) he cannot sit still long enough while working at near-point tasks; (5) he cannot concentrate or has a short attention span; (6) he cannot read without pointing or using a marker (he still needs tactile clues or a hand to lead his eyes in reading). These are some of the familiar descriptive phrases used by teachers in pointing out the difficulties of the slow learner or poor reader. They all refer to the same basic problem—lack of sufficient tactile and visual experience with objects, forms, and spatial relationships. Related symptoms which teachers commonly observe but do not recognize as part of the syndrome are inability to identify verbally right or left in space or in parts of the body of the self or others, difficulties with cross-identification of a facing body, and inability to reproduce simple two-dimensional forms or designs (unless these are first named verbally, as the square or triangle, in which case the child produces a stereotyped model).

Despite the beliefs of some writers, these symptoms of disturbances of visual perception are not readily explained by handedness, cerebral dominance, crossed-dominance, mixed eye–hand dominance, and similar theories. These theories completely fail to explain visual perception or the most irritating symptom, reversals in reading. Nor is there any reason to believe that these behaviors have a neurological basis, in the average normal or non-brain-damaged child. Poor visual perception is found among children with any and every combination of preferences for hand, foot, and eye. Moreover, recent extended brain surgery research shows that cerebral dominance has nothing to do with language functions or visual perception. Reversals in reading are a common reading behavior among beginners in reading in any language or even among older persons who are learning to read for the first time. The simplest proof that reversals arise from immaturity in visual discrimination or perception is the fact that, without any special attention, they spontaneously disappear among successful readers as the accuracy of their word discrimination increases or, in other words, as perception improves. The fact that some of these symptoms persist among ineffectual readers is a better argument for perceptual training, in our opinion, than for classifying such pupils as ineducable, neurological problems.

At the present time, increasing attention is being paid to perception in writings on readiness and early reading. Readiness tests are beginning to include various measures of this fundamental process. Vernon (58) has intensively reviewed the research on perception in a very readable fashion. Goins' dissertation study confirms Vernon's identification of two general types of perceivers at first-grade level—those who can recognize and hold the total configuration or symbol in mind and those who can apparently discriminate among the significant details. Good readers, in Goins' experiment, were found to be those children who were successful in both these types of perception (14). Barrett (2) has made a careful review of the available studies involving tests of visual perception and discrimination. He concluded that the best tests for predicting early reading ability have not yet been identified. He therefore recommended that the assessment include measures of discrimination among words, letters, and geometric designs as well as tests of letter names.

Teachers generally recognize the perceptual limitations of grossly brain-damaged or mentally retarded children, children with cerebral palsy, or even posttraumatic aphasic* children, although they see very few of this last type outside the reading clinic. At the same time, teachers fail to recognize that similar handicaps may hinder the reading success of apparently normal pupils. The assumption is often made that since the child is now of school age, he must have passed through all the stages of neuromuscular development which result in visual perception. Fortunately, as we learn more about perception and improve our diagnostic abilities, we are recognizing that this assumption is often false.

With the current increase in interest in visual perception there has also come a distinct looseness in the use of the term. All sorts of tests are being called measures of visual perception, including copying letters, numbers, words, and geometric forms; matching these same symbols; and drawing or reproducing letters or forms while viewing or from memory. Figure–ground perception, as it is called, is measured in many ways—pictures embedded in a loose or highly structured background, intersecting geometric forms or other figures, marble board figures against a background. Tests involving part–whole relationships, hand–eye coordination in a tracing task, tests of arranging cutouts or marking pictures by size, tests involving memory for geometric forms, and such tests free of the memory factor, discrimination and memory for single letters, bigrams, and trigrams—all are considered tests of visual perception. And the concept is also broadened by some to include left–right orientation in space and in relation to one's own body. Some writers link this left–right orientation to laterality and handedness, to cerebral dominance, and to reversals in the act of reading, with very little research justification.

* Children who have lost certain language functions as a result of cerebral injury.

Visual perception obviously means different behaviors to different authors; furthermore, they often do not bother to discover the influence of memory, drawing skill, coordination, and intelligence upon the results of the tests they create. Often several such tests are thrown together into a battery, à la Frostig and de Hirsch, with little concern for duplication, overlap, or intercorrelations between subtests as great as their reliability.

Table 6–1 offers comparative information on the eight most widely used standardized tests of visual perception. Briefly, they may be described as follows.

Bender Visual–Motor Gestalt Test.   This test requires the reproduction of nine complex geometric forms from memory. It is interpreted by some as a test for brain injury, emotional problems, perceptual handicaps, immaturity, or general intelligence. Still others consider it a test of personality or of ego strength of the child. It was originally designed to detect organic pathology among adults and was later adapted for use with children by employing various scoring systems. It does seem to yield results somewhat similar to readiness tests in some populations but it is a poorer predictor of reading achievement than such tests, particularly when the factor of intelligence is removed from the correlation.

Frostig Test of Developmental Perception.   This test includes subtests of motor coordination, figure–ground, constancy of shape, position in space, and spatial relationships. It was standardized in southern California with middle-class white children exclusively. There are several questionable aspects in the battery, as subtest V does not function when it is used to test children under the age of five but the instructions are to score the child as succeeding at this level, even when he achieves a zero score. This same arbitrary scoring for zero scores is also used in the

TABLE 6–1. Scoreboard on Visual Perception Tests

Test	Validity for Reading	Reliability	Control of		
			Speed	Memory	Intelligence
Bender	− .16 to − .17	.54 to .71	None	None	None; .48 to .79
Frostig	.32 to .615 total; − .03 to .49 subtests	.69 to .98 total; .29 to .74 subtests	Yes	Yes	None; .318 to .460
MPD	Uses cutoff scores; r's not known	.74 to .85	Yes	Yes	Yes (?); norms corrected for IQ
Graham–Kendall	Unknown	.72 to .90	None	None	Yes (?); − .60
Winter Haven	.24 to .44	Unknown	Yes	Yes	None
Beery	.33 to .50	.80 to .90	Yes	Yes	None; .37 to .70
Benton	Unknown	ca. .85	Yes	Yes	Yes; norms corrected for IQ
de Hirsch	.55, .63		Yes	Yes	None

other subtests. The reported reliability of the test drops markedly when it is given by teachers or others who are not highly trained in its use. Subtest III is more reliable than any others and, in fact, is more reliable than the entire test. Intercorrelations among the subtests are higher than their reliabilities in some cases, implying that the various subtests resemble one another more closely than two administrations of the same subtest.

Summaries of the studies on the validity of the Frostig test in predicting reading achievement show that in most populations this relationship is very low. Several researchers have seriously questioned whether there is any justification for the subtest labels, or in fact for use of any of the tests in predicting reading success (35,36).

Predictive Index Tests.   This is a battery of tests tried out on fifty-three kindergarten children to eliminate the less discriminative subtests. Ten of the thirty-seven tests assessed in this fashion seemed desirable to the authors. They include measures of pencil use, the Bender, the Wepman auditory discrimination, the number of words used in a child's story, a categories and a reversals test, a word matching test, a word reproduction test, and two-word recognition tests. The procedure has been severely criticized for the minute size of the population and the faulty assumption that given a large number of tests we can select out a few, with any certainty that the present relationship is anything more than chance. The tests appear to predict about as well as the better readiness tests except in overpredicting failures. It is also an error to assume that the subtest correlations or their predictive abilities would be equally effective in all populations, until they have so tested.

Other available tests of visual perception include the *Graham*–Kendall Memory for Designs, the *Beery Developmental Test of Visual Integration,* the *Revised Visual Retention,* and the *Minnesota Percepto-Diagnostic Test.* In content these instruments are all very similar to the Bender in requiring the reproduction of two to twenty-four geometric forms, usually from memory. Like their parent, none of these has shown strong relationships with reading success, although some seem relatively efficient in identifying brain-damaged children, which was the original purpose for their creation.

We described the Bender and the Frostig only because they are widely used, the first by school psychologists, the second, by classroom teachers. The Winter Haven Perceptual Forms Test was designed for teacher use and interpretation and, if we believe hand–eye coordination relevant to beginning reading, does help to identify those pupils likely to have problems in handwriting, letter formation, and word recognition because of this factor. Its value is not specifically in predicting reading failure but rather in finding pupils who would benefit from coordination training.

It is quite clear that most of the published tests of visual perception leave a great deal to be desired. Of these eight, none is entirely satisfactory in its ability to predict readiness or reading achievement; in reliability, which should be .90 or above for individual diagnosis; in control of the speed, memory, or intelligence factors; or in the possibility of alternative administrations to analyze the child's performances. We need a test that consistently predicts reading as well as the Bender sometimes does, a test with the higher reliabilities of the Beery, Benton, or Graham–Kendall, none of which relates well to reading achievement, or a test which can be scored for several different ways of testing, in the manner of the Benton. Only then could we distinguish children's ability to trace, to match, to copy at sight, and to reproduce from memory and perhaps thus determine whether a perceptual difficulty was present or whether the child simply lacked basic visual–motor abilities. In our opinion, these popular tests of visual perception, most of which were built for the different purpose of detecting brain damage among adults, are not ready to make a real contribution to the teacher's attempts to decide which of her pupils need visual–motor training.

Intelligence

The child's mental age and intelligence quotient are often considered among the most important factors in their significance for reading success. Many early studies of the intelligence of beginning readers led to the conclusion that a mental age of approximately six was essential before the child could be successfully introduced to reading. Under most classroom conditions this is probably a reasonably accurate statement. A mental age of six is highly desirable because the teacher is unable or unwilling to differentiate instruction according to pupil needs. Under optimum classroom conditions, as Gates' almost forgotten study (11) shows, children of much lower mental age can learn to read adequately. Gates' classroom studies indicated that the necessary mental age for successful reading was related to the size of the group and the flexibility of the program. In small groups and with differentiated procedures some children with mental ages of four and one-half to five may well learn to read. At the other extreme, some teachers operate in a manner that makes it very difficult for pupils of even seven years of mental age. Like these authors, Gates considers statements regarding the necessary mental age for beginning reading to be meaningless, unless we state the prevailing classroom conditions. Schools in other English-speaking countries commonly admit children as young as five and experience no great difficulties in teaching them to read. It is the stereotyped, inflexible, and mass-oriented reading program which demands a higher mental age, and makes intelligence so important a factor in reading success, in our primary classrooms. The demands of the average or poor classroom in effect create a condition in which only the fittest (the brightest) can survive and meet these demands. This is why intelligence seems to be an important factor in early reading success.

Many other research studies of school beginners show that intelligence test results are not highly predictive of early reading success. If pupils are arranged in the order of their reading test scores after a period of training, the order just does not neatly parallel a ranking based on mental age or intelligence quotient. Only the extreme cases, the very superior and the mentally retarded pupils, tend to agree in their ranks in reading and intelligence. The degree of reading success for most pupils is determined not by their exact level or rank in intelligence but by other, more influential factors.

In these writers' opinion, altogether too much dependence is placed upon mental test results as predictors of reading progress. First, mental tests are not per se very accurate predictors of reading achievement, particularly at primary levels. Any broad intelligence test samples facets such as concrete reasoning, spatial relations, and quantitative thinking, which have little relationship to reading. The broader the sampling of intellectual abilities, the less accurate is the test in specific predictions in reading.

Second, the test results represent a sort of average of the child's cognitive abilities. This average could not be equally related to such diverse abilities as handwriting, spelling, language usage, and arithmetic fundamentals. These school subjects require different mental abilities and, besides, they develop dissimilarly as the child grows. The variation in both mental and school abilities constantly increases for both individuals and groups. One test offering an average estimate of mental ability cannot possibly predict accurately in these varying school abilities.

Practically all intelligence tests currently available for classroom use, particularly those that emphasize verbal intelligence, are keyed to the middle-class culture in the language development, information, and experiences which they assume the testees have. Many minority children tend to test low, thus reducing teacher expectations and often underestimating their actual potential for learning. The intelligence test result ignores the very potent factors of pupil and parental aspirations, which are often more significant in academic success than the actual level of ability. Even if the test items did reflect the backgrounds of minority children, such elements as negativism, lack of drive, poor response to timed tasks, plus the possible effect of an examiner from a different race or culture militate against accurate results in many cases. The mental age obtained from a test does not indicate the level of school performance to be expected, for the test just is not that good a predictor. Nor does the intelligence quotient show the probable rate of learning of new material, since those behaviors depend upon the nature of the task in many instances.

Some indication of relative strengths and weaknesses in attention, informational background, verbal ability, and nonverbal ability can be derived from certain individual intelligence tests when interpreted by trained examiners. But pattern analysis of the test results is often overworked and based on very subjective grounds in attempts to detect brain damage, dyslexia, educational disabilities, and the like. At best, the intelligence test is a crude estimate of the child's learning abilities, divorced from consideration of his cultural and language background, his self-concept, the attitudes of his family, and the other factors that tend to influence his school progress. If used, the implication of the results must be combined judiciously with other measures, such as auditory comprehension and learning style, and the possible effects of the influential elements we have mentioned.

Yet many studies of the relationships between mental test results and reading achievement seem to support the belief in the predictive values of intelligence measures. We are inclined to believe, however, that the relationship reflects the climate and procedures of the classroom more than the limiting effects of intelligence upon reading achievement. Several observations derived from the twenty-seven first-grade studies of 1964–1966 support this opinion. These studies are reviewed in detail in a later chapter. But a general overview of their results indicates that relationships between intelligence or other readiness factors did not vary considerably from one instructional method to another, or from one classroom to another. Other studies show that teachers' expectations based on the intelligence test results tend to limit their pupils' achievement accordingly. Finally, such teacher characteristics as overall competence and fitting the difficulty of her lessons to pupil progress do make a real difference in pupil achievement regardless of the initial readiness and ability of the pupils (6).

Language Facility

Many parents and teachers believe that the early development of language skills, such as the breadth of the child's speaking vocabulary and his fluency in using it, is a strong indication of readiness. Observations of first graders indicated that the development of these and other language skills followed individual patterns, and that they were unrelated to each other, to readiness, or to early reading achievement. The child's total number of words used in oral communication, his average sentence length, and the number of different words he used all had negligible significance.

This is not the observation of many other writers, who have emphasized the positive relationships between language and speech development and reading success. Group data tend to conceal the true relationships. Children at the lower end of the continuum in language development—those with very limited vocabularies, poor articulation, and poor ability to communicate—will obviously have difficulty with reading. At the upper end children with advanced language skills will probably experience success. But the great mass of children with average language skills do not show a marked relationship of these abilities to reading.

In other words, these language abilities are most significant when they differ greatly from the average. Most school beginners probably show sufficient language development to be ready to read or to achieve success in the average early reading program. Most beginners will succeed reasonably well in reading without extended or intensive language training in the readiness program. In the average American community retardation in language abilities will be a crucial factor for only that small number of children who have had a bilingual or dialectal background or extremely isolated environment, and thus deviate markedly in language development.

We have already mentioned the disagreement among language specialists regarding the nature and extent of the handicap among economically disadvantaged children. Since it is at the readiness level that the reading teacher begins to become concerned about these language differences, it is appropriate to review some of the studies that describe and evaluate the differences.

In a population of Mexican-American pupils, one study claims to have found minimal attention span, auditory and visual discrimination, and experiential background for early reading materials; fear, apathy, or insensitivity toward school; inadequacy in simple cognitive abilities such as directions, labeling, classifying, and discrimination of differences among objects; and marked nutritional deficiencies. Several studies have shown that average length of sentence and range and diversity of vocabulary were slightly related to reading tests of word recognition and comprehension but not to measures of vocabulary or oral reading. Raph (39) claimed that economically disadvantaged children are deficient in range and level of vocabulary, use of syntactic variations within sentences, and such structures as clauses, infinitives, verbals, linking verbs, and complete sentences. These children tended to use a restricted code, as in fast speech, reduced articulatory clues (wat-cha-dn?), and confused word meanings. These differences vary with geographical regions of the United States but are present in parallel studies in England. Another study compared the oral language with that of upper-social-status groups and found that children of the poor used shorter sentences, fewer words, less variety, less mature and complete sentences, and showed more syntactical errors. The children apparently used only about 50 percent of the words in basals for the first two grades and a similar proportion of the words in common vocabulary lists. The pertinent question, of course, is whether these differences are as general as these authors imply, and whether they must be treated before we can expect children to succeed in early reading.

Other samples of economically disadvantaged children indicate that these apparent handicaps may not be as great as claimed. Sherk (46) has found, for example, that poor black children used about 75 percent of the Dolch list, or the basic vocabulary of beginning readers. There were differences in types of words in using fewer adjectives and adverbs, comparatives, animals, flowers, and foods, perhaps an indication of lack of richness in experiences and vocabulary rather than a real lack in words of high frequency. Several studies have shown that the variety of sentence types or structures among these pupils is not significantly different from the usage of middle-class whites (25,46).

One of the problems in interpreting the studies of the language of these pupils is the nature of the testing instruments and the manner in which language is analyzed. We see that sentences may be shorter but are as varied in type and structure as those of other children. We see that the variety of words may be limited in some categories, yet most of those essential to beginning reading are present. Syntactical variations are interpreted as a handicap by some and by others as simply characteristic of a dialect which we do not believe is really an interference with reading success at all. Moreover, the use of unstandardized measures of various language aspects for which there are no norms, the use of test items that are unfamiliar to poor children, the lack of knowledge of what really is an adequate vocabulary for a first grader, plus the possible effects of being tested by a person of another race or culture, in a school setting which is strange and threatening, tend to yield confusing and contradictory observations.

Perhaps the best conclusion we can reach is that there are differences between the language of economically disadvantaged children and the standard English of the school. These differences must be carefully observed and evaluated, perhaps in the manner described later and, where it can be justified, training instituted as suggested in a later chapter.

Certain other language skills, however, have shown greater relationships in several studies. Iver Moe's dissertation study (*31*) found that the first grader's ability to answer questions based on standardized reading selections read to him—or in other words, his auditory comprehension—was more efficient in predicting early reading achievement than several common readiness or intelligence tests. Earlier studies confirm the importance of this language ability as a predictor. Auditory comprehension is a far more complex ability, of course, than other simple skills. Therefore, it is not easy to isolate the reason for its predictive value. The relation of auditory comprehension to intelligence is quite high and probably reflects the intellectual stimulation and the level of oral communication in the home (*44*). If early reading is presented as a thinking process, it is obvious that the child who has been previously stimulated to employ his reasoning abilities in verbal contexts and to listen thoughtfully will show greater progress in reading achievement.

In our opinion, a measure of auditory comprehension is superior to a general group or individual intelligence test in indicating a child's readiness for reading or, in other words, predicting his degree of success in early reading. A measure of auditory comprehension makes a particular demand upon the intellectual processes of memory, cognition, and reasoning as well as the verbal factor of intelligence. Skill in auditory comprehension probably reflects more faithfully the language factors and the intellectual factors in the child's background that influence his readiness and early reading success.

Auditory vocabulary, or the breadth of words that a child recognizes when he hears them, is significantly related to readiness. Measures of this language skill are often included in readiness tests and, in some instances, comprise the entire test. The degree to which a test of auditory vocabulary predicts precisely future reading success varies from one test to another and varies also according to the nature of the readiness training and the early reading program. In his review of readiness tests Starr (*52*) found a range of correlations between various auditory vocabulary tests and reading. These correlations imply a moderate tendency for children with good auditory vocabularies to show high reading scores.

The child's articulation, or his tendency to use baby talk or to make substitutions for certain sounds, relates to his early reading because these difficulties affect his oral reading. Since oral reading is commonly used to such a great degree in beginning programs, children with articulatory defects suffer constant comparison, embarrassment, and correction. Their early reading experiences at the hands of unsympathetic teachers and classmates are often unhappy and frustrating.

The *Monroe Reading Aptitude Test,* a readiness test originally constructed in 1935, includes simple tests of speed and accuracy of articulation. The fact that defects in such areas need not be a barrier to reading success is shown by the very moderate mathematical relationship Marion Monroe (*32*) found between her tests and reading success. Her correlation of .57 indicates only a moderate tendency for children of poor articulation to fail in reading—or the reverse, for children of good articulation to show strong reading scores. Overemphasis upon perfect oral reading and constant criticism of the child's speech errors will produce reading failure for some of these children. Other children with the same problems will succeed in reading when given speech help, and when the attitude of the teacher (and consequently that of the class) is more helpful than derogatory.

Auditory Factors

Auditory acuity refers to the ability to hear sounds of varying pitch and loudness. We are not referring here to the condition of being hard-of-hearing, which implies loss of acuity over a wide range of tones, or extreme losses. The various research studies indicate that losses in auditory acuity, particularly of high tones, are related to reading success in the primary program.

Such losses in acuity affect the child's ability to hear such consonants as *p, b, s, t, k, v, c* and such blends as *fl, ch, th.* The child hears most of the vowel sounds, however. Losses of acuity in the high tones have obvious implications in the phonics training involving consonants and in word discrimination by auditory means.

Auditory discrimination refers to the abilities to hear likenesses and differences among letter sounds as they occur in words. Pupils with normal auditory discrimination are able to detect that words begin or end with the same sound, that they rhyme, that they contain a given sound, and that they are composed of a sequence of sounds in a certain order. These abilities enable the normal pupil to match his pronunciation of an unknown printed word with his auditory memory of the word. Good auditory discrimination helps the beginner to match words he is learning with his previous auditory experiences with the same words.

Auditory discrimination may, in a few cases, be poorer because of actual hearing losses for certain tones or pitches. Because of loss in auditory acuity, the child may be unable to discriminate, for example, between several sounds that vibrate at similar pitches. He may not be able to hear any difference between *t* and *d, s* and *z, m* and *n,* or other sounds which are close together on the scale of pitches. However, in most cases of poor auditory discrimination the problem is not an obvious hearing loss.

Poor auditory discrimination is most frequently related to musical abilities such as pitch discrimination, recognition of auditory rhythms and beat, discrimination of tonal quality, timbre, and loudness. Various research studies differ in their identification of the most important of these auditory skills, probably because they are interrelated or interdependent. Children with weak auditory discrimination tend to be unskilled in several or most of these abilities rather than simply defective in one. Observing such children, the primary teacher notes that they seem to lack an alertness or awareness of the auditory characteristics of words. They seem unable to hear small differences between words, to recognize rhyming, and even to distinguish differences in loudness or pitch in everyday sounds. They readily miscall or mispronounce words, substitute or transpose sounds or syllables in words, and have trouble with complex or polysyllabic words. Sometimes these same auditory errors appear in a child's speech and his spelling. Poor auditory discrimination may interfere with the child's development of accuracy in word recognition, particularly while he is in the primary grades. These auditory difficulties assume lesser significance as pupils above the critical level become less dependent upon relating their auditory vocabulary to word recognition, are less needful of phonic clues, and develop other word recognition clues such as word form, context, and structural analysis.

A research study conducted by one of the writers gave strong evidence of the importance of auditory discrimination in early reading. Some six tests of visual discrimination, auditory discrimination, and auditory vocabulary were used in this study. Each of the tests was repeated four times at two-month intervals. Thus data for predicting first-grade reading success were gathered on what amounted to twenty-four tests. In these predictions, the measures of auditory discrimination were the best single predictors in sixteen out of the twenty-four possibilities. This observation reinforces the primary significance of auditory discrimination in some first grades using the basal reader approach (50).

Several problems, however, cloud our interpretation of the exact significance of auditory discrimination in reading. Dykstra (8), for example, found seven such tests, each of which claimed to measure auditory discrimination in a different manner. The tests varied greatly in their intercorrelations and in their relevance to reading. In fact, combinations of five or six or these tests had only a moderate relationship with reading (multiple coefficient of about .60). As a result of his data, Dykstra concluded that auditory discrimination was not a highly significant factor in beginning reading. Perhaps this conclusion should have been tempered by relating it to the kind of test and reading program offered to the children. It undoubtedly varies in significance according to the demand for phonic analysis in the program and the teacher's attitude toward accurate pronunciation in oral reading, as well as the nature of the test.

In testing with the common measure of distinguishing pairs of words that differ in a single sound, many studies report the inferior performance of minority or economically disadvantaged children. As a result of their findings, most of these researchers recommend intensified training for extended periods in auditory discrimination for these populations (1). In contrast, Venezky (57) and other language specialists feel that auditory discrimination is not a cause of poor reading among dialect users. Their poor reading might just as readily be due to other lacks in attention and in cognitive and verbal development, Venezky argues. Besides, the common discrimination of pairs of words demands distinctions not commonly present in dialectal speech, and not really necessary in reading because of the clues supplied by the context. Moreover, the test is quite unreliable in these populations. Thus, although auditory discrimination may be poorer for dialect speakers, their inferior performance is largely due to the nature of the test and does not affect the reading comprehension of these pupils.

There is also the evidence that such sounds as *l, sh,* voiced *th, v, s, z, j,* and *r* are not yet fully developed in the average primary child's speech, but continue improving spontaneously during this period without speech therapy. Since this is so, overemphasis upon correct discrimination of these sounds would seem pointless. In other words, articulation and auditory discrimination are related and are not completely developed until the age of eight or nine, or perhaps later for some children, and thus reflect the child's development rather than a defect to be corrected. Perhaps the best we should say for auditory discrimination training is that the child probably needs no more than he has to have to deal with the phonics or decoding aspect of the reading program. We should also recognize that there is a difference between teaching children to make the sounds of letters and apparently to recognize differences—and the ability to use these learnings in obtaining meaning from the printed page by phonic analysis.

Further evidence of this interpretation of the lack of auditory discrimination was presented when Karlsen and Blocker (*21*) tested black children on the final consonant blends in the Stanford primary test. They found that their pupils who were drawn from the upper lower and lower middle class equaled the norms for the test. It appears that although they may not say these final consonant blends in speech or oral reading, these pupils could hear and discriminate among them. This ability to discriminate is further shown in Williams's study (*59*) in the pupils' success with initial phonemes in a common test, although not with finals. Groff (*15*) also argues strongly against a significant relationship between auditory discrimination and reading, repeating these same criticisms of the tests used and their low relationship with early reading, and he points out the very small proportion of children for whom this ability is really a problem.

It is essential to recognize that the use of a test of auditory discrimination does not neatly divide pupils into those who need training and those who do not. Among the relevant facts that affect the interpretation of the test are:

1. The child's performance may reflect a hearing loss among high tones—certain consonants and their blends; or among low tones—the vowels *m, n, b, h* and their blends.
2. The child's articulatory development: the sounds of *z, zh, s, sh, r, th* (thin or the), *wh,* and *l* are not commonly mastered by the age of six or seven. If this is the explanation for the test result, what is the point in training him to discriminate sounds not yet present in his speech? Seek the advice of a speech therapist.
3. If the errors are due to dialect, as in final consonants in particular, is training really essential for the reading program because of its emphasis upon phonics?

Or, will the teacher accept his dialect and recognize that he can read and comprehend without modifying his speech?

4. Auditory discrimination is not an independent ability; it is linked with auditory span and intelligence. Is it possible that these account for the test results? Perhaps repeated testing and some observation of the apparent attention span are needed to obtain a more meaningful assessment. All three of these traits will effect the child's progress in a heavily phonic oriented reading program, in the negative sense if they are less than average. What modification of such a program will be made for this type of pupil? What alternatives to discrimination and phonics training can be used with this pupil? (See Chapter 11.)

Preschool Learning

Under certain circumstances the child's preschool learning seems to be an important factor in his readiness and early reading success. Some upper-class homes provide a wealth of experiences with language and books. Beginning as early as twelve months of age, some children develop important concepts of books. Among these are the following: books contain pages to be turned; pictures resemble familiar objects; pictures and books have a top and bottom, a front and a back; books give information and pleasure; and language adults use in reading is constant for each page; this language can be remembered and related to specific pages or pictures; the printed smbols tell the reader what to say. These concepts facilitate the gradual development of children from a nonreading status to that of actual reading.

Many different tests are included in readiness tests in an attempt to sample these preschool learnings. Among these are matching or naming letters, giving sounds of letters, writing letters, matching beginning and ending sounds in words, and speed in learning words, to mention just a few. Some of these tests give a fair prediction of reading achievement at the middle or end of the first grade, and thus their use tends to persist in common readiness tests. The assumption is that they are measuring the child's status in developing readiness for reading. Because the tests seem of some use in predicting early reading success, some of their authors jump to the conclusion that these skills with letters and letter sounds should be greatly emphasized in the reading program of the first year (7). Actually, these tests merely sample bits of information that some children, particularly the bright ones, have acquired. Careful review of these readiness studies shows that the tests of preschool learning are loaded with the intelligence factor. In a roundabout way they are simply measuring mental ability, which, as we have pointed out, tends to be an important factor under the conditions present in the average or the poor classroom. Moreover, it is fallacious to insist that the skill involved in a certain readiness test should be highly emphasized in the reading training as an essential part of the reading process. By the same logic it would be wise to train intelligence, if this is conceivable, because in many classrooms this factor seems to affect ultimate reading achievement. Many reading programs put very little emphasis on letters, and yet their pupils learn to read adequately. Like John Downing, the British researcher, we refuse to believe that knowledge of letter names is very important in first-grade reading, until it has been shown that this ability is not merely a reflection of intelligence and socioeconomic status (5).

The long process of preschool learning of concepts about language and books is certainly helpful in creating a readiness for reading. But its lack can be readily overcome by a competent teacher in a first-grade program. This is shown by the comparable reading success of pupils who vary widely in their preschool learning and experiences. Unless there are other significant handicaps, most of these pupils learn to read as well as the average when the readiness program is keyed to their needs.

Another aspect of preschool learning that assumes importance in some studies of beginning readers is the child's range of information. A few commercial readiness tests include a measure of this range. Like the other tests of preschool experiences, this random sampling of the child's information is, in all probability, another test of his mental ability. Tests of general information have been used to distinguish degrees of intelligence ever since the first so-called intelligence test was built. In fact, it is one of the basic assumptions in intelligence testing that the retention of information is a major evidence of intelligence.

It is probably true that the child's range of information assumes real significance as the content of his reading material broadens in the intermediate grades. Holmes and Singer's detailed studies (16) of the factors underlying success in reading at the fourth grade and higher levels confirm the importance of the informational background the child brings to his reading. But, at the primary levels, the reading materials are so simple and the demands for background so slight that the extent of the child's informational background is not often a crucial factor. The average child has sufficient informational background to understand the usual basal reader program, with the exception perhaps of a few children from bilingual or particularly isolated or barren environments. Furthermore, the few concepts he may lack are readily supplied by direct instruction or the exchange of ideas and information in classroom discussion.

Emotional Adjustment

Every experienced primary teacher has taught children whose lack of emotional adjustment to the classroom has hindered their reading success. She has seen excessive timidity or fearfulness, hyperactivity, overaggressiveness, and such personality traits constantly handicap these children in their attempts to function in the group. The average teacher does the best she can to meet the needs of maladjusted children, sometimes with success, sometimes without avail. Unfortunately, the research on personalities of beginning readers has not had very much to contribute to this situation. We do not know which traits are most handicapping or conducive to reading failure; nor do we have any simple, effective tools to aid the teacher to make this judgment. In fact, our best diagnostic tools for teacher detection of the emotionally maladjusted child are still in a research stage. We know very little about the appropriate corrective or preventive steps for the teacher to take in dealing with personality problems. Thus, despite its importance for reading success, this is one area still highly dependent upon the individual teacher's subjective judgment. This is not exactly a hopeless situation, for many research studies of beginning readers show that teacher appraisal is still the most effective predictive tool we have. Apparently, the average teacher can identify and help children whose maladjustments predestine them to failure even if the psychologists have not been able to teach the teacher how to prevent this failure.

WHEN IS A CHILD READY TO READ?

Readiness to read does not occur at a certain point in a child's development in the sense that a child is ready to read one day but not the day before. The child is not necessarily ready for reading instruction the day he completes a readiness workbook or when he finishes a readiness program offered to the class as a whole. Readiness is a gradual development from nonreading to beginning reading. Or, as Wilson et al. (60) phrased it, readiness is, in reality, *reading progress in the initial stages of learning to read.* The child gradually develops interest in words as meaningful symbols that resemble the words he hears. He shows increasing ability to make accurate discriminations among these symbols and to relate them to words in his auditory vocabulary. These visual and auditory realizations or learnings gradually result in the act of actually reading and understanding words. Boney (3) also recognizes the continuity of this developmental process and suggests that perhaps the best way to determine readiness is to try reading instruction at intervals until the child begins to show regular progress. This trial process is probably a fair description of what occurs in many first-grade classrooms.

Most teachers, however, feel the need for some guidelines to help them judge a child's readiness. This is perhaps a more realistic viewpoint than simply deciding in the negative when the child shows a poor response to repeated attempts to teach him to read. Some teachers will use these guidelines to initiate active readiness training related to the child's individual needs. Thus checklists and readiness tests have a twofold value—to suggest the type of readiness training that will promote the child's development and to suggest that the child is about ready to profit from formal instruction in reading.

As we have pointed out, teachers' judgments of their pupils' readiness status are usually quite effective. In many studies, teachers have demonstrated their skill in differentiating between children who would succeed in reading and those who would not. In some cases, after only a few weeks with their kindergarten or first-grade classes, teachers can predict the probable reading success of their pupils with about as much accuracy as a readiness test. Is this, however, proof that teachers can substitute their global judgments or ranking of pupils for readiness tests, as one writer suggests?* In our opinion, definitely not. The purpose of teacher judgment of each child's readiness is not, as some seem to think, a global, overall judgment—"This child is ready, this is not." "This is an excellent risk, this is not." Both teacher observation and readiness tests are supposed to yield detailed information regarding the child's specific instructional needs during the readiness period. Global judgments of pupils imply that readiness is a thing, a specific stage the child reaches on a certain day, or that at a certain time he is mentally, visually, auditorily, and linguistically ready to begin reading. Such an interpretation of readiness is nonsense.

Perhaps each first-grade teacher evolves some standards of readiness of her own or depends upon an intuitive feeling about when a child is ready for instruction in reading. But it is also essential to enumerate a number of behaviors which readiness research indicates are characteristic of this stage of reading development.

Perhaps the most efficient way to use this checklist would be to make a chart listing the items to be observed in the left-hand column. Draw three or four vertical lines about a half inch apart on the chart. Reproduce one of these charts for each child in the class. The three or four spaces enable the teacher to record her observations (check positive, cross if negative) at intervals during the school year. Some items, of course, need only one recording, as the results of the vision and hearing screening tests, while others, such as the speech, listening, and other areas, will need repeated observations. Plans for corrective attention can be made for each child as soon as a negative recording appears on the chart. Group corrective efforts can be begun as soon as the records for a half dozen or fewer children indicate an area of need.

A few minutes spent writing the observations made during each day's activities will suffice for keeping the record. Observations of incidents which raise doubts in the teacher's mind can be very briefly summarized on the back of a child's chart. To illustrate, on Johnny's chart, "Seemed withdrawn and tense in group" might appear (with the date). This type of entry would alert the teacher to make subsequent notes on Johnny's group behavior and thus reach a decision regarding the approach to use in the future. If similar statements appeared as the year progressed, a clearer idea of the seriousness of the problem or the child's positive progress would become possible. Anecdotal records of classroom incidents and pupil behaviors, as these are called, stimulate the teacher to action and to seeking the advice or help of other school personnel, such as counselors, school psychologists, and principals. In parental interviews, these brief descriptions of unusual behavior enable the teacher to explore specific areas of a pupil's adjustment and progress, both positive and negative. This exploration will be intended to elicit parental reaction, to determine whether similar behavior is present at home, whether home conditions are contributing, how such incidents are handled by the parent, to suggest steps that might be taken by the parent to aid or reinforce the teacher's approach, and to decide jointly on a course of action to help the child.

* Samuel B. Kermoian, "Teacher Appraisal of First Grade Readiness," *Elementary English,* 39 (March 1962), 196–201.

Vision

Good binocular acuity, near
Good binocular acuity, far
Able to shift focus easily and accurately
Good binocular coordination
Good visual discrimination
Good hand—eye coordination, near

Speech

Free from substitutions and baby talk
Able to communicate in conversation and with group
Reasonable fluency and sentence structure

Listening

Able to hear and respond in class or group situation
Normal hearing indicated in screening test
Able to attend to and recall story
Able to answer simple questions
Able to follow simple directions
Able to follow sequence of story
Able to discriminate sounds of varying pitch and loudness
Able to detect similarities and differences in words
Sufficient auditory vocabulary for common concepts

Social and Emotional Behavior

Able to work independently or in group
Able to share materials
Able to await turn for teacher's attention
Able to lead or to follow

Interest in Learning To Read

Shows interest in signs and symbols
Is interested in listening to stories
Can tell some stories and recite some poems or rhymes
Likes to look at the pictures in books
Can attend to the continuity in a sequential picture book
Makes up stories about a picture
Asks to take books home; brings some to school
Tries to identify words in familiar book

FIGURE 6–1. Readiness Checklist

These suggestions for follow up on the observations based on the checklist may be interpreted as though we were expecting each first-grade teacher to function like a guidance counselor or school psychologist. We have no illusion that all such teachers are competent in interpreting child behavior or are sufficiently professionally motivated to record, follow up, and take corrective action when it appears desirable. On the other hand, we do know that many are concerned about the 20 percent or so of school entrants who show problems in school adjustment and that the child's overall adjustment and achievement during the first grade is highly predictive of his success for a number of years later. We know that this aid will be rejected by some and adopted and improved upon by others. It is offered solely because it draws attention to the significant factors which are likely to influence the child's success in early reading. It is offered as a diagnostic aid during the entire first grade, not as a series of criteria to determine when the child is completely ready for formal reading.

In evaluating pupil readiness, the experience of having attended nursery school or kindergarten is usually interpreted as a favorable factor. Children without this previous training are often expected to perform more poorly in beginning reading. But Morrison and Harris (33) have shown that the effects of kindergarten vary with the method of instruction. Kindergarten or no kindergarten made no difference for pupils taught by a basal or language experience approach. Only when an ultraphonic method was used were these children without kindergarten experience handicapped, evidencing again the greater demands of this type of program. Of course, whatever value kindergarten experience has for progress in early reading is related to the extent that its program is keyed to that goal in providing language and experiential stimulation in terms of pupil needs. Kindergarten or no, each child's readiness will have to be assessed by the teacher on an individual basis. There has been a surge of interest in the past few years in attempts to identify "learning disabled" or "at risk" or "high risk" children, as they are dubbed, prior to school admission, and in some instances even during nursery school ages. The theory is offered that if we identify children early who will later experience severe difficulties in school learning we could prevent many school failures. The concept is certainly laudable, but the possibility of implementation is presently very dubious, as we shall demonstrate.

Early prevention programs usually involve giving preschoolers a battery of tests of visual, auditory, and cognitive abilities, often including the Illinois Test of Psycholinguistic Abilities. Specific deficits supposed to be fundamental to school learning are thus presumably found, and the "at risk" children are given training programs intended to repair each deficit and thus ensure their success in school in subsequent years. Critics of these programs point out that (1) we have little or no research indicating that the abilities tested are really significant for predicting early school success; (2) the tests and instruments used, including the Illinois Test of Psycholinguistic Abilities, are of dubious relationship to later success, and often have very low reliabilities because of the immaturity of the children or the construction of the tests themselves; (3) besides, we have very little evidence that the abilities can be developed by training at these ages, or by the programs in common use. Shipe and Miezitis (48), for example, tested a number of five-year-olds, offered apparently appropriate training programs, but found no substantial improvement related to either of two types of training. Like Stott (53) and Clark (4) and others, these authors concluded that large-scale preventive programs as a prophylactic educational measure have, as yet, no solid research foundation. Stott is of the opinion that the factors to be identified, at about the kindergarten level, are inappropriate learning style, impulsivity, and lack of self-confidence. He has, in fact, evolved rather intriguing materials involving peer monitoring, conditioning, careful scaling of tasks, and intensive social reinforcement intended to modify these three traits. His materials, a Programmed Reading Kit (Scott, Foresman Co.) and "Flying Start to Learning" kit (Brook Educational Publishing), may be helpful in this readiness context, if subsequent research supports their use.

As the research cited earlier, and a great deal more in England, Sweden, and other countries shows, handicaps in visual, auditory, language, and cognitive abilities can be discovered and ameliorated at the readiness level. High-risk children can be identified and their needs met with subsequent positive results in reading achievement. But there is very little evidence that prevention of failure programs can be profitably or rationally begun in the preschool years.

Vision Tests

Until better tests of vision are universally available in schools, some of the responsibility for detecting the visual difficulties of pupils falls upon teachers. It is possible to improve the results of the present inadequate vision testing by careful teacher observation of pupil behavior and posture. Several authorities have suggested rather long lists of visual symptoms to be noticed by teachers. These impractical lists represented only opinions and until recently were unverified. A study by Gertrude Knox has attempted to evaluate the symptoms shown by elementary school children which may indicate visual difficulties that are verified by complete professional examinations. She found that both observation and screening should be used to refer pupils to an eye specialist. This combined method resulted in referring some children who were not in need of visual help, but, on the other hand, no child needing such help was overlooked (23).

The significant symptoms that were found to indicate probable visual difficulties fell into definite patterns such as these: (1) facial contortions and forward thrusting of head, (2) facial contortions and tilting of head, (3) facial contortions and tension during close work, and (4) forward thrusting of head and holding book close to face.

Other significant symptoms that may be observed by teachers are these: (1) tension while looking at distant objects, (2) posture that may indicate strain, (3) excessive head movements while reading, (4) rubbing eyes often, (5) avoiding close work, and (6) tending to lose place in reading. A number of other symptoms were investigated but they were not found to be closely related to true visual difficulties.

None of the commercial vision screening batteries available are complete tests of all important visual skills. Some of these tests omit measures of near-point visual acuity, farsightedness, depth perception, and convergence difficulties at near-point. Many of the commercial tests are based upon, and are no better than, the Snellen test. Because of this situation, we shall point out the specific limitations of the various vision screening tests.

We would recommend these tests:

- *Keystone Visual Survey Tests,* Keystone View Company, Meadville, Penna.
- *Orthorater,* Bausch and Lomb Optical Company, Rochester, N.Y.
- *Professional Vision Tester,* Titmus Optical Company, Petersburg, Va.
- *Spache Binocular Reading Test,* Keystone View Company, Meadville, Penna. This is a necessary supplement to measure the child's use of both eyes in the binocular act of reading.
- *Stereotests,* Titmus Optical Company, Petersburg, Va. This test of depth perception at near-point is a necessary supplement to the batteries listed above since none of them includes such a test.

We would not recommend the following batteries because they are largely simple imitations of the Snellen test:

- *American Optical School Vision Screening Test,* American Optical Company, Southbridge, Mass.
- *Eames Eye Test,* Harcourt Brace Jovanovich, New York.
- *King Sight Screener,* King Sight Screener, P.O. Box 391, Quincy, Ill.
- *Massachusetts Vision Test,* Welch Allyn, Inc., Auburn, N.Y.
- *New York School Vision Tester,* Bausch and Lomb, Rochester, N.Y.
- *School Vision Tester,* Titmus Optical Company, Petersburg, Va.

Visual Discrimination

True tests of visual discrimination, which do not simply measure the child's previous knowledge of letters and words, are offered in the *Harrison–Stroud Reading Readiness Test,* the *Murphy–Durrell Reading Readiness Analysis,* and the *Reading Aptitude Tests* by Marion Monroe. It is important to note, however, that these tests of visual discrimination show significant relationships with later reading achievement in a great many research studies.

The simplest test of visual discrimination to administer and interpret is probably the *Winter Haven Perceptual Achievement Forms (61).* It does reveal those children who are likely to have difficulties in writing and reading letters and words, and it can be used by the teacher without requiring special training. Moreover, it leads directly to a corrective program of definite effectiveness in promoting better hand–eye coordination.

Readiness Tests

There are several basic limitations in the use of most reading readiness tests. First, most tests are limited in the sampling of abilities they include. Some measure only auditory vocabulary; others omit any evaluation of such significant factors as visual or auditory discrimination, articulation, or auditory comprehension. A second common limitation in readiness tests is the tendency to depend upon measures of preschool learning such as matching or even reading words and letters. Because of this content, many readiness tests are not much more than concealed measures of intelligence determined by sampling the child's preschool learning. Finally, most readiness tests do not yield very accurate predictions of later reading success. Their correlations with reading are usually about .5 or .6, a relationship which gives a prediction 25 to 30 percent better than sheer chance. Is it surprising that careful teacher observation and judgment often yield predictions just as accurate as any readiness test?

Several studies indicate that, like other commercial instruments, readiness tests are not so reliable nor as effective in predicting future pupil achievement when used with minority pupils (30) as their standardization data imply. When analyzed item by item, only 35 percent of the tasks in the Metropolitan Readiness test had acceptable levels of difficulty and validity in predicting reading in one study. This is the same type of problem we discussed earlier in the use of intelligence tests with minority pupils. Another analysis of the Lee Clark Readiness and the Metropolitan did not find that the various subtests were measuring different abilities, nor that they were assessing facets unlike those in a common intelligence test.

Some of these inherent difficulties in the use of readiness tests could be overcome by more intelligent planning for interpretation of the results. The norms or standards given by the publisher are seldom appropriate to the particular class being tested. Norms based on many classes drawn from both rural and urban areas, from industrial and agricultural communities, from large school systems and small, and from high and low socioeconomic groups are seldom meaningful in any one particular class. Predictions based on these general norms are more inclined to predictive error the more individual the class is. One solution to this problem is the accumulation of local norms based on all the first grades or kindergartens in the local school system or, if the number of classes in one year is very small, on the accumulation of norms based on successive years. This type of norm, like all others, assumes that the different groups are sufficiently similar in intelligence and socioeconomic background to warrant combining the scores.

Sometimes the major differences in the backgrounds of different classes, or the small number of cases that can be accumulated, make the formation of local norms unfeasible. Even then, however, it is possible to use the reading readiness test scores for the maximum accuracy in prediction despite the inherent weakness of the test in this respect. Scores in the various portions of the test as well as the total score may be used, as the items of the *Readiness Checklist* are employed, to make separate and combined judgments regarding the children's readiness. If the scores of the children are arranged in rank order from lowest to highest, those in serious difficulty are identified, and necessary corrective steps are implied. It is not essential to compare each child's score with the hypothetical standard which is supposed to apply to all children, the test norm, in order to discover those pupils in need of a particular type of readiness training.

Furthermore, by accumulating scores from successive years for classes that are offered a program that is consistent in its methods and philosophy, predictions of pupil success may be further refined. Both by teacher observation and noting the ranked scores of pupils, cutoff scores or minimum scores in the various parts or the total test can be established. These cutoff scores will be the next highest scores above those achieved by children who failed to learn to read successfully. The cutoff scores separate the successful pupils from those who fail. Thus without falling into the errors induced by the use of national norms it is possible to find the individual needs of pupils in the readiness program, and, as scores accumulate, to increase the predictive accuracy of the tests by the use of cutoff scores.

With these possibilities of overcoming the common limitations of readiness tests, let us review the major characteristics of the leading tests.

Gesell Institute Readiness Tests (see *School Readiness* by Ilg and Ames, Harper & Row) are a series of readiness tests employing a developmental schedule rather than standardized norms for evaluating pupil readiness among children from five to ten years in the areas of visual perception, directionality, and language.

Clymer–Barrett Prereading Battery (Personnel Press, Inc.) is a diagnostic battery of six subtests in reading letters, word matching, discrimination of beginning and ending sounds in words, form completion, and copying a sentence for use at the end of kindergarten or the beginning of grade one. A checklist of readiness behaviors is also included. Continued study of this test supports its validity as a reasonable predictor of first-grade reading (*19*). However, like the other readiness tests it is influenced by the socioeconomic status and intelligence of the pupils. Children tend to score in keeping with their social ranking from upper middle class to lower and their relative intelligence. Even when the intelligence factor is held constant, there is still, as we might expect, a significant relationship between socioeconomic status and visual discrimination, reflecting the preschool experiences of the children, in this and the other readiness tests (*34*). This is not an argument against their use, for the results can still be interpreted at face value as indicating children in need of some specific training to ensure their success in early reading. Unlike most of the others, the subtests of the Clymer–Barrett are reliable enough for individual prescriptions.

Harrison–Stroud Reading Readiness Test (Houghton Mifflin Company) has subtests of (1) visual discrimination, (2) using the context, (3) context and auditory clues, (4) auditory discrimination, and (5) using symbols. No data are offered by the authors to support the validity of this test. A study by Spaulding (*51*) showed a correlation of the total score with achievement on a later reading test of 46. The visual discrimination test and the context and auditory clues were least effective; the remaining tests were fair to poor in prediction of reading success.

Lee–Clark Reading Readiness Test (California Test Bureau) includes measures of (1) discrimination of letters, (2) selection of pictures according to verbal descriptions, and (3) discrimination of printed word forms. Various reports of validity studies by Starr (*52*) indicate a range of correlations between this test and later reading success from .43 to .68. Correlations with intelligence tests as high as .65 have been reported for this test.

Metropolitan Readiness Test (Harcourt Brace Jovanovich) measures (1) general reading readiness, (2) number readiness, and (3) total readiness. Starr (*52*) reports various validity correlations of this test, with a later reading test ranging from .27 to .69, with the majority in the .5 to .6 level. Spaulding (*51*) reported a correlation of .59, while Karlin (*20*) found only .36 when chronological age and intelligence were held constant. As Starr (*52*) noted, and Karlin's data indicate, many studies of this test show that scores on it are highly related to intelligence.

Murphy–Durrell Diagnostic Reading Readiness Test (Harcourt Brace Jovanovich) purports to measure (1) auditory discrimination, (2) visual discrimination, and (3) learning rate. No data on the reliability or validity of this test are reported by the authors. The test of learning rate is unique in that it requires twenty minutes of group instruction and three individual retests of the child's retention of words during the same day. While there is other evidence of the significance of visual and auditory discrimination for reading success, we have no indication of the values of these tests as they appear in this battery. Nor do we know the significance or true meaning of the learning rate test.

Reading Aptitude Tests (Houghton Mifflin Company) by Marion Monroe includes eight tests of (1) motor coordination, (2) perception of forms, (3) visual memory for forms, (4) auditory discrimination, (5) maze tracing, (6) blending of sounds, and (7) auditory vocabulary. In addition, individual tests of articulation, auditory memory for a story, and name writing are used. Starr's review of studies (*52*) of this test shows validity coefficients in predicting later reading success of .38, .41, and .75. These tests sample significant readiness factors more widely than any other available readiness test, thus yielding more diagnostic information for the teacher. Unfortunately for the validity of the norms, the test was standardized over twenty-five years ago and the norms are relatively meaningless today. However, the test can be utilized intelligently if local norms or cutoff scores are established. As Starr remarks, the broad sampling of readiness factors in this test and the consequent diagnostic advantages appeal to many teachers.

Gates–MacGinitie Readiness Skills Test is an eight-subtest battery of listening comprehension, auditory discrimination, visual discrimination of words, following directions, letter recognition, visual–motor coordination in completing letters, auditory blending of word parts, and word recognition. The emphasis upon beginning reading skills as compared with readiness skills is apparent here.

The coauthor of this test, MacGinitie (*26*), has severely criticized other readiness tests for (1) low subtest validity; (2) failure to provide diagnostic information; (3) lack of factor analysis to discover the true components of the test, as opposed to just labeling its parts; (4) subtest reliability too low for individual prescriptions; (5) using weights in scoring subtests which are not applicable from one population to another; and (6) ignoring that the predictive validity of any readiness measure will depend upon the particular reading method, and hence will vary from one class to another. These are certainly accurate criticisms of many readiness tests. But they were apparently conceived after the Gates–MacGinitie test was constructed, for most of them apply to this test also. The authors of this test have not yet supplied us with sufficient information to determine whether their subtests are very valid or reliable enough for diagnosis of individual needs.

Other readiness tests are, of course, available but these have not yet had sufficient use for us to judge their merits and include them here. Some publishers of reading series also offer their own readiness tests for use with their instructional system. Usually, these are unstandardized and unnormed, which means that no one knows what levels of performances are normal for any particular type of children. They tend to lack any of the basic elements of good test construction such as item analysis for validity and difficulty, field trials to establish overall validity in predicting later reading performances, and analysis of the subtests to determine their values in discrimination, prediction, and validity. These criticisms are particularly relevant in view of the flaws even in the better-constructed tests described above.

One other aspect of the use of readiness tests, or indeed of any other standardized test, must be emphasized. The testing of young children is obviously more fraught with error than is the testing of older children. The reliability of the measures is often quite low because tests are administered in groups larger than four or five children, which is about as large as any adult can carefully monitor. Young children are more disturbed and their responses more inhibited or distorted by a cold testing atmosphere. Sometimes teachers recognize these problems and think to ease the situation by ignoring test timing limits or changing the directions, or even by helping or coaching young children in the hopes of stimulating their best performances. While the test should be presented as a game situation, in a very small group, using several settings if fatigue or distractions intervene, the test must be given exactly as the manual dictates. The only legitimate variation is in providing pretest explanations or examples to be certain that the pupils understand each task clearly. After being certain that each pupil understands what "the game" is and what he is to do, the teacher should move among the group to be sure that they are moving along from one item to the next, are keeping their place, and are working on the correct item. Quiet comments such as, "That's good. Go on with the next one" are permissible. Comments indicating recognition of a poor performance or attempts to correct these are not permissible. Timed limits may not be ignored simply because the pupils seem to have done only a small portion of a subtest, for that may be all they can be expected to do. Following these suggestions, if the test is well made, will result in obtaining some accurate indications of the pupils' needs to ensure their reading success.

Auditory Discrimination

One or two simple tests of auditory discrimination are suitable for use by the primary teacher, such as the *Auditory Discrimination Test* by Joseph M. Wepman of the Department of Surgery, University of Chicago. A similar test could be constructed by the teacher using twenty-five pairs of monosyllabic words with some of the pairs differing in a single sound, such as the beginning consonant. The test words may be real or nonsense words composed on a consonant or consonant blend, a vowel, and a final consonant, as *pin–tin, kate–gate*. The pairs of words are read to each child while he is seated with his back to the teacher. The child simply tells whether the pair of words sounds the same or different. In such a test, the child with normal auditory discrimination is likely to make no more than two or three errors. The most reliable way to handle the scores on an unstandardized test like this would be to make further careful observation of those children making the greatest number of errors to watch for the speech and hearing errors that would confirm the test results.

Identification of children with mild to severe hearing losses can be done by teacher observation with some small degree of accuracy, according to some studies (24). But when hearing loss is suspected or the child's behavior raises some doubt in the teacher's mind, it is wisest to refer the child for a professional hearing examination. The average medical practitioner is not equipped to perform this examination. The best referral is to a medical hearing specialist, an otolaryngologist or otologist, a speech or hearing clinic, or, if it is properly equipped, a reading clinic in a nearby college. If the teacher knows of no such sources of help, he may seek advice from the Volta Bureau, 1537 35 Street, N.W., Washington, D.C., or from the state or National Society for Crippled Children or Adults, 11 S. LaSalle Street, Chicago, Ill.

It must be remembered that this type of test is quite unreliable with young children and may need to be repeated several times. Also, it may demand discrimination of sounds that are not normally present in the child's dialect, and thus it is testing the child's ability to hear discriminations he does not naturally make. It may also be testing sounds that have not yet appeared in the child's speech development. As we pointed out earlier, accuracy in a test of auditory discrimination is not significant in a dialect speaker, for if he can recognize and interpret a word, it does not really matter whether he pronounces it differently. Reading orally with a dialect produces as much comprehension as reading in standard English. Perhaps auditory discrimination tests have their best use in detecting middle-class children whose poor performance would militate against their profiting from the phonics instruction of the reading program. Since there are alternative methods of instruction for these cases that we will discuss later, the test results may not really be significant for this group either, unless a heavy phonics program is mandatory.

There are a number of group tests of auditory discrimination in the commercial readiness tests listed above. A study by Robert Dykstra (8) which analyzed and compared seven of these tests yielded some very interesting insights. Auditory discrimination is measured in a half-dozen ways in these batteries, and these tests obviously do not measure the same factor. The discrimination between spoken words which may or may not begin with the same sound, as in the Harrison–Stroud battery, was consistently effective in predicting reading achievement. Monroe's subtest of selecting the correct pronunciation of a word from among three versions was also relatively good. At the same time, the *Gates Rhyming Test,* the Monroe blending, and the Harrison–Stroud measure of context and auditory clues were poor predictors. The two Murphy–Durrell samples of discrimination of beginning and ending sounds were the poorest of all. Dykstra's conclusions were that girls were better than boys in initial discrimination ability, as well as learning this skill, and in reading achievement; various tests do not measure this ability similarly, for some were good, some poor, and all less efficient than the intelligence test used. Further research seeking the most effective tests, the values of specific training, and the true nature of the components of auditory dicrimination is needed, according to Dykstra.

Auditory Comprehension

The child's abilities to listen to, understand, and react to story material may be sampled by an auditory comprehension test such as that included in the *Spache Diagnostic Reading Scales* (California Test Bureau) or the *Durrell Reading Capacity Test* (Harcourt Brace Jovanovich). Or, if the teacher prefers, he may construct his own test in the manner used in our *Diagnostic Reading Scales (49).* Short units of story material, ranging from one hundred to two hundred words in length and offering a relatively complete story, may be selected from a basal reading series. Selections are chosen and graded by formula to represent each reading level, as preprimer, primer, first reader, low second, high second, low third, high third. After the story has been read to the child, he is asked eight to ten questions previously prepared on the facts of the story, the sequence of events, and the characters. These questions should be phrased so that they must be answered in the child's own words rather than by a simple yes or no. At this level it is advisable to avoid questions involving interpretation of the motives of the characters, the purpose of the author, or others demanding any depth of interpretation. The purpose of the testing is to discover the level of the material the child can recall and comprehend. Adequate comprehension is indicated by the ability to answer 60 percent or more of the questions.

The higher the level of the selections for which the child can answer with at least the minimum degree of comprehension, the greater his auditory comprehension and, all other things being equal, the more favorable the prediction of his later reading achievement. Most middle-class pupils can listen to and show comprehension of selections scaled more than a year above their school or reading status. But any successful performance much above a child's grade level is a favorable sign.

SUMMARY

In this chapter we have reviewed present knowledge about factors that influence readiness for reading instruction and current testing practices. Theories of readiness, the values of the training, and readiness activities not yet in common use are presented in the next chapter. We intend that this chapter will introduce readers to the truly significant influences upon early reading success insofar as available research clarifies them. Review of these factors will demonstrate the necessity for a diagnostic approach to children's needs, an approach which may then be implemented by later suggestions.

DISCUSSION QUESTIONS

1. Has your definition of readiness been modified by reading this chapter? How has it changed?

2. In view of the contradictory research, why do schools continue to justify their demand of a certain chronological age for admission to school?

3. What measures of language facility are described in this chapter that will be useful to you?

4. Why do you suppose people are so violently debating whether reading should be begun in the kindergarten or nursery school? What are some of the arguments pro and con? What do you believe?

5. What do you think can be effective in the effort to recognize and help children with perceptual difficulties?

6. What is your reaction to the authors' interpretation of the true significance of sex differences in reading success?

7. What are the limitations in most current readiness tests? How might these be overcome?

8. What are some of the applications and uses of the *Readiness Checklist?*

9. How does early language development of the child influence his success in early reading?

10. What is your concept of a good preschool readiness program?

REFERENCES

1. Arnold, Richard D., and Wist, Anne H., "Auditory Discrimination Abilities of Disadvantaged Anglo- and Mexican-American Children," *Elementary School Journal,* 70 (March 1970), 295–299.

2. Barrett, Thomas C., "The Relationship Between Measures of Prereading Visual Discrimination and First-Grade Reading Achievement: A Review of the Literature," *Reading Research Quarterly,* 1 (Fall 1965), 51–76.

3. Boney, C. DeWitt, "A New Program for the Late Reader," *Elementary English,* 38 (May 1961), 316–319.

4. Clark, Richard M., "The Risk in Early Identification," paper presented at the National Reading Conference, St. Petersburg, Fla., December 1975.

5. Downing, John, "Specific Cognitive Factors in the Reading Process," in *Reading: The Right to Participate,* Twentieth Yearbook, National Reading Conference, 1971, 38–45.

6. Durkin, Dolores, *Children Who Read Early.* New York: Teachers College Press, 1966.

7. Durrell, Donald D., et al., "Success in First Grade Reading," *Journal of Education,* 140 (February 1958), 1–48.

8. Dykstra, Robert, "Auditory Discrimination Abilities and Beginning Reading Achievement," *Reading Research Quarterly,* 1 (Spring 1966), 5–34.

9. Fallon, Berlie J., and Filgo, Dorothy J., eds., *Forty States Innovate To Improve School Reading Programs.*

Bloomington, Ind.: Phi Delta Kappa Educational Foundation, 1970.

10. Friskey, Margaret, *ABC, 123, The First Step.* Chicago: Children's Press, 1969.

11. Gates, Arthur I., "The Necessary Mental Age for Beginning Reading," *Elementary School Journal,* 37 (March 1937), 498–508.

12. Georgiady, Nicholas P., Romano, Louis, and Baranowski, Arthur, "To Read or Not To Read—in Kindergarten," *Elementary School Journal,* 65 (March 1965), 306–311.

13. Gesell, Arnold, Ilg, Frances L., and Bullis, Glenna E., *Vision: Its Development in Infant and Child.* New York: Harper & Row, Inc., 1949.

14. Goins, Jean T., *Visual Perceptual Abilities and Early Reading.* Supplementary Educational Monographs, No. 87. Chicago: University of Chicago Press, 1958.

15. Groff, Patrick, "Reading Ability and Auditory Discrimination: Are They Related?" *Reading Teacher,* 28 (May 1975), 742–747.

16. Holmes, Jack A., and Singer, Harry, *The Substrata Factor Theory: Substrata Factor Differences Underlying Reading Ability in Known Groups.* Washington, D.C.: Office of Education, 1961.

17. Jackson, Walter M., "Visual Screening in City Schools," *Optometric Weekly* (April 16, 1953).

18. Johnson, Dale D., "Sex Differences in Reading Across Cultures," *Reading Research Quarterly,* 9 (1973–1974), 67–86.

19. Johnson, Roger E., "The Validity of the Clymer-Barret Prereading Battery," *Reading Teacher,* 22 (April 1969), 609–614.

20. Karlin, Robert, "The Prediction of Reading Success and Reading Readiness Tests," *Elementary English,* 34 (May 1957), 320–322.

21. Karlsen, Bjorn, and Blocker, Margaret, "Black Children and Final Consonant Blends," *Reading Teacher,* 27 (February 1974), 462–463.

22. Kelley, Marjorie, and Chen, Martin K., "An Experimental Study of Formal Reading Instruction at the Kindergarten Level," *Journal of Educational Research,* 60 (January 1967), 224–229.

23. Knox, Gertrude, "Classroom Symptoms of Visual Difficulty," Master's thesis, University of Chicago, 1951.

24. LaConte, Christine, "Reading in Kindergarten," *Reading Teacher,* 23 (November 1969), 116–120.

25. Levy, Beatrice K., "Is the Oral Language of Inner City Children Adequate for Beginning Reading?" *Re-search in the Teaching of English,* 7 (Spring 1973), 51–60.

26. MacGinitie, W. H., "Evaluating Readiness for Learning To Read: A Critical Review and Evaluation of Research," *Reading Research Quarterly,* 4 (Spring 1969), 396–410.

27. Malmquist, Eve, "An International Overview of Primary Reading Practices," *Journal of Reading,* 18 (May 1975), 615–624.

28. McDill, Edward L., McDill, Mary S., and Sprehe, J. Timothy, *Strategies for Success in Compensatory Education: An Appraisal of Evaluation Research.* Baltimore, Md.: The Johns Hopkins Press, 1969.

29. McNeil, J., *ABC Learning Activities.* New York: American Book Company, 1965.

30. Mishra, Shitala, and Hurt, M., Jr., "The Use of Metropolitan Readiness Tests with Mexican-American Children," *California Journal of Educational Research,* 21 (1970), 182–187.

31. Moe, Iver A., "Auding Ability as a Measure of Reading Potential Among Pupils in Primary Grades," Doctoral dissertation, University of Florida, 1957.

32. Monroe, Marion, *Manual for Reading Aptitude Test.* Boston: Houghton Mifflin Company, 1935.

33. Morrison, Coleman, and Harris, Albert, "Effect of Kindergarten on the Reading of the Disadvantaged Child," *Reading Teacher,* 22 (October 1968), 4–9.

34. Mortenson, W. Paul, "Selected Pre-Reading Tasks, Socioeconomic Status and Sex," *Reading Teacher,* 22 (October 1968), 45–49.

35. Niedermeyer, Fred C., "Parents Teach Kindergarten Reading at Home," *Elementary School Journal,* 70 (May 1970), 438–448.

36. Olson, Arthur V., "School Achievement, Reading Ability and Specific Visual Perception Skills in the Third Grade," *Reading Teacher,* 19 (April 1966), 490–492.

37. Peters, Henry B., "Vision Screening with a Snellen Chart," *American Journal of Optometry and Archives of American Academy of Optometry,* 38 (September 1961), 487–505.

38. Prescott, George A., "Sex Differences in Metropolitan Readiness Test Results," *Journal of Educational Research,* 48 (April 1955) 605–610.

39. Raph, Jane Beasley, "Language Development in Socially Disadvantaged Children," *Review of Educational Research,* 35 (December 1965), 389–400.

40. Robertson, Jean E., "Kindergarten Perception Training: Its Effect on First Grade Reading," in *Perception and Reading,* Helen K. Smith, ed. Proceedings Annual

Convention, International Reading Association, 12, no. 4 (1968), 93–98.

41. Robinson, Helen M., "Vision Screening Tests for Schools," *Elementary School Journal,* 53 (December 1953), 217–222.

42. Robinson, Helen M., and Huelsman, Charles B., Jr., "Visual Efficiency and Learning To Read," in *Clinical Studies in Reading II,* Helen M. Robinson, ed., Supplementary Educational Monographs, No. 77. Chicago: University of Chicago Press, 1953, 31–63.

43. Rosen, Carl L., and Ohnmacht, Fred, "Perception, Readiness and Reading Achievement in First Grade," in *Perception and Reading,* Helen K. Smith, ed. Proceedings Annual Convention, International Reading Association, 12, no. 4 (1968), 33–39.

44. Rystrom, Richard, "Caveat Qui Credit (Let the Believer Beware)," *Journal of Reading,* 16 (December 1972), 236–240.

45. Scherwitsky, Marjorie, "Reading in the Kindergarten: A Survey in Virginia," *Young Children,* 29 (March 1974), 161–169.

46. Sherk, John K., Jr., "A Word Count of Spoken English of Culturally-Disadvantaged Preschool and Elementary Pupils," University of Missouri, Kansas City, 1973.

47. Sherman, Arnold, "Vision Screening of School Children: Time for a Change?" *Optometric Weekly,* 66 (September 4, 1975), 817–819.

48. Shipe, Dorothy, and Miezitis, Solveiga, "A Pilot Study in the Diagnosis and Remediation of Special Learning Disabilities in Preschool Children," *Journal of Learning Disabilities,* 2 (November 1969), 579–592.

49. Spache, George D., *Manual for the Diagnostic Reading Scales.* Del Monte Research Park: CTB/McGraw-Hill, 1972.

50. Spache, George D., Andres, Micaela C., Curtis, H. A., et al., *A Longitudinal First Grade Reading Readiness Program.* Cooperative Research Project No. 2742, Florida State Department of Education, 1965.

51. Spaulding, Geraldine, "The Relation Between Performance of Independent Pupils on the Harrison–Stroud Reading Readiness Tests and Reading Achievement a Year Later," *1955 Fall Testing Program in Independent Schools and Supplementary Studies.* Educational Records Bulletin, No. 67. New York: Educational Records Bureau (February 1956), 73–76.

52. Starr, John W., III, "Analysis of Reading Readiness Tests," *Curriculum Bulletin,* 13, No. 180 (December 10, 1957), 1–10. Eugene, Ore.: School of Education, University of Oregon.

53. Stott, D. H., "A Preventive Program for the Primary Grades," *Elementary School Journal,* 74 (February 1974), 299–308.

54. Sutton, Marjorie Hunt, "Children Who Learned To Read in the Kindergarten: A Longitudinal Study," *Reading Teacher,* 22 (April 1969), 595–602.

55. Sweeting, Orville J., "An Improved Vision Screening Program for the New Haven Schools," *Journal American Optometric Association,* 30 (May 1959), 657–677.

56. Swenburg, Sandra L., and Dykstra, Robert, "A State-Wide Survey: Reading Readiness Instruction in Minneapolis Public School Kindergartens," *Minnesota Reading Quarterly,* 11 (1966), 44–51.

57. Venezky, R. L., *Nonstandard Language and Reading.* Madison, Wis.: Wisconsin Research and Development Center for Cognitive Learning, 1970.

58. Vernon, Magdalen D., *Perception Through Experience.* New York: Barnes and Noble Books, 1970.

59. Williams, Peggy E., "Auditory Discrimination Differences Versus Deficits," in *Help for the Reading Teacher: New Directions in Research,* Wm. D. Page, ed. National Conference on Research in English, 1975, 91–99.

60. Wilson, F. T., et al., "Reading Progress in Kindergarten and Primary Grades," *Elementary School Journal,* 38 (February 1938), 442–449.

61. *Winter Haven Perceptual Achievement Forms.* Winter Haven, Fla.: Winter Haven Lions Research Foundation.

SUPPLEMENTARY READING

Beck, Joan, *How To Raise a Brighter Child: The Case for Early Learning.* New York: Trident Press, 1967.

Cullinan, Bernice, ed., *Black Dialects and Reading.* Urbana, Ill.: National Council of Teachers of English, 1974.

Downing, John, and Thackray, Derek, *Reading Readiness.* London: University of London Press, 1971.

Durkin, Dolores, *Teaching Young Children To Read.* Boston: Allyn and Bacon, Inc., 1976.

Emery, Donald G., *Teach Your Preschooler To Read.* New York: Simon & Schuster, Inc., 1975.

Mountain, Lee Harrison, *How To Teach Reading Before First Grade.* Highland Park, N.J.: Drier Educational Systems, 1970.

Pilon, Barbara, and Sims, Rudine, *Dialects and Reading: Implications for Change.* Urbana, Ill.: National Council of Teachers of English, 1975.

Smethurst, Wood, *Teaching Young Children To Read at Home.* New York: McGraw-Hill Book Company, 1975.

Stevens, George L., and Orem, R. C., *The Case for Early Reading.* St. Louis, Mo.: Warren H. Green, Inc., 1967.

Tinker, Miles A., *Preparing Your Child for Reading.* New York: Holt, Rinehart and Winston, Inc., 1971.

7
Readiness Training

PREVIEW

Theories and training materials offered to promote readiness for beginning reading differ widely in philosophy and in effectiveness. Some self-appointed experts would dispense with any readiness program in order to speed up, they think, the introduction to formal reading. Some teachers place their faith in a whole class use of a readiness workbook. After all, if the authors of this workbook are to be believed, the pupils will now be ready to proceed successfully with learning to read—or so some teachers interpret the use of this device. Currently, a few writers are emphasizing the learning of the names of the letters of the alphabet as an essential, and sometimes, a complete, readiness preparation. Just how this knowledge actually affects the word recognition act has not yet been demonstrated. But after all, these writers say, the alphabet must be important, for children who tend to succeed in reading have learned some letters before entering school. But is this the reason for their success, or is it simply a reflection of their intelligence and socioeconomic background?

Our concept of readiness needs, while not unique or original, is based on attention to those factors found significant in the research literature. Few would dispute the fact that visual perception is based on such visual–motor skills as form perception, directionality, and ocular motility. Some might question the nature of the training programs we recommend. But this criticism would be based on unfamiliarity with their effectiveness, not on any negative research results. After more than five years of trial with these procedures in about 150 first-grade classrooms, we are quite convinced of their efficacy, when the programs and their duration are fitted to individual pupil needs.

There are a number of views regarding the proper type of readiness training. One view, offered by Glenn McCracken (*32*), coauthor of the Lippincott readers, is that such training is wasted effort. Regardless of mental test results, which McCracken does not believe in anyway, and without any pretense of grouping for individual differences, McCracken would have the teacher begin reading instruction with the total class. Some years ago McCracken had his teachers sit the first graders in front of a few frames of a filmstrip for forty minutes, while they memorized the story. In the afternoon, the children read the same pages in the basal reader. Although he has since dropped the filmstrip session, early editions of the Lippincott readers offered no readiness program. And they still emphasize whole-class instruction in one reader as well as the same brief readiness workbook for all the children. This concept of how to begin reading instruction is unique among those current today.

A second concept of beginning reading might be entitled the "do nothing" school. Sheer maturation of the first grader will take care of all his needs and deficiencies, according to this view. If we just wait, all the problems will disappear, and if they do not, we'll just raise the entrance age a bit higher next year, or we'll let the child repeat the first grade. After all, everyone knows that children need time to grow and mature before they will be ready for reading. It never seems to occur to the followers of this school that those characteristics of the child that might interfere with his early progress could be overcome by instruction or some adaptation of teaching procedures.

The third and largest school of thought regarding readiness has found a complete answer to all the problems in the readiness workbook. These are purchased for every child and appear to provide all the necessary training preliminary to beginning reading. Most basal reading series offer such a workbook presumably directly keyed to future needs during the early reading program. Or, similar workbooks are available in bound or ditto form from other publishers. After completion of this workbook, practically all children except the most immature will be ready to begin the basal program, the authors of some of these imply.

Despite the widespread dependence upon readiness workbooks, there has been extremely little research demonstrating their supposed values. For the most part the exercises they contain have been selected empirically because they seemed related to significant readiness factors. As Allen et al.'s analysis (*1*) of a number of workbooks shows, most contain activities such as the following, in order of their frequency: (1) language development through the medium of sequential pictures; (2) visual discrimination (matching) involving pictures, common objects, geometric forms, letters, and words; (3) motor training through tracing, copying, drawing, dot pictures, and mazes; (4) auditory training with common sounds, rhyming, and initial consonants; and, in a very few cases, (5) discrimination of outlines of word shapes.

A study by Ploghoft (38) found no real difference in the readiness preparation of children with or without nine weeks of workbook training during the kindergarten. Blakely and Shadle (7) showed the inferiority of a basal readiness workbook program to one based on interest and a wide variety of activities. Oral activities were similar in both programs, but the control group substituted an activity period centered around an interest unit for the readiness workbook. End-of-year results in the kindergarten indicated that the workbook program produced inferior readiness among boy pupils but not among girls.

Studies such as these and the varying interpretations which may be made of investigations like that of Allen have led many authorities to question seriously the validity of many of the exercises in current reading readiness workbooks. As the Iowa State Elementary Teachers Reading Handbook (27) suggests, the experiences inherent in the use of a readiness workbook may not be as significant as those planned by the teacher herself to meet individual pupil needs. If we have also conveyed this impression, we have succeeded in the primary purpose of this chapter. Readiness for the beginning reading program is not achieved by waiting for nature to speed up maturation, by a stereotyped filmstrip program, or by simply following current readiness workbook exercises. The differentiation of individual pupil needs in significant readiness factors that we have already stressed should lead inevitably to a differentiated training program in which teacher judgment will play a significant role.

IS READINESS TRAINING PROFITABLE?

Perhaps the best answer to the do-nothing school of readiness is the evidence of the values of planned training during this period. Literally dozens of studies of the outcomes of readiness programs might be cited to show these values. These include investigations like those by Allen et al. (1), Blakely and Shadle (7), Ploghoft (38), and Powell and Parsley (39), which demonstrate that readiness for reading and consequent success in early reading are markedly improved by a prereading preparatory program. A second type of readiness study contrasts the ultimate success of pupils with and without readiness training. This approach is typified in the two-year experiment described by Beatrice E. Bradley (9). First graders were divided into two matched groups. One followed a program based on the concept of readiness; the other began formal instruction immediately. Small groups were formed in the readiness class according to the results of readiness, verbal ability, general ability, and other tests. One subgroup was given five months of readiness training, a second, eight months; and a third group, ten months of training before instruction in reading was begun.

In the control class, high, average, and low groups were formed according to the children's progress in beginning reading. All pupils used the same basal materials and advanced as rapidly as they could with the aid of forty-minute daily reading lessons. Thorough testing during the first three years of school indicated that, despite the delay in introduction of formal instruction, the readiness class caught up in reading achievement by the end of the second year. During the third year the group showed equal or better progress in reading than the control pupils. In such skills as work study, language abilities, and arithmetic, the readiness group exceeded the controls.

Sister Mary Nila's experiments (35) showed even more immediate and dramatic results in favor of readiness training. In two studies with matched experimental and control groups, those receiving readiness training before formal instruction showed greater reading achievement at the end of the first grade. These results are fairly typical of many similar studies. Collectively they imply that readiness training keyed to pupil needs promotes greater academic success than formal reading instruction offered immediately upon entrance to the first grade. Even when readiness training is substituted for reading instruction for a major part of the first grade, the effects of this delay are overcome by the end of the second grade or before and the benefits of the readiness training begin to manifest themselves. Lack of readiness training may not be harmful, but it may well prevent or deter success for a sizable number of children.

We have referred several times to the research study conducted by one of the authors, but it is most appropriate to repeat its description again here, for it is a dramatic demonstration of the values of an extended, intensified readiness program. Thirty-two first-grade classes in which the usual basal reading program was employed served as the control group. In an equal number of classes, reading instruction was supplanted by small-group training in visual discrimination, auditory discrimination, or auditory vocabulary. The children's needs were determined every two months by repeated use of six readiness tests, two in each area. Special training was offered each child for periods of two, four, or six months as his test results warranted. Children performing in the upper quartile of scores on all tests were introduced to basal reading at the beginning of the year or after each retesting.

The training materials in visual discrimination employed the chalkboard exercises described later in this chapter and the seatwork *Visual Discrimination* and *Visuo-Motor Skills* workbooks of Continental Press. The auditory training included a wide variety of group activities selected from Russell and Russell— *Listening Aids Through the Grades* and for seatwork, the *Blending and Rhyming* workbooks of Continental Press. The auditory vocabulary training was drawn largely from Russell and Russell and other standard sources.

Some of the significant results of the experiment were as follows (47):

1. Growth in visual discrimination was significant during four months of the special training, and greater after two months than that present among control groups after six months in the basal program.
2. Growth in auditory discrimination was significant but similar in both experimental and control groups. Only among older black boys was the experimental training more effective than that present in basal programs.
3. Growth in auditory vocabulary, as measured by tests of auditory comprehen-

sion, was significantly greater in the experimental classes among white pupils.

4. There were no significant differences in the overall reading achievement of the control and experimental groups (despite the two to six months' less reading instruction in experimentals).

5. Reading achievement was greatest among the white pupils in the control classes, but also among black pupils in the experimental classes, evidencing the marked advantages in the experimental training for black children, particularly those of lower mental ability.

6. Level of mental ability was significantly related to reading achievement, for (a) at upper levels of ability, the experimental training enabled white boys to equal the achievement of girls; (b) black experimentals of lower mental ability exceeded white experimentals of similar ability; and (c) white pupils of upper mental ability profit more from the basal program than do black pupils of similar ability.

Our readiness experiment, like that recently reported by Jo Stanchfield (49), emphasized a number of significant readiness factors. Both training programs enabled economically and language-handicapped children, those obviously most in need of such experiences, to exceed the achievement of matched control groups. In our study, black children given extended readiness training and the pupils of the lowest quartile in intelligence profited most, and surpassed in reading the control basal reader groups. In Stanchfield's experimental kindergarten group, Mexican-American and black children given an intensive readiness training excelled the control white children in readiness testing. Surely readiness training seems profitable for those with the greatest needs.

Since readiness is not a simple global trait such as maturation, the training program must be multifaceted, and its application differentiated to the pupils' needs as determined by readiness tests, teacher observation, a checklist of behaviors, and the responsiveness of the child to training. The overview of the readiness program given in Table 7–1 does not, of course, mention all the procedures and materials which the teacher may utilize. Space does not permit such a complete listing. But we know that the interested teacher will extend these few suggestions as her judgment dictates, and from the discussion of the rationale and results of various programs which follows the chart.

TRAINING IN VISUAL PERCEPTION

In the words of G. N. Getman, the prominent optometrist, "the concepts of our world are learned. . . . Visual perception, which should become the supreme skill for more complete and adequate concepts of our world of people, objects, words, pictures, direction, distance, size, shape, color and texture, develops out of the sensory-receptor mechanisms of actual contact."* As we have suggested earlier,

* Unnumbered references will be found in the resources bibliography at the end of the chapter.

TABLE 7–1. *Overview of the Reading Readiness Program**

Perceptual–motor

Body image	Jointed dolls, Simon Says, mirror, rhythmic activities to music, movement games, skipping rope, Angels-in-the-Snow, trunk and leg lifts, sit-ups
Laterality and directionality	Etch-A-Sketch, balance beam and balance disc, chalkboard exercises, creeping obstacle course, walking obstacle course, stepping games
Hand–eye coordination	Templates, chalkboard exercises, coloring, cutting, pasting, jacks, marbles
	Swinging ball, finger play, straight line and rotary pursuits with flashlight or eyes, eye-movement charts, Space Masks, Space Sighters

Form perception:

Three-dimensional	Puzzles nested cubes, pegboards, parquetry, mosaic tiles, pattern boards, block designs, clay
Two-dimensional	Ditto masters, tracing and reproducing forms, matching forms, likenesses and differences, desk templates, drawing
Small-muscle coordination	Bead stringing, paper and pencil activities, tracing, dot pictures, pick-up sticks
Large-muscle coordination	Bean bags, dart games, ball throwing, catching and bouncing, nail pounding, ring toss, rhythm bands, Lummi sticks, hoops, jump board
Word and letter discrimination	Sandpaper letters, magnetic letters, flocked letters, ditto masters for matching and reproducing
Sensory discrimination	Identifying by feel, taste, smell, and sight, describing sensations, as in Feel Box, Smell Box
Auditory awareness	Identifying sounds of the earth, animals, man-made sounds; imitating and responding to inflections; distinguishing·intensity or loudness, pitch, duration, and sequences of sounds; What Is It Game
Auditory perception	Expressing sounds as in dances, marching, rhythmic activities, finger snapping; alliterative play with rhymes and jingles; games such as Sound of the Day
Auditory memory	Echo game, reproducing tapping patterns, following one-, two-, and three-step directions,

* Adapted from *The Teaching of Reading* by George D. Spache (Bloomington, Ind.: Phi Delta Kappa Educational Foundation, 1972), by permission of the publisher.

TABLE 7–1 (continued)

	Whispering Game, Restaurant Game, You Must Game, Bring Me Game
Auditory discrimination	Identifying sounds, words, rhymes on records; anticipating words or sounds in storytelling; imitating animal noises as in *Billy Goats Gruff, The Three Bears;* identifying sounds or number of syllables in names and other words; practicing rhyming in poetry, songs, and jingles
Language and thinking	
Receptive language	Listening to stories, dramatizing antonyms, following directions, detecting omissions or absurdities in stories, rhymes, or jingles, categorizing pictures, matching pictures and story sequence, enacting action words.
Expressive language	Telling Time, Sharing Time, social games, interpreting pictures and picture sequences, telling rote or cumulative tales, talking games such as Gossip Game, I Am Thinking of a Word That Tells Game, composing group experience charts, retelling stories, composing original stories, rhymes, and riddles

visual perception grows out of visual–tactual experiences. These experiences are multitudinous and require four to six years for sufficient development to the levels which will permit the child to read. They begin with the first visually directed reach and grasp of the infant, his first visual–tactual learning. Their number and variety determine most of the child's nonverbal or kinesthetic learning and also form the basis for his verbal learnings, speech or reading.

Visual–tactual experiences eventually are substituted for by visual movements, communication and speech patterns, which in turn yield to visualization and symbol manipulation (reading). Restriction of these experiences retards the child's entire physical and intellectual development to a point below his inherited potential.

Riesen (42) reared three chimpanzees for seven months in situations controlling the exercise of their normal vision. One chimpanzee was never allowed any light. A second was permitted ninety minutes of light, but his vision was obscured by a plexiglass mask. The third was allowed ninety minutes of clear vision per day. Both of the chimpanzees whose visual–tactual experiences were obstructed showed such losses as the inability to fixate on objects, absence of response to play objects or to the feeding bottle, and lack of the blink response. This experiment demonstrates dramatically the tremendous importance of visual–tactual experiences for the normal development of perception and the individual's concepts of the world about him. Probably very few children ever experience so severe a deprivation of the opportunity to react to their environment. But this experiment and others of similar implication remind us how dependent the child is upon adequate visual–tactual experiences.

In view of these facts, it is not surprising that we emphasize teacher observation, diagnosis, and training of visual–tactual development, visual perception, and functional visual skills as absolute prerequisites to reading instruction. Space does not permit us to treat this subject adequately, but we sincerely hope our readers will fill this lack by consulting some of the resources mentioned in the bibliography.

The act of reading demands such visual discriminations and perceptions as an orientation to left and right, up and down, front and back; accurate binocular shifts from point to point; accurate focus and accommodation to distance; and a fine degree of parallel or coordinated action of both eyes, or binocular coordination. To read, the child must be able to note similarities and differences among words by the clues given by the shapes of their beginning and ending letters, by letters that ascend and descend above the line, and by the patterns or outlines formed by combinations of these elements of words. The child must learn to make quick, accurate discriminations among a host of words, perhaps a more demanding visual task than any other he has experienced. Reading is first and foremost a visual task for the beginning reader and almost impossible for him to accomplish without the perceptual and discriminative abilities we have stressed.*

Therefore, when the child's behavior and quality of performance during near-point tasks indicate lack of visual perception or hand–eye coordination, developmental training should be given. In fact, the research on perceptual training shows that the entire third of the class which is lowest in general ability, readiness, or reading progress will probably benefit from this training. The values of developmental work in visual perception and hand–eye coordination are attested by many optometric and educational studies. Office records of hundreds of optometrists who specialize in visual training, and of orthoptists, their medical counterparts, show that training such as we will outline results in greater comfort and success in near-point activities as well as in reading and other academic tasks. Lillian Hinds' longitudinal study showed that first graders receiving this training were decidedly more successful in reading than might have been expected by reason of their intelligence or readiness (25). Goins' first-grade pupils showed improvement in discrimination after training given in the second semester, if they were already reading well in the first semester. In other words, her tachistoscopic training with geometric forms and digits was not very helpful for the less successful perceivers and readers either in improving discrimination or reading. Cox and Hambly (13) employed a variety of training procedures, such as we shall describe later, with low achievers. The trained pupils showed significantly greater gain in tests of visual skills given a year and a half after the three-month training period. The interdependence of the visual skills was shown by the fact that those children who improved in all three skills stressed showed the greatest gain in learning rate

* See the discussion of reading as a visual and a perceptual act in Chapter 1 for a complete description of the visual skills demanded by reading.

or achievement quotient. Improvement of only one visual skill did not produce greater learning ability. Halgren (24) gave training to both ninth graders and first graders, although he gives detailed results only for the older group. Since the training procedures are very similar to those we will describe, the marked gains in academic achievement for low achievers are significant to the primary school teacher. Baskin (4) also used these techniques with older, mentally retarded children with favorable results in reading.

Space does not permit a detailed review of all the evidence pro and con on visual-perception training experiments, for there are dozens and dozens of studies. For those who feel a need to evaluate this area more in depth before accepting some of our later suggestions, we may point out that intensive reviews of the outcomes of perceptual training programs are offered in the senior author's most recent books.*

One approach to this area in the readiness program is the use of commercial programs advertised for the development of visual perception or discrimination. Two popular programs of this type are the Frostig Visual-Perceptual Program based on the test by the same author, and the Delacato neurological organization training (14,20). Because of their wide use and, in our opinion, questionable results, we have tried to find as many studies of the outcomes of these two programs as a search of the literature would reveal. Those relevant to the Frostig program are summarized in Table 7–2.

It is apparent that using the Frostig program in the hopes of improving pupil readiness or reading is not likely to succeed. Four of the five studies testing the effects of the program on a readiness test gave nonsignificant gains. Seven of the eight studies testing the effects of the Frostig training on reading again gave insignificant gains in reading. The only result of this visual perception program appears to be in raising scores on the Frostig test, a finding in five out of seven experiments. In other words, when children are practiced in materials patterned on the Frostig test, they improve, as we expect, in that test, but there is little or no transfer to readiness or reading achievement. In the only study in which the training produced gains in reading, two other perceptual training programs were also used, so that we cannot really attribute the good results to the Frostig.

The Delacato program is supposed to be based on a theory of neurological organization, or developing complete sidedness in the child. The brain, presumably, is retrained and the sidedness induced by a variety of creeping and crawling exercises. Glass and Robbins have reviewed twelve reports from schools which adopted this program (21) but find that all of them lacked careful research designs and the usual scientific controls of a true experiment. O'Donnell (36), McCormick et al. (31), and Stone and Pielstick (50) used the program, but only McCormick claimed any favorable results. Unfortunately, his study was faulty in selecting children from a larger group, and failing to control the teacher inspiration or in-service training variables.

---

* *Investigating the Issues of Reading Disability* and *Diagnosing and Correcting Reading Disabilities* by George D. Spache (Boston: Allyn and Bacon, Inc., 1976).

TABLE 7–2. *Scoreboard on the Frostig Perceptual Training Program*

Source; grade level; number of cases	Gains on Frostig test	Gains on readiness test	Gains in reading test	Frostig versus
Alley et al. (2); disadvantaged kindergarten; N = 108	Significant	Significant		Eight months on Frostig vs. no Frostig
Arciszewski (3); grade one; N = 34	Significant		Not significant	Phonics program
Beaupre and Kennard (5); kindergarten; N = ca. 75		Not significant		Five other programs all superior to Frostig
Buckland (10); grade one; 16 classes	Not significant		Not significant; controls superior	Listening to stories and discussion
Cohen (11); grade one; N = 155	Significant		Not significant	
Cohen (12); grade one; N = 120			Not significant	
Faustman (18); kindergarten; 14 classes			Significant	Frostig plus Winter Haven plus Kephart programs
Fortenberry (19); grade one			Not significant	Frostig plus usual readiness
Jacobs et al. (28); prekindergarten, kindergarten, and grade one; N = 300		Not significant		
Jacobs et al. (28); prekindergarten to grade three; N = 300		Not significant	Not significant	
Pumfrey and Anthony (40); physically handicapped; N = 24	Not significant			Frostig training keyed to initial subtest vs. total Frostig vs. none
Rosen (44); grade one; N = 637	Significant		Not significant	
Wingert (53); kindergarten; N = 54	Significant	Not significant		

Robbins (43) studied the program under Delacato and applied it to second graders in comparison with one group given unpatterned physical activities and a control group given no training. The results did not support the neurological reorganization theory or its relationship to reading or its effect upon sidedness of children. Like the American Academy of Pediatrics (15), Robbins rejects completely both the theory and the treatment program as being relevant to reading or any other type of language difficulty.

On the positive side of visual perception training experiments, there are many other studies. We cannot possibly review all the individual studies here, but we will attempt to categorize them into types of programs and summarize their results. One group of studies emphasizes training with letters and words. In toto, these seem to indicate that using color in letters or backgrounds, letter names or letter discrimination, or matching geometric forms or words seems to contribute little to eventual skill in word recognition. Another group indicates that it is possible to stimulate whatever is measured by popular perception tests, like the Bender or the Frostig, but these results do not seem to transfer to readiness or reading. Among brain-damaged or mentally retarded children even these gains are only temporary and not much greater than the effects of mental maturation.

Readiness training intended to facilitate word recognition should move toward the meaningfulness of words rather than word form, or sound, or both, and toward training in letter discrimination without stressing letter names. Pretraining trials should probably be conducted to discover the individual differences among children so that perceptual training can be matched to their development and aptitudes. One group of studies has emphasized the chalkboard and template exercises we will describe later. This training seems profitable for children in low-socioeconomic groups or those of low intelligence rather than those of the middle or upper class. In fact, used as tests to predict reading achievement, the form perception, the chalkboard, and the walking beam programs proposed by Kephart and Getman show good relationship to reading through the second grade.

Other experiments which failed to influence reading achievement include those stressing tachistoscopic training in form recognition, noting likenesses or differences in words or pictures, tracing textured word forms, matching word forms, and rearranging plastic letters. These activities do not readily transfer to the act of word recognition.

There are three major types of visual training for perception and discrimination that any teacher can conduct. These include (1) directionality, or orientation to direction; (2) ocular motility, or promoting coordinated movements of both eyes; and (3) form perception, or discrimination of similarities and differences in designs, figures, and wordlike forms. A few children may also need more fundamental training in body coordination or motor development such as the exercises described by Getman et al.,* Kephart,* and in a book written particularly for parents, *Success Through Play* by Radler and Kephart.* These outline exercises

* Unnumbered references will be found in the resources bibliography at the end of the chapter.

and tests for general physical fitness of children which are widely accepted by physical educators and other experts. This basic body conditioning is highly desirable for brain-damaged and cerebral-palsied children, and also for a small proportion of grossly incoordinated normal children. It is not highly related to success in reading; hence we will not review the exercises and tests in detail here. But every primary teacher should be thoroughly familiar with this gross coordination training program, as outlined in the government bulletin *Games and Self-Testing Activities for the Classroom*.

Directionality

A well-developed sense of directionality to left–right, up–down, front–back, as well as to curves and angles in both three-dimensional and two-dimensional representation, is fundamental to successful reading. While reading is only a two-dimension task, with words having length and height but not thickness, visual skill in depth perception* is still highly important for reading. Many careful studies of child vision show that loss of depth perception is a significant symptom of subsequent academic difficulties (*30*). The relationships of other types of directionality skill must be quite obvious. The child must stabilize a constant left-to-right movement and an accurate return sweep for successful word recognition and forward progress along the lines of print. He must recognize and retain the patterns made by the curved and straight lines of letters and whole words. For fluent reading, the recognition of these shapes or patterns must constantly increase in speed and accuracy. Without adequate development of these directional skills, the child's reading is retarded by frequent reversals, inversions, word confusions, and substitutions.

The research study conducted by one of the authors employed a number of chalkboard exercises in directionality as part of the training for the first graders who were lacking in accurate visual perception. About fifteen minutes per day of this training, accompanied by seatwork in similar discriminations offered by the Continental Press workbooks, was offered. The training in the experimental classes was substituted for the usual reading instruction for periods ranging from at least two months to as long as six months. Despite the shorter time for reading training, the experimental classes equaled in reading achievement the classes not receiving such training. Moreover, the experimental children in the lowest quarter in intelligence and those in the lowest levels of socioeconomic status benefited most from this training, for both these groups excelled their matched control groups in the regular basal reading program.

In the area of directionality, the chalkboard exercises used in this study were as described below. These practices were drawn from the recommendations

---

*Depth perception—the visual recognition of thickness, depth, or solidity of objects arising in part from a blending of the images received by the separate eyes, and originating in visual–tactual experiences.

of Getman and others and are adapted from the description in the leaflet *Proper Chalkboards Properly Used* (37).

When child is facing the chalkboard at a distance of about ten inches, an X is placed on the board at a point directly in front of the tip of his nose. The child is to fixate on this mark while doing these preliminary exercises:

Space Organization

The child holds the chalk between the thumb and the inside of the first finger (inside the palm, not like a pencil) and scribes with both hands back and forth from the X, as far as the arms will extend. The child scribes repeated lines at points about as high as the hairline, at the level of the X, and again opposite the hips. When scribing at or above eye level, the thumbs are opposite each other, the back of the hands up; below eye level, the hands are rotated with the thumbs outward and the back of the hands underneath.

The teacher draws a vertical line through the X, and draws horizontal lines through the center of the child's lines. If the child's lines deviate or slant upward or downward, he should continue practice until appropriate bimanual control is achieved.

Motor Equivalence

The child scribes bimanual circles with both hands, at the same levels on the chalkboard, as above. Circles are scribed with both hands simultaneously, first outward from the X, then inward with both hands, and then alternately with both hands scribing toward the right and then the left.

Bimanual Straight Lines

The teacher places a large circle of dots on the chalkboard (with a felt-tip pen) with a large center dot opposite the child's nose. The dots around the circle are lettered or numbered, or if the child cannot read these symbols, the teacher indicates the two dots for the starting points. Using both hands, the child tries to draw from the opposite dots on the edges of the circle to the center dot, or from the center dot to the two opposite outer dots. Extend this training so that the child can scribe simultaneously from any two dots to the center or the reverse. In this exercise, as in those above, the teacher should continue with short daily practice sessions until the child's movements become comfortable and fluent, and the performances with both hands are relatively similar.

Unimanual Training Procedures

A. Make a vertical row of dots on the chalkboard with a felt-tip pen at about ten inches to the right of the center position and a similar row of dots to the left of the center position. Label each dot on the same horizontal line similarly and the vertical spacing between the dots should be about three inches.* Your chalkboard would have this type of pattern:

```
A  .                                                      .  A
B  .                                                      .  B
C  .                                                      .  C
```

About five pairs of dots are sufficient. The child is given his piece of chalk and told to place it on the dot by the letter A on his left. He then scribes a chalkline from the left A to the right A in a straight line *without stopping.* When he has completed drawing the lines, erase the lines, and have the child continue the training. If these lines can be drawn easily, continuously, and accurately (start precisely from one dot and end right on the other dot), begin using the next exercise.

B. Construct two rows of horizontal dots with a vertical spacing of about twelve inches apart. In the horizontal row the dots should be about three inches apart. The chalkboard pattern will now be:

```
A   B   C   D   E
.   .   .   .   .

.   .   .   .   .
A   B   C   D   E
```

The child is asked to start with his chalk at the dot below the letter A and draw a *continuous* line to the lower A. This is done for all the different letters, so that you end up with a series of vertical lines. Now have the child reverse the procedure *and* again make a series of vertical lines starting with the lower dots and going upward to the top dots. When the child can perform adequately on the horizontal and vertical lines, we advance to the oblique lines.

C. Again two rows of dots are constructed and labeled but placed at an oblique angle:

The child scribes lines from a left-to-right, upward direction.

*If the child is unfamiliar with letters or numbers, use stars or asterisks to mark the points in each pattern.

The child scribes from left to right downward. The child must make a continuous line starting from one dot and ending at the other dot before we consider that he has developed adequate performance ability.

D. Combining straight and oblique lines. Using the rows of dots as in exercises *A, B,* and *C,* ask the child to draw both horizontally (as in *A*), and obliquely, from the dot at the right to the second dot at the left.

Repeat using the vertical spacing of dots, as in exercise *B,* and the oblique spacing as in *C.*

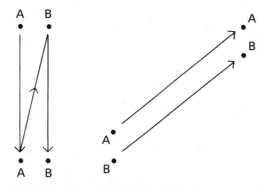

The child should make a continuous, rapid line from each dot to the next. Please note that these lines are drawn straight, quickly, and with a single free motion, *not* painstakingly, slowly, with only hand or wrist movement.

E. Repetitive forms. This technique develops rhythm, shape, or form, and the ability to maintain constancy of size. Two parallel lines are constructed across the board with a separation of about six inches and at the nose level of the child. The child starts with his chalk about four inches from the left edge of the lines and makes circles in a counterclockwise direction moving slowly toward the right as he scribes his circles. It looks as follows:

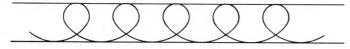

As a variation of this, have the child scribe vertical lines in the same manner.

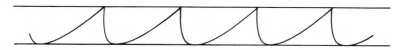

When the child can perform these visual-kinesthetic procedures with ease and accuracy we proceed to chase the leader.

F. Chase The Leader. You construct a series of three dots or more on a chalkboard and label them A, B, C . . . M. The child must go in the proper direction and continuously scribe a line from A to B and on to the last letter on the chalkboard. This develops ability to rapidly scribe lines in all directions. It teaches the child to be able to make a rapid shift in direction (to draw angles) and it also enables the child to develop the ability to stay on his primary target in spite of the distraction of other lines in his field of view. Start with three dots, then increase to five, seven, etc.

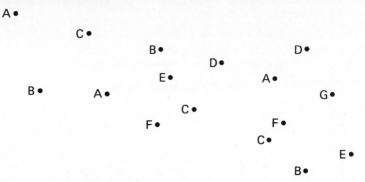

G. Dot Pictures. Drawing from dot to dot to form the outlines of objects is another directionality exercise found in some readiness workbooks and children's playtime or coloring books. These are desirable near-point unimanual exercises only if the child is held to a standard of straight, fluent movements.

H. Visual projection. Directionality training should be extended to include visualization of objects, distances, and directions. Games of describing his route to and from school, to the store or church, or while on a common auto trip, which require the child to visualize and describe direction, are excellent. Other variations include describing the directions necessary to complete an errand at school or home, or the contents of a room or a store.

Almost any teacher can devise variations of these basic directionality exercises by using her imagination. She must keep in mind that the primary purposes are to produce recognition of directions, pursuit of these directions by coordinated hand and eye movements, and, eventually, the ability to verbalize directions or translate directions into words.

These exercises, as well as those that follow, are not designed exclusively for beginning readers. Many poor readers, of all ages, show their need for directionality training by excessive regressions or repetitions and losing their place.

Ocular Motility

Many children entering school have not developed coordinated movements of the eyes. Their eyes do not follow an object in motion with equal binocular movements of the eyes. One eye may lag behind the other, or overreach, or even remain still while the other is reaching out in space. Visually speaking, because of lack of binocular coordination the child may not receive exactly the same images from both eyes since they may not bear upon the same object. These conflicting images are reflected in inaccurate perception and discrimination and if persistent or severe, lead to a tendency to suppress or ignore one of the images. To accomplish this the child may permit one eye to drift or it may turn away almost constantly in what is called strabismus, cockeye or walleye. Practically every thorough study of child vision indicates that these various difficulties in binocular coordination are highly significant in reading failure at almost all ages of children.

Among the exercises commonly employed by visual training experts to improve ocular motility are these:

1. Swinging Ball. Suspend a small rubber ball (or any similar object) from a doorway, light fixture, or the hand, at the child's eye level. Gently swing the ball to and fro, in a circle, and from side to side a foot or two from his face, while he follows it with his eyes. To vary this exercise, hang the ball about three feet from the floor, and have the child watch it while lying directly beneath it. Or, have the child try to follow movement of ball with a jar four or five inches in diameter, without hitting sides of jar. This can be varied by asking child to reach out with his forefinger to touch the ball in flight, from beneath or the side.
2. Finger Play. Have the child jump his eyes back and forth to the tip of each of your or his forefingers, held a foot apart at a foot from his face. If he needs assistance, pace his eyes with your finger swinging slowly between the tips of his forefingers.
3. Flashlight. To vary these straight line and rotary pursuits, use a small flashlight or other bright object in place of the ball or fingers. Or, have the child point with a flashlight to crosses on the blackboard arranged in a large circle. He holds flashlight at side, points on signal.
4. Point to Point. Hold a pencil twelve to fourteen inches from the child's face, and have him look from the pencil to a picture on the wall. Be sure that he sees each clearly when his eyes are at rest on either target. As this exercise becomes easier, move the pencil closer to his face. Or, using primer or pica typewriter, prepare two sheets of capital letters in rows, five spaces between each letter. Hold the sheets in each hand, and have him jump his eyes back and forth from letter to letter without moving his head. Have him move along the lines and down the page in this fashion.

The purpose of these ocular motility exercises is to promote equal, coordinated, and quick binocular movements. If the child shows any difficulty in these activities after a half-dozen ten-minute practice sessions, the wisest course would be to recommend a complete professional examination, preferably by an optometrist or ophthalmologist who is interested and trained in visual training. The classroom teacher should realize that this training is not intended as a substitute for professional care, and it is not intended to correct or repair severe visual problems. It simply provides practice in several visual functions which are essential to the act of reading for all pupils.

As Kephart notes, some children may need the reinforcement of hand action in these exercises in ocular motility. They may need to follow the swinging ball or the flashlight at first with their pointed finger as well as with their eyes. Thus they may lead their eyes with their fingers or hands, as a small child does in exploring space. Some children show this dependence upon tactual contact by using their finger to point as they read. If so, they should be permitted to use this method of reinforcement or be supplied with a marker until they spontaneously discard it because of increasing visual coordination. It is unnecessary to note that this reading behavior is strong evidence of the need for training in directionality and ocular motility.

Since the child is most experienced in ocular control in a restricted central area, it is highly desirable to extend the action gradually into periphery. The child should learn both to cross the midline of his body to the opposite side with accurate movements and to extend this binocular coordination outward in all directions. Most children and adults show better control in an area opposite the center of the body and extending toward the preferred right or left side. On the other side of the body and toward the outer edges of our visual or manual reach, more training may be necessary for accuracy.

In ocular motility training the child has no real way of judging whether he is following the target accurately and binocularly. The teacher should watch closely to be certain that the child is fixating constantly on the target. If there is any doubt that he is seeing the target sharply and clearly, check by asking him to point to it or touch it. If it appears that he is following with only one eye, cover that eye and ask him to look again at the target. When the wandering eye has fixated, uncover the other eye and resume the exercise. By these two checks the child can be helped to maintain binocular fixation in the training exercises.

Although it is not always recognized as such, practice on the walking beam or rail is an extension of the training in ocular motility and control. It is based on the fact that binocular control of one's own vision while in motion is related to reading progress (23). Thus fixation on the target during these exercises is an essential part of the training. The specific exercises are adapted from the program outlined by G. N. Getman and his collaborators.

Exercise on the Walking Beam

General Instructions: The teacher should have a fixation target, such as X on the blackboard or a small picture, at eye level, opposite the end of the beam. Children should always look at this target when exercising on the beam, and should practice in stockinged feet.

Indian Walk: Children walk, Indian fashion, heel touching toe, along the beam. The teacher instructs them to keep eyes fixed on the target.

Butterflies: Using the Indian walk, children spread arms out like a butterfly, moving them up and down slowly, while moving along the beam.

Backward Walk: Children walk backward on the beam, toe-to-heel fashion, keeping eyes on the target.

Backward Butterfly: Children walk backward on the beam, moving arms up and down slowly, like a butterfly.

Forward and Backward: Children walk forward until teacher or other pupil says "Stop," then reverse, moving backward. They use Indian walk, heel to toe, in each direction.

Giant Steps: Children repeat forward and backward movements upon command, using giant steps. The teacher can vary the exercise by using the game, "Captain, May I _____?" or "Rover, Red Rover _____."

Learning Distances: The teacher puts a red stripe across the beam at the middle, and green stripes at the one-quarter and three-quarter points. The teacher uses the Forward and Backward movements upon command and uses the words—one-half, one-fourth, two-fourths, three-fourths, etc.

Peripheral Targets: The teacher places the Walking Beam parallel to the wall or chalkboard, positions the beam about two feet from the wall, and puts a red circle at the child's eye level, on the wall or board at a point opposite the halfway mark on the beam.

The teacher should have the children try to walk the beam, with arms extended to the side, until they think they are even with the red circle and can touch it, without looking in that direction.

The exercise is repeated with beam placed at an angle (45 degrees or less) to the wall. Again the teacher should have the children try to touch the red circle without looking at it. They should practice touching the side targets while walking backward as well as forward and should practice starting from either end of the beam.

A class record sheet listing the eight types of exercises on the walking beam at the top of the page and spaces for each child's name in a vertical column at the left will be useful to keep track of pupil progress. The exercises are arranged in order of increasing difficulty. As each can be performed comfortably by the child, perhaps after related brief trials scheduled daily, he may progress to the next exercise. To save the teacher's time, an aide or a parent can direct other children through the sequence, judge their performances, and record their progress by check marks on the record sheet, as each exercise is accomplished.

Form Perception

Discrimination of wordlike forms is, of course, desired as the ultimate outcome of all visual training, as well as all readiness training. But, like the other visual skills, form perception is a complex, learned act which has not yet been completely analyzed by vision and reading specialists. Training materials which are supposed to increase accuracy of form perception are commonly found in readiness workbooks. Children are asked to detect slight differences among a series of drawings of common objects, geometric forms, designs resembling objects or words, and actual letters and words. Frequently, the training begins with large drawings and continues through a series which is gradually reduced in size. There is some evidence that this logical arrangement aids some beginning readers to achieve greater reading success (29). But it is not clearly understood why and how this training is helpful. We are not certain how to identify the pupils who need the training, the amount needed, or the most effective types.

Several rather brief experiments on kindergarten children have been attempted to discover the best type of form perception training for learning a few words. Muehl (33) and Staats et al. (48) gave a short training period in discriminating geometric forms, or letters, or words. One control group had no discrimination training whatever. The letters or words used as practice material were identical with those found in the final test of word recognition. All groups, including the controls, showed learning of a similar degree in the test. There was only slight evidence that practice in discriminating words was most effective for immediate learning. Final retention of the test words was similar for all types of discrimination training. These are rather inconclusive results for a number of reasons. They seem to support the logic that form perception training should involve the discrimination of words or wordlike forms. But they leave us with no explanation for the variations in learning among the individuals in these groups. Do some children need more of this particular type of training, or do they need some other more basic type? Some of the children undoubtedly began the experiment with good form perception, while others were quite undeveloped in this skill. Which of these children profited from the training? Goins' first-grade study (22) involving tachistoscopic training with geometric forms and gradually increasing groups of numbers again showed marked individual differences, with the greatest benefit being shown by pupils whose pretraining form perception was high. What type of form training do the poor perceivers need to prepare them for accurate discriminations among words? Perhaps these are the only tentative conclusions we may draw from these experiments: (1) pupils will vary a great deal in the amount of form perception training they need; (2) the training should probably proceed from gross discriminations to fine; (3) the more closely the final perceptual tasks resemble word forms, the more effective they are likely to be; and (4) emphasis upon speed in discrimination should probably occur late in the training process, after a high degree of accuracy has first been developed.

We have attempted to list a sequence of form perception activities that observes these tentative conclusions drawn from the research.

1. Tracing around simple pictures, coloring within the lines, and cutting out simple forms are basic types of form discrimination. (But they are certainly not as necessary for all children as the extent of their use in readiness and reading workbooks would imply.)
2. Practice with tridimensional objects such as puzzles, nested cubes, and peg boards is highly desirable. Peg-board play can be varied by varying the picture

the child tries to produce or by reducing the number of pegs used for each object or form.

3. Tracing geometric forms, designs, words, or his own name on a magic slate or carbon paper fosters comparison and discrimination.

4. Using templates of geometric forms aids in perception training. Templates can be made from Masonite, plastic, pressed board, or artist board with cutouts of the geometric forms: circle, square, rectangle, diamond, triangle. The template should be 10 by 12 inches and the cutout extend to one inch of the edges on three sides. The cutout is centered in the upper two-thirds of the template. This allows a solid portion of about four inches for the child to hold the template with the nonwriting hand. Some teachers fix a wooden spool to the solid portion to provide a more positive grip.

   The template is held against the chalkboard with the nonwriting hand below the cutout. The X placed on the board opposite the child's nose should appear through the cutout slightly above the center of the opening. The child traces around inside the form, continuously for five to six times, with the chalk constantly touching the edges of the shape. The tracing should be done smoothly and rhythmically. Practice may be scheduled daily for five to ten minutes with a number of children at the blackboard.

   The order of difficulty is from circle, square, rectangle, triangle, to diamond. When the child can repeatedly trace within the template fluently, he should progress to making the same shape on the board without the aid of the template, and then go on to the next-most-difficult form.

5. Having the child attempt to draw forms, patterns, or shapes you put on the blackboard is helpful. After he has seen these for a few seconds, erase them and let him reproduce your drawing. Use simple geometric forms at first, then reduce size and increase complexity.

6. Encouraging the child to make line drawings of persons, objects, and common events (and to tell the story of his drawings) is a useful training procedure.

7. As actual introduction to reading begins, pencil or chalk outlines of common words, emphasizing the ascending and descending letters and cued by context and initial letters or blends, should be used. Begin with pupils' names, your name, and objects in the classroom.

8. See such sources as Spache for other training activities.

Another possible extension is by the use of small-size templates for seat-work on blank newspaper sheets and later paper of ordinary sizes. This approach has been intensively studied in the Winter Haven (Florida) schools as a means of helping poor achievers acquire patterns and freedom in hand–eye coordination. Results are reported to show that trained first graders exceeded matched controls by six to nine months in reading, four months in arithmetic, three to four months in spelling, and seven months in vocabulary (41). The differences were greatest between matched low-socioeconomic groups but also marked in high-socioeconomic groups. One of the obvious values of this template training is the relationship to the child's learning to write. He is, in effect, practicing the strokes which comprise written letters as well as learning to direct his hands and eyes in tracing and reproducing basic shapes. The value of learning to write as an aid to progress in early reading was redemonstrated in the results of the Cooperative First-Grade Studies (8). If extended training seems necessary for some children, as shown in the research study of one of the present authors (47), the ditto masters of Continental Press of Elizabethtown, Pennsylvania, entitled *Visual Discrimination* and *Visuo-Motor Skills* are relevant.

Another basic effort to improve perception would consider the child's posture during the act of reading and writing. Faulty posture will distort the child's perception of objects in space or, more significant for our concern, result in faulty interpretation of printed symbols. Tilting of the head, or shoulders, improper distance from the printed page, partial suppression of the vision in one eye because of these postural distortions—all may cause distorted perception despite our training efforts. To aid the child to secure the proper posture for reading, the desk should be tilted at approximately 15 degrees. This slant tends to promote a balanced, bilateral approach to the reading and writing task.

The proper working distance from the paper or book is approximately equal to the distance between the middle knuckle of the child's clenched fist and elbow joint, measured on the outside of the arm. In other words, both of the child's eyes should be about as far from the working task as the length of his forearm and the back of his hand combined. The paper may be turned slightly to the right or left to favor his preferred writing hand, but this turn should not be so exaggerated as to force him into one-eyed reading.

Another source of training in form perception, on rather advanced levels, is the *Learning To Think Series* by Thelma G. Thurstone (Science Research Associates). The research of these authors shows that these exercises are beneficial for some beginning readers. Perhaps their greatest values are for children with obviously mature visual skills, or for children in later stages of the program subsequent to the more basic training we have outlined.

The obvious questions in using these exercises in improving visual skills are which children need the training and how long they should continue to receive it. In the absence of any standardized tests of these visual skills other than those employed in a professional optometric examination, these decisions must be based on the observations and judgment of the teacher. The exercises themselves and some trained observations offered by the staff of the Gesell Institute of Child Development of New Haven, Connecticut, will be helpful in selecting children for training and deciding when to terminate the exercises. Try the first few exercises in directionality, ocular motility, and form perception with each child or group of children. When the child can do each exercise readily with speed and accuracy, progress to the next exercise. If the child evidences incoordination or any other type of difficulty in an exercise, continue to repeat it in varied ways until his performance shows distinct improvement.

From their many observations of reading and visual behaviors under controlled conditions, Ilg and Ames* suggest that the child's visual skills show a

---

*Frances L. Ilg and Louise Ames, "Developmental Trends in Reading Behavior," *Journal of Genetic Psychology,* 76 (June 1950), 291–312.

sequential development. These stages may be observed during some of the exercises or in a teacher–pupil conversational setting or while looking at a book together:

1. Eye movements are more circular than direct, more disorganized than orderly or methodical.
2. The eyes tend to make wide horizontal sweeps from one side to another, rather than many small disorganized movements. (See particularly the first three ocular motility exercises.)
3. The eyes can make planned oblique movements upward and downward.
4. The child can combine both oblique and horizontal movements into a single coordinated movement.
5. The eyes can move quickly and accurately from point to point horizontally, vertically, or obliquely. They can also repeatedly shift focus from near point (reading distance) to far point (any distance greater than three or four feet) with speed and accuracy).
6. The child can trace, copy, match, reproduce from memory, discriminate differences among outlines of simple geometric forms, designs, symbols, or word forms. Do not, however, expect reproduction of the diamond or other forms involving oblique lines or complex internal diagonals or other details.

Visual Perception Training Materials

The current interest, and confusion, regarding training materials for improving visual perception demands special treatment. We cannot define visual perception simply here, if at all, for it is still in the process of being identified in laboratories, clinics, classrooms, and research centers. However, despite incomplete definition, it is possible to suggest activities and devices which will contribute to the ability to make the discriminations which underlie word recognition and writing.

Visual perception represents, in our opinion, an ultimate performance in the acts of reading and writing, at the end of a long continuum of bodily, hand, and visual experiences. In Gesell's terminology, we might say that the child learns to recognize abstract symbols first with the mouth and hand; later with the hand and body; then with the hand and eyes; and only eventually with the eyes alone. In this long development, the learning of finger, hand, and bodily coordination, of directionality, of the properties of objects in space or depth perception, and of tridimensionality form foundations for the child's functioning in the two-dimensional media of reading and writing.

Although the research evidence is not entirely clear, it is possible that development of rhythmic bodily movements, of bodily balance, of auditory rhythms, and of orientation to laterality in one's own body or in that of other bodies may be significant steps in this development of visual perception. In the belief that future research may give some support to these latter experiences, we have included some related training materials. As this research appears, this eclectic list will be refined accordingly.

These perceptual training materials are offered without reference to special types of children exhibiting learning difficulties. We are not concerned here with such meaningless categories as the "minimal brain damaged," "slight cerebral dysfunction," "dyslexic," "incompletely lateralized," "poorly neurologically organized," or the like. We are concerned here only with children (or adults) who show marked difficulties in discriminating among forms, letters, or words despite exposure to ordinarily effective instruction. In our opinion, the job of teachers, clinicians, and reading specialists is to find appropriate developmental tasks, no matter what diagnostic labels are offered by this or that cult or school.

In our judgment, the logical sequence in the testing-training program in visual perception extends from hand–eye and bodily coordination, to spatial relationships, to three-dimensional and later two-dimensional form discriminations, and finally to word and letter discrimination. In addition to the specific training suggestions offered earlier, we would offer a list of readily obtainable materials. Included are trade books which offer experiences with physical and/or verbal concepts of size, directionality, spatial relationships, self-concepts, and the like.

Hand and Bodily Coordination

Chalkboard Templates. St. Louis, Mo.: Webster. Opaque templates of geometric forms to be used at the chalkboard.

Creative Playthings, Inc., Princeton, N.J.
  Rubber peg board and pegs
  Rhythm band set
  Balance blocks and boards
  Peg-board tiles
  Kikit

Desk Templates. St. Louis, Mo.: Webster. Similar in form to those for chalkboard use, but smaller in size.

Developing Body-Space Perception Motor Skills. Freeport, N.Y.: Activity Records. Offers two albums and activities to improve sense of form, structure, laterality, and directionality.

Eye Movement Charts, Space Masks, and Space Sighters. St. Louis, Mo.: Webster. These charts and masks enable the child to develop control and accuracy of eye movements.

Introducing the Rhythm Instruments. Educational Record Sales, 157 Chambers Street, New York. A pair of albums that offer an introduction to rhythm activities through percussion instruments.

Judy Clown Bean Bag Set. Minneapolis, Minn.: Judy. Large wood clown and bean bags intended to improve hand–eye coordination.

Listening and Moving. Freeport, N.Y.: Activity Records. A pair of LP records provide a training program in development of body awareness and position in space; perceptual-motor skills involving body balance.

Perceptual-Motor Development Kit by Fairbanks and Robinson. Boston: Teaching Resources. This kit includes a number of training materials for improving hand–eye coordination, as (1) lines-movement exercises; (2) coloring exercises; (3) cutting exercises; (4) spatial relations, which involves drawing from point to point.

Tootie-A-Go-Go. Hawthorne, Calif.: Creative Ideas Co. A game of toss and catch with small bean bags and a hand-operated net catcher.

Walking Beam. St. Louis, Mo.: Webster. A wooden beam on blocks, for developing bilateral balance, peripheral awareness, and related abilities. Targets for visual fixation are also available.

Webstermasters and Movable Melvin. St. Louis, Mo.: Webster. Melvin is a doll character with movable parts. Its use plus the two-dimensional duplicating masters are intended to aid children in exploring movement patterns.

Words and Movement About Myself. Dansville, N.Y.: F. A. Owen. A record for relating physical movements and language concepts of directionality, laterality, and the like.

Spatial Relationships

Creative Playthings, Inc., Princeton, N.J.
Geometric Metal Insets
Parquetry Blocks
Graded Circles, Squares, and Triangles
Rubber Oversized Parquetry
Geometric Mosaic Tiles
Pattern Boards

Parquetry Design Blocks. Beckley-Cardy. Forms in smooth wood for making designs in color.

Stick-O-Mats. Minneapolis, Minn.: Judy. For discrimination of geometric forms at the flannelboard. Another set, *Color-Shapes,* provides experiences with both forms and colors.

Sticks for Laying. Beckley-Cardy. Sticks from one to five inches long in separate or assorted sets. For spatial relationship development.

Visual-Perceptual Exercises. Boston: Teaching Resources. This group of exercises and a *Perceptual Bingo* game are part of the *Erie Perceptual-Motor Kit.* Offers variety of exercises in form and color discrimination.

Form Discrimination—Three-Dimensional

Creative Playthings, Inc., Princeton, N.J.
Stringing Beads
Shape Sorting Box
Wood Snap Blocks

Building Letters. Ideal School Supply, 8312 S. Birkhoff Avenue, Chicago, Ill. Pieces of straight lines, arcs, etc., which can be put together to form letters. Wool felt for flannelboard use, or suitable for seatwork.

Perceptual-Motor Development Kit by Fairbanks and Robinson. Boston: Teaching Resources. Offers one section on spatial relations in puzzle form involving the matching of three- and two-dimensional forms.

Form Discrimination—Two-Dimensional

Creative Playthings, Inc., Princeton, N.J.
  Design stamps
  Playskool community activity puzzles
Come and See. Chicago: Follett. A supplementary readiness workbook particularly emphasizing visual discrimination and eye–hand coordination in a two-dimensional medium.
Fruit and Animal Puzzles. Boston: Teaching Resources. These forty-two puzzles and others termed *Formed Puzzles* are part of the Cheves Visual-Motor Perception materials. Aided by pictures or colors, the child assembles these simple two- to four-piece puzzles.
Perceptual Motor Development Kit by Fairbanks and Robinson. Boston: Teaching Resources. The kit contains several sets of training exercises in form discrimination: (1) shapes—recognition and discrimination; (2) spatial orientation; (3) constancy of form and size; (4) figure–ground discriminations.
Perceptual Readiness. Huntington, N.Y.: Educational Developmental Laboratories. Twenty strips for use in the Tach-X to promote rapid visual discrimination of forms, etc. Similar materials are offered for the hand Flash-X.
Primary Reading Master Duplicators by Ethel S. Chaney. Elizabethtown, Penna.: Continental. Workbooks in Visual Discrimination, Visuo-Motor Skills, Rhyming, Beginning Sounds, Thinking Activities, and others which are useful for readiness and beginning reading training as well as visual or auditory perceptual training.
See-Quees. Minneapolis, Minn.: Judy. Each formboard is divided into four to twelve sequential pictures portraying a logical sequence or story. Useful in building physical and mental concepts of sequence and directionality.
A Simplified Reading Readiness Program. Chicago: Follett, 1966. Offers separate workbooks for visual discrimination and spatial discrimination.
Visual Memory Filmstrips. St. Louis, Mo.: Webster. Fifteen filmstrips for visual discrimination of forms are offered. Intended for tachistoscopic use.
Visual Perception Skills. Educational Record Sales, 157 Chambers Street, New York. Seven filmstrips offering structured activities in various facets of visual discrimination.

Word and Letter Discrimination

Creative Playthings, Inc., Princeton, N.J.
  Magnetic Letters and Board
  Sandpaper Letters
  Kinesthetic Letters on Board
  Word building box
Cut-Out Letters and Figures. Darien, Conn.: Teachers Publishing Corp. Sets of letters and numbers in two-, three-, or four-inch sizes for flannelboard or kinesthetic use.
Flocked Assortment. Darien, Conn.: Teachers Publishing Corp. Over 200 pieces of card stock for flannelboard or kinesthetic use. Includes forms, pictures, letters, etc.

Geake, R. Robert, and Smith, Donald E. P. *Visual Tracking.* Ann Arbor, Mich.: Ann Arbor Publishers, 1962. A practice book in visual discrimination among letters of decreasing size.

Judy Manuscript Letters. Minneapolis, Minn.: Judy. Heavy stock letters, manuscript capitals or lowercase, for flannelboard or kinesthetic use.

Magnetic Assortment. Beckley-Cardy, 1900 N. Narragansett Ave., Chicago. Plastic letters, assorted capitals or lowercase, with built-in permanent magnets for use with metal chalkboard or bulletin board.

Smith, Donald E. P., *Symbol Tracking.* Ann Arbor, Mich.: Ann Arbor Publishers. Supplementary to the *Visual Tracking* noted above.

Stolpen, Beulah Harris, et al., *Linguistic Block Series.* Chicago: Scott, Foresman. Plastic blocks engraved with letters or words can be arranged to form words or sentences.

Related Books*

Borten, Helen, *Do You See What I See?* New York: Abelard-Schuman, 1959. Shapes, forms, and colors merge into common objects.

Borten, Helen, *Do You Hear What I Hear?* New York: Abelard-Schuman, 1960. Discrimination of common sounds.

Borten, Helen, *Do You Move as I Do?* New York: Abelard-Schuman, 1963. Bodily movement experienced through imitation.

Budney, Blossom, *A Kiss Is Round.* New York: Lothrop, Lee & Shepard Company, 1954. Forms and shapes are contrasted.

Grayson, Marion F., *Let's Do Fingerplays.* Washington, D.C.: Robert B. Luce, Inc., 1962. Rhymes and games to introduce finger play to improve coordination.

Kessler, Ethel, and Kessler, Leonard, *Are You Square?* New York: Doubleday & Company, Inc., 1966. Common shapes are contrasted.

Kohn, Bernice, *Everything Has a Size.* Englewood Cliffs, N.J.: Prentice-Hall, Inc., 1966.

———— *Everything Has a Shape.* Englewood Cliffs, N.J.: Prentice-Hall, Inc., 1964. Relative sizes and shapes of everyday objects and animals.

Krauss, Ruth, *I'll Be You—You Be Me.* New York: Harper & Row, Inc., 1973. Explorations in self-concept.

Munari, Bruno, *Bruno Munari's ABC.* Cleveland: World Publishing Company, 1960. Relates common objects to the alphabet.

Palazzo, Tony, *The Magic Crayon.* New York: Lion Books, 1967. Creative experiences with common shapes and forms.

Schneider, Herman, and Schneider, Nina, *How Big Is Big?* New York: Scott, 1950. Relative sizes.

Shapp, Charles, and Shapp, Martha, *Let's Find Out What's Big and What's Small?* New York: Franklin Watts, Inc., 1975.

*A more complete list of perceptual training material is available in *Good Reading for Poor Readers*, ed. 8, by George D. Spache (Champaign, Ill.: Garrard Publishing Company, 1974).

A Footnote to Training in Visual Perception

Some reviewers of the results of perceptual-motor training programs, including Helen M. Robinson* and Stephen E. Klesius,* are disturbed by the poor and contradictory research, and the unproved nature of the tests of this area. These reviewers agree in concluding that a direct effect upon reading achievement or readiness has not been shown for such programs. Even when the more careful research studies only are considered, as by Klesius, the evidence is about equally positive or negative. In some experiments, readiness is improved or reading is increased or both results appear. In almost as many other studies, only the scores on some perceptual-motor test or other are increased, and there are no observable effects in readiness or reading.

Thus our research on perceptual-motor programs is often inconclusive or doubtful. Is it possible that this is due to the confusion in defining the basic elements of perceptual-motor development, the extreme variations in the types of training given, the unproven validity of many of the tests of perception offered, as well as to the lack of careful control of many of the studies? Are the indefinite results also influenced by the fact that the experimenters try to isolate the effect of perceptual-motor programs from other normal readiness activities with which they are interrelated? It is apparent that the field of perceptual-motor training is in a very early stage of evolution. We do not really know all the skills that are significant, how to test their development, what types of training produce the most valuable results, or what influence the skills we should train will have on school success.

If perceptual-motor training constituted the entire readiness program, it would certainly be difficult to justify it in the reading program, at this stage of our knowledge. But the same could be said of other readiness factors, such as auditory discrimination or language development. If one of these were the sole content of readiness activities, the results would be just as inconclusive. Success in early reading, as we have pointed out earlier, is not based entirely upon the child's development in just one of these areas, but rather depends upon overall development in all of them. To say this another way, we could ignore visual perception or auditory discrimination or language development entirely in the beginning reading program, and yet some children would learn to read. At the same time, we know that many would fail because of deficits in directionality, visual discrimination, auditory confusions, inadequate speaking or listening vocabulary, or the like.

It may not yet be possible to show a direct impact of perceptual-motor training on some aspects of readiness or reading. On the other hand, we do know that these activities are appropriate in early childhood education to increase body

---

* Helen M. Robinson, *Perceptual Training—Does It Result in Reading Improvement?*, pp. 135–150, and Stephen E. Klesius, "Perceptual Motor Development and Reading—A Closer Look," pp. 151–159, both in *Some Persistent Questions on Beginning Reading*, Robert C. Aukerman, ed. (Newark, Del.: International Reading Association, 1972).

awareness, balance, locomotor, and manipulative skills. We all acknowledge the relationship between hand–eye coordination and handwriting, which in turn influences letter formation, letter and word recognition, and early reading success. We know that this type of training is developmentally sound for many disadvantaged children as a preventive program, or as a remedial program for some with learning disabilities. Perceptual-motor programs that more closely resemble classroom tasks do tend to transfer to academic performances. Moreover, the programs have a positive influence in developing attention, impulse control, and self-concept, probably more so for younger than older children. These values are reiterated in the publications of a number of national organizations of optometrists, physical educators, and early childhood specialists.* These specialists firmly believe that a sequential perceptual-motor program integrated with the other important readiness activities, and emphasized only for those children who appear to need such training, will make a greater contribution to child development than the prevailing free play or game-oriented programs now used in many kindergarten, nursery, or primary-grade classes.

As we tried to imply in the preceding section, the exercises in directionality, ocular motility, and form perception will contribute to the overall development of the children who need such training. In the absence of very valid tests, the exercises themselves can function as screening devices to identify children lacking in each area. Thus we would give intensive practice beginning at the point of the child's failure in any series of exercises, and no training to any child who can successfully perform the entire sequence. Five years of experience in several hundred classrooms in the schools of Jacksonville, Florida, in training teachers in these techniques and observing the results has convinced these authors of the values of these specific exercises. They do not prevent all reading failures, nor do all the children given extensive training always score high in reading. Reading success or failure is not determined by any such single factor in the child's experiences or backgrounds. But, like our colleagues in the other disciplines, we see young disadvantaged children given a better chance of school success when aided in this fashion.

TRAINING IN AUDITORY DISCRIMINATION

The purpose of auditory training in the readiness program is the development of the child's ability to hear similarities and differences in sounds. The ultimate goal

* Steven B. Greenspan, "Research Studies of Visual and Perceptual Motor Training," *Optometric Extension Program,* 44 (October 1971–August 1972), Duncan, Okla.: Optometric Extension Program Foundation; Lorena Porter, *Movement Education for Children* (Washington, D.C.: American Association of Elementary-Kindergarten-Nursery Education, 1969) and Margaret D. Robb, ed., *Foundations and Practices in Perceptual-Motor Learning A Quest for Understanding* (Washington, D.C.: American Association for Health, Physical Education and Recreation, 1971).

is, of course, preparation of the child for the auditory discriminations present in the word recognition process. Such discriminations are essential for effective use of letter sounds in word attack or phonics. Because of the obvious relationships of auditory training to the child's early training in phonics, some authors assume, logically enough, that the training should begin with attention to letter sounds as they occur in isolation or in whole words. This approach ignores the fact that there are auditory discriminations basic even to these that some pupils cannot make when they enter school. Some children cannot discriminate (although they may hear) differences in common sounds of widely varying pitch and loudness, much less make the fine distinctions among letter sounds.

The values of auditory training for reading achievement are demonstrated particularly by the experiments of Helen A. Murphy (34). All groups given training showed superior reading achievement, on the average, throughout successive tests in the first grade, except for one very low ability class which did not exceed its matched controls. In one study this superior reading achievement attributed to the auditory training was still present at the end of the second year in school. Training continued throughout the first year, as contrasted to that during the first semester only, showed very small differences in average reading achievement at the end of the first or second grade. Other outcomes noted by the teachers were greater success in sight reading early in the reading program, better listening skills, and increased comprehension. Murphy noted that sex differences in reading achievement were lessened among trained groups. In neither experiment, however, did all children benefit from these particular exercises, nor did all the trained children react with increased reading achievement.

Rosner, who has authored a training program in what he terms auditory analysis (45), was unsuccessful in producing accelerated reading for groups of kindergarten or preschool ages. However, he still considers this skill closely related to reading achievement. As we have pointed out in our discussion of auditory factors, discrimination training is probably essential only for programs that emphasize sound–symbol associations as the primary word recognition technique. The experiments of Murphy cited above appeared to be successful mainly because the reading programs stressed this auditory skill. The auditory training programs, it should be noted, were heavily loaded with phonics training. The senior author's finding that auditory discrimination tests were apparently good predictors of first-grade reading success (46) similarly reflects the nature of the reading program rather than the inherent value of such training for all primary children.

In another chapter we question the belief that intensive auditory discrimination training is so essential for dialect-speaking pupils who appear to lack this ability. Because of the variations in their enunciation of speech sounds from standard English, such children may not respond to or need the usual phonics program. Because they speak the dialect of their families and communities, they have perhaps not learned to hear the differences between sounds commonly demanded in phonics training. Nor is there strong evidence that dialect users really cannot learn to read well, or even to use some phonics as a minor aid to word recognition. In fact, there is the contradictory evidence that children from the white majority groups in various parts of our country also speak dialects, such as the Bostonian, the New England, the Southern, the Midwestern, and others. Yet most of these children learn to use phonics sufficiently for their purposes, even though they vary greatly in the enunciation of vowel sounds.

In our opinion, the most practical steps to help young children who speak any sort of dialect likely to interfere with reading, and who test poorly in auditory discrimination because of the dialectal variations, are as follows:

1. Accept the child's dialect just as you do his other individual traits, without criticism or constant correction.
2. Provide alternatives in standard English for his dialectal expressions casually, as you would in writing his language experience chart. Speak of these as simply other ways of saying a thought. Elicit these alternatives (as during a group language experience chart) from the rest of the class as often as you can. If they cannot supply any which approximate standard English, then offer several from which they may select one. Treat this activity as a game, not as an instructional procedure.
3. Provide as much opportunity for oral composition, playing roles, telling stories, and engaging in real or make-believe conversation as you can to build auditory memories of language. Play an active part yourself in these activities so as to provide a constant model of standard English (if you speak it) that the children will hear and, perhaps, imitate. Keep your language spontaneous and natural, not stilted and formal.
4. If the dialect does not greatly interfere, teach children the sounds of initial consonants and digraphs. Skip the endings, the inflectional forms, and the vowel sounds, all of which are often affected by dialect. Children can read and understand sentences containing these forms, even though they do not repeat them in their own speech or oral reading.
5. Teach your children, if they seem to be able to profit from it, to use the context and the sound of the initial letter or digraph as basic clues to word recognition. Do not attempt to teach blending or synthesis of sounds, or letter-by-letter phonic analysis, for all of these demand good auditory discrimination.
6. Remember that most of your pupils can learn to read to the limits of their potential, even though they speak a dialect, if you provide a reading program that emphasizes getting ideas from the printed page—not just letter sounds and word calling.

Provide other types of auditory training as outlined below for all your beginning pupils, omitting only those in auditory discrimination which are too demanding for pupils with dialectal speech and poor auditory discrimination.

Auditory Training Exercises

Dorothy B. Butt, adjunct professor of Jacksonville University, has made a detailed outline of auditory training activities. Space does not permit the reproduction of the entire outline, but we can describe briefly the sequence Butt has evolved and the auditory aids she recommends.

Auditory Training Activities

Auditory Awareness

1. Sounds of the earth—wind, thunder, rain, waves. Records: *Spook Stuff for Halloween,* MP-TV Services, Inc. *Spotlight on Sound Effects,* Pickwick International, Inc. Long Island City, N.Y. *Sounds Around Us,* Scott, Foresman and Co. *Listening Time Albums,* Webster Publishing. *Auditory Training,* Greystone Corporation. *Sounds for Young Readers,* Educational Record Sales.
2. Sounds of animals—birds, dogs, cats, ducks. Records: *Muffin in the City; Muffin in the Country; Noisy Book; Muffin at the Seashore,* E. M. Hale Company, Eau Claire, Wis. Pete Seeger—*Bought Me a Cat; Frog Went A Courtin; Jim Crack Corn; All Around the Kitchen; American Folk Songs for Children,* Folkways Records and Service Corp., New York. Burl Ives—*The Fox; Woolie Boogie Bee; Bluetail Fly,* Decca. Josef Marais—*Songs of the South African Veld; Stellenbosch Boys,* Decca. *Warbler's Serenade,* Victor Records. *The Whistler and His Dog,* Victor.
3. Man-made sounds—bouncing ball, crunching, cars, planes, trains, bells.
4. Varying inflections of a single word—*PLLLL-ease! PlEEEase! PleaSSe! Oh! OOOOh! OOOOOhhh!* Use also the story of the little engine, *Little Toot.*
5. Intensity of sounds—stamping versus tiptoe; loud and soft sounds of bell, clapping, closing door.
6. Pitch—contrasting high and low tones to show monotony and variation, alarm—reassurance, anger—pleasure. Use such stories as *Three Bears, Billy Goats Gruff.*
7. Duration and sequence—how successive sounds make music or words or sentences; contrast staccato rhythm with legato time; keeping time in skipping, marching, galloping; contrast short and long notes on piano; same with two or three syllable words exaggerating the accented syllable; imitating tapping sequences.
8. Quality—contrasting same tone on different rhythm instruments; resonance of tuning fork versus piano; using natural and disguised voices in games such as Who Said That?
9. Recognizing rhythm and rhyme—use a wide variety of poems, limericks, jingles, and rhymes from any good anthology of children's literature. See *Riddle-a-Rhyme,* Eye Gate House.

Auditory Perception

1. Experiential background—provide firsthand experiences through trips and visits.
2. Expressing sounds—provide opportunities for children to express the ways sound affects them in dances, rhythmic activity, tapping, finger snapping.
3. Alliteration—play with rhymes and jingles—*Lucy Locket; Hickory, Dickory, Dock; Baa-Baa Black Sheep;* use pictures cut out or drawn to show alliteration—pig in a

pen, house on a hill, boy on a bike; composite pictures to use for finding similarities and differences in sounds; games as Sound of the Day—children listen for or offer words with the sound of *b* as in *baa.*

Auditory Memory

1. Play echo game—children attempt to reproduce three tones (words or numbers) given by child behind screen.
2. Children repeat tapping pattern given by teacher.
3. Children attempt to follow one-, two-, and three-step directions.
4. Have children think sounds and tell or reproduce what they hear.
5. Play gossip game—one child whispers a sentence to his neighbor, who whispers it to his neighbor, who whispers it to his neighbor, etc.
6. Play the restaurant game—children choose foods from picture display, give orders to waiter, who must remember them and serve.

Auditory Discrimination

1. Draw attention to common sounds in and around the classroom, such as children walking or running, bells ringing, dogs barking, and the like. Encourage descriptions and comparisons by the children.
2. Have short listening periods for the pupils to identify sounds they hear. Use recordings such as *Sounds Around Us* (Scott, Foresman), *Listening Time Albums* (Webster), and recordings of poetry and children's stories. Or read selections to the group. Ask pupils to anticipate sounds in the records or words in the story.
3. With their eyes closed, have children identify noises you make such as tearing paper, tapping with pencil, snapping fingers, bouncing ball, etc.
4. Have one child imitate animal noises (big bear, little bear, angry bear) or human noises (father, mother, baby) while group tries to identify sources. Play same game using airport sounds, street sounds, farm sounds, train and automobile noises. Stress differences in pitch, loudness, and timbre.
5. Pronounce children's names, names of common objects, and actions letter by letter or syllable by syllable. Have children identify and indicate number of separate sounds.
6. As discrimination of pitch and loudness increases, introduce sounds of initial consonants. Draw attention to beginning sounds in pupils' names, classroom objects, pictured objects. Ask children to note similarities and differences and to make discriminations. Stress commonly recurring consonants such as *b, k* or hard *c, f,* hard *g, h, j, l, m, n, p, r, s, t, w;* speech blends *wh, ch, sh, th;* and consonant blends *fr, tr, br, st, pl, gr,* etc. Identify letter sound by its name (*m* has sound of the beginning of *Mary*) in dealing with single consonant sounds, but do not emphasize an isolated letter sound such as *muh.* Introduce blends by analogy with common sounds (*drip, splash, pulp, gr-r-r,* etc.) Use recordings such as *Let's Listen* (Ginn), *Listening Time Albums* (Webster), *Phonics for Children* (Audio-Education, American Book Co.).
7. Continue with auditory exercises on letter sounds as outlined in readiness workbooks or other easily available sources, such as Russell and Russell, and Spache.

8. Introduce concept of rhyming by riddles, jingles, nursery rhymes, and poetry. Permit children to suggest rhyming words for such selection.
9. Ask children to supply a rhyming word for a given word or to choose one of a given group that does not rhyme.
10. To sharpen discrimination, ask children to listen for similar sounds in the beginning, middle, or end of words. Again, use children's names, common objects and actions, and pictured objects. Proceed slowly, asking for discrimination of similarity or difference in only one area, as beginnings, at a time. Then move to a different area of a word as task is consistently accomplished correctly by group.
11. As the introduction to reading begins, emphasize the use of sounds to derive the word implied by the story, as in guessing the word you omit or the word that rhymes.

LANGUAGE TRAINING

A number of reports on the vocabularies of children entering school imply that the average child is familiar with at least several thousand words. He does not necessarily employ this number in his speech but recognizes them when he hears them and has meaningful associations for them. Since the child has this relatively large auditory vocabulary, it is apparent that he is auditorily familiar with most of the words, and hence the concepts, that are introduced in the vocabulary of the beginning readers. His primary language needs in the readiness period are not those of introduction to the words and concepts presented in the readers. Rather, he may need help in developing fluency, depth, and facility in the language patterns in which the basal reader concepts are to be presented. If the child speaks and thinks in monosyllables or fragments, he will have difficulty with the sentence and paragraph structure of beginning reading materials. Although basal readers are not noted for the depth of their content, the child must have more than rudimentary understanding of the words of the basal vocabulary if he is to become more than a mechanical word caller. The child's own output and language usage must be comparable to that found in the beginning reading materials or his intake will be severely limited.

Basically, language training in the readiness and early reading stages is based upon firsthand experiences with words and ideas through the medium of pictures, trips and excursions, story material, and games. A wide variety of such experiences broadens and deepens the child's language skills, thus ensuring a greater degree of success in the verbal task of reading.

Fluency

School beginners may exhibit a number of levels of fluency or expressiveness ranging from practically no response to a veritable flood of ideas. When the teacher uses such stimuli as a story, picture, or conversation, she may observe these variations in fluency:

1. Monosyllabic words, simple pointing or naming of objects in the picture, or even no response at all. Example: "Boy," "There's boy."
2. One or two short sentences, offering a simple description of the picture. Example: "Boy and girl are running. That's all."
3. Response to prompting questions, simple interpretation. Example: "The boy and girl are running a race."
4. Free, fluent response, perhaps with own story. Example: "One day a boy said, 'I can beat you.' . . ."
5. Reaction to teacher as well as the stimuli offered; evaluation of the picture or story, morals or conclusions. Example: "You know, girls shouldn't race boys because boys always win."

The school beginner's output and expressiveness can be stimulated in many ways by the alert teacher. She can ensure ample opportunity for each child to speak or take his turn in small-group work. Talking games, in which children take turns finishing a sentence or a story, played in a group of lesser fluency, provide excellent practice. Talking with the teacher about his own art work or some other familiar topic provides an opportunity for the child who is not sufficiently fluent for group games, or for participating in "Telling Time" or other audience situations. Face-to-face work with the teacher or a very small group may be preferable and less threatening for the child lacking in fluency.

Children who are reluctant to talk to an adult will often talk to a hand puppet. With this aid, they may be led to retell a story that has been read to them, or to offer an original playlet or dramatization of an actual incident they have experienced. Acting out the meanings of words, as verbs; labeling and classifying objects, pictures, and action; talking about the attributes, such as color, size, and use, are stimuli to growth in dealing with words or, in other words, with ideas (51, 52). The primary purpose of this training is to promote the child's ability to express his own thoughts and thus to grow in power of handling ideas. Many games and activities which will contribute to these language skills may be found in Russell and Russell, Spache, and other sources.

Sentence Structure

Children differ not only in the quantity and content of their language but also in the complexity of the patterns in which it is expressed. They may employ any of the following:

1. Monosyllables, simple nouns: "Boy."
2. Simple sentences with subject and one verb: "Boy runs."
3. Simple sentences with compound subject or predicate: "The boy and girl are running," or a run-on sentence: "The boy is running, the girl is running."
4. Compound or complex sentences: "The girl is running but the boy is beating her."
5. Complex sentences with more than one dependent clause: "The girl is running but I think the boy will win because boys can run faster."

There has been a development toward prepared oral language programs for primary pupils often imitating the procedures used in teaching English as a second language to adults. Many of these stress oral exercises in sentence patterns in varying, enlarging, and elaborating on simple expressions. Others suggest teaching pupils word order, word function, and other aspects of structural linguistics. We have referred to these programs in other parts of this text in discussing the effect of this training upon reading comprehension. We have serious doubts about the essentiality of such programs for dialectal speakers, or of the impact upon reading comprehension. Undoubtedly, some of these types of training would result in greater fluency in speech and increased ability to manipulate words to express ideas, and would perhaps help pupils move toward a greater use of standard English—all desirable goals. But to our knowledge there is no conclusive evidence that the formal programs in oral language and/or linguistics produce better reading comprehension. Nor do we see any justification for ignoring the individual differences present in a group of dialect speakers in the use of a preplanned program. As we have expressed our view before, dialect is not a real barrier to learning to read standard English nor is its eradication, assuming these programs can produce such an effect, a guarantee of success.

Auditory Comprehension

To a large degree, the child's use of more mature language patterns reflects the quality and complexity of the language to which he is exposed. We have already pointed out the significance of auditory comprehension as a predictor of early reading success. Growth in auditory comprehension can be markedly promoted by persistent efforts of the teacher. The sentences she uses in speaking with them, the directions she offers, the stories she reads to them, the reasoning demanded by the questions she asks—all help children to grow in comprehension of and development of sentence structure. While it is true that reading involves learning to recognize many words, success in word recognition is strongly dependent upon the child's sentence sense, his feeling for or expectation of the appropriate words for each idea or thought. Success in contextual analysis, as it is called, demands a sentence sense—a familiarity with the language patterns through which ideas are expressed. The child who truly reads does not simply name each word as he meets it, but having read the first few words, anticipates the rest of the thought. He logically expects certain words to occur next because they would follow the train of events or ideas. In anticipating the sentence pattern he helps himself to read an unknown or unfamiliar word because he senses the word which would be most logical. He has heard and reacted to similar patterns of language many times and, once he has acquired a reasonable sight vocabulary, readily makes the transition from listening to sentence patterns to reading sentence patterns.

The extent of thinking or reasoning the child does in listening is based upon the facts and relationships he is asked to report. In other words, depth of auditory comprehension is determined by the questions proposed by the teacher before she reads to the group, while she is reading, and after she has finished. It is important here to stress the significance of the pattern of comprehension established by the demands upon the child listener. One of the frequent criticisms of current early reading instruction is that it fails to promote creative, critical thinking among children. Teachers are apparently satisfied when children can simply parrot back the facts given. Seldom are children asked to answer such questions as "Why? What will happen next? Why will it happen? What will he do? What would you do? Why?" Or such reactions as "Why did the author write this story? What did he want to tell you? How did he expect you to feel? How did you feel?" are not demanded.

Auditory comprehension, or the child's ability to understand, retain, and reason about material he hears, can certainly be promoted by planned classroom activities. Answering questions on stories read by the teacher, or another child, or presented through records or tapes is, of course, the most obvious method of training auditory comprehension. Listening to and reacting to directions, explanations, descriptions, and conversations are other good training activities. Many appropriate games and activities are described in Russell and Russell's *Listening Aids Through the Grades* and other sources.

The aim of auditory comprehension training is not only to provide experiences with words, to deepen and broaden the child's knowledge of words or his auditory vocabulary. It provides these stimuli to language development to be sure, but even more significantly the training promotes the child's verbal reasoning, memory, critical thinking, and other intellectual processes. These are the processes he must employ in dealing with ideas encountered later in reading. These are the processes which underlie that rather vague ability, comprehension. Training in auditory comprehension is, in effect, training to think with words. For this reason, early skill in auditory comprehension is a good predictor of the child's later success in reading. For the same reason, training in auditory comprehension is one of the essential facets of the prereading and beginning reading stages of the child's development.

Articulation

Several aspects of the child's speech may militate against his success in reading if they are not corrected. Substitutions of one sound for another as *w* for *l*, and *d* for *th* (*dat* for *that*), baby talk, and stammering are among these handicaps. Correction of these speech difficulties is properly the work of the speech correctionist or therapist, but there is much that the teacher can do in the absence of professional help. The pattern of speech that the teacher herself exhibits to the children is an important influence. Individual help in correct formation of the proper sounds, the placement of the tongue and teeth for correct sound formation, is of primary value. These children will also need assistance in hearing the differences between their enunciation and the proper models. Simple recordings by disc or tape are useful in this effort. Then with correct use of speech mechanism and a proper auditory image of the desired sound the child is prepared for individual or small-group work. This may include such devices as choral reading and listening to and imitating jingles, poems, and rhymes that emphasize the sounds.

Since a number of speech sounds usually do not appear to be used correctly by many six- and seven-year-olds, but do develop later, speech correction efforts by the teacher should be approached cautiously. The advice of the school speech therapist should be used as a guide to the nature and amount of any training offered. Sometimes auditory training in hearing the differences among these late-appearing speech sounds, without much emphasis upon reproducing them, may be all that is desirable. As we have repeatedly pointed out, this type of training is necessary only if letter–sound discrimination is going to be stressed in subsequent reading lessons. Persistence of articulatory substitutions beyond primary ages is, however, a cause for concern and treatment, perhaps not so much for reading success as for social communication and self-concept.

READING CONCEPTS

There are fundamental concepts about books and pictures which children must acquire if they are to be successful in reading. Many of these concepts may be established early in the preschool years if children are given sufficient experiences with books. Among these concepts, the following are the most significant:

1. There is a directional orientation to book and pictures. The flow of ideas is from left to right, from top to bottom, or from the beginning of the book to the end.
2. Pictures and books tell stories. They suggest action and events which occur sequentially. The action seems to move from one picture to the next, from one page to the next. The action often evokes emotions in the reader or listener.
3. When reading, adults constantly use the same words or the same language patterns for each particular picture or page. They say the same thing each time they read the story. This story often may be remembered, particularly if it has rhythm or rhyme.
4. Sharing pictures and books with others is a pleasant experience. Stories can be told about the picture sequences. Other children react to these stories as the storyteller did.
5. Pictures and books stimulate their user to suggest ideas of his own, to react to them, to ask questions, and perhaps even to compose similar stories.
6. The words used to tell the story in a picture sequence or book are natural and familiar. They resemble the oral language one would be likely to use in telling the story. The words on the page are, in effect, talking written down.

These concepts can be built by firsthand experiences with books and pictures:

1. Ample opportunity to handle books in a library corner.
2. Helping to assemble a picture file organized under various headings; using this as a source for portraying stories, cartoons, and action sequences.

3. Making scrapbooks of pictures selected by the children to illustrate topics of interest to them; to tell a story.
4. Listening to stories and following the story by seeing the accompanying pictures.
5. Pictures on the bulletin board, changed each day or two after directed discussion.
6. Picture sequences (or picture books) which illustrate nursery rhymes.
7. Small-group discussion of pictures, books, and stories read by the teacher or a child.
8. Picture study as outlined in various readiness books and manuals.
9. Using films, filmstrips, or slides as a basis for storytelling and class discussion.
10. Sharing books from home by leaving them in the library corner, by telling or reading a story from them, or by lending them to other children.
11. Drawing picture sequences to illustrate a class trip or experience. These may be made into simple movies and used as a basis of sharing with other classes or to review together a pleasant group experience.
12. Labeling or writing on children's art work the interpretation they offer for the material.

A significant warning about training in reading concepts is implied in the studies of John Downing in England (16), Meltzer and Herse* in this country, and parallel studies in Canada. Interviews and observations of first graders show that these children often do not comprehend the terms the teacher uses. In listening to a tape or cutting up a sentence strip, many could not demonstrate that they understood what a letter, a sound, a word, a phoneme, a phrase, or a sentence really was. Teachers use these terms glibly, often assume that their pupils comprehend their meanings, and then attribute irrelevant or incorrect answers to inattention or mental dullness. Certainly teachers must ensure that children have concrete experiences with materials that represent these abstract terms (matching cutouts of letters, words, sentences, composing from letter or word cards, writing and editing their own stories, etc.) if the child is to understand this process of learning to read.

Downing has stressed the need for child understanding of the reading act in pointing out the marked relationship between confusion in these concepts and reading failure even beyond the primary levels (17). Of course, clarification of all these concepts will just be begun during the readiness period, for many of them become relevant only as the reading program advances. We are not suggesting teaching technical terms, such as word, sound, and the like, for this only leads to verbalism, parroting back to the teacher what she has just said. Rather, it is through actual experiences with reading materials, as suggested above, that beginning concepts of the reading act are conveyed.

Elsewhere we have suggested means of identifying the children who are in need of the training activities described here. It is apparent, however, that available tests and observation procedures do not always completely reveal each child's needs. For this reason, trials with the exercises outlined here, particularly in

* N. S. Meltzer and R. Herse, "The Boundaries of Written Words as Seen by First Graders," *Journal of Reading Behavior,* 1 (Summer 1969), 3–13.

visual perception and auditory discrimination, may be necessary for further diagnosis and final determination of individual and group needs. The time consumed by these trials may appear to be considerable, and some teachers (or administrators) may be concerned about the effects of the delay of the introduction to reading. But the ultimate success of children trained by these methods, and the elimination of reading failures caused by too rapid introduction of the reading act, more than compensate for any initial loss of time due to careful diagnosis and planning of the readiness program. Moreover, using the training exercises as supplementary diagnostic tools eliminates the obvious inefficiency inherent in offering all types of training to all pupils suggested by so many workbook-oriented readiness programs.

DISCUSSION QUESTIONS

1. How do the authors' concepts of a readiness program differ from those described earlier, or from those with which you are familiar?

2. Why do you suppose that it is suggested that the emphasis in readiness should be given to training in visual perception, auditory abilities, and language? Do you agree?

3. What other factors would you stress in a readiness program? Why?

4. Why do you think the authors do not suggest a variety of outdoor, large-muscle activities as essential to readiness?

5. What types of training outlined here do you believe might be helpful for primary pupils who make very poor progress in reading? Why?

REFERENCES

1. Allen, Ruth J., et al., "The Relationship of Readiness Factors to January First Grade Reading Achievement." Master's group thesis, Boston University, 1959.

2. Alley, G., et al., "Reading Readiness and the Frostig Training Program," *Exceptional Children,* 35 (September 1968), 68.

3. Arciszewski, Raymond A., "A Pilot Study of the Effects of Visual Perception Training and Intensive Phonics Training on the Visual Perception and Reading Ability of First Grade Students," paper presented at American Educational Research Association, New York, February 18, 1967.

4. Baskin, Jacquelyn White, "Teaching Reading to Older Mentally Handicapped Pupils," *Chicago Schools Journal,* 39 (January–February 1958), 152–153.

5. Beaupre, R. G., and Kennard, Ann, "An Investigation of Pre- and Post-Metropolitan Readiness Test

Scores for Differing Motor Education Programs," *Illinois School Research,* 5 (1968), 22–25.

6. Bernetta, Sister M., "Visual Readiness and Developmental Visual Perception for Reading," *Journal of Developmental Reading,* 5 (Winter 1962), 82–86.

7. Blakely, W. Paul, and Shadle, Erma M., "A Study of Two Readiness-for-Reading Programs in Kindergarten," *Elementary English,* 38 (November 1961), 502–505.

8. Bond, Guy L., and Dykstra, Robert, "The Cooperative Research Program in First-Grade Reading," *Reading Research Quarterly,* 2 (Summer 1967), 5–142.

9. Bradley, Beatrice E., "An Experimental Study of the Readiness Approach to Reading," *Elementary School Journal,* 56 (February 1956), 262–267.

10. Buckland, Paul, "The Effect of Visual Perception

Training on Reading Achievement of Low Readiness First Grade Pupils." Doctoral dissertation, University of Minnesota, 1969.

11. Cohen, R. R., "Remedial Training of First Grade Children with Visual Perceptual Retardation." Doctoral dissertation, University of California at Los Angeles, 1966.

12. Cohen, S. A., "Studies in Visual Perception and Reading in Disadvantaged Children," *Journal Learning Disabilities,* 2 (October 1969), 498–507.

13. Cox, Brian J., and Hambly, Lionel R., "Guided Development of Perceptual Skill of Visual Space as a Factor in the Achievement of Primary Grade Children," *American Journal of Optometry and Archives of the American Academy of Optometry,* 38 (August 1961), 433–444.

14. Delacato, Carl H., *Neurological Organization and Reading.* Springfield, Ill.: Charles C Thomas, 1966.

15. "The Doman–Delacato Treatment of Neurologically Handicapped Children," *Journal of Pediatrics* (May 1968), 750–752.

16. Downing, John A., "How Children Think About Reading," *Reading Teacher,* 23 (December 1969), 217–230.

17. Downing, John, "A Summary of Evidence Related to the Cognitive Clarity Theory of Reading," in *Diversity in Mature Reading: Theory and Research I*, Phil L. Nacke, ed. Twenty-second Yearbook National Reading Conference, 1973, 178–184.

18. Faustman, Marion N., "Some Effects of Perception Training in Kindergarten on First Grade Success in Reading," in *Perception and Reading,* Helen K. Smith, ed. Proceedings Annual Convention, International Reading Association, 12, no. 4 (1968), 99–101.

19. Fortenberry, Warren Dale, "An Investigation of the Effectiveness of the Frostig Program upon the Development of Visual Perception for Word Recognition of Culturally Disadvantaged First Grade Students." Doctoral dissertation, University of Southern Mississippi, 1968.

20. Frostig, Marianne, and Horne, David, *The Frostig Program for the Development of Visual Perception.* Chicago: Follett Publishing Co., 1964.

21. Glass, Gene V., and Robbins, Melvyn P., "A Critique of Experiments on the Role of Neurological Organization in Reading Performance," *Reading Research Quarterly,* 3 (Fall 1967), 5–52.

22. Goins, Jean T., *Visual Perceptual Abilities and Early Reading Progress,* Supplementary Educational Monographs, No. 87. Chicago: University of Chicago Press, 1958.

23. Grattau, Paul E., and Matin, Milton B., "Neuromuscular Coordination Versus Reading Ability," *American Journal of Optometry and Archives of American Academy of Optometry,* 42 (August 1965), 450–458.

24. Halgren, Marvin R., "Opus in See Sharp," *Education,* 81 (February 1961), 369–371.

25. Hinds, Lillian R., "Longitudinal Studies of Certain Visual Characteristics, Readiness and Success in Reading," *Reading in a Changing Society,* Proceedings Annual Convention, International Reading Association, 4 (1959), 84–86.

26. Hurst, W. A., "Vision and the Retarded Reader," *Canadian Teacher's Guide,* 10 (Winter 1960), 3, 7.

27. Iowa Elementary Teachers Handbook, II, *Reading.* Des Moines, Iowa: Department of Public Instruction, 1943, 34.

28. Jacobs, J. N., et al., "A Follow-up Evaluation of the Frostig Visual-Perceptual Training Program," *Educational Leadership Research Supplement,* 26 (1968), 169–175.

29. Junkins, Kathryn N., "The Construction and Evaluation of Exercises for Developing Visual Discrimination in Beginning Reading." Master's thesis, Boston University, 1940.

30. Kelley, Charles R., *Visual Screening and Child Development: The North Carolina Study.* Raleigh, N.C.: Department of Psychology, School of Education, North Carolina State College, 1957.

31. McCormick, C. C., et al., "The Effect of Perceptual-Motor Training on Reading Achievement," *Academic Therapy Quarterly,* 4 (1969), 171–176.

32. McCracken, Glenn, *The Right To Learn.* Chicago: Henry Regnery Co., 1959.

33. Muehl, Siegmar, "Effects of Visual Discrimination Training on Learning To Read a Vocabulary List in Kindergarten Children," *Journal of Educational Psychology,* 51 (August 1960), 217–221.

34. Murphy, Helen A., "An Evaluation of the Effect of Specific Training in Auditory and Visual Discrimination on Beginning Reading." Doctoral dissertation, Boston University, 1943.

35. Nila, Sister Mary, "Foundations of a Successful Reading Program," *Education,* 73 (May 1953), 543–555.

36. O'Donnell, P. A., "The Effects of Delacato Training on Reading Achievement and Visual–Motor Integra-

tion." Doctoral dissertation, Stanford University, 1969.

37. Optometric Extension Program, "Optometric Child Vision Care and Guidance," 37 (December 1964), Series 9. Duncan, Okla.: Optometric Extension Program Foundation.

38. Ploghoft, Milton H., "Do Reading Readiness Workbooks Promote Readiness?" *Elementary English,* 36 (October 1959), 424–426.

39. Powell, Marvin, and Parsley, Kenneth M., Jr., "The Relationships Between First Grade Reading Readiness and Second Grade Reading Achievement," *Journal of Educational Research,* 54 (February 1961), 229–233.

40. Pumfrey, P. D., and Anthony, D. A. S., "The Use of the Frostig Programme for the Development of Visual Perception with Children Attending a Residential School," personal communication from the authors, 1972, from University of Manchester, Manchester, England.

41. Rice, Arthur H., "Rhythmic Training and Body Balancing Prepare Child for Formal Learning," *Nation's Schools,* 69 (February 1962), 2–11.

42. Riesen, A. H., "The Development of Visual Perception in Man and Chimpanzee," *Science,* 106 (August 1947), 107–108.

43. Robbins, Melvin Paul, "The Delacato Interpretation of Neurological Organization," *Reading Research Quarterly,* 1 (Spring 1966), 57–78.

44. Rosen, Carl L., "An Experimental Study of Visual Perceptual Training and Reading Achievement in First Grade," *Perceptual and Motor Skills,* 22 (1966), 979–986.

45. Rosner, Jerome, "Auditory Analysis Training with Pre-Readers," *Reading Teacher,* 27 (January 1974), 379–384.

46. Spache, George D., *The Teaching of Reading.* Bloomington, Ind.: Phi Delta Kappa Educational Foundation, 1972.

47. Spache, George D., Andres, Micaela C., and Curtis, H. A., et al., *A Longitudinal First Grade Reading Readiness Program.* Cooperative Research Project No. 2742. Tallahassee, Fla.: Florida State Department of Education, 1965.

48. Staats, Carolyn K., Staats, Arthur W., and Schutz, Richard E., "The Effects of Discrimination Pretraining on Textual Behavior," *Journal of Educational Psychology,* 53 (February 1962), 32–37.

49. Stanchfield, Jo M., "The Development of Pre-Reading Skills in an Experimental Kindergarten Program," *Elementary School Journal,* 71 (May 1971), 438–447.

50. Stone, M., and Pielstick, N. L., "Effectiveness of the Delacato Treatment with Kindergarten Children," *Psychology in the Schools,* 6 (1969), 63–68.

51. Vukelich, Carol, and Matthais, Margaret, "A Language Process for Use with Disadvantaged Children," *Elementary English,* 51 (January 1974), 119–124.

52. Yawkey, Thomas D., Aronin, Eugene L., Street, Michael A., and Hinjosa, Olga M., "Teaching Oral Language to Young Mexican-Americans," *Elementary English,* 51 (February 1974), 198–202.

53. Wingert, Roger C., "Evaluation of a Readiness Training Program," *Reading Teacher,* 22 (January 1969), 325–328.

54. Young, Lula Mae, Kane, Burton M., et al., *Marion Hill School Motor Coordination–Visual Perception Study.* Duncan, Okla.: Optometric Extension Program, 1971.

RESOURCES FOR THE TEACHER

Bryngelson, Bryng, and Mikalson, Elaine, *Speech Correction Through Listening.* Chicago: Scott, Foresman and Company, 1962.

Games and Self-Testing Activities for the Classroom. Washington, D.C.: Government Printing Office, 1961.

Getman, G. N., Kane, Elmer R., Halgren, Marvin R., and McKee, Gordon W., *Developing Learning Readiness.* Manchester, Mo.: Webster Publishing Company, 1968.

Henderson, Lillian R., *Lesson Plans for Use of Geometric Shapes in Perceptual Training.* The Author: Box 6, Pablo Island, Groveland, Florida 32736.

Ilg, Frances L., and Ames, Louise Bates, *School Readiness.* New York: Harper & Row, Inc., 1965.

Kephart, Newell C., *The Slow Learner in the Classroom.* Columbus, Ohio: Charles E. Merrill Publishing Company, 1960.

Manual of Primary Perceptual Training. Johnstown, Penna.: Mafex, Inc., 1971.

Motor Perceptual Handbook. La Porte, Tex.: Perceptual Development Research Associates, 1969.

Perceptual Training: Teacher's Manual. Winter Haven, Fla.: Winter Haven Lions' Research Foundation.

Radler, D. H., and Kephart, Newell C., *Success*

Through Play. New York: Harper & Row, Inc., 1960.

Robb, Margaret D., ed. *Foundations and Practices in Perceptual-Motor Learning: A Quest for Understanding.* Washington, D.C.: American Association for Health, Physical Education and Recreation, 1971.

Russell, David H., and Karp, Etta E., *Reading Aids Through the Grades.* New York: Teachers College Press, 1951.

Russell, David H., and Russell, Elizabeth F., *Listening Aids Through the Grades.* New York: Teachers College Press, 1959.

Spache, Evelyn B., *Reading Activities for Child Involvement.* Boston: Allyn and Bacon, Inc., 1976.

Van Witsen, Betty, *Perceptual Training Activities Handbook.* New York: Teachers College Press, 1967.

8
The Combined Program for Primary Grades

PREVIEW

It is apparent that the authors' concept of a reading program is not one that is carefully prescribed with daily plans that are supposed to fit all situations. If we believed this, we would have spent our time in preparing a basal reading series. Rather, we believe that the effective reading program is a flexible instrument based on what is clearly demonstrated by the research on reading instruction.

A good reading program shows that degree of individualization that is possible within the framework of the teacher's planning and organizing capacities. It is not determined by the materials provided by the state, nor can it be prescribed exercise by exercise, skill by skill, as many reading experts believe. The variety of learning activities and teacher-made materials, the possibility of differentiation into small groups, and the needs of the particular class are the true determinants of a reading program.

In her teaching, the good teacher brings to bear everything she knows about child development, learning, and materials. She combines these elements into a program which meets the needs of every pupil, insofar as her experience and skill in teaching permit.

Constance M. McCullough has said*:

Much of the knowledge we now have about the teaching of reading has been developed by a curious and—in terms of the lives of students—wasteful pattern of extremes. We learned a great deal about oral reading by having too much of it, about silent reading by neglecting oral reading, about extensive reading by neglecting intensive reading, about sight vocabulary by neglecting phonics, about phonics and speed by neglecting comprehension. . . . One would think that it should finally have dawned on us that all of these practices have value and that the sensible, most efficient program encompasses them all.

The purpose of the earlier reviews of various approaches to beginning reading was to point out their strengths and weaknesses. Now we shall presume to offer a combined approach which will avoid the flaws and build on the advantages of each. As the reader will soon recognize, ours is not, strictly speaking, a new approach but an attempt to capitalize on the strengths of other methods and to avoid their weaknesses. All the techniques that we shall suggest have been used before by teachers who were prone to experiment. Our contribution consists of the emphasis, rationale, and justification we shall offer for these techniques, as well as an organizational plan within which they may operate.

READINESS FOR READING

Our concept of readiness implies a pacing of the introduction to beginning reading according to the child's abilities to profit. By observation, readiness tests, and evaluation of the child's development in vision, speech, listening, and social and emotional factors, the teacher decides when an introduction to formal reading is appropriate. Depending upon her diagnostic judgments, the teacher delays reading instruction for varying periods of time for different pupils. Meanwhile she offers preparatory training in directionality, ocular motility, form perception, auditory discrimination, language fluency, oral language, and auditory comprehension as well as articulation and reading concepts, as pupils evidence their needs. With repeated observations she notes the increasing skill with which various pupils handle these fundamental exercises and their decreasing need for continued readiness training. At intervals she permits these rapidly developing pupils to participate in the reading activities of the class and notes their successes. With

* Constance M. McCullough, "Individualized Reading," *NEA Journal,* 47 (March 1958), 163.

these observations as a basis she arranges for some of these pupils to join the type of group reading for which they appear ready. For certain pupils she will continue to offer visual, auditory, language, or speech training because of their needs and in order to ensure their success in beginning reading. Thus, as they demonstrate the ability to participate successfully in simple reading activities, first graders will be introduced to beginning reading.

The reader will note the lack of reference to a formal readiness program such as that commonly offered in readiness workbooks. In our opinion such workbooks do not, and cannot, accomplish their avowed purpose of providing essential prereading training for most pupils. Their treatment of the important readiness traits is too brief, too superficial, and too stereotyped to serve the needs of any large number of pupils. As we have pointed out earlier, there is little evidence of the validity of the workbook, even if we did believe that readiness for most pupils could be achieved within a set period of time. Readiness implies development, and development differs significantly among individuals.

Rather, a wide variety of workbook-type exercises, whether drawn from commercial sources or teacher-made, will be an essential aid in several readiness areas, as well as later development of reading skills. There are a number of collections or kits of these materials available mentioned in the chapter bibliography. If desired, the expense of these can be avoided by the construction of the teacher's own kits of materials, an approach we think permits more flexibility and relevance to the teacher's own goals and procedures. The construction of this kit is described in detail in *Reading Activities for Child Involvement* by Evelyn B. Spache (Boston: Allyn and Bacon, Inc., 1976). Briefly stated, the kit is made by selecting exercises from a variety of sources, and other collections like the Wagner and Hosier book mentioned in the bibliography. Exercises of different types or workbook pages which, preferably, present a single exercise are collected, collated in a rough order of difficulty, color coded according to their type, and placed in a convenient box. Acetate folders are made available in which the exercise is placed, as the child indicates his answers by a crayon or felt-tip pen. If desired, pages may be mounted permanently in the acetate folders. After the child has completed an exercise, he checks it with an answer key in the file, removes his writing from the acetate by a moist tissue, and replaces the material in its proper place, as indicated by color coding. To construct such a kit, the teacher will need a plan for the sequence of exercises, such as that offered later in this book in the areas of phonics and structural and contextual analysis. With this approach, a teacher can provide training in depth for any specific skill for any child in accordance with his needs.

BEGINNING READING

We suggest that the introduction to reading occur through the medium of experience charts. For those unfamiliar with this term, an experience chart is an original composition arising from children's common experiences. With the help and guidance of the teacher, the group or child composes materials based on a trip, the weather, a holiday, a greeting, a message, classroom rules, and the like.

We suggest that experience charts constitute the beginning reading program for at least several months, or until the pupils demonstrate sufficient reading vocabulary to read independently. Some pupils, of course, are ready to read when they enter school and should be permitted to do so. But they should also participate in the group work in composing experience charts. As we have implied, experience chart work would continue throughout the primary grades.

In addition to providing reading materials of timely and interesting nature, the chart approach serves a number of other functions. The child's first experiences in composing and learning to read a chart provide opportunities for judging his readiness for reading instruction. His difficulties with directionality, word discrimination, recall of words, his fluency and sentence structure, and his concepts of the reading act are manifest in these early trials at reading.

It is also probable that by its very nature the language experience technique makes a real contribution to clarifying the child's concepts of the reading process. It may thus help avoid the confusions about such terms as word, sentence, letter, sound, and about what goes on when one reads that John Downing (4) and Meltzer and Herse (17) have shown to be so prevalent. The act of composing, writing, editing, rewriting, and arranging stories in book format, followed by the use of these materials for a variety of word recognition and word analysis activities—all of which are part of this approach—should obviate these difficulties that arise from other methods of instruction.

When the reading materials are the child's very own experiences, the concept that written or printed words convey meaning is inherent. With this approach, we may be able to avoid the naive interpretation of the reading act present in these quotes from intermediate-grade children about reading (13):

a book. If you don't know the words, sound them out.

when you see a group of words in a sentence

something you do from books

words have names and they have certain letters you look at the letters and you put them together and you read a whole bunch of words together

when you say a whole bunch of words

Some idea of the nature and composition of these charts may be gained from the following samples.

I saw a sun
in the sky.
It was hot
up there.

Hot.
hot up there.

THE RESTROOM

The restroom smells
like a skunk when it has
been disinfected. But when
it has worn off it
smells better.

Two little monkeys, jumping on a bed.
One fell off and hurt his head.
The other called the Doctor
And the Doctor said.
"That's what you get for jumping on beds."

Once upon a time
I found a shiny dime.
I tried to make a rhyme
About my shiny dime.
But before I made the rhyme
I lost my shiny dime.

MY FISHY

I have a little fishy,
And her name is Mishy.
She swims around
in a little dishy.

Children's stories are a natural source for skill development. Most compositions contain word endings, compound words, descriptive words and phrases, action words, long and short vowels, and the like.

There was a little wild canary outside who flew into our room because it
was raining. It fluttered around the room in two circles then flew straight
into the blackboard. Down he went! Our teacher put him in a box to keep
him warm. When we were at reading she let him fly far away. The canary
was green, yellow, and it had orange feet, too.

Elizabeth Olsen

HURRICANE GLADYS

On October 19th, Hurricane Gladys came into Jacksonville Beach. It didn't
do much damage—just blew a lot of fronds off palm trees. The elec-
tricity went out a few times so many people went outside to look at the
neighborhood.

Ricky Pettis

Other compositions are rich in words that tell what, how, when, and name substitutes (I, his, mother, him, she, my), and words to express feelings (scared, sorry).

I hit John with a rock
yesterday.
Blood came out of his
head.
Boy was I scared!
His mother said I had
to tell him I was sorry.
Shucks. She didn't have
to do that.
John's my best friend.
I WAS sorry!

Charts are composed in connection with special days or seasonal changes.

AN EASTER BUNNY

Once there was an Easter bunny,
He came out when days were sunny.
Long pink ears and funny legs.
He delivered Easter eggs.
Around the bushes and in the trees,
And around the houses where nobody sees.
Some are pink and some are blue.
And some are even just for you.

WALKING THROUGH THE WOODS

When we were walking thru the woods we took our magnifying glass and
our butterfly net. We looked at some berries under the magnifying glass.
We saw different kinds of tree bark under the magnifying glass too. When
we were walking through the woods a black cat kept following us. Her
name was Muchacha.

THE ORANGE CITY

The sun was shining in the blue sky. An old witch and a cat came and sat
on the boat. The bats started to fly around them. A ghost spreaded his
arms and legs out and frighten the witch. The witch banged her pumpkin
down, and everything turned orange, even the dog. From that time on ev-
erything was orange.

A group composition fully explains the recipe for preparing the Thanksgiving turkey.

Kill the turkey.
Chop off its head.
Take out the blood, guts and heart.
.Pull out the feathers.
Put him in a pan.
Pour on salt, pepper and sauce.

Put him in the oven.
Take him out.
Carve the turkey.
Put it on the table.
Pour the Kool-Aid.
Say a prayer of thank-you.
Then eat!

A graduate student, observing in a fourth-grade class, found this note left for her:

TO THE NICE LADY

I hope you will come back before school is out because I like you a lot you is very nice. I like ti when you said I can read well because no one never said I can read well I don't think and I love everybody and I hope to see you soon again.

yours Iruely,

Children collaborated on this story:

How old is Miss Pippin?
Joan says she's 15.
But Mark says "No!
My sister is younger and
she's 15."
"She's not married so she
can't be very old" says Alan.
"I think she's 79," said Mark.
"Ha-ha-ha," we all laughed.

A first-grade repeater who could seldom remember any written word read this personalized story to his principal two days after it was recorded on the back of his drawing of a hot rod.

I brung my toy.
I brung my hot rod.
And I don't want nobody
to touch it!

Simple charts for following directions:

To feed the fish we:
1. Get the food from the shelf.
2. Open the box.
3. Shake it 3 times over the fish.
4. Close the box.
5. Return the box to the shelf.

To feed the birds we will bring:
  Apple—Maryanne
  Raisins—Margaret
  Chopped nuts—Carl
  Corn—George
  Stale bread—Jane and Nancy
  Pumpkin seeds—Nina

We will:
  LISTEN for their kind of talk
  WATCH what they do
  SEE what kinds come
  LOOK UP pictures of them

Classification charts (may be illustrated):

Words for Halloween
  pumpkin
  jack-o-lantern
  black cat
  witch
  broomstick
  trick-or-treat
  costume

Observation charts:

Watch our beans grow
  Mar. 2—We planted the seeds in cups.
  Mar. 10—We can see the sprouts.
  Mar. 12—The sprouts have leaves.
  Mar. 16—We planted them outdoors.
  Now we must care for them every day.
  Soon we will have beans to eat.

Kaper charts:

We all do our share
  Messenger—Jean
  Librarian—Ann
  Gardener—Stephen
  Aquarium—Della
  Host or hostess—George

Display charts (with realia attached):

THE MYSTERY TOOTH

This tooth was found by Ray.
He found it at Sandy Bluff.

What kind is it?
How can we get more information?

The following story was painstakingly typed by a sixth-grade eleven-year-old from a Mexican-American family.

THis IS for when I get my check.
I am to post to do this with my check.
Pay 7 dollers on my tapereqrter. That leves 12

$$\begin{array}{r} 12 \\ -7 \\ \hline 5 \end{array}$$

IAM going to spen 2 dollers on my family.
I have left.

$$\begin{array}{r} 5 \\ -2 \\ \hline 3 \end{array}$$

I will give my Ma Ma 1 doller. And I will give my Daddy 50¢. And I will give baby 25¢ each.
Buy Mrs. Mc something. And spen the writ for me. Andy Maybe buy my Mama a bannan spit.
xx xxandx
By Angel Flores

To aid this very poor family, the principal had arranged a job for the boy with specific duties around the school. This plan, the boy's first real attempt at composition, was typed in the office in anticipation of his first weekly check. Unfortunately for the boy's progress in English, this school did not employ the language experience method.

THE METHOD

The younger child's first compositions are usually told to the teacher, who writes or types them directly. This is to prevent the mechanics of writing or typing from hindering the fluency of the child's contribution. Later, the material is often written by hand or typewritten by the child himself, unless it is apparent that these methods of reproduction interfere with the child's expression. Best results are obtained if the processes of composition and reproduction are distributed over a number of sessions and alternated with varied uses of the child-made materials.

The experience charts may be the initial reading materials, as we suggest, supplanting the usual basal readers. This program is distinctly preferable for a number of reasons. Unlike most preprimers, charts provide interesting, varied reading materials which resemble the language forms and structures already known to the children. The direct connection between reading and other forms of language activity is made obvious to the children, for they see the very words they have spoken written on paper. The chart approach makes realistic use of the pupils' auditory memories for speech, and promotes the set toward thought getting from printed words. A feeling for sentence structure and sequence is fostered as well as the habit of reading from left to right. Word recognition, comparison, and discrimination are promoted by the fact that the children see their words take form as they are written. In contrast to the content of the basal reader, the experience chart is real, familiar, concrete, and spontaneous.

This approach to beginning reading through the experience chart capitalizes upon the strongest value of the technique. It equates reading progress with the child's verbal skills in a realistic fashion. Certainly no child can learn to read faster than his own auditory and speaking vocabularies permit. This limitation is truly recognized most clearly in the experience chart or language experience approach. The reading materials the child uses are created out of his own language backgrounds and daily experiences. Each child learns to read the very words he knows best from his auditory and speaking experiences.

The experience chart approach is functional not only for average children but is particularly appropriate for children with language handicaps. The bilingual child who may have heard and spoken a language other than English during much of his preschool years, the child with delayed language development because of isolation, timidity, or cultural difference, the child who comes from a home that employs nonstandard English or a marked dialect—all these benefit markedly from the realism of the experience chart approach to reading. As studies show when taught by this approach, these children show increased reading achievement and interest, more rapid development of vocabulary in speaking, reading, writing, and listening, and early development of independence in using such aids as the dictionary and reference books.

As children mature in their ability to compose independently, a number of other values appear in the use of the language experience chart. A graduate student of the authors, Carolyn Hendrix, has offered a number of observations on her employment of the child's compositions in understanding their personal problems. These are the provocative titles for such efforts, and some of her pertinent comments:

> *"What I Think Heaven Is Like"*—seems to be a subject that draws out the child's wants and needs; and often the thing he misses most in his home life will be present in his description of heaven.
> *"The Way I Feel on Dark, Rainy Days"*—a subject to find causes of moodiness (on an appropriate day).
> *"The First Thing I Remember"*—brings forth some very interesting memories.
> *"The Reason I Like My Best Friend"*—helps children realize the qualities they like in others and want to develop in themselves.
> *"Why I Am Happy"*—often reflects a picture of home life.
> *"Why I Am Sad"*—is also often a picture of the child's home life.
> *"Ten Rules for Mother and Daddy"*—may provide a very interesting insight into parent–child relationships.
> *"What I Want Most To Do When I Grow Up"*—a discussion before this

paper can lead it to be more than a simple description of occupational
goals, for there are other aims in life than simply vocational goals.

"If I Were a Turkey"—is usually done at some time near Thanksgiving,
again to reflect child's needs and wants.

"What Makes Me Bad?"—an obviously leading subject.

"My New Year's Resolutions"—excellent for revealing children's
feelings about right and wrong, and their consciousness of their own
shortcomings.

"The World I Live In"—may be used following a discussion of moon, stars,
and space, as an imaginary conversation with one we might find on
another planet. Also reflects the child's view of his world.

Other story starters are:

"People should remember that . . ."—may show insight into actions of
people which bother the child that may not fit into a particular category.

"If I could go to . . ."—may lead to some research on places of interest
locally or perhaps foreign countries.

"I was calmly waiting for my friend, when suddenly . . ."—opens the mind
to try an action-packed account of an imaginary event.

"If I had only known . . ."—may release some guilt feelings, or help him
(or the teacher) to make better plans for future events.

Another aid to stimulate use of descriptive terms is to introduce metaphors,
explaining that a metaphor makes something more real by giving it live action,
even though it is not alive. Children can supply the nouns or objects, then supply
some action words. These words can be combined into sentences or incorporated
into stories.

Inanimate Nouns	Metaphors
furnace	lick, burped, belched, gobbled, ate, sizzled
truck	leaped, slid, skip, purr
light	bounced, flitted, filtered, danced
limbs	claw, snap, scratched, tore, clung
floor	jerked, swam, slanted
radiator	paled, brightened, flirted

Examples:
The limbs clawed and scratched at me as I ran. The old truck burped,
leaped, and slid, then purred down the road.

The ability to react to these provocative story titles will, of course, reflect the
maturity of the pupils. We would not expect first graders, for example, to offer very
long compositions or to show deep self-insights as a result of these stimuli. Second
or third graders, or older children, are more likely to react in depth in their
compositions. But subjects dealing with the feelings about self, the family, friends,
one's future, and the like can be used with children of any school age to enable us

to gain insight into the child's self-concept. This is another way of learning more about each child as an individual in order that we may relate to him more effectively.

The language experience approach has many mental hygiene advantages, often lacking in other reading methods. It fosters an informal, helping relationship between teacher and pupil, as we aid children to get their ideas on paper. Working this closely together promotes personal, physical contact with the pupil, again reassuring him of our liking for him as a person. The frequent use of children's stories by other pupils strengthens the child's positive self-concept as a worthy member of the group, because of the peer recognition of his contributions. Hence, our emphasis upon the constant sharing of each child's compositions with others has many different advantages. Through the child's stories and drawings, we gain insights into his likes, dislikes, fears, family, and sibling relations. His feelings of restriction or freedom are also manifest in the size and placement of his drawings on the page, and the length and fluency of his stories. Sharing of one another's chart stories, working together in pupil teams, using children of other races and other lands as subjects of compositions about such topics as homes, schools, and families around the world have mental hygiene implications. Feelings about other races, prejudices, and misconceptions can be affected through the language experience medium to a far greater degree than in most other methods, if the teacher provides the appropriate resource materials, stimulating story titles, and classroom climate.

The curiosity of the child is increased by his participation in the firsthand experiences arranged by the teacher in nature study, science, social studies, community life, etc. This observation is supported by the results of studies which show the superior test performances of these pupils in these areas, by the third grade. Second, the teacher does not constantly dominate the classroom with lecturing at children, thus reducing their opportunities for learning by discovery as well as their ultimate academic achievement. Other strengths are the actual transcription of talking into writing, an essential realization by pupils for true progress in reading, and the strengthening of recall of words by the feedback through auditory and visual media, as the chart story is read aloud to others.

General principles to guide the teacher in the preparation of experience charts are:

1. Charts should be done in manuscript with words clearly spaced. A dark crayon or felt-tip pen is probably best for visibility.
2. The chart can be any size. If the story is only a sentence or two, 12- by 18-inch drawing paper is sufficient. For longer stories 24- by 36-inch chart paper is best.
3. Lettering should be large—capitals double-spaced (two inches) and lowercase single-spaced (one inch).
4. The actual story may be written on anything, as chart paper is not often handy when a spontaneous story erupts; later the story can be rewritten on chart paper.
5. The story should be written as the child relates it. In the beginning stages of this approach, errors in grammar or sentence structure should not be corrected.

6. The words should be visible to the child, or children, as the teacher writes them. A left-to-right direction should be emphasized by moving the pointer or hand to guide the pupil's rereading. The return sweep to the next line should be similarly pointed out.
7. When rewriting the story, the teacher may want to question the child as to which event happened first, next, or later and rearrange some sentences to show sequence of events.
8. The teacher should help the child realize when good stopping points arrive in his story to complete a sentence, and take advantage of natural breaks in phrasing.

In the 1930s there was considerable debate about the values of manuscript versus cursive writing for beginning readers. Eventually, the research both in this country and England demonstrated the superiority of manuscript for legibility, for promoting reading because of its similarity to printed words, for individuality in writing style, and its lesser demands for fine coordination in the writing act. The arguments that it was slower than cursive, unacceptable in business as a legal signature, or that it prevented children from learning to read cursive were readily disproved. Manuscript writing has persisted in use in the early grades in many school systems (11). But the tendency to discard it in favor of cursive as soon as possible, as after perhaps only a year or so, is quite common. To remind school systems of its basic values, Eve Malmquist (15) has reported a series of studies in the schools of Sweden. He shows that when introduction to cursive was delayed until the latter half of the third grade, children using manuscript were superior in silent comprehension, clearer and more legible in handwriting, and better in spelling for the whole three-year period. The delay until the second half of the third grade, instead of the current practice of changing the mode in the latter part of the first or second year, did not interfere with learning cursive as well as that done by those who changed over earlier.

We illustrated many types of experience charts earlier, but this list may serve as a quick reminder of the variety possible.

Chart of Charts

1. Picture story	Child draws picture, dictates one or two sentences about it. Teacher writes sentences and attaches them to picture.
2. Sharing	One of the sharing stories told by the children is selected by group and retold for chart. Group may jointly or alternately contribute to this story.
3. Seasonal	Rhymes, slogans, greetings appropriate to holidays or season are used; may include short stories about the weather, season, calendar.
4. Instructions	Lists children's rules for lunchroom, for listening behavior, for fire drill, etc.

5. Kaper	Includes step-by-step directions for classroom duties, as care of chalkboard, feeding fish or animals; to be read by child chosen for each duty.
6. Classification	Employs vocabulary lists of concrete (not abstract) words children need for their stories; spelling words needed, etc.
7. Informational	Centers around steps in science experiments, nature study; social science materials (with context).
8. Phonics	Key words for consonant or vowel sounds, supplied by the *children,* with or without illustrative pictures; same for blends, phonograms, syllables, roots, and affixes.
9. Display	Shells, rocks, insects, leaves mounted and accompanied by identifying words, phrases, or labels.
10. Letters	Letters written to another class, an absentee, an author, to express thanks, regrets, or other communication; may be composed in individual or group session. For older children, provide model of letter noting address, salutation, body, close, punctuation, etc.
11. Maps	Includes maps of playground, school, home, classroom, community, town, state, appropriately labeled.
12. Time lines	Uses listing of school holidays, children's birthdays, school events, or those related to social science units.
13. Phonics	Words in stories containing any designated phonic element may be identified; copied in classified lists; read aloud to another pupil to demonstrate control of the phoneme or morpheme; used in initial consonant substitution exercises or as illustrative words in the teacher's lesson on an element.
14. Structural analysis	Compound words, words with specific endings, prefixes or suffixes, syllables or phonograms, may be identified by the children and used as the material for a variety of exercises and teaching approaches.
15. English mechanics	Before transferring his handwritten story from the paper to a large chart that others may also read, or before binding them into a book of stories, the child should be helped to edit his punctuation and spelling. He can gradually learn to do much of this editing himself with the aid of a picture dictionary, or his buddy or helper, or his word bank. Children's stories are at first written exactly as dictated without censorship. However, in the writing, endings, spelling, and punctuation are used as in standard English, without particular emphasis. Later, alternative expressions and appropriate idioms are offered as "other ways of saying that," inserted in the dictated story between lines to be read or not by the child, as he chooses. This editing is not present in the initial efforts of the child,

since it may interfere with his spontaneity and recognition that you are writing exactly what he says.

These are a few of the activities by which experience charts may be directed toward skill development.

Some Ways of Using Experience Charts

1. Small-group reading	Each child may read a part of the chart (that portion he contributed or another part). In the group, a child may share his chart with the others by reading to them.
2. Individual reading	Charts may be read to oneself, to a buddy or helper, or to the teacher during a conference.
3. Sequence strips	Cut copy of chart into strips, each one line long. Child reassembles chart by arranging strips in sequence, then reads.
	Draw sentences from large, illustrated shopping bag. Use strips from different charts. Child goes to chart and matches strip, then reads it. Child separates strips and assembles them in proper story sequence for each story. Use also sentence strips depicting action: Roar like a lion, cry like a baby. Child reads and enacts action.
4. Word discrimination	All the words of a chart are written on small cards. Child reassembles entire chart, word by word, then reads. Words may be filed by placing them in an envelope stapled to the chart. New stories may be made using the word cards.
	Draw words from a large pumpkin, Santa's sack, etc. Match each word to those in a chart nearby. Group takes turns drawing cards.
5. Copying charts	Small-group or individual charts may be recopied by the child, with an illustration. Chart should be one composed by the children, not one phrased by the teacher for handwriting drill.
6. Story book	Collections of child's or group's charts are brought together into a booklet with illustrations. This story book may be read by child to himself, to group, to another class, to teacher, to parent. Stories may be duplicated and copies of books placed in the classroom library.
7. Movies	Series of related charts depicting the events of a story are taped together in one long strip. The strip is mounted on dowels and drawn past opening in a large box, while group takes turns narrating story.

Components of the Program

Among the major elements of a language experience program are:

1. Dictating to teacher.
2. Listening to stories and content material daily.
3. Discussing common experiences.
4. Sharing personal versions of common experiences.
5. Constructing group charts (with labeling by child's name in color of each child's contribution).
6. Writing stories independently.
7. Compiling individual stories on a common topic in a book to be placed in the classroom library.
8. Compiling a child's own stories in a book, suitably inscribed to be read to other classes or to parents or to be taped for others to listen to while they attempt to read.
9. Using resource books, pictures, and other audiovisual aids for information to be incorporated in one's own stories; include books on animals, other lands, nature study, simple science, picture dictionaries, etc.
10. Supplying art and construction materials for preparing charts, murals, dioramas, models, etc., to illustrate a story.
11. Providing charts of words to aid in spelling—on current themes, holidays, hard words, interesting words, and the like.
12. Preparing collections of narrative and informational books, poems, records, filmstrips, word recognition games, and constantly replenishing the classroom library.
13. Arranging work centers in the classroom for art, library, music, construction, science, and nature study materials.
14. Using the vocabulary of the stories as a basis for training in many significant skills.
15. Promoting individual vocabulary development by use of a card-file word bank.

It is apparent from the variety of activities suggested above that a primary goal of the language experience approach is the development of the child's language by speaking, writing, and reading. We firmly believe that progress in early reading is promoted by exercise of all these media of expression, not by reading alone.

Genevieve S. Lopardo (14) prepares a cloze version of her children's stories after they have been read several times. By removing every fifth or tenth word, and asking the children to fill in the missing words, this teacher finds that quicker word recognition, particularly of structural words, is stimulated.

Ross (23) uses cutouts and a flannelboard to tell a story to a child or a group and then asks one to tell the story or one of their own using the board. The story told by the child is copied exactly as he delivers it. If the child is a poor reader, he is asked to underline the words he knows in the written story. Then teacher and child read together, with the child reading those words he has underlined. With children lacking in fluency or self-confidence this supportive variation should be very helpful. Smith and Morgan (26) have shown that simply having children record their stories on tape, which were then typed and placed in their folder to be read a number of times later, produced superior reading for groups of pupils in a basal program in both first and second grades. In our opinion, the obvious contribution of the language experience strengthens basal programs. The novelty effect of using a recorder could be retained by having children also read them into the machine, for other children to listen to while following a typewritten copy.

Because the language experience technique includes instruction in many aspects of language, it should be apparent that it will require a larger block of time in the day than is usually devoted just to reading instruction. This need not be a continuous period of writing stories, correcting mechanics, learning phonic, structural, and contextual clues from the stories, practicing manuscript, listening to the teacher read, and all the other adjunctive classroom activities that characterize the method. Rather, the teacher may schedule these as she chooses in terms of the maturity of attention span of the pupils, and the periods of time needed for other curricular areas and for school routines. Because it is child-centered and small-group-oriented, the technique can be scheduled much more flexibly than methods which tend to demand set periods, more or less of a specific length of time.

Some object to the extended use of experience charts because, they claim, the compositions lack vocabulary control, repetition of the basal vocabulary, and depth and variety of organized content matter (5). As a result, these critics recommend that experience stories be employed for only a short part of the beginning reading program, or only as an interesting supplement to the basal reading program, or for occasional lessons in creative writing. It is apparent that our concept of the language experience approach is as a relatively complete method of teaching early reading through the primary grades.

As for the lack of repetition of the basal vocabulary, if there is such a group of words, it is probably no more than the 200 or so most frequent words in our language (and as we have pointed out earlier, these words are not necessarily present in basal readers). These few most frequent words (largely prepositions, adverbs, conjunctions, and such structure words) are important, but it is also true that they are present even in children's stories (see earlier samples of chart stories). In fact, one cannot form English sentences without using these words, which mark the structure of such sentences. To manipulate children's compositions to include some list of "basal vocabulary" in preparation for the use of a certain reader is self-defeating and a distortion of the true purpose of the language experience approach. Overconcern about these service words will destroy the meaningfulness and vitality which characterize experience charts. The appropriate methods to ensure learning of this list of words are illustrated later in this chapter, not by censoring or editing children's spontaneous material.

As for experience charts lacking organized content material, the same criticism could be made of most primary reading materials. In contrast, as we have stressed several times, children taught to read by language experience do learn more organized content matter than other pupils.

In fact, using various types of instructional charts can strengthen the teaching in content areas a great deal. Time lines; directions for class or individual routine activities; classification of products, rivers, cities; collections of leaves, rocks, and shells mounted and labeled; reports on animal life—food, habitat, life cycle; information on community workers, are but a few of the ways of reinforcing learning in these fields.

Another point made by those who object to language experience is that the charts often include words of only immediate value, such as satellite, astronaut, or antimissile. Children should not be exposed to these mature terms, the critics say. This thinking reflects, in our opinion, the common basal author's overconcern with spoon-feeding of vocabulary. We know better than this today, for we have finally realized that when given any skill in word attack, our children learn hundreds of words beyond those presented in the reader. If these difficult words are significant to the child's composition, why shouldn't he learn them, even if only temporarily? Knowledgeable language experience teachers do not expect pupils to learn these technical terms permanently, knowing that the context, the unusual lengths and shapes will suffice for temporary reading of the charts. In a word, we believe the chart should reflect truly the child's thoughts, vocabulary, and feelings, without undue adult manipulation.

ORAL READING IN THE PRIMARY PROGRAM

Despite the criticisms of reading authorities and the trend in basal reader manuals away from oral reading, this activity still occupies much of the class time in our primary classrooms. Over two-thirds of the first- and second-grade teachers observed or questioned by Austin and Morrison* admit to spending "Considerable" time on this form of reading. Although there is a shift in emphasis to silent reading in the third and fourth grades, 30 percent of such teachers still devote *most* of their instructional time to oral reading. As observers note, these teachers are aware of some of the objections to oral reading as they employ it, but persist in overemphasizing and misusing the practice, perhaps because of inertia or simple resistance to change. Others cling to the habit with a sincere but mistaken belief in its effectiveness as an instructional technique.

Few reading experts would argue that oral reading has no legitimate

---

* Mary C. Austin and Coleman Morrison, *The First R* (New York: Macmillan Publishing Co., Inc., 1963).

functions or goals in the total program. Rather, their objections center upon the manner in which oral reading is conducted in the average classroom. In many schools, the most frequent oral reading activity consists solely of round-robin recitations of pupil after pupil reading a small portion aloud to his group or the entire class. This practice is used not only in the basal reader but also in many other schoolbooks, particularly in intermediate grades.

Some teachers make the oral reading more functional by using it largely to permit children to answer questions or substantiate their answers. A few utilize oral reading in play acting, asking children to assume roles and to read only the dialogue. Occasionally one sees oral reading functioning in choral reading of poetry or prose in which groups of children enact roles or the contrasting voice levels of boys and girls are used to add enjoyment to the story. And, of course, oral reading is sometimes used in the classroom to convey messages and to share selected portions of the children's recreational reading. Whether all of these oral reading activities are justifiable and whether they actually accomplish the aims teachers attribute to them is the heart of this issue.

In the following chart we have tried to present as objectively as possible the usual claims made for or against oral reading. These pros and cons arise from many sources, including both classroom teachers and reading authorities. Each claimed advantage or justification for oral reading is contrasted with a contradictory statement which attempts to question each claim. The reader should try to keep in mind that the point of discussion is oral reading as it is commonly practiced, not oral reading per se. A discussion of each pro and con is offered following the chart to clarify the antagonistic viewpoints.

Pros and Cons of Oral Reading

Assumptions	Refutations
1. Reinforces the child's effort to recognize words by their sounds.	1. Assumes that reading vocabulary, particularly the new or unknown sight words, are within child's auditory vocabulary.
2. Permits teacher observation of child's knowledge of reading vocabulary.	2. Emphasizes word calling at the expense of comprehension.
3. Permits teacher observation of error tendencies in pupil's reading (i.e., confusion of word form, meaning).	3. Assumes that teacher hears and records most of child's errors for subsequent analysis.
4. Permits observation of pupil's word attack habits and techniques.	4. Assumes that teacher analyzes errors and plans corrective steps.

5. Provides repetitive practice for rest of the group or class, thus strengthening their reading development.

5. Actually requires children to follow closely a pupil who often reads worse than they do.

6. Centers attention of group upon the reader and the teacher; promotes group spirit and identification.

6. Promotes boredom and inattention among the better readers of the group.

7. Provides opportunity for practice in listening skills for the rest of the group.

7. Promotes inattention, for unless questions are used to focus attention of the other members of the group, no real training in listening occurs.

8. Gives child practice in proper phrasing, pitch, inflection, and other speech habits, thus promoting skill in oral communication.

8. Assumes that teacher actually directs and corrects speech habits; rather it emphasizes oral reading at sight, thus promoting what is basically an inferior and unnatural oral performance.

9. Offers opportunities for role playing, dramatization, choral reading, and other practices leading to oral communication skill.

9. Overemphasizes the learning of the reading vocabulary and thus provides little practice in individual or group communication situations.

10. Helps emphasize the relationship between the printed word and normal speech—that "reading is talking written down."

10. Assumes that printed prose and normal speech are quite parallel.

11. Provides opportunity for personal contact between the pupil and teacher, thus strengthening his ego and social adjustment.

11. Offers basically a threatening, anxiety-producing experience for the poor reader or even the child with slight speech handicaps.

12. Provides foundational training for present and future development of silent reading ability.

12. Assumes that silent and oral reading are similar processes and mutually supporting.

The Pros and Cons of Oral Reading Reviewed

1. Auditory Reinforcement—As a child reads aloud, assuming that he pronounces the words in a manner natural to him, the sounds he says help to reinforce the visual impressions of the words. In a sense, he strengthens his visual recognitions with auditory memories for the same words, thus promoting a multisensory impression. However, this reinforcement occurs only when (1) he has previously heard and understood the words, and (2) he analyzes the words correctly and pronounces them the same way he has usually heard them. If the

word is not in his auditory vocabulary, in other words, is not one he remembers from the classroom or normal conversation, he may not be able to say it correctly and certainly is unable to deduce its meaning just because he can pronounce it.

For example, you can probably read and pronounce *Deltamatic*. But what does it mean? Does the ability to say it clarify that this word refers to the electronic system of handling reservations on Delta Air Lines? Teachers often justify a great deal of oral reading in and above primary grades by claiming that it helps word recognition and even comprehension. Unfortunately, this assumption is true only in material that is easy for the reader, with very few unfamiliar words and few technical terms. The claim is entirely true perhaps only at the beginning stages of reading and then only if the material resembles normal conversation in its selection of words (which it seldom does). Others who insist that early reading is highly dependent upon auditory memories for speech forget that reading is taught successfully to many without such memories, as the deaf, hard-of-hearing, bilingual, and foreign born. In fact, in some experiments, children have been taught to read for as long a period as the first six years without any practice in circle reading. Many types of oral reading were permitted, but only for obvious communication. At the close of the experiment, these children read as well as any others in every respect. To paraphrase Constance McCullough's remarks, "How essential is this oral reading?"

2. Learning Basal Vocabulary—Teachers often believe that oral reading permits them to determine a child's command of the basic vocabulary in the basal reader or his understanding in content field books. It is obvious, however, that first, the ability to read a sentence (that is, to pronounce all the words correctly) does not prove anything about comprehension. If we could be certain that the reader understood the material because he read it aloud reasonably well, we would never have to ask questions testing his comprehension. But every experienced teacher recognizes the falsity of assuming understanding of material just because it is read aloud. In fact, practically all research studies on the subject indicate that comprehension is relatively weak in oral reading. The reader has too many other demands to meet in delivering the sentences well to be able to listen comprehendingly or to spend any time really thinking about what he is saying.

What we see in most classrooms in the oral reading circle is really a worship of word calling, with the implicit belief that if the child reads the words correctly, he has learned these basic words and he is comprehending. We cannot assume that saying the words correctly once, twice, or a dozen times proves that the child really understands them, or even that he can now easily recognize them. Words are learned as sight words or in terms of their various meanings quite gradually in a process that extends over a long time, perhaps a lifetime. Learning sight words (and their meanings) is not a simple additive process accomplished by so many repetitions per new word. Words are known some days and forgotten other; their command is irregular and almost unpredictable. No teacher could guarantee which of the basic words she overemphasizes in this type of oral reading her pupils really know on any single day.

Furthermore, the stress is upon saying the words precisely in this circle reading, as shown by the fact that the teacher's main effort is spent in correcting the child's word-naming efforts. Children are not permitted to substitute words despite the fact that such words might convey the same sense or meaning as the original words. They are not supposed to think their way through the material, calling on their previous learning or associations to aid in interpreting the ideas. They are simply supposed to call the words correctly and that act, of course, is supposed to result in comprehension. We know that teachers try hard to build a mental bank of ideas or words in children's minds. Yet in this type of oral reading, pupils are not permitted to call on these memories, integrate them with the concepts offered by the printed page, and, in reading, present a mixture of both. Obviously, the practice of circle oral reading as usually practiced promotes word calling rather than comprehension.

A recent study (21) required children to read orally under two conditions: reading without any interruptions or corrections, and with the teacher correcting all word recognition errors. The correction of errors, as most teachers might, actually produced slower rate and poorer comprehension. Even when simply asked to "pay closer attention to the words," these trends were present. Thus this common practice acts as a deterrent to oral reading progress.

A much sounder practice would lead the children to read each portion silently first, in order to answer leading questions. This usage would provide opportunities in independent word attack in keeping with the training given previously and would emphasize comprehension rather than word calling. Later, if oral reading still seems desirable, it might be used in answering the prereading questions or in some of the other ways, such as play acting, choral reading, or sharing selected portions mentioned earlier.

3. Correcting Errors—Oral reading is often justified as an opportunity for the teacher to observe the child's word error tendencies and thus to plan corrective steps. It is claimed that the teacher will note whether the child readily recognizes the basic vocabulary or whether his errors involve word form, meaning, or both. However, as most observers of classroom practices know, few teachers follow through on this opportunity. Few teachers ever keep any records of pupil reading errors in the circle or do any more than correct the errors orally as the child reads. Most teachers apparently depend upon their overall impressions of the child's oral reading and use these to make whatever readjustments in materials or instruction seem indicated.

4. Diagnosis—Circle reading is also supposed to provide the chance for the teacher to diagnose the child's abilities in word attack—in phonics, or in structural or contextual analysis. If this were true, two conditions would have to be present. First, teachers would have to be skilled in analyzing the child's reading, and second, they would have to make some type of detailed record of the child's errors which would later be analyzed. Unless the teacher is well practiced in recording errors and has a duplicate copy of the selection on which errors can be marked, no adequate record is possible. Few teachers have such training, and fewer still actually attempt to record and analyze the child's word attack habits. Most commonly, what really takes place is that the teacher notes mentally a few errors, draws a quick conclusion, and proceeds to take some corrective measures

she deems appropriate. The proportion of retarded readers who exhibit poor word attack techniques is evidence that this particular value of oral reading as an aid to diagnosis is very doubtful in the ordinary classroom.

Most teachers would frankly admit that in group reading the necessity for the teacher to supervise the group, try to maintain the attention of the members, direct questions, and the like precludes any real possibility of carefully analyzing the reader's errors. Such diagnosis is probably feasible only in a one-to-one situation of teacher and pupil.

5. Following a Model—Most teachers assume, almost without question, that oral reading in a group with each pupil reading in turn provides some sort of helpful practice for the entire group. Presumably it helps the others when they read along with the child reading aloud. As a matter of fact, this group practice results in requiring children to follow and imitate someone who often reads more poorly than they. Gilbert's* eye-movement studies of children reading in this fashion indicate that they actually read with many more errors, poorer phrasing, and excessive fixations while following another child. The type of reading done in this situation is much worse than that done by children reading similar material silently and independently.

Requiring other children in the group to read along silently as each child reads aloud is *not* a sound instructional technique. It obviously does not provide training in quick, accurate word recognition (even though children are permitted to call out a word on which the reader stumbles). It does not provide a helpful repetition of the basic vocabulary, for all the fumbling, mispronunciations, or miscalling that the child hears certainly do not reinforce a correct impression of the words. This type of oral reading practice does not strengthen children's word analysis techniques since the context which should assist such analysis is often distorted by the fumbling oral reader. How, then, can it contribute to the development of better oral or silent reading? Perhaps the only result is to strengthen the child's impression that the most important goal in reading is calling the words correctly, a view apparently shared by many teachers.

A much sounder approach would substitute listening for reading along silently as the group activity. Then the questions on the content would be addressed not to the reader, but to the listeners. Any benefits in following another reader are achieved only when he is a superior, fluent performer or when the teacher, a tape recording, or record provides the model.

6. Attention—Some say that the oral reading circle helps to center the attention of the group upon the child reading; to give him a sense of importance and strengthen his ego. It also serves to build a group spirit among the members, a sense of belonging. However, when we see the group in action, it is apparent that only a few actually listen to or read along with the reader; the others appear bored and inattentive because of the poor performance of the reader. The majority sit apathetically (or impatiently) waiting their turn. Only one or two follow the reader carefully enough to note his errors and to flap their arms for a chance to call out

---

* Luther C. Gilbert, "Functional Motor Efficiency of the Eyes and Its Relation to Reading," *University of California Publication in Education,* 11 (1953), 159–232.

corrections. Even the teacher's efforts to focus their listening by calling on those she deems inattentive seldom suffice to maintain more than sporadic listening.

Yet children seem to want this type of reading activity, to feel neglected or disappointed if they do not get a turn at reading. They may complain to their parents that "they didn't get a chance to read today," although they have read silently several times during the day in other lessons. This attitude implies that there is a moral or ego-building value to be found here, if we could only eliminate some of the wasted time. Perhaps the answer lies in a smaller reading group and better selection of children of equal abilities to compose a group. Other arrangements preferable to the usual practice include more opportunity for reading to the teacher alone, or to another child, or to a small group which simply listens to and enjoys the story without attempting to follow silently. Reading to an audience that is attentive is a highly gratifying experience, but teachers must try to ensure that the situation is truly rewarding and not a farcical imitation.

7. Listening Skills—Group oral reading may be intended to provide an experience in listening while one member reads aloud. As we have pointed out, this experience is seldom realized, for most of the listeners tune out the reader or only pretend to listen while they wait for their turns. If listening training is to occur, it must be planned and directed. Leading questions should be presented to the group before the reading to direct their listening toward the types of ideas to be gained from the material. After the reading, or at intervals during it, if it is a long selection, the prereading questions should be answered and discussed. At the end of the reading, questions may be answered either orally by the group or in the accompanying workbook material. These pre- and postreading questions should parallel the type of questions used to direct reading comprehension.

Such a listening activity provides practice in the kinds of thinking that are supposed to occur in the act of reading—various types of reasoning, memory or recall, evaluation, and the like. There is ample evidence that this activity helps children to read (and to listen) more effectively when it is carefully directed, somewhat as we have suggested.

8. Speech Training—Oral reading in turn in a group is claimed to offer practice in acquiring good speech habits, such as proper inflection of sentences, modulation of the pitch of the voice, and correct phrasing of the elements of sentences. If this is true, then this type of reading would have value in improving the oral communication abilities of children. But does the average teacher use the situation for these constructive purposes? Does she even know very much about improving the children's reading habits? Is she really concerned that the reading sounds like good, natural speech, or does she spend most of her time correcting word recognition errors?

If oral reading is to result in the improvement of speech, the teacher's instructional activities will have to change a great deal. Except among superior readers, oral reading at sight is apt to be a halting, unnatural activity. The teacher will first ask the children to read the material silently so that their later oral reading will be a better, more fluent performance. She will also stress playing roles by various children with each child reading only the appropriate dialogue of the character represented. After having practiced each bit silently, the oral reading of the part of each character will tend to resemble natural speech with its intonations, inflection, pitch, and rhythm. Frequent use of simple plays as a substitute for the basal stories, or employing recreational materials selected by the members of the group (and practiced silently and orally before presentation), are superior ways of promoting better and more natural speech habits in oral reading. Oral reading can contribute to improve speech habits in other oral communication acts, but if it is to do so the group reading must be structured to achieve this goal.

9. Communications Skills—We have emphasized several times in the preceding discussions of the claims for group oral reading that it can indeed contribute to speech habits and oral communications skills. If the modifications in the usual procedures are made, and if the more appropriate oral reading activities are frequently substituted for round-robin reading, then these particular values certainly can be achieved. On the other hand, when teachers persist in pointless reading in turn around the circle, it is very doubtful that there is ever any such value.

10. Reading and Speech—Some reading specialists and some linguists insist that oral reading strengthens the relationship between reading and speech. It is supposed to help children realize that printed matter is simply speech written down, and thus foster the transition from speaking to reading. This assertion depends strongly on several assumptions which are seriously questioned by other reading and language specialists.

The first and most obvious of these assumptions is that printed prose and normal speech are parallel, or at least sufficiently parallel to promote easy transition to reading. However as Marquardt (16), a language specialist, has pointed out, these media are more different than parallel or similar. They differ in these ways:

1. Printed material is not a complete representation of spoken matter, for these are oral sounds for which there are not possible printed symbols.
2. Speech is accompanied with a variety of exclamations, grunts, sighs, and other sounds that help communication but are seldom present in prose.
3. Facial changes, silences, gestures, shrugs, and many nonverbal signs clarify speech and are completely lacking in print.
4. Sentence length and structure differ markedly in the two media, for those in speech are often fragmentary, run-on, faulty in grammatical features, monosyllabic, and the like. These characteristics are absent in prose. Moreover, printed or even handwritten sentences are longer, more formal, and more complex, even in children's writings from about third-grade level on.
5. Pitch, intonation, and inflection help carry the meaning of the speaker, as well as volume and tone of the voice. None of these can be produced in prose.
6. In appropriate settings, accent, dialect, and regional variations help convey the speaker's meanings. Each group of listeners tends to understand and react to these familiar nuances more readily than to standard English. These differences in speech either cannot be or seldom are conveyed in print.
7. As critics of basal readers indicate, the content seldom resembles normal

speech as the child knows or uses it. The sentences tend to be artificially short, stilted, and limited in variations of their patterns when compared with the oral language most children hear and use.

For all these reasons, spoken and written language differ, and we cannot assume that the reading of written prose is simply a type of speaking or the reading of "talking written down." If he is ever to read intelligently, it may be essential for the reader to recognize that written prose and speaking involve the same kinds of thinking and processing of ideas. But to assume that any child is ready to read because he can speak reasonably well, or that he move easily from speaking and listening to reading because of the parallelism is manifestly absurd, as almost any primary teacher can testify.

Perhaps the only situations in which prose and spoken language are really alike are those in which the material is actually composed by the children, as in experience charts. If the chart follows faithfully what the children are saying, it comes as close to being "talking written down" as it is possible for prose to be. Yet it still lacks the gestural, facial, and inflectional signs of spoken language.

11. Ego Building—As we have said, oral reading can be a gratifying, ego-strengthening experience. But for some children it may be a threatening, anxiety-producing task. When children who know they read poorly are required to read aloud before others, the results may well be tension, fear, and other types of unwholesome emotional reactions. Pupils who suffer from minor speech difficulties, such as baby talk, substitutions, lisp, or stuttering, may also react badly to required oral reading. The unsympathetic laughter or ridicule of classmates, or sometimes even of the teacher, makes oral reading a nightmare for some children. Need we point out the obvious necessity for teachers to prevent these disturbing experiences for such children by permitting them to read silently whenever possible? Sometimes the morale-building effects of oral reading may be better achieved by extending to these children the privilege of reading aloud to the teacher alone, or permitting them to read aloud to an audience only when they have had ample previous practice with the material.

Unwholesome, frightening experiences in oral reading are not uncommon among children. Almost any experienced reading clinician can recount the stories of such children whom she has later almost vainly tried to help recapture some enjoyment in reading. On the other hand, alert, sympathetic teachers can capture the positive values for the child's personality in the oral reading situation and help build self-confidence and a strong foundation for future academic success.

12. Oral Versus Silent—Perhaps the most frequently repeated justification for group oral reading is that it is the essential experience upon which future silent reading activity is based. Unfortunately, this is an almost completely mistaken belief, for the two ways of reading are not interdependent but rather almost antagonistic to each other. Some of the common basic goals of oral reading are (1) correct pronunciation of the words; (2) delivery in a proper speech manner; (3) communication with the listeners; and (4) proper use of pitch, volume, inflection, rhythm, and enunciation. In contrast, none of these goals for which we practice

oral reading functions significantly in the silent reading act. Rather, silent reading training is intended to produce (1) adequate comprehension; (2) an integration of the reader's background of information with the content of the reading; (3) a rate of reading comparable to the reader's capacity for speed in associating ideas; (4) an intelligent use of the context to help derive the meanings of new or difficult words; and (5) successful use of a variety of methods of word analysis resulting in the deduction of word meanings (not necessarily their pronunciation).

There are, of course, other goals for both types of reading which stress enjoyment; growth in use of reading as a tool for personal, social, and academic needs; reading tastes and interest; and so forth. But we are emphasizing the dissimilarities between silent and oral reading rather than their common goals.

None of the aims of oral reading function in silent reading. In fact, if we try to have some of them transfer, such as the need for careful reading of each word, we would block silent reading development. Silent reading must involve the skipping of words, the omissions of unimportant words, and an emphasis upon the basic ideas of the sentence or the paragraph. A careful word-by-word emphasis as is characteristic of good oral reading would destroy comprehension in silent reading. If one reads this slowly and carefully, his comprehension as well as his concentration would be minimal. Silent reading demands a thinking act, a reaction to ideas, at the rate of thinking and associating of which the reader is capable. If he moves through the material at a slower rate, his mind wanders; he deals with words not ideas, with consequent loss in comprehension.

Furthermore, studies of the errors in reading indicate more omissions and substitutions among sixth graders than at beginning levels. These errors reflect the pupil's attempt to read more rapidly and fluently—a normal developmental trend at about high-third-grade level—and to associate his knowledge with the ideas of the material. They are typical behaviors in the silent reading act and, moreover, essential to it. But when a child uses these same behaviors in oral reading, he is likely to be considered a poor reader. He cannot transfer the behavior characteristics of each type of reading back and forth—slow word reading from oral to silent or rapid idea gathering with little attention to the exact words—from silent to oral.

Practice in oral reading promotes that type of reading but, except for the development of sight vocabulary, tends to retard the development of silent reading ability. Practice in silent reading may interfere with good oral reading if silent habits are carried over. Perhaps each type of training has its place in the total reading program, but it is obvious that oral reading, if justified in the early stages, must be greatly deemphasized at later levels if eventual development of silent abilities is to be promoted. This trend is present in most surveys of classroom practices.

Yet we see the confusion of the two processes persisting in many classrooms. For example, intermediate-grade as well as junior and senior high school teachers show lack of complete understanding of this problem. They often ask students to read materials aloud at sight, such as textbooks which have proven rather difficult, under the impression that they are promoting comprehension. Such oral reading is supposed to make it easier for the reader to understand the content when, as a matter of fact, it benefits only those listening carefully (not the reader or necessarily those following him in their own book). Any gain in comprehension from this approach arises from the discussion of each portion, not from the oral presentation, which could, therefore, be entirely omitted.

In this and other classroom practices, and in their attempts to judge probable silent reading ability from oral informal or formal tests, teachers and even some reading clinicians demonstrate their confusion over the two processes. When oral reading is accompanied by many errors or weak comprehension, it is assumed that the silent reading of the pupil is similarly poor. As many reading clinic personnel can testify, a large number of pupils are referred to reading centers because of this assumption of parallelism between the two reading behaviors. However, as we have tried to point out, oral and silent reading are not very similar performances in rate, comprehension, use of word attack or word recognition techniques, or thinking processes.

Using the standardized oral–silent reading test, Rowell (24) showed that a large sample of third- and fifth-grade boys showed higher reading performance in oral than in silent reading. The reading level was higher also in whichever ability was tested second. The author justly raises questions about the validity of judging silent reading behavior from an oral test, and is concerned with the implication in his data that oral reading is apparently being emphasized at the expense of silent in many of our schools, despite the general acceptance of the opposite goal in most reading programs.

Uses of Oral Reading

We are sure that by this time some of our readers are certain that we are most antagonistic toward oral reading. Perhaps we can dispel this illusion by repeating that there are many legitimate types of oral reading and that a small degree of this practice is necessary in a good reading program. But we differ almost violently with common oral reading practices and the manner in which this skill is fostered in the usual basal reading program. Rather, we see many possible uses of oral reading for functional purposes, as in the following list.

Substitutes for the Oral Reading Circle

1. Read story to children. Discuss its ideas, new words, its meaning, and the children's reactions. Have children relate their own parallel stories or experiences.
2. Plan and write together an experience chart about a recent common experience or happening. If children can, let them copy the chart on paper and take it home to read to their parents.
3. Ask children to select a story from a supplementary reader. Let them read it

The individualized approach has shown us the fallacy of following a basal program written for average learners when dealing with gifted pupils. These are the fortunate children who learn to read earlier and more easily than the average. These are the pupils of high verbal ability, strong vocabularies, and quick learning aptitude. These are the pupils who can and do read more widely and deeply when the reading program is stimulating and challenging. Therefore, we suggest that the reading program for the fastest-learning third or quarter of the class follow the individualized approach, after introduction to reading through experience charts. These children may be permitted to read the basal materials, if they choose them. But formal instruction in the basal in the usual manner would be eliminated in order to permit the rapid progress of which these pupils are capable. They may function as a group for chart reading and writing, project work, special reports, training in skills, and many other purposes. But the content of their reading program would be determined basically by self-selection under the guidance of the teacher in individual and group conferences.

Despite their superior learning aptitudes, the fast learners, like other children, need help in planning and organizing their reading efforts. They should not simply be turned loose in the classroom or school library to fumble their way toward satisfying reading materials. They will need help in developing discrimination, purpose for reading, criteria for selecting books they can read and enjoy, and instruction in how to organize their reporting on books and record keeping. As several studies have shown, children permitted to do individualized reading do not necessarily read easier books first and then progress directly to the harder. Their reading records are more likely to show a kind of alternation between easy and hard books, not because they cannot discriminate, but perhaps because of their motivation to reach out for more challenging materials or because of their interest in the content. Children spontaneously evolve such clues to the reading difficulty of a book as familiarity of vocabulary, details of format such as size of type or book, amount of text on page, and the relevance of pictures to text. Some teachers make a definite attempt to facilitate the child's discriminative ability by pointing out these differences early in the individualized program. Children may be trained to judge the vocabulary difficulty of a book by practice in previewing it before attempting to read.

Early in the individualized program for gifted pupils the teacher must help the children evolve some methods of record keeping. These will differ, of course from class to class in terms of the teacher's philosophy and goals. But she must decide on the types and kinds of child records that will enable her to observe pupil progress, guide and develop reading interests, and permit observation of growth in skills. Does she want a running record of the titles of books they are reading, their reactions to these, a list of the vocabulary they encountered, or other facts? Does she wish children to keep a notebook for these facts, or report them verbally in the conference, or demonstrate their learning by projects reported to the group or class? These decisions must be made before individualized reading begins, and the details must be worked out with the children. Other preliminary steps in organizing for individualized reading are suggested in another chapter.

We will point out at length elsewhere the different types and purposes of individual conferences, and the inventorying and diagnosis of pupil reading skills which may be attempted in certain of these conferences. In our opinion, the effective conference is the heart of the individualized approach and must be studied most carefully. Other problems inherent in individualized reading, such as planning beforehand, use of conferences, judgment of pupil readiness for this method, planning follow-up, and the keeping of pupil and teacher records will be discussed in detail.

It is obvious that we are attempting to capture the peculiar values of the individualized approach in our suggested program for fast-learning pupils. But this method is most feasible with children capable of rapid, individual progress. These children, in our opinion, do not require the measured pace of the basal program, the cumulative repetitions, and the careful doling out of new words. With adequate teacher support and guidance to ensure well-rounded development of word recognition skills, of sight and meaning vocabularies, and of comprehension, these pupils may grow at their potential accelerated rates. Avoidance of the basal program with these pupils does not imply that they do not need diagnosis of their skill development and appropriate training. The syllabi of skills we offer are intended for these pupils as much as for the slow and average groups.

THE PRIMARY PROGRAM WITH AVERAGE PUPILS

The second large segment of the class is composed of pupils of average verbal skills and learning capacities. For these pupils we suggest a modified basal reader approach, involving introduction to reading by the experience chart, followed by the use of basal materials, and later, individualization. There are a number of sound reasons for this type of program, in our opinion. These are the pupils for whom the basal program has primarily been devised. The controlled vocabulary is offered at a rate commensurate with the learning capacities of average pupils. Yet most of these children can reach out toward individualized reading after completion of the basals, if they are given the opportunity. During the period that is needed to complete the basal books, teacher skill in individualizing will grow because of her experiences with the fast reading group. For the average group, individualization can begin gradually with recreational materials and, as children grow in independence and reading skill, can be extended to their entire reading program. The exact point at which extended, individualized reading is begun is not critical in the children's reading development. This decision can well be a matter of teacher judgment and experience.

Individualized reading may be introduced to the average readers in a variety of ways: by releasing individuals from the group work, by special reading assignments, by urging children to prepare themselves for sharing time by special reading, by substituting individualized reading on the topic for a basal unit, by using the parallel readings suggested in the basal as a substitute for a basal lesson, by using the group lesson as an occasion for sharing best-liked books, and most of all, by providing ample time, motivation, and materials for self-selected reading. All average pupils will not necessarily be ready for individualized reading at the same time. Despite their gross similarities in capacity, the average pupil will differ in the breadth of sight vocabulary, in the rate with which they can learn new words, in their independence in word attack and other important reading behaviors. Teacher judgment based on observations of group work and of the child's success in his first trials in self-selected materials will indicate when each child is ready for some degree of individualized reading. Detailed suggestions for making this judgment of pupil readiness for individualized reading are offered later.

We would depart drastically from several of the common practices in using basals. First, we would not repeat the mistake in some manuals of coaching the children in the new vocabulary prior to their reading of the story. Children will grow much more in independence in word attack when their spontaneous efforts are not stifled by prereading coaching. A setting for the main idea of the story and a structuring of children's purposes for reading should certainly precede actual reading. If desired, the new vocabulary may be woven into this discussion, but it should not be written on the blackboard or chart for memorization. Children should be permitted and urged to attempt independent word attack and given assistance only when this is unsuccessful, or when it is apparent from their answers to questions on the material that their techniques were inadequate to the task.

In many classrooms, use of the basal workbook is the primary type of follow-up activity, whether or not the child needs to do these exercises. Here again we would depart from a fairly common practice. Certainly every child does not need to do every exercise that parallels each basal story. The teacher can and should be selective in her use of this basal tool, in terms of her observations of the child's need for further practice. Reinforcement of learning by use of the workbook can be ensured by selecting only the exercises related to the pupil's needs in such skills as word recognition, word attack, recall, and interpretation. This matching of workbook exercises and pupil need is readily based on the teacher's observation during the basal reading lesson. Further reinforcement of vocabulary and concepts may be achieved by the continued supplemental use of experience charts, thus adding some degree of spontaneity and creativity to the program.

The selective use of workbook materials can readily be effected within the average school budget for such items. Instead of ordering multiple copies of a workbook to parallel each basal reader, we suggest ordering a few copies each of a half-dozen workbooks from different series of books or from other sources. Certain workbooks are available for practice in particular skills as in word attack—Stone, *Eye and Ear Fun* (Webster); Brake, *New Phonics Skill Texts* (Merrill); Feldman and Merrill, *Ways To Read Words* (Teachers College Press), *Phonics We Use* (Lyons and Carnahan)—as well as the spirit masters of Continental Press, Elizabethtown, Pennsylvania, and those of Jenn Publications, Louisville, Kentucky. These sheets and the unbound pages of the sample workbooks can then be collated into related groups of exercises for each facet of the reading process. If children are taught to place each sheet in a heavy acetate folder, obtainable from most school suppliers, they can indicate their answers in crayon or marking pencil on the acetate. Thus the worksheets may be used again and again, for each child will wipe off his markings after completing each exercise, and checking with his group leader or neighbor. This plan enables the teacher to provide a wide variety of practice materials as needed by each group or pupil, for as long a period as it seems necessary.

A third major departure from the basal approach that we would recommend is in the tempo of the program. Many observers are amazed at the amount of time that some teachers manage to devote to covering basal materials of trifling content. The spoon-feeding pace arises, in our opinion, from several faulty assumptions often unwittingly made by classroom teachers. Because the manual and the workbook are so highly organized, teachers fear to slight the most minute details and undoubtedly waste much time in implementing most of the suggestions of the manual and in ensuring use of the entire workbook by every pupil. While it is true that repetition is essential for overlearning, there is no real evidence that this present degree of overlearning is necessary for ultimate reading progress of the pupils of average ability. If we may judge by the progress of pupils in other countries, particularly those in English-speaking lands, we realize that much more rapid progress is quite feasible. The crucial point that many classroom teachers have failed to recognize is that there is nothing particularly sacred or perhaps even essential in the vocabulary of any one preprimer or other basal reader. The repetition needed for eventual skill in sight vocabulary may also be achieved in a breadth of reading materials, with the added advantages of interest and vitality. Rapid completion of the basal materials followed by individualized reading, with both being reinforced by judicious selection of workbook and teacher-made exercises, will accomplish the teacher's ultimate goals for average pupils.

When children have passed the primer stage, or in other words have learned one to two hundred words, they are quite capable of reading many of the easy-reading books now available. In our opinion, routine reading of the basal, story by story, is no longer essential or even desirable at this stage. There is no magic in a particular reader's vocabulary and probably very little vocabulary that will not be encountered in most of the materials of suitable level of difficulty. Beyond the first two hundred most frequent words in English, there is *no real basic vocabulary* essential for all children. Rather, the vocabulary of each reading series varies more and more from each of the other series with the list of words determined not by some mythical master list but by the nature of the content of the readers. For all these reasons, slavish story-by-story following of any reading series is naive. Other materials may be used alternately or substituted for the basal in a dozen ways, as we have already suggested. Children should be allowed to select stories of interest to them, both from the basal and their recreational books as often as possible.

If, as will probably be the case, the teacher wishes to operate with small groups, she may either order several copies of various trade books or paperbacks, or use such resources as the *Reading Round Table* of the American Book

Company, which does furnish five copies of each of the six paperbacks in the kit for each reading level. In this manner, the use of the basal becomes selective and the tempo of the program is accelerated, as we have urged.

Another departure from the usual basal approach, which would inevitably follow if our earlier suggestions are accepted, is in the type and number of lesson preparations attempted by the teacher. It is our strong impression that one of the basic reasons for the small number of reading groups present in the average classroom is the teacher's concept of the role she must play with each group. Many teachers feel that they must conscientiously prepare a lesson for each group each day. Or, conversely, the teacher believes that a group really cannot progress unless she has personally worked with them each time they engage in a reading activity. Some critics of the basal program would say that the average teacher acts as though she thinks that children cannot learn unless the teacher sits and listens to them say the words, preferably in a round-robin reading circle.

If the teacher attempts the type of program which is moving toward many small groups and individualization, she will have to abandon some of these illusions about her indispensability to child learning. If the teacher diversifies instruction according to needs, she will soon find that even in the first grade she is promoting the formation of a half-dozen groups and, eventually, perhaps even more groups than this. Obviously under these circumstances a teacher cannot possibly prepare formal reading lessons for each group each day. At best, time will permit her to work intensively with only two or three such groups and to deal with the others only briefly. We have tried to suggest many ways in which the teacher may move toward this more flexible program by listing alternatives to the oral reading circle, and by mentioning different ways of conducting group reading.

In today's publishing market, there are a wide variety of kits and boxes of varying types and merits. Many of these would lend flexibility to the reading program by fostering independent work by small groups of children. Among the more widely known are the *SRA Reading Laboratories* (Science Research Associates); the *Macmillan Spectrum* (Macmillan) for skill development; the *Ginn Word Enrichment Program* (Ginn) for programmed word study; the Merrill *Reading Skilltexts* and their accompanying *Skilltapes* (Charles E. Merrill) and *New Reader's Digest Skill Builders* (Reader's Digest). These are but a few of such available tools for independent work. The ingenious and creative teacher will, of course, create her own supplementary practice materials and tapes in order to ensure their relevance to her own instructional practices.

We could list dozens of others which offer some sort of reading instruction by drill books, tapes, records, kits, paperbacks, computers, and the like. But, unlike some compilers, we feel an obligation to list only those aids which we or the teachers we work with have found effective. To some, this may appear to be a limited viewpoint, but since the authors spend more than half of their time working in and with clinics and classrooms throughout the country, we offer no apologies.

Although we have spoken of our combined program as a flexible plan, or an individualized program, it is apparent that we envision the use of basal readers for definite purposes, particularly with average and slow-learning readers. To promote the best possible use of this teacher tool, we have already suggested some deviations from the usual basal procedures. Among those discussed were the presentation of new vocabulary, the constant sequential following of the basal content, the preparation of reading lessons, and the tempo of the reading program. One final suggestion is now pertinent regarding the basal reading lesson itself.

In our judgment, the effective reading lesson, in which multiple copies of any type of reading material are employed, includes these components:

1. Prereading discussion of related children's experiences.
2. Prereading questions to direct the thinking of the pupils.
3. Silent reading to answer the prereading questions.
4. Oral reading of these answers, as their discussion proves necessary.
*5. Evaluation of the material to elicit children's personal reactions, to discuss its point or purpose, etc.
*6. Applications—a follow-up activity providing reinforcement for the ideas, facts, vocabulary, or other necessary skills; or using these aspects of the material in a spontaneous, creative manner, as in planning a mural, play, debate, or puppet show.

Grouping.   A word about groups and grouping would be most appropriate here. We have already criticized the practices commonly utilized in the basal approach and should point out how these can be improved. A natural group is formed by children or adults because of a common interest or need. Goals are shared, members become more efficient in working toward these, and a hierarchy of leaders and followers soon appears. The cohesiveness of the group is fostered by developing intereactions and influences among the members in their movement toward their goal. But ability grouping as employed in our classrooms tends to lack these normal group characteristics. In fact, studies show that this cohesiveness or group esprit with its inherent efficiency of achievement is present only in the top reading groups, perhaps because of their recognition of their superiority (1).

If we are to profit from these known facts about group dynamics and are to promote groups that are efficient, goal-seeking entities, it is apparent that teachers should be promoting group action on bases other than reading level alone. Temporary groups should be fostered to help children share a common reading interest, to work on projects, as well as to develop skills. Particularly in this last type of group, the members must see their work as meaningful and profitable for reading progress and class status. The work must also be recognized as valuable by members of other groups. Interaction among the members of a group should be stimulated when working with the teacher by skillful questioning and discussion in which all members are led to participate. Growth of cohesiveness will be stimulated by emphasizing cooperation and democratic leadership by both example and suggestion from the teacher. The authoritarian concept of the

---

* The fifth and sixth components would not necessarily occur during the first approach to the material, but more often would provide the activity for small-group independent work.

teacher, as shown in children's imitative play, may well be perpetuated in these groups, unless the teacher provides a more democratic model. The size of the group promoted should be relevant to the task or project in that all members can have responsibilities and contribute to the goal. Obviously these groups are not formed by arbitrary designation of the members by the teacher, for self-selection of members is most desirable. As the teacher identifies pupil needs for a certain skill, the nature and importance of this should be clarified for the pupils. A concrete goal permitting self-evaluation would then be established by discussion with the pupils and a way of sharing the outcomes with the rest of the class agreed upon. Finally, the pupils would be invited to form a working group or two by mutual selection.

In brief, the teacher plays the role of stimulating group formation by proposing projects and accepting those suggested by the children; by arranging for children to select helpers to aid them in skill development; by asking for volunteers to assist in a needed class activity; and by suggesting reading interest groups and providing materials and sharing a goal.

Boys Versus Girls. There is ample research to indicate that the difference between the reading achievement of boys versus girls is not simply a matter of psychological or physiological maturity. Rather, boys achieve less in reading because of lower teacher expectations for them, poorer relationships with female teachers, and, because of their masculine interests, motivations, and goals that tend to make for poor adjustment to the routines of the school.* Probably more than any other reading authority, Jo M. Stanchfield (27) has explored this problem and tried to find solutions. Among the characteristics of boys which she identifies are these in personality style: more aggressive; less conforming; lower frustration level for boredom and monotony; more inner-directed in reading to find out, not just to please the teacher; less adaptable and flexible to new situations. In language development, boys are poorer in fluency, articulation, auditory discrimination, and listening skills (except when really interested). They show a shorter attention span, and in terms of motivation are less anxious to please or to achieve, but more tenacious in trying to solve a problem. In terms of reading interests, they prefer unusual and dramatic, active and exciting stories, unlike those usually offered in the basal. Stanchfield has conducted a number of experiments intended to elicit greater achievement among boys by sex grouping, a basal series keyed to boy interest, and classroom instruction enriched by a variety of audiovisual aids and auditory discrimination training, as well as special reading materials. But although boys showed accelerated growth in these programs, it was equaled by the girls in the groups. In fact, very few experiments have overcome this differential achievement for any great length of time. However, there is the implication here that boys do respond to an enriched program with a masculine emphasis. Even greater response is present when teachers are cogni-

---

* See *Reading Teacher,* 29 (May 1976), for contrasting viewpoints on this interpretation of the reasons for differences in the achievement of boys and girls.

zant of their differences, acceptant of these deviations, but still hold high expectations for their male pupils.

Doris V. Gunderson* has pointed out that the reasons for the greater proportion of failures among boys (a ratio of about three to two) are still in need of intensive research. Fewer male than female teachers, lesser verbal facility, the effect of teacher expectations, and the perception of this attitude by boys probably do contribute to the failure rate among boys, although explicit proof is lacking. Practices that might change the picture, such as longer, more intensive readiness and language development programs for boys, special reading materials, a study of the differences in women's and men's use of language, the creating of a male-role model for reading, and the exploration of a possible difference in learning style in boys and girls, all remain to be researched before we can find the causes and cures for this American problem.

THE PRIMARY PROGRAM WITH SLOW LEARNERS

Every classroom has a number of pupils who progress slowly in beginning reading. They may be handicapped intellectually or in verbal skills; they may be bilingual or lacking in some of the major aspects of readiness; or they may be simply more dependent. For this group, no completely satisfactory program of reading materials is yet available. But we shall attempt to describe a realistic approach that will utilize the present tools in the best possible manner.

An extended readiness program is often essential for these pupils. Their visual, speech, auditory, listening, and language skills need considerable reinforcement if their efforts in beginning reading are to be attended with any degree of success. Although progress may be slow, we still believe that beginning reading instruction should utilize the experience chart with these pupils. Perhaps more so than for any other type of pupil, the basing of reading materials on the child's own language experiences is a realistic recognition of this child's readiness or capabilities for reading. Using the slow learner's own compositions we can be fairly certain that we are moving into reading at an appropriate pace. We will probably not progress faster than the child's own speaking and auditory vocabularies permit. If these vocabularies are really quite limited, the child's compositions will tend to be repetitious, very simple, but meaningful to him. Overlearning of words may have to be ensured by careful teacher planning, but the child's own limited vocabularies help in achieving this need.

These pupils will be introduced to the basal materials as soon as the teacher judges that they are ready. This decision may be based upon the readiness characteristics outlined in the checklist in Figure 6–1. Meanwhile, during the children's experience chart stage, the teacher will continue efforts to increase readiness for success in early reading.

* Doris V. Gunderson, "Sex Differences in Language and Reading," *Language Arts,* 53 (March 1976), 300–308.

Although it is not specifically written in terms of their learning rates, the basal reading program is the only organized body of materials that is even remotely suitable. These pupils need the carefully controlled introduction of new vocabulary, the simple concepts, and the high-frequency repetitions of the basal reader. Programmed instructional materials with their step-by-step, repetitive presentations and constant reinforcement of learning may eventually prove particularly valuable for this class of pupils, or such programmed texts may also help to individualize the progress of average or gifted children. But until a variety of programs for primary readers is available, we shall have to do the best we can with the present basal materials.

Even when the basal reading program is pursued at a decelerated rate, the slow-learning group is in constant need of reinforcement, review, and reteaching. The basal workbook, teacher-made exercises, visual aids, and repetitive games are important aids in promoting learning in this group, perhaps even more than with average and above-average pupils.

Enriching the basal by including all the skill and other activities and materials recommended in the basal manual or otherwise available may delay the completion of the readers offered for a grade, but it definitely produces much greater reading development than use of the reader and its workbook only. Simple parallel reading materials keyed to the vocabulary of the basal series—as available in some reading series—are needed for the slow-learning group. Materials emphasizing concrete words—nouns and transitive verbs rather than abstract words, such as adjectives, adverbs, prepositions, and conjunctions—must be provided for this relatively nonverbal group. Charts emphasizing concrete, pragmatic learning, such as the vocabulary of traffic and street signs, store signs, school and classroom rules, numbers, children's names, the calendar, and names of holidays, should be given special emphasis for this group.

THE PRIMARY PROGRAM WITH THE DISADVANTAGED CHILD

The basic facts we need to know to be able to teach reading effectively to the economically or language-handicapped child are just beginning to appear in our professional literature. At this time we cannot stipulate a best method or even a number of special activities for such children with certainty of their values. But we can overview those concepts of dealing with the problems of the disadvantaged child upon which there is relatively general acceptance.

Bilingual Education

We have mentioned earlier the divergence of opinion regarding the language of the minority groups in our culture. Some insist that there are deficits in the language and therefore in cognitive growth that must be repaired if schooling is to be successful. Another group points out that a dialect is an organized, effective language that differs from standard English but is not inferior or a handicap unless the school makes it so by its rejection of dialect speakers. A third group addresses itself to the problem of those pupils whose native language is a tongue other than English. These educators promoted the idea of bilingual education, that is, education in both the native language and English, and were successful in securing the Bilingual Education Act of 1968 (5). They offered research to prove that children taught to read first in Spanish were later able to move into reading in English with greater success (2, 18), and that learning to read in Spanish was easier than in English. The Act was ambiguously worded to imply that schooling could be continued in the native language into the secondary level, thus presumably producing students who were truly bilingual. However, pupils eligible for its benefits were defined by a poverty criterion, as though the special education was intended only for the economically disadvantaged, rather than to promote development of superior children from the Spanish or other cultures.

Projects of great variety were undertaken in an effort to realize the benefits of the Act. But it soon became apparent that school administrators and some legislators interpreted the goal to be the development of programs to teach English to the pupils—not to develop or maintain the mother tongue or to employ members of ethnic groups in instruction. As Gaarder has pointed out (7), the only justifiable rationale for the Act, namely that every group has a basic right to rear its children in its image and culture, was inevitably lost in the implementation. First, our society is not pluralistic but rather one in which the assimilation for the purpose of national unity means that the cultures and languages of minority groups must be eliminated. The power structure, both political and economic, as well as the prestige of the languages concerned, forces us toward monolingualism. True collective bilingualism, in which two languages are accorded equal status, does exist in a few countries, but even in some of these one language tends to dominate the other, as French over Flemish in Belgium, English over Afrikaans in South Africa, and English over Maori in New Zealand.

Second, all the preparatory steps essential to bilingual instruction were ignored by our school systems. Native speakers of Spanish who might have been expected to provide the instruction were not available or their educational qualifications were judged insufficient. Few training programs were initiated to equip teachers to function in a non-English tongue. Instructional materials in Spanish proved to be too difficult, both for the teachers and the pupils. Attempts to teach in both languages by switching back and forth demonstrated that the supposed quick learning of a language by young pupils either in conversation or in the reading act just did not happen. The difficulties with articulation, syntax, word recognition, sentence structure, and letter sounds were significant obstacles to acquiring bilingualism (9). Additional research in teaching English by grammar rules, English as a Second Language, intensive introduction to English before beginning schooling, dialect training, structural linguistics, aural–oral language training, linguistic readers, and specially created instructional materials gave no really positive results (7, 10, 19, 22, 25).

If we agree that these inconclusive experiments in some twenty-four languages and dialects and the social forces present in our society make collective bilingualism an impractical ideal, what steps can be taken to aid the economically disadvantaged and linguistically different pupils to succeed in school? Wilson (28) and others suggest that the solution lies in quality education—abundance of teaching materials in all media; stronger home—school relationships; extensive use of aides, parents, and community volunteers; strong staff development; and integration of the child's cultural heritage in the classroom activities. A number of writers stress use of the language experience technique with stories in the child's own words, with gradual introduction of idioms, inflections, and other elements of standard English, as we have suggested earlier. Follow-up activities emphasizing the child's cultural background (6), involving pictures, slides, foods, and native prose and poetry are also recommended. Attitude changes and reduction of prejudice toward minority groups can be promoted by the use of minority litera-ture and multiethnic readers and stories (12). Some persons suggest using folk tales and materials grouped around a central theme, such as the art, music, poetry, or beliefs of a minority group, with intensive use of real materials from the culture. Reading to children and discussing the content has been shown to be a worthwhile contribution to language development.

It is unrealistic to expect that complete command of standard English or perfect articulation is readily achieved with bilingual or dialect speakers. The true goal of the emphasis upon language development is not "correct" English, but skill in communicating with others and achieving comprehension in reading. The proper goal of the teacher is not trying to teach the child to speak in her dialect, but providing opportunities for hearing and using language as a tool for self-expression and the exchange of ideas, and broadening experiences as a basis for the symbols (words) by which they are represented.

Self-Concept.   In every way, children whose basic problem is adjusting to the middle-class milieu of the classroom must be given opportunities to feel secure, to feel accepted, to receive peer recognition and to achieve success in reading. To accomplish these goals, we make the following suggestions:

1. Both by actions and words, by physical contact and praise, the teacher must show the child that she trusts him, respects his judgments, expects him to succeed (in a task selected to be within his capacities), and believes that he is making progress and that he wants to relate to the teacher.
2. Carefully planning the reading tasks to ensure success, praising frequently, and coordinating facial and physical actions to reinforce this praise are important. The teacher should make the actions of her hands, her face, and her body reinforce what she is saying to the child.
3. It is important to seek materials with which the child can identify racially, ethnically, and culturally. (See the senior author's lists of books of this type, suitable for each American minority group. *) Reinforce this self-identification by

---

* George D. Spache, *Good Reading for the Disadvantaged* (Champaign, Ill.: Garrard Publishing Company, 1975).

room decorations, pictures, songs, and so forth, as outlined in the same resource book.

4. The teacher should provide many opportunities for these children to share their reading with their peers, to assume minor responsibilities in the management of the classroom, and to learn how to function as leaders for groups, for the class, in pupil teams, and in other capacities.

5. The use of standardized tests should be deemphasized, for these represent largely middle-class standards of performance. Almost all are culturally biased in their language, time limits, and content (8). Use local standards rather than national norms, if such tests must be used to measure progress. Judge children's progress by the growth in their uses of books, the breadth and variety of their reading, their ability to use library resources and other reference materials, and, above all, their abilities in talking and writing about what they have read rather than their sheer recall of the facts or their skill in reciting on a book.

6. It should be recognized that one of the major problems in adjusting to the middle-class school is the child's lack of standard English language experiences. Stimulate language in every conceivable way of speaking, listening, reading, and writing; reactions to pictures; role playing; writing and acting plays; discussing films, filmstrips, records, and other audiovisual aids; visits to community resources such as the library, fire station, police station, zoo, a farm, the newspaper office, and whatever else is available. Prepare the children before the trip, discuss it at length afterward, and, if there is sufficient interest, make the trip the basis of a group or individual experience chart. These stories can be collected into a book for the library, embellished by a colored cover cut in the shape of the fire engine, a barn, or whatever is relevant.

7. The teacher must be aware that the attitudes toward self and progress in reading during the early primary stages are very significant in the child's later success in school. Reading achievement in the first grade is a strong predictor of reading success at least until the sixth grade (20). In other words, we are not only teaching beginning reading but also laying a foundation in feelings of worthiness and competence which will support the child's efforts over a long period. If you program the child toward success, as by using his own language development in the language experience approach (rather than his efforts to deal with the language of adults as written for children in readers), no child will experience the devastating effects of failure, no matter how slow his progress in reading development.

8. Promote identification with the children's own racial and cultural backgrounds by exhibiting reproductions of painting, sculpture, and architecture done by members of their racial group; by collecting newspaper clippings on national figures; by showing artifacts or handicraft by artisans of their community; by making collections of stamps, coins, etc., from the countries of their origins. Help them to make dioramas, models, or papier-mâché figures depicting common life activities characteristic of their group, as in a shoebox or shadowbox display. Weave in the plays, music, poetry, and prose of their culture, appropriate to the grade level and the subject matter being studied, as in social sciences. Capitalize on the opportunities for oral expression in the activities of collecting, assembling, labeling, and displaying examples of their culture.

9. Raise their self-ambitions by examples of successful persons of their racial or ethnic groups. Use simple biographies, pictures of local or national heroes and

sports and political figures. Even more realistically, invite local persons who are successful in some line of endeavor to visit the classroom, and to talk about their work. Thus provide real-life experiences with fortunate or prosperous members of their group.

10. Recognize that these children are not motivated by vague comments about progress, or statements that their good work will result in something good or pleasant in the future (such as grades, school awards, a better job). They are present-oriented in time, not future-oriented as middle-class individuals are. Rewards must be constant, immediately after the act, and material or physical. Other children may be motivated to continued effort by the knowledge that they have just succeeded in a task that may count toward a future reward; but disadvantaged children need extrinsic motivation, through the immediate reactions via the voice or actions of the teacher.

DISCUSSION QUESTIONS

1. How does the program for primary grades attempt to combine characteristics of the individualized, the basal, and the language experience approaches?

2. What possible improvements could you suggest for this eclectic program?

3. Do you really believe that this proposed program would be more successful than one based entirely on one of the common major approaches to reading? Why?

4. What is your reaction to the author's division of children into three types—gifted, average, and slow? Can you suggest other arrangements?

5. If you were a primary teacher following the program outlined here, about how much of your instructional time would you devote to the development and uses of experience charts (in contrast to the time spent with readers and other books)?

6. Make a tentative weekly plan which would encompass elements of the individualized, basal, and language experience approaches. Be prepared to explain and defend your choice of activities and instructional sessions.

REFERENCES

1. Alexander, J. Estill, and Filler, Ronald Claude, "Group Cohesiveness and Reading Instruction," *Reading Teacher,* 27 (February 1974), 446–450.

2. Bauer, Evelyn, "Teaching English to North American Indians in BIA Schools," *The Linguistic Reporter,* 10 (1968), 2.

3. Cramer, Ronald L., "Dialectology—A Case for Language Experience," *Reading Teacher,* 25 (October 1971), 33–39.

4. Downing, John, "Children's Developing Concepts of Spoken and Written Language," *Journal of Reading Behavior,* 4 (Winter 1971–1972), 1–19.

5. Garcia, Ricardo L., "Mexican American Bilingualism and English Language Development," *Journal of Reading,* 17 (March 1974), 467–473.

6. Garcia, Ricardo L., "Mexican Americans Learn Through Language Experiences," *Reading Teacher,* 28 (December 1974), 301–305.

7. Gaarder, A. Bruce, "Bilingual Education: Central Questions and Concerns," *New York University Education Quarterly,* 6 (Summer 1975), 2–6.

8. Hammill, D., and Wiederholt, J. L., "Appropriateness of the Metropolitan Tests in an Economically

Deprived, Urban Neighborhood," *Psychology in the Schools,* 8 (1971), 49–50.

9. Hatch, Evelyn, "Research on Reading a Second Language," *Journal of Reading Behavior,* 6 (April 1974), 53–61.

10. Horn, Thomas D., "Three Methods of Developing Reading Readiness in Spanish-Speaking Children in First Grade," *Reading Teacher,* 20 (October 1966), 38–42.

11. Huitt, Ray, "Handwriting: The State of the Craft," *Childhood Education,* 48 (January 1972), 219–220.

12. Jenkins, Esther C., "Multi-ethnic Literature: Promise and Problems," *Elementary English,* 50 (May 1973), 694–700.

13. Johns, Jerry L., "Reading: A View from the Child," *Reading Teacher,* 23 (April 1970), 647–648.

14. Lopardo, Genevieve S., "LEA-Cloze Reading Material for the Disabled Reader," *Reading Teacher,* 29 (October 1975), 42–44.

15. Malmquist, Eve, *Research Reports, No. 3.* National School for Educational Research in Linkoping, Karlshamn, Sweden, 1964.

16. Marquardt, Tom F., "Language Interference in Reading," *Reading Teacher,* 18 (December 1964), 215–218.

17. Meltzer, N. S., and Herse, R., "The Boundaries of Written Words as Seen by First Graders," *Journal of Reading Behavior,* 1 (Summer 1969), 3–13.

18. Modiano, Nancy, "Bilingual Education for Children of Linguistic Minorities," *American Indigena,* 28 (1968), 405–414.

19. Morrisroe, Michael, and Morrisroe, Sue, "TESL: A Critical Evaluation of Publications, 1961–1968," *Elementary English,* 49 (January 1972), 50–61.

20. Newman, Anabel P., "Later Achievement Study of Pupils Underachieving in Reading in First Grade," *Reading Research Quarterly,* 7 (Spring 1972), 477–508.

21. Pehrsson, Robert S. V., "How Much of a Helper Is Mr. Gelper?" *Journal of Reading,* 17 (May 1974), 617–621.

22. Rosen, Carl L., and Ortega, Philip D., "Language and Reading Problems of Spanish Speaking Children of the Southwest," *Journal of Reading Behavior,* 1 (Winter 1969), 51–72.

23. Ross, Ramon Royal, "Franme and Frank and the Flannelboard," *Reading Teacher,* 27 (October 1973), 43–47.

24. Rowell, E. H., "Do Elementary Students Read Better Orally or Silently?" *Reading Teacher,* 29 (January 1976), 367–370.

25. Rystrom, Richard, "Linguistics and the Teaching of Reading," *Journal of Reading Behavior,* 4 (Winter 1971–1972), 34–39.

26. Smith, Lewis B., and Morgan, Glen D., "Cassette Tape Recording as a Primary Method in the Development of Early Reading Material," *Elementary English,* 52 (April 1975), 534–538.

27. Stanchfield, Jo M., "Differences in Learning Patterns of Boys and Girls," in *Reading Difficulties: Diagnosis, Correction and Remediation,* William K. Durr, ed. Newark, Del.: International Reading Association, 1970, 202–213.

28. Wilson, Herbert B., "Quality Education in a Multicultural Classroom," *Childhood Education,* 50 (January 1974), 153–156.

PROFESSIONAL REFERENCES FOR THE TEACHER OF THE DISADVANTAGED

Chase, Judith Wragg, *Books To Build World Friendship.* Dobbs Ferry, N.Y.: Oceana Publications, Inc., 1964. A bibliography.

Cheyney, Arthur B., *Teaching Culturally Disadvantaged in the Elementary School.* Columbus, Ohio: Charles E. Merrill Publishing Company, 1967. A program for language development, emphasizing the language experience approach.

Children and Intercultural Education. Washington, D.C.: Association for Childhood Education, 1974.

Cullinan, Bernice, ed., *Black Dialects and Reading.* Urbana, Ill.: National Council of Teachers of English, 1974.

Gordon, Ira J., *Children's Views of Themselves.* Washington, D.C.: Association for Childhood Education, 1972.

Hall, MaryAnne, *The Language Experience Approach for the Culturally Disadvantaged.* Newark, Del.: ERIC/CRIER and International Reading Association, 1972. A review of values for beginning readers.

Learning To Live as Neighbors. Washington, D.C.: Association for Childhood Education, 1972.

von Maltitz, Frances Willard, *Living and Learning in Two Languages.* New York: McGraw-Hill Book Company, 1975.

Millen, Nina, *Children's Games from Many Lands.* New York: Friendship Press, 1965.

Orem, R. C., *Learning To See and Seeing To Learn.* Johnstown, Penna.: Mafex Associates, Inc., 1972. Collection of articles on visual and perceptual training.

Pialorski, Frank, ed., *Teaching the Bilingual.* Tucson, Ariz.: University of Arizona Press, 1974.

Pilon, Barbara, and Sims, Rudine, *Dialects and Reading: Implications for Change.* Urbana, Ill.: National Council of Teachers of English, 1975.

Scott, Louise Binder, *Learning Time for Language Experience with Young Children.* Manchester, Mo.: Webster Publishing, 1968.

Selakovich, Daniel, *Social Studies for the Disadvantaged.* New York: Holt, Rinehart and Winston, Inc., 1970. A text.

Spache, Evelyn B., *Reading Activities for Child Involvement.* Boston: Allyn and Bacon, Inc., 1976. Offers 472 reading and language development activities.

Spache, George D., *Good Reading for the Disadvantaged Reader.* Champaign, Ill.: Garrard Publishing Company, 1974. A list of graded and annotated books and instructional materials for the minority pupils of America of all types.

Stauffer, Russell G., *The Language Experience Approach to the Teaching of Reading.* New York: Harper & Row, Inc.: 1970. The author's own combination of the language experience approach with directed reading–thinking activities.

Trela, Thaddeus M., *Getting Boys To Read.* Belmont, Calif.: Fearon Publishers, 1974.

Zintz, Miles V., *The Reading Process.* Dubuque, Iowa: William C. Brown Company, 1975.

ORAL LANGUAGE DEVELOPMENT

These are largely collections of dramatic pictures which may serve to stimulate oral expression, or plays for enactment by children, or other such programs to promote language development and improve self-concepts.

Black, Millard, et al., *Visual Experiences for Creative Growth.* Columbus, Ohio: Charles E. Merrill Publishing Company.

Carroll, Hazel Horn, *Play Like Series.* Dallas, Tex.: Taylor Publishing. Pictures, scripts, records, and filmstrips.

Docu Drama. New York: Harcourt Brace Jovanovich, 1968. Play collection.

Dunn, Lloyd, and Smith, James O., *Peabody Language Development Kit.* Circle Pines, Minn.: American Guidance Services. Two graded kits of puppets, pictures, etc.

Durrell, Donald D., and De Milia, Lorraine A., *Plays for Echo Reading.* New York: Harcourt Brace Jovanovich. A play collection.

Evertts, Eldonna L., and Wiggins, Antoinette, *Storytelling, Oral Reading and the Listening Process.* Urbana, Ill.: National Council of Teachers of English, 1974.

Experiential Development Program. Chicago: Benefic Press.

First Talking Storybook Box. Glenview, Ill.: Scott, Foresman and Company. Storybooks and accompanying records.

Lancaster, Louise, *Introducing English: An Oral Prereading Program for Spanish-Speaking Primary Pupils.* Boston: Houghton Mifflin Company, 1966.

Let's Learn Sequence. Philadelphia: Instructo. Picture-story sequences, ten per box.

Let's Start—Picture Box. New York: Scholastic Book Services.

Little Picture Cards. Glenview, Ill.: Scott, Foresman and Company.

Martin, Bill, Jr., *Sounds of Language Series.* New York: Holt, Rinehart and Winston, Inc., Language development readers.

Phono-Viewer Programs. Morristown, N.J.: General Learning Press. Synchronized strip projector and record player present variety of songs.

Rector, Douglas, and Rector, Margaret, *The Story Plays—Self-Directing Materials for Oral Reading.* New York: Harcourt Brace Jovanovich. Multiple copies of forty plays for children.

Walden, James, ed., *Oral Language and Reading.* Urbana, Ill.: National Council of Teachers of English, 1969.

OTHER PROFESSIONAL REFERENCES

Allen, Roach Van, and Allen, Claryce, *Language Experiences in Reading: Teacher's Resource Book, Levels I, II, III.* Chicago: Encyclopaedia Britannica, Inc., 1966.

American Association for Health, Physical Education and Recreation, *Foundations and Practices in Perceptual-Motor Learning: A Quest for Understanding.* Washington, D.C.: The Association, 1971.

Arena, John I., *Teaching Through Sensory-Motor Experiences.* San Rafael, Calif.: Academic Therapy, 1969.

Ashton-Warner, Sylvia, *Teacher.* New York: Simon & Schuster, Inc., 1963. A New Zealand teacher discovers the language experience approach.

Barsch, Ray H., *A Perceptual-Motor Curriculum: Volume I—Achieving Perceptual-Motor Efficiency.* Seattle, Wash.: Special Child Publications, 1967.

Cratty, Bryant J., *Movement, Behavior and Motor Learning.* Philadelphia: Lea & Febiger, 1967.

Goodman, Yetta, Burke, Carolyn L., and Sherman, Barry W., *Strategies in Reading.* New York: Macmillan Publishing Co., Inc., 1974.

Hafner, Lawrence E., and Jolly, Hayden B., *Patterns of Teaching Reading in the Elementary School.* New York: Macmillan Publishing Co., Inc., 1972.

Hall, MaryAnne, *Teaching Reading as a Language Experience.* Columbus, Ohio: Charles E. Merrill Publishing Company, 1970.

Labuda, Michael, ed., *Creative Reading for Gifted Learners: A Design for Excellence.* Newark, Del.: International Reading Association, 1974.

Landrum, Roger, and Children from P.S. 1 and P.S. 42 in New York City, *A Day Dream I Had at Night.* New York: Teachers and Writers Collaborative, 1974.

McCracken, Robert A., and McCracken, Marlene J., *Reading Is Only the Tiger's Tail.* San Rafael, Calif.: Leswing Press, 1972. An attractively illustrated presentation of the authors' ideas on the language experience method.

Perceptual-Motor Task Force, *Approaches to Perceptual-Motor Experiences.* Washington, D.C.: American Association for Health, Physical Education and Recreation, April 1970. Reprint of articles from Journal of Health–Physical Education–Recreation.

Porter, Lorena, *Movement Education for Children.* Washington, D.C.: American Association of Elementary–Kindergarten–Nursery Education, 1969.

Shafter, Fanny, and Shafter, George, *Words and Action: Role-Playing.* New York: Holt, Rinehart and Winston, Inc., 1967. Twenty dramatic pictures to stimulate oral expression and role playing.

Slingerland, Beth A., *Training in Some Prerequisites for Beginning Reading.* Cambridge, Mass.: Educators Publishing, 1967. A list of large photographs.

Talkstarters. Glenview, Ill.: Scott, Foresman and Company. Colored pictures in sets of six.

Thomas, Hadley A., and Allen, Harold B., *Oral English.* Oklahoma City, Okla.: The Economy Company, 1972. A one-book program in speech and articulation for non-English-speaking pupils. No reading involved.

Visual-Lingual Reading Program. East Orange, N.J.: Tweedy. Forty-eight color transparencies for discussion purposes.

Walker Plays. New York: Walker Educational Book Corp. A collection of simple plays.

Bank Street Readers. New York: Bank Street College of Education and Macmillan Publishing Co., Inc.

Baugh, Dolores, and Pulsifer, Marjorie P., *Chandler Language Experience Readers.* San Francisco: Chandler Publishing Company, 1964–1966.

Brown, Virginia, et al., *Skyline Series.* St. Louis, Mo.: Webster Publishing, 1965.

Common Signs of Community Service and Safety. Dinuba, Calif.: Fern Tripp.

Cornerstone Readers. San Francisco: Field Enterprises. High-interest stories at primary reading levels.

Franco, John, *Afro-American Contributors to American Life.* Westchester, Ill.: Benefic Press. A social studies text of which one edition is at the primary level.

Myers, Walter M., *Where Does the Day Go?* New York: Parents Magazine, 1969. A multiethnic group of children try to explain night and day.

New York, N.Y. New York: Random House, Inc. Simple newspapers on current events, for five levels of inner-city children.

Rollins, Charlemae, *City Starter Books.* Glenview, Ill.: Scott, Foresman and Company. Eight-page picture books for city children.

Schueler, Nancy, et al., *The City Is My Home.* New York: The John Day Company. Inner-city readers.

The Urban School News. Detroit: Urban Educational Publications. A biweekly newspaper for intermediate-grade urban children.

Wyndham, Robert, *Tales the People Tell in China.* New York: Julian Messner, 1971. Sixteen Chinese tales for storytelling.

* This list includes only specially prepared, multiethnic materials. There are hundreds of trade books suitable for children of each ethnic and minority group. See George D. Spache, *Good Reading for the Disadvantaged Reader* (Champaign, Ill.: Garrard Publishing Company, 1974), for graded lists of such books.

9
The Combined Program for Intermediate Grades

PREVIEW

Basal reader-oriented teachers will undoubtedly be disturbed by the reading program outlined here for the intermediate grades. Where is the sequential skill development that is supposed to be so essential? How could such a program ever accomplish the all-important goals of the basal reader? Obviously the authors do not share the belief that many basal programs offer foundational training in reading. In fact, we think that many contribute very little to the development of the reading and study habits essential to junior and senior high school students. In our opinion, some intermediate-grade basal reader programs are simply training in reading in literature. Such training may have some values, but it is certainly inadequate to the future demands for effective reading in other subject areas.

Reading instruction in the intermediate grades should begin to emphasize learning the special content field vocabularies, the organization and retention of facts, and the types of reasoning peculiar to each field of study. The content vocabularies offer not only a group of essential words with new and significant meanings, but also a second group of known words with new meanings. These vocabularies are the idea or concept core of each subject area and are fundamental to its comprehension. Organization and retention of facts by summarizing, outlining, and notetaking are an integral part of content study, and their acquisition cannot be left to trial-and-error learning. Each content field demands somewhat different reasoning processes—cause and effect, formulation of principles, recognition of a chain of events, etc. Children do not spontaneously develop these processes without the stimulation of appropriate questions, discussion, illustration, and other attempts at teacher direction of pupil thinking.

In previous editions we have criticized basal reader programs for their failure to provide the special reading skills necessary for content fields. Most programs stressed narrative material heavily and only occasionally offered watered-down samples of science, social science, or other areas. Today's readers, speaking generally of course, have improved greatly, in our opinion, in recognizing pupils' needs for training in study skills. But the materials representing various fields and the accompanying skill practice that can be presented within the framework of a basal program is necessarily limited. We could not expect a basal to do more than offer samples from various curricular fields and to initiate the study skill training. For these reasons, we emphasize development of the abilities in reading with flexibility, study skills, and essential reading behaviors in the content fields so strongly in our intermediate-grade program.

We suggest the following for training in the content reading skills: use the available content textbooks, as science, health, history, geography, and arithmetic, assuming of course that these are suitable for the independent reading levels of the various types of pupils. We recognize that many teachers are limited to a narrow range of textbooks in teaching the content fields. Some teachers will not have science books of different grade levels to match their pupils' reading abilities. In these cases, it is imperative that the teacher gradually secure a wide variety of booklets, pamphlets, brochures, maps, charts, and the like, of varying difficulty. To aid in finding these and securing them within a limited book budget, we have included a number of source lists of free and inexpensive materials. These sources offer a great variety of teaching materials on almost every topic normally touched upon in the intermediate-grade curriculum. In addition to this assumption that the teacher will have or will get varied content field materials, we are certainly expecting that much of the instruction and practice in content skills will occur in small groups, perhaps arranged according to reading levels and abilities. We cannot conceive of effective content skill teaching being conducted with a single piece of reading matter being used for all pupils regardless of their abilities. Exceptions to this might occur in the teaching of certain skills in map and chart reading or simple library skills.

There are a number of compelling reasons for the emphasis upon content reading skills in these grades (21). Any of the daily reading tasks in the classroom involves the study of content textbooks beginning in the fourth grade and during the rest of the child's school career. Not only must the pupil learn to use these materials effectively, but he must also learn that each area demands certain unique types of thinking, approach, and study habits. Even those pupils whose fundamental skills are well developed vary considerably in their effectiveness in reading in different fields. Some excel in science or in social science but are ineffectual in another field, such as mathematics. Good general reading ability such as that stressed in the basal program tends to support learning in the subject matter areas. But simply because a pupil continues to develop in basic reading skills, we cannot assume that he will therefore also grow in subject matter achievement. Content fields differ too widely in vocabularies, fact relationships, types of reasoning, and background information for us to expect similar progress in all areas.

The manner in which the study of content fields is approached also determines the nature of the reading skills demanded. Some teachers use a single textbook and expect only direct recall with a minimum of interpretation. Other teachers use a variety of sources and reference materials, thus demanding that their pupils show some organizing ability as well as skill in comparing and combining sources. Some teachers utilize a great deal of independent work and small-group activity, expecting that their pupils will be able to collect and collate materials, organize them, and prepare reports based on a critical evaluation of the available resources. Still other teachers approach the content of a field through problem-solving activities which require the pupil to collect and organize facts, recognize principles, and discover and defend solutions.

It is true that most content textbooks are highly organized and offer a great many aids to the child's learning. Texts commonly employ such devices as headings, summaries, illustrations, glossaries, indexes, diagrams, charts, and other graphic aids. Both the authors of these texts and the teachers who use them often assume that the textual aids simplify the reading task for the pupil and assist him in his learning. Unfortunately, this assumption is not true, for research shows that these visual and graphic aids do not ensure better understanding or retention for most pupils (1). Only when pupils are carefully trained to read and use them effectively do these aids function as intended. Without such training, the average pupil finds common content textbooks more difficult because of the inclusion of a variety of so-called aids. No available basal reading program offers complete training for these complexities of content field reading.

Several writers have tried to discover what teachers understand and believe about reading in the content fields. Some of these reports are encouraging, for they seem to indicate that we are affecting teachers' thinking and practices in this area. Brother Leonard Courtney observes that teachers who are now alert to student reading problems: (1) do recognize conceptual and experiential deficiencies; (2) contend with poor motivation and strive to develop pupil interest; (3) differentiate between general and technical vocabulary and try to establish conceptual understanding beyond the mere recognition of the word; (4) differentiate levels of instructional materials to meet reading needs of the pupils; (5) find time for individual work with pupils; (6) try to extend the extra-class reading of the pupils; (7) use a variety of media to interest and instruct; and (8) adapt their expectations to pupil's abilities. These are certainly hopeful signs that, when teaching subject matter, teachers are more aware of the individual differences in the reading abilities of pupils and the impact of these differences upon content learning (2).

Other surveys show that teachers are, as we have stressed, beginning to believe that the teaching of reading skills can be incorporated into content presentations without interfering with the learning of the field. A corollary opinion, that any teacher who gives assignments should teach his pupils how to read and study the assignments, is also gaining acceptance. Most teachers no longer believe that all the reading training should be taken care of in the formal "reading lessons" or by remedial teachers.

At the same time, there are gaps and weaknesses in the implementation of these ideas, for many think their textbooks are suitable for most of their pupils, without even knowing or trying to find out how difficult the textbooks really are, nor how their readability levels compare with those of the pupils exposed to them. Many still accept the publishers' labels for the levels of textbooks and would be shocked to read the analyses of textbook difficulty, which almost uniformly indicate that many, if not most, content textbooks are written at reading levels much higher than the grade levels for which they are offered (12).

BASIC SKILLS FOR CONTENT READING

Before pupils may read efficiently in the content area, they must be skillful in a number of fundamental reading practices. Some of these are promoted by the training given in the average basal reading program, but most of them must be developed in realistic practice with content materials.

Previewing

Essentially, previewing is an organized, rapid coverage of reading materials, such as a chapter in a book, a report, a newspaper article, or other source. In practice, it involves reading some or all of the following before deciding how or whether to read the entire selection: title, headings and subheadings, summary or introductory statements, illustrative and graphic materials, and opening and closing sentences of each paragraph.

The purpose of previewing is to answer such questions as the following: What information may be obtained from this material? How is this information organized? Is this information significant to the readers' purposes? Should the entire selection be read? What are the main ideas presented? A large number of research studies show that previewing is an important initial step in reading almost any type of content material. When used before actual reading, comprehension and retention of the material is greatly increased, and the reader's time is conserved by eliminating irrelevant materials; after sufficient practice the reader learns to handle materials more rapidly and economically. Previewing should be taught as a preliminary step to all textbook study and as an effective device for reviewing for a test, as a quick brush-up before recitation, and for evaluating materials collected for a report. Since most narrative or basal material does not lend itself to this technique, it is apparent that this practice must be used extensively in content textbooks, reference, and resource materials.

Simple, repetitive practice of previewing, or other reading techniques we shall discuss, is pointless unless the purpose of the training is apparent to the pupils. The teacher must not only demonstrate how to preview and provide practice, but also prove to the pupils the values of this device. She may demonstrate these by testing pupil comprehension and retention in two halves of a chapter—with one half studied after previewing and the other studied without any previewing. She may provide a number of possible resource materials on a topic for each child and then ask him to decide after a few minutes which of these are most important to the topic. She may provide an unfamiliar textbook or other resource to the children and allow only a few minutes for them to find the main ideas of a certain chapter. Or, she may provide two versions of a current event as found in different newspaper articles and ask the pupils to see how quickly they can find any facts present in one article but not in the other. These sample exercises will, with teacher guidance, demonstrate the values of previewing as contrasted with unplanned reading. From these introductory exercises she may proceed to directed practice in previewing in the pupils' different textbooks and in other materials she commonly expects them to use. The Coronet film, "Reading with a Purpose," is particularly useful in introducing previewing to intermediate-grade pupils.

Four out of five sixth graders and even many college students do not use previewing even when their purpose is simply to identify main ideas. The lack of development of this essential skill among mature students emphasizes two implications for the classroom teacher. This skill does not appear spontaneously merely because the pupil continues to mature in general reading skills. In addition, students do not learn to use this skill without extensive, realistic practice in content field materials.

The need for instruction in how to read and interpret subheadings when previewing is shown by an investigation by Hvistendahl (11). The paragraph headings in newspaper articles were modified to repeat facts, or to be almost irrelevant, to be contradictory, or omitted entirely. The experimenter found that the variations had no differential effect upon the readers' recall of information given by them. In fact, less than half of the readers recognized that some headings were contradictory! In other words, headings of any of these types did nothing for the students to aid in previewing the material. The need for practicing reading subheads and discussing their meaning or implications is very real if the pupil is to be successful in gaining an overview of the material before reading it thoroughly.

Before leaving discussion of this important basic skill, it would be wise to stress one other important facet of the training. The teacher often fails to realize that the manner in which his pupils handle reading tasks is a direct reflection of his structuring of the problem. The crux of the matter is not whether the teacher poses "thought questions" or "memory questions." The significance of the practice lies in the way in which the student is led to handle the answer, to organize the facts, to attack the reading materials. If the teacher hopes to teach children previewing and the other basic skills we will discuss, then her presentation of the reading task must impel pupils to use the particular skill she is stressing. In practicing previewing, for example, the assignments or questions she proposes must be such that they can best be accomplished by previewing. Imposing time limits in these tasks, and asking for a variety of performances—rapid identification of main ideas, quick comparisons of sources, evaluation of relevance of a source to a given topic, discovery of the presence of a given fact or topic, quick reviews before recitation, rapid summaries of the content of a selection, frequent comparisons of retention with and without previewing—are reading tasks which push children in the direction of the desired practice. This purposeful practice is essential if the student is to adopt and use effectively the technique we are offering him.

Skimming and Scanning

These rapid reading techniques, like previewing, are fundamental to effective reading in the content fields. Skimming, as we define it, is actually a broadened previewing in which not only the main ideas are discovered but also some of the supporting details. When the pupil has learned to preview, we suggest teaching him to skim by adding to his previewing the reading of some of the details within each paragraph. In previewing, the pupil usually reads the opening and closing sentences of each paragraph, for in textbook materials these sentences commonly include the main ideas of the paragraph. To skim, we teach the pupil to extend this to include the details within the paragraph as these may be discovered by cue words or phrases. Having read the opening and closing sentences, the pupil looks quickly for such cues as italicized words, numbered sentences, or such words as *first, second, because, in addition to, also,* and *but.* These words serve as signals to point out the various supporting details that the author is offering. By reading these details, the pupil strengthens his understanding of the main ideas but saves the time that would be needed for complete reading.

Scanning is that type of reading used in locating quickly specific information in printed materials without reading the entire page. We use scanning constantly in such tasks as reading an index, a telephone directory, a dictionary, and in finding a word, a date, a number, or a certain phrase. Three steps are involved in scanning: (1) knowing clearly what it is that is being sought and the form in which it is likely to appear; (2) looking swiftly over the page, list, or column, expecting the fact to stand out from the rest of the page; and (3) verifying the answer when it is found by reading it carefully.

Skimming and scanning are not superficial types of reading which may result in weak comprehension. Rather, they are specific techniques for definite purposes in certain reading tasks. By learning to skim, the pupil develops skill in strengthening the comprehension of main ideas which he might have grossly identified by previewing. Skimming ability promotes flexibility in reading: it increases skill in shifting to high speed in familiar material for quick exploration of an idea to determine its relevance; it promotes ability to select portions for more careful reading and to eliminate portions that are not related to the reader's purpose. By learning to scan, the pupil reads lists or columns intelligently or can find with ease a specific fact somewhere in the printed page. He learns that the single fact he is seeking can be found without reading the entire page.

As suggested earlier, practice in these skills should be carefully planned. Skimming may be practiced in timed reading tasks such as finding the number of details in a certain paragraph, finding the facts offered to support a certain main idea, deciding on the relevance of a certain portion, and comparing details found in two or more sources. Scanning may be practiced in finding a given fact in a textbook page or chapter, index, table of contents, dictionary, glossary, table or chart, street directory, and other sources. Imposing time limits and comparing the time required by various pupils helps keep these skills functioning as rapid reading techniques.

Skimming is not a type of random or casual reading, or just a "looking over" of materials, as we conceive of it. To prevent skimming from deteriorating into this unplanned, ineffectual approach, we suggest a definite sequence in the training efforts. Having established the habit of previewing, begin practice in skimming a single paragraph to find such facts as a certain detail, the number of details, the nature of the author's proof or support to the main idea, the order of presentation of these proofs or details. Practice in a variety of materials from science, social science, and arithmetic, varying the practice according to the organization of the material. Gradually extend the skimming practice to several paragraphs, a whole page, a section, and finally a chapter.

Scanning is also a selective, not a random, type of rapid reading. Early practice should include only a paragraph or two of material in which the reader attempts to find a single fact—a name, a date, a number, or a phrase.

The length of the material to be scanned can be gradually increased and thus the reader's search made longer, with the result that he retains more of the desired information as well as incidental facts (6). Each practice exercise is introduced by a question which clearly indicates that fact to be found. Multiple-choice or true–false questions are preferable at first, since they help to point out the form in which the answer is likely to be found. Children will be more successful in their early efforts if the form in which the answer is likely to appear is pointed out to them—in capital or italicized letters, in numbers, and so forth. The exact pattern of the movements of the eye in scanning is not very significant, provided it, in general, proceeds from the top to bottom of the page. The research studies which have been made of children scanning indicate that most employ a kind of Z-shaped movement over the lines and paragraphs. Both the amount and type of material in which scanning is practiced should gradually be increased from a paragraph or two, to a page, to several pages, to a whole chapter. In dealing with the longer selections, pupils should be helped to realize that the tasks will be done more quickly if they preview the material before scanning for the fact desired. By the previewing, they can quickly find the most likely section or page in which the fact will be and then scan only that portion. Scanning should be practiced in textual materials, lists, directories, charts, tables, indexes, glossaries, and any of the other elements of a textbook in which it is feasible.

All three of these techniques—previewing, skimming, and scanning—help pupils develop flexibility in rate and skill in adapting the form of reading to the reader's purpose. Flexibility results in greater comprehension, economy of study time, and greater enjoyment of work-type reading. As a result the flexible reader is more effective in his handling of study tasks, more successful in retention and achievement in the content fields.

Reading Graphic Materials

There are relatively few studies which clarify the desirable sequence of training in such tasks as reading maps, graphs, charts, diagrams, and tables. Thus most of our suggestions for teaching pupils how to read these difficult materials must be based on logic rather than research. Studies give some clues regarding the map-reading abilities of pupils in the intermediate grades (1,23). The tests employed in these studies were used on a sufficient number of children to indicate the probable difficulties of various skills, and therefore some indications for the logical sequence in which they might be taught. The indications of these tests are combined in Figure 9–1 in the order of difficulty from easier items to harder.

A. Reading a key or legend to find:

desert	products
capital of country	rivers
minerals	population
railroads	scale of miles
rainfall	seaports
swamps	flow of rivers
mountains, plateaus, lowlands	capitals of states

B. Knowledge of globe
  Recognizing
    distance and direction
    distortion in polar equal-area projection
    distortion in any given map
    distortion in Mercator projection

C. General skills
  1. Longitude and latitude
     of a city
       naming city at given longitude and latitude
       reading latitude of given place
       reading longitude of given place
  2. Rivers
       recognizing junction of rivers
       identifying source and mouth
       recognizing a delta
       finding a tributary
       locating a city in reference to a river

3. Zones
    naming geographical circles
    describing general climate
    locating continent
    locating tropical areas
    meaning of "arid"
4. Coastline
    identifying adjoining oceans
    finding city on coastline
    distinguishing regular and irregular coastlines
    finding protected harbor
5. Continents
    finding lake within continent
    finding city serving as railroad center
    identifying oceans surrounding each
    recognizing boundary lines of largest states
    recognizing continents by shape
    finding city on peninsula
6. Directions
    on a globe
    on make-believe road map
    on Mercator projection
    in long and complicated journey
    use meridians and parallels
    on world or sectional map
    on polar map
    on partial, globular map

FIGURE 9–1. **Map-Reading Skills** [After Louise Durkee Wagner, "Measuring the Map-Reading Ability of Sixth-Grade Children," *Elementary School Journal,* 53 (February 1953), 338–344. Copyright © 1953 by the University of Chicago; reprinted by permission of the University of Chicago Press.]

According to Wagner (*23*), the accuracy with which sixth-grade children exercised these map-reading skills varied considerably. The order of their difficulty from easiest to hardest was: continents, globe, rivers, zones, directions, coastlines, reading a key or legend, and longitude and latitude. The average scores on the test items ranged from 82 percent down to 57 percent. It is surprising to discover that the ability to read the key or legend of a map, for example, was still so difficult for children of this grade level. This essential element of reading and interpreting a map apparently needs much more training than it has received in the past.

This study of children's map-reading skills was conducted almost twenty-five years ago. We can find no more recent studies which might indicate whether the data are true today. Hence Wagner's study is probably useful only for indicating the relative difficulty of these map-reading skills, not for showing how well children can perform them in today's schools.

A bulletin, "Skills in the Social Studies," issued by the Board of Education, Prince George's County, Upper Marlboro, Maryland, offers a very helpful list of map and globe skills. The items listed under each skill correspond in number to their respective grades.

Map and Globe Skills

Ability To Orient One's Self and One's Position in Relation to the Environment

1. Relationship of furniture, door, and windows to child.
2. Relationships of lunchroom, hall, office to own classroom.
3. Showing on community map, relation of child's home to school and other community landmarks.
4. Locating one's community on county map in relation to other communities and landmarks.
5. Locating own town, county, and state on map of United States. Same for United States on a world map.
6. Locating home, community, county, state, and country to rest of the world in terms of cardinal directions.

Ability to Orient One's Self in Terms of the Cardinal Directions—N., S., E., W.

1. & 2. Distinguishing directions by own shadow in the A.M. and P.M.
3. Locating directions in relation to the sun.
4. Locating north by a compass and thus identifying other directions, cardinal and intermediate.
5. Locating cardinal and intermediate (N.E., S.E., N.W., S.W.) on a community map. Using compass to lay out community map.
6. Tracing route on map or globe, identifying each change of direction in terms of cardinal and intermediate directions, parallels, meridians, latitude and longitude.

Reading a Map According to Cardinal Directions

1. Using cardinal directions on a street map. Tracing and telling directions in a route from the school to a landmark.
2. Using directions on a community map, or road map of the area. Reading directions for trip to nearest community.
3. Using a road map for directions on a simulated trip through several cities of the state or elsewhere.

Developing a Feeling for Direction and Distance

1. Walking to specified area of building, telling directions followed.
2. Giving directions for trip to school, store, fire house, etc., from home. Use picture map of community for similar activity.
3. Follow diagram of route for short field trip, as drawn by teacher. Telling directions of route from own to neighboring community.

Finding General Directions on a Globe or Map

1. Discovering and discussing the north and south poles.
2. Discussing the poles and the equator.
3. Relating poles and equator to hot and cold lands.
4. Poles, equator and earth's axis, network of lines on globe and rotation.
5. Locating positions using parallels, meridians, latitude, longitude, north and south poles. Locating S.O.S. position with reference to latitude and longitude.
6. Locating cities, answering S.O.S. when latitude and longitude are given. Using polar projection maps.

Recognizing Scale and Distances on Maps

1. Observing relative distances, time for travel on community maps.
2. Noting shortest distances between points on community map drawn to scale by teacher.
3. Noting distances between points on road maps, estimating time.
4. Recognizing linear units and their relative lengths: foot, block, mile, etc. Estimating distances and travel time between given points. Drawing to scale plan of such objects as desk, window, classroom.
5. Exploring ways of expressing scale: graphic, inches to miles, one-half inch to one foot, etc. Studying aerial maps and comparing with ground, linear units.
6. Drawing scale maps of the community. Using scale to measure distances on maps. Comparing map areas.

Locating Designated Places on Maps and Globes

1. Comparing shape of globe to earth. Locating own community on globe. Comparing areas of land and water.
2. Comparing sizes of oceans and continents. Locating familiar states and communities.
3. Locating areas related to social studies content. Making large-scale community map. Using and coloring outline maps to show given areas.
4. Locating equator, hemispheres, parallels, latitude, longitude, Prime Meridian. Locating countries and states with reference to bordering land and water bodies. Making a relief map of given area, noting boundaries, terrain, etc.
5. Locating points by latitude and longitude.
6. Using atlas grid to locate places on road map. Recognizing different grid systems.

Understanding and Expressing Relative Location

1. Make model representation of school grounds. Using map terms to locate equipment, buildings, etc.
2. Using community map to show relative locations of school, home, and other landmarks.
3. Using large town and county map for relative locations.
4. Recognizing significance of physical features: bays, harbors, rivers, peninsulas,

etc., for growth of a city. Expressing relative position by latitude, longitude, distance, and terrain.

5. Discussing growth effects of mountains, water bodies, distances, resources, etc.
6. City development in relation to trade routes, climatic conditions, physical features, resources and market areas. Importance of great circle air routes.

Drawing Maps Oriented to True Direction

1. Sketching a route.
2. Sketching rough map of town showing main streets.
3. Drawing maps to scale: room, playground, state.
4. Drawing maps using grids furnished by teacher. Comparing with wall map.
5. Drawing maps based on own grid of latitude and longitude.

Reading and Using Map Symbols, Key, or Legend

1. Using large-scale map of play area, placed in line with true cardinal directions, place cutouts of equipment, etc., to convey concept of symbolic representation. Devise key.
2. Introduce symbols for rivers, lakes, oceans, bays, continents, etc. Match these with pictures of same. Make pictorial map of community, later substituting with symbols.
3. Study firsthand differences in land and water forms. Make models of these and match with pictorial symbols.
4. Compare pictures of landscapes with aerial photographs and later with symbols on a large-scale map.
5. Using dots, lines, and color to show physical features, as streets, buildings, land forms, railroads, etc. Chart routes of explorers, discoverers, and other figures from social studies.
6. Constructing and reading transportation maps to show routes of steamships, railroads, airplanes, major highways, covered-wagon routes. Reading weather maps for atmosphere and climatic information.

Comparing Maps and Drawing Inferences

1. Using pictorial maps, note placement of gas stations, schools, cemeteries, etc., at strategic locations.
2. Noting location of shopping centers, housing developments, suburbs in logical sites.
3. Comparing simple community maps for size, industries, growth, etc.
4. Comparing area relationships, and rainfall and temperature maps for inferences regarding climate.
5. Comparing colonial and present-day population maps, topography of large regional areas.
6. Using symbols to infer patterns of rainfall, soils, growth of cities, railroads, location of industries, etc.

Chart and graph reading skills are outlined in the same bulletin in this brief fashion.

Reading Charts and Graphs

1. Using and interpreting simple pictorial charts. Making such charts.
2. Using pictorial bar graph to show sunny and rainy days, or temperatures.
3. Using circle graph to show child's own daily program [i.e., hours in school, at play, at sleep, at meals (by clock faces)].
4. Interpreting and comparing pictorial, bar and circle graphs. Reading and making charts showing geographical resources, products, etc.
5. Making bar graphs regarding mean temperature, rainfall, population. Making pictorial charts to illustrate lives of famous personages, etc.
6. Using circle graphs to show use of taxes, child's own daily schedule, etc.
7. Practice interpreting newspaper cartoons, particularly those without words.
8. Make large current events map by placing pictures of recent happenings on large world wall map.
9. Make time lines to show chronology of series of events.
10. Use charts to depict organization of the school, local, state, or national governments.

Reading Tables and Diagrams

1. Read and interpret simple tables drawn from daily newspapers, such as guide to sections, index, TV and radio programs, etc.
2. Discuss structure of tables; their types; headings; marginal, head, or tail material.
3. Read and interpret railroad, airline, and bus timetables.
4. Read and interpret baseball or football records, shipping reports, weather forecasts.
5. Practice with various types of diagrams found in magazines, newspapers, and texts.
6. Make simple tables and diagrams to illustrate facts drawn from materials available.
7. Practice scanning in tables.
8. Make diagrams based on outlines or list of directions constructed by group.

There are only a few sources of practice materials for training in map reading. These are listed among the resources at the end of this chapter. In addition to these, intensive use of the maps available in classroom textbooks is certainly desirable. Commercial and industrial sources of wide variety of free and inexpensive maps to supplement classroom materials are also listed in the resources bibliography.

In learning to read maps of various types, children should be made aware of the inherent limitations in flat maps. Such maps inevitably distort areas, shapes, size, distances, and even directions. Recall, if you will, your own mental picture of the size of Greenland on the usual classroom map of the Western Hemisphere. Other limitations of maps are their essential selectivity in the amount of detail any one map can offer; their variation in accuracy according to the information available in different parts of the world; and the use of representative or completely symbolic legends. Children (and the teacher) should be aware that certain projections introduce constant errors. For example, the Mercator map exaggerates size as distance increases from the equator (see earlier reference to common impressions of Greenland); the Van der Grinten projection also exaggerates but to a lesser degree; while the Mollweide and other elliptical projections are correct in size but distort true shapes near the poles.

Other graphic materials in which intermediate-grade pupils must be trained to read effectively include graphs, charts, diagrams, and tables. One basic tool in reading many of these, scanning, has already been described. In many instances, the reading of a chart or table is basically a scanning art. The reader quickly reads the title and the column headings and then looks within the material to find the facts he is seeking. Pupils should have practice in a variety of these items by following a systematic scanning, including the title, headings, and left-hand column of items, thus identifying the correct line and column in which to read. Inexpensive practice materials in reading a variety of graphic, tabular, chart, and pictorial items in grade science and social science materials are available in the *EDL Study Skills Library*. Each of these kits consists of eleven complete lessons in science or social science for one of the intermediate and upper elementary grades. Each lesson includes practice in reading several graphic or pictorial aids, as part of a complete science or social science lesson. Other study skills are also stressed in these materials, as we shall note later.

Single kits of practice materials for intermediate and upper elementary grades combined are available in the *SRA Graph and Picture Study Kits* and the *SRA Map and Globe Skills Kit*. Each of these kits offers a wide variety of exercises in different types of graphs or maps, respectively. Each exercise is an independent, brief task in reading and interpreting a type of graphic aid.

Two other alternatives are possible, if the commercial kits are not available. Collections of maps, charts, diagrams, and tables may be made from newspapers and magazines by the children and the teacher. Having those who bring in samples try to explain them to the class, then mounting them around the room in groups according to their types, and using them later as the occasion arises as resources for the children to consult as they construct their own is an inexpensive and realistic way of strengthening pupil learning in this area. Second, as each type of chart or graph is introduced, having children execute a very simple example of it and adding these to the display areas reinforces reading skills with graphic materials. As implied in the lists of types earlier, the subject portrayed need not be complex. Almost any recurring phenomenon of life in the classroom or community will lend itself to graphs, charts, and diagrams. Almost any body of facts shown in a graph can be transmitted to a table, and most arithmetic problems can be represented by a chart or diagram (which also aids in understanding the problem). Almost any series of events can be represented by a time-line chart, as cause-and-effect relationships can be portrayed by drawings and charts. Even without extraordinary resources, the interested teacher who recognizes the importance of the development of these thinking–reading processes can supply a wealth of experiences for the pupils.

Most teachers and reading authors agree that growth in effective use of the library is essential for success in reading in the content fields. However, there is little unanimity of opinion as to who shall assume the responsibility for this training. Some teachers attempt some training; others leave this task to the librarians. In the final analysis, the responsibility for training in library skills really rests upon both, according to the facilities, opportunities, and abilities they possess. When librarians are available and capable of offering such training, some division of responsibility must be agreed upon between the teaching staff and the librarian. When librarians are not available or their time is already completely occupied, the classroom teacher must assume complete responsibility for such training, with whatever guidance she may be able to solicit from the professional librarian. Just how this ideal can be accomplished is very problematic when, as we have already noted, intermediate teachers allow only about an hour per week for library activities and independent reading in the room or school library.

Conferences at the University of Nebraska and the University of Miami have emphasized the role of the teacher in stimulating growth in library skills in these basic principles: the teacher must understand the nature and content of reference materials and their uses; the teacher must be interested in teaching the use of reference materials; such materials must be readily available; the skills of reference must be systematically taught; and, finally, the teacher must encourage independent exploration of a variety of sources of information. Principles such as these do not imply that children learn locational and library skills by doing a few simple exercises in a workbook (without ever actually using the reference tool for which they are presumably practicing). As in every other type of learning, practice in locational and library skills will have to be realistic, varied, and purposeful.

Library Skills

At Primary Levels

1. Title, title page.
2. Copyright page, acknowledgments.
3. Preface, table of contents.
4. Lists of tables, maps, illustrations.
5. Chapter headings or titles.
6. Index.
7. Graphic and pictorial aids.
8. Picture captions, picture credits.
9. Introduction to the dictionary, atlas.
10. Arrangement of the library.

At Intermediate Levels

1. Sectional heads, side and other headings.
2. Chapter or section summaries.
3. Card catalog.
4. Dewey Decimal System.
5. Simple practice in finding desired book.
6. Glossary, appendix, footnotes.
7. Almanac, yearbooks.
8. Picture and clipping files.
9. *Guide to Periodical Literature*.
10. Indexes.
11. Simple projects in finding resource materials related to given topic.
12. Projects involving (a) compiling bibliography; (b) preparing outline of research paper; (c) summarizing various materials on given topic; (d) preparing brief paper incorporating quotations from several sources.

Most of this training should center around the resources available in the classroom or be conducted in the school library, if it is to be effective. If desired, it can be supplemented by some of the materials listed in the resources bibliography. One of these, the *EDL Study Skills Library—Reference Skills,* merits special mention. Each of these kits offers a graded sequence of library training exercises for one of the intermediate or upper elementary grades. Practice in most of the specific library skills mentioned above is included. The kit is relatively inexpensive and has sufficient materials to permit every child in the classroom to practice each lesson. The lessons are brief, independent of each other, and permit each child to progress sequentially at his own rate of learning. To our knowledge, this is the only multilevel, individualized body of materials available for training in library skills.

Even more important than the teaching of library skills are the teacher's efforts to establish a good working relationship with the librarian and to motivate children to use a library. Cooperation between librarians or media specialists and teachers is often poor largely because of lack of planning on the part of classroom teachers. Before making an assignment or initiating a project that will require use of the library or media center, the teacher certainly ought to (1) inform the teacher in charge of his plans, (2) make sure that the materials needed are available there, and (3) clarify his directions to ensure that the children know what resources they will be seeking. If the project will require extended time or resources, the specialist should be informed to help the teacher schedule his activities and those of other groups of children working there in order that the needed resources will continue to be available. When we suggest that the librarian or media specialist should be informed of the teacher's plans, we imply that this request should be forwarded to these specialists at least several days prior to their beginning.

Particularly in the individualized reading program, motivating children to library use should develop naturally from the program. The library is the major source for the replenishing of the classroom library and is an obvious step to leading children to go to the library to seek other books that are like those they have enjoyed. Because of the heavy demands upon them and the frequent understaffing (only 17 percent have a full-time librarian), school libraries and media centers must often maintain what appears to be a rather rigid schedule for different grade levels. Children should know the schedule and, after having been introduced to the arrangement several times jointly by teacher and specialist, be permitted to avail themselves of these opportunities in small groups or even independently.

A very significant aspect of motivating children's reading is the example offered by the teacher. She should demonstrate her own appreciation of reading by reading while the children are also so engaged in the classroom and center, by reading to them with obvious pleasure and expression, by familiarizing herself constantly with children's books that may appeal and presenting them dramatically, by giving books as prizes for contests or exceptional achievement, by encouraging children to bring their own library books to loan to other pupils, and by keeping parents informed of children's reading needs and interests. When their class is scheduled for the library, as is the custom in some schools, many teachers seize the opportunity to disappear quietly to the teacher's lounge. In this and other instances, their negative attitudes may work against the primary goal of all reading instruction—the development of lifelong use and enjoyment of the ability to read. Even at the sacrifice of some personal free time, teacher behavior must be consistent with their avowed intentions. Going to the library or center with children, and using its resources frequently in the classroom library, will produce significantly more reading among children than just sending them off on their own.

Organizing and Reporting

The research on organizing and reporting skills makes two points quite clear: (1) success in content field reading is improved by training in these abilities; and (2) many junior and senior high school students show great inadequacy in these important skills. On the other hand, the available research clarifies neither what the content of training in these skills should be nor the best sequence of steps. Very few prepared materials are available for this essential training.

A suggested sequence of steps is offered in the *SRA Organizing and Reporting Skills Kit*. This collection of short exercises is offered for intermediate and upper elementary grades and by its individualization permits students to progress at their own rates. The kit offers the following training in the skills of reporting.

Organizing and Reporting Skills

A. Form of the Report

1. Identifying portions of a report as beginnings, middles, or ends.
2. Arranging parts of a report in proper order.
3. Recognizing which part of an incomplete report is missing.
4. Judging simple reports for completeness and order.

B. Sticking to the Point

1. Finding irrelevant statement in reports.
2. Identifying statements of opinion or feeling.

C. Order in the Paragraph

1. Correcting the sequence or time order of details in a paragraph.
2. Detecting the omission of opening or closing sentence.
3. Identifying topic sentences or recognizing omission of such.

D. Quality in the Paragraph

1. Locating repetitious words or phrases.
2. Identifying repetition of ideas or contradictions.
3. Identifying paragraphs as objective or subjective opinion.

To each of these aspects of reporting, the experienced teacher will undoubtedly wish to add other kinds of practices. It is apparent also that training in reading, writing, and analyzing paragraphs, summaries, book reviews, and magazine and newspaper articles will have to precede and accompany the report training offered in this kit. Some of these applications are suggested in the kit.

Among the basic skills of note taking that should be taught are the following:

Note-Taking Skills*

1. Summarizing a paragraph with a single sentence.
2. Summarizing the main ideas or topic sentences of a group of paragraphs by single sentences.
3. Summarizing the answer to a specific question by a short note.
4. Summarizing successive paragraphs by single sentences.

*Training in the concepts of main ideas, and topic and summary sentences, will precede this program.

5. Summarizing an entire passage by a paragraph.
6. Given a topic, choose relevant notes from a group of such.
7. Arrange these selected notes in logical sequence under the given heading.
8. Given a group of notes, select a possible topical heading and choose relevant items.
9. Arrange selected items in a sequence under a heading supplied by a student.
10. Given the topic and a number of relevant sentences, arrange the sentences in a paragraph, including a topic and summary sentence.

This type of training in note taking and outlining can be expanded in a number of ways. The various steps can be practiced in the pupil's content textbooks of all types and in listening as well as reading situations.

Practice in taking summarizing notes while listening is an essential type of training. These notes can be improved by discussing them and comparing them with the teacher's outline of her lesson. Practice in varying the amount of detail taken in notes, as well as the degree of originality, should be given. Some areas demand more careful, detailed notes than do others; some require exact notes, while others may be freely paraphrased by the student. Notes including the summaries of main ideas, selected while reading or listening, should be practiced. The habit of revising or reorganizing notes shortly after they have been written, of combining notes from several sources into a single outline, and of evolving time-saving abbreviations which can later be readily interpreted should be given attention. Other types of practice and application of note-taking and outlining skills will suggest themselves as this training progresses.

As every teacher knows from his own experiences in high school and college, note taking tends to be a very personal kind of practice. Probably because of the lack of formal training, each student's system tends to have its own peculiarities. Some underline, some do not; some write a great deal, others have no systematic arrangement. Some copy the words of the text or speaker; others paraphrase ideas in their own words. Some can reuse their notes for review, while others find their notes too scanty or incomplete (or even unreadable). Some evolve abbreviations for frequently recurring terms, or even use incomplete writing of words to speed up the task. Are some of these practices ineffectual or even useless for retaining information? Should we give some sort of training in note taking to overcome these inefficient habits?

Unfortunately, most of the research on note taking does not give very definite answers to guide our instruction. The studies are based largely on experiments with high school and college students who have already evolved their own peculiar systems. When these students are instructed in a type of note taking, and the retention compared with another system, the results are often inconclusive. Possibly new note-taking systems conflict with their own systems and temporarily retard learning, or possibly the new system is not maintained long enough in these experiments to demonstrate its values.

Undoubtedly, disorganized, unsystematic notes are of less value than clearer arrangements. Reorganizing notes shortly after making them is profitable. But the other idiosyncratic variations in shorthand systems, or brevity versus direct quotations, do not appear to be significant, or, at least, we have not been able to show that they matter (*16*). Recent studies have strongly supported the use of underlining as a note-taking device superior to outlining (*3*). We are not certain exactly how the student's previous habits might have affected these studies, but they are quite clear-cut in their results. Not only does this procedure seem to result in better retention, but the more extensive the pupils' underlining, the better the results. Other writers, however, continue to experiment with note taking (*16*), to defend it as a profitable study technique (*15*) and to devise new systems (*8*). With this kind of research to guide us, we should probably compromise by introducing our pupils to both note taking in various ways and to underlining, and let them, as we have in the past, evolve their own systems. We would, of course, review these systems from time to time to point out ways they could be improved in permanence, clarity, organization, and speed.

A more complete program of training in outlining would include the following steps.

Outlining Skills

1. Group words under an appropriate given heading. Later practice same with children supplying the heading.
2. Group words under two headings.
3. Detect irrelevant words in a given classification.
4. Classify sentences under given heading.
5. Group words under three headings.
6. Arrange series of sentences as they appear in the reading material.
7. Arrange subtitles as in given material.
8. Arrange events in chronological order.
9. Select sentences that tell about the main idea.
10. Collect sentences bearing on a given question in a short selection.
11. Group such statements under one, two, or later, three headings.
12. Find subtopics in a paragraph.
13. Find subtopics in a longer selection.
14. Select main points to complete skeleton outline of given details.
15. Add main ideas and one or more subheadings to given skeleton outline.
16. Select main ideas for an outline.
17. Select main ideas and subheadings for an outline.
18. Outline more than one paragraph.
19. Organize notes from several sources under main ideas, subheadings, and details.

All of these study skills must eventually be woven into the fabric of instruction in the content fields. In other words, if these skills are to function realistically in the future, there must be ample opportunity for their use as a part of the class study of content materials. Thus, a typical content field lesson follows.

PLAN FOR A CONTENT AREA UNIT

Our suggestions for teaching content areas makes several assumptions. First, we are talking about the presentation of a unit of material in a series of lessons. Second, the instructional materials are relatively limited. Third, some of the pupils cannot read and comprehend the textbook.

Teaching a Content Area Unit

Teacher Preparation

1. If a manual is provided, read this to make a list of the concepts to be taught, for teaching suggestions, and for teaching aids.
2. With the help of the librarian or media specialist, assemble pertinent materials, including books and other matter for supplementary reading. Preview these aids. Complete the selection and assembling of these aids at least several days before you are to present the unit to be certain of their availability.
3. Make a time schedule for the unit, indicating the major sections, approximate time required for their presentations, and for the use of the aids previously collated.
4. Preview the unit to identify general and technical terms probably new to your class. Add these to your overall plan, listing them in relation to the concepts they clarify.
5. If you will need any apparatus, maps, etc., for the unit, check their readiness for use and assemble them in a convenient place. Plan also, at least tentatively, for follow-up activities for each day's lesson.

Presenting the Unit

1. *Motivation*—Attempt to create interest by initiating a discussion of pupil-related experiences and knowledge about the topic. If unit is closely related to previous one, spend some time reviewing concepts already learned and the association between the units. In other words, try to establish the relevance of the unit concepts to the body of knowledge of this field, and, if possible, to life itself.

   If certain reading skills are to be demanded by the nature of the unit, point this out to the pupils in the unit in the textbook. With the relevant section before them, discuss the use of scanning, map reading, interpretation of chart or diagram, etc. Remind them or elicit from them the basic reading procedures to be used. Remind them to give full attention to these graphics during their previewing.
2. *Vocabulary and concept development*—Using the chalkboard, present the new

vocabulary and concepts to be gained from the first day's lesson on the unit. Repeat this at the opening of each subsequent lesson. In presenting new terms, elicit pupil definitions and related knowledge, as possible. Clarify structure, derivation, and meaning of each term, as well as pronunciation. Discuss the interrelationship of vocabulary and unit concepts.

3. Present your demonstration, experiment, or visual aids according to your schedule. Some, of course, will be done before pupil study, others after their reading, and still others at a strategic point during the lesson.

4. Preview the textbook material which is to be covered in that day's lesson. As pupils read silently the headings, subheads, graphic aids, etc., discuss possible interpretations or implications of these, as they relate to the group of concepts presented earlier. Ask pupils to suggest questions which seem likely to be answered in a full reading. Place these on the chalkboard in an order related to the organization of the textbook.

5. *Silent Reading*—Have pupils read textbook paragraph by paragraph. As they finish each portion, ask appropriate questions which stress interpretation, analysis, synthesis, and similar reading skills.* If certain material must be memorized, have pupils copy the principle, formula, or other item and point out various ways in which this might be memorized. As the answers to the questions on the chalkboard appear, discuss them.

   Remember that some of your pupils cannot read this textbook easily. Spare them embarrassment by directing your questions to other pupils, unless the poor readers volunteer. Whatever these pupils learn about the topic will probably be through the medium of listening to the answers to your questions, the discussion of those answers, and the teaching aids or demonstration you use, unless you can supply some parallel easier materials for them to read.

   As the new vocabulary terms appear during the silent reading, point them out; ask for definitions or interpretations.

   Use oral reading only as needed to cite facts, clarify disagreements, show chronology, or to supply supporting facts in response to your questions—*not* for reading whole paragraphs.

   As graphic aids such as charts, tables, and diagrams or pictures appear in the text, discuss these in terms of their clarification of the text, their relevance, and any additional information they offer.

6. *Application*—You will have been helping pupils apply such reading skills as comprehension, scanning, previewing, and vocabulary development as you presented each segment of the unit. Obviously you intended that some of the concepts presented were to be retained in long-term memory. For this to occur, some reinforcement, some application of the ideas and facts gained, must follow each presentation. Use any of the following, matching the task to pupil ability: outlining main facts and details; constructing a time line to show a sequence of events or cause–effect or enumerative relationships; group construction of a mural; individual drawings, charts, diagrams, or a simple map. Ask a group to plan a spontaneous role-playing session depicting one of the events in the lesson; suggest resources (from your list); allow pupils to select one to deepen their knowledge; plan for a

*See detailed suggestions on questioning strategies in Chapter 13.

sharing with the class. Distribute the supplementary books you borrowed from the library, trying to match their reading difficulty to pupil ability. Here again, permit pupils to make their own selection and discuss with them their ideas about sharing the book with the class. If this supplementary material is nonnarrative, remind the pupils that this is another opportunity to practice their content reading skills, such as previewing, scanning, and learning new vocabulary.

7. *Review*—If it is essential for pupils to retain some of the concepts presented in a unit, then review of these must be planned. You can arrange some types of reviewing, such as discussing the concepts of the previous or other units, when introducing a new one. Group reviews can be accomplished by tests from time to time (as immediately after a unit, a few days later, and a few weeks later). Other types of review can be arranged by helping children repeat their previewing of all the segments to be included in a test; by aiding them in preparing an outline of the concepts and the supporting details. This is, in itself, a review, whether or not it is followed immediately by a test.

Keep in mind, in writing your review tests, that your poorer readers will have trouble reading these, too. Frame your questions as briefly and simply as possible; use true–false, completion, matching, and even multiple-choice questions in preference to essay types. Use open book questions which require use of the text to find answers. And you may still find that you will have to read or interpret your questions to the poor readers, if you are going to give them a fair chance to show what they have learned.

Review your tests with your pupils by returning their papers to them and discussing why certain answers were correct or incorrect. This is an important means of correcting misconceptions and reinforcing learning.

In an earlier chapter we mentioned an experiment in which we were involved that attempted to teach content fields to middle-school pupils who could not read the usual textbooks. The teaching took the form of collating all the ideas and information pupils and the teacher could bring together on the chalkboard, somewhat as we have described the previewing step of a content lesson above (except that the textbook was not the basic resource in these classes). These concepts were discussed, reorganized with the aid of the class, and, at the end of the day, duplicated to form, in effect, the textbook for the next day. Since the material was phrased by the pupils, even the poor readers could read and discuss the notes. Demonstrations and audiovisual aids were, of course, frequently used to reinforce the learning. Tests and quizzes were adapted to the content presented, and grades were utilized as usual. Thus, with the textbook serving only as an occasional resource book, practically the same content of English, science, social studies, and mathematics was taught to this disadvantaged group.

We have oversimplified our description of this successful attempt to teach content matter to poor readers. But the basic implication is true that content field learning can be taught to poor readers if teachers will make the adjustments in approaches and objectives that are necessary, and will lessen their dependence upon a textbook as the basic or only tool for instruction.

READING IN SCIENCE AND SOCIAL SCIENCE

The reading of science and social science materials presents an opportunity for the exercise of a variety of reading skills and techniques. Many writers have suggested that these skills be combined into a systematic approach to study-type reading. For example, *The EDL Study Skills Library* utilizes these steps in each science and social science lesson.

1. Readiness—The title, cover illustration, and a leading question under the illustration serve to stimulate the student's interest and curiosity.
2. Preview vocabulary—A list of the technical vocabulary is also offered on the cover page. These terms will occur in the article. Their pronunciations and meanings are given.
3. Survey—The student is asked to survey or preview the selection by reading the headings and looking at the illustrations and the captions.
4. Purpose—A purpose-setting question is offered on the cover page. For example, the student is asked "to read carefully to find out: 1. What makes magnets behave as they do? 2. Is a compass a magnet? 3. Why is the earth like a magnet?"
5. Reading—The student now reads the selection, presumably for the purposes previously defined.
6. Comprehension—Ten questions on general recall, main ideas, information from illustrations, and inferences are then answered.
7. Study skill—The back of the four-page folder offers further practice in a specific study skill such as outlining, summarizing, recognizing cause and effect, map reading, reading an experiment, a time line, or a diagram.

This particular sequence of steps is, of course, keyed to the format of the folders in the *EDL* kit. It is apparent, however, that the pattern of approach is adapted to transfer to the reading of other content field materials, such as the classroom textbooks. The steps of readiness, previewing vocabulary, survey or previewing the material, planning purpose, reading, and comprehension check can be used in the study of most science and social science materials.

Studying a Textbook

It has been a widespread practice to teach students to follow a definite sequence of steps when they are studying a textbook. This system, often called *Survey Q3R* or *PQRST,* led students to frame questions through surveying or previewing (*Survey Q* or *PQ*), then to read to answer these questions. Following these steps, the student would recite to himself the answers to the questions he proposed and test himself by reviewing answers without the text or his notes. Serious questions have been raised about this system by the research on the effect of reading to answer prereading questions. As we have pointed out in our discussion of ways to stimulate comprehension, detailed prereading questions tend to direct pupils to read only for the answers, and thus to achieve very limited comprehension. To overcome this hindrance to total comprehension, if students are to be urged to use a study method, it should probably take this form:

- Preview—Read title, headings, opening and closing of paragraphs, and introductory or summary paragraphs.
- Summarize—Begin to organize your comprehension of the material by making a rough outline of the main ideas as you were able to identify them by previewing. (Or, underline main ideas as you preview.)
- Read—Read through the chapter, either filling in your outline as you go, or underlining the facts which support the main ideas.
- Test—Ask questions like those your teacher might ask, or quiz yourself. Check your answers by looking at the text or your outline.

This is a relatively idealistic plan for studying a textbook which students do not necessarily adopt just because the teacher recommends it. Moreover, brighter students eventually modify the system in terms of their experiences with it, as indeed they should. If the whole idea is worth teaching to students, and we believe it does aid in their organization, it will have to be presented, and practiced many times, step by step, under teacher guidance.

For those who question our rejection of the popular *SQ3R*, we may cite the research of Crewe and Hultgren (*3*), who have shown that, as logical as it may seem to be, there is little or no research to show that student learning is improved by adopting the system. Indeed, underlining has proved superior in several investigations of comparative study methods. The ineffectualness of reading to answer prereading questions has been demonstrated by a number of research experiments discussed in Chapter 13. This conclusion is reaffirmed by Goudey's comparison of directed reading. At all levels of reading ability among fourth graders, retention of information was better under nondirected conditions (*7*).

General reading skills are important in reading in science and social science, but in addition there are a number of special skills that are demanded in these content fields. Some of the special reading skills and ways in which they may be promoted are listed below.

Reading Skills in Science and Social Science

Vocabulary—The technical terms and the general terms which are used with special meanings must be given strong emphasis. Their meanings may be approached by discussion, by teacher or pupil definition, by resorting to the glossary or dictionary, or the context, or by analysis of their structure and derivation. Similar attention must be given to terms involving concepts of distance, time, space, and the like.

Comprehension and Interpretation

1. Details—ability to recall details, to see relationships among them, to combine them into generalizations, concepts, or laws; to discriminate between significant and

insignificant or irrelevent details; to be able to scan quickly to find specific details when needed; to follow detailed directions.

2. Main ideas—ability to recognize, or formulate from details or observations; to select or make the best restatement of the main idea; to apply the main ideas in new contexts.

3. Reasoning—deducing generalizations from a series of observations, applying the generalization in new problems, recognizing cause-and-effect relationships among details or events. Using critical thinking such as evaluating sources, recognizing author's purposes, distinguishing opinion and fact, making inferences, forming judgments, and detecting propaganda devices.

Organization—Collating, summarizing, comparing materials from several sources; previewing; skimming, scanning, and careful reading. Using parts of a book, reference materials, and the library for own purposes. Taking notes and making outlines.

Use of Graphic Materials—Using common graphic and tabular materials with profit. Making such aids based on own reading. Reading, interpreting, and making maps.

In addition to these reading performances, some authors feel that pupils must learn to recognize and react to various patterns of writing in science and social science. Among the patterns commonly present are (1) directions for carrying out an experiment or creating a time line or map; (2) classification of main ideas versus details; (3) explanation of a technical process or a governmental structure by a diagram or chart; and (4) detailed statement of facts. In teaching a lesson in these contents; it would be feasible to help pupils recognize these patterns during the previewing step of the lesson, as we have outlined it earlier.

The value in such an emphasis upon the structural organizational pattern of the textbook lies in the fact that it helps to create a reading set or attitude. In other words, the reader focuses his attention on reading directions, or memorizing facts, or seeing relationships in a chart, etc. Speaking of memorizing, the teacher must be alert to detect pupils who constantly attempt to substitute memorization for real understanding. They have a constant set to try to learn all the facts, almost in a rote fashion, conceiving of this as the best type of studying. Of course, some teachers promote this set for memory of facts by their questions, which demand exact quotations from the printed material rather than reader reactions or interpretation. Two treatment approaches are appropriate: (1) pointing out the pattern of the segment of the material and discussing ways of understanding and retaining it during the previewing; and (2) focusing questions of analysis, synthesis, interpretation, and similar skills rather than sheer recital of facts. When readers who are overdependent upon sheer memory are detected by the teacher, and they are many, a few personal sessions with them in discussion of their set for reading will be profitable.

This prereading discussion of the structural characteristics of the study material helps organize the reader into a frame of mind that is receptive to learning. Like the other advance organizers we mentioned above, this preparation for reading or studying makes a direct contribution to comprehension and retention.

READING IN MATHEMATICS

The introduction of what is termed the New Mathematics has created an acute problem in terms of pupil reading ability. Analysis of a number of these new curricula indicates that at each grade level the reading difficulty of the text is much above the average reading levels of children of that grade (9,18). Both in complexity of sentence structure and breadth of vocabulary, these new materials tend to be more difficult than normal instructional materials in the field of reading. It is obvious that their use will demand extraordinary efforts on the part of teachers to help pupils read and comprehend them.

In the primary grades, and to a decreasing degree, in the intermediate, the comprehension of arithmetic problems is largely a reading rather than a mathematical task. The simple arithmetic problem presents the basic reading tasks of word recognition, word meaning, and comprehension. Thus, in the lower grades, the improvement of fundamental reading skills reflects in improved reading in arithmetic. However, as arithmetic relationships and processes become more complex, good general reading ability becomes less significant and specific training in arithmetic reading skills is necessary.

Some teachers try to meet this problem of training for reading in arithmetic by teaching pupils a pattern of thinking in problem solving, involving such steps as: "What is given? What is to be found? What arithmetic steps shall I take? Approximately what will the answer be?" A number of research studies have shown that this logical type of training is not very profitable. The average pupil does not naturally follow a specific pattern of thinking such as this recommended procedure. Nor do the experiments show that training in trying to follow a pattern always results either in greater success in problem solving or a channeling of the student's thinking. A more general training in how to read in arithmetic is probably more effective.

Pupils should be taught a general pattern in problem solving: (1) a rapid first reading (or preview) of the problem for general understanding; (2) a second, slower reading to identify the details and relationships. After the first, or certainly after the second reading, the pupil should be able to restate the problem in his own words, and should attempt this mental paraphrasing before beginning computation. If the problem involves several steps, the student should be able, after the second reading, to visualize or express the computation steps he will take. These two types of reading should be practiced frequently with the pupils giving orally their restatement of the problem and their description of the computational steps they intend to take (1).

Many reading skills are present in the reading of mathematical materials of expository, computational, and problem-solving nature. When pupils are using these materials, the teacher must be alert to recognize the reading skills being demanded and do the direct teaching that will result in improved reading in arithmetic. Some of the significant arithmetic reading skills and supporting activities are these:

1. *Vocabulary*—By illustration, definition, analysis of structure or discussion, the technical vocabulary of arithmetic must be taught before the lesson, during the lesson, and in reviews. Anticipating the need for this instruction should be an integral part of the arithmetic lesson plan. Symbols such as $+$, $-$, $\times$, $\div$; abbreviations such as ft, in., yd, sq ft, % are an important part of the arithmetic vocabulary.

2. *Reading for details*—Pupils must be able to distinguish significant and insignificant details, and see relationships among details. They must also be able to scan quickly for details in order to begin computations and check correctness of their copy. Repeated practice in indicating the significant details and their relationships, and in detecting the insignificant, is essential for these skills.

3. *Interpretation*—Arithmetic problems make great demands upon deductive and inductive reasoning, upon the child's ability to generalize a process from a group of details or to recognize a familiar type of problem by previewing it. Many problems demand the divergent reasoning which proceeds from a group of given facts to a visualization embodying these, as in problems of area, measurement, and the like. Practice in reading problems without numbers, 'or in interpreting them without attempting computation, and in attempting to visualize them on paper or to explain them in the pupil's own words promotes growth in the skills of interpretation.

4. *Use of graphic and tabular materials*—Charts, drawings, graphs, and diagrams are frequent in arithmetic and require special training. Practice in constructing and reading these proceeding from the simplest types to those testing the most complex situations that the child is capable of handling is essential. As we have noted before, graphic materials without adequate explanation in the text are not handled readily by most pupils. When this textual explanation is lacking, the teacher's obligation is obvious. The making of sketches, diagrams, and other types of drawings in practicing visualization, as recommended above, is a realistic approach to learning to read the graphic materials encountered in texts and tests.

   The reading of tables represents a task which differs from most conventional reading. The material is not necessarily arranged to be read from left to right. Sometimes tables are to be read vertically, sometimes both vertically and horizontally simultaneously. Headings may be at the top, side, bottom, or several of these places in the table. Observation of the habits of children, or even of adults, in reading tables often indicates a haphazard approach. Intermediate-grade children should be trained in an organized previewing and scanning of tables, which involves some of these steps: reading the title, reading the columnar headings, reading the left-hand headings or footings, as the case may be. This previewing of the organization of the table enables the reader to identify the probable location of the fact he may be seeking. Then he is ready to run his eye down or across (scanning) to find that fact.

To facilitate reading in mathematics, many other teacher efforts are recommended. Muelder (*13*) suggests that the teacher must be cognizant of the pupils' reading test scores and give special assistance in reading text or problems as indicated. He repeats the suggestions we have given earlier regarding how to read a problem, and adds the idea that pupils should be given an opportunity, when working in a group with the teacher, to ask questions about the problem—an excellent idea. Earle (5) recommends intensive study of the technical vocabulary at the chalkboard, with interrelationships shown by their arrangement or a sketch. Betty Willmon (24) reminds us that mathematics books use a large number of new terms (473 in primary levels), over half of which are repeated infrequently in each series of books.

Our list of suggestions for teaching a content area unit (given earlier in this chapter) is relevant to this area when using a textbook as the basis for instruction. The steps outlined under Teacher Preparation, Motivation, Vocabulary and Concept Development, Silent Reading, and Application may be used with such a text. In mathematics, of course, much of the application will be the solving of problems that illustrate the relationships taught in the lesson or unit. Other detailed steps to be followed in teaching this content are given above.

READING IN LITERATURE

Basal readers form the fundamental source of literature in many classrooms. Their manuals usually provide lists of suggested readings, a wide variety of reading selections, units of selections to stimulate child interest, and activities intended to promote understanding and appreciation of library materials. As commendable as this program is, it is a mistake to consider the reading series as a complete or even a broad literature program. Studies of teachers' implementation of this material as well as the quality of its content are not very encouraging. For example, the poetry in basal readers varies greatly both in quantity and quality. One series neither includes poetry nor even mentions it; another suggests its exploration but offers no examples or resources for the teacher. Most series offer one or two poems per unit, but these vary greatly from largely jingles or dull selections to sparkling, contemporary pieces accompanied by attractive illustrations (17).

Some basal authors consider the poetry they present as silent reading practice material, thus failing to realize the oral characteristics of melody, movement, rhythm, or rhyme. The poetry is also used to polish word analysis or phonic drills, a practice almost certain to destroy its appeal. Detailed analysis is suggested in some materials, desiccating the poem (as well as destroying its unique qualities). All of these criticisms imply that in approaching the poetry portion of the basal reader program at least, teachers should probably follow their own ideas in presentation.

They should attempt to create a climate in which children can enjoy prose and poetry. Formal lessons on a story or poem intended to stimulate enjoyment, understanding, and the desire for further exploration surely are desirable in contrast to those we have criticized above. Reading enthusiastically to children every day from their choices not only promotes the development of their breadth and their reading interests but also improves their reading and listening abilities. The reading of classics to pupils, with the excuse that they are "good" for children or will elevate their literary tastes, does not produce these desirable outcomes or promote reading interests (4). Leading stimulating discussions of their emotional and personal reactions to your presentations as well as to their own chosen readings again stimulates their taste for literature. Arranging for many creative reactions through movement, writing, musical, and construction activities adds distinct values to the program. Assigning writing tasks or expecting creative writing after every experience, however, detracts from the positive attitudes we are trying to create (19). Oral responses to literature are more fluent and spontaneous than written.

In dealing with poetry, choose many selections that have action, story line, nonsense, or humor and very little description (14). Then allow the pupils to make their own choices from among all that you have collected. These ideas presume that the teacher will have made the effort to bring a large number of poems to the classroom, and that she will provide opportunities for their sharing, in a planned program. Since no one really knows whether simply exposing children to interesting poetry or conducting lessons discussing and exploring them is better for promoting interest and enjoyment, the teacher will probably have to learn by trial and error and the reactions of the pupils which is most effective in the particular situation (17).

Because of its availability, the basal reading series may often serve as the initial teaching materials in the literature program. The directions and aids for the teacher, if they are present, will help inexperienced teachers in this area of instruction. But we would expect that, after each unit or theme in the basal is firmly under way, both teacher and pupils would broaden their presentations and reading, respectively, to include many other selections. The cost factor sometimes interferes with the attempt to provide a wealth of reading matter in the classroom. Fortunately, however, there is strong evidence that the less expensive paperbacks not only help solve this problem but also provide a strong impetus to children's reading. Some writers have shown that increasing markedly the number of books available in this manner certainly stimulates pupil reading, even as early as the fourth grade. Comparative groups with access to the same books in clothbound editions in the classroom or school library did not show this positive response.

These suggestions assume that the teacher either knows or has ready means of determining her pupils's reading interests so that she may maintain a constant supply of appropriate materials. To accomplish this, some suggest the use of checklists of titles or questionnaires about the pupils' leisure-time activities. Responses to these are supposed to reflect the pupils' reading needs. But reading interests and free-time activities do not necessarily arise from the same motivations. Checking titles assumes a sophistication about the relationship of title to content not often present in elementary pupils. Reading interests are often motivated by desires for escapism, vicarious experiences, identification of self, information, and the like. These differ significantly from the need for peer recognition, physical prowess, and other motives for the participation in sports, hobbies, or the use of television. Rather, we suggest that the teacher be guided by the information she obtains in individual and group conferences, pupils' reading records, and other spontaneous choices. Although we often generalize about the reading interests of children according to their ages or sex or intelligence, these are only rough guides, for reading interests tend to be highly individualized and even crystallized by about the fifth grade. Interests reflect socioeconomic status, sex, and the influence of the times, as in space travel, science, etc. The best source for teacher guidance in selecting books for the pupils is her own observations. She must also be cognizant of the fact that peer choices are often more influential than her suggestions and capitalize on this in supporting and promoting interest groups.

Teaching Literary Reading

What Works	*What Does Not Work*
Selecting books according to expressed interests of pupils	Selecting books according to pupil ages or mental ages
Offering books in terms of pupil interest, not their exact difficulty	Offering low-level books to poor readers
Permitting self-selection	Offering books that children ought to read; books that you like
Allowing pupils to read very simple books, if they choose to	Expecting pupils to read only books at or above their reading levels
Recognizing that many books vary in interest level and in difficulty enough to be rejected	Expecting pupils to finish each book they borrow
Realizing that girls may read almost any type of book	Designating books as those for boys or for girls
Offering the child several books to choose from	Choosing a book for the child to read
Reading portions of interesting books aloud to class	Expecting children to develop fresh interests
Setting the example by reading while they do	Sending children to their seats to read while you do paper work
Permitting children to choose when and how they will share	Making sharing of books required each time
Arranging for children to sign up for a conference when they feel a need to	Asking children to report to you personally on each book
Making a wide variety of books available in the classroom, by borrowing frequently from the school or public library	Sending children to the school or public library to bring back a book

Teaching Literary Reading (*continued*)

What Works	*What Does Not Work*
Teaching children how to select a book they can read and thus perhaps enjoy	Permitting complete freedom of choice, as in the school library
Realizing that self-insight may not come spontaneously, without guidance and discussion	Expecting pupils to find answers to their own personal problems in books you select for them
Recognizing that many other media which bring ideas to children also strengthen their background for reading.	Believing that only reading results in the improvement of reading ability
Arranging for use of the library resources for specific tasks related to classroom learning	Offering formal instruction in library usage and expecting this to promote it with children
Recognizing that many children feel very little need for reading, until they can learn to relate reading to their own goals	Expecting all children to want to read and to learn to read better
Perceiving the individual differences among pupils in verbal skills, as reflected in quantity and quality of their reading	Using stars, charts of the number of books read, presumably to motivate children
Offering better material in the areas of their interests and capitalizing on television presentations to evoke further reading	Warning children against excessive use of comic books, cheap magazines, and television
Encouraging reading by supplying many paperbacks as well as the others	Expecting children to read and offering them only high-quality books
Understanding that some books are read for escape or fun, not for retention	Quizzing children for comprehension on each book they have read
Emphasizing development of racial identity and self-concept by offering books on their own people	Offering a diet of books dealing with white middle-class family life
Influencing racial beliefs and prejudices by offering books on many races and minority groups (and discussing them)	Trying to affect prejudices by direct order or instruction
Strengthening learning in science and social science by biographies, stories of explorers, scientists, adventurers, etc.	Using library books only for recreational reading

What Works	*What Does Not Work*
Scheduling free reading time regularly to be spent in reading or preparation for sharing	Expecting children to read at home, and failing to provide time in class
Encouraging debates, panel discussions, mock interviews, choral reading, creation of plays as means of deepening appreciation	Emphasizing analysis of characters, writing forms and styles, memorization of teacher-selected poetry
Promoting enjoyment of the library by making it a center for book-related activities	Discouraging children by many library regulations about quiet, opening hours, number of books allowed, etc.
Promoting enjoyment of poetry by providing a wide selection, sharing children's choices	Choosing poetry for children to listen to or read (*14*)
Reading aloud from many types of books to stimulate interest, relating your selection to contemporary events, time of year, holidays, weather, etc.	Limiting your selection for reading to children to "useful" books, as those related to social science (*10*)
Stimulating open discussion of author's intentions, feelings of the characters, realism of the book, etc. (*10*)	Discussing books in detail rather than in depth (*10*)
Making careful selection of book to read to children, based on their choice; reading only selected portions each day	Reading aloud an entire book, part by part, because it is "good for them"

DISCUSSION QUESTIONS

1. What are your reactions to the deemphasis upon the basal reader and the substitution of reading instruction in content fields?

2. Prepare a unit in social science or science such as that illustrated in this chapter. Be prepared to explain your ideas on combining content and reading instruction for pupils of varying reading abilities.

3. Experiment in your class with instruction and practice in more efficient ways of reading and studying in a content area. Be prepared to report your observations and evaluation of the outcomes.

4. Discuss the possibilities of individualizing reading in the intermediate grades. For what types of pupils, in what kinds of materials would this be possible, in your opinion?

REFERENCES

1. Christensen, E.M., and Stordahl, K. E., "The Effect of Organizational Aids on Comprehension and Retention," *Journal of Educational Psychology,* 46 (1955), 65–74.

2. Courtney, Brother Leonard, "Meeting Special Reading Needs in the Content Area Classroom," in *Fusing Reading Skills and Content,* H. Alan Robinson and Ellen Lamar Thomas, eds. Newark, Del.: International Reading Association, 1969, 26–36.

3. Crewe, James, and Hultgren, Dayton, "What Does Research Really Say About Study Skills?" in *The Psychology of Reading Behavior,* 18th Yearbook, National Reading Conference, 1969, 75–78.

4. Cullinan, Bernice E., "Research Report—Teaching Children's Literature," *Elementary English,* 49 (November 1972), 1028–1050.

5. Earle, Richard A., "Reading and Mathematics Research in the Classroom," in *Fusing Reading Skills and Content,* H. Alan Robinson and Ellen Lamar Thomas, eds. Newark, Del.: International Reading Association, 1969, 162–170.

6. Frase, Lawrence T., and Silbiger, Francene, "Some Adaptive Consequences of Searching for Information in a Text," *American Educational Research Journal,* 7 (November 1970), 553–560.

7. Goudey, Charles E., "Reading-Directed or Not?" *Elementary School Journal,* 70 (February 1970), 245–247.

8. Hanf, M. Buckley, "Mapping: A Technique for Translating Reading into Thinking," *Journal of Reading,* 14 (January 1971), 225–230.

9. Heddens, James W., and Smith, Kenneth J., "The Readability of Elementary Mathematics Books," *Arithmetic Teacher* (November 1964), 466–468.

10. Huck, Charlotte S., "Strategies for Improving Interest and Appreciation in Literature," in *Reaching Children and Young People Through Literature,* Helen W. Painter, ed. Newark, Del.: International Reading Association, 1971, 37–45.

11. Hvistendahl, J. K., "The Effect of Subheads on Reader Comprehension," *Journalism Quarterly,* 45 (1968), 123–125.

12. Johnson, Roger E., and Vardian, Eileen B., "Reading, Readability and Social Studies," *Reading Teacher,* 26 (February 1973), 483–488.

13. Muelder, Richard H., "Reading in a Mathematics Class," in *Fusing Reading Skills and Content,* H. Alan Robinson and Ellen Lamar Thomas, eds. Newark, Del.: International Reading Association, 1969, 75–80.

14. Nelson, R. C., "Children's Poetry Preferences," *Elementary English,* 43 (March 1966), 247–251.

15. Palmatier, Robert A., "Notetaking: Do We Heed Expert Advice?" *Journal of Reading Behavior,* 2 (Spring 1970), 105–113.

16. Palmatier, Robert A., "Comparison of Four Notetaking Procedures," *Journal of Reading,* 14 (January 1971), 235–240.

17. Rudie, Helen N., "Poetry in Basal Readers: Perished or Cherished?" *Elementary English,* 52 (January 1975), 136–140.

18. Smith, Kenneth J., and Heddens, James W., "The Readability of Experimental Mathematics Materials," *Arithmetic Teacher* (October 1964), 391–394.

19. Smith, Richard J., and Hansen, Lee H., "Integrating Reading and Writing: Effects on Children's Attitudes," *Elementary School Journal,* 76 (January 1976), 238–245.

20. Spache, George D., "Improving Reading in the Subject Matter Areas," *Seventh Annual Yearbook Southwest Reading Conference.* Fort Worth, Tex.: Texas Christian University Press, 1958, 30–38.

21. Spache, George D., "Types and Purposes of Reading in Various Curriculum Fields," *Reading Teacher,* 11 (February 1958), 158–164.

22. Spache, George D., "Effective Reading in the Content Fields," 15–36, and "The Development of Work-Study Habits and Skills," 37–60, in *Reading Attitudes and Skills Needed for Our Times,* Paul C. Berg, ed. Columbia, S.C.: School of Education, University of South Carolina, 1960.

23. Wagner, Louise Durkee, "Measuring the Map-Reading Ability of Sixth-Grade Children," *Elementary School Journal,* 53 (February 1953), 338–344.

24. Willmon, Betty, "Reading in the Content Area: A New Math Terminology List for the Primary Grades," *Elementary English,* 48 (May 1971), 463–471.

RESOURCES FOR THE TEACHER

Professional References

Association for Childhood Education, *Literature with Children*. Washington, D.C.: The Association, 1972.

Catterson, Jane H., ed., *Children and Literature*. Newark, Del.: International Reading Association, 1970. Collected articles.

Chase, Judith Wragg, *Books To Build World Friendship*. Dobbs Ferry, N.Y.: Oceana Publications, Inc., 1964. A bibliography.

Cheyney, Arthur B., *Teaching Culturally Disadvantaged in the Elementary School*. Columbus, Ohio: Charles E. Merrill Publishing Company, 1967. A program for language development emphasizing the language experience approach.

Cheyney, Arthur B., *Teaching Reading Skills Through the Newspaper*. Reading Aids Series, Newark, Del.: International Reading Association, 1971.

Earle, Richard A., *Teaching Reading and Mathematics*. Newark, Del.: International Reading Association, 1976.

Fenton, Edwin, ed., *New Social Studies for the Slow Learner*. New York: Holt, Rinehart and Winston, Inc., 1970. Teaching strategies with examples.

Gillespie, John, and Lembo, Diana, *Introducing Books: A Guide for the Middle Grades*. New York: R. R. Bowker Company, 1970. How to help pupils relate books to their developmental needs.

Herber, Harold L., *Teaching Reading in the Content Areas*. Englewood Cliffs, N.J.: Prentice-Hall, Inc., 1970. A how-to-do-it text.

Huus, Helen, *Children's Books To Enrich the Social Studies for the Elementary Grades*. Washington, D.C.: National Council for the Social Studies, 1961. An annotated bibliography.

Keating, Charlotte M., *Building Bridges of Understanding*. Tucson, Ariz.: Palo Verde. Annotated bibliography of books dealing with various ethnic groups.

Millen, Nina, *Children's Games from Many Lands*. New York: Friendship Press, 1965. Anthology from sixty-five countries.

Painter, Helen W., *Reaching Children and Young People Through Literature*. Newark, Del.: International Reading Association, 1971. Collection of articles.

Robinson, H. Alan, *Teaching Reading and Study Strategies: The Content Areas*. Boston: Allyn and Bacon, Inc., 1975.

Robinson, H. Alan, and Thomas, Ellen Lamar, eds., *Fusing Reading Skills and Content*. Newark, Del.: International Reading Association, 1969. Collection of articles.

Shaker Heights Public Schools, *A Curriculum Guide for Work-Study Skills* and *Suggested Activities to Follow Up Work-Study Skills Lessons*. Shaker Heights, Ohio: Shaker Heights City School District, 1964.

Simpson, Dorothy M., *Learning To Learn*. Columbus, Ohio: Charles E. Merrill Publishing Company, 1970. How to develop fundamental abilities for learning success.

Spache, George D., *Good Reading for the Disadvantaged Reader*. Champaign, Ill.: Garrard Publishing Company, 1975. Many graded and annotated books to promote reading and the self-concept for each American minority group.

Spache, George D., *Good Reading for Poor Readers*. Champaign, Ill.: Garrard Publishing Company, 1974. Ninth edition of a resource book in many different instructional and reading materials.

Taba, Hilda, and Elkins, Deborah, *Teaching Strategies for the Culturally Disadvantaged*. Chicago: Rand McNally & Company, 1968. Outlines approaches, questioning, and discussion techniques.

West, Gail B., *Teaching Reading Skills in Content Areas*. Orlando, Fla.: Sandpiper Press, 1974.

Instructional Materials and Aids—Content Fields

Bernstein, Theodore M., *Get More Out of Your Newspaper*. New York: *The New York Times*.

Bolinger, Willeta R., *You and Your World*. Palo Alto, Calif.: Fearon Publishers. Simplified social studies text and workbook.

Book and Educational Division, New York Times, *School Times*. New York: *The New York Times*. Special edition for upper elementary grades.

Branley, Franklyn M., ed., *Reader's Digest Science Reader*. Pleasantville, N.Y.: Reader's Digest Association. Six books.

Brown, Jack, and Brown, Vashti, *Proudly We Hail*. Boston: Houghton Mifflin Company, 1968. Elementary black history text.

Ervin, Jane, *Reading Comprehension*. Cambridge, Mass.: Educators Publishing. Content reading workbooks for grades three to eight.

Greenwood, Rosalie, and Williams, James V., *Looking Ahead*. Columbus, Ohio: Charles E. Merrill Publishing Company. Content reading workbook.

Liddle, Wiliam, ed., *Reading for Concepts*. New York: McGraw-Hill Book Company. 1970. Eight-book series in reading in social and physical sciences.

Martin, Bill, Jr., *Sounds of Language*. New York: Holt, Rinehart and Winston, Inc. Poetry, stories, etc., for emphasis upon the sounds of language (i.e., rhythm, rhyme, sentence patterns, onomatopoeia).

New York Times, *The New York Times Introduction to a Good Reading Habit*. New York: The New York Times. Analysis of the parts of a newspaper, a guide for teachers and students.

Reader's Digest Science Reader. Pleasantville, N.Y.: Reader's Digest Association. Science reading selections and exercises for grades four to six.

Scholastic Book Services, *Curriculum Unit—Prejudice*. Englewood Cliffs, N.J.: Scholastic Book Services. Kit of sixty-one paperbacks for intermediate-grade social science.

Skill File. New York: Reading Laboratory. Box of 175 exercises at eight levels in content field reading.

Smith, Edwin H., et al., *Reading Development*. Menlo Park, Calif.: Addison-Wesley Publishing Company, Inc. Kit of content field readings.

Springboards for Learning Programs. New York: John Wiley & Sons, Inc., 1968. Collections of brief reading selections and accompanying exercises in social studies.

Thinking Skills Development Program. Westchester, Ill.: Benefic Press. Three hundred skill developmental activities on cards for content reading.

Thomas, Lydia, *New Reader's Digest Skill Builders*. Pleasantville, N.Y.: Reader's Digest Association. Reading selections and exercise workbooks, in wide variety of areas, for grades two to eight.

Young Pegasus Packets. Pleasantville, N.Y.: Reader's Digest Association. Packets of picture book, games, puzzles, and pictures for primary social studies.

Zachar, Irwin J., and Sailer, Carl, *Toward Better Newspaper Reading*. Newark, N.J.: The Newark News, 1969. Pupil and teacher activities for a unit on the newspaper.

Graphic Materials—Instructional Materials and Aids

Anderzohn, Mamie Louise, *Steps in Map Reading*. Chicago: Rand McNally & Company. Learning sequences.

Denoyer-Geppert Co., Chicago, Illinois. Write for list of free brochures and pamphlets.

Hammond's Illustrated Atlas for Young America and *Hammond's My First World Atlas*. Maplewood, N.J.: C. S. Hammond and Co., 1962.

Latitude and Longitude. Chicago: Coronet Instructional Films. Programmed text for sixth grade.

Map Skills for Today, Map Skills for Today's Geography, and *Readiness for Map Skills*. Columbus, Ohio: American Education Publications, 1965. Three brief booklets.

Maps: How We Read Them. Chicago: Coronet Instructional Films. Programmed workbook.

Marsh, Susan, *All About Maps and Mapmaking*. New York: Random House, Inc., 1963. For grades four to six.

McFall, Christie, *Maps Mean Adventures*. New York: Dodd, Mead & Company, 1973.

Naslund, Robert A., et al., *SRA Graph and Picture Study Skills Kit and SRA Map* and *Globe Skills Kit*. Chicago: Science Research Associates, 1962. Collections of exercises for independent work.

Rand McNally Readers World Atlas. Chicago: Rand McNally & Company.

Reading Latitude from Maps and *Reading Longitude from Maps*. St. Louis, Mo.: Webster Publishing, 1964. Programmed exercise books.

Rinkoff, Barbara, *A Map Is a Picture*. New York: Thomas Y. Crowell Company, Inc., 1965. Primary reading level.

Robinson, H. Alan, et al., *The EDL Study Skills Library in Social Sciences*. Huntington, N.Y.: Educational Developmental Laboratories, 1961. Separate kits for each grade.

Sholinsky, Jane, *Map Skills Books*. Books 1 to 3. New York: Scholastic Book Services, 1974.

Table and Graph Skills. Columbus, Ohio: American Education Publications. Four workbooks for grades three to six.

Tannenbaum, Harold E., et al., *Math Projects—Map Making*. Brooklyn, N.Y.: Book-Lab, Inc., 1968. Mapmaking projects.

Thralls, Zoe A., *Map Symbols Pictured*. Chicago: A. J. Nystrom and Company. Five large charts.

Use of Maps and Globes. Indianapolis, Ind.: George F. Cram Company. A teacher's guide.

Library Skills

Barnes, Donald L., and Burgdorf, Arlene B., *Study Skills for Information Retrieval*. Boston: Allyn and Bacon, Inc., 1971.

How To Use a Library. Niles, Ill.: Moreland-Latchford. Four filmstrips, two cassettes for intermediate-upper elementary.

Library Skills. Atlanta, Ga.: Colonial. Two sets of transparencies.

Library Skills. Holyoke, Mass.: Technifax. Thirty transparencies and teacher's guide.

References. Cambridge, Mass.: General Education, Inc. Offers twelve brief programmed exercise booklets on library skills for elementary pupils. Require special machine.

Robinson, H. Alan, *E.D.L. Study Skills Library in Reference Skills.* Huntington, N.Y.: Educational Developmental Laboratories. Kits of ten to twelve study-type exercises in library skills are offered for grades three to nine.

Using the Library Skill Text. Columbus, Ohio: Charles E. Merrill Publishing Company. Four workbooks at successive grades beginning with the fourth.

Your Library: How To Use It. Niles, Ill.: Moreland-Latchford. Five cassettes, filmstrips, and teacher's guide for upper elementary.

Organizing and Reporting

Naslund, Robert A., et al., *SRA Organizing and Reporting Skills Kit.* Chicago: Science Research Associates, 1962. Kit of exercise materials for independent work.

Reading Improvement for the Disadvantaged Pupil

Many of these items are written to appeal to disadvantaged or minority children or to aid them in their development of reading abilities. See similar list for primary pupils in our earlier chapter.

Ashcorn, Maimon, and Reynolds, E., *Stories of the Inner City.* New York: Globe Book Company, Inc.

Bank Street Readers. New York: Bank Street College of Education and Macmillan Publishing Co., Inc.

Baugh, Dolores, and Pulsifer, Marjorie P., *Chandler Language Experience Readers.* San Francisco: Chandler Publishing Company, 1964–1966.

Branley, Franklyn M., *Gravity Is a Mystery.* New York: Thomas Y. Crowell Company, Inc., 1970. A black boy and a white boy puzzle together over gravity.

Challenger Books. New York: Hill & Wang, 1970. Ten paperbacks, five on blacks, five on Spanish-Americans. With teacher's guide and study cards.

Common Signs of Community Service and Safety. Dinuba, Calif.: Fern Tripp.

Crazy Horse and Nau Gale. Philadelphia: Madden Publishing Co., 1972. Story book, manual, and worksheets to accompany this Indian story.

Detroit Public Schools, *First Steps in Language Experience.* Detroit: Division for Improvement of Instruction.

Docu Drama. New York: Harcourt Brace Jovanovich, 1968. A collection of plays.

Durrell, Donald D., and Crossley, B. Alice, *Favorite Plays for Classroom Reading and Thirty Plays for Classroom Reading.* Boston: Plays, Inc., 1966. For oral reading and role playing.

Durrell, Donald D., and De Melia, Lorraine A., *Plays for Echo Reading.* New York: Harcourt Brace Jovanovich, 1970.

Ethnic Drama Series. New York: New Dimensions, 1971. Nine biographical plays at fourth- to fifth-grade reading level, on black and other minority figures. Activity book and teacher's guide available.

Farquhar, Margaret C., *The Indians of Mexico: A Book to Begin On.* New York: Holt, Rinehart and Winston, Inc., 1967.

Gilford, Henry, *Plays for Today.* New York: Walker Educational Book Corp. Twelve original short plays.

Glass, Gerald G., and Klein, Muriel Walzer, *From Plays into Reading.* Boston: Allyn and Bacon, Inc., 1971. Fourteen plays.

Hall, Richard, *Discovery of Africa.* New York: Grosset & Dunlap, Inc., 1970. A simple history.

Humphrey, Henry, *What Is It For?* New York: Simon & Schuster, Inc., 1969. City life.

Lampman, Evelyn Sibley, *The Year of Small Shadow.* New York: Harcourt Brace Jovanovich, 1971. Story of a present-day American Indian boy.

Marvin, Stephen, *World Studies—Africa.* San Francisco: Field Enterprises. Fifth-grade-reading-level history book.

Meltzer, Ida S., *Black History.* Brooklyn, N.Y.: Book-Lab, Inc., 1972. Brief story booklets, some in semiprogrammed format

New York, N.Y. New York: Random House, Inc. Newspaper on current events, at different levels, for inner-city children.

Rector, Douglas, and Rector, Margaret, *The Story Plays—Self-Directing Materials for Oral Reading.* New York: Harcourt Brace Jovanovich. Offers multiple copies of forty plays.

Reluctant Reader Libraries. Englewood Cliffs, N.J.: Scholastic Book Services. The fifth- to sixth-grade library offers fifty paperbacks, at a low reading level.

Schueler, Nancy, et. al., *The City Is My Home.* New York: The John Day Company. A group of inner-city readers.

Schwartz, Melvin, *Exploring American History*. New York: Globe Book Company, Inc. A fifth-grade-reading-level American history book.

Smith, Frances C., *Men at Work in Alaska*. New York: G. P. Putnam's Sons. Social studies material at intermediate-grade level.

SRA Dimensions Series, *We Are Black*. Chicago: Science Research Associates. Four-page reading selections on blacks, with skill development cards.

Weeks, Douglas, *Blacks in Time*. Syracuse, N.Y.: New Readers Press, 1969. Human interest stories about blacks in America before the Civil War, with suggested activities.

Young, Margaret B., *The First Book of American Negroes*. New York: Franklin Watts, Inc., 1967. Black history in America.

Audiovisual Materials—For the Teacher

Teaching Map Reading Skills in Elementary Schools. Nineteen-minute color film of classroom activities. Los Angeles: Bailey Film Associates.

Teaching Reading Skills for the Social Studies. Twenty-three-minute color films depicting small-group instruction. Los Angeles: Bailey Film Associates.

Audiovisual Materials—For Pupils

Constructing Reports. Six filmstrips on preparing reports for middle and upper grades. Chicago: Encyclopaedia Britannica Films, Inc.

Exploring Through Maps. Five elementary filmstrips. New York: McGraw-Hill Book Company.

Globes: An Introduction. A ten-minute color film using animation to illustrate physical features of the earth, for primary-intermediate. Bloomington, Ind.: Indiana University Audio-Visual Center.

How Far? A short, primary-level film on finding distances on a map. Bloomington, Ind.: Indiana University Audio-Visual Center.

How To Study. Filmstrips for upper elementary grades. New York: Curriculum Research Associates.

How To Use Maps and Globes. Six strips for elementary pupils. New York: McGraw-Hill Book Company.

How To Use an Encyclopaedia. Elementary-grade strip. New York: McGraw-Hill Book Company.

How We Know the Earth's Shape. A ten-minute color film with sound. Bloomington, Ind.: Indiana University Audio-Visual Center.

Learning To Use Maps. Six filmstrips for intermediate grades. Chicago: Encyclopaedia Britannica Films, Inc.

Library Series. A large group of filmstrips on various library resources. New York: McGraw-Hill Book Company.

Library Services. A series of strips for elementary grades. New York: Eye Gate House, Inc.

Maps: An Introduction. A simple twelve-minute film in color with sound for primary–intermediate grades. Bloomington, Ind.: Indiana University Audio-Visual Center.

Maps Are Fun. An eleven-minute color film with sound, offering fundamental concepts of map reading in a story setting. Chicago: Coronet Instructional Films.

Our World. An eighteen-minute color film with sound, depicting classroom activities in constructing a globe. Bloomington, Ind.: Indiana University Audio-Visual Center.

Reading Maps. An eleven-minute color film with sound, showing the values of ability to read types of maps, for intermediate- and upper-grade levels. Chicago: Encyclopaedia Britannica Films, Inc.

Study and Reading Skills. Each strip emphasizes a study skill, such as summarizing or outlining, for intermediate- and upper-grade pupils. New York: Eye Gate House, Inc.

Understanding a Map. A twelve-minute sound film in black and white, illustrating simple map reading. New York: McGraw-Hill Book Company.

Using the Library. Six filmstrips to acquaint elementary pupils with library resources. Chicago: Encyclopaedia Britannica Films, Inc.

Using Maps—Measuring Distance. A ten-minute sound film in black and white for primary–intermediate pupils. Chicago: Encyclopaedia Britannica Films, Inc.

What Is a Map? A ten-minute sound film in black and white, offering fundamental ideas on how a map is born. Bloomington, Ind.: Indiana University Audio-Visual Center.

Which Way? Primary film on finding directions. Bloomington, Ind.: Indiana University Audio-Visual Center.

Your Lesson Plan Filmstrips. Several strips on study and library skills. Philadelphia: Morehouse Associates.

10
Steps Toward Individualized Reading

PREVIEW

Teachers who are familiar only with group instruction in reading find it difficult to conceive of other approaches or to visualize the ways in which they might begin to use these unfamiliar individualized procedures. Teachers accustomed to following the planned routine of a basal system or some other structured approach tend to doubt their ability to achieve a thorough skill-building program within the framework of an individualized program. For some these are probably legitimate doubts, for they have become so dependent upon the teacher's manual for planning that they have lost the teaching skills of flexibility and creativity.

The teacher who moves toward individualization must show initiative and judgment in acquiring and familiarizing himself with children's reading materials. In some instances, she will even create some of these materials or stimulate the pupils to do so. The teacher must gradually learn how to utilize the information gained in individual and small-group conferences as a basis for planning for materials, for small-group instruction, and for individual pupil needs. Even before this, she must learn how to initiate, to schedule, and to conduct meaningful, profitable conferences with individuals or a small group. This teacher will gradually evolve record-keeping techniques which satisfy her needs, and teach her pupils how to maintain useful records of their reading and skill development.

No proponent of individualization suggests that such a program makes fewer demands upon teaching skill than other instructional approaches. But at the same time, practically all teachers who learn this approach find it a stimulating professional experience which they wish to continue.

ORGANIZATIONAL STEPS

The primary problem for a teacher who is beginning to use individualized approaches is an adequate supply of reading and instructional materials. Some experienced teachers suggest a minimum class library of three to five trade books per child. In addition, there must be a continued flow of books borrowed from such sources as the school or public library, children's home libraries, or a school depository. Available materials should include not only a relatively constant supply of trade books but ample supplies of a wide variety of other materials. Among these are stacks of old child and adult magazines, an atlas or two, an almanac, an encyclopedia, several different dictionaries, a sampling of science and social science textbooks and reference books, a picture file, a clipping file, and a pamphlet or leaflet file. A variety of basal and supplementary readers and a selection of basal reader workbooks, both extending over several grade ranges, are highly desirable. Current subscriptions to children's newspapers and magazines and, perhaps, to an inexpensive child's book club are most useful. A variety of games for skill building may be selected from among those listed in *Good Reading for Poor Readers (41)* or constructed according to the suggestions of Evelyn B. Spache. If the budget permits, the materials list may include an *SRA Reading Laboratory (31)*, several of the *EDL Study Skills Kits (37)*, and the other kits useful in content field reading mentioned earlier. The average teacher will supplement the skill-building exercises present in his collection of basal reader workbooks by selections of phonics, word recognition, word attack, and vocabulary workbooks perhaps chosen from the list in *Good Reading for Poor Readers (41)*.

To keep abreast of new trade books, the teacher should have access to such sources as the book reviews in *The Reading Teacher, Elementary English, The Horn Book, Bulletin of the Center for Children's Books* (Graduate Library School, University of Chicago), and the listings in the *Children's Catalog*. Excellent guides to children's literature include those by Larrick, *A Parent's Guide to Children's Reading* (Doubleday & Company, Inc., and Pocket Books, Inc., 1958), and *A Teacher's Guide to Children's Books* (Charles E. Merrill Publishing Company, 1960); Tooze, *Your Children Want To Read* (Prentice-Hall, Inc., 1957); Arbuthnot, *Children and Books* (Scott, Foresman and Company, 1957); Fenner, *The Proof of the Pudding* (The John Day Company, 1957); and Anne Thaxter Eaton, *Treasure for the Taking* (The Viking Press, Inc., 1957).*

---

* See also bulletins from your State Department of Education on books recommended for elementary school libraries.

Even more readily available as sources of new books are the annual children's book review sections of leading newspapers, such as the following:

- *Book Week* (*World Journal Tribune, The Washington Post, Chicago Sun-Times*) The Fall Children's Issue of October 30 (Business Office, *Book Week,* 230 W. 41st St., New York, N.Y. 10036)
- *Boston Herald Traveler and Record American* Children's Book Fair Supplement of October 30 (Subscription Dept., *Boston Herald Traveler and Record American,* 300 Harrison Avenue, Boston, Mass. 02106)
- *Chicago Tribune* Books for Children Supplement of November 6 (Tom Tincher, Rm. 1212, *Chicago Tribune,* Chicago, Ill. 60611)
- *Christian Science Monitor* Children's Book Week Feature of November 3 (Circulation Dept., *Christian Science Monitor,* 1 Norway St., Boston, Mass. 02115)
- *Cleveland Press* Book Fair Supplement of November 1 (Public Service Counter, First Floor, *Cleveland Press,* 901 Lakeside Ave., Cleveland, Ohio 44114)
- *The Columbus Dispatch* Special Children's Book Section of November 6 (Circulation Dept., *Columbus Dispatch,* Columbus, Ohio 43216)
- *Denver Post* Children's Book Section of October 30 (Mail Subscription Dept., *Denver Post,* Denver, Colo.)
- *Detroit Free Press* Children's Book Section of October 30 (William Benson, Advertising Dept., *Detroit Free Press,* Detroit, Mich. 48231)
- *Louisville Courier-Journal* Children's Book Section of October 30 (Dispatch Room, *Courier-Journal,* Louisville, Ky. 40202)
- *The New York Times* Children's Book Section of November 5 (Subscription Mgr., *The New York Times,* 229 W. 43rd St., New York, N.Y. 10036)
- *San Francisco Chronicle* Children's Book Section of November 6 (Book Dept., *San Francisco Chronicle,* 860 Howard St., San Francisco, Calif. 94103)

It would be presumptuous of us to try to list the films, filmstrips, flat pictures, recordings, plays, and poetry collections that are an essential part of instruction in reading. Each teacher will use these devices according to the facilities and budget available. In the opinions of many observers, she may use them too infrequently and haphazardly. She may even ignore those constructed as special aids to the basal materials, such as those offered by a number of basal reader publishers. Among other tools, these publishers offer free series of bulletins on reading, filmstrips correlated to their texts, newsletters, and monographs. A great many reading lists are given in Chapter XI of the senior author's book *Good Reading for Poor Readers* (Garrard Publishing Company). Space does not permit the reproduction of these various types of lists, but they are readily available in most college libraries.

No teacher should be naive enough to believe that a materials collection such as we have outlined will be waiting for her the first day of school. She will acquire these supplies slowly as her gradual approach to individualization makes them increasingly necessary.

Even the ordering of new trade books during the first year may be delayed until she is asked to suggest a list for purchase for the classroom or the school library. Meanwhile she will be dependent upon the existing materials in those and other sources. Her experiences during the year, however, will help her to learn the types of books and reference materials she should request.

A good part of the problem of selecting and grading the classroom library is being met by book collections offered by various publishers. Among those listed at the end of the chapter, the following have the advantages of graded books, prepared questions on vocabulary and comprehension, and suggestions for follow-up activities: Jacobs's *One-to-One,* Jacobs and McInnes's *Venture Books,* Random House's *Pacemakers,* and *Yearling Reading Centers.* A few others, such as the Hoffman *Gold Series, Prime-O-Tec,* and Random House's *Sights and Sounds,* offer parallel books and tapes or records, for whatever values a two-way presentation has in learning to read.

These book collections, and the others mentioned later, can be of great assistance to teachers moving toward individualization. None of them has enough variety or breadth to supply the total needs of an ordinary class of thirty or so pupils for an entire year. But, at the beginning of the individualized program, they do offer books of known reading levels, aid in assessing the pupils' reactions and learnings from the books, and help in planning related follow-up activities.

The teacher must have some estimate of the relative difficulties or grade levels of these books. If the books are part of the classroom library, the teacher may wish to paste colored stickers on them or make a secret mark somewhere in the book to indicate the grade level to her. The fact that children may recognize that the books with a pink sticker are more difficult than those marked with another color is not greatly important. They would soon evolve their own methods of estimating the difficulty of books, in any event. They learn that the difficulty of a book is often an individual matter dependent, in a large degree, upon their interest in the content. Pupils are not overly concerned about the exact level of each book they read, for they do not progress directly from easy to more difficult books but tend to alternate in levels. The major purpose of the labeling or grading of books is not to promote competition among the pupils but to facilitate the teacher's record keeping. This information is significant to the teacher to enable her to observe progress, guide children's choices, suggest other books of appropriate difficulty, select additional books for the classroom library, and the like.

In general, some basal readers are reasonably accurate in their labels, but unfortunately textbooks and trade books may often be incorrectly graded or even lacking in any indication of their grade levels. Estimates may be made by applying appropriate readability formulas such as the Spache (*41*) formula for primary grades or the Dale–Chall (*6*) for intermediate grades. These formulas or other methods of evaluation have been applied to a great many books in the lists by one of the present writers (*41*), Condit (*4*), Dees (*10*), Groff (*18*), Guilfoyle (*19*), Sister Julitta (*24*), and Heller (*20*). Cataloging and labeling of the classroom library, as well as suggestions for book orders, can be greatly facilitated by use of these evaluations.

Some writers suggest that a child should estimate the difficulty of a book by counting the number of words in a page that he does not understand, when previewing the book. They say he should count on the fingers of one hand and that if all the fingers are used, the book should be discarded as too difficult. This advice is, of course, ludicrous without reference to the number of printed words on the page. Five unknown words could represent anywhere from about 5 percent, as in a primer, to 1 to 1.5 percent in an intermediate-grade book. Are we to believe that any book in which the child would not know these minute proportions is really too difficult for him? Are we to believe that most children have no ability to derive meanings for words not in his sight vocabulary from the context? On the contrary, there is ample evidence that pupils can derive meanings from context and also can read books that interest them even when they are distinctly more difficult than their measured reading levels as used in the classroom. It will be more sensible to allow children to make their evaluations of books on the basis of their own reactions to the content, style, and format.

HOW TO START INDIVIDUALIZING

Perhaps one of the chief advantages of the individualized approach is the flexibility with which it may be adapted to teacher or pupil readiness. Conferences may be introduced gradually into any type of classroom organization and thus eventually substituted for more conventional procedures. Some teachers are capable of planning and organizing the procedure rather readily. Other teachers find it difficult to adjust to a relatively large number of individualized or small-group activities. But it is quite feasible for all teachers to develop a personal program at their own pace beginning at first, as we have suggested earlier, with a few of the better readers. Later the approach may be extended to more of the superior group and then gradually to average pupils, as teacher skill in planning and directing the program increases.

Pupil readiness for individualized methods is second only in significance to teacher readiness. Pupils accustomed to basal reading procedures vary in their abilities to adjust to and profit from more individualized methods. Lack of experience with small-group or independent work or dependence upon constant teacher supervision and support may militate against initial adjustment to the new procedures for some pupils. Dependent pupils need constant support and encouragement, ask for assistance frequently, and show uncertainty and lack of adaptability in new situations. Withdrawn pupils lack initiative, persistence, and good qualities of attention. Our own research (40) into the personalities of children who experience reading difficulties indicates that the number of depressed or withdrawn pupils is relatively small. But they do present problems that the teacher must attempt to solve for successful classroom management.

In planning the experiences necessary for introducing pupils to independent work, Edwards (14) has emphasized the importance of conveying to pupils some understanding of the reasons for the new procedures. Teachers should clarify the purposes of the individual conference, the reasons for the freedom of choice of materials, as well as the plans for the working procedures of small groups, teams, or committees.

The problem of providing leadership and direction for the small-group work that is characteristic of the individualized approach is often met by the training of pupil leaders. Initially pupils who are qualified both by personality and reading skill may be selected by the teacher to function as team or group chairmen. As the program expands, these positions are rotated among the other pupils to extend the leadership experiences to all. Among the responsibilities that pupil leaders may be helped to assume are the following:

1. Helping the group to secure needed materials at the beginning of the work period and to replace these at the close.
2. Answering questions of the group or relaying these to the teacher when convenient for her.
3. Helping the group to have a clear-cut idea of their purpose and of the directions outlined earlier by the teacher.
4. Checking progress of the group, giving assistance or directions where needed. Reporting special problems to the teacher.
5. Helping members of the group to learn to function as chairmen or leaders.

Teachers vary greatly in the manner in which they initiate the use of individual conferences. Some begin by substituting a small-group conference for the reading circle. The children assemble as usual but use silent reading in place of oral. Each child may be questioned privately on his comprehension and reactions. A variant of this is the substitution of a book chosen by the child, for the usual basal reader, followed by a group or teacher–pupil conference or both. Other teachers begin by using the parallel readings suggested in the basal reader manual as a substitute or supplement to the basal reader unit. Or, children are permitted self-selection of books which are related in content to the unit. These selections may then form the basis of small-group or teacher–pupil conferences. Another approach is through encouragement of self-pacing by the pupils in the basal material. As a result of permitting self-pacing, simultaneous reading of the same story in the group rapidly becomes impossible and the group activity gravitates toward individualized conferences. Special reading assignments for an individual or a committee and projects involving self-selected reading, both of which are later shared with the class and with the teacher in conferences, are other initiating steps.

Individualizing with Learning Stations. A currently popular way of individualizing is the development of learning centers. Each center occupies a small area in the classroom and contains the basic equipment, furniture, directions, and work utensils for independent study and group interaction. Screens, mattress boxes, bookcases, or even a sheet hung from the ceiling act as dividers to set off the area from the rest of the classroom. Noisy areas (those with record players or typewriters or those intended for discussion purposes) are separated widely from quiet areas. Each center is intended to promote study in a particular skill area—word attack, comprehension, sustained silent reading, creative writing, decoding skills. Many teachers also eventually utilize science centers, math centers, art centers, music centers, etc.

Each center offers specific directions as well as written purposes or objectives for a variety of tasks that extend over a range of levels. Choices of activities intended to meet the same objective should be offered. These guidelines may be inscribed on a large chart or small cards in a file box or form the headings on worksheets. Manipulative activities beyond just paper and pencil work are most desirable and may be provided in the form of group games, puzzles, sorting and classifying, flannelboards and cutouts, and construction materials. It is not essential that all the tasks be completed at the center, for some may be done at the child's seat or elsewhere. All the materials needed for the planned activities, including such items as filmstrips and projector, kits, transparencies, tapes, records, typewriter, worksheets, etc., are filed at the learning center.

Criscuolo (5) offers a number of options and alternatives in this approach to individualizing. Each center he describes is labeled with a catchy title. Peck Deck—creative writing; Tabletop Acres—plant care and study, etc. Waynant and Wilson offer many valuable hints and examples in their guidebook on learning centers. Kaplan et al. provide a number of time-saving ideas and techniques to aid the teacher.

Obviously, as in all efforts to individualize, this approach can develop no faster than the teacher's and the pupils' readiness for the idea. Teachers cannot try too many centers at once, before their pupils are prepared for the flexibility of movement, maintenance of acceptable noise levels, and demand for independent study habits. Starting with one or two well-planned centers which the children become accustomed to using effectively before adding others is the usual sensible approach. The time and effort required for the preparation is well repaid in the growth of independent creative abilities of children. Learning centers take children beyond the repetitive use of commercial or teacher-made kits to a wide variety of purposeful, self-pacing, and highly motivated learning tasks.

There are many indications and clues for the teacher who is attempting to initiate individualized reading with gifted or average pupils or, when it is feasible, with some of the slow-learning pupils. We have outlined our suggestions of criteria for judging pupil readiness for this type of program in Figure 10–1. The characteristics and behaviors that the teacher would observe certainly differ with the grade placement and reading level of the pupil.

In later primary and intermediate grades, pupil readiness for individualized reading naturally demands different behaviors and skills. During the early reading stages in which experience charts are used, the teacher must again make judgments regarding pupils who may be ready for individualized reading. At this level, we have suggested a group of reading behaviors, evidences of learning and of interest to help distinguish such pupils. Continually throughout subsequent grades, the teacher must make judgments before she introduces pupils to individualized reading. These judgments require again a slightly different group of criteria, for the child is no longer a beginning reader nor in the very early stages. At these levels, the teacher's judgments will be based largely on the child's demon-

Reading Behaviors (Experience Chart Level)

Does the child –

show recall or recognition of words and phrases on charts or in isolation, and almost daily learning of sight vocabulary?

ask for identification of words or letters he is interested in – as in signs, book titles, magazines – and identify some spontaneously with increasing frequency?

try to identify some words by spelling orally, and practice copying words, without demand; make some reversals in reading or writing, tending to correct them spontaneously or when queried?

enjoy books, pictures, picture sequences, scrapbooks, etc.; choose them during free time; select favorites and use them over again; ask the teacher to read from them; share findings with group?

Reading Behaviors (Primary and Intermediate Grade Levels)

Is the child able to –

care for materials, borrow and return, take turns?

read, study, complete assignments independently or in small groups?

share materials, work cooperatively, wait turn with teacher, lead small–group work constructively and without undue friction, or follow another leader?

follow through on individualized reading assignments or group projects, and show realistic self-selection when given the opportunity?

show independence in word recognition skills, and reasonable command of sight and meaning vocabulary, insofar as these have been taught in the program?

show reasonable comprehension (60 to 70 percent) in materials at his instructional and independent reading levels?

evidence distinct reading interests or tastes; does he want to explore certain areas, to contribute or share his findings with the group?

FIGURE 10—1. Checklist for Readiness for Individualized Reading

stration of independence in working habits and his command of fundamental or basal reading skills.

Some teachers would prefer us to describe exactly the type of behavior which satisfied each of our suggested criteria. But these descriptions would only succeed in spelling out the author's peculiar ideas about child development and classroom management. No one can really dictate or even suggest to a teacher precisely how she should operate, how much independent child activity she can successfully stimulate and direct, how many groups and subgroups she can instruct efficiently, how many effective conferences she needs to or can give each pupil per week, etc. These are skills that vary greatly from one teacher to another, as teachers differ in competence, organizing ability, experience, and many related abilities. The checklist provides some criteria for judgment, but teachers must interpret and apply these judgments and follow their implications as their own personal operational skills permit.

It is obvious that the successful use of conferences includes adequate follow-up of the conference observations. In fact, lacking a manual to suggest appropriate follow-up activities, the teacher's effectiveness in devising her own applications is of crucial significance. Some would regard the lack of a manual as most fortunate, for this frees the teacher to employ her own originality in creating follow-up activities. Many others, including the authors, are somewhat skeptical of the thoroughness of the average teacher's efforts to provide opportunities for the practice of various reading skills. It is for this reason that we have attempted in other chapters of this book to provide detailed outlines of the sequential development of various groups of skills. The phonics syllabus, the structural elements, the types of contextual clues, and the approaches to sight and meaning vocabularies offered in these chapters are intended to aid in planning the follow-up on skills training.

Teacher's manuals are an excellent source for ideas on how to teach various skills. They differ, of course, in their inclusiveness and sequences, but this is not a great handicap. Beginning teachers are well advised to try to make a collection of these guides and use them for teaching tips and procedures in skill development. The manuals will have to be previewed perhaps before each school week to select those ideas that are immediately relevant to the lessons the teacher plans to use for the pupil needs she has observed. If the workbooks written to accompany these manuals have also been gathered, the appropriate parts may be used for independent, follow-up work. The most efficient use of the workbooks would be to assemble them in a teacher-made kit that has been organized and indexed or color-coded, in the manner we have described earlier in discussing the individualized approach.

There are many helpful suggestions regarding grouping for teachers who are about to depart from a rigid three-group plan. Strang et al. (44) discuss six types of intraclass grouping: (1) achievement grouping according to reading levels; (2) research grouping of two or three pupils to explore and answer specific questions; (3) interest grouping of pupils with similar or related reading tasks; (4) special needs grouping formed for development of a specific skill; (5) team grouping—three or four pupils, including a team leader and a recorder, who undertake a specific task resulting in materials and ideas that will be shared with the class; and (6) tutorial grouping, in which a particularly competent pupil helps one or several others in skill-building activities. Lanning (27) speaks of dyadic groups of two based on common interests or abilities. The pair of children read the same book, poem, or story, and question each other orally (or by written questions if the pupils are sufficiently mature). Lanning emphasizes such outcomes of this pairing as mutual enjoyment and empathy, as well as better comprehension and retention. Such interest grouping may readily arise from a class experience such as a movie, filmstrip, or trip. Following the class discussion, volunteers may be secured who will work together to answer some of the questions raised by the class. Guided by the questions and the teacher's suggestions regarding resource materials, the interest group (or research group or team) may prepare exhibits, a mural, a picture or book collection, graphic aids; present a formal, informational report or an entertaining pseudo-TV panel or debate; or share their findings in any of a multiplicity of ways (*22, 23, 33*).

Here are thirty of the book-sharing activities that may be used as a follow-up to children's reading.

1. Listen to a prepared tape with earphones. Good readers tape the informational material.
2. Make up new endings to stories. Children read their versions to the class.
3. Prepare a brief biography of the author. Present to class.
4. Prepare a monologue from a story. Putting themselves in others' places helps in understanding social relationships.
5. Children bring in objects made at home. They demonstrate step-by-step procedures to the group by either oral or written directions. This increases their ability to give and follow directions.
6. Have children read only dialogue in a story, while a good reader provides the narrative background material.
7. An excellent group project to provide opportunities for socialization, sharing ideas, and participation in simple drama is to allow the children who have read the same story, book, or play to give a performance based on their common reading.
8. Children enjoy tape recording a poem, episode, or story, which is then available to others for a variety of uses.
9. Collecting and reading newspaper articles related to social studies and science can be of great value. See later suggestions.
10. Reading stories to younger children is enjoyable for reader and listeners.
11. Preparing a report with accompanying questions for the listeners. Report should be brief.
12. A vivid oral description of a character in a book stimulates other children to want to become better acquainted with the character.
13. Reading the saddest part, the most exciting event, the part most enjoyed, or a very humorous incident helps children seek certain types of material.
14. Reading a story to the musical accompaniment of a tape or recording gives pleasure to the audience as well as skill to the performer in selecting music, controlling volume, etc.
15. Reading beautiful descriptive passages and displaying a painting or drawing of the scene stimulates imagery and enlarges vocabulary.
16. To stimulate interest in a book, the student may write, and share, a letter to the librarian or a friend recommending the book.
17. Several children reading the same book can check each other's comprehension by writing sets of questions and checking each other orally.
18. Book reviews, given to a lower-level class, are an excellent experience in storytelling.
19. A book review broadcast over the school intercom requires careful reading and speech. This activity also provides opportunities for creative use of sound effects, background music, etc.

20. A commentator may narrate a story during the display of a tableau or series of paintings.
21. Writing and sharing letters asking for various types of information or materials from outside sources gives opportunities in writing and oral reading skills.
22. Oral reading of captions on filmstrips (after previewing it) as an illustrated lecture.
23. Choral reading of dramatic material or poetry can involve almost all the class. Children may conduct choral reading in unison, in two-part (high and low, boy and girl voices), by a line-a-child, with one solo part and the rest reading the refrain, and by arranging for a number of parts.
24. Using informational materials, notes, and pictures to make a scrapbook, which is then shared with others, stimulates interest in such projects.
25. Set aside a daily time for sustained silent reading. In some schools everyone—teachers, administrators, and pupils—reads a book of their choice at this time. The length of the reading period is, of course, adapted to the attention span of the pupils. But the attitude toward reading as a meaningful, enjoyable activity is certainly strengthened by this practice.
26. Invite the school librarian to visit your class and give a series of book talks. She may bring several copies of each book she discusses for children to borrow, or invite the pupils to come to the library to secure a copy, or to make their own choices. This idea will have to be adapted to the librarian's schedule.
27. Read to your class every day, at a time that seems appropriate. Perhaps let them choose the book that they would like to hear. Some groups prefer listening to successive parts of the same book; others will prefer a different book every few days. Make certain that a copy or several are available to those children who can read the book.
28. Arrange a schedule for pupil storytelling or reading orally to others. Preview their selections before they present the book. Suggest that they choose an exciting or interesting portion (as you would in reading to them). Promote group reactions to the story—not evaluation of the pupil reader.
29. Use various types of charts for pupil recording of the books they have read and their reactions. Small cards, for example, may be tucked in the back of the book, or mounted on a bulletin board, or displayed in any of a dozen ways. Thus the comments of those who have read a book may be shared with others. These will strongly influence other pupil's choices (*33*).
30. Spontaneous dramatization of a story by one or several children with hand puppets or a more elaborate puppet theatre, or as a playlet, is both enjoyable for the class and highly motivating.

Using Newspapers.　Newspapers should be an integral part of the reading program, for the ability to read them intelligently and critically is of lifelong value. They can often be obtained from the local newspaper office without cost, are highly contemporary, contain a wide diversity of materials, and are readily disposable. The creation of a class newspaper to be shared with other classes in the school, an excellent medium for the development of reading and other language abilities, may evolve from this activity.

　　The newspaper may be used to develop reading skills, such as using an index; finding the main idea; recognizing a sequence; outlining an article; learning to use graphs, charts, maps, and tables; and reacting critically to news reports, editorials, and advertisements, to mention only a few. Small groups (committees) or individuals may carry on such extended activities in the use of the paper as creating a map showing the travels of an important personage, such as the president or secretary of state, and attaching brief notes on the reasons for the trip; a weather chart showing daily changes; a record of the progress of a sports team; and a file of articles on a topic related to class study in social science or science. Others are planning a balanced menu and its daily cost from the information in store advertisements; screening the listing of television programs for features related to classwork and announcing these on a bulletin board; comparing the articles on a news item in several newspapers and leading a critical discussion of the contrasts; locating significant world events on a large world map; and making a calendar of local events of interest to the class. Still other uses of a newspaper are: comparing prices in the advertisements of competing stores and supermarkets; checking the For Sale columns for items of interest and for comparing prices; making a display collection of different maps or tables, or graphs or cartoons, to serve as a resource in children's own writing. Obviously, if this ready source of interesting and often vital information is explored, it may serve a wide variety of learning experiences. Other sources of ideas in using newspapers are listed in the bibliography.

GROUPING BY LEARNING APTITUDES

Noting that pupils differ in their aptitudes for various approaches to word recognition, some primary school teachers will form groups or teams based on this criterion. Using the *Learning Methods Kit* distributed by Mills (*29*) they will conduct a series of diagnostic lessons in word recognition to differentiate those pupils who learn best by visual, phonic, kinesthetic, or combined approaches, and initiate different types of follow-up activities for each. Teachers who are attempting to deal with retarded readers who seem unresponsive to ordinary classroom methods will certainly find this diagnostic approach very fruitful.

It is true that some group experiments in teaching to the child's learning modality in this fashion have not shown strong results. On the other hand, when a child has been experiencing slow or poor progress, a dramatic change in the mode of teaching, as in word recognition, may well be responded to very positively. The effects may be only temporary, but they do influence the learner's self-concept and attitude toward learning to read. We are not suggesting that, if a preferred modality can be identified, it be followed indefinitely. Rather, the new approach should be dramatized and exploited to produce as positive a child reaction as possible, for as long as any real progress in its use seems to be present.

We have barely outlined the planning of follow-up activities at this point. Subsequent chapters will offer much more detailed suggestions. But the teacher will also find many helpful descriptions of meaningful activities in such sources as

Darrow and Allen (7), and the various lists of games we have mentioned earlier, and those listed in the chapter bibliography.

SCHEDULING

The number of conferences and small-group sessions that a teacher can manage per week is an individual matter. The recommendation of two to four conferences per child per week suggested by some writers may be ideal but it is almost impossible for some teachers. If the daily time devoted to reading ranges from ninety to one hundred minutes in the first grade to forty-five to sixty in the intermediate grades, a minimum of two ten-minute conferences per week per pupil would occupy all the time allotted to reading instruction, in a class of twenty-five to thirty pupils. It is apparent that conferences must be less frequent than twice per week, or extremely brief, or limited to one segment of the class—for example, to the superior readers. These are some of the reasons for having recommended that individualized reading be offered at first only to the better readers. Even with this arrangement, which assumes that about one-third of the instructional time is devoted to this segment of the class, scheduling of the teacher's time is a problem.

Some teachers meet this situation by making a schedule which ensures that all pupils will have conferences in turn. Other teachers offer a schedule sheet on which children may write their names when they feel the need for a conference or wish to report on a book they have read. A third approach involves permitting children to ask the teacher for a conference at any time during the day that she is not otherwise engaged. As a fourth solution, some teachers conduct group conferences with pupil teams or committees. In our opinion the use of inventory and diagnostic conferences offers a real contribution to efficiency in scheduling conferences. Careful analysis of skill development will be made at planned intervals by this approach. Thus the teacher will be relieved of the impossible task of using most conferences for diagnostic purposes. She will not feel pressured to have the child read orally to her each time under the mistaken illusion that this procedure is the best method of keeping her finger on the pulse of the child's reading development. Rather she will devote her conferences to the more significant purposes of evaluating silent comprehension, stimulating interests, and planning follow-up and group activities with each pupil.

We are not implying here, as some might assume, that each child must be quizzed in detail on every book or selection he reads. Such a picayune attitude would probably help to destroy children's enjoyment of their reading rather than promote it. Evaluation of comprehension should occur often enough to create a set toward intelligent, critical reading; thus the evaluative techniques will be used with varying frequency from pupil to pupil. Furthermore, this method is also promoted by those activities which require sharing or reporting to the group as much as by "telling" the teacher. In the final analysis, each teacher will have to work out her own solutions to the problems of frequency and content of individual conferences, perhaps with due recognition of the true purposes we have tried to indicate above.

RECORD KEEPING

If the teacher follows our earlier suggestions, she will collect five basic types of records for each child. Whether these are placed in a notebook, a card file, or a folder is a matter of personal choice. The first records will include the facts acquired from the school's cumulative record-keeping system, and from informal discussions with the previous year's teacher. These should include the child's age, IQ, mental age, reading interests, and general comments on his interest, progress, and difficulties. Recent reading test results from both standardized and informal testing may be included. Some teachers will want to add notes on the child's personality and needs, as well as any health problems and family conditions that are likely to affect his schoolwork. A second record of the child's instructional, independent, and potential reading levels will be obtained during the initial inventory conferences. A third record will be that of his oral reading behaviors. These observations will be based on a number of conferences and classroom notes.

A fourth record will contain an analysis of the pupil's oral reading errors as observed during the inventory conferences and several subsequent conferences during which the child reads orally. For the sake of securing a fairly reliable picture of the child's oral reading errors, the total number of errors analyzed in this fashion should probably be close to a hundred. This particular record would, of course, include a summary statement of the child's apparent needs for follow-up activities in word recognition skills and sight vocabulary.

The final set of records will include those notes that each teacher deems adequate for judging and guiding the progress of the pupils. These may include a page or card for each child on which he notes such items as titles of books read, degree of and types of comprehension shown, child's reactions to the book, books suggested to the child, plans for sharing his selections, plans for follow-up activities, and the like. The breadth and depth of these records will vary according to the teacher's concepts of their purposes and their values to her.

Some teachers tend to keep both individual and group records of pupil needs and progress. The individual records may note the particular skills in which the child shows weaknesses, such as contextual, structural, or phonic analysis, and breadth of sight vocabulary. The group records may note the skills to be stressed, the pupils forming the group, the materials used, and the dates upon which the group has met. Both group and individual records may be compared with the teacher's overall written plan for skills development outlined in her notebook or some such guide.

Typical records kept by the teacher might resemble this sample.

	Title of book Page number		
Date	Level	Comments	Follow-up
2/2	*Jed Smith* by Lathan (Garrard) pp. 7–14 3rd	John is impressed by Jed's freedom and out-door ability. Read aloud p. 10 and we discussed story. Expression excellent.	Suggested he add new words from each chapter to his word bank.
2/8	pp. 15–41	Help needed with long *a* as in w*ei*ghing, wa*i*ted. Give definitions of words added to word bank.	Worksheets Nos. 14–17 phonics file A (*ei*, *ea*, *ue*, *ai*).
2/11	Finished book	Worksheets O.K. Sup-plied synonyms for several words. Needs some help. Wants book on Lewis and Clark.	File B: worksheets 60–61, synonyms. Marking map with Jed's route for talk to small group. Use *Scholastic Map Skills* for help.
2/15	*George Rogers Clark* by DeLeuw (Garrard) to p. 50 3.5	Excited about westward movement. Found film-strip for class. Worked on compounds and in-flectional endings. Easy reading — urge more difficult one next time.	Is making trail in dif-ferent color on same map. Worksheets file A 23–24 plurals *s—es*.
2/20	Finished book	Found answers to ques-tions — narrated film-strip yesterday.	Alphabetize word bank by second letter.
2/24	*Jim Bridger: Mountain Boy* by Winders (Bobbs-Merrill) p. 20 4.4	Book difficult but interest high — reading carefully. Need con-ference again soon. Trouble recalling sequence of events.	Made comprehension questions to answer after next chapter. Keep word bank up to date. Worksheets B41–42, sequence.

Name: *John*   Instructional: *3.5*   Independent: *4.5*   Potential: *7.5*

(continued)

Date	Title of book Page number Level	Comments	Follow-up
2/27	p. 45	Questions answered O.K. — read orally exciting part. Asked questions about Mormons.	Library for reference on Mormons. Making model cabin. Writing short article to explain model for display.

Or, the teacher's record may be of this type:

Teacher's Record for Small Group

Date: 10/9/76		Book read: Tuffy and Boots	
Sherry	Read us an excerpt from her book	Finished — *Green Eggs and Ham*	Suggested she present one of the humourous incidents to the class
Karen	Still absent		
Rosanna	Still anxious about status in group	Splash	Give individual help in preparing for sharing time
Paul	Still guessing wildly on new words	Animal riddles	Select exercises on contextual clues

Other teachers maintain an overall reference list of exercises for skill building in the available workbooks, exercise books, teacher-made exercise file, and similar sources. This catalog of skill training aids is consulted after diagnostic interviews and again from time to time after other conferences. The list permits quick prescription of an exercise or series which would correct the observed pupil weaknesses. If desired, these exercises may be cut from their sources, filed in folders or envelopes, or bound in manila folders to be drawn as needed.

Eucyle W. Spaulding, of Fort Lauderdale, Florida, accomplishes the recording of her pupils' skill progress in a unique fashion. She constructs a large wall chart which depicts a number of satellites and space stations in orbit around the classroom. Each station is labeled in terms of a specific word recognition skill, such as sounds of initial consonants, consonant blends, long vowel sounds, vowel digraphs, and silent e rule. With the teacher's assistance each child draws materials from the exercise file to help him acquire these various skills. When he has completed using the skill-building materials, the pupil asks the teacher to check him out. If he is successful, he adds a drawing of his profile labeled with his name to the appropriate place on the space chart. Thus the children are kept aware of the skills they are attempting to master and their progress. The nature of this wall chart could, of course, be adapted to the particular level and interests of the class to depict a trip around the world, a time line of historical events, or a wagon train, etc.

Record keeping by the children is usually initiated by a class discussion of the needs for such records and by developing with the children the forms to be used. The pupil records, which may be kept in an easily accessible card file or in the child's own folder, commonly include a mimeographed form for listing titles, authors, dates of reading, and pupil comments. Some intermediate-grade teachers ask pupils to record also the types of books they are reading to encourage greater breadth and variety. This record may take the form of a large wheel in which the spokes represent various categories. As a child finishes each book, he writes its title or a key word on the proper spoke of the wheel. Other teachers have their pupils maintain a list of various categories and simply check each type as the pupil completes a book. A few teachers prefer their pupils to keep a list of unusual words or phrases, or unknown words, interesting or exciting words encountered in their reading. These lists may form the basis for vocabulary-building exercises, picture dictionaries, or various word games. Older children may write short summaries of books and place these in a file to be consulted by any child who is considering a book. These peer comments are often significant influences upon pupil selection. At primary school levels when children's writing abilities are not highly developed, pupils often keep records of their reading in the form of art work. These records might include a painting or drawing of a particularly interesting incident, a series of drawings or pictures cut from old magazines depicting the chief characters of the book, or a make-believe cover of the book illustrated by the child. For these pupils, most of the record keeping will be in the form of teacher's notes on their follow-up activities, as book sharing by puppetry, dramatization, or oral report. Pupils at these levels can and should be expected to keep a list of the new words encountered in each book to stimulate their word consciousness. These lists may well be incomplete, for the average child or even college student does not know accurately with which words he is really unfamiliar. But keeping the list promotes a set toward learning words, an attitude or habit which is fundamental to continued vocabulary growth. If, as we have suggested earlier, these lists are used in a variety of ways by the child and teacher, this important set is strengthened.

If desired, individual records for each book read might take this form.

Name _____

Date _____

1. *Write the title of your book.*

2. *List the main characters and describe book.*

3. *Choose one character and tell what you liked most or least about him.*

4. *Make a list of some of the new words you met and learned.*

Or, an individual's record might look like this:

Name _____

Date _____

Summarize the story.

How did this story make you feel?

Make a list of some of the interesting words that the author used.

Write a phrase that answers each of the following questions: who, what, where, when.

Individual records kept by the children may take a variety of forms, such as this example.

Child's Record

Title of book	*Begun*	*Finished*	*Comments*	*New words learned*
Abigail Adams	April 29	May 2	Very good story about the girl growing up to be a fine lady	pinafore, petticoat

Name:

This type of record could be varied by using separate pages for different types of books, as famous people, fun and fancy, life in other places, etc.

USING THE CONFERENCE FOR EVALUATION

The individual conference between teacher and pupil is obviously the cornerstone of any approach to individualization of reading instruction. Teacher skill in the conference determines whether there will be effective diagnosis of the pupil's instructional needs or any continuous evaluation of his overall reading development. The conference is a crucial opportunity for observation of the child's reading interests and his skills in word recognition, comprehension, oral and silent reading. In effect the recurring conferences become the major means of communication between the teacher and pupil in the area of reading instruction. On the one hand, the conference is the basis of teacher diagnosis, planning, and instruction; on the other, it is the prime pupil opportunity for receiving personal instruction, guidance, and support.

We are not suggesting that in the individualized approach no instruction is offered other than in the conference. Nor are we implying that there is no pupil–teacher interaction except that in the conference. Communication between teacher and pupil certainly occurs in a variety of settings. But for two significant reasons, the conference is the most important contact between teacher and pupil. First, the conference is the basis upon which most other contacts between teacher and pupil are planned. The nature, type, and frequency of the other kinds of teacher–pupil interaction are based on the teacher's findings in the conference. Second, the conference is the main opportunity for warm, personal communication between teacher and pupil, and hence a highly significant factor in the child's school adjustment and academic progress.

Elsewhere we have noted a number of interpretations of the purposes and conduct of the individual conference. To some writers, the conference is simply an opportunity for casual discussion of the child's reading selections, his enjoyment of the material, and his probable future choices. To other teachers, it is a substitute for the oral reading circle, for the teacher's major observation is the child's growth in sight vocabulary. To still others, the conference involves a number of factors—diagnosis of the pupil's skill development, planning for related instruction, careful recording, review of the child's current and future reading—all occurring almost simultaneously during each brief conference.

Judging by the reports in most individualized reading literature, oral reading during the conference is the chief interaction between teacher and pupil. This type of oral reading is, in effect, merely a substitute for the old oral reading circle. Like the oral reading in conventional classes, the practice is based upon two presumptions. It is obvious that many teachers and pupils believe that oral reading is the most important application or practice in reading, a very questionable assumption. It is equally obvious that teachers who depend heavily upon oral reading, either in the conference or the circle, believe that this practice affords a good opportunity for overall evaluation of reading progress. At several places in this book we have attempted to point out the errors in these beliefs.

In our opinion, oral reading is not an essential part of every individual conference. There are many other better reasons for conferences. The teacher could spend time discussing the child's current reading choice, determining his readiness for sharing, discussing future choices, giving instructions regarding the child's role in small-group work, discussing the progress of his research activities, reviewing his reading records, checking comprehension of his silent reading, and providing individualized instruction in reading skill, to mention only a few.

In assessing the child's comprehension in a conference, the questions should range over all of the book insofar as the child has read it. We could not consider comprehension questions based only on that portion he might read aloud in the conference (assuming that the teacher persists in using oral reading to observe the child's progress). Comprehension in oral reading is not efficient and is not indicative of the types or degree of understanding achieved through silent reading. These questions could be prepared early in the school year with relevance to each book in the classroom library and, as one of the commercial book collections has done, they could be placed on a small card and inserted in a holder on the back cover.

But if the supply of books is replenished from time to time, and the total number of books read by the pupils is quite large, and these conditions are very probable, there may be little teacher time to prepare a set of questions for each and every book. The teacher could, of course, just ask leading questions which would elicit a rehash of the story, or the child's personal reactions. But these are useless as measures of comprehension despite their recommendation by several sources (5). Those who are accustomed to follow the questioning strategies outlined in a basal manual raise such doubts as: How does a teacher who has not read the book sample the child's comprehension? We believe that these problems can be solved by developing teacher skill in questioning, beginning perhaps with questions such as the following:

Questions for a Conference

Comprehension

1. Which character in the story did you like best? Why?
2. Would you like to trade places with any of the people in the story? If so, why?
3. What would you have changed in the ending of the story, if you had been the author?
4. If you close your eyes and think about the story, is there any part you can recall? What do you see or think of?
5. Which character in the story would you like to have as a friend? Why?
6. Do you believe that everything in the book could have happened? Why or why not? Was the story intended to be true to life?
7. What part of the story was hardest for you to understand? Let's turn to that part and talk about what puzzled you.
8. Who in our class do you think would like to read this book? Why? Will you tell him about it?
9. Would you like to meet the author? If you could, what would you talk about?
10. Is there any part of the story that you would have left out in order to make it more interesting? If so, what part?
11. Was there any person in the story whom you didn't like? What kind of person is he?
12. What other titles could you think of for this story?
13. What did you learn from this book? Something about people? Some new ideas? Something about the way people used to live?

Follow-up

1. Could you think of another way this story could have ended? Will you write down your ending and share it with me later?
2. You know that sometimes an author writes several stories about the same person. Could you pick a character in your story and write a short story about him?
3. Do you think that there is a part of the book that could be made into a short play that the class would enjoy? What part? How would you like to ask some of your friends to help you present that part as a play? Let me know when you have practiced once or twice and I'll arrange a time for you to give the play.
4. Would you make a group of drawings showing some of the things that happened in the story? You could paste them together in a long strip and unroll them as you tell the class about the book.
5. Were there any funny parts to your book? Could you make a picture of that part, and write enough of the story so that others could enjoy the funny part? We could put it on our bulletin board.
6. Do you have a friend or a relative who is not in our class who might like to hear about this book? Will you write a letter telling him why you think he would enjoy the book, and we'll arrange to mail it.
7. Was there a character in the book who was anything like you? Imagine that you were in his place in one part of the story, and write down what you would have done or said then.
8. Would you write a short paragraph telling why you liked this book and why you think others would like it? We'll put your review on the bulletin board.
9. Would you like to read another book like this? Or by the same author? Look through our library and let me know whether you find one you think you will like.

Skill Development

1. While you were reading you met some words you didn't know, didn't you? Did you make a list of these? Let's look at your list and talk about their meanings.
2. An author usually tells about his characters by describing them, their looks, their behavior. Can you find a place in the book where the author is describing one of his characters? Let's see whether we can use other words to give the same ideas (synonyms) about that person.
3. Did your author use any large words in his story? Can you find some of them and divide them into syllables? Then we'll try to pronounce them and talk about their meanings.
4. Let's just pick a page from the book at random. On this page, try to find (adapt to pupil's previous training):
   a. Any compound words.
   b. Any with the short *i* sound.
   c. Any with prefixes.
   d. One with a soft *c*, and another with the hard *c* sound.
   e. Any with silent vowels.

f. A sentence with two adjectives in it.

g. Five words that have initial consonant digraphs.

h. A three-syllable word.

i. Two words with a vowel digraph.

j. Any with suffixes.

k. A word you cannot pronounce.

l. A word that refers to clothing; a way of moving; a color word; one that tells time.

m. A word that begins with each letter of the alphabet. (Write them down, beginning with one starting with *a,* then with *b,* and so on.)

5. Can you arrange all the words on this page that begin with *c* in the proper alphabetical order?

We have offered, of course, more questions than would be needed for a conference to show the types possible. Each teacher would choose those questions she felt relevant, stress the area of the child's apparent needs, and soon enlarge this collection by adding her own questions.

Like Darrow and Howes (8) we believe that the conference may take different forms and serve different purposes from time to time. One type of conference is diagnostic: it involves observation of the child's skill development and planning for future instruction. Even before the diagnostic conference, some attempts to inventory the child's initial status in various reading skills must be made. Thus the first individual conferences may serve the unique purpose of evaluating the child's instructional, independent, and potential reading levels, and his present abilities in a number of reading skills. A third type of conference, mentioned most frequently in reading studies, involves the evaluation of the child's growth in reading interests. This type answers questions regarding the development of new interests, the child's insights into the deeper meanings of his readings, his growth in informative background, his attempts at self-evaluation of his reading, and his groping efforts to explore new areas with his skills.

If these various types of individual conferences are to be effective in accomplishing their purposes, it is obvious that they must be carefully planned. The purpose of the conference must be clear-cut and the record keeping relevant and accurate. The form of the conference should certainly not be inflexible, for each is an opportunity for strengthening the relationships between teacher and pupil. But, on the other hand, neither is the conference a casual contact resulting in only incidental observations or information.

In the average-sized classroom, the opportunities for conferences are too infrequent and too brief for a casual approach or for a laissez-faire attitude which allows the conference to become a purely social contact. Because we believe that the individual conferences are extremely important in the success of individualized reading, we shall attempt to point out in detail our concepts of their organization and conduct.

Is this kind of inventory of reading skills a practical, economical device for determining children's reading performances? Why can't the results of a simple reading test accomplish the same goals in less time? These are some of the questions which will certainly arise in the minds of many teachers who are concerned with the amount of time demanded by our suggestions. Despite the extra teacher time required, there is little doubt in the minds of most reading authorities of the superiority of the inventory approach. Group tests, largely because of their brevity, fail to supply an adequate sampling of the skills the teacher is concerned about and thus fail in their primary purpose of supplying diagnostic information. Few commercial tests sample adequately the very skills the teacher will emphasize. Moreover, if their results are used to distinguish the working reading levels of pupils, as in preparation for tentative grouping, the scores are often greatly inaccurate and misleading.

John Emerson Daniel* compared several group tests and two versions of an informal inventory with teacher judgments of pupils' instructional levels. The *Gates Advanced Primary Reading Test* (Teachers College, Columbia University) provided adequate differentiation for planning for three or five reading groups but overestimated teacher judgment *constantly by two full grades.* The informal inventory, however, was superior in that it was equally efficient in indicating groups and in addition yielded significant diagnostic information. This inventory, incidentally, was scored in a modified manner rather than by the artificially high standards suggested by Betts, a necessary precaution we have already mentioned. Group tests have values for group studies, for school surveys, and the like, but most are inadequate for diagnosis, for pupil–pupil comparisons, or for classroom planning and grouping.

TAKING INVENTORY IN THE CONFERENCE

At the beginning of the school year, in many classrooms the available records of pupil reading progress are scanty or inaccurate. The appropriate levels of reading materials needed for instructional purposes, the possible recreational or independent reading levels of the children, and the potential of the pupils for reading growth possibly may not be noted in the previous year's records. It is true that schools employing the more sterotyped basal reader approach often supply a list of the basal books read by each child. But to the current year's teacher, who intends to employ largely individualized procedures, such a list simply hints at the child's present reading status. The teacher still must discover the pupil's capacities for independent reading, estimate his potential for the future, and evaluate his reading skills. Despite the good intentions responsible for it, a list of basals previously read by each pupil gives no clues to his present instructional needs.

Similarly, the score on a general reading test given near the close of the previous year is often of no real value to the current year's teacher. Aside from the inherent inaccuracy in group testing, which tends to result in misleading estimates

---

* John Emerson Daniel, "The Effectiveness of Various Procedures in Reading Level Placement," *Elementary English,* 39 (October 1962), 590–600.

of pupil reading status, the score on the average reading test is of little diagnostic significance. It is merely a gross sum of the pupil's performances in a half-dozen skills operating simultaneously with varying degrees of effectiveness, transmitted into a meaningless grade level.

Use of some diagnostic tests that sample pupil ability in significant subskills is much more useful than the usual end-of-year general reading test. Among those of merit are: Word Analysis—*McCullough Word-Analysis Tests* (Ginn); *Stanford Diagnostic Reading Test* (Harcourt Brace Jovanovich). *The Diagnostic Reading Scales* (CTB/McGraw-Hill) contain a fairly complete group of phonic measures that must be administered individually.

In many sources teachers are being urged to construct their own informal inventories. In brief, the directions suggest selecting samples from an unfamiliar basal reader series at successive grade levels. One such sample is used to test oral reading; another, to measure silent. In the oral reading, that level at which the child reads with no more than one error per twenty running words (95 percent accuracy) and at least 75 percent comprehension is called the instructional level and represents the level of reading matter to be used in classroom instruction. The sample in which the child reads with 99 percent oral accuracy and at least 90 percent comprehension is called the independent level, or that which may be used for supplementary and recreational reading. Some authorities assume that the comprehension exhibited in the oral reading is also true for silent and give no test of this ability. Others use both silent and oral reading samples and average the percentages of comprehension to estimate these levels. Reading orally with more than ten errors per hundred running words and comprehension of 50 percent or less is supposed to represent the frustration level. The simplicity of this arrangement and the apparent realism of the testing material, as contrasted with that in many standardized tests, has given the Informal Reading Inventory (I.R.I.) wide appeal.

But when we explore the history of the I.R.I. and examine it, as we would any other test, for evidence of validity and reliability, its appeal diminishes markedly. The whole idea is based on a single study of forty-one children tested in reading selections *first silently, then orally.* With these two exposures to the same passages, their oral reading was, as we would expect, quite good, averaging 93 percent accuracy. This single study was accepted at face value by Emmett A. Betts, who then coined the terms and announced the standards for the three descriptive levels we have mentioned. Needless to say, the whole procedure has been severely criticized by a number of writers. Among the flaws they emphasize are (*32, 24, 43*):

1. Any basal series is not a good source of reading selections, for the books are not graded accurately nor similar from one series to another. A sample may or may not reflect a specific grade level (*43*).
2. Basal material is not the best possible for sampling reading ability among children in other types of reading programs.
3. The standards for oral reading accuracy in the I.R.I. are completely arbitrary. A study by Powell and Dunkeld (*35*) comparing these standards with actual child

reading performances in the five leading oral reading commercial tests and a sample of their own shows a great divergence. Children just don't read as well as the I.R.I. expects them to, particularly in reading orally at sight, as in the current testing procedure (not silently first, then again orally as in the original study). Their real oral reading accuracy ranges from about 80 percent at the first grade, to 85 percent at the second, and gradually increases to about 90 to 95 percent by the sixth grade (32).

4. Kasdon (25) has shown that the original testing method produced much higher oral accuracy than today's oral reading at sight, as well as a very different profile of errors, thus again challenging the I.R.I. standards.

5. Limiting children's independent reading to a level below classroom instructional materials fails to recognize the influence of interest on children's choices. Many children read some harder materials with good comprehension. The fact that they may not be able to read these harder materials with the exaggerated degree of accuracy demanded by the I.R.I. also ignores pupil ability to derive meanings from the context for words not in their sight vocabulary (39).

Since many classroom teachers do not have access to better oral reading tests, and there is some merit in trying to supply them with a usable instrument, we offer the following suggestions for constructing an informal test.

1. Draw the graded reading samples from the basal reader series to be used in your classroom. Its levels may not be accurately labeled but, realistically, this is what you and your children are going to live with. If you have the time, apply a primary- (41) or an intermediate-grade readability formula to be certain of the reading levels of these samples (6).

2. Each reading selection should be long enough to require three or four minutes of reading and be a complete story or at least the beginning of such in order to be coherent. One set of selections will be needed for oral reading, a second set for silent, and a third for auditory comprehension or measuring potential. These parallel selections should be as comparable as possible.

3. With older pupils, you may wish to assemble a similar series of samples for science and social science texts to evaluate these reading areas. For each selection, frame questions that appear to measure recall of details, interpretation or inferences, and main ideas, preferably in almost equal numbers. Do not try to count the number of each type of question answered in an attempt to pinpoint a type of comprehension weakness. The number the child will attempt is too small for significance and besides, as we will point out later, there is strong doubt that there are really different comprehension skills. Try out these questions on a number of children to determine those that can be answered *without reading the selection,* and eliminate those so answered by 20 to 30 percent or more of the pupils you use in this trial. Rewrite and retry the questions in this fashion until you have at least eight to ten for each selection.

4. Ditto or mimeograph a number of copies of the test selections and questions, double- or triple-spacing the lines to permit recording of errors as the child reads orally. Use the error recording system outlined later in this chapter.

5. Consider your pupils' performances as adequate if they read orally with (a) no more than fifteen to twenty errors per one hundred words in the first or second grade, with at least 70 percent comprehension; (b) no more than ten errors per

one hundred words in other grades, with at least 70 percent comprehension; and (c) at least 70 percent comprehension in silent reading and in answering the questions on a selection after you have read it and the questions to the pupil.

6. Use the highest level of pupil success in oral reading for instructional materials (if you follow a basal system). Use the highest level of success in silent reading to guide you in offering supplementary recreational and reference materials. Use the auditory testing result as a rough estimate of the child's language background readiness and his potential for progress. In most middle-class pupils this estimate will be about one to two years above the instructional level. When this difference is not present, recognize and implement the child's need for language and firsthand experiences to develop his vocabulary and thinking capacities.

Using Cloze.   An alternative to the construction of an informal test is the use of the cloze procedure.* This approach to estimating the child's functional silent reading level eliminates the difficulty of creating comprehension questions that really function. Briefly, the steps are:

1. Use a set of passages selected as described above. Each should be at least 500 words in length. Delete every tenth word, leaving constant blank spaces of at least five or six letters in width. The deletions begin in the second sentence and should number at least fifty. Retype and mimeograph the material in multiple copies.
2. Give the passage to the pupils, in a group or individually, asking them to write a word for each blank space in the margin or, if they are mature enough, on numbered lines of a separate piece of paper. Make certain that they understand they are to leave a blank line if they cannot supply a word for a blank space in the passage.
3. Allow the pupils ample time to try all the items. Score for the total number of words *exactly* like those deleted that they can supply. Synonyms are not acceptable; misspelled words are. Multiply the score by two to find the percentage of correct answers, if you have prepared fifty test items.
4. Those passages in which the children score 40 to 44 percent indicate their functional silent reading level, assuming that the passages actually reflect the various grade levels. For some children it will be necessary to administer several test passages to find their proper level. You may expect that this silent reading performance will often be higher than the Instructional Level found by the oral reading test.

THE DIAGNOSTIC CONFERENCE

Most individual conferences described in reading studies are intended to be diagnostic in that the teacher determines the child's needs for skill instruction by

---

* John R. Bormuth, "The Cloze Procedure: Literacy in The Classroom," in *Help for the Reading Teacher: New Directions in Research,* William D. Page, ed., National Conference on Research in Reading, 1975, 60–90.

listening to his oral reading. This diagnostic effort appears to be the most common activity in the conference, if we may judge from current reports on individualized programs. There are several assumptions inherent in this approach to the diagnosis of pupil reading needs. First, there is the obvious belief that oral reading performances are a good indicator of general reading ability. Second, there is, of course, the assumption that the average teacher is capable of judging each pupil's training needs by listening to his oral reading—that he can make appropriate judgments and accurate evaluations and then plan the best types of instruction for each pupil. Let us first explore the question of whether oral reading errors are a good indicator of other reading skills, such as silent comprehension. Preston's study (36) of elementary school children considered retarded in reading by their teachers raises a number of doubts about teacher judgment. He found that from 40 to 60 percent of these children were not actually retarded when their silent reading levels were compared with the expected performance according to their mental ages. Teachers' judgments were most inaccurate at primary levels, not only because teachers ignored the child's mental ability, but also because the judgments were based largely on oral reading. Most teacher estimates of reading ability were related to the grade-level expectation and not to the true capabilities of the children. Preston decries the teacher habit of equating oral reading with silent reading and of drawing hasty conclusions about the child's overall progress solely from observation of oral reading errors.

Gilmore's dissertation (15) offers evidence which tends to substantiate Preston's complaints. He found that the correlations between oral reading errors and silent comprehension drop rapidly from a high level (.918) in the second grade to only moderate levels (.631 to .693) in the third to sixth grades and still lower levels (.572 and .561) in the seventh and eighth grades. Predictions of the pupil's silent reading ability from observing his oral reading errors are about 36 percent better than a sheer guess in intermediate grades and about 25 percent better at the junior high school level. This trend toward an increasingly smaller relationship between oral and silent reading continues as skill in these two types of reading matures. In fact, among good college freshmen readers one study found a high negative relationship between oral and silent comprehension. Good silent comprehenders tended strongly to score poorly in oral comprehension, while good oral comprehenders tended to be poor in silent comprehension. Among poor college freshmen readers there was very little relationship between oral and silent comprehension.

The obvious implication of this research is that the teacher cannot judge the overall reading progress of pupils simply by observing their oral reading. Pupils may be significantly better (or worse) in such silent reading skills as rate, vocabulary, and comprehension than their oral reading implies. If teacher observation of oral reading has any useful purpose, it is certainly not that of overall evaluation. The proper function of an oral reading test is the observation of oral reading skills and word recognition skills, as we shall point out later.

For judging silent reading ability, only a silent reading sample is appropriate. Comprehension may be evaluated by the quality and quantity of the child's response to such questions as we have listed earlier; not by an oral informal inventory or an oral standardized test, as we have previously emphasized.

Teacher observation of oral reading assumes accurate recording and interpretation of oral errors, as we have suggested earlier. Several studies cast serious doubt on these diagnostic skills of the average teacher. For example, in a broad cross section of elementary teachers, Adams (1) found that 96 percent were doubtful that even experienced teachers were able to diagnose their pupils' reading problems. Sixty-two percent were also doubtful of the teachers' ability to plan appropriate remedial steps, even when their pupils' problems had been diagnosed. After a three-month experience with individualized reading, Sartain's second- and third-grade teachers (38) complained of their diagnostic inadequacies in the individual conference. A third study, by Eleanor M. Ladd (26), points up even more strongly these teacher difficultiies in recording and interpreting oral reading errors. Ladd found that groups of untrained teachers recorded incorrectly 34 to 39 percent of the oral reading errors they were trying to observe. After thirty hours of training with recorded tests or actual children or both, teachers were still missing 33 to 37 percent of the errors. Collectively, these studies imply that diagnosis based on errors in oral reading in the individual conference is not made very accurately by the average teacher.

Most of the negative result, however, was due to the fact that the teachers were attempting to follow a recording system which was literally impossible. They had been asked to record hesitations of two seconds or more as well as apparent errors in ignoring punctuation. As the figures above show, scoring of these so-called errors was no more accurate after training than in the initial trial. We hope it is possible to aid teachers in this diagnosis by outlining a more practical system for recording oral errors.

Recording Oral Reading Errors and Behaviors

A number of studies have made careful records of oral reading errors and skills. The authors of these used different checklists and hence recorded somewhat different patterns of errors and difficulties. Despite these differences it is possible to observe some trends in oral reading behaviors as children mature in this skill. Duffy and Durrell (12) listened to the oral reading of a number of third-grade children and made certain general observations. A few years later Daw (9) used the same checklist of difficulties in observing a number of fourth- and fifth-grade children.

These data are, of course, general observations of oral reading rather than a detailed analysis of oral errors. Although they are only crude diagnostic observations, they demonstrate certain definite trends. According to these studies, the average third grader tends to ignore punctuation and shows lack of sight word accuracy by many additions, omissions, and inaccurate guesses. The fourth and fifth graders may have been reading at sight in relatively difficult materials, for their difficulties were marked in poor word attack, poor phrasing, and lack of expression. In the opinions of these observers, pupils of all three grades were guilty of poor enunciation, many mistakes on small words, and excessive head movements.

Using a much smaller number of pupils, but a similar checklist, Barbe et al. (2) observed somewhat similar trends. They also noted the tendencies to poor sight vocabulary, guessing at words, and ignoring punctuation as characteristic of poor primary readers. Their upper-elementary-grade pupils, like those in the other studies, showed marked problems in phrasing, monotony of tone, frequent repetitions, and ignoring punctuation.

In her classic study of poor readers in grades one to six, Marion Monroe (30) used a more diagnostic checklist of oral reading errors, for she was concerned about planning specific remedial steps. Madden and Pratt (28) employed a somewhat similar checklist in observing the oral reading of over a thousand pupils in the third to ninth grades. The data collected in these two studies again permit us to observe significant trends in the patterns of oral reading errors as children advance in age and reading development.

Both studies show increasing omissions as children mature and their speed of oral reading increases. Madden and Pratt detected the same trend in error of additions of words. Both studies note the decrease in words aided or told to the child because of his failure to analyze them successfully. We would expect this trend to appear as sight vocabulary grows and skill in word analysis improves.

Collectively, these studies indicate that the pattern of oral reading errors and the child's general oral reading skills change in many respects as his reading development continues. It is apparent also that there are two distinct ways of approaching the observation of oral reading: one by noting general difficulties in fluency, word attack, and posture; the other, by carefully recording the exact errors made by the child while he reads. General observations, such as those which would be made by using the accompanying checklist, may represent the teacher's impressions accumulated during a number of individual conferences and other classroom activities. The detailed analysis of oral reading errors would, on the other hand, probably be made during one of the conferences early in the school year and repeated perhaps at the middle and again toward the end of the school year. If the early conferences include taking an inventory of the child's reading skills, as we have suggested earlier, a record of oral reading errors will be included.

Several relatively recent studies of oral reading errors have moved away from the detailed count of mistakes on vowels, consonants, and the like to other interpretations. One new emphasis is upon the graphic similarity between the printed word and the child's response (3,45). In other words, each error is counted according to whether it resembles the given word in the beginning or ending letters. Another new trend is to interpret each error according to first, its graphic similarity to the printed word; second, whether the two words sound alike; third, whether the response is grammatically the same; fourth, whether the sentence produced by the child is syntactically correct; and fifth, whether the sentence is acceptable semantically (meaning). This type of analysis is exemplified in the

Reading Miscue Inventory of Yetta Goodman and Carolyn Burke (*17*). Based on his studies of oral reading errors, Kenneth S. Goodman (*16*) also emphasizes the need for a careful tabulation of the child's self-corrections.

While noting that graphic similarity is, in effect, an analysis of the child's phonic skills, it is apparent that the other types of reading behaviors observed move dramatically away from the older systems of recording. This linguistic-oriented system of analysis is concerned almost entirely with the child's success in dealing with the grammar and meaning of the sentence, not his reactions to letters or their sounds. Analysis of oral reading errors is intended to reveal whether the child is really reading for meaning rather than naming the words correctly, certainly a very significant observation that should be incorporated into our diagnoses.

A doctoral study by Herlin (*21*) attempted to establish contemporary norms for oral reading errors by testing children on Monroe's battery of tests and by the *Durrell Analysis of Reading Difficulty* (*13*), a fairly recent series. Surprisingly, Herlin found that today's children made the same proportions of errors in the Monroe tests as the children of forty years ago. At first, this seemed to imply that children's oral error tendencies had not changed in almost half a century. But when he compared the error profiles from the two tests, they were quite different. Moreover, the reading levels achieved in the two batteries differed by more than six months for the average child.

The most striking implications of this study are that, first, the kinds of reading errors that pupils seem to make are often peculiar to the particular test selections employed. Second, reading-level estimates from two tests, even though standardized, are very apt to differ significantly. How, then, does the teacher determine what the true errors of a child are and therefore what retraining procedures she should employ? Since no norms for proportions of errors are available, except those for several standardized tests, how does the teacher judge a child's profile of errors to determine his needs? How does she know whether the testing reveals an accurate estimate of the reading levels the child can deal with profitably?

The best answers we can offer to these problems are not very strong. We suggested that she might employ an oral reading test in which the selections are at grade levels and the selections extend over a number of levels. Oral reading errors should be recorded in the manner described later. Lacking norms for proportions of errors, the teacher can identify probable needs by the frequency of each type of error. Della-Piana and Herlin (*11*) have shown that this gives a reasonable indication of a pupil's error tendencies. Even though the profile of errors may be peculiar to the test, if she uses the same test with all the pupils she wishes to evaluate, the results will, at least, be comparable from one child to the next.

Except for beginning readers, each reading selection should be close to two hundred words in length, for short samples do not yield an accurate profile. Sufficient test samples should be administered to permit collecting about seventy-five to one hundred errors, to ensure a reliable profile. The errors collected to form the profile should not be a combination of those from easy to difficult selections since pupil errors vary with different levels of materials. The oral reading sample should be accompanied by comprehension questions for which some standard of accuracy has been established. Without such questions, good word callers will be judged to be good readers at levels they really cannot comprehend.

Standardized tests which meet most of these criteria are the *Diagnostic Reading Scales* (CTB/McGraw-Hill), the *Individual Reading Placement Inventory* (Follett), and the *Classroom Reading Inventory* (William C. Brown). If some measure of the breadth of sight vocabulary is desired, test lists are offered in the *Diagnostic Reading Scales* and the *Dolch Basic Sight Word Test* (Garrard). Oral reading errors in reading these word lists are sometimes added to those present in the reading selections, but this is a dubious procedure. Several studies show that children can recognize many words in context that they cannot on lists (*16*). Hence the judgment of which basic words the child still needs to learn is more accurately made from his performance with selections containing these words, such as those formed by the teacher or simple materials from basals or other sources. This difference in word recognition in lists and in context is less in the first grade than later primary grades because beginning readers vary so little from isolated words to contextual reading. Word lists at that level are therefore a reasonable sample of sight vocabulary. Above this beginning level, word lists tend to force the pupil toward phonic analysis, since other clues to the words are lacking. Thus, although his performance does give some clues regarding his phonic skills, it does not reflect his actual word recognition or word analysis skills, when reading in context. Above the first-grade level, sight vocabulary recognition must be tested both by list and contextual reading if we are to secure an accurate picture.

We have regrouped and rephrased the checklists used in the studies described earlier to permit the teacher to make somewhat more detailed observations. With the checklist at hand, during conferences or classroom oral reading activities, the teacher may note the difficulties shown by each pupil. The category of speech difficulties provides an opportunity to note the child's needs for correction of such hindrances as stammering, lisping, or constant sound substitutions. The items losing place, skipping lines, or using finger to keep place are combined because they are related symptoms of poor directional attack.

Fluency

Poor phrasing or word by word
Speech difficulties
Monotone, lacking inflection
Pitch: too high or too low
Volume: too loud or too soft
Loses place, skips lines, uses finger
Ignores punctuation

(continued)

Word Attack

Skips over unknown words
Needs frequent prompting
Substitutes by guessing from context
Substitutes irrelevant words
Spells or sounds letter by letter
Blends poorly
Mistakes mainly on small words
Fumbles, repeats frequently

Posture

Book too close, too far
Moves head
Cocks head or book
Squints or frowns

The list of items under *Word Attack* is expanded to include more of the specific difficulties shown, as we have seen, by primary school children and poor readers. Since the purpose of the checklist is to help the teacher plan corrective instructional steps, not simply to describe how well the pupil reads, the list includes only symptoms of poor reading habits and skills.

If an inventory test, such as we have mentioned earlier, is given, the teacher will have a duplicate of the reading selection in her hands. She can record the types of oral reading errors shown at the top of the next page.

If the pupil corrects himself in any type of error, do not count that error, unless his correction involves a repetition. For example, the child reads "a red house" for "a house." Realizing he has inserted a word, he repeats the phrase correctly as "a house." Cross out or check the addition error as no error, but score the repetition by an arrow under the words he has repeated.

Do *not* attempt to record hesitations, phrasing, word stress, or the child's observation of punctuation. Ladd's study (26) indicates that even after thirty hours of training, teachers could not record these accurately. Moreover, other research indicates that the tendencies to make these errors are inconsistent and unreliable.

Interpreting Errors

Attempting to assign an exact reason for each oral reading error or type of error that a pupil makes is literally impossible. The same type of error may occur several times during a reading, but for a different reason each time. Therefore, the diagnosis of a pupil's instructional needs is not directly related to his pattern of oral

	Examples
Additions. Insert a caret ∧ wherever the pupil adds a sound or a word. Write the addition above the line.	red s a ∧ house ∧
Omissions. Put a circle around each sound or word omitted.	a (red) house
Repetitions. Put an arrow under a repetition of two words or more. Ignore one-word repetitions.	It was difficult
Substitutions. Cross out any word that the pupil substitutes for or mispronounces. Write in the word as he pronounces it.	run Mary ~~ran~~ down the street.
Reversals. Show reversals of whole words or a letter sequence by a transposition symbol, ⊔⊓.	John was a friend John was a friend
Words aided. When pupil blocks on a word, wait five seconds for him to attempt it. If he says nothing, tell him the word and cross it out.	Paul ~~Revere~~ was a

reading errors. To make the best diagnosis, we can note the proportions of various errors, the types that are excessive, the portion of the word in which his errors are concentrated, then assume certain explanations for his more frequent errors and begin the logical corrective steps. We can give only general suggestions of the meanings of various types of errors to aid the teacher in the interpretation of each pupil's pattern.

In general, when errors are concentrated on the beginnings of words, as they tend to be, they indicate either failure in sight vocabulary or difficulty with consonants and consonant blends. In the middle of words, vowel sounds may be the problem, while errors on endings may arise for several reasons, as we shall point out.

Additions. Additions of whole words may represent the pupil's attempt to embroider the author's ideas, as "the big old red house" for "the red house." This tendency is more common among intermediate-grade and older pupils, for it demands quick reactions, rapid reading, and a degree of verbal fluency. Other additions of this type tend to occur when, in trying to correct another error, the pupil adds a word or two to smooth out the phrase. When excessive, additions of whole words may represent superficial reading and an overdependence upon context with consequent loss of accuracy in comprehension of fine details.

Additions at the end of words which change the tense or number may well indicate lack of training in structural analysis, especially among primary-grade pupils.

Omissions. Omissions of whole words, particularly among intermediate-grade and older pupils, may indicate either excessive speed or a tendency to skip over unknown words. If we ask the child to reread a list of the omitted words after he has finished the reading selection, it is readily possible to distinguish between these two probable causes. Omissions of endings may again reflect poor structural analysis, or the influence of dialect.

Repetitions. Frequent repetitions may reflect poor directional attack, or lack of consistent left-to-right movement in reading. In some cases they represent the pupil's fumbling with recognition of a difficult word or thought occurring several words later in the sentence. While processing or attacking mentally the hard word, the reader repeats the preceding word or phrase, once or several times. Meanwhile he gains time to recognize the difficult word. This mental fumbling, resulting in an error of repetition, is a frequent and normal part of the reading act. We do not believe that the overall estimate of the child's reading should be unduly penalized by counting every single repetition he makes. After all, the habit of analyzing new, hard words while reading is a very desirable one. Therefore, we count repetitions only when two words or more are involved, to reduce the artificial frequency of this error. Another possible explanation of repetitions may be the tension or nervousness of the child, who is insecure in the threatening situation of reading aloud to another person, or his attempt to correct a miscue.

Substitutions. Substitutions of whole words take four forms: (1) The substituted word has the same shape or form and the same idea, as "house" for "home." This type implies that the reader is attending to the meaning of the context and word form, but probably not using phonics or syllabication for word identification. (2) The substitution is a whole word, same form, different idea, as "horse" for "house." This error may indicate overdependence upon gross word form as the chief means of word identification. It is the most frequent of the whole-word substitutions, especially among primary-grade readers. (3) The substitution is a whole word, different form, different idea, as "house" for "there." This implies little attention to word form, context, or any other method of word attack. (4) The substitution of a whole word, same idea, different form, as "can" for "will." This implies good use of context but little attention to word form or phonics.

Among primary grade and poor readers, the partial substitution error involving a letter or sound is the most revealing regarding the pupil's phonic and other word attack skills. As we have indicated earlier, the concentration of a high proportion of errors in one area of words may reveal the extent of the pupil's knowledge and use of consonants, consonant blends, vowels, and endings.

Reversals.   If they occur in initial consonants or in other letter sequences, reversals may indicate lack of directional attack, especially among primary-grade or poor readers. If errors occur within certain letters, as *p* for *q, b* for *d,* they may show lack of knowledge of letter sounds or poor letter recognition. If reversals appear in word sequences, they may imply haste or carelessness, in some cases. They may also reflect the difference in word order in standard English and the child's mother tongue, as in the case of Spanish, in which adjectives follow the noun.

Reversals are seldom present among individuals who read above primary levels. Their frequency drops markedly as the reader matures, demonstrating that they are not due to handedness, mixed eye–hand dominance, or lack of cerebral dominance, as some writers suggest. If reversals were due to anatomical relationships, they would not disappear while handedness, eyedness, and the like persisted. In fact, most research studies show no consistent relationship between reversals and these physical factors. The error is characteristic of the beginning reader and it spontaneously disappears as skills improve.

Words Aided.   A large proportion of errors of this type implies dependence in the reader. Lack of a habit of independent word attack or lack of training in phonics and word analysis is usually responsible for this error.

Graphic Similarity.   Noting whether the response resembles the printed word in the first or first few or last letters is an indication of the child's use of phonic or graphic clues. Whether the word he produces is similar in sound is an additional indication. Beginning readers use these cues in almost half of their oral reading errors. Gradually they begin to combine graphic and meaning cues, using such substitutions as *didn't* for *did not, blue* for *black,* and *many* for *most.* When combined with the error count on vowels, consonants, and the like, as in partial substitutions, the child's skill and knowledge of phonics is denoted.

To a degree the extent of errors in which there is a graphic similarity between the printed word and the response is influenced by the amount of phonics instruction. Children trained in a sight-word approach make relatively few errors of this type, substituting instead by configuration, word form, or using irrelevant words drawn from their reading or auditory vocabularies. Children trained in a phonics-oriented system make more errors of this type, as well as more mispronunciations, omissions, and repetitions, because of their emphasis upon phonemes as cues to word recognition.

Self-Corrections.   As children mature in the reading act, their dependence upon the teacher lessens and the attempts to maintain meaning increases. Efforts at self-correction increase gradually with reading skill; thus the greater their number, the closer the child is toward meaningful reading. The repetitions that occur as a result of an attempt at self-correction would, of course, not be considered as oral reading errors, according to this interpretation. Much of the time these self-corrections either correct the initial miscue or involve substituting words of similar function, as a noun for a noun, a verb for a verb. This is the attempt by the maturing reader to maintain the syntax—the word order, tense, and word function—according to several observers (3,16,45). Only when the reader is not comprehending or his dialect interferes does he tend to violate syntax.

Dialect.   What to do about dialect in oral reading testing becomes a very complex problem. If the teacher is not to downgrade the child's reading ability because the oral reading is delivered in dialect, he must be able to distinguish between what is a miscue due to lack of phonic skill or word recognition and a dialect pronunciation. Changes in word order; omissions of helping verbs and of word endings signifying tense or number; omissions of medial consonant sounds, as in *hep-help* and others involving *t, d, s, z, g,* and *k;* substitutions for vowel and consonant sounds, such as *pin–pen, breav–breathe, bref–breath* may characterize the black dialect reader. Spanish–English speakers may show many vowel confusions and substitutions, as *s* for *th, sh* for *ch, j* for *y,* as well as differences in word order, verb forms, and in dealing with negatives.

Teachers will have to familiarize themselves with these differences in time to make their decisions regarding the pupils' real needs. Until this ability is achieved, the judgments will have to be based on evaluations of the child's comprehension. Questioning will show whether the child has the message or, in the case of specific words, whether he clearly understands the terms. As we have pointed out elsewhere, the teacher cannot jump to the conclusion that, because certain phonemes are missing or changed in the child's enunciation, he is in need of further training in auditory discrimination or more phonics or exercises calculated to eradicate the dialect. If he understands and can interpret the material, the fact that he reads it aloud in dialect is insignificant. The presence of dialect in oral reading is not evidence of a decoding failure but rather demonstration of successful decoding plus recoding into his own speech pattern.

Gaining Skill in Recording Errors

The recording of the errors of an individual who reads to us is not a very simple matter. Most teachers, reading clinicians, and psychologists who are learning to perform this task require a good deal of training before they achieve a high degree of accuracy. Ladd's study (26) indicates that this training is more effective if tape recordings are used at first, followed later by trials with live readers. The practice with taped readings is apparently easier for the teacher and more conducive to accuracy, probably because the teacher can give her full attention to the recording rather than to the social interactions necessary in a live reading. The taped readings may also be reviewed as often as desired, and thus the accuracy of the recording of errors will be increased. Therefore, we suggest that wherever possible the teacher employ a tape recorder in her initial attempts to record oral reading errors.

In this chapter we have tried to describe the various types of conferences intended to yield information regarding the child's needs for specific instruction. We have suggested that the first few conferences be used for the purpose of making an inventory of the child's overall development. The use of an informal reading inventory or a standardized inventory will be essential to these evaluation conferences. By their careful application, the teacher may make judgments regarding the level of her instructional materials, the levels the child can read independently, and the child's potential for growth, as measured by listening comprehension. Other tests reviewing the child's word attack skills may also be employed.

Diagnostic conferences will serve two basic functions—observing the child's general reading behaviors in fluency, word attack, and posture; and making a record of the oral reading errors that the child characteristically makes. We have offered checklists to guide these detailed diagnostic observations. With a little conscientious practice, most teachers can utilize these plans to guide decisions about pupils' instructional needs.

Some readers are concerned that our checklists do not give specific standards for error counts, comprehension level, word recognition counts, and other items. We did not supply such statistics, for they could not possibly apply in all types of reading selections and school populations. If teachers construct their own informal inventories, or even if they use those published, they will find that the standards for average reading performances will vary from one group of selections to the next, certainly from one school to the next. When the teacher feels the need for standardized testing, we recommend our *Diagnostic Reading Scales (42)* for making comparisons with the general population.

The *Diagnostic Reading Scales* are a series of standardized reading selections and word lists for use from first grade to junior high school. The first step is the use of a sight vocabulary list to estimate the child's probable reading level. The child then reads appropriate selections orally until he fails to achieve a satisfactory level in either oral reading errors or comprehension. This point is designated as his instructional or classroom working level. Continuing with the next most difficult reading selection silently, the limits of the child's independent reading ability are tested in successive selections until his comprehension fails. The next higher levels of selections are then read to the child to determine his potential for reading performance through his listening comprehension. Finally, a series of simple phonics tests are given to assess the pupil's skills in this area. The *Diagnostic Reading Scales* were constructed to give a fuller picture of pupil abilities than other oral reading tests by a group of measures that almost any classroom teacher could easily administer.

When using her own informal tests, the teacher must form her own standards and judgments of what is average performance in her class and on her reading selections. The real purpose of this testing is not to assign a grade-level score in each major reading skill, or to determine how well children read in terms of some hypothetical normal population. The basic purpose of the tests is to yield diagnostic information: In what reading skills does this child perform poorest in comparison with his other skills? What type of training does he now seem to need most? Which one or two major skills should we now emphasize in our instruction to help improve his overall reading growth?

It is true some teachers will evolve standards that are too low, while others will expect almost perfect reading. Some will tell the child almost every word on which he hesitates, even while testing to discover his word attack and word recognition abilities. Others watch sternly, letting the child struggle by himself, without offering any encouragement or assistance. But the teacher with common sense will try to elicit the child's best effort, compare the child's performances to determine weaknesses, and, using her own experience and the group's average performances as guides, try to make judgments and plans.

A FOOTNOTE ON INDIVIDUALIZING

Some seem to think that individualized reading is taking a new form—that of using programmed workbooks, sequential worksheets, tapes, or filmstrips. (See the bibliography for a list of these.) Another apparently simple answer to the problems inherent in individualizing is sought in the use of one or the other of the skill development kits listed later. To be sure, many of these prepared materials are reasonably sound. They certainly can be used to provide independent work in skill development, in using tapes or records that parallel books, and similar learning activities. But, despite the claims of their producers, are they really individualized instruction?

As we understand the term individualized, it has connotations which are ignored in the manner in which these highly organized, sequential materials are often offered and used. To us, individualization means that instruction and follow-up practice materials are based on the actual needs of the pupil as determined by teacher observation and testing. Certainly, after small-group instruction, the pupils may use any of a number of these prepared materials to reinforce their development. But the crux of the difference between our concept of individualizing and that displayed in the use of many of these commercial programs is in the matching of reinforcing practice to observed need.

What we often see happening ignores this basic principle in the recognition of individual differences. Rather, the commercial program is offered as a relatively complete, basic reading skill development plan, an integrated, sequentially organized program *from which practically all pupils would benefit*. The teacher is led to believe that the program is "individualized" since, after all, the children go off to their own seats to do the exercises. Other principles and terms borrowed from individualized reading, such as self-pacing, self-instructional, diagnostic, and prescriptive, are alluded to in the advertising literature. Finally, the producers manage to convey the implication that the program will produce successful reading for most pupils for, as they claim, it is (1) adequate to produce development of most or all important reading skills, (2) carefully patterned and organized to produce sequential learning, (3) self-pacing, and (4) individualized.

Convinced of its merits, the teacher begins to use one of these basic skill development programs. Does she choose only certain components of the program, as some of the phonic skills, or sight vocabulary, or visual discrimination, and assign only those exercises to those pupils whom she has determined need such practice? Or, does she simply start pupils somewhere in the sequence according to a placement test furnished by the producer, or some other such criterion, and then let the pupils continue indefinitely with the successive exercises? Does she direct pupils only to those elements of the sequence obviously related to their developmental needs, as she has determined by observation and testing? Or, do practically all pupils do the same exercises at their own speed, whether or not every one of the pupils needs all the exercises?

Where is the reading research that proved that any reading program ever designed was effective for most or all of the pupils on whom it was tried? What research supports the use of precisely the same sequence of learning activities, whether through one or several modalities, with most or all of the pupils in the average class? Where is the research that proves that, as promoted in some of these programs, a multimedia approach is best for most or all pupils?

The only legitimate sense in which these programs are individualized is the fact that each child works alone at his desk, or at the projector, the listening center, or the record player (doing exactly what every other child is doing or has done, in the same order of learning activities, through the same modality).

Obviously, we are criticizing the assumptions underlying the most common use of these carefully planned materials, and the misleading implications found so frequently in the sales literature. These are *not* individualized programs; they are *not* complete plans for skill development; they are *not* effective with most or all pupils. At best, they are adjuncts to a *teacher-planned* sequence of diagnosis of need and prescription of reinforcing practice for individual pupils. Some, such as many of those listed later, can be part of the teacher's instructional plans, if they are used in part selectively, as needed by pupils according to the teacher's judgment. With the purchase of several such kits, plus perhaps one of her own, the teacher can refer pupils to certain corrective or developmental activities for many reading skills when, in the teacher's judgment, that practice is needed.

DISCUSSION QUESTIONS

1. What do you think would be your greatest problem in learning how to make conferences an integral part of your teaching? How might you approach this problem?

2. If you were to begin using conferences, with what type would you start? Why?

3. Arrange a role-playing situation in which you will be the teacher conducting some definite type of conference. Use a pupil, or even another member of the class, if necessary. Discuss your strengths and weaknesses with the group.

4. How could you arrange for practice in recording and analyzing oral reading errors? How might a tape recorder contribute to improving your accuracy?

5. Is having the child read aloud to the teacher necessarily part of an individual conference? Why or why not?

6. Discuss the possibility of a series of conferences for purposes other than simply diagnosis. What might these be planned to accomplish?

7. In your experience, what are the characteristics of pupils who are ready for individualized reading? How would you approach this method with these pupils?

8. What do you think are the most difficult tasks for the teacher to learn when she attempts individualization in reading?

9. Assuming that you have never attempted this way of teaching reading, what do you foresee as problems for you?

10. Since individualized reading demands a wide variety of reading materials, how might this problem be attacked when school funds or library facilities are limited?

11. In what ways may a teacher who is accustomed to group instruction initiate individual and small-group conferences?

12. How do individualized reading teachers ensure and check on the sequential development of important reading skills?

13. Plan a role-playing session in which one member of your class defends the basal reading method while another supports individualized reading.

REFERENCES

1. Adams, Mary Lourita, "Instructional Needs of Elementary Teachers in Teaching Reading with Implications for Televised In-Service Education." Doctoral dissertation, University of Florida, 1962.

2. Barbe, Walter B., Williams, Thelma, and Ganaway, Virginia, "Types of Difficulties in Reading Encountered by Eighty Children Receiving Instruction at a Reading Clinic," *Journal of Educational Research,* 51 (February 1958), 437–443.

3. Clay, Marie M., "Reading Errors and Self-Correction Behavior," *British Journal of Educational Psychology,* 39 (1969), 47–56.

4. Condit, Martha O., "Trade Books for Beginning Readers," *Wilson Library Bulletin,* 34 (December 1959), 284–301.

5. Criscuolo, Nicholas P., "Mag Bags, Peg Sheds, Crafty Crannies and Reading," *Reading Teacher,* 29 (January 1976), 376–378.

6. Dale, Edgar, and Chall, Jeanne S., "A Formula for Predicting Readability," *Educational Research Bulletin* (Ohio State University), 27 (January 21 and February 18, 1948), 11–20, 28, 37–54.

7. Darrow, Helen Fisher, and Allen, R. Van, *Independent Activities for Creative Learning.* New York: Bureau of Publications, Teachers College, Columbia University, 1961.

8. Darrow, Helen Fisher, and Howes, Virgil M., *Approaches to Individualized Reading.* New York: Appleton-Century-Crofts, 1960.

9. Daw, Seward Emerson, "The Persistence of Errors in Oral Reading in Grades Four and Five," *Journal of Educational Research,* 32 (October 1938), 81–90.

10. Dees, Margaret, "Easy To Read for Beginning Independent Readers," *Elementary English,* 39 (May 1962), 418–420.

11. Della-Piana, Gabriel M., and Herlin, Wayne R., "Are Normative Oral Reading Error Profiles Necessary?" in *Improvement of Reading Through Classroom Practice,* J. Allen Figurel, ed. International Reading Association Conference Proceedings, 9, 1964, 306–309.

12. Duffy, G. B., and Durrell, Donald D., "Third Grade Difficulties in Oral Reading," *Education,* 56 (September 1935), 37–40.

13. Durrell, Donald D., *Durrell Analysis of Reading Difficulty.* New York: Harcourt Brace Jovanovich, 1955.

14. Edwards, D. Lewis, "Teaching Beginners the Purpose of Reading," *Elementary English,* 39 (March 1962), 194–195, 215.

15. Gilmore, J. V., "The Relationships Between Oral Reading Habits and Silent Reading Comprehension." Doctoral dissertation, Harvard University, 1947.

16. Goodman, Kenneth S., "A Linguistic Study of

Cues and Miscues in Reading," *Elementary English*, 42 (October 1965), 639–643.

17. Goodman, Yetta, and Burke, Carolyn, *Reading Miscue Inventory.* New York: Macmillan Publishing Co., Inc., 1972.

18. Groff, Patrick J., "Recent Easy Books for First-Grade Readers," *Elementary English*, 38 (December 1960), 521–527.

19. Guilfoyle, Elizabeth, *Books for Beginning Readers.* Champaign, Ill.: National Council of Teachers of English, 1962.

20. Heller, Frieda M., *I Can Read It Myself.* Columbus, Ohio: Center for School Experimentation, College of Education, Ohio State University, 1962.

21. Herlin, Wayne R., "A Comparison of Oral Reading Errors on the Monroe Diagnostic Reading Examination and the Durrell Analysis of Reading Difficulty." Doctoral dissertation, University of Utah, 1963.

22. Jensen, Amy Elizabeth, "Attracting Children to Books," *Elementary English*, 33 (October 1956), 332–339.

23. Johns, Jerry L., and Hunt, Linda, "Motivating Reading: Professional Ideas," *Reading Teacher*, 28 (April 1975), 617–619.

24. Julitta, Sister Mary, "A List of Books for Retarded Readers," *Elementary English*, 38 (February 1961), 79–86.

25. Kasdon, Lawrence M., "Oral Versus Silent-Oral Diagnosis," in *Reading Diagnosis and Evaluation,* Dorothy L. DeBoer, ed. International Reading Association Conference Proceedings, 13, 4, 1970, 86–92.

26. Ladd, Eleanor Mary, "A Comparison of Two Types of Training with Reference to Developing Skill in Diagnostic Oral Reading Testing." Doctoral dissertation, Florida State University, 1961.

27. Lanning, Frank W., "Dyadic Reading," *Elementary English*, 39 (March 1962), 244–245.

28. Madden, M., and Pratt, M., "An Oral Reading Survey as a Teaching Aid," *Elementary English Review*, 18 (April 1941), 122–126, 159.

29. Mills, Robert E., *The Learning Methods Test.* The Author: 1512 E. Broward Boulevard, Fort Lauderdale, Fla.

30. Monroe, Marion, *Children Who Cannot Read.* Chicago: University of Chicago Press, 1932.

31. Parker, Donald, *SRA Reading Laboratories.* Chicago: Science Research Associates.

32. Pikulski, John, "A Critical Review: Informal Reading Inventories," *Reading Teacher*, 28 (November 1974), 141–151.

33. Pillar, Arlene M., "Individualizing Book Reviews," *Elementary English*, 52 (April 1975), 467–469.

34. Powell, William R., "Reappraising the Criteria for Interpreting Informal Inventories," in *Reading Diagnosis and Evaluation,* Dorothy L. DeBoer, ed. International Reading Association Proceedings, 13, 4, 1970, 100–109.

35. Powell, William R., and Dunkeld, Cohn G., "Validity of the I.R.I. Reading Levels," *Elementary English*, 48 (October 1971), 637–642.

36. Preston, Ralph C., "The Reading Status of Children Classified by Teachers as Retarded Readers," *Elementary English*, 30 (April 1953), 225–227.

37. Robinson, H. Alan, Taylor, Stanford E., and Frackenpohl, Helen, *The EDL Study Skills Library.* Huntington, N.Y.: Educational Development Laboratories, 1961.

38. Sartain, Harry W., "The Roseville Experiment with Individualized Reading," *Reading Teacher*, 13 (April 1960), 277–281.

39. Shnayer, Sidney, "Some Relationships Between Reading Interests and Reading Comprehension." Doctoral dissertation, University of California at Berkeley, 1967.

40. Spache, George D., "Personality Patterns of Retarded Readers," *Journal of Educational Research*, 50 (February 1957), 461–469.

41. Spache, George D., *Good Reading for Poor Readers.* Champaign, Ill.: Garrard Publishing Company, 1974.

42. Spache, George D., *Diagnostic Reading Scales.* Monterey, Calif.: McGraw-Hill–California Test Bureau, 1972.

43. Spache, George D., *Investigating the Issues of Reading Disabilities.* Boston: Allyn and Bacon, Inc., 1976.

44. Strang, Ruth, McCullough, Constance M., and Traxler, Arthur E., *Improvement of Reading,* 3rd ed. New York: McGraw-Hill Book Company, 1961, Chap. IX.

45. Weber, Rose-Marie, "A Linguistic Analysis of First-Grade Reading Errors," *Reading Research Quarterly*, 5 (Spring 1970), 427–451.

RESOURCES FOR IMPLEMENTING
INDIVIDUALIZATION

General References

Crutchfield, Marjorie, *Individualized Reading: A Guide for Teaching Word Analysis Skills.* Los Angeles: Gramercy Press, 1975.

Darrow, Helen Fisher, and Van Allen, Roach, *Independent Activities for Creative Learning.* New York: Teachers College Press, 1961.

Darrow, Helen Fisher, and Howes, Virgil M., *Approaches to Individualized Reading.* New York: Appleton-Century-Crofts, 1960.

Duffy, Gerald G., and Sherman, George B., *Systematic Reading Instruction.* New York: Harper & Row, Inc., 1972.

Hennings, Dorothy Grant, *Smiles, Nods and Pauses.* New York: Citation Press, 1974.

Hoetker, James, Fichtenau, Robert, and Farr, Helen L. K., *Systems, Systems Approaches and the Teacher.* Urbana, Ill.: National Council of Teachers of English, 1972.

Howes, Virgil M., *Individualizing Instruction in Reading and Social Sciences: Selected Readings on Programs and Practices.* New York: Macmillan Publishing Co., Inc., 1970.

Kaplan, Sandra, Kaplan, Jo Ann B., Madsen, Sheila K., and Taylor, Bette K., *Change for Children: Ideas and Activities for Individualizing Learning.* Pacific Palisades, Calif.: Goodyear Publishing Co., Inc.

Mandell, Muriel, *Games To Learn By.* New York: Sterling Publishing Co., Inc., 1972.

Musgrave, Ray, *Individualized Instruction: Strategies Focusing on the Learner.* Boston: Allyn and Bacon, Inc., 1975.

Spache, Evelyn B., *Reading Activities for Child Involvement.* Boston: Allyn and Bacon, Inc., 1976.

Spache, George D., *Good Reading for Poor Readers.* Champaign, Ill.: Garrard Publishing Company, 1974.

Spache, George D., *Good Reading for the Disadvantaged Reader.* Champaign, Ill.: Garrard Publishing Company, 1975.

Spice. Stevensville, Mich.: Educational Services, Inc. One of several collections of learning activities.

Veatch, Jeanette, *Reading in the Elementary School.* New York: The Ronald Press Company, 1966.

Wagner, Guy, and Hosier, Max, *Reading Games: Strengthening Reading Skills with Instructional Games.* Darien, Conn.: Teachers Publishing Corp., 1960.

Using Newspapers

Bernstein, Theodore M., *Get More Out of Your Newspaper.* New York: *The New York Times,* 1970.

Cheyney, Arthur B., *Teaching Reading Skills Through the Newspaper.* Newark, Del.: International Reading Association, 1971.

New York Times, The, *Introduction to a Good Reading Habit.* New York: *The New York Times.*

Sailer, Carl, *Toward Better Newspaper Reading.* Newark, N.J.: *The Newark News,* 1969.

Zachar, Irwin J., and Sailer, Carl, *Toward Better Newspaper Reading: A Students' Guide.* Newark, N.J.: *The Newark News,* 1969.

Learning Centers

Greff, Kasper N., and Askov, Eunice N., *Learning Centers.* Dubuque, Iowa: Kendall/Hunt Publishing Co., 1974.

Morlau, John, et al., *Classroom Learning Centers.* Belmont, Calif.: Fearon Publishers, 1974.

Peterson, Gary Y., *The Learning Center.* Hamden, Conn.: Linnet Books, 1975.

Waynant, Louise F., and Wilson, Robert M., *Learning Centers: A Guide for Effective Use.* Paoli, Penna.: Instructo Corp., 1974.

Instructional Materials—Book Collections

These are packaged kits of books usually graded in reading difficulty, and sometimes offering questions on vocabulary and comprehension, and follow-up activities.

Bantam Books Classroom Reading Library. New York: Bantam Books, Inc.

Bowmar Primary Reading Series. Glendale, Calif.: Bowmar.

Classroom Library Series. Oklahoma City, Okla.: The Economy Company.

Coburn, Doris, ed., *Messner Classroom Library.* New York: Julian Messner. Ten titles on the winning of the West.

Gold Series Reading Program. Arcadia, Calif.: Hoffman. Paperbacks, records, and synchronized strip-record machine.

House of Books. Chicago: Benefic. Three different collections.

Invitations to Personal Reading. Glenview, Ill.: Scott, Foresman and Company.

Invitations to Story Time. Glenview, Ill.: Scott, Foresman and Company. Five collections, some with records.

Jacobs, Leland B., *One-to-One—A Practical Individualized Reading Program.* Englewood Cliffs, N.J.: Prentice-Hall, Inc., 1970.

Jacobs, Leland B., and McInnes, John, *Venture Books.* Champaign, Ill.: Garrard Publishing Company. Primary collection, with manual offering suggestions for evaluation and follow-up.

Learning To Read While Reading To Learn. Chicago: Century Consultants. Collection ranging from third to fourth grade in difficulty.

Literature Sampler. Chicago: Learning Materials. Brief excerpts from 144 books in ten interest areas. Some of these are available in a complete edition from the publisher.

Martin, Bill, Jr., *Kinder Owls.* New York: Holt, Rinehart and Winston, Inc. This and three other sets, *Wise Owls, Little Owls,* and *Young Owls,* offer picture and simple reading materials for beginners.

Miniature Libraries. New York: Multimedia Education, Inc. Offer four collections of twelve story booklets each for each primary grade, with skill cards and comprehension questions.

Nolen, Barbara, and Parker, Don H., eds., *SRA Pilot Libraries.* Chicago: Science Research Associates. Each of the three collections offers seventy-two excerpts of elementary-level books.

Pacemakers. New York: Random House, Inc. Six collections of books, with comprehension checks.

Pauk, Walter, and Harris, Raymond, *Jamestown Classics.* Providence, R.I.: Jamestown Publishers. Eleven classics adapted to fifth-grade reading level; with student booklet, guide, and cassettes.

Prime-O-Tec. New York: Doubleday & Company, Inc. Offers tapes and records to parallel the book selection.

Read As You Listen. Winchester, Mass.: Cooper Films and Records. Each kit offers a record paralleling the stories. Ten kits comprising sixty-nine classics for first four grades.

Scholastic Book Services. Englewood Cliffs, N.J. This publisher offers wide variety of paperbacks, plus selected collections of these for social studies and literature.

Sights and Sounds. New York: Random House, Inc. Eight copies each of ten titles, with tapes.

Skillstarters. New York: Random House, Inc. Primary books with seatwork exercises, picture–word cards, etc.

SRA Basic Reading Series Satellites. Chicago: Science Research Associates. Four-page selections, graded in levels.

SRA Classroom Libraries. Chicago: Science Research Associates. Thirty or so paperbacks per kit beginning at the fourth-grade level.

TTC Classroom Libraries. Van Nuys, Calif.: Teaching Technology. Six kits of paperbacks of sixteen titles each.

Whitman Classroom Bookshelf. Chicago: Science Research Associates. 1962. Beginner and Junior series of eighty-eight and forty-four books, respectively, for beginners and other elementary pupils.

Yearling Reading Centers. New York: Noble & Noble Publishers, Inc. Kits for grades three to six include two to three copies each of twenty-five to thirty books, teacher guides to aid in the individual conference, skills development folders, worksheets, and tests.

Skill Development Kits

Most of these are packaged kits or workbooks to permit children to work independently in an effort to develop their own reading skills.

Croft–NEI, *Reading Resource File.* Waterford, Conn.: Croft–NEI Publications. Fifty cards offering game activities.

Dimension 99. New York: New Dimensions. Science kit.

Dimension 120. New York: New Dimensions. Science kit.

Dimensions in Reading. Chicago: Science Research Associates. American history.

Gates, Arthur I., and Peardon, C. C., *Practice Exercises in Reading.* New York: Teachers College Press, 1963. Series of four booklets for three to six, respectively.

It's Your World. Elizabethtown, Penna.: Continental Press. Brief practice materials in general and science reading.

Jenn Publications, *Primary Worksheets.* Louisville, Ky.: Jenn. Many printed or master ditto exercises.

Johnson, Eleanor M., ed., *New Reading Skilltext Series.* Columbus, Ohio: Charles E. Merrill Publishing Company, 1970. Six workbooks in reading skills.

Kaleidoscope of Skills: Reading. Chicago: Science Research Associates. 1966. Individualized workbooks for grades five to seven.

McCall, William A., and Crabbs, Lelah Mae, *Standard Test Lessons in Reading.* New York: Teachers College

Press. Five graded workbooks of short readings with questions.

New Reader's Digest Skill Builders. Pleasantville, N.Y.: Reader's Digest Association. Eight-story collections similar to those in parent magazine plus skill development workbooks.

Niles, Olive S., et al., *Tactics in Reading.* Glenview, Ill.: Scott, Foresman and Company. Two boxed sets and one workbook in corrective skill exercises.

Parker, Don H., et al., *SRA Reading Laboratory.* Chicago: Science Research Associates. Boxes of multilevel selections and skill exercises, for all elementary grades.

Reading Skills Lab. Boston: Houghton Mifflin Company. Offers diagnostic tests and follow-up practice materials in content fields.

Robinson, H. Alan, et al., *E.D.L. Study Skills Library.* Huntington, N.Y.: Educational Development Laboratories. Each kit has ten to twelve self-directed, study-type reading exercises. Kits for grades three to nine, in science, social science, and library skills.

Smith, Edwin H., et al., *Reading Development.* Menlo Park, Calif.: Addison-Wesley Publishing Co., Inc. Kit of skill development materials.

Taylor, Frank D., et al., *Individualized Reading Skills Improvement.* Denver, Colo.: Love. Individualized worksheets for skill development. May be reproduced.

11
Word Recognition Techniques and Skills

PREVIEW

For most nonprofessionals writing on the subject of reading and for some teachers and authors of phonics materials, phonics skill is the most important area of all reading instruction. If we were to believe some of these, we would be led to think that the effectiveness of the entire reading program depended upon the manner and extent of phonics teaching. In reality, phonics is just one of several basic word recognition techniques. It is of only moderate importance in early reading success and must be replaced by more advanced, permanent skills such as use of context, if overall reading development is to occur.

The recent research we have cited should help to clarify the proper role of phonics in the reading program. We now have objective evidence of the values of phonic generalizations during the first six years of schooling. Future phonics teaching should, therefore, be much more functional and pragmatic than formerly. We now know by reason of the overall results of the First-Grade Reading Studies and those extended into the second and third grades that no one system of teaching phonics is significantly better than any other, nor are reading systems based strongly on phonics superior. Furthermore, as we discovered in updating our analysis of the phonics in basals, such programs are earlier and more intensive than formerly. This trend is directly parallel to the indications of the need for such a revision as found in the First-Grade Studies. These research studies and trends in phonics teaching should result in somewhat more effective primary reading programs in the future. Whether they will quiet the chronic critics or the ultra-phonic-minded authors, however, remains to be seen.

Since about 1910, the recognition program has been the subject of more heated debate than any other element of the entire reading program. Most of the arguments have centered around the question of the values of teaching phonic analysis, or, as it is more commonly but incorrectly termed, phonetic analysis.* Reading instruction gradually shifted from a system which stressed phonics as the chief method of word recognition to a method involving practically no phonics at all in some schools. By the late 1920s, this trend was reversed and since then phonics has been presented in practically all American basal reading series as one of the significant word recognition skills. It is commonly taught not as the basis of learning to read but is introduced as one type of aid.

Before they are introduced to phonics, children spontaneously employ a variety of clues for word recognition. Among these are word shape, word length, context or sense of the sentence, pictorial clues, and details within the word. For example, once they have been identified in reading, such words as *elephant, Christmas,* and *rabbit* are subsequently easily recognized by their striking patterns or shapes, for example, ⊓_⌐⌐_⌐ ⌐_____⌐_ ⌐_____⌐. Other words, for example, *grandmother, automobile,* and *policemen,* offer clues to recognition not only by their distinctive shape but also by their unusual length. Many other words may be recognized by the inherent structure and thought of the sentence, particularly when the concept is supported by an accompanying picture. For example, few primary school children would be unable to supply the missing word in the sentence, "The cat likes to drink _____," if the adjoining picture shows a mother pouring a fluid from a quart bottle into a pan placed in front of a cat. Finally, elements of a word, such as double letters, capitals, and details which lend themselves to a mental association between the word and its meaning, as "the two eyes in *look*," "the curly tail on *dog*," contribute other clues to word recognition.

The intention of the authors of many basal reading programs was the promotion of the development of these quasi-spontaneous clues to word recognition. Beginning instruction was deliberately planned to stimulate the pupils' use of these means of word discrimination and recognition. The justifications offered for this *whole-word* method are the following:

1. There is some evidence that early instruction in phonics is apt to be ineffectual with children under the mental age of six and one-half to seven.
2. Too early introduction of phonics may tend to make children dependent upon letter sounds as their major or only technique of word recognition. Rapid recognition and, hence, rate of reading are impaired by this dependency.

*Phonics, the practice of using letter sounds as an aid to word recognition, is a minor element of the field of phonetic analysis.

3. Too early or too great an emphasis upon phonics may make pupils read over-cautiously, slowly, and too analytically. These habits are difficult to overcome and may interfere with the normal development of rate and comprehension.
4. The habit of rapid word recognition by a variety of clues is of permanent value in reading development. Therefore, it should be established early and none of the several clues taught, such as phonics, should be permitted to interfere with or displace this essential habit.

However, shape or length as a basis for word recognition promotes rapid initial learning but does not promote transfer to learning new words. It soon becomes a guessing game, as shown by the tendency to substitute for the printed word, words that are drawn from the child's auditory vocabulary or words learned earlier. Today the early training directs the child's attention to the sounds of first letters, final letters, and middle letters, in that order of preference. Instruction that forces attention to more than a single-letter basis for discrimination aids the learning of new words. Color cues promote rapid learning at first but cannot transfer to ordinary print and, besides, they lead pupils to ignore the other cues present and hamper transfer of learning new words.

Letter name learning, although popular in a number of programs, does not facilitate learning to read, for names of letters are not functional in word recognition. It is true that some studies show that knowledge of letter names upon entering school is a good predictor of early reading success. But such knowledge obviously reflects the child's intelligence, socioeconomic and language backgrounds, and parental aspirations, for the learning is not present among economically disadvantaged or linguistically different children. Learning letter names does not foster learning new words, even when they are composed of the letters just learned (28,41,46).

Many critics of current reading programs write as though there is a dichotomy between a phonics method and the whole-word method. They claim that the latter is the only word recognition skill offered in today's programs and that phonics is almost completely ignored. Our later analysis of the phonics content of several widely used basal programs completely refutes this false argument. The teachers' manuals and other guides to training in word recognition clearly outline extensive programs in phonics. If these guides were followed carefully, every child would receive adequate training in this important skill. But, in the minds of some, there is doubt regarding the thoroughness and competence with which teachers follow the suggested program.

Disturbed by the attacks upon schools, a number of educators have reexamined the phonics program. Rather than assume that teachers understood the skills and were teaching phonics as outlined in the basal manuals, a number of investigators began to assess how much knowledge teachers had in this area. The results of these surveys were disturbing, for it became apparent that in the early 1960s teachers did not know much about phonics. Average scores on phonics tests in large samples were only about 50 to 60 percent correct, and apparently even this knowledge was gained only by classroom experience in teaching phonics to pupils (and learning it at the same time!) (50). The impact of these studies on preservice training of teachers was dramatic, and more intensive training of teachers in this area has become common. Testing teachers with the generalizations listed later in this book, Fleming (20) found that today's teachers could give examples of many of these, particularly those of superior validity, certainly an encouraging sign. This study does not, of course, prove that phonics is well taught everywhere, but the bulk of evidence in this and many other surveys at least supports the belief that it is being taught more effectively than a decade ago, for whatever values it has.

One of the implications of the First-Grade Reading Studies was that the program of the basal readers of the late 1960s would be strengthened by a stronger, earlier functional phonics program. The children achieved better reading scores at the end of the first grade in those programs in which the basal was supplemented by an emphasis upon phonics. This result produced dramatic changes in the attention to phonics in basal readers published after the First-Grade Reading Studies reports became available in 1965–1967. These changes are noted in detail in our later discussion of the phonics content in the leading basal readers. Critical review of the early studies which supported a delay in phonics teaching until late first or early second grade has also cast doubts upon this practice.

A third series of questions concerning the current phonics program deals with its content and the proper programming of instruction. There is a tremendous diversity of opinion on these topics among reading authorities, authors of reading series, and self-appointed popular writers on the subject. The diversity of practice in basal reading programs is apparent in a comparison of the generalizations in Figure 11–2 (p. 375). Other programs insist upon the presentation of some phonics training before any reading instruction, such as given in the *Phonetic Keys for Reading* (The Economy Company). Content in various phonics textbooks varies from teaching only the single sounds of seventeen consonants and nothing else regarding letter sounds to a program which offers over five hundred letter sounds and combinations to primary school children. Most of the popularized programs completely ignore the necessity for teaching pupils any rules which might guide their efforts and omit any training in blending sounds which might result in enabling the child to produce some resemblance of the true word (47).

For many debated points, the research gives somewhat conflicting results. These include the questions of phonics before reading (51), of complex phonics programs versus simple or extra phonics versus the basal system (21), or the true importance of knowledge of the alphabet for early success in reading. Finally, although the research definitely does not support them, there are the current beliefs that phonics is particularly good for children of below-average mentality; that there is an exact sequence in which various letter sounds and combinations should be taught; that the ability to sound the letters of a word is equivalent to word recognition or even the complete reading act; and that the memorization of phonic elements will transfer automatically to the act of continuous reading, and the child will therefore read better.

Jeanne Chall's book *Learning To Read: The Great Debate* (New York: McGraw-Hill, 1967)* triggered a tremendous amount of attention to contrasting phonics systems which enlivened the field of reading for some time. After reviewing many studies of comparative methods, Chall reached the conclusion that intensive or systematic phonics, as she termed it, was superior to gradual phonics, as commonly taught in the basals. Actually, her definition was expanded to include a number of different phonics systems as well as the phonological approach of the linguists. In brief, she supported an approach which includes at least these characteristics (*40*):

1. Letter–sound relationships before rhyming or alliteration.
2. Teaching isolated letters and their sounds.
3. Finding letters in words representing certain sounds; writing, pronouncing words by sounding letter after letter.
4. Teaching a few prefixes and suffixes and a bit about the dictionary.
5. Lots of letter naming, more letters, and more specific sounds.
6. Little attention to deriving word recognition from context.

As we shall see, these practices contrast greatly with most basal programs (as well as with most linguistic programs). And many reviewers of this book did not feel that Chall had proved her theory, particularly when she depended so strongly upon studies over a long period of time from a wide variety of sources which often differed in their instructional practices from Chall's definition. Strangely enough, Chall did not refer to the 1965–1967 reports of the First-Grade Reading Studies, which would have contradicted much of her argument.

But the book did stimulate many school boards and laymen to turn to a type of phonics which apparently would make instruction more efficient. However, as in the past, the results were disappointing, for it was soon obvious that although a heavy emphasis upon phonics did produce better scores on word recognition tests, the system did not result in better comprehension, word meaning, or spelling, particularly among lower-ability pupils, nor did it appreciably reduce failures in reading. Harris et al. found no advantage in an intensive phonics system (Phonovisual) over each of three consecutive school years. In fact, their data show a negative correlation of $-.61$ between the time spent in phonics teaching and word knowledge and $-.75$ between phonics time and reading comprehension (*32*).

DeLawter's comparison of the reading miscues of children taught by a linguistic decoding system (Miami and Merrill readers) versus a sight-word approach (Chandler Language Experience) indicated dramatic differences after two years of instruction. The meaning-oriented children tended toward miscues which were real words while the decoding-trained children produced a high percentage of mispronunciations or nonwords. The errors of the latter showed strong graphic

* See our review in *Journal of Reading Behavior,* 1 (Winter 1969), 71–74, and William Rutherford, "Learning To Read: A Critique," *Elementary School Journal,* 69 (November 1968), 72–83.

similarity between the miscue and the printed word, but many were semantically (meaning) inappropriate. Moreover, their self-corrections were usually on the basis of graphic cues not meaning or contextual cues (14).

Phonics seems to be like a pendulum that swings our instruction from one extreme to another in which the ultimate goal of comprehension often seems forgotten. Ignoring often the broader implications of the research, because of the temporary spurt in word recognition, we grasp at any new (?) system which seems to offer solutions for our reading problems.

This brief review of its many debated or unsolved questions may help to show why phonics has received so much attention, even though it is probably not the most important word recognition skill. All these conflicting theories and experiments certainly imply that a careful review of our present program and methods is highly desirable.

As Emans has shown in his brief history of phonics (17), its teaching and rationale have been in and out of fashion repeatedly since the sixteenth century, and these differences in opinion and practice will probably continue to stimulate debate.

HOW WE NOW TEACH PHONICS

In each edition of this book we have attempted to summarize current practices in the teaching of phonics or decoding. A brief review of these summaries will illustrate the marked changes in content and instructional practices which have characterized this facet of the reading curriculum. In 1964 none of the leading programs attempted to teach pupils how to use letter sounds at the readiness or preprimer stages. Auditory discrimination of these sounds was all that was offered then. During the ensuing decade more and more emphasis has been placed on the application of letter sounds in phonic analysis at these earliest stages of reading development. Today a child is commonly being taught to use the sounds of all twenty-one initial consonants, some final consonants, and perhaps some vowel sounds during the readiness–preprimer levels.* This training is in addition to learning to name and match lowercase and capital letters and to recognize similarities and differences among letter sounds.

As a result of this downward shifting of the content of the decoding program, much less time is now spent on the prereading auditory training that many authorities believe is so essential. Just what effect this decrease in prepara-tory steps to phonic analysis will have on children's reading progress remains to be seen.

There is, of course, the argument we have referred to earlier, that auditory discrimination training is not highly significant for early reading success, particu-

---

* The reader should note that a number of current basal programs are substituting the term "levels" for such words as "readiness, preprimer, primer," and the like. The development stages are similar, however, and we shall continue to use the more descriptive terms until they disappear from use.

larly among linguistically different children. It has been shown that these bilingual or dialectal speakers may not hear differences or observe these differences in their own speech, and yet they can comprehend standard English. Thus there may be some justification for the lesser emphasis upon auditory training in recent programs.

A decade ago the instruction in phonics continued through the third grade and sometimes even into the fourth. Today practically all the content of the program, including consonant and vowel sounds, short and long vowels, consonant and vowel digraphs, and vowel diphthongs, has been taught by the end of the second grade. Only a few of the more difficult letter–sound combinations are delayed until the third grade, in most series.

A third trend has been the tremendous increase in the presentation of word patterns, or phonograms as they once were called. These are largely two- to four-letter units of frequent occurrence in primary reading materials. A few years ago only a few of the basal reading programs presented any great number of these units. Today the number of word patterns being taught in most basal series is vastly greater than formerly. In fact, these letter combinations form the heart, if not the total content, of the decoding program in some series.

These words, or spelling patterns as they are sometimes called, were largely derived from a computer analysis of the frequency of various letter combinations in our language. The linguistic analysis of these word patterns has shown that the sounds of vowels are often determined by the consonants preceding or following them. For example, the medial vowel in a consonant–vowel–consonant (CVC) unit is often a short vowel, while the vowel in a CVCe (consonant–vowel–consonant–silent *e*) is frequently a long vowel. Some basal series now emphasize the learning of these word patterns exclusively and offer no instruction in the sounds of individual letters or letter combinations. For example, the decoding objectives of the Merrill Linguistic Reading Program are:

- Decode words of the consonant–vowel–consonant (CVC) spelling pattern. (Pre-primer through first half of second grade.)
- Decode words of the consonant–vowel–consonant–silent *e* (CVCe) spelling pattern. (Second half of second grade through first half of third grade.)
- Decode words of the consonant–vowel–vowel–consonant (CVVC) spelling pattern. (Second half of second grade through first half of third grade.)
- Decode minor spelling patterns and irregular spellings. (Second half of second grade through third grade.)

This, of course, is an extreme example of this trend. As shown in Figure 11–1, most basal series are combining the emphasis upon word patterns with the usual training in individual letters and letter combinations that was once the entire phonics program.

The great variations among these decoding systems is another indication of the state of flux characteristic of this area of the reading curriculum. The basic research is lacking to tell us when to teach the sound of individual letters and letter combinations, or whether it would be better to teach these in the larger units called word patterns. The computer can tell us, of course, the frequency of occurrence of the letter sounds and the spelling patterns in which these variations occur. But it cannot tell us which phonemes are most easily learned or the best sequence of presentation. Hence these decisions are often made on the basis of the words used in the reading selections of the basal series. As a result we see that the scope and sequence of decoding instruction varies from one series to the next and may extend over anywhere from two to six grade levels.

There is, of course, more content to this program than can be presented in tabular form. Practically all these basal series teach children to deal with compound words, contractions, silent letters, and such spelling conventions as doubling the final consonant, dropping a final *e*, and changing *y* to *i* when adding an ending.

The decoding or phonics content of six leading basal series is outlined in Figure 11–1 (p. 369). The figure does not include, of course, the details of methodology, the generalizations or rules presented, or a description of the readiness training which may precede these programs.

This listing of the content of the average basal phonics program must be expanded by a description of the approach to convey an accurate picture. Letter sounds are not taught in isolation but as an integral part of words. *B* is not *buh* but "the sound of the letter *b* as in *boy*." Initial consonant sounds are closely tied to the adjoining vowel and cannot readily be separated without distortion of the pronunciation of the word. Listen carefully to yourself as you say aloud the hard sound of *c*, then the phonogram *at*. Compare this with the distinctly greater resemblance to the true word as you say aloud the sound of *ca*, and then add the *t* sound. Initial consonants, blends, and digraphs are stressed in the phonics program somewhat more than the final ones, and the final ones more than those occurring in a medial position. This emphasis reflects the known significance of these portions of words for word recognition. Because of the difficulty in pronouncing a single consonant sound without adding some sort of *uh* or vowel sound to it, a few of the most common short vowel sounds are usually taught with the first consonants. Again there is strong support for this practice because of the frequent occurrence of monosyllables containing the short vowel sound in most primary reading materials.

MacGinitie (37) has severely criticized the instructional procedures suggested in basal manuals for phonics lessons for their undue complexity and lack of research basis in the logic and concepts they demand. He also notes the lack of cognitive clarity regarding the teacher's terms—letter, word, sound—that we have referred to earlier. He describes several typical teacher presentations which are unreasonably difficult, particularly because of emphasis upon linguistic detail. For example, in such apparently simple tasks as recognizing and identifying the same phoneme that is present in the two words *now* and *nor*; or supplying a word that ends with *ed* and begins with the same sound, as in *be, but,* and *ball,* MacGinitie points out that we do not really know what process the child uses to do these tasks nor do we know how to advise him if he fails. Each of these common tasks and the terms they employ should be approached step by step, for the relation between the phonemic element and its sound is very complex. But we do not have the basic research to tell us how to present these concepts and analytic

Series	Word patterns	Consonants	Short vowels	Long vowels	Vowel digraphs and diphthongs
Preprimer and Primer Levels					
Allyn and Bacon	*ay, at, and, ate, VC, VCC, CVCe, VCV, VCCV*	*b, c(k), k, ck, qu, ss, c(s), ch, d, f, ph, g, g(j), j, h, l, m, n, p, r, sh, t, v, w, y, z, s(z)*	*a, e, i, o*	*a, e, i, o*	*ea, ew, oy, oi*
American Book	*et, en, ot, op, ish, ay, at, it, an, eed, ess, ed, en, un, up, ud, ug, alk, oll, ell, all, ill, ar, art, arn, ark, arm, i-e*(ride)*, ir, o-e*(home)*, or, er, ake, ent, and, ird, ine, ain, one, ose, ice, ace, eg, ound*	*g, h, m, y, wh, s, w, b, c, pl, p, t, n, th, l, tr, t, m, f, d, b, sh, p, r, ll, lk, j, st, th, nt, nd*	*i, o, e, a*	*e, o, a, i*	*ee, ow, aw, ai, oo, ou, oo*
Ginn 720	*ill, ide, id, it, im, ike, ite, in, ine, ip, ipe, en, ell, ed, et, eet, eel, eed, eek, eep, ead, eat, ean, ing, at, an, ack, ad, ake, ame, ade, CVC, CVCe, CVVC, CV, CVCC*	*b, l, r, h, j, c(k), f, y, n, d, g, t, v, m, s, w, p, d, ck, g, s, ss, z, l, ll, s(z)*	*i, e*	*i, e*	*ee, ea*
Harper & Row: Design for Reading		*h, n, y, f, l, k, b, v, z, t, n, g*	*i, a*	*y*	
Houghton Mifflin	*et, at, an, op, ay, ing, ick, un, ook, est, ack, er, ot, ell, ed, in, en, ake, qu, squ, ide, ight, all, ame, es, ock, ad*	*w, g, h, c, t, p, r, b, m, j, d, f, k, l, n, v, s, y, ck, tr, st, ch, sh, th, wh, z, pl, sm, c(s), fl, sc, fr, pr, gr, x, cr, nk, br, g, thr,*	*a, i, e, o, u*	*y*	*oo, ai, oy, oi, aw, oa, ee*

(continued)

FIGURE 11-1 (continued)

Series	Word patterns	Consonants	Short vowels	Long vowels	Vowel digraphs and diphthongs
		ge, dge, sl, cl, sk, str			
SRA Basic Reading Series	an, ad, ag, at, ap, am, ab, al, it, in, ig, id, im, ip, CVC, CVCC, CCVC, CCVCC	c, d, f, m, r, n, p, v, b, s, d, w, g, h, t, l, j, k, z, y, x, ss, ff, ck, nd, nt, st, mp, ft, pt, xt, lf, lk, lp, bl, cl, fl, gl, pl, sl, sk, sn, sp, sw, tw, br, cr, dr, fr, gr, tr, sm, pr			

First Reader Level

Series	Word patterns	Consonants	Short vowels	Long vowels	Vowel digraphs and diphthongs
Allyn and Bacon	VCle, VCre, VCste	ch (k), wh, th, ng			ow, ou, ai, ee
American Book	ost, ight, ind, old, ere, ong, ear, ur, ould, air, ore, ing, in, een, ix, ink, other, ool, oom, oot, orn, ox, ail, ip, ad, any, ack, ick, ock, uck, eep, eam, ean, ast, end, ate, owl, ave, ich, inch, oad, oat, ade, age, ame, ane, ate, am, ey, be, ad, ange, ease, elf, ic, oose, ump, ap, oke, eek, ob, ale, ance, uch, ge, ung, umb, pe, tor, ze	k, bl, gr, dr, fl, u, br, pr, str, sm, cl, fr, x, ck, ch			oa, ow, ea, oy, ou, ow, ea
Ginn 720	ook, all, ar, ang, ung, ink, ing	c (city), pl, sm, ch, nd, nt, bl	o (top), a (call), u	o-e (rope), o	oo (wood), aw, oo (moon)

FIGURE 11-1 (continued)

Series	Word patterns	Consonants	Short vowels	Long vowels	Vowel digraphs and diphthongs
Harper & Row: Design for Reading	er, ar	zz, sw, cl, pl, gl, br, fr, sn, str, scr, thr, nt, mp, nd, ld, th, ch, tch	u	y	ai, ea, oa, oo, ew, ow, ay, oi, oy, ow
Houghton Mifflin	ir, ur	kn, wr, s(z), sh			ou
SRA Basic Reading Series	CCVCC, CVCCC	ng, nk, sh, th, ch, wh, qu, tch			

Second-Reader Level

Series	Word patterns	Consonants	Short vowels	Long vowels	Vowel digraphs and diphthongs
Allyn and Bacon	VCC	sk, sh, ll, ff, gh(f), gh(g), gg, mb, mm, nn, kn, pp, rr, wr, wh, x	er, or, ir, ar, ur		ea, oa, ie, ui, ie, oa, ow, oo, au
American Book	ever, ear, ger, ought, ire, orn, ank, em, est, own, fly, ead, ive, arr, err, ar, sun, to, qu, ard, orr, od, ope, our, oor, ang, ther, ove, igh, eet, se, oss, are, aught, eer, eight, ier, al	sk, cr, v, thr, wr, kn, sn, sc, ff, tw, mb, nch, ny, tch, ly, es, te, dge, le, nce, sw, spr, gl, ph, squ, gry, gh, it, ft	o, a(swap), a(palm)	u, y	ew, oi, oe, ie, ou, ue, ei, au, ui
Ginn 720	ing, at, an, ack, ad, ake, ame, ade, CVC, CVCC, CVCe	tr, qu, v, x, st, wh, th, gs, sh, gr, fr, f, ff, th	a	a	
Harper & Row: Design for Reading		sh, th, wh, p, m, d, s, l, r, k, ss, ll, fl, sp, tr, sl, ck, ch, wr, kn, nk, ng, b, s(z), x, ff, cr, gr, sc, dr, sm, bl, sk, st, pr, spr, st, sh	e, o, u	a, e, i, o, u	

(continued)

FIGURE 11-1 (continued)

Series	Word patterns	Consonants	Short vowels	Long vowels	Vowel digraphs and diphthongs
Houghton Mifflin	en, est, old	dr, sn, bl, sp, spr, gl	a, e, i, o, u	a, e, i, o, u	ow
SRA Basic Reading Series	CVCe, CVVC, CVVCe	c(city), gh(f), g(j), s(sh)	a(ball), o(cost), u(bush)		ee, ea, oo, ai, ay, oa, ou, ow, au, aw, oi, oy, oo, ea
Third-Reader Level					
Allyn and Bacon	CCV	ps, c(ch), dg, gn, hr, z(zh)	y		au, ei, ew, oo, io, ion, ue, aw
American Book	ur(church)		a(map), a(all), a(talk), o(boss), y(crystal)	i, y, e, i, o, u	ow, ou
Ginn 720	igh, eigh	sp, ft, str, pt, squ, pr, spr, sw, lt, sc, scr, tw, mp, wr, gu, gue	o(dog), or, ar, u(bull), a(watch)	y, u	ea, ew, ie, ew, au, augh, ei, oi, oy, ou, ough, ou, ou(four)
Harper & Row: Design for Reading	gu, qu, squ, igh, ight, ir, ur, or, ough, ought	g(j), c(s), tw, spl, sch, shr	y		ie, ey, aw, ea
Houghton Mifflin	or, ible, age, ally, ant, able, ous, ish, ate, ent, ive				
Fourth-Grade Level					
American Book					ei

FIGURE 11-1 (continued)

Series	Word patterns	Consonants	Short vowels	Long vowels	Vowel digraphs and diphthongs
Ginn 720		c(sh), ch(sh), ch(k), gn, gh, ph(f), t(fortune)	y	ue(clue)	ei
Harper & Row: Design for Reading	ai, aigh, ea, ei, eigh, es, ey, qu, uy, ear, ar, le, arr, cqu	dg(j), ph, s(zh), sc(s), ss(z)			ui, ue, ie, oo, ew, ou, ough, au
Fifth-Grade Level					
Harper & Row: Design for Reading	er, or, inc, ink	rh, x(gz), sc, cc(k), gn, bt, pn, ps, pt, mn			ae, ei, us
Sixth-Grade Level					
Harper & Row: Design for Reading	ge, gue, ur, ien	ch(sh), ll			ough

FIGURE 11–1. Decoding in the Basal Reading Program

processes in the logical steps children can utilize. In a sense, each child is left to his own resources in learning and applying phonic analysis.

The vowel sounds are the most difficult to teach because of their many variations and combinations. Most basal programs try to aid the child by leading him inductively to recognize that there are a number of basic rules which can assist him in recognizing the vowel sounds in unknown words. Unfortunately, there are a disturbing number of exceptions to almost any generalization which can be framed. As a result there is considerable debate about the values of these rules. The obvious answer to this question, of course, would be found by examining the vocabularies of a number of basal series for the number of applications and exceptions to each principle. But the authors of most basal series have been loathe to perform this analysis, perhaps for fear of what they might discover.

Theodore Clymer (*11*) and his students analyzed the manuals, workbooks, and readers of four basal series to determine the phonic principles taught. Amazingly, over 121 different statements were offered: fifty on vowels, fifteen on consonants, and twenty-eight each on endings and syllabication. The variation from one basal series to another was remarkable, ranging from thirty-three principles in one series to sixty-eight in another. Of the fifty vowel principles, only eleven were found in all four programs. Many principles were trite or repetitious and, as Clymer notes, almost useless as an aid to word recognition.

Clymer selected forty-five reasonably useful principles for evaluation and counted the number of examples and exceptions to each in the entire word list of the four combined basal series, plus the words in the *Gates Reading Vocabulary for the Primary Grades*. We have grouped his results from the data he has so kindly supplied, omitting for the moment those rules dealing with syllabication.

Two more recent studies have repeated Clymer's study by extending the analysis of the utility of phonic generalizations in reader vocabularies above the primary grades. Emans sampled 10 percent of the words beyond primary levels in *The Teacher's Word Book of 30,000 Words* by Thorndike and Lorge (16). Bailey's sample included words that were found in two or more of eight leading basal series for the first six grades (2). Thus one of the possible objections to Clymer's study, that his observations about phonic generalizations might not apply above the primary level, may be answered by these complementary studies.

We have combined the results of the three studies into one chart in Figure 11–2 (p. 375), since all three tested the value of the same phonic generalizations. The figures for each study represent the percent of utility, or the percent of the times that each principle actually held true in relevant words.

Clymer suggests that the validity of a phonic generalization should fall no lower than 75 percent utility: it should be true in at least three out of four words to which it is applicable. Perhaps another way of evaluating these principles would be to note the total number of words in which they function. Clymer's original table contains the number of examples and exceptions to each principle, and we shall use these facts in further evaluation.

It is apparent from Figure 11–2 that the generalizations concerning the sounds of vowels and vowel combinations are not only more numerous but also more variable in utility. If we expect a principle to work three out of four times, only the first three of those dealing with the sounds of single vowels are valid. The second, however, applied to only thirty-one words or about 1 percent of the 2600-word basal vocabulary studied by Clymer. There is some disagreement between the figures of Emans and Bailey regarding this principle. But, since Bailey could find only thirty-eight examples in the vocabulary of the first six grades, it is apparent that the principle, no matter how often it works, has no practical utility. The first and third of these valid generalizations function in 84 percent of 201 basal words and 76 percent of 112 words, respectively. The fourth in our list is widely taught in phonics and basal programs but functions in only 62 percent of 657 words. In other words, for every two words in which this principle works, there is one word which is an exception. We have modified Clymer's statement by adding the phrase "ending in a consonant" to distinguish from one-syllable words which

	Percent of utility		
	Clymer	Emans	Bailey
Vowel Principles			
1. When *y* is the final letter in a word, it usually has a vowel sound.	84	98	89
2. If the only vowel letter is at the end of a word, the letter usually stands for a long sound.	74	33	76
3. When there is one *e* in a word that ends in a consonant, the *e* usually has a short sound.	76	83	92
4. When a vowel is in the middle of a one-syllable word, ending in a consonant, the vowel is short.	62	73	71
5. When there are two vowels, one of which is final *e*, the first vowel is long and the *e* is silent.	63	63	57
6. When words end with silent *e,* the preceding *a* or *i* is long.	60	48	50
7. One vowel letter in an accented syllable has its short sound.	61	64	65
8. In many two- and three-syllable words, the final *e* lengthens the vowel in the last syllable.	46	42	46
9. The letter *a* has the same sound (*o*) when followed by *l, w,* and *u*.	48	24	34
10. When *a* follows *w* in a word, it usually has the sound of *a* in *was*.	32	28	22
11. When *y* is used as a vowel in words, it sometimes has the sound of long *i*.	15	4	11
12. When *y* or *ey* is seen in the last syllable that is not accented, the long sound of *e* is heard.	0	1	0

(continued)

FIGURE 11-2 (continued)

	Percent of utility		
	Clymer	Emans	Bailey
Vowel Digraphs			
13. When the letters *oa* are together in a word, *o* always gives its long sound and the *a* is silent.	97	86	95
14. Words having double *e* usually have the long *e* sound.	98	100	87
15. In *ay* the *y* is silent and gives *a* its long sound.	78	100	88
16. When *ea* come together in a word, the first letter is long, the second silent.	66	62	55
17. The first vowel is usually long, the second silent in the digraphs *ai, ea, oa, ui.*	66	58	60
18. When there are two vowels side by side, the long sound of the first one is heard and the second is usually silent.	45	18	34
19. *W* is sometimes a vowel and follows the vowel digraph rule.	40	31	33
20. In the phonogram *ie,* the *i* is silent and the *e* has a long sound.	17	23	31
Vowel Diphthongs			
21. The two letters *ow* make the long *o* sound.	59	50	55
22. When *e* is followed by *w*, the vowel sound is the same as represented by *oo.*	35	14	40
Vowels with *r*			
23. The *r* gives the preceding vowel a sound that is neither long nor short.	78	82	86
24. When *a* is followed by *r* and final *e*, we expect to hear the sound heard in *care.*	90	100	96

FIGURE 11-2 (continued)

	Percent of utility		
	Clymer	Emans	Bailey
Consonants			
25. When *c* and *h* are next to each other, they make only one sound.	100	100	100
26. When the letter *c* is followed by *o* or *a*, the sound of *k* is likely to be heard.	100	100	100
27. When *ght* is seen in a word, *gh* is silent.	100	100	100
28. When a word begins with *kn,* the *k* is silent.	100	100	100
29. When a word begins with *wr,* the *w* is silent.	100	100	100
30. When a word ends in *ck,* it has the same last sound as in *look.*	100	100	100
31. When two of the same consonants are side by side, only one is heard.	99	91	98
32. When *c* is followed by *e* or *i,* the sound of *s* is likely to be heard.	96	90	92
33. *Ch* is usually pronounced as it is in *kitchen, catch,* and *chair,* not like *sh.*	95	67	87
34. The letter *g* often has a sound similar to that of *j* in *jump* when it precedes the letter *i* or *e.*	64	80	78
Phonograms			
35. When the letter *i* is followed by the letters *gh,* the *i* usually stands for its long sound, and the *gh* is silent.	71	100	71
36. When *ture* is the final syllable in a word, it is unaccented.	100	100	95
37. When *tion* is the final syllable in a word, it is unaccented.	100	100	100

FIGURE 11–2. *Analysis of the Utility of Phonic Generalizations*

end in *e*, as governed by principle 5. This change does not, however, affect the functioning or utility of principle 4. The fifth is also a very popular generalization, despite the fact that it works only two out of three times even in primary words. Some would suggest that the only defensible way of using this principle is by teaching simply that the final *e* on most words is silent. This might be a feasible phonic principle, but we have no data of how often it is true. Thus, of the twelve phonic principles governing the sounds of single vowels in primary-grade vocabularies, only two appear to be functional and to justify teaching—the first and the third. The additional data from Emans and Bailey confirm almost exactly Clymer's observations about these vowel phonic principles and offer no suggestion that they would function any more effectively above the primary level than they do there.

In a study by Burmeister (*8*), the fifth principle was again examined for its validity. In a 17,000-word list, 2715 examples were found. The validity of the principle varies from 61.1 percent of the words with medial vowels, to 100 percent for *y*. Burmeister suggests that if children were taught that the medial vowel may be long *or* short, the principle would function 85.6 percent of the time. Two exceptions should also be taught, she recommends, of *a–e* with the *a* having a short sound of *i*, and *i–e*, with the *i* having the short sound of *e*, as in *furnace* and *machine,* respectively.

Eight principles governing vowel digraphs, or double vowels forming a single sound, were analyzed by Clymer. Of these, only the first three meet his utility criterion of validity in three out of four applications. The thirteenth, however, applies to only thirty-five primary words and to a total of sixty-six in the vocabulary of the first six grades. Principle 15 occurs in thirty-six primary basal words and in fifty words in the first six grades. In other words, the principles apply in about 1 percent of basal words, which is hardly frequent enough to justify their teaching. On the other hand, the fourteenth of this group appears defensible since it has 148 examples during the first six grades.

Although it is very popular with the authors of basal and phonics series, principle 18 is very ineffectual, with more exceptions than examples. This result could readily be anticipated, for it makes no distinction between two adjoining vowels, which are simply a double vowel or digraph, and vowel diphthongs, which are the blending of two vowel sounds into a pair of new sounds, such as *oi, oy, ow.* The more limited statements of this double-vowel principle, as in principles 13, 16, and 17, are more valid, but still not acceptable. Perhaps a careful study of the exceptions might result in improving the validity of this principle. None of the other vowel digraph principles appear to be justifiable.

The studies of Burrows and Zyra (*10*) and Burmeister (*7*) concentrated on these vowel pairs. Burrows and Zyra investigated their frequency and adherence to this principle among the first 5000 words of highest frequency in children's own writing. They found 1728 words with adjacent vowels, of which 23 percent were diphthongs, as *oy, oi, ow.* In the remaining examples, 49 percent followed the principle, 51 percent violated it!

Burmeister counted the frequency of vowel pairs that yielded a single phoneme in a 17,000-word list of common words. She found that the most common sound of each vowel pair was present in anywhere from 36 to 100 percent of the words in which it occurred. A vowel pair might have from one to nine common sounds! She distinguished four types of vowel pairs: long vowel plus a silent; a blend as in *au, aw;* a new sound, as *ou's* most common sound being schwa, and *ew* being *u;* and a type in which the vowel pair separates into two phonemes, as in *extraordinary, science.* To deal with these varying sounds, Burmeister suggests that *au, aw, oi, oy* and the two sounds of *oo* be taught as diphthongs; the second most common sounds of *ea* as short *e; ow* be taught with the most common sounds, as in *town* and *own. Ou's* most common sound, as we pointed out, is a schwa, with *ou* as in *out* being second in frequency for this pair. The combinations *ei* and *ie* are equal to so many sounds that any generalization is impractical, in her opinion (and ours).

The two vowel diphthong principles are relatively weak in validity and, moreover, function in only fifty words and nine basal words, respectively. On both counts, these seem hardly worth teaching. Of the two principles on vowels with *r,* the first, a very popular version, shows high validity and functions in 484 words, according to Clymer. The number of exceptions is large, 134 words, but it works in four out of every five words to which it can be applied. Although it works well, principle 24 applies to only nine basal words and probably should be eliminated for this reason. Even in the six-grade vocabulary sampled by Bailey, it applied to only twenty-four words.

The ten consonant principles show, on the whole, much greater validity than those concerning vowel sounds, reflecting the greater consistency and fewer variants in English consonant sounds. Nine of the ten are completely justified by the utility criterion. However, principles 27, 28, 29, and 30 apply to very small proportions of words. In Clymer's 2600-word basal vocabulary, these affected the pronunciation of thirty, ten, eight, and forty-six words, respectively. In the interests of simplicity, it would seem more logical to teach these few words as sight words than by these generalizations. This evaluation of these four generalizations is not altered by our consulting Bailey's study, for each item is found to apply to less than 1 percent of the words.

Principle 35 concerns the *igh* or *ight* phonogram. In the form stated here, it applies to only thirty-one words, of which nine are exceptions. The same combination is treated in the 27th principle and is more valid in that version. The small number of words in the basal vocabulary governed by this principle indicates that the phonogram *ight* can more profitably be taught as such, without burdening the pupil with another generalization with almost one exception for every two examples. Principles 36 and 37 refer to four and five basal words, respectively, and thus are hardly worth the effort of learning. The broader study by Bailey does not alter the picture of the relative infrequency of these three generalizations, for none of them applies to more than about 100 words in a six-grade vocabulary.

To summarize Clymer's highly significant study of phonic generalizations, we see that of the thirty-seven, only nine are sufficiently valid and widely applicable. Two of these, 1 and 3, concern vowel sounds; one deals with vowel digraphs, principle 14; one concerns vowels with *r,* principle 23; and five control consonant sounds, principles 25, 26, 31, 32, and 33. Neither of those regarding vowel diphthongs is acceptable. The additional data extending Clymer's type of study to a representative vocabulary of basal readers for the entire six grades, as offered by Emans and Bailey, do not change Clymer's implications in the slightest.

These studies also illustrate one of the factors contributing to the general confusion about the values of phonics teaching. Both teachers and pupils must certainly be confused: the teachers, by the great variations from one reading program to another in numbers of generalizations and the manner in which they are stated; the children, by the many exceptions to most of the principles they are being taught. Clymer's type of study has been most useful in clarifying this aspect of the phonics program, even though the implications will not be acceptable to some authors. But the onus of proof that other personal versions of phonics principles are more valid than Clymer's versions rests upon those who disagree with the implications.

HOW WE OUGHT TO TEACH PHONICS

Our concepts of the way in which phonics should be taught, in contrast to present practices, are neither very original nor revolutionary. Although we may not agree with many aspects of the present system, a research basis to support drastic changes is lacking. Our proposals will differ, however, from current practices in many details, such as sequence, time of introduction, and principles.

Suggested Phonics Syllabus

Simple Consonants

b, p, m, w, h, d, t, n, hard *g* (gate), *k,* hard *c* (cake), *y* (yet), *f* (for)

More Difficult Consonants

v, l, z (zoo), *s* (sat), *r, c* (cent), *q* (kw), *x* (ks), *j, g* (engine), *s* (as)

Consonant Blends and Digraphs

ck, ng, th (the), *zh, sh, th* (thin), *wh, ch*

Simple Consonants with l, r, p, or t, as bl, pl, gr, br, sp, st, tr, thr, str, spl, scr, and others as they appear

Short Vowels

a (hat), e (get), i (sit), o (top), u (cup), y (happy)

Long Vowels

a (cake), e (be), i (five), o (old), u (mule), y (cry)

Silent Letters

k (knife), w (write), l (talk), t (catch), g (gnat), c (black), h (hour)

Vowel Digraphs

ai (pail), ea (each), oa (boat), ee (bee), ay (say), ea (dead)

Vowel Diphthongs

au (auto), aw (awful), oo (moon), oo (wood), ow (cow), ou (out), oi (oil), oy (boy), ow (low)

Vowels with r

ar (car), er (her), ir (bird), or (corn), ur (burn)
Same with L and w.

Phonograms

ail, ain, all, and, ate, ay, con, eep, ell, en, ent, er, est, ick, ight, ill, in, ing, ock, ter, tion
Alternates—ake, ide, ile, ine, it, ite, le, re, ble

The order of presentation of our syllabus follows our knowledge of the development of the articulation of consonant sounds (42). All the simple consonants will have developed in the speech of the average child by the age of five and one half. The more difficult consonants normally are not fluent or accurate in the speech of the average child until the ages of six and one half to seven and one half. This would seem to argue for their teaching and the relevant generalizations to be delayed until the latter half of the first grade or the beginning of the second, assuming that most children enter school at about the age of six. The order of the consonant blends and digraphs [which Groff suggests should be called consonant clusters (27)] similarly follow the known order of their appearance in speech development. Groff suggests a sequence for teaching consonant clusters based on their ease of spelling, frequency of use, reading difficulty, and the total number of words in which they are found. The sequence he offers does not differ greatly, however, from that we give, although he includes a number of other clusters, such as *qu, nt, ss, ll, rm,* and the like, that are not commonly stressed in basal programs as significant phonemes. Most of those he would add would be more functionally taught, in our opinion, as phonogram elements, such as *ent, all,* and *ill.* Dependence upon frequency counts to suggest instructional sequences, as Groff (27) and Johnson (35) and a number of other writers have done, is unrealistic in our opinion. Frequency counts based on a large corpus of words tend to ignore first, the articulatory development of children; second, the abstractness or complexity of the combinations in which some letters are sometimes silent, sometimes sounded, sometimes blended, sometimes separate. Third, frequency of occurrence does not indicate learnability of the items, for we have practically no data on this important aspect. We cannot see the logic of a sequence which suggests teaching phonemes the child cannot yet articulate well, and thus probably cannot read, for their enunciation is not likely to be present in his auditory memory bank.

Phonics syllabi commonly include a list of rules which are to be taught inductively at various stages. Our review of the Clymer, Emans, Bailey, and Burmeister studies of the utility of these generalizations resulted in the reduction of such a list to a defensible minimum. We would eliminate the weaker or esoteric principles and suggest only the following:

Consonants

1. When *c* is frequently followed by *e, i,* or *y,* it has the sound of *s,* as in *race, city, fancy.*
2. Otherwise, *c* has the sound of *k,* as in *come, attic.*
3. *G* followed by *e, i,* or *y* sounds soft like *j,* as in *gem.*
4. Otherwise *g* sounds hard, as in *gone.*
5. When *c* and *h* are next to each other, they make only one sound.
6. *Ch* is usually pronounced as it is in *kitchen,* not like *sh* (in *machine*).
7. When a word ends in *ck,* it has the same last sound, as in *look.*
8. When two of the same consonants are side by side, only one is heard, as in *butter.*
9. Sometimes *s* has the sound of *z,* as in *raisin, music.*
10. The letter *x* has the sounds of *ks* or *k* and *s,* as in *box, taxi.*

Vowels

11. When a consonant and *y* are the last letters in a one-syllable word, the *y* has the long *i* sound, as in *cry, by.* In longer words the *y* has the long *e* sound, as in *baby.*
12. The *r* gives the preceding vowel a sound that is neither long nor short, as in *car, far, fur, fir.* The letters *l* and *w* have the same effect.

Vowel Digraphs and Diphthongs

13. The first vowel is usually long and the second silent in *oa, ay, ai,* and *ee,* as in *boat, say, gain, feed.*
14. In *ea* the first letter may be long and the second silent, or it may have the short *e* sound, as in *bread.*

15. *Ou* has two sounds: one is the long sound of *o;* the other is the *ou* sound, as in *own* or *cow.*
16. These double vowels blend into a single sound: *au, aw, oi, oy,* as in *auto, awful, coin, boy.*
17. The combination *ou* has a schwa sound, as in *vigorous,* or a sound as in *out.*
18. The combination *oo* has two sounds, as in *moon* and as in *wood.*

We have adapted and simplified these generalizations from the forms in which they were offered by Clymer and Burmeister *(6,7,9).* This attempted simplification is amply justified by MacGinitie's criticism of their unnecessary complexity. Yet the rules are still sometimes phrased for adults, not for children, as in the case of 11 and 17. Would that we knew how to simplify them further, and how to lead children through the logical steps that result in their understanding.

When we analyze the words in basal series or in larger samples by computer, these generalizations seem to be justified by the frequency of their appearance in such sources and by the infrequency of their exceptions. Mary Ann Dzama *(15)* has also tested them in a random sample of the sight vocabulary of first graders in a language experience program. In general, she found similar results, except that fewer words fitted the generalizations in the childrens' sight vocabulary than in the Clymer study of a basal vocabulary, perhaps reflecting the breadth of the childrens' vocabulary resulting from use of the language experience method.

Inspection of our list of recommended phonics principles will show the exclusion of many generalizations commonly taught. Some reading teachers may feel that we have so drastically reduced the number of principles that children will be handicapped in attempting to apply phonics to word recognition. For example, it would seem that children taught in accordance with our syllabus and principles would have no clues in the following situations:

1. Pronouncing the vowel sound in monosyllables, as *get, man, go.*
2. Recognizing long or short vowel sounds, as in *pin–pine, cap–cape,* and the like.

It is certainly not our intention to deprive primary-grade children of any effective, functional aids to word recognition and thus to make the task of learning to read more difficult. On the contrary, we hope to make the process as painless as possible, but also as pragmatic as we can. Certainly, teaching children a number of generalizations which frequently fail to function or work only in a relatively small number of words cannot be justified. Phonics can be taught effectively without dependence upon such generalizations.

Our syllabus suggests the teaching of the long and short vowel sounds, the common and variant sounds of consonants, a number of vowel digraphs and vowel diphthongs, the effect of *r, l,* and *w* on adjoining vowels, and the recognition of silent letters. If these phonic elements are taught as we shall outline later, no pupil will actually be unable to deal with these when the word demands. But the question remains in the minds of some whether this knowledge will enable pupils to recognize the correct pronunciation of the vowels and vowel digraphs they encounter in primary words. For example, without some generalization to guide them, how do pupils know whether the vowel is long or short in *ate, five, get,* and *sit?* How will they approach such words as *seat, paint,* and *go?*

Without actually teaching children to depend upon poor generalizations, we would teach children a system of approach, a series of steps that capitalizes upon the known vagaries of English pronunciation.

In effect, when meeting an unknown word, the child would ask himself:

1. What is the sound of the first letter or blend? (This may be sufficient to trigger off or recall the entire word, because of the contextual clues.)
2. What word beginning with this sound would make sense in this sentence?
3. How many vowels are there? Where are they?
   a. If there is one vowel in the beginning or middle, try the short sound of the vowel.
   b. If there is one vowel and *e* at the end, try the long sound.
   c. If there is one vowel at the end, try the long sound.
   d. If there are two vowels in the middle or at the end, try the long sound of the first vowel, except in *oi, oy, ou, ew, au, aw, oo, ow.*

These four possibilities would result in an approximately correct pronunciation of the vowel sound in better than two out of every three words. If the first attempt does not result in a recognizable word, the child would simply try again as in steps 4 and 5.

4. Say the whole word. Do you know it? If not, try the other vowel sound.
5. Now do you know the word? If not, write it down and get help later from the teacher or your dictionary. Go on with your reading.

This systematic approach plus the generalizations we have recommended and the phonic facts suggested in the syllabus given earlier would, we believe, give the child sufficient phonics knowledge to be successful in this particular word recognition technique.

The syllabus and the generalizations are only the content of the phonics program. More significant by far than these are the principles which should guide the teacher in his methods of presentation. Among these principles, we think the following are justified (*48*).

1. Precede and accompany phonics training by instruction in auditory discrimination as outlined elsewhere in this volume. Continue this auditory training as long as necessary, particularly for slow-learner groups, if profitable.
2. Begin informal phonics at the experience chart or preprimer level, teaching simple consonant sounds as they appear in a number of words in the pupil's reading vocabulary. Use games and, perhaps, M. Lucile Harrison's approach by auditory and context clues, as we describe later in this chapter. Make small cards for each letter in capitals and lowercase and picture cards for games in matching letters to beginning sound of pictured objects.
3. Although gifted pupils may not be learning a vocabulary identical with that in the basals used with other groups, they also need planned, small-group phonics

instruction. If necessary use the chart vocabulary as the basis, if words known to all are needed. In other words, despite the fact that these pupils apparently learn many words very quickly, give them the same phonics training outlined in our syllabus.

4. For economy of time, introduce study of an element or a principle to a small group or the entire class. Follow up with workbook or teacher-made exercises, a phonics workbook, or several such applications. Place greatest emphasis upon promoting use of phonics skills during small-group reading or individual conferences. Ability to parrot sounds is useless. Constant use of the elements in attacking unknown words is the only purpose for their teaching. Try not to separate phonics learning from the act of reading by teaching phonics only at certain periods. Help children to transfer their phonics knowledge by (a) using words drawn from their current reading materials in your phonics instruction; (b) refraining from telling children the unknown words when they are reading and instead urging them to try to use whatever phonics they know; (c) asking them to list new words they meet that contain a known phonic element, such as the initial consonant *m,* the long sound of *e,* etc.; and (d) using these children's lists in your phonics lessons.

5. In teaching each phonic element, deal only with words as units, not with sounds isolated from words. Approach each sound in a systematic fashion, perhaps in the manner suggested by Harrison, which we will describe later. Remember that phonic analysis is only one type of clue to word recognition. Urge children to use others by asking questions about the significance of the word length, shape, details, probable contextual clue, and the like.

6. When teaching a particular phonic element, present it at first in only one part of the illustrative words. After it is easily recognized both visually and auditorily in its initial position, its function in medial or final positions may be taught.

7. Teach phonic elements in initial, medial, and final positions in words, except for those phonograms which normally do not occur in initial positions. In other words, after introducing *s* as an initial consonant, help children to recognize it anywhere in a word by using a variety of words containing *s* in your phonics lessons.

8. Teach children to utilize any or all other clues to word meaning simultaneously with phonics, such as word form, picture, context, and structure clues. The goal of phonics training is not to train children in a letter-by-letter, sound-by-sound approach to word recognition. Pupils should be taught to use as few phonic clues as possible in the effort to recall or recognize the word. In many instances, the simple sound of the initial consonant or blend should suggest a word that makes sense in that sentence. Ideally speaking, most of the practice with phonic elements should occur with words in context to stimulate the reading act and promote use of other clues. Most available teaching materials ignore this principle, unfortunately.

9. To be completely functional, phonics skill must operate in reading, spelling, and writing. Phonic elements must be readily recognized and translated from one medium to the other. Therefore, complete phonics training will result in these associations: (a) knowing name and common sound of element, (b) seeing and writing the element, (c) seeing and sounding while writing or tracing, (d) responding by sound when letter name of element is given, (e) responding by writing when letter name is given, and (f) responding by writing when sound and illustrative word are given.

Two fundamental phonics skills, often ignored in popular systems, are blending and substitution. Pupils must learn to recognize a phonic element, sound it, and then blend it with the rest of the word. Simple knowledge of phonic elements does not ensure successful blending so that the final pronunciation corresponds to the auditory memory of the word. Substitution involves recognition of an element present in an unknown word, as *ight* in *bright,* reasoning by analogy with a known word, *light,* substituting *br* for *l,* and pronouncing the word. Both of these skills must be given ample attention and practice in order that other phonics learnings will function.

Railsback (*44*) questions strongly whether young children, particularly those below average in ability, have more difficulty than teachers or authors of basals realize in trying to use consonant substitution. The task demands having a good mental image of a word resembling the unknown word except for the initial letter; then mentally dropping the first letter of the known word and substituting the initial letter or letters of the new word. His observations of second graders attempting to attack new and real and nonsense words (in which consonant substitution based on their known reading vocabulary was possible) showed that only one child used this technique in any words, despite training in it since the primer level. Again, our inadequacy in knowing how to teach these phonic skills so that they really function for children is manifest.

Steps in Teaching a Phonic Element
(Such as Short a Sound)

Auditory Discrimination. Use a key word containing the new sound, preferably a word that can be illustrated by a concrete object (*apple, hat*). Use other objects for comparison, the names of which do not contain the short *a* sound (*eraser, pencil, light, seat*). Ask pupils to give the key word and compare it with the names of these classroom objects. Which has the short *a* sound?

Reproduction. Children repeat the names of objects in the classroom after the teacher in varied order. Repeat this, with teacher pointing to objects while children pronounce the names, without any auditory cue from the teacher. Make a game of the exercise by having children give the name of the object only when it contains the new sound. When the name does not contain the sound, the pupils respond by a greeting to the teacher.

Illustrative Words. Pupils look around the room to find items illustrating the short *a* sound (*map, Alice, bat, Jack, record rack*). These words are written on the chalkboard as children offer them. It is important, we feel, that these lists of words illustrating the new sound should *not* be prepared by the teacher or offered from a printed list. The words must be discovered and offered by the pupils as a result of discussion, observation, or their reading.

Reinforcement Activities. Items from home may be brought by the pupils and teacher, and arranged in a table display. Also, pictures from magazines may be used for charts illustrating a sound, or for a picture–sound dictionary.

An exercise challenging the children's thinking is one in which the teacher asks questions leading to answers containing the new sound: "What could we use to hit a ball?" or "What is sticky and oozes from a tree?"

To promote transfer of the phonics learning to the reading act, ask the children to locate printed words illustrating the new sound. These words may be written on slips of paper, as they are reading, and brought to the group session later, to be added to the list. The writing component of this activity helps pupils to match the sounds representing letters with their written forms, an essential phonics skill for spelling (an area even more demanding of phonics skill than reading).

While building these lists of illustrative words, it is essential to initiate discussion of these words, their multiple meanings, their opposites, and other associations related to them. Learning the pronunciation of these words and reacting to the presence of a certain phonic element is desirable, but not as important as understanding their meanings. Only by the building of many associations with each word can we be certain of their storage in long-term memory.

For extended reinforcement, use teacher-made or commercial worksheets in such activities as:

1. Answering riddles with words containing the new sound.
2. Supplying missing words in a sentence with word containing the new sound.
3. Circling words in a given list.
4. Doing crossword puzzles composed of words with the new sound.
5. Drawing a picture containing some objects whose names illustrate the sound; labeling those objects in the drawing.
6. Classifying or grouping words, from the list already assembled, in such categories as foods, household items, toys, actions, etc.
7. Adding words containing the new sound to spelling exercises.

ALTERNATIVE APPROACHES TO PHONICS

Two experiments by Hillerich (*33,34*) in the first and second grades were concerned with teaching vowel sounds. In the first grade, children taught the vowel rules were better in a test of nonsense words but not in a reading test. In fact, the nonvowel group showed better reading comprehension. In his second-grade report, Hillerich contrasted a group taught all vowel sounds with one trained in auditory perception and only the long and short vowels and a control group given no instruction on vowels. The second group, with minimal vowel training, achieved the highest reading scores; the group with complete vowel training had the lowest scores of all groups.

Wylie and Durrell (*56*) have suggested another way of dealing with the difficulties inherent in the variable vowel sounds. They would stress teaching phonograms rather than vowel sounds and claim that is it easier for the child to learn these than even the short vowel sounds. We have been emphasizing the values in teaching phonograms (three- to four-letter units of consistent pronunciation) since our original study of this field of phonics in 1939 and are glad to discover that there is now some evidence to support this viewpoint. Wylie and Durrell's first-grade pupils were able to identify whole phonograms by analogy with known words better than by having a knowledge of short vowels. In effect, most phonograms are closed syllables with a consonant or two following the vowel. A few involve a final *e* and a medial long vowel, but even these appeared to give little difficulty to these pupils. When the vowel was followed by *r, l,* or *w,* the change in the vowel sound did give some difficulty because the children, by this time, were expecting a short vowel sound.

This procedure might well be a type of instruction given to those pupils who have difficulty reading vowel combinations and distinguishing the long from the short sound. If taught the three- to four-letter phonograms and practiced in generalizing from one word to another by initial consonant substitution, such pupils would indeed be enabled to recognize and pronounce many words, such as *band, sand, land, cake, make,* and *take,* without fumbling with the unpredictable vowel combinations.

This review of various methods of systematizing phonics teaching would include the approach suggested by M. Lucile Harrison and Paul McKee. This method has been tried out extensively with preschool, kindergarten, and primary-grade pupils. A television course addressed to parents of preschool children with a special manual, "Preparing Your Child for Reading," has been prepared to promote wide use of the method in the Denver area. Preliminary results indicate that children taught by this system show marked success in early reading in the primary grades.

The program leads the child to make great use of initial consonant sounds and context for word recognition, through the following steps:

1. Begin training in auditory discrimination in kindergarten by emphasizing comparison of initial sounds of objects, children's names, and the like.
2. Teach children to relate name of initial consonant and its sound, for example, "Mary's name starts with an *M,* doesn't it?"
3. Develop a key word for each initial consonant sound. Select a drawing of an object beginning with a particular sound. Outline drawing with heavy lines, forming the initial letter. For example, an upright bat and an adjacent ball can be thus transformed into a lowercase *b.* In using the key word chart, refer to a letter by name only, not by its sound: for example, letter *b,* as in *ball,* not *buh* as in *ball.*
4. Practice recognizing words from context by allowing children to supply a word in a sentence of a story you are reading to the class. Select words beginning with a particular consonant in each story, thus practicing with only one consonant sound at a time, in words that are in the pupil's auditory and speech vocabularies.
5. Help children to associate both use of context and sound of initial consonant in act of recognizing words in oral context read to them.

6. Begin simple reading materials, experience charts. Urge children to use their two-word attack skills for word recognition.
7. Expand usefulness of initial consonant approach by teaching the substitution technique; for example, "This boy's name is just like the word *back* except for the first letter. His name begins with the *j* sound like *jump.* Put the *j* sound in place of the *b* in *back,* and tell me the boy's name."
8. Do not attempt to teach vowel sounds.

Trial of this method in the Denver Public Schools shows that if taught at beginning or middle of kindergarten or beginning of the first grade, children are reading successfully, some even at the first reader level, after half a school year. Furthermore, these children show marked independence and skill in word attack.

It is apparent that certain steps in the selection and preparation of the reading materials, as well as further training in word attack skills, are necessary to ensure the ultimate success of this approach. Stories to illustrate contextual use of words beginning with a certain sound must be carefully selected. Beginning reading materials will certainly need stronger narrative and expository characteristics than are present in the preprimers and primers of many basal reading series to permit frequent successful contextual analysis. However, the many new easy-to-read books for beginners will be helpful in solving this problem, as will experience charts and teacher-made materials. Many teachers will feel the need to extend their pupil's knowledge of phonics to initial consonant blends, endings, phonograms, and the like (as Harrison probably does also) and perhaps to short and long vowel sounds (as Harrison apparently does not).

The strength of this approach to facilitating success in initial reading and independence in word attack lies in its provision for a two-pronged system of word recognition. The simultaneous use of rudimentary phonics and context strengthens the possibilities of accurate word recognition. Anticipation of a particular word from the sense of a sentence is completely natural and linguistically defensible. Success in the use of this logical approach to word recognition is further ensured when the child confirms his contextual guess by comparing it with the actual sound of the beginning of the word. If the beginning reading materials are natural and resemble the sentence the child usually speaks and hears (as they would in experience charts, teacher-made materials, and some trade books), successful word attack in the early stages of reading is greatly enhanced.

The rationale for teaching decoding (phonics) varies from one author to the next. Some think of it as the most essential tool for learning to read, and that skill in this area should be manifest at all ages up to and including the college level. In truth, its justification lies in the fact that it helps *beginning readers only* to pronounce and thus recognize words for which auditory memories are already stored. In other words, decoding functions with simple, known words but not with harder or technical terms that are unfamiliar. It is a distinct aid in early reading stages but deteriorates as the normal reading vocabulary expands beyond the individual's auditory vocabulary. Decoding produces a pronunciation of a word which is helpful in its recognition—*if* the pronunciation is similar to the spoken version of the word and *if* some meaningful associations to that word have already been stored in the reader's memory. Without previous knowledge of the word, decoding produces only a meaningless group of sounds.

There is, of course some question whether good auditory discrimination is essential to reading progress and even if it is somewhat related, whether all children can benefit or profit from auditory training. We have already pointed out that dialect speakers do not normally show good discrimination in the common tests, for their dialect has not prepared them to make these distinctions. There is also evidence that these children can still learn to read reasonably well, when judged in terms of their intelligence and socioeconomic backgrounds. We also know that some children do not exhibit a preference for learning through auditory avenues, and, in fact, learn better when other facets are emphasized.

In effect, we are questioning whether auditory training and phonics of the usual sorts are as important for some beginning readers as we have previously assumed.

It is fairly well accepted that phonics is not a great aid to children of less than average ability, or in some studies, for black pupils or other dialect speakers. For example, Hackney found that his high reading group was superior to the average, which, in turn, was better than the poor reading group in all eleven of the Doren phonics skills tests (30). Benz and Rosemier report a similar observation using the Bond–Hoyt–Clymer phonics skills battery (3). In general, then, good readers do seem to test better in phonics than do poor or average readers. But in both these studies it was noted that the correlations between phonics skills and reading were relatively low, with only a small part of the variation in reading scores being accounted for by the phonics skills. Furthermore, the variations in the phonics scores as measured by their standard deviation increased from high to average to poor readers. This implies that average and poor readers, in particular, vary greatly in their possession of phonics knowledge, and possibly even more in their application of these skills in the act of reading. Other studies indicate that not all phonics skills are mastered by normal readers even by the sixth grade (4).

Boyd's study showed that the most rapid growth of the fifteen phonic skills tested was in the second and third grades but that their development thereafter was much slower (4). A similar testing in grades three to six found that phonic skills, such as recognizing phonic elements in a word, beginning sounds, rhyming sounds, and letter sounds grew progressively worse. Yet the children tested achieved expectancy levels in reading of 89 percent in the third grade and 80 to 81 percent in the fourth to sixth grades.

These studies seem to indicate that, as we have suggested, the decoding skills first taught in the primary grades were deteriorating or falling into disuse in the intermediate levels. Moreover, the relationships among skill subtests and with reading comprehension were quite low by the middle grades (3,29). Several inferences are possible in view of these facts: first, phonic skills are helpful or functional only in primary reading materials; second, other more relevant word analysis techniques should be stressed in the middle grades; and third, good readers, although generally better in phonics tests, vary in their knowledge and use of phonic skills beyond the second grade, while average and poor readers vary from skill to skill even more.

These studies are limited in scope and in the extent to which they can be generalized. But there is little doubt that there are some children who do not profit from much of our phonics instruction for a variety of reasons. If we grant this obvious fact, we are obligated to offer alternative types of training which will enable these children to deal with new or strange words and to read successfully. The alternatives we see as feasible are as follows:

1. If children can learn some of the initial consonant sounds, teach them these and use them as a clue to word recognition. Stress the thinking of "What word beginning with that sound would make sense in this sentence?" This is the most common word recognition technique used by children.
2. As a reinforcing method to word recognition (or as an alternative method for children who cannot distinguish initial consonant sounds accurately), substitute intensive training in contextual analysis by the cloze procedure and other exercises outlined later in this chapter.
3. If children respond favorably to that technique (as discovered by use of the Mills Learning Methods Test or observation), teach them to use the kinesthetic procedure of tracing words in order to learn them. Reinforce this learning modality by providing ample practice in writing, as by the language experience approach.
4. Provide intensive practice for these pupils in classifying words to build depth of meanings, perhaps in the fashion we have described in earlier chapters. There is some evidence that this emphasis is effective for poor readers, and more so than training in phonics and syllabication for some.

OTHER APPROACHES TO PHONICS

There are, of course, a great many other approaches to phonics teaching. Many of these have their own coterie of devout followers who apparently feel that it is their mission to rescue the schools from the look–say method. Each group has its own rigid program which admits no merit in any other sequence, timing, or methodology than its own. The more attention given to these programs, the more confused the anxious teacher becomes, for she finds great contradictions and conflicting claims. The adherents of each phonics system are positive that they alone have the proper answers to all problems in this area.

As we have tried to point out, most reasonable American reading authorities are certain of only one fact—that they do not know the correct answers to all questions about phonics. Despite the best efforts, the available research does not prove any particular system superior to all others. Nor is our knowledge certain enough to determine the exact sequence, timing, methods, or content that is best. Since this is the true situation, any system offered to teachers which claims to have the answers to all the unsolved questions is likely to approach being a cult rather than a phonics program (47).

Like phonics, training in structural analysis is founded upon the primitive recognition of words by configuration or shape as well as minor details. Young readers may identify words by a certain element, such as a curved letter at the end of *dog* reminds them of the dog's tail. Mature readers also use outlines of words but tend to recognize larger details, such as common syllables and affixes. The purpose of training in structural analysis is, then, the development of the habit of recognition by larger, more meaningful units within words. Among the units commonly included in a structural analysis program are inflectional endings, compound words, syllables, prefixes, roots, suffixes, and contractions. Phonic analysis aids in structural analysis, for the final recognition of the structural elements is often dependent upon successful pronunciation derived from sounding the letters present. However, most of the word elements taught in structural analysis are composed of several letters and have a pronunciation which is not dependent upon the successive sounds of the letters present. Children trained in letter phonics alone are handicapped in attempting recognition by structural elements, unless they discard this approach and learn to deal with larger units. The necessity for this development of new word recognition skills is just another reason against overemphasis upon letter phonics and a reason for the teaching of many phonograms in the phonics program.

In Figure 11–3 the structural analysis content of the primary levels of six well-known basal reading series is presented. These are fairly representative of other basal programs.

In the teaching of these structural units, several principles which function also in spelling and writing are commonly emphasized. Among these are the following:

1. When a base word or accented last syllable of a word ends in a single consonant preceded by a single vowel, the final consonant is doubled when adding a suffix beginning with a vowel, for example, *hop–hopped.*
2. When a base word ends in *e,* the *e* may be dropped before adding an ending beginning with a vowel, for example, *hope–hoping.*
3. When a base word ends in *y,* preceded by a consonant, the *y* is changed to *i* before the ending (unless the ending begins with *i*), for example, *hurry–hurried–hurrying.*
4. When a base word ends in *f,* or *fe,* in which the *e* is silent, the *f* sometimes is changed to *v* before the ending, for example, *calf–calves, knife–knives.*

These principles are not phrased in the oversimplified versions preferred by most authors because the common versions are inaccurate and open to too many exceptions. The phrasing here is that proposed long ago by Wheat (55). Emphasis on full comprehension of the more accurate definitions probably should be postponed until intermediate grades. But they should eventually be understood in their entirety if they are to function in spelling and writing. Other structural relationships, learned more or less informally, include these: the formation of plurals of nouns by adding *s* or *es,* the use of the apostrophe and *s* to show possession in most words, the use of the apostrophe alone in words ending in *s,* the use of the hyphen in numbers and the combining form *self,* the use of the apostrophe to show the omission of a letter or letters in a contraction.

Figure 11–3 includes, of course, only the inflectional endings, prefixes, and suffixes taught in these particular primary-grade programs. Compound words and contractions are also stressed in all these programs as they occur in the basal vocabulary. Roots or stems which are the core of polysyllabic words are also presented in these programs, beginning in about the fifth grade, as are rules for syllabication. We shall discuss these elements of a structural analysis program in greater detail later.

Even a casual inspection of the table reveals the marked variations from one series to another. Some do not stress any prefixes or suffixes until the second grade (Allyn and Bacon, Harper & Row); some teach only a few of these structural elements, as in the two-grade SRA Basic Reading Series. Since the Allyn and Bacon is in the writing process at this moment, we can report on its program only as far as the third grade. In all probability, its suggestions for structural analysis will extend into the intermediate grades, as in the Ginn 720, Harper & Row, and American Book programs.

The point is obvious that there is no constant sequence or content that can be observed in all these series. These word elements are taught, apparently, if and when they occur in the reading selections, rather than in any preplanned order. This basis of selection for the items in a structural analysis program can be justified, perhaps, on a practical basis. But, does the appearance of a suffix, prefix, root, or inflection once or even several times in a certain reading selection justify its instruction at that time? Are there no differences among these elements in learnability, difficulty, or meaningfulness? Should not their frequency in the total vocabulary encountered in the average child's reading, for example, in the first six years, be considered?

Beyond the primary levels, the selection of a syllabus of prefixes, suffixes, and roots is made in many ways. The possible criteria for choosing these items include their frequency in various word lists, such as basic reading or spelling vocabularies, their frequency in children's own writing; and their simplicity and infrequency of multiple meanings. Breen (5), for example, lists the thirty prefixes, fifty-four roots, and nineteen suffixes which were of greatest frequency in the Rinsland study of pupils' writing. This selection would seem to indicate those items pupils should learn in order to facilitate their writing. But the list ignores the question of multiple meanings. Are we to assume that children need to know most of the meanings of these affixes? Or are they simply elements that pupils recognize visually and by ear and thus can use them in writing? Deighton (13), on the other hand, would eliminate all the roots suggested by Breen because they have multiple meanings. He includes in his syllabus only those structural elements which have single meanings, except for a few items. The total list includes twenty-six combining forms, seven word prefixes and suffixes (*out, over, under,* etc.), eleven other prefixes, and fifty-seven suffixes. While simplicity of meanings

Series	Prefixes	Suffixes and inflections
Preprimer–Primer Level		
American Book		*ing, s, ed*
Harper & Row Design for Reading		*s, ing, 's*
Houghton Mifflin		*s, ed, ing, ly, ful*
First-Reader Level		
American Book	*be*	*er, y, le, et*
Ginn 720		*es, ed*
Harper & Row Design for Reading		*ed, er, est, ly, y*
Houghton Mifflin	*un*	*ness*
SRA Basic Reading Series		*ing*
Second-Reader Level		
Allyn and Bacon	*de*	*ly, ed, ible*
American Book		*er, es, est, ly, el, on, en, n, ful, or, en, tion*
Ginn 720		*er, est, ly, y*
Harper & Row Design for Reading	*un*	*n, en*
Houghton Mifflin	*re, ex, dis*	*tion, ment, less, al, ture*
SRA Basic Reading Series		*en, er, ed, est, ness, es, y, ies, ied, ly, ily, le, el, al, on, et, it, ic, ish*
Third-Reader Level		
Allyn and Bacon	*dis, tele, un, super*	*ier, er, ous, ish, est, ful, fully, ness, ied, less, ing*

Series	Prefixes	Suffixes and inflections
American Book	un, pre, ex, re, de, dis, mis, in	ish, ern, an, ian, like, ment, less, ness, ure
Ginn 720	a, be, de, re, pre, un, under	ful, tion, sion, ion
Harper & Row Design for Reading	re	ward, some, ous, ship, ment
Houghton Mifflin	mis, de, pro, pro, ad, pre, com, in	ance, en, ence

Fourth-Reader Level

Series	Prefixes	Suffixes and inflections
American Book	col, com, con, pro	ant, al, ion, age, some, ology, ous, able, ship
Ginn 720		ment, ness, ful, fully
Harper & Row Design for Reading	mis, in, anti, inter, trans	al, ate, dom, ity, ure, ance, ion, ish, ty, ian, or, an, ism, ive
Houghton Mifflin		en, er, est, s, es, ies

Fifth-Reader Level

Series	Prefixes	Suffixes and inflections
American Book	sub, trans, non, mid, en, ad, co	hood, ward, ive, ist
Ginn 720	over, fore, out, uni, bi, tri, ad, at, ex, pre, pro, sub, super, trans, com, con	miss, tract, less, scrib, spect, vis, port, ology, aud
Harper & Row Design for Reading	semi, co, im, ir, fore, il, mid, over, vice	ant, ic, ent, ee, ize, ster, age, ess, err, cy

Sixth-Reader Level

Series	Prefixes	Suffixes and inflections
American Book	inter, fore, im	most, wise, ic, ary, ery, cy, ical, ance, ence
Ginn 720	post, inter, intra, mono, octa, dec, duo, quad, quart, sex, centi, anti, counter	aqua, hydro, ward, ize
Harper & Row Design for Reading	en, non, sub, mal, a, pre	

FIGURE 11–3. *Structural Analysis in the Basal Reading Program*

is a practical criterion, it ignores the significance of the frequency of appearance in reading and writing vocabularies. Thus Deighton's list includes many items which function in only a few of the words the average elementary pupil will probably read or write.

In our opinion, two lists of these structural elements must be evolved. One list will include those items with singular meanings, the knowledge of which would aid the pupil in word recognition and understanding word meanings. These elements would, of course, also function as familiar units in the pupil's spelling and writing. The second list will include those items which would function as common units or syllables in reading, spelling, and writing, but without knowledge of their meanings. Pupils would learn to recognize visually these latter units, know their common pronunciations, but need not learn their multiple meanings. Both lists of meaningful and visual units, as they may be termed, must include only these items of reasonably frequent occurrence in the pupil's learning experiences.

By combining a number of studies of frequency with Deighton's list of simple affixes, we can derive the list of meaningful units. Items of high frequency in reading materials, plus Breen's list of those frequent in pupil writing, may be combined into the second list of visual units in Figure 11–4.

In addition to these structural elements to which we have referred, the structural analysis program includes the teaching of the principles and practices of syllabication. Syllabication functions as an aid in word recognition by helping the pupil break words into smaller units, pronounce these, blend, and thus recognize words in his auditory vocabulary. Syllabication helps pupils in spelling and writing. Moreover, as has been indicated, most normal readers, as they mature in reading in intermediate and upper elementary grades, become increasingly dependent upon their knowledge of syllables and less upon letter phonics.

In question in the teaching of syllabication is the utility of the various rules. Should pupils be taught a number of stable, consistent principles? If so, which principles? Is a knowledge of rules essential for reasonable success in syllabication or can the skill be learned by rule of thumb (42)? In other words, is precise syllabication needed for a functional use of syllables in reading, spelling, and writing? Is there evidence that mature readers use the rules they have been taught, or are they reasonably successful in discriminating syllables without such knowledge? Unfortunately, there are very few conclusive answers to these questions.

Our unpublished studies of the syllabication skills of college freshmen indicate little value in the knowledge of rules at this level. A comparison of the ability to complete the statements of thirteen principles showed very little relationship to a test of ability to indicate the number of syllables in fifty difficult words. Generalizing from these studies, we believe that most college freshmen and adults have probably long since forgotten the rules they once learned. Yet they are able to syllabify well enough for their own purposes. Perhaps syllabication would be of greater use and accuracy if they remembered the rules. But this is doubtful, since the correlation between knowledge of rules and accuracy in syllabication was very low in our studies.

This same question of the pragmatism of rules has been raised by a

Meaningful units	Visual units
Combining Forms	
auto- (self)	*aqua-*
micro- (small)	*audio-*
phono- (sound)	*bene-*
poly- (much, many)	*cred-*
tele- (far off)	*junc-*
	mit-
	pon-, pos-
	scrib-, scrip-
	vert-, vers-
	vide-, vis-

Meaningful units	Visual units	
Prefixes		
circum- (around)	*a, ab-*	*per-*
extra- (outside, beyond)	*ad-*	*peri-*
in- (in, into)	*ante-*	*post-*
intra-, intro- (inside)	*anti-*	*pre-*
mis- (wrong)	*con-, com-, col-*	*pro-*
non- (not, the reverse)	*contr-*	*re-*
out- (more than, beyond)	*de-*	*sub-*
over- (too much)	*dis-, di-*	*super-*
self-	*e-, ex-*	*trans-*
syn- (together)	*inter-*	
under- (below)		
up- (up, above)		

Meaningful units	Visual units
Suffixes	
-self	Noun
-wise (manner)	*-ance, -ence, -tion, -cion, -sion, -ism, -ment,*
	-al, -ic, -meter, -scope, -fer, -ity, -gram,
	-graph
	Agent ("one who")
	-eer, -ess, -ier, -ster, -ist, -stress, -trix
	Adjectival
	-est, -fic, -fold, -from, -wards, -less, -able,
	-ible, -ble, -most, -like, -ous, -ious, -eous,
	-ose, -ful, -way, -ways

FIGURE 11–4. Syllabus of Roots and Affixes

number of other authors. Brother Leonard Courtney (*12*) has made the observation that syllabication principles appear of decreasing value above elementary school levels because of the increase in exceptions. He also notes that teaching absolute rules makes the process an end in itself, for these are soon learned informally. In his experience, the use of context and the aid of the dictionary serve more effectively in word recognition than formal syllabication principles. After all, as Deighton (*13*) points out, the aim of syllabication is an approximately correct pronunciation which may aid in recalling the auditory memories of the word in reading or writing. Therefore, he would teach only the principles that (1) each syllable has a vowel sound, (2) prefixes are separate syllables, and (3) doubled consonants may be split. All other rules, he says, are of doubtful value because of their exceptions.

Recent studies at the intermediate-grade levels tend to support this tendency to deemphasize rules as the most effective way of learning syllabication and other forms of word analysis. Children given practice in categorizing and grouping words showed good progress in word recognition skills and word pronunciation. Such pupils showed progress as great as those taught rules, and poorer readers showed even greater progress under this approach.

To turn to the objective studies of the utility of syllabication principles, we must refer again to the studies of Clymer (*11*), Emans (*16*), and Bailey (*2*). Among those principles they analyzed are the following:

		Percent of Utility		
		Clymer	*Emans*	*Bailey*
1.	In most two-syllable words the first syllable is accented.	85	75	81
2.	If *a, in, red, ex, de,* or *be* is the first syllable in a word, it is usually unaccented.	87	83	84
3.	In most two-syllable words that end in a consonant followed by *y*, the first syllable is accented and the last is unaccented.	96	100	97
4.	If the first vowel sound in a word is followed by two consonants, the first syllable usually ends with the first of the consonants.	72	80	78
5.	If the first vowel sound in a word is followed by a single consonant, that consonant usually begins the second syllable.	44	47	50
6.	If the last syllable of a word ends in *le,* the consonant preceding the *le* usually begins the last syllable.	97	78	93

7. When the first vowel element in a word is followed by *th, ch,* or *sh,* these combinations are not divided and may go with either the first or second syllable.	100	100	100
8. In a word of more than one syllable, the letter *v* usually goes with the preceding vowel to form a syllable.	73	40	65

Using Clymer's criterion of utility that a generalization should work at least three out of four times would definitely eliminate the fifth and eighth principles and raise doubts about the fourth principle. The second principle is unnecessarily complex and functions in a total of only ninety-nine words. It hardly seems justified. Similarly, the third principle applies to only 105 words, the sixth to sixty-four words, and the seventh to thirty words in the 2600-word vocabulary analyzed by Clymer. There is, of course, the possibility that if the entire reading, writing, and spelling vocabulary of the elementary grades were analyzed, certain of these principles might have much wider application and perhaps even greater utility. In the case of the second, Bailey's recent study does tend to alter our estimate of the functional value of this principle in basal vocabularies. In the six-grade vocabulary, this principle applies to 398 words with only sixty-two exceptions. Thus it would appear to have some significance if taught after the primary grades. In the remainder of the principles, the data of Emans and Bailey confirm the indications of the Clymer study.

Many authors writing on the teaching of syllabication would retain the fifth generalization because it functions more efficiently in the total vocabularies. It also is very useful as a complement to the fourth principle. The seventh, which suggests that consonant digraphs are not divided but rather move toward the syllable in front of or behind them, is often recommended because of its consistency and eventual wide applications.

Burmeister, in contrast, is inclined to follow the older system and teach that (6):

1. Every single vowel or vowel combination means a syllable (except for final *e* in a *VCe* setting).
2. Divide between prefix and root, between two roots, and between a root and a suffix. (If the reader doesn't know the word, how does he know where these parts begin or end?)
3. Divide at a consonant pair in *VCCV* but consider *ch, sh, ph,* and *th* as a single consonant.
4. Divide before the consonant in a *Cle* pattern (*ble, tle,* etc.).

It may be interesting to note that the fourth rule above in Clymer's list, and Burmeister's third rule, contradict the phonic principle that two similar, adjoining consonants should produce only one sound. If we follow this syllabication principle, we would probably produce two identical sounds. Which is correct?

The problem of phrasing generalizations that are consistent and functional is still being attempted by many writers. Johnson and Merryman (36), for example, tried to rephrase the VCCV principle by suggesting that the syllabic division should be before the two consonants if they are the same, as *bu-tter*. This would produce a pronunciation closer to actual speech patterns, but so would dividing after the two similar consonants, as *butt-er*. McFeely (39) has tested eight syllabication principles in a basal and social studies vocabulary and rephrased them in keeping with his findings. And this exploration will probably continue, for despite the difficulties with rules and exceptions, syllabication continues to be accepted as an important word analysis scheme by many.

In a comprehensive study of the usefulness of syllables, Groff (26) concluded that the teaching of generalizations is not worth the effort because most of them are only spelling conventions, and besides, the syllable is almost indefinable (and by this time, we are sure the reader is inclined to agree with Groff). Limits of syllables, Groff says, should be determined by the aural–visual perceptions of the word in units that seem logical, and seem to fit growing familiarity with the recurring patterns of spelling. Groff insists, and we are inclined to agree, that syllabication is largely intuitive, although he does seem to see some sense in helping children to distinguish open and closed syllables.

Groff believes that syllabication taught in this graphonemic fashion will help in both word recognition and spelling. Other writers reject syllabication on the grounds that the reader must know how to pronounce the word (or a great many rules) before dividing it into syllables, and that principles are too variable and difficult to remember (22, 52). These legitimate criticisms would seem to be met by Groff's natural approach, particularly since special help is given children in blending syllables (rather than letter sounds).

Waugh and Howell (53) are similarly critical of present practices in teaching syllabication. They point out that a syllable is a unit of speech (á la Groff), not a unit of letters. Moreover, the rules imply that consonants are significant in determining the boundaries of syllables (see rules 3 to 8 in Clymer's list or rules 3 and 4 of Burmeister). In actuality, pronunciation ignores these artificial boundaries, as in the common reading of *butter, trample,* and many others. Even dictionary editors use pronunciation as a guide to syllabication, say these authors. Rather, these writers would stress the recognition of meaningful units in words as in our earlier list; deemphasizing syllabication to the goal of obtaining meaning for words; and teach only the principle that each syllable (part?) has a vowel sound.

Glass and Burton (23), who have criticized syllabication teaching before, tried to resolve the question by intensively interviewing and taping good readers of the second and fifth grades as they attacked thirty unknown words. Eighty-five percent of the pupils, as Groff predicted, used strategies falling into the general category of sound cluster analysis. If syllabication was used, it was employed only *after* decoding the words. Only one child attempted to decode any words letter by letter. In answer to the question of what they had looked for first, all the pupils said they looked immediately for familiar parts formed by letter clusters.

A recent study compared the gains in tests of syllabication with those in comprehension in a middle-school population. The correlation between the gains in syllabication and comprehension was extremely low ($r = .13$), indicating very little relationship between these reading skills. The authors conclude that there is hardly any justification for teaching syllabic rules.*

We are much impressed with these objections to formal instruction in syllabication rules, which result in teaching pupils how to divide words at the end of the line rather than how to attempt their pronunciation. The concepts that we would try to convey to children in this area are:

1. Each important part of a word has a vowel or a vowel combination as part of it.
2. We call these parts of a word that we can recognize and pronounce, syllables.
3. Look at the word and try to say it slowly, part by part.
4. If a syllable seems to begin and end with a consonant, with a vowel between them, try the short sound for the vowel.
5. If a syllable seems to be only a vowel, or to end with a vowel, try the long sound of the vowel.
6. Do you now recognize the word?
7. If not, read the sentence all the way through again and try to guess what word that begins like the new word would make sense.
8. Try to say the word again, if you still have no clues, trying long vowel sounds instead of short in some of the syllables. Now do you recognize it?
9. If not, mark it by underlining or a check in the margin. Go on and finish your reading.
10. If you still have not figured out the word, and you need it to understand the selection, go to the dictionary.

Clinical records of retarded readers clearly demonstrate the weakness of many such pupils in these word recognition skills. Many writers feel that the chief reason for this weakness is the failure of teachers to recognize the interdependence of auditory, phonic, and structural analysis skills. Another contributing case is the tendency to separate instruction in these successive skills into definite periods during the primary and intermediate grades—auditory training during the readiness period only, phonics in the first or second grades, syllabication in the intermediate grades, and so forth. This dichotomizing of related skills probably results in producing many reading failures among pupils in the intermediate and later school years. These pupils, despite their exposure to successive groups of skills, fail to develop the ability to relate their auditory discrimination to the recognition of letter sounds, base simple structural analysis and syllabication on letter sounds, abandon letter phonics gradually as familiarity with larger, syllabic

* Robert J. Marzano, Norma Case, Anne De Booy, and Kathy Prochoruk, "Are Syllabication and Reading Ability Related?" *Journal of Reading,* 19 (April 1976), 545–547.

and structural units grows, and learn gradually to use base words and affixes as a mature word recognition skill.

HOW WE TEACH CONTEXTUAL ANALYSIS

From the very beginning of his reading efforts, the child spontaneously tries to identify unknown words by the sense of the sentence. This process is known as contextual analysis and should be constantly strengthened by planned instruction throughout the elementary and secondary years. Linguists speak of this ability in somewhat different terms, as grammatical sense, or reaction to linguistic structure. They are disturbed that reading authors do not specifically refer to the significance of grammatical structure and its influences upon word function, word meaning, and comprehension. But this difference is simply a matter of semantics. No matter what we term the process or whether we describe examples in reading or linguistic terms, we are talking about the reader's ability to determine word recognition and word meaning by the position or function of a word in a familiar sentence pattern.

Contextual recognition of a word is accomplished by a number of clues. Constance McCullough (*38*), for example, distinguishes ideas and presentation clues. "Idea" clues give some help in recognizing the word: (1) Pictorial illustrations. (2) Verbal—The sentences before or after that sentence containing the unknown word give some indication of its probable nature and meaning. (3) Experience—Concrete experiences of the reader enable him to assume or guess the difficult word. For example, "Sally gave the cat _____ to drink." Most children would recognize that the omitted word was *milk,* or perhaps, *water.* (4) Comparison and contrast—"Mary was *happy* but John was *sad.*" The implied contrast, plus knowledge of the word *happy,* enable the reader to sense the meaning and probably identify *sad.* (5) Synonym—A sentence involves a repetition of the same idea and employs a synonym for the unknown word. "The girls were happy and *gay* at the party." (6) Summary—The strange word is a summary of several ideas already presented. "Oranges, pineapples, and lemons are some of the *fruits* grown in Florida." (7) Mood—The tone or mood of the sentence suggests the nature of the new word. "The happy boy's face was *wreathed* in smiles." (8) Definition—The unknown word is defined in the surrounding sentence or sentences. "A *triangle* is a closed figure with three straight sides." (9) Familiar expression—The word is recognized by its use in a familiar language pattern or verbal experience. "When he picked up the phone, he said, *'Hello.'* "

More mature readers are aided by what McCullough calls presentation clues, such as (*13,38*):

1. Position of word within a sentence
   "This portion of the_____ you are reading deals with contextual analysis." (book? chapter? obviously a noun)

2. An appositive phrase or clause

"On her head she wore a *tiara,* a circlet of gold and precious stones, which complemented her beautiful hair."

3. A nonrestrictive clause

"*Humus,* which is food upon which plant life depends. . . . "

4. Figures of speech

"Such a *cyclopean* doorway could only have been built for the admission of a horse and carriage." (gigantic? huge?) "His argument was as *specious* as the words of the snake who beguiled Adam and Eve in the Garden of Paradise." (deceitful? untruthful?)

5. Inference

"The pillars were almost immediately *contiguous,* with scarcely space enough between them for a hand to enter, much less a person." (adjoining? in contact?)

Other writers mention the contextual clues offered by typography: italics, capitalization, boldface type, parentheses, quotation marks, and footnotes. These serve to call attention to new words for which meaning may be derived from other contextual clues.

Apparently most context clues demand some degree of inferential thinking. As a result, some teachers assume that contextual analysis is not much more than guesswork and therefore should not be promoted. The truth is that such inferential thinking is an essential part of the reading process at all maturity levels and should be strongly encouraged. Pupils should not be burdened with learning the technical terms which might be employed to describe the types of context clues. Rather the emphasis should be placed upon helping the reader use the sense of the sentence or the surrounding sentences as an aid in identifying the probable meaning of a difficult word. The goal of contextual analysis is not always an exact recognition of a word or its pronunciation. These may be approached by other means, such as phonic or structural analysis. But when these techniques are successful, they do not necessarily result in the derivation of the meaning of the word, for it may not be encompassed in the reader's auditory vocabulary. Thus contextual analysis takes the reader beyond pronunciation to meaning, which in many situations is more significant for his ultimate comprehension.

Primary-grade children learn to use contextual analysis of simple types quite effectively, as Porter's experiments (43) with good third graders show. When words were completely omitted from the context, these pupils correctly deduced the exact word omitted 23 percent of the time. They were able to deduce probable meanings of the omitted word 82 percent of the time. In other words, they were successful in contextual analysis for meanings in eight out of ten attempts. Contextual analysis is a very real help to comprehension among good readers, even when they have had no special training in its use. Since we cannot assume that skill in contextual analysis will increase spontaneously for all children, planned training is highly desirable.

Eventually, contextual analysis becomes one of the most frequently used methods of derivation of word meanings, as phonics and structural analysis decrease in use. Most college and adult readers use letter sounds or structural elements very little. They have discovered that although these help pronunciation, they do not aid in deriving meanings, unless the word is familiar auditorily. Since the reading vocabulary rapidly increases far beyond the average student's auditory vocabulary during the secondary school years, the pupil is constantly meeting terms he has never heard. Phonics and structural analysis which may aid in pronunciation are relatively useless in deriving meaning, for the student just does not know the meanings of many of these words. Thus contextual analysis (or perhaps constant use of the dictionary) becomes the reader's main tool for comprehending strange words.

Training in contextual analysis is part of the complete program in word recognition and word meaning skills. It should be begun during the early reading efforts of the child and continued indefinitely. Among primary school children, the following practices are appropriate:

1. Read a sentence, rhyme, jingle, or story in which obvious words are omitted. Encourage children to supply the missing word as you come to it. Discuss with them their reasons for selection of the words they offer. This practice may be combined with a given phonic clue, such as a constant initial sound, in the manner of M. Lucile Harrison described earlier.
2. Have children read a new selection silently. Then question them on the meanings of new words present in the story. Discuss reasons for their deductions.
3. Supply reading material with words occasionally omitted. Leave out every tenth word or a number of words of the same part of speech. Encourage children to infer the missing words and to defend their selections. Accept as correct any answers consistent with the sense of the sentence.
4. Insert a nonsense word in place of a certain noun or verb several times in a paragraph. Ask children to infer the word substituted for, to describe it, and to explain their selection.
5. Vary the nonsense word game by using the correct initial sound, blend, or syllable present in the true word, thus promoting simultaneous use of phonic and contextual, or phonic and structural analysis. Use such games for oral or written responses by the children.
6. With children as young as first-graders, Mary K. Gove (25) used such cloze procedures as deleting every fifth or tenth noun or verb; every fifth or tenth word; or portions of nouns, verbs at these intervals. Children's ability to deduce the omitted or incomplete word was practiced first while listening, later in reading the selections, as their reading ability permitted. Their answers and their reasons were discussed and answers synonymous, identical, or semantically correct were accepted. Yetta Goodman (24) proposes similar modified cloze exercises as important in emphasizing the semantic element in reading.

Other examples of cloze exercises to be used in building meaning vocabulary are offered elsewhere in the book. For contextual analysis training at the intermediate-grade level, use similar exercises but increase the difficulty of the material by using selections from content field textbooks.

In these texts, wherever possible, also help children to use charts, maps, tables, and diagrams as contextual clues to word meanings and comprehension. Also, vary the types of contextual clues described earlier. Ask children to make lists of words approached by contextual analysis, and discuss their inferences and lists. Encourage the use of phonic and structural analysis in these lists, as well as contextual analysis, by questioning pronunciation as well as meanings. See also the games and exercises suggested by Evelyn B. Spache.

Based on the reading behaviors of a number of graduate students, Ames (1) has offered a classification of contextual clues to meaning. He suggests that this process is supported by:

1. Experience with language and familiar expressions.
2. Modifying phrases and clauses.
3. Definition or description.
4. Words connected in a series.
5. Comparison or contrast.
6. Synonym clues.
7. Time, setting, and mood.
8. Referents or antecedents.
9. Association clues.
10. Main idea and supporting details.
11. Question–answer pattern of paragraph.
12. Preposition clues.
13. Nonrestrictive clauses or appositive phrases.
14. Cause–effect patterns.

The significance of this identifying of contextual clues by introspection of mature readers is not immediately apparent for our instruction of elementary pupils. Are these same clues used by children? If so, at what ages and with what degree of facility? Earl F. Rankin and Betsy M. Overholzer (45) have done an initial study seeking answers to these questions. They tested Ames's series of contextual clues on fourth to sixth graders in cloze tests. The material was arranged so that each deleted word could be derived with the aid of one of these clues. The pupils were reasonably successful in supplying the expected words, with increasing scores from grade four to grade six. Most important of all, Rankin and Overholzer ranked the clues from easiest to most difficult as shown by the pupils' ability to supply the missing words in each type of context. In order from easy to difficult, as numbered above, the clues were 4, 2, 1, 14, 9, 8, 6, 3, 12, 11, 5, 10, 13. The last four yielded less than 50 percent accuracy in supplying deleted words, a performance lower than normally expected.

We could base instruction in using contextual clues on the implications of these studies. We might supply cloze exercises exemplifying each type of deduction, have children attempt to supply the missing words, and then discuss their reasons for their answers. Without giving the structures formal labels, we could follow the order suggested by Rankin and Overholzer from easiest to most difficult types, thus to increase children's skill in this most important of all tools for word recognition.

Emans (*18*) has recommended several additional types of contextual analysis training based on his study of the information given by configuration and graphic clues to contextual derivation of words. Emans would employ the cloze and discussion steps we have suggested and add to these exercises by (1) including pictures; (2) supplying the beginning letter in the blank space; (3) showing the length of the word by the size of the space; (4) giving the beginning and ending letters; (5) giving four words as possible answers from which the child would select the best; and (6) printing only the consonants in the blank.

These types of practice, all using the cloze arrangement, do make use of the pupil's phonics knowledge as well as his inferential thinking, and probably could be introduced earlier than the intermediate grades. In terms of children's ability to use these clues, the order given above is from most difficult to easiest, or from least helpful to most helpful.

In constructing the practice exercises in training pupils in each type of contextual clue, a simple approach is to prepare dittoed or mimeographed reading selections, leaving out every tenth word. Variations following Emans' ideas would require leaving in the clue of the beginning or ending letter or all the consonants, etc. These cloze exercises may also be varied by omitting a particular kind of word as every fifth noun, verb, or adjective. Deleting every tenth word in this other kind of cloze would probably require too long a reading selection for a brief classroom activity.

Preparing training exercises to follow Ames' types of contextual clues would, of course, involve much more preparation and rewriting of the reading selections to ensure the repetition of each clue. Or, prior to deleting words, the teacher would identify the probable contextual clue by which every fifth noun or other type of word might be deduced by pupils. Then later the nature of the clue and the thinking necessary to employ it could be brought out in the class discussion.

Studies have been made of the contribution of various portions of a sentence to derivation of the meaning of an unknown word (*54*). It appears that the words which follow a strange word are more likely to aid in contextual analysis than those which precede it. These studies confirm the desirability of teaching pupils to read the entire sentence (and perhaps the rest of the paragraph) before attempting to derive the meaning of an unknown word. The use of a dictionary or any other aid to finding meaning should also be delayed until after the complete sentence or more has been read. This pattern of delayed attack in contextual analysis is also conducive to better overall comprehension, for it prevents interruptions in the continuity of the thinking process.

DISCUSSION QUESTIONS

1. Is it possible that some pupils cannot learn to use phonics and yet can learn to read adequately? Discuss such types of pupils and their habits of word recognition.

2. Discuss the possible reasons for the often observed lack of word attack skills among retarded readers.

3. Would you emphasize phonics skills for a retarded reader of junior or senior high school age who was functioning at the fifth- or sixth-grade level? Give the reason for your answer.

4. If you have observed or used any published systems of phonics teaching, describe them and compare them with the approaches suggested in the text or in other sources.

5. What are the implications of Porter's research on contextual analysis regarding the importance of this skill compared with other word attack skills?

6. Which of the word recognition skills contributes most to accurate pronunciation, to recognition of meaning, or to both? How do these outcomes of the various ways of analyzing words differ when the word is familiar or unfamiliar to the child's auditory vocabulary?

7. Discuss the statement that phonics is of great value only at primary reading levels when the reading vocabulary includes only words already familiar to the child.

REFERENCES

1. Ames, Wilbur S., "The Development of a Classification Scheme of Contextual Aids," *Reading Research Quarterly,* 2 (Fall 1966), 57–82.

2. Bailey, Mildred Hart, "The Utility of Phonic Generalizations in Grades One Through Six," *Reading Teacher,* 20 (February 1967), 413–418.

3. Benz, D. A., and Rosemier, R. A., "Concurrent Validity of the Gates Level of Comprehension Test and the Bond–Hoyt–Clymer Reading Diagnostic Tests," *Educational* and *Psychological Measurement,* 26 (1966), 1057–1062.

4. Boyd, R. D., "Growth of Phonic Skills in Reading," in *Clinical Studies in Reading III,* Helen M. Robinson, ed. Supplementary Educational Monographs, 97 (1968), 68–87.

5. Breen, L. C., "Vocabulary Development by Teaching Prefixes, Suffixes and Root Derivatives," *Reading Teacher,* 14 (November 1960), 93–97.

6. Burmeister, Lou E., "Usefulness of Phonic Generalizations," *Reading Teacher,* 21 (January 1968), 349–356, 360.

7. Burmeister, Lou E., "Vowel Pairs," *Reading Teacher,* 21 (February 1968), 445–452.

8. Burmeister, Lou E., "Final Vowel-Consonant-*e*," *Reading Teacher,* 24 (February 1971), 439–442.

9. Burmeister, Lou E., "Content of a Phonics Program Based on Particularly Useful Generalizations," in *Reading Methods and Teacher Improvement,* Nila B. Smith, ed. Newark, Del.: International Reading Association, 1971, 27–39.

10. Burrows, Alvina Treut, and Lourie, Zyra, "When 'Two Vowels Go Walking'," *Reading Teacher,* 17 (November 1963), 79–82.

11. Clymer, Theodore, "The Utility of Phonic Generalizations in the Primary Grades," *Reading Teacher,* 16 (January 1963), 252–258.

12. Courtney, Brother Leonard, "Methods and Materials for Teaching Word Perception in Grades 10–14," in *Sequential Development of Reading Abilities,* Helen M. Robinson, ed., Supplementary Educational Monographs, No. 90 (1960), 42–46. Chicago: University of Chicago Press.

13. Deighton, Lee C., *Vocabulary Development in the Classroom.* New York: Teachers College Press, 1959.

14. DeLawter, Jayne A., "The Relationship of Beginning Reading Instruction and Miscue Patterns," in *Help for the Reading Teacher: New Directions in Research,* Wm. D. Page, ed. National Conference on Research in English, 1975.

15. Dzama, Mary Ann, "Comparing Use of Generalizations of Phonics in LEA, Basal Vocabulary," *Reading Teacher,* 28 (February 1975), 466–472.

16. Emans, Robert, "The Usefulness of Phonic Generalizations Above the Primary Grades," *Reading Teacher,* 20 (February 1967), 419–425.

17. Emans, Robert, "History of Phonics," *Elementary English,* 45 (May 1968), 602–608.

18. Emans, Robert, "Use of Context Clues," in *Reading and Realism,* J. Allen Figurel, ed. Proceedings International Reading Association, 13, Part 1, 1969, 76–82.

19. Emans, Robert, and Fisher, Gladys M., "Teaching the Use of Context Clues," *Elementary English,* 44 (March 1967), 243–246.

20. Fleming, James T., "Teachers' Understanding of Phonic Generalizations," *Reading Teacher,* 25 (February 1972), 400–404.

21. Gates, Arthur I., "Results of Teaching a System of Phonics," *Reading Teacher,* 14 (March 1961), 248–252.

22. Glass, Gerald G., "The Strange World of Syllabication," *Elementary School Journal,* 67 (March 1967), 403–405.

23. Glass, Gerald G., and Burton, Elizabeth H., "How Do They Decode? Verbalizations and Observed Behavior of Successful Decoders," *Education,* 94 (September–October 1973), 58–64.

24. Goodman, Yetta M., "Reading Strategy Lessons: Expanding Reading Effectiveness," in *Help for the Reading Teacher: New Directions in Research,* Wm. D. Page, ed. National Conference on Research in English, 1975, 34–41.

25. Gove, Mary K., "Using the Cloze Procedure in a First Grade Classroom," *Reading Teacher,* 29 (October 1975), 36–44.

26. Groff, Patrick, *The Syllable: Its Nature and Pedagogical Usefulness.* Portland, Ore.: Northwest Regional Educational Laboratory, 1971.

27. Groff, Patrick, "Sequences for Teaching Consonant Clusters," *Journal of Reading Behavior,* 4 (Winter 1971–1972), 59–65.

28. Groff, Patrick, "The Topsy-Turvy World of 'Sight' Words," *Reading Teacher,* 27 (March 1974), 572–578.

29. Guthrie, J., "Models of Reading and Reading Disability," *Journal of Educational Psychology,* 65 (August 1973), 9–18.

30. Hackney, Ben H., Jr., "Reading Achievement and Word Recognition Skills," *Reading Teacher,* 21 (March 1968), 515–518.

31. Hanson, Irene W., "First Grade Children Work with Variant Word Endings," *Reading Teacher,* 19 (April 1966), 505–507, 511.

32. Harris, Albert J., Serwer, Blanche L., and Gold, Lawrence, "Comparing Approaches in First Grade Teaching with Disadvantaged Children Extended into Second Grade," *Reading Teacher,* 20 (May 1967), 698–703.

33. Hillerich, R. L., "Vowel Generalizations and First Grade Reading Achievement," *Elementary School Journal,* 67 (March 1967), 246–250.

34. Hillerich, R. L., "Teaching About Vowels in Second Grade," *Illinois School Research,* 7 (1970), 35–38.

35. Johnson, Dale D., "Suggested Sequences for Presenting Four Categories of Letter-Sound Correspondences," *Elementary English,* 50 (September 1973), 888–896.

36. Johnson, Dale D., and Merryman, Edward, "Syllabication: The Erroneous VCCV Generalization," *Reading Teacher,* 25 (December 1971), 267–270.

37. MacGinitie, Walter H., "Difficulty with Logical Operations," *Reading Teacher,* 29 (January 1976), 371–375.

38. McCullough, Constance M., "Context Aids in Reading," *Reading Teacher,* 11 (April 1958), 225–229.

39. McFeely, Donald C., "Syllabication Usefulness in a Basal and Social Studies Vocabulary," *Reading Teacher,* 27 (May 1974), 809–814.

40. Mason, George E., "Word Recognition Practice: Basal Versus Phonics Programs," in *Improvement of Reading Through Classroom Practice,* Proceedings International Reading Association, 9, 1964, 309–310.

41. Muller, Douglas, "Phonic Blending and Transfer of Letter Training to Word Reading in Children," *Journal of Reading Behavior,* 5 (Summer 1972–1973), 212–217.

42. Poole, I., "Genetic Development of Articulation of Consonant Sounds in Speech," *Elementary English Review,* 11 (1934), 159–161.

43. Porter, Douglas, "The Instrumental Value of Sound Cues in Reading." Paper read at the AERA Convention, Atlantic City, N.J., February 17, 1960.

44. Railsback, Charles E., "Consonant Substitution in Word Attack," *Reading Teacher,* 23 (February 1970), 432–435.

45. Rankin, Earl F., and Overholzer, Betsy M., "Reaction of Intermediate Grade Children to Contextual Clues," *Journal of Reading Behavior,* 1 (Summer 1969), 50–73.

46. Samuels, S. Jay, "Modes of Word Recognition," in *Theoretical Models and Processes of Reading,* Harry Singer and Robert B. Ruddell, eds. Newark, Del.: International Reading Association, 1970, 23–37.

47. Spache, George D., "A Phonics Manual for Primary and Remedial Teachers," *Elementary English Review,* 16 (April-May 1939), 147–150, 191–198.

48. Spache, George D., "Limitations of the Phonetic Approach to Developmental and Remedial Reading," in *New Frontiers in Reading,* Proceedings International Reading Association, 5, 1960, 105–108.

49. Spache, George D., Andres, Micaela C., Curtis H. A., et al., *A Longitudinal First Grade Reading Readiness Program.* Cooperative Research Project, No. 2742, Florida State Department of Education, Tallahassee, Fla., 1965.

50. Spache, George D., and Baggett, Mary E., "What Do Teachers Know About Phonics and Syllabication?" *Reading Teacher,* 19 (November 1965), 96–99.

51. Sparks, Paul E., and Fay, Leo C., "An Evaluation of Two Methods of Teaching Reading," *Elementary School Journal,* 57 (April 1957), 589–596.

52. Wardhaugh, Ronald, "Syl-lab-i-ca-tion," *Elemen-*

tary English, 43 (November 1966), 785–788.

53. Waugh, R. F., and Howell, K. W., "Teaching Modern Syllabication," *Reading Teacher,* 29 (October 1975), 20–25.

54. Weaver, Wendell, "The Predictability of Word Meanings," in *New Developments in Programs, Training Aids and Procedures, for College–Adult Reading,* 12th

Yearbook, National Reading Conference, 1963, 152–157.

55. Wheat, Leonard B., "Four Spelling Rules," *Elementary School Journal,* 32 (May 1933), 697–706.

56. Wylie, Richard E., and Durrell, Donald D., "Teaching Vowels Through Phonograms," *Elementary English,* 47 (October 1970), 787–791.

RESOURCES FOR THE TEACHER

Professional References*

Curry, Robert L., and Rigby, Toby W., *Reading Independence Through Word Analysis.* Columbus, Ohio: Charles E. Merrill Publishing Company, 1969. A pretest and manual of exercises.

Dawson, Mildred A., compiler, *Teaching Word Recognition Skills.* Newark, Del.: International Reading Association, 1971. A collection of articles.

Dechant, Emerald, *Linguistics, Phonics and the Teaching of Reading.* Springfield, Ill.: Charles C Thomas, 1969. Contrasts viewpoints on phonic methods.

Durkin, Dolores, *Phonics and the Teaching of Reading.* New York: Teachers College Press, 1965. A review of the phonics curriculum.

Gans, Roma, *Fact and Fiction About Phonics.* Indianapolis, Ind.: The Bobbs–Merrill Co., Inc., 1964.

Gray, William S., *The Teaching of Reading and Writing,* 2nd ed., Ralph C. Staiger, ed. Glenview, Ill.: Scott, Foresman and Company, 1969. A worldwide review of methodology.

Groff, Patrick, *The Syllable—Its Nature and Pedagogical Usefulness.* Portland, Ore.: Northwest Regional Educational Laboratory, 1971. A research-based challenge of the present-day methods and content.

Heilman, Arthur W., *Phonics in Proper Perspective.* Columbus, Ohio: Charles E. Merrill Publishing Company,

1968. A rational review of phonics.

Henderson, Ellen C., *Phonics in Learning To Read: A Handbook for Teachers.* Boston: Exposition Press, 1967.

Hull, Marion A., *Phonics for the Teaching of Reading.* Columbus, Ohio: Charles E. Merrill Publishing Company, 1969. Programmed self-instruction for the teacher.

Schell, Leo M., *Fundamentals of Decoding for Teachers.* Chicago: Rand McNally & Company, 1975.

Schell, Leo M., and Winters, Constance, *Resources for Word Identification.* Manhattan, Kans.: College of Education, Kansas State University, no date. Extensive list of teaching activities.

Spache, Evelyn B., *Reading Activities for Child Involvement.* Boston: Allyn and Bacon, Inc., 1976.

Trela, Thaddeus M., *Sensible Phonics: A Self-Teaching Guide-Book for Teachers.* Belmont, Calif.: Fearon Publishers, 1975.

Waller, Carl J., *Word Attack Skills in Reading.* Columbus, Ohio: Charles E. Merrill Publishing Company, 1969. A general guide.

Wilson, Robert M., and Hall, Mary Anne, *Programmed Word Attack for Teachers.* Columbus, Ohio: Charles E. Merrill Publishing Company, 1968. To help teachers to learn phonics.

INSTRUCTIONAL MATERIALS

Games, Workbooks

Alcock, Dorothea, *Blendograms.* Covina, Calif.: The Author.

* Many other word recognition skill games and activities may be found in the resource books listed in Chapter 10.

Alcock, Dorothea, *Grab.* Covina, Calif.: The Author. A card game.

Alpha One: Breaking the Code. New York: New Dimensions.

Alphabetic Phonics. Cambridge, Mass.: Educators Publishing.

Armstrong, Leila, and Hargrave, Rowena, *Building*

Reading Skills. Wichita, Kans.: McCormick-Mathers. A six-book series.

Bennet, May, *Sound Tunes Kit.* Freeport, N.Y.: Educational Activities, Inc.

Decoding Games. New York: Multimedia Education, Inc.

Dolch, E. W., *Consonant Lotto.* Champaign, Ill.: Garrard Publishing Company. One of a dozen or so games for early phonics. See catalog.

Durrell, Donald D., et al., *Word Analysis Practice.* New York: Harcourt Brace Jovanovich. One of several kits of cards, worksheets by the author.

Fillmore, Nadine, *Steps to Mastery of Words.* Benton Harbor, Mich.: Educational Service. Four workbooks plus five records.

Gifford, Margaret, *Learning the Letters.* Cambridge, Mass.: Educators Publishing, 1963. A six-workbook series.

Goldman-Lynch Sounds and Symbols Development Kit. Circle Pines, Minn.: American Guidance Services, 1971. A program for ages four and one-half to nine in individual speech sounds, for introduction to reading through phonics or speech therapy. Uses diacritical marks to indicate vowel sounds, learning which cannot be transferred to normal reading.

Junior Listen–Hear Classroom Package. Chicago: Follett Corporation. Books to be read to pupils to promote auditory discrimination and phonics.

Key-Lab. Boston: Houghton Mifflin Company. Puzzles and alphabet cards for sound–symbol learning.

La Coste, Roberta, *Patterns, Sounds and Meaning.* Boston: Allyn and Bacon, Inc., 1971. Work texts.

Meighen, Mary, and Pratt, Marjorie, *Phonics We Use.* Chicago: Lyons and Carnahan. Seven-book series of workbooks.

Pepper, Wilma Del, *Read with Me.* Ann Arbor, Mich.: Ann Arbor Publishers. Poetry for alternate or choral reading, with emphasis upon phonics.

Phonic Lingo. Chicago: King. Two sets of cards for Bingo-like games with letter sounds.

Phonics We Use—Learning Games Kit. Chicago: Lyons and Carnahan. A box of ten phonic games for small-group use.

Phonovisual Method. Washington, D.C.: Phonovisual Products. Group of charts, workbooks, texts, and games offering a systematic phonics program.

Spelling Learning Games Kit. Chicago: Lyons and Carnahan. Twenty-five games on phonics in spelling.

PROGRAMMED MATERIALS

Bishop, Margaret M., *Making Sounds Work, with Write and See.* New York: New Century.

Bishop, Margaret M., *Phonics with Write and See.* New York: Appleton-Century-Crofts. These are five- and three-book workbook series with special crayon which indicates correct answers by evoking color from the page.

Bondanza, William J., and Bacci, William A., *Phonics for Pupils.* New London, Conn.: Croft Educational. Two brief programs covering the whole phonics curriculum.

Carroll, Lucy, *Programmed Phonics.* Cambridge, Mass.: Education Publishing. Tape or script read by teacher gives directions for programmed workbook.

Cyclo-Teacher. Chicago: Field Enterprises. Phonic wheels forming words to be inserted in special machine.

Fitzhugh, Loren, and Fitzhugh, Kathleen, *Fitzhugh Plus Program.* Galien, Mich.: Allied Education Council. A program in phonics for beginning readers.

Lepehne, Renate, *Building Words.* Cambridge, Mass.: Honor Products. A short program in structural analysis.

Loretan, Joseph O., ed., *Building Reading Power.* Columbus, Ohio: Charles E. Merrill Publishing Company, 1964. Offers several programmed booklets on contextual clues and structural analysis for fifth grade and up.

Markle, Susan Meyer, *Words.* Chicago: Science Research Associates. A lengthy structural analysis workbook for upper elementary grades.

Mott Reading Programs. Galien, Mich.: Allied Education Council. Semiprogrammed phonics workbooks for each grade level.

SELECTED AUDIOVISUAL MATERIALS

Bremner, Al J., and Davis, Josephine T., *The Sound Way to Easy Reading.* Wilmette, Ill.: Bremner-Davis

Phonics. Records and cards for repetitive drill.

Bulletin Board of Basic Phonics. Fremont, Calif.: Educational Aids.

Dialog I. Chester, Conn.: Chester Electronic Labs, 1963. Tapes, booklets, and record forms.

Direct Approach Audio-Visual Method to Phonetics. Buffalo, N.Y.: Kenworthy Educational Service. Three long-playing records, charts, and worksheets for primary grades.

Directional Phonics Program. North Hollywood, Calif.: Teaching Technology. Tapes, strips, records, and workbooks.

Discovery Phonics. Glenview, Ill.: Psychotechnics. Color transparencies and worksheets.

Easy Way to Difficult Sounds. Kankakee, Ill.: Imperial Productions, Inc. Tape of six stories, each emphasizing a consonant sound.

Edson, Ann, *Phonics and Word Development.* Freeport, N.Y.: Educational Activities, Inc. Tapes or records.

Elligson, Dolly K., *Seals, Sea Gulls and Other Sounds.* Chicago: Systems for Education. Kit of records and booklets.

First Talking Alphabet. Glenview, Ill.: Scott, Foresman and Company. Twenty records and sound–picture cards.

Foster, Lawrence J., et al., *Singing Sounds.* North Hollywood, Calif.: Bowman Records. Records and workbooks.

Hardwick, Bettie L., *New Auditory Visual Response Phonics.* Shafter, Calif.: Polyphone. Tapes, textbook, and workbooks.

Hear-See-Say Phonics Approach. Hawthorne, Calif.: Teaching Aids Institute. Records and wall charts.

Independent Word Perception. New York: Association Films. Three sets of twelve strips each.

Insel, Eunice, *Ear-Eye-Hand Phonics.* Freeport, N.Y.: Educational Activities, Inc. Five albums, ten activity books on initial consonants.

Instructional Tapes. Kankakee, Ill.: Imperial. Tapes, charts, and workbooks.

Jones, Ernest A., *Phonics in a Nutshell.* Oklahoma City, Okla.: Educational Electronics. Nine strips and records.

Landon, Alline, *Landon Phonics Program.* San Francisco: Chandler Publishing Company, 1967. Tapes and worksheets.

Learning To Read with Phonics. Hawthorne, Calif.: Teaching Aids Institute. Three records and their workbooks.

Listening with Mr. Bunny Big Ears. Freeport, N.Y.: Educational Activities, Inc. Six long-playing records to promote dramatic play based on stories emphasizing consonant sounds.

McAuliffe, Garth L., *Decoding for Reading.* New York: Macmillan Publishing Co., Inc., 1969. Sixteen records and workbooks.

McIntyre, Barbara M., and Irwin, Eleanor C., *Countdown for Listening.* Freeport, N.Y.: Educational Activities, Inc. Six records for phonics and listening skills.

McKee, Paul, ed., *Listen and Do.* Boston: Houghton Mifflin Company, 1963. Sixteen records and ditto masters, emphasizing context and initial consonant sounds as clues.

O'Connor Remedial Services, *Audio-Visual Charts.* Birmingham, Mich.: O'Connor. Fourteen phonics charts in this set, plus six more in "Corrective Reading Roll-Up Charts."

Percepta-Phonics. Los Angeles: Rheem Califone, Inc. Twenty-five taped lessons on vowel sounds.

Phonic Talking Letters. Chicago: Ideal. Story cards presenting phonic elements.

Phonics. St. Paul, Minn.: Visual Products Division, 3M. Six sets, each of twenty-two transparencies or spirit master copies.

Phonics Charts. Chicago: Ideal. Large charts presenting objects related to letter sounds.

Phonics—Initial Consonant Sounds. New York: Multimedia Education, Inc. Six sets of three records and six filmstrips each to present beginning phonics in narrative materials.

Phonics and Word Development. Freeport, N.Y.: Educational Activities, Inc. A set of records and tapes for first six grades in phonics, structural analysis, and spelling.

Primary Picture Alphabet. Tremont, Calif.: Educational Aids. Cards offering letter, picture, and word associated with phonic elements.

Smith, Mary C., *Reading Made Easy with Phonics.* Chicago: King. Fourteen phonics lessons on one long-playing record, with flash cards.

Sounds and Stories. Oklahoma City, Okla.: The Economy Company. Twenty cassettes and worksheets for exercises.

Sounds for Young Readers. Freeport, N.Y.: Educational Activities, Inc. Six long-playing records for primary grades, two for review with older children.

Starter Set. Boston: Houghton Mifflin Company. A kit for relating the names and sounds of letters to objects, pictures, etc.

Wheel Transparencies. Boston: Camboso Scientific. Twenty-one transparencies for phonics. Other sets for syllabication and context clues.

12
Building Sight and Meaning Vocabulary

PREVIEW

Like many other facets of reading instruction, the task of vocabulary development is undergoing reexamination and reevaluation. The drill procedures, the dependence upon sheer repetition, even the criteria of success as word calling or matching words and definitions are being questioned. The factors which influence vocabulary growth most significantly may lie in the classroom or school climate, the language experience in the family or community setting, as well as in the directed teaching efforts of the teacher. For all these reasons, classroom development of sight and meaning vocabularies in reading is undergoing change.

New concepts about vocabulary include the realization that there are a number of different vocabularies. To mention only a few, there are distinctly different groups of words in the child's speaking, listening, writing, and reading vocabularies. Promotion of each of these vocabularies requires differing experiences which must be presented in the medium in which new terms are to be used. Knowledge of words does not readily carry over from reading or listening to speaking or writing, or from any one medium to the other.

Another basic concept which is beginning to influence vocabulary training is the recognition that words are not learned as of a certain date because of a certain number of repetitions. Rather, words are thoroughly understood only as a group of associations is built around each word, associations which include multiple meanings, and visual, auditory, and perhaps kinesthetic imagery. Accepting this concept of vocabulary growth makes the teacher's task one of providing multifaceted experiences with words—their meanings and their usage—in a variety of settings and contexts, rather than a task of providing drill and massive repetitions.

Many writers and teachers use the term "vocabulary" as though it referred to a single kind of learning with words. They may be speaking of the child's speech—his sentence length, choice of words, and fluency. Or, if he is in the primary-grade reading stages, they may be discussing the number of words he recognizes without analysis or help—his sight vocabulary. The same general term is also used to describe the variety of words that the pupil uses in his spontaneous writings—his writing vocabulary, or those words whose meanings he ultimately understands in reading—his meaning vocabulary. At other times the term "vocabulary" is used to mean the words that a child can hear and understand—his listening vocabulary. But every teacher knows that a pupil has these several vocabularies which differ in breadth, accuracy, and the fluency with which the child uses each.

These various vocabularies are not equivalent or synonymous at any time in the child's development. Before he learns to speak, he often demonstrates a sizable listening vocabulary, and even after he has begun talking, his ability to comprehend auditorily exceeds his own speech vocabulary markedly. In fact, the average person can listen to and understand more words and more complex language patterns than he uses in his ordinary speech probably throughout his entire lifetime. Similarly, his listening vocabulary exceeds his meaning and sight vocabularies in reading until he reaches secondary school age. At this point, if he has developed good reading abilities, he begins to read more complex material than he can listen to. At the same time, the child's writing vocabulary lags far behind his speaking, reading, and listening vocabularies, and probably continues to be inferior indefinitely. Thus at no time in his life is his growth precisely similar in the various types of vocabulary.

Just what is the significance of our interpretation of the term vocabulary? It is important to recognize the differences among various kinds of vocabulary growth simply to avoid the loose thinking and faulty teaching practices based on the assumption that a pupil has a "vocabulary." Understanding and use of words does not transfer readily from one language medium to another. The child does not easily write the new words he has learned by listening or reading, and he does not tend to incorporate these same words into his daily speech. New words learned from reading or listening are often only imperfectly understood. Moreover, the school climate is not conducive to oral experimentation with new words, for such attempts are likely to meet with ridicule from peers. Pupils and adults tend to depend upon commonplace, conversational terms rather than on the more precise words they learn from reading or listening. Because of these almost universal tendencies, classroom practices which assume that vocabulary is a unitary trait or that a pupil will use in speech or writing the words he is taught by certain reading exercises fail to accomplish their purposes. Classroom practices which attempt to teach a child to write or spell most of the words he learns in reading or listening or to use these in his speech are not realistic. Listening to a teacher explain new terms, looking up lists of new words in the dictionary, completing artificial exercises in workbooks, and similar common practices do not necessarily help to increase the child's reading vocabularies. This is a matter of concern when we are discussing methods of improving reading ability.

In the activity of reading, there are two basic vocabularies—sight vocabulary and meaning vocabulary. Sight vocabulary includes those words that the primary-grade pupil recognizes visually and by the aid of his auditory memories for each word. His recognition is aided by his training in phonics and structural and contextual analysis. Meaning vocabulary includes those words for which the child has a number of meaningful mental associations. The word may not be in his listening vocabulary, and he may not be able to pronounce it correctly. Knowledge of the meanings of roots and affixes, and recognition of a known base word may aid in clarifying the meaning. But he finally recognizes the meaning of the word as used in each particular reading context. When we speak of the child's reading vocabulary at the primary-grade levels, we usually mean his sight vocabulary. When we refer to his reading vocabulary in the intermediate and upper elementary grades, we are really referring to his meaning vocabulary.

We make these distinctions between sight and meaning vocabularies deliberately, because in many classroom practices, particularly in primary grades, they are assumed to be synonymous. If a child can recognize and name a printed word, it is often presumed that he must be familiar with its meanings. For this reason, observers since the time of Horace Greely have been disturbed by the fluent word naming of many children that is not accompanied with the comprehension of the message. Word calling is rampant in our schools at all educational levels and in every field of learning. Teachers and some reading experts who attempt to judge comprehension by the fluency, phrasing, and expression of the oral reader are similarly misled. As we point out in our discussion of oral reading, very good oral performances are not proof of comprehension, either in oral or silent reading. Being able to read lists of words at sight does not prove that these same words are correctly interpreted in the context of a passage. The performance is evidence only that these words have become familiar visually and auditorily as printed symbols, not necessarily as meaningful ideas. For these reasons, we will emphasize the differences between these two types of reading vocabulary throughout this discussion of vocabulary development.

INFLUENCES UPON READING VOCABULARY GROWTH

The school is certainly not the only or even the major influence upon the child's development of sight and meaning vocabularies. The ability of the primary school child to develop a sight vocabulary in early reading is highly dependent upon his auditory memories for words. If he is limited in verbal intelligence or in experiences with words because of bilingualism, poor family or cultural background, narrow preschool verbal experiences, and the like, the child will lack an auditory background for acquiring an adequate sight or meaning vocabulary. The intellectual interests of the family and the level of its verbal intercommunication also condition the child's readiness for reading vocabulary growth. Throughout the elementary years the pupil's play and reading interests, hobbies, and pastimes influence his vocabulary development. Although in general they tend to lag behind girls, boys' vocabularies show distinct breadth in their areas of interest such as sports and science. Girls tend to show greater overall development in vocabulary and less tendency to excel in specific areas of high interest. Thus we see that a number of factors other than the school's efforts influence the development of vocabulary both before and after the child enters school.

Direct efforts to promote vocabulary development begin almost the day the child enters school. By providing many verbal and visual experiences, and listening and speaking opportunities, the school attempts to strengthen the average child's auditory readiness for reading. The vitality and spontaneity of the curriculum offered to the pupils as well as the very atmosphere of the classroom exert powerful influences upon vocabulary development. The freedoms to explore, to be curious, to question and discover determine ultimately the breadth and depth of this development, or by their absence stifle and restrict it. Other classroom efforts to promote sight vocabulary at the primary-grade levels— acquiring a broad classroom library, training in word recognition skills, language activities which reinforce the reading vocabulary, and the prolific use of word games and audiovisual aids—are reasonably effective in supporting early sight vocabulary development. Training in the use of the dictionary, varied exercises in manipulating word meanings, workbooks and games emphasizing word study probably make a small contribution to growth of meaning vocabulary. But in our opinion these planned efforts on the part of the school have much less effect than the cultural and socioeconomic backgrounds. Some children respond to the school's planned and indirect influences upon vocabulary development but probably are more conditioned by extra-school factors to function close to a level commensurate with their cultural and social backgrounds. A few are driven by their own efforts or by the school's training to function on distinctly higher linguistic levels than those from which they started. On the other hand, most eventually learn to read about as well as might be expected in view of their verbal intelligence and sociological backgrounds, a level probably adequate to their ultimate vocational and cultural interests.

HOW PUPILS LEARN WORDS

The bases for all early vocabulary learning are the child's firsthand experiences. For example, hundreds of tactile, visual, and psychomotor observations underlie the words *rough* and *smooth*. These nonverbal contacts must also be reinforced and associated with a number of auditory and speech experiences with the same words in varying language patterns and contexts. Collectively, these multisensory concepts determine and are essential to understanding of the tools we call "words." Contrast this variety of experiences, if you will, with the common five-minute prereading blackboard or flash card drill that the primary school teacher sometimes offers in the naive belief that she is teaching the group the new sight vocabulary of the reading lesson. How effective can this superficial presentation be in the absence of multisensory experience with these words? The presentation of these words is pointless unless the children already know the words from previous auditory or firsthand experiences. Since they usually do know the words, what is accomplished by the prereading presentation, other than associating the visual and auditory image which might be better accomplished in the context of the story?

However, direct teaching of vocabulary probably produces superior growth to incidental methods. Intensive emphasis at primary-grade levels pays dividends in increased sight and meaning vocabularies and improved comprehension. In fact, at these early stages of development such training may appear to produce quite dramatic gains, insofar as these are measured by common vocabulary and reading tests. With older elementary school pupils and at secondary and collegiate levels, intensive vocabulary programs show gains but usually of a much less striking nature. Improvement is often linked to verbal intelligence, with the brighter pupils showing the greater gains. In one experiment duller pupils did not profit from the abstract word parts but did appear to improve in the more primitive skill of visual discrimination of words and word parts. But careful review of much of our direct training for meaning vocabulary shows there is still much to be desired. Drills with synonyms and antonyms, matching, categorizing, and the like ignore the multiplicity of meanings of many words and the basic fact that the meaning intended is often dependent upon the context. For example, many exercises tend to emphasize only the commonest meaning of a word such as *fast,* a word for which most dictionaries offer six or eight different definitions. These word drills also assume that there is a direct transfer of the learning to the reading situation. How do exercises with singular or common meanings help the pupil to interpret the uncommon, multiple meanings he encounters in his reading? Despite these limitations and weak assumptions, these planned efforts probably produce more development and transfer to various language media than the incidental learning which results simply from casual classroom word activities or general reading. Extensive or intensive reading undoubtedly also makes some contribution to reading vocabulary but probably less than planned, direct teaching.

There are many natural ways in which pupils learn correct or incorrect meanings of words, by their auditory or visual similarity to other words: assumption of total meaning from recognition of one major part of the word—*earnest* means earn something; the influence of a figure of speech—*brawny* means smart because of confusion with the common expression "brains and brawn"; and associations with familiar experiences—"that boy dawdles." Certainly most reading authorities agree in recognizing these naturalistic contributions to vocabulary development but favor direct, inspirational teaching. Teachers, on the other hand, tend to prefer those vocabulary activities which involve little or no direct teaching—dictionary use, context, and incidental and informal attention. These same teachers consider vocabulary card files, lists given by the teacher or from the textbook, exercises in classifying, grouping words, or writing them in sentences as least effective, an opinion shared by many reading experts. To sum up this discussion of how pupils learn words, we may repeat that the foundations of voabulary are (1) vital firsthand experiences, (2) direct teaching which provides many meaningful associations, and (3) incidental learning from casual contact with words through one or several language media.

LEARNING SIGHT VOCABULARY

The Experience Chart

Our approach to beginning reading emphasized the use of experience charts as the initial reading medium. We suggested that such charts form the basis of common language experiences for the gifted readers until they are ready for individualized reading and thereafter serve as a type of group reading activity. In the average and slow-learning groups, the chart approach would serve as a group activity during the readiness period and thereafter as a supplement to the basal program. In our opinion the experience chart can continue to be useful in a variety of purposeful group activities during the intermediate grades.

Before formal reading activities and also after these have begun, the chart is a prime means of promoting growth in sight vocabulary. In the fast-moving group, it helps provide a common core of words among those pupils pursuing their own reading interests. In all the reading groups, the chart offers the teacher an opportunity to observe pupils' knowledge of sight words and their use of word recognition skills. Charts offer also an opportunity for repetition and reinforcement which are necessary for permanent learning. The teacher can arrange for repetition in interesting ways by emphasizing sensory appeals such as repetitive sounds, rhythm, rhyme, and words stressing color. This principle can be kept in mind and approached carefully without stifling the spontaneity and creativity of the pupils' compositions. Similarly, the important service words, as listed by Fry (7) or Dolch (5), will be repeated frequently in children's charts. These lists tend to include the connectives, conjunctions, prepositions, and the like that play so large a part in all written materials. These words are more difficult to learn than the nouns, verbs, and even many of the polysyllabic words that find their way into the charts. Because of their frequency, difficulty, and significance for comprehension, these service words should (and probably will be) frequently repeated in the charts but not at the expense of stultifying their content.

Words that should be learned are best approached in meaningful pairs, as "the *cow* chased the *ball*" or "the *cow* behind the *ball*." This linking is more effective using verbs and prepositions than conjunctions, as "the *cow* and the *ball*." Grouping words to be learned according to common experiential bases, as *moon–night–dark* or *sun–light–day* are effective presentations. Also, grouping and learning words that are related in meanings, as *talk–speak–shout;* or in rhyming, as *I–eye* is more effective than grouping based on structural or spelling patterns, as *age, ago, fat, pat (25)*.

Sight vocabulary learning will also derive from the pupil's self-help efforts, such as keeping a list or notebook or card file of new words. With the aid of another pupil, the child may use these words for the basis of reviews, games, a picture dictionary, a resource list for his writing, exercises in categorizing or classifying words according to their type (name of something showing action or description—for example, vegetable, animal, mineral, or zoo, farm, school) or the number of syllables or phonic, suffix, prefix, or root elements, and other activities. There is recent evidence that these inductive self-help exercises in analyzing and sorting words are very effective, especially for poorer readers. In some instances this approach is even more effective than exercises in learning vocabulary based upon knowledge of phonic and syllabication rules.

Meeting Individual Differences

We have referred from time to time to the *Learning Methods Test (16)* as a means of meeting individual differences in aptitude for learning sight vocabulary. Robert E. Mills *(15)* has adequately described this testing–teaching technique, but it bears repeating. After testing pupils for their sight knowledge of a group of words, the teacher selects several that are unknown to each pupil or largely unfamiliar to a group of pupils. This list of words is not a random selection but a group carefully selected for similarity of difficulty in length, degree of abstractness, and other comparable elements. A list for each of the primary-grade levels is available on small cards from Dr. Mills, The Mills Center, 1512 E. Broward Blvd., Ft. Lauderdale, Fla. A group of fifteen unknown words is taught by the visual method, another group, by the auditory method, a third group, by the kinesthetic method, and a fourth, by the combination approach. Immediately after each twenty- to thirty-minute lesson, each pupil's learning of the words is tested by having him try to read each word at sight. His learning is tested again one day later and the number of words learned at this time by each type of lesson is recorded. Differences as small as two or three more words learned by any one method indicate a reliable aptitude for that method. The indication of the *Learning Methods Test* can then be followed with individual pupils or small groups to ensure most effective learning of sight vocabulary. Pupils who show distinct aptitude for visual, phonic, or kinesthetic learning probably should be grouped and taught accordingly.

As Mills and others who have followed this testing–teaching approach have found, no one method of teaching word recognition is intrinsically superior to the others. Gifted children, as a group, learn words easily by any of these presentations; slow learners seem to learn with the most difficulty by the phonic approach.

But for children in general, one presentation is as effective as another. The point of the sampling of methods by the *Learning Methods Test* is to discover the individual pupils who demonstrate an unsuspected aptitude for more effective learning by some one method of presentation. Those teachers who have used this diagnostic procedure are extremely gratified by the clarity of its indications. Pupils who would learn much more effectively by a particular presentation are readily identified and their success in early reading thus fostered.

The controlled conditions used in the *Learning Methods Test* and its reliable results cannot readily be duplicated in imitative experiments in the classroom. The test words must be carefully selected for equality in several characteristics that influence their learning. The controls of teaching time, purity of the type of presentation, and rotation of methods among groups cannot be observed without very careful planning. For these reasons we do not recommend that teachers attempt this procedure without the detailed directions and word lists supplied in the inexpensive *Learning Methods Test Kit* (16). Extensive experimentation in the use of the kit in the individual or group diagnosis demonstrates that even the inexperienced teacher has no great difficulties in using or interpreting the materials (20).

John Paul Jones (10) has written a comprehensive review of the research on modality testing and teaching. Several of the studies he cites followed the Mills technique, with various results. Among the conclusions possible are (1) that the Mills test can identify the preferred modality for some children, (2) modality preference does not seem as significant for good readers as for poor readers, and (3) modality preference is an individual matter, not a group or class phenomenon. In a group situation, the individual differences tend to cancel each other, so that one method does not seem more efficient than another based on group results (3).

Modality preferences seem to vary over time among both good and poor readers. Thus we have very little evidence that teaching the apparently preferred modality over a long term is profitable. Another problem in interpreting the effectiveness of modality teaching is the fact that the child may be translating the approach and learning through other channels than we intend. Because words are not a unimodal experience as simply a visual memory, or an auditory memory, or a kinesthetic gestalt, or a tactile sensation, the child may actually be learning the words by some combination of cues that may or may not include the modality stressed in the lesson (29).

Following the indications of the Mills technique does not offer a complete solution to difficulties in word recognition. But, changing from the previous method to the modality apparently preferred by the child will provide a degree of success, at least temporarily, if for no other reason than because of the newness of the method. The sense of failure that the child may be experiencing can thus be relieved. As this Hawthorne effect wears off and the initial success diminishes, other modality cues may be introduced (or appear spontaneously in the child's learning) to restimulate his progress. We believe it is most essential to explore new, stimulating approaches in this fashion to try to maintain the child's positive self-concept as a reader.

In our opening chapter on reading as a perceptual process, we emphasized the variety of ways in which children learn sight vocabulary. Because some authors of reading materials for primary-school children ignore these natural word recognition techniques, we think it important to review their implications again. Some writers tell us that our current methods are faulty; they say that children do not recognize words by their shape, their context, and such clues. They believe that children read the letters, recognize the sounds for which they stand, translate the letter sounds into words, and thus recognize words (2,4). To these authors, the clues given by a familiar sentence, the outline of the word formed by the ascending and descending letters, the stimulus of the recognition of sounds of the first letter or two plus the sentence, the recognition of two familiar words in a compound, and similar perceptual stimuli just don't matter, or don't even exist. Only the recognition of the separate letters or the sounds of all of these are significant, they say. In keeping with his particular reasoning, we see primary-grade reading materials offered which carefully control the appearance of letters, doling these out, as it were, a few at a time (8). Other readers offer sequences of words one group at a time, each of which contains the same vowel sounds or a particular two- or three-letter combination (2). Still others offer a complete new alphabet in which each new symbol represents all the possible spellings of a sound, such as the long sound of *i* (6). All of these, and others still to appear, depend exclusively upon the assumption that letter–sound recognition is essential before word recognition can occur.

A few minutes spent in the average American primary-school classroom observing children's spontaneous efforts to identify words should dispel this absurd assumption. Every day, children who do not know one letter of the alphabet from another, or any of the variant sounds for which one letter may stand, or any of the many ways in which a sound or phoneme may be represented orthographically, learn to read. Children recognize words by a wide variety of clues ranging from one extreme—an inspection of some letters and details—to the other extreme—simply guessing that so-and-so would make sense in the sentence. Numerous experiments in analyzing the word recognition techniques of older students and adults confirm the persistence of this variety of word recognition techniques. Even pupils trained in a method emphasizing recognition solely by letter sounds gradually abandon this technique and adopt a variety of approaches. Studies of the eye-movement photographs of readers of all ages and of the elements and parts of words perceived when words are exposed for a fraction of a second unmistakably prove these facts. The values for word recognition and spelling of mechanical training by tachistoscopes, filmstrips, and other devices which expose words too rapidly for a letter-by-letter translation again demonstrate that the true nature of the word recognition process is not a letter-by-letter or a sound-by-sound recognition.

It is true, of course, that letters stand for speech sounds. Even the primary-school child eventually recognizes that reading is simply talking written down. We did not have to wait for the new science of linguistics to discover that reading is an extension of speech. But we should not attempt to explain the entire process of word recognition as a matter of translating words letter by letter into the speech sounds they represent. Children can learn to read by a letter-by-letter sounding approach but almost every objective study of the results of this method shows that it delays or prevents the very goal it claims to accomplish—rapid, facile word recognition and letter comprehension.

These divergent interpretations of the true nature of word recognition are the basis for the current conflict between the "sight-word" and "phonics" schools, as we have pointed out elsewhere. More recently, the disagreement has been used as the basis of an attack upon current reading instruction by certain groups of linguists, as we have also pointed out in reviewing the thinking of these groups. The heart of the argument lies in the interpretation of the significance of the alphabet. The phonics and linguistic schools argue that since letters represent speech sounds they must be the basis of every act of word recognition. We believe, in company with many other reading specialists, that this is *confusing the reading process with the reading unit.* Certainly, letters represent speech sounds and reading is, in one sense, a process of recognizing the meanings of speech sounds set down in symbolic fashion. But we have proven that word recognition is not often accomplished by a unit translation of the symbols for speech sounds into mental words or spoken sounds. This is not to say that children need never learn the alphabet or its many sound equivalents, for these skills are essential to phonic and structural analysis, which in turn are foundational to full development of word recognition skill. But the translation of written letters into sounds is not *the basis* of early or mature word recognition, however useful it may eventually become as a supplementary skill.

Early Cues to Word Recognition

Children spontaneously discriminate among words by similarities and differences in the following ways:

1. Unusual length—as *grandmother*.
2. Shape—as ⌐‿‿⌐ *beautiful*.
3. Base words—as *smile* in *smiled*.
4. Context—The kitten likes to drink _____.
5. Picture clues.
6. Compounds—as *milkman*.
7. Initial letters or sounds—as *boy, box, ball*.
8. Internal details or cluster analysis—as in *apple, look*.

One other word recognition technique is used by primary-school children and sometimes mistakenly promoted by teachers. This is the attempt to recognize small words within other words, and use these small words as a guide to pronunciation. Unfortunately, the lack of consistent relationship between sounds and symbols in our language makes this technique impractical. The common little words which appear to be present in larger words vary considerably in their pronunciation within different contexts. For example, contrast the sounds of *in* when it appears in *line, tin, ring, singing, drink,* and other such words. The small words—*on, an, is, it, at, are, be,* and the like—are not sound guides to the pronunciation and recognition of the words within which they may be found.

The eight other word recognition techniques comprising the sight-word approach should be strengthened as much as possible in the daily reading lesson. In promoting sight vocabulary from experience charts, basals, or trade books, these recognition clues should constantly be emphasized. Children should be urged to compare lengths, shapes, details, base words, and other characteristics of words visually, auditorily, and kinesthetically. The last of these comparisons may include drawing word outlines, laying them upon or next to or under others, tracing outlines through transparent paper, and trying to read words when only the outline, or the outline and the initial letter or two, are given *in a sentence.* Speed in recognition of familiar words is desirable and may be promoted through judicious use of games (*26*) and far-point or hand tachistoscopes, provided that speed of presentation is emphasized only after a high degree of accuracy is obtained.

These sight-word recognition techniques naturally lead to and blend with phonic, contextual, and structural analysis as outlined earlier. But these clues are never completely displaced by the more structured technique. The clues are refined and made more discriminative by the formal training in other word recognition skills, but they are still present in mature, adult reading.

LEARNING MEANING VOCABULARY

The goals of meaning vocabulary training as suggested by reading textbooks, workbooks, and professional articles are apparently very diverse. Judging by the exercise materials offered in some sources, the primary goal would seem to be the memorization of the meanings of a certain list of words collected by a teacher or author. How realistic is a specific list of a certain number of words which are supposed to be taught at each grade level? Beyond the first thousand or so commonest words in printed or handwritten materials, who really knows just what words most pupils need to learn during a particular school year? In the authors' opinion many lists are offered on very questionable grounds, for there is no agreement among their authors upon the proper sources for compiling such lists. Some lists are drawn from the study of child or adult writing, some by sampling a certain dictionary, others by sampling the textbooks and teaching materials used at a certain grade level. A few lists seem to represent simply the author's concepts of pupils' needs, without reference to any objective criterion. Are the words used in the spontaneous writings of adults, or even those of children, the words most necessary for reading comprehension, or are they really the words children should learn to spell in order to express themselves in writing? While there is an overlap in these two vocabularies, the one which functions in reading must obviously be much larger than the writing vocabulary. How does sampling every nth word from a dictionary prove that these are essential for reading success? Of these various sources of words for meaning vocabulary study, only current textbooks and other reading materials would appear to be related realistically to pupil needs for reading development.

Much of the research and training materials seem to be predicated on the assumption that simply enlarging the reading vocabulary by any means is the desired goal. Little attention is paid to the breadth of concepts with which the words are linked. In our opinion, this common approach to vocabulary building can result only in word calling or verbalism, not in the development of words (or ideas) with which the individual thinks.

There is another conflict of opinion among the authors of meaning vocabulary exercises concerning the aims of the exercises. Some authors apparently think that the goal is for the pupil to learn the commonest meanings of a certain number of words which, as we have seen, may be drawn from a questionable source. Other writers, ourselves included, believe that the training is intended to equip the pupil with efficient methods of attacking, analyzing, and comprehending word meanings. This latter group has grave doubts about the validity of most lists of words and about exercises that tend to deal with words apart from meaningful contexts.

Studies from reading clinics and other sources offer strong support for the emphasis upon word analysis skills. The difficulties of poor readers are frequently observed to be due to their lesser skill in word attack, rather than to less exposure to lists of words. Weaknesses in phonic, structural, and contextual analysis are often the basic explanation of the poor sight and meaning vocabularies of these pupils.

Approaches to Training

Olive S. Niles, a secondary school reading specialist, and many others (17) have suggested that meaning vocabulary training must (1) be interesting and challenging to pupils; (2) provide positive reinforcement for learning; (3) be self-pacing or otherwise individualized to pupil needs; (4) stress a wide variety of activities with words, most frequently in contextual settings; and (5) emphasize words of permanent value. These authors also stress the need to teach the multiplicity of meanings of most words, the need to provide for application of the learning in other language activities such as writing and speech, and the need to teach word meanings by a variety of visual, auditory, and kinesthetic experiences with each word.

Probably the best sources of the words to be stressed in meaning vocabulary training are the daily reading and study materials of the classroom, if we assume that there is reasonable breadth in these materials. Words from the experience charts, the basals and trade books, as well as the technical vo-cabularies of the texts are appropriate. Teachers who are unsure of the significant technical terms to be stressed in each content field may make temporary lists based on the glossaries and indexes of their pupils' textbooks and by inspection of the classroom textbooks. To these primary sources may be added children's own lists of the difficult and interesting words they have encountered. It is true that many pupils, even college students, may be unaware of their inability to define or use accurately many of the difficult words they meet. They often just don't know what words they don't know well and fail to add such to their personal lists. But this ignorance may be combated by the emphasis on words of permanent value as drawn from readers, textbooks, and the like. Despite their limitations, personal lists provide a necessary element of interest and individuality to word study. Teachers must try to develop an interest in words and stimulate independent study. Teachers should ensure frequent opportunities for pupils to report on findings and progress in building personal lists and for sharing these lists with others.

Several writers stress, and properly so, the desirability of training pupils for a more-or-less systematic approach to new, difficult words. Niles (17) suggests that pupils should be helped to recognize that practically all polysyllabic words fall into one of these types:

1. Compound words, as *honeydew, Yellowstone.*
2. Known words with affixes, as *unsystematic, unbreakable.*
3. Familiar syllable is largest recognizable element, as *laboratory, foundation.*
4. Sufficiently nonphonetic to need dictionary, as *louver, ricochet, quay.*

In effect, Niles is suggesting that a pupil should analyze a word first by its major elements or most recognizable part; second, by adding to this base word the variations given by his knowledge of the meanings of the affixes; and third, if this analysis plus the context does not lead to recognition of the word, by turning to the dictionary. One author offers a series of steps by which pupils should approach a word for its meaning:

1. Check or underline it. Try to get the meaning from context. Go on reading.
2. Break it up. Try to recognize parts, guess at total meaning.
3. Sound it out. Perhaps then the word may be recalled.
4. Look it up in the dictionary. Pronounce it, notes its parts and various meanings. Select the appropriate meaning for the context.

Use of the Dictionary

It is apparent that these systematic habits of word analysis are built upon phonic, structural, and contextual training such as we have outlined earlier. In addition, these approaches imply that pupils have been trained in effective use of the dictionary. This reference tool involves at least two real problems—the vitality of the teaching and the number of subskills involved. Many studies show that stereotyped training in use of the dictionary fails in its purposes. Simply looking up teacher-made or personal lists of words for their meanings does very little to improve vocabulary. Such words are divorced from their contexts and their connotative associations in reading. Furthermore, the practice limits the child's concepts of the values of a dictionary by failing to help him to realize that it may also be a source for assistance in pronunciation, derivation, spelling, and usage. Once the skills needed to handle a dictionary effectively have been taught, further practice should be varied among these possible uses.

Our research with a dictionary test for secondary school pupils indicates that these various skills overlap and interrelate markedly. The abilities to use a dictionary for pronunciation and spelling, and for spelling and derivation, are particularly related, for obvious reasons. Skills in dealing with meanings and derivation are only slightly less interdependent. Perhaps the implication here is that related uses might be taught simultaneously.

Dictionary Skills

Needed To Locate Words

1. Knowledge of alphabetical order, from A to Z.
2. Knowledge of alphabetical sequences or relative position of each letter in the entire order, for example, *D* is in the first quarter, *M* is in the middle, *V* is in the last quarter, etc.
3. Ability to alphabetize by first, first two, or first three letters.
4. Knowledge of the value of thumb indexes.
5. Ability to interpret guide words and their clues to alphabetic position, for example, the word *strong* would be found somewhere between the guide words *strange* and *structure*.
6. Knowledge that derived or inflected forms do not necessarily immediately adjoin the root word, for example, *streaky* may not immediately follow *streak*.
7. Knowledge that complete meanings may not be given for all inflected or derived forms of root words and that it may therefore be necessary to consult the entry under the root word.

Needed To Derive Pronunciation

1. Knowledge of consonant and vowel sounds and their combinations, and ability to recognize the symbols for each in the pronunciation key.
2. Ability to blend letter sounds into syllables or pronunciation units, and these, in turn, into complete words.
3. Recognize the meanings of common diacritical marks as used to indicate vowel sounds.
4. Recognize the syllabic divisions and the effect of primary and secondary accents.
5. Ability in reading phonetic respelling.
6. Willingness to pronounce word aloud in order to create an auditory memory for it.

7. Recognition of the possible effect upon pronunciation of words that vary in usage, or in pronunciation of inflected forms, for example, *ac'cent* versus *accent'uate*, *pro'gress* versus *pro gress'*.

Needed To Derive Appropriate Meaning

1. Ability to comprehend the definitions offered.
2. Ability in using illustrations, pictures, diagrams, or examples given in comprehending the meaning.
3. Recognition that a word may have many meanings, that the first definition is neither necessarily relevant to given context nor the most common meaning in some dictionaries.
4. Ability to try several definitions in the given context and to select the most appropriate.
5. Ability in adapting the appropriate definition to the context in which the word occurs.
6. Comprehension of the approved usage of the word, as a noun, verb, etc.

Needed for Use of Dictionary for Spelling

1. Knowledge of variant spellings of common sounds.
2. Knowledge of common silent initial letters, such as *kn, gn, wr, pn*.
3. Recognition of dictionary's method of handling compounds, separates, hyphenated words, and plurals.
4. Ability to recognize dictionary's method of indicating syllabic division.

Needed for Use of Dictionary for Usage

1. Knowledge of meanings of usage terms and abbreviations, for example, *n, t.v.*
2. Knowledge of functions of various parts of speech, for example, transitive verb denotes action.
3. Understanding of possibility of multiple functions of a word, as one which may function both as a noun and a verb, for example, *progress.*
4. Understanding of abbreviations used to indicate standards of usage, for example, *obs (olete), arch (aic), rare, slang.*
5. Ability to interpret information on idiomatic usages, for example, "pick a bone with."

Needed for Comprehension of Derivation

1. Knowledge of meaning of common abbreviations used to indicate etymology, for example, *Lat., Engl.*
2. Knowledge of meaning of abbreviations used to indicate words or meanings of technical nature, for example, *Mus., Chem., Bot., Zool.*

Needed for Permanent Learning

1. Interest in the details of the derivation of the word, its source and history, and variety of meanings.
2. Forming of several mental associations with known words derived from the same root or bearing some other structural relationship.
3. Recognition of the effect of the affixes present upon the root word.

4. Attention to any unusual orthographic details, such as words which are examples or exceptions to common spelling rules, or which present uncommon spellings of common sounds.

A recent article suggests that children prepare their own brief dictionaries, as a slang dictionary, and in so doing learn more about how a dictionary functions. Other interesting variations on this idea are preparing a dictionary with pictures cut from magazines and grouped to illustrate a sound, a setting (a farm), or a theme (transportation). A dictionary may represent a collection of words from the child's personal reading or interests, such as the Civil War, baseball, dog training, or some other subject, with or without pictures. The arrangements within the child's collection of words may be alphabetical or as in many beginning dictionaries, thematic (words that name things, express action). The formality of these dictionaries will, of course, be related to the maturity of the pupils and will range from simple picture collections to productions offering meanings, derivations, and illustrative sentences.

Use of the Context

Earlier we offered an explanation of the role of contextual analysis in word recognition. When the unknown word is within the listening vocabulary of the reader, context analysis functions as an aid in word recognition. When the word is not within the reader's auditory experiences, contextual analysis may continue to be helpful by revealing the probable meaning. Thus even when the reader does not know the word by ear, context may reveal enough of the word meaning to permit comprehending reading.

In the intermediate grades and increasingly thereafter as reading vocabulary exceeds listening vocabulary, context analysis becomes more significant in the development of meaning vocabulary and reading comprehension. It functions not, as some critics of the whole-word or sight method think, as sheer guessing but as a constant tool to inferential derivation of deeper meanings. Among intermediate-grade pupils, exercises such as the following promote greater facility in contextual analysis.

1. Select a half-dozen difficult words from a future reading assignment. Have pupils write their definitions of these words without any exchange of ideas or discussion. After the reading has been completed, permit pupils to correct or revise their earlier definitions. Discuss their reasons for their revisions and their justifications for their final definition. Ask pupils to discuss the ways meanings were clarified by the context.
2. Give a series of sentences using a word in several contextual meanings. Ask pupils to explain the exact meaning of the key word as used in each sentence. For example—

a. We made the boat *fast* to the dock.

b. In the morning, we broke our *fast* before beginning the journey.

c. The horses ran a very *fast* race.

Use the dictionary as a source of these contrasting meanings. If pupils have any difficulty in deriving the various meanings, allow them to use their dictionaries.

3. Vary the second exercise given above by requiring students to attempt to supply a synonym appropriate to the meaning of the key word in each sentence.

4. Duplicate an explanatory or descriptive paragraph from some uncopyrighted teaching materials. Choose a paragraph in which a word is used several times. Delete this word in your reproduction. Ask pupils to read the paragraphs and to attempt to supply the missing word. Discuss the various answers offered, their accuracy, and the tendency to introduce synonyms. Ask for explanations of the ways in which they deduced the unknown word.

5. Vary the fourth exercise by inserting a nonsense word in the paragraphs at each point where the key word originally appeared. Before attempting to identify the true word, ask pupils to describe and tell the functions of the nonsense term: What does it look like? What does it do? What action does it have? How do you know? How did the paragraph support these ideas?

6. Give pupils a series of sentences in each of which a key word is underlined. Give also three or four words, one of which means the same as the underlined word. Have the pupils choose the best synonym.

7. Vary the preceding exercise by supplying a group of sentences in which the underlined word is to be replaced by a synonym supplied by the pupil. Compare and discuss their answers. Use the same exercise in the pupil's own sentences.

These and other exercises in contextual analysis suggested by Russell and Karp (*21*), Wagner and Hosier (*28*), Kingsly (*11*), and Spache (*27*) are intended to strengthen the deductive thinking characteristic of successful use of contextual analysis. Exercises such as the fourth and fifth given above strengthen pupil efforts to deduce probable meanings of an unknown word. The sixth and seventh exercises promote the searching for mental associations, for synonyms, for probable meaning from context which are the heart of this skill.

Programmed Learning and Vocabulary

There are many aspects of word study which lend themselves to highly organized sequential learning steps. Prefixes, affixes, and roots, base and derived words, words related in derivation, relationships among words such as antonyms, homonyms, and synonyms exhibit very logical and interdependent interactions. Learning of these facts and relationships might well be readily accomplished by the use of programmed materials and teaching machines.

Programmed materials are built on a theory of learning emphasizing the stimulus–response relationship, reinforcement of the correct response, and very careful, logical arrangement of the learning materials.

The pupil proceeds through the program progressing by steps of very slight difficulty, learning at his own rate of speed. Some programs include built-in progress tests at various intervals and end-of-program tests to evaluate the learning. Motivation is promoted by ensuring the constant success of the learner, by confirming his success immediately after each response, by the freedom in pacing his own learning, and by coaching clues in the frames which constantly support his success.

Currently available programs for teaching sight or meaning vocabulary are listed at the end of this chapter. There are a number of unsolved questions regarding the use of these in reading instruction, as Riegel (19) has pointed out. Is the conditioned learning involved in this stimulus–response–reinforcement framework as effective for humans as for animals? Are not higher processes—inductive generalizations, self-criticism, deductive applications, and evaluative or creative activities—more profitable and permanent? Are programs really appropriate for slow, average, and rapid learners, or should they be differentiated for these groups? Is the learning really more active than in the formal classroom, or does the repetitive nature result in bored, passive reactions? What is the proper role of programmed materials in the learning process—an initial presentation of facts, a review, a supplement to more usual materials? When may programs substitute for direct teaching and pupil–teacher interaction? Despite these problems we would urge reading teachers to consider the possible advantages of programmed materials in various areas of reading instruction. These carefully planned, repetitive teaching devices may release teachers from drill work and its correction, permit each student to proceed at his own pace, reinforce each step by correction or reward, and reveal pupil's errors for corrective steps or revision of the program. Levine also points out that the program exhibits an infinite degree of patience, introduces teachers to a detailed analysis of skills, and helps them to discover more about the learning of each skill and the proper sequences of presentation when they use or prepare programs (13). The amount of research done on the subject of programmed learnings indicates that these approaches may make some real contribution to both pupil and teacher learning.

Learning Vocabulary

What Works	*What Does Not Work*
Categorizing or classifying words according to type, function, rhyme, sounds, etc.	Attempting to learn lists of words
Recognizing that the needed writing vocabulary is much smaller than in reading and teaching spelling only of those words child needs to communicate	Expecting transfer from one medium to another, e.g., from reading to spelling

Learning Vocabulary

What Works	*What Does Not Work*
Recognizing that words are symbols for ideas or experiences which must precede the learning of the related word	Teaching "vocabulary" or teaching "words"
Fostering vocabulary development by permitting children to read widely, and in depth in their areas of interest	Structuring or planning a similar reading program for all children
Encouraging children to work out new words in each piece of reading material	Presenting new words prior to child's attempt to read them in a context
Presenting, gradually, a word in many contexts which emphasize its many meanings	Teaching a word and its meaning
Recognizing that different children show varying aptitudes in learning modality as visual, auditory, or kinesthetic	Presenting new words in a repeated, static fashion to all the group
Realizing that some children are confused by multisensory impressions of words and would learn better if only one avenue was employed, at least at a time	Assuming that a multisensory presentation of a word is superior to use of a single medium
Helping children to recognize which strategies work best for each of them and then strengthening their use of this technique	Placing dependence for vocabulary growth upon one strategy, as phonics or dictionary use
Recognizing that small words in large words are often not true words and that their pronunciation differs widely from the true word	Teaching children to look for known small words within a new word
Stimulating interest in words, collecting interesting words, displaying and discussing them, finding opportunities to use them	Limiting word study to the list offered in a reader or some such source
Offering pictures and actions and relevant adjective to reinforce lexical words; teaching structural words only in phrases: *to* the store, *in* my desk (24)	Teaching lexical words (nouns and verbs) in same fashion as structural words (prepositions, conjunctions, etc.)
Trying to build relationships among the words, as *cows* eats *hay*, the *rope* is	Teaching several unrelated new words

What Works	*What Does Not Work*
around the *jug*. Including related words, as *moon–night–dark* to strengthen retention of the desired word (*24*)	
Using pictures only in the initial presentations, then practicing without pictures (*22, 23*)	Using pictures as a constant reinforcement to word recognition over and over again
Strengthening word recognition by variety of exercises in classifying same words (i.e., according to size, color, shape, setting, common word elements, etc.) (*1*)	Reviewing word recognition largely by workbook exercises emphasizing matching of word and picture
Encouraging children to use only the sound of the first letter and the context to derive the word	Expecting children to react to pattern of separate letters, e.g., spelling patterns
Realizing that word recognition is much more successful in context than in lists (*9*)	Using a test on a list of words as a final indication of a child's recognition of these
Being aware that this list of commonest words demands differentiated instruction for nouns and verbs than for conjunctions and prepositions, for which a variety of associated meanings is very difficult to assemble	Teaching some list, such as the Dolch, as essential to all future reading (*5*)
Realizing that long-term learning of words necessitates forming generalizations and associations, as suggested above in this column (*12*)	Repeating words over and over again as primary strategy for learning
Recognizing that associations are stimulated better when words are heard than when they are seen, as in reading to children, then discussing (*18*)	Relying on blackboard presentation of new words as basic technique
Stimulating deduction from context by the cloze procedure, by discussing their reasons for their choices (*24*)	Discouraging children from guessing what a word is
Postponing practice in quick recognition until much practice in classification and forming associations has occurred	Moving quickly to rapid drill on words with flash cards, or some machine soon after their initial presentation

DISCUSSION QUESTIONS

1. What is your reaction to the current emphasis upon language development in preschool and primary-grade federal and state programs for culturally and linguistically different children? Why is language development thought so significant for reading and school success?

2. How do the authors' basic concepts of pupil learning of words contrast with common classroom methods of stimulating growth in reading vocabulary?

3. Is there really a core or basal vocabulary that children need to know in order to read adequately? What is the best source of such a list—a particular reading series, some word count, the Dolch or Barbe lists, or what?

4. Select types of word recognition exercises from workbooks and textbooks that agree or disagree with the viewpoint expressed in this text. Compare and justify these various approaches.

5. What sources should be used for words to be added to the meaning vocabulary of the average pupil in intermediate and upper elementary classrooms?

6. When can it be said that a child "knows" a word? When he can read it in context or isolation, or use it in speech and writing, or interpret its multiple meanings, or all of these? When is this process of learning a word completed?

REFERENCES

1. Bickley, A. C., Dinnan, James A., and Jones, J. P., "Oral Associates and Reading Readiness," in *Reading: The Right to Participate,* 20th Yearbook National Reading Conference, 1971, 14–16.

2. Bloomfield, Leonard, and Barnhart, Clarence L., *Let's Read: A Linguistic Approach.* Detroit: Wayne State University Press, 1961.

3. Cooper, J. David, "A Study of the Learning Modalities of Good and Poor First Grade Readers," in *Reading Methods and Teacher Improvement,* Nila B. Smith, ed. Newark, Del.: International Reading Association, 1971, 87–97.

4. Diack, Hunter, *Reading and the Psychology of Perception.* Nottingham, England: Peter Skinner Publishing, 1960.

5. Dolch, E. W., *The Dolch Word List.* Champaign, Ill.: Garrard Publishing Company.

6. Downing, John A., *The Augmented Roman Alphabet.* London: Sir Isaac Pitman & Sons Ltd., 1962.

7. Fry, Edward, "Teaching a Basic Reading Vocabulary," *Elementary English,* 37 (January 1960), 38–42.

8. Gibson, C. M., and Richards, I. A., *First Steps in Reading English.* New York: Pocket Books, Inc., 1957.

9. Goodman, Yetta M., "Using Children's Reading Miscues for New Teaching Strategies," *Reading Teacher,* 23 (February 1970), 455–459.

10. Jones, John Paul, *Intersensory Transfer, Perceptual Shifting, Modal Difference and Reading.* ERIC/CRIER and International Reading Association Information Series. Newark, Del.: International Reading Association, 1972.

11. Kingsly, Bernard, *Reading Skills.* San Francisco: Fearon Publishers, 1958.

12. Lane, John Manning, Jr., "Verbalization and Learning of Paired Associates," in *Reading: The Right to Participate,* 20th Yearbook National Reading Conference, 1971, 272–282.

13. Levine, Jane, "Let's Debate Programmed Reading Instruction," *Reading Teacher,* 16 (March 1963), 337–341.

14. Manzo, A. V., and Sherk, John K., "Some Generalizations and Strategies for Guiding Vocabulary Learning," *Journal of Reading Behavior,* 4 (Winter 1971–1972), 78–89.

15. Mills, Robert E., "An Evaluation of Techniques of Teaching Word Recognition," *Elementary School Journal,* 56 (January 1956), 221–225.

16. Mills, Robert E., *Learning Methods Test Kit.* The Mills Center, Fort Lauderdale, Fla., 1970. (Available from the author.)

17. Niles, Olive S., "Improving General Vocabulary," *High School Journal,* 39 (December 1955), 147–155.

18. Reynolds, Richard J., "Effects of Modality on Response in Word Association Tasks," in *Reading: The*

Right to Participate, 20th Yearbook National Reading Conference, 1971, 300–303.

19. Riegel, Paula, "Programmed Learning and Reading," *Elementary English,* 40 (March 1963), 251–254.

20. Rivkind, Harry C., "The Development of a Group Technique in Teaching Word Recognition To Determine Which of Four Methods Is Most Effective with Individual Children." Doctoral dissertation, University of Florida, 1958.

21. Russell, David H., and Karp, Etta E., *Reading Aids Through the Grades.* New York: Teachers College Press, 1951.

22. Samuels, S. Jay, "Attentional Process in Reading: The Effect of Pictures on the Acquisition of Reading Responses," *Journal of Educational Psychology,* 58 (1967), 337–342.

23. Samuels, S. Jay, "Effects of Pictures on Learning to Read, Comprehension and Attitudes," *Review of Educational Research*, 40 (June 1970), 397–407.

24. Samuels, S. Jay, and Chen, C. C., "Comparison of Word Recognition in Strategies of Adults and Children," in *Reading: The Right to Participate,* 20th Yearbook National Reading Conference, 1971, 73–77.

25. Schoer, Lowell, "Effect of Similarity in Structure, Meaning and Sound on Paired Associate Learning," *Journal of Educational Psychology,* 58 (August 1967), 189–192.

26. Schubert, Delwyn, G., "Reading Games: Why, How, When," *Elementary English,* 36 (October 1959), 422–423.

27. Spache, Evelyn B., *Reading Activities for Child Involvement.* Boston: Allyn and Bacon, Inc., 1976.

28. Wagner, Guy, and Hosier, Max, *Reading Games: Strengthening Reading Skills with Instructional Games.* Darien, Conn.: Teachers Publishing Corp., 1960.

29. Wolpert, Edward M., "Modality and Reading: A Perspective," *Reading Teacher,* 24 (April 1971), 640–643.

RESOURCES FOR THE TEACHER

Dale, Edgar, and O'Rourke, Joseph, *Techniques of Teaching Vocabulary.* San Francisco: Field Educational Publications, 1971.

Filmstrips

Beginning Dictionary Skills. Four color strips on entry words, pronunciation, and usage for intermediate grades. American Book Company.

Better Reading Series. Seventy strips for word and phrase recognition. Pasadena, Calif.: Still Film, Inc.

Controlled Exposure Series. Strips for use in the Tach-X, a special projector for training in rapid word recognition and spelling. Huntington, N.Y.: Educational Developmental Laboratories.

The Dictionary and Other Reference Books. Single strip on the dictionary, encyclopedia, and telephone directory for primary grades. New York: Eye Gate House, Inc.

Dictionary Skills. Three sets of transparencies on dictionary usage, plus spirit masters, for intermediate grades. Morristown, N.J.: Silver Burdett Company.

Dictionary Skills. Ten color strips and thirteen spirit masters on dictionary skills of the third- to fourth-grade levels. Chicago: International Film.

Learning To Use the Dictionary. Eight strips to promote vocabulary. San Francisco: Pacific Productions.

Reading Speed-i-o-Strip Series. Many strips for rapid word and phrase recognition. Chicago: Society for Visual Education.

Some Words Mean Two Things. Strips for primary grades. New York: McGraw-Hill Book Company.

Tachisto-O-Filmstrips. Strips for rapid word recognition. Chicago: Learning Through Seeing.

Using a Dictionary. Strips for intermediate grades. Manchester, Mo.: Webster Publishing.

What's the Word. Twelve strips to promote vocabulary and dictionary skills for intermediate grades. Boston: Houghton Mifflin Company.

Word Mastery. Three strips stressing recognition and derivation. Chicago: Learning Through Seeing.

Words. Their Origin, Use and Spelling. Six strips on derivation, structure, and usage. Chicago: Society for Visual Education.

Your Dictionary and How To Use It. Six strips for intermediate grades. Chicago: Society for Visual Education.

Films

Better Choice of Words.   Coronet.
Look It Up.   Coronet.
We Discover the Dictionary.   Coronet.
Who Makes Words?   Coronet.

MEANING VOCABULARY
DEVELOPMENT MATERIALS

Anwyll, B. Jean, *Word Clues: Be a Word Detective.* Cambridge, Mass.: Honor Products. A brief program in context clues.

Bierman, Emanual, and Schure, Alexander, *Vocabulary Building I and II.* New York: Cenco Educational Aids.

Deighton, Lee C., and Sanford, Adrian B., et al., *Macmillan Spectrum of Books.* New York: Macmillan Publishing Co., Inc., 1964. The kit includes vocabulary development workbooks.

Learning, Inc., *David Discovers the Dictionary.* Chicago: Coronet Instructional Films. A short fourth-grade program.

Learning, Inc., *Using the Dictionary.* Chicago: Coronet Instructional Films. For elementary pupils.

Loretan, Joseph O., ed. *Building Reading Power.* Columbus, Ohio: Charles E. Merrill Publishing Company. Kit includes vocabulary development programs.

Markle, Susan Meyer, *Words: A Programmed Course in Vocabulary Development.* Chicago: Science Research Associates, 1962. Program in roots and affixes for eighth grade or above.

Moreda, Natalie, ed. *Grow in Word Power.* Pleasantville, N.Y.: Reader's Digest Association. For upper elementary grades.

Roberts, Clyde, *Word Attack.* New York: Harcourt Brace Jovanovich, 1956. For upper elementary grades.

Rosenberg, Ruth B. *Fun with Words.* Cambridge, Mass.: Honor Products. A reusable program in homonyms.

Smith, Donald E. P., et al., *Word Attack.* Ann Arbor, Mich.: Ann Arbor Publishers. An elementary-level program.

Taylor, Stanford E., Frackenpohl, Helen, and McDonald, Arthur S., *EDL Word Clues Series.* Huntington, N.Y.: Educational Developmental Laboratories. Programs in vocabulary development through context clues for grades seven and up.

Vocabulary Enrichment. Cambridge, Mass.: General Education, Inc. A brief program for vocabulary building.

Vocabulary III. Chicago: Science Research Associates. For upper elementary grades.

Instructional Materials—Sight Words

These devices are primarily intended to promote the beginning reading skill of sight word recognition without phonic or other kind of word analysis. See also Skill Development Kits listed in Chapter 10.

Alcock, Dorothea, *Grab.* Covina, Calif.: available from the author. A card game for developing sight-word vocabulary.

Concepto-Charts. Ridgefield, N.J.: Reporting Service Co. Charts offering words and pictures grouped around a common concept.

Dolch, E. W., *Basic Sight Word Cards.* Champaign, Ill.: Garrard Publishing Company.

Dolch, E. W., *Group Word Teaching Game.* Champaign, Ill.: Garrard Publishing Company.

Dolch, E. W., *Match.* Champaign, Ill.: Garrard Publishing Company.

Dolch, E. W., *Picture Word Cards.* Champaign, Ill.: Garrard Publishing Company.

Dolch, E. W., *Popper Words.* Champaign, Ill.: Garrard Publishing Company.

Dolch, Marguerite P., and Astrofsky, Lillian, *My Puzzle Book I and II.* Champaign, Ill.: Garrard Publishing Company, 1964. These last six items are word cards and card games for sight-word vocabulary.

Educational Developmental Laboratories, *Flash-X.* Huntington, N.Y.: Educational Developmental Laboratories. A hand tachistoscope for rapid word recognition.

Fry, Edward B., *Instant Words—Line Up* and *Instant Words—Pairs.* Sunland, Calif.: Learning Through Seeing. A pair of word games.

Jenn Publications, *Primary Worksheets*. Louisville, Ky.: Jenn Publications, Inc.

Leavell, Ullin W., *Reading Essentials Teaching Aids*. Austin, Tex.: Steck-Vaughn Co. See catalog for various materials.

Little Picture Cards. Glenview, Ill.: Scott, Foresman and Company. Picture–word cards.

Match and Check. Glenview, Ill.: Scott, Foresman and Company. Four sets of disks for picture–letter–word matching.

Milton Bradley Reading Aids. Springfield, Mass.: Milton Bradley Company. See catalog for a variety of word-learning devices.

Phelps, Victor N., and Arrowsmith, Jessie M., *Primary Playhouse Corrector Tests*. Sherwood, Ore.: Primary Playhouse. Pads of worksheets.

Rhyming Pictures. Darien, Conn.: Teacher's Publishing Corporation. Forty pictures for flannelboard.

Rhyming Puzzles. Chicago: Ideal School Supply Company. Sixteen puzzles in matching rhyming pictures and words. See catalog for others.

Ruddell, Robert B., Graves, Barbara W., Davis, Floyd W., and Shuy, Roger W., *Build*. Lexington, Mass.: Ginn and Company, 1975. Color-coded blocks for word recognition and sentence structure practice.

School Material Company, *Individual Reading Apparatus*. Chicago: School Material Company. See catalog for a number of word-teaching devices.

Speed Up! Columbus, Ohio: Charles E. Merrill Publishing Company. Sets of cards offering practice in sentence reading.

Stand Up! Sound Off! Columbus, Ohio: Charles E. Merrill Publishing Company. Set of 210 picture cards representing a beginning vocabulary.

Tachistoscopic Training Series. Meadville, Penna.: Keystone View Company. Slides for words and phrases.

Wonder Words. New York: Educational Games, Inc. A bingo-like sight vocabulary game.

13
Developing Comprehension and Critical Reading Skills

PREVIEW

The term "comprehension" is one that is used glibly by many teachers and reading experts. Yet the meaning given the word differs greatly from one user to the next. Despite the research analyses of the process, comprehension is often hypothesized as a long list of subskills. The logical assumption is then made that each of these skills must be practiced separately—that eventually all the skills will function simultaneously while the individual is reading. Some teachers stress a certain few of these subskills; other teachers emphasize others. Both are quite sure, however, that they are promoting the development of comprehension.

Recent studies by tests and interviews are beginning to raise questions about this multiplicity of comprehension subskills. It appears that what the reader retains while reading reflects such influences as (1) his purpose in reading or what he intends to retain; and (2) the instructions he is given before reading, which may lead him to find only the precise answers to specific questions or to secure a broader comprehension if the questions are more general (3). Comprehension is affected even more, however, by the pattern of questions the child learns to anticipate. He learns to read with only those types of thinking that the teacher's questions demand. Since teachers' questions appear to be limited in type and depth, children's thinking (or comprehension) tends to be superficial and stereotyped, and lack critical thinking.

Interviews of students with good and poor comprehension reveal one other significant element. This is the degree of involvement of the reader, his interaction with the author's ideas, the depth and variety of the associations he reacts with to the material. Active reacting to reading is, again, a habit promoted by classroom practices which foster stimulating, interesting follow-up to the child's reading. Thus, again, it seems that the comprehension achieved by pupils is largely determined by what associations the teacher stimulates.

Despite the wealth of materials suggesting ways of developing comprehension and critical reading skills, it is quite clear that we still lack basic definitions of these terms and clear differentiation between them. Some authorities give long lists of comprehension skills and other lists of critical reading skills with considerable overlap. Others define these reading behaviors as an encoding process, a thinking process, a cognitive procedure, or a process operating simultaneously at four levels—word perception, comprehension, reaction and evaluation, and assimilation of the new ideas and previous information.

For the sake of simplicity, we will consider separately these two aspects of understanding and reacting to what is read. But, as we shall point out, we consider critical reading a type or degree of comprehension—a type of reading behavior that appears as a natural application of comprehension, if the reader is so trained.

COMPREHENSION AS SKILL DEVELOPMENT

As part of an attempt to provide better reading instruction for migratory children, Roy McCanne of the Colorado State Department of Instruction has listed comprehension skills. His list enumerates fifty-five supposedly separate comprehension skills. A parallel list of thirty-three critical reading skills was compiled by Gertrude Williams from the basal reading series (31). Twenty-seven of the skills in the two lists are identical. Not only is there considerable duplication between these two areas as seen by these reading authorities, but many of the items are very vague and ill defined.

What we have tried to illustrate is the great difficulty any reading expert experiences in trying to name the specific reading skills that constitute comprehension or critical reading. First, because of the problem of semantics, authors of any two lists would probably disagree. What one calls "establishing cause and effect" the other calls "recognizing cause and effect" or "perceiving relationships," and so forth, until the teacher of reading becomes thoroughly confused.

Perhaps this confusion between what is critical reading and what is comprehension, if there is a distinction, can be recognized by carefully defining each of these areas. Let us review various concepts or definitions of these high-level reading skills.

COMPREHENSION AS A DECODING PROCESS

Recently, reading teachers have been urged to conceive of comprehension as a decoding process—a translation of graphemes into phonemes—a recognition that "reading is talk written down." Reading is apparently synonymous with spoken language or simply a matter of (1) making discriminative responses to graphic symbols, and (2) decoding graphic symbols into speech. Encoding or obtaining meaning, receiving communication from the printed page, and integrating former experience with the concepts offered in a printed form are generally ignored in this linguistic type of definition.

We have dealt with this oversimplified concept of the reading process at length in an earlier chapter. We have questioned whether a grapheme-by-grapheme decoding ever really occurs; have pointed out the significant differences between spoken and written language; have shown that the control of vocabulary by its spelling patterns is irrelevant to the question of word meaning or word difficulty; and have demonstrated that linguistic analysis of the frequency of letter combinations has almost nothing to do with a sequential presentation of beginning vocabulary. The interested reader may refer to these rebuttals in our discussions of the linguistic approach and of reading as a psycholinguistic process.

COMPREHENSION AS A THINKING PROCESS

If we conceive of comprehension as a thinking process, there are two immediate and striking implications for instructional procedures. These are the nature of the operations in thinking and the possible ways of stimulating these cognitive processes. Guilford (*10*) has offered his well-known model of the structure of the intellect, in this fashion:

Operations	*Products*
Cognition—recognition of information	Unit—the word
Memory—retention of information	Class—the sentence
Divergent Production—logical, creative ideas	Relations—literal main ideas of a paragraph
Convergent Production—conclusions, inductive thinking	Systems—paragraph organization and structure
Evaluation—critical thinking	Transformations—analyzing and manipulating paragraph content
	Implications—recognizing, selecting, implementing implied ideas

In an earlier book, Spache (*27*) has shown how this model of reading as a thinking process could be translated into specific reading behaviors. For example, at the word level, these processes might result in these behaviors:

- Cognition—the recognition that the word has meaning; is a symbol for an object or event.
- Memory—the recall of specific word meanings.

- Divergent Production—obtaining the meaning of a word from context by inference.
- Convergent Production—obtaining the meaning of a word from the structure of the context, as by an appositive clause.
- Evaluation—acceptance or rejection of the author's use of this particular word to convey a certain meaning.

Donald L. Cleland (1) has another interesting analysis of the thinking processes inherent in the comprehension act. He believes the reader uses:

- Perception—a meaningful response to the graphic symbols we call words, sentences, paragraphs, etc.
- Apperception—relating new material to one's background of experience; matching the reader's experiences to those offered by the writer.
- Abstraction—selecting, choosing, and rejecting perceptions, concepts, images.
- Appraisal—estimating the validity of these poor processes.
- Ideation—inductive reasoning or generalizing opinions, conclusions, or judgments

    deductive reasoning or examining the facts in the light of a known principle or fact

    critical reasoning—interaction between the reader and the writer involving evaluation by the reader

    problem solving—(1) becoming aware of a problem; (2) orienting to the problem; (3) forming a tentative solution; (4) evaluating or testing the solution; (5) testing the final solution by use or application

    creative thinking—the making of new syntheses or seeing new relationships.
- Application—the uses that a reader makes of the ideas acquired by reading.

One other model of comprehension offered by William S. Gray and modified by Helen M. Robinson (19) might be described. The five major aspects of reading may be distinguished in this manner.

- Word Perception—at the center or beginning of the process and involving recognition as well as pronunciation and meaning.
- Comprehension—a "clear grasp of what is read" at the levels of literal meanings, implied meanings, and possible applications beyond the author's meanings.
- Reaction—standards of judgment, reaching conclusions, and emotional responses as well as an inquiring attitude.
- Assimilation—using critical judgment, creative thinking, and combining one's own experience with the information offered by the author.
- Speed of Reading—demanding flexibility and adjustment to the reader's purpose and the nature and difficulty of the material.

It is widely accepted by teachers and reading authorities alike that reading employs the higher intellectual processes. Just what this implies for classroom practices and reading methodology is not quite so obvious, however. Exactly what mental processes does the reading act emphasize? Can these thinking abilities be stimulated or even trained to function more effectively? Which are the most significant for comprehension, or for speed, or both? Are these processes the same for good and poor readers? Are the processes of equal significance at different school ages? As yet, the available research gives us only partial answers to these questions.

What are the implications of these studies for the classroom teacher? The most obvious implication is, of course, the dependence of the development of the child's thinking efforts in reading upon the direction given by teacher demands. As is true of many facets of the reading act, higher types of thinking do not spontaneously appear or develop simply because the pupil progresses in reading levels. In reading, children and adults employ only those types of thinking that enable them to meet the minimal demands imposed on them. If the purposes for reading are superficial or vague, so is the thinking and retention of the reader.

A simple experiment by Keislar (14) demonstrates how superficial reading can really be when the purposes are inadequately defined. A group of pupils was trained to expect a number of questions stressing only main ideas when they completed each daily reading assignment. A second, comparable group was required to answer questions which consistently emphasized only the details of their reading. After a period of training, the questions were switched one day and each group was asked to answer the other's type of question. When faced with a different question most of the children were completely at a loss. They simply had not employed that kind of thinking. How much thinking or reasoning does the average reader use spontaneously? Apparently only that degree or kind that enables him to fulfill the minimum of the demands upon his comprehension. Later we will offer specific suggestions regarding the teacher's role in stimulating complete development of this skill. But the point has been made here that although certain higher mental processes may be important in reading, they are not always present in every pupil's reading act. In fact, the more advanced reading habits, such as we speak of in critical reading, may never appear unless the student is specifically trained for them.

COMPREHENSION AS DEFINED BY TESTS

In the average American school, the most frequent measure of the success of the entire reading program is the annual or semiannual reading test. Administrators as well as classroom teachers seem to accept these instruments as meaningful evaluations of the outcomes of their instructional efforts. If, in so-called reading comprehension tests, their pupils test at or above grade, everyone assumes that the pupils are developing facility in this area. It is assumed that such results prove the validity and effectiveness of the usual skills-drill procedure.

But what do reading comprehension tests really measure beyond the ability to obtain literal meanings from printed materials? Do any reading tests actually sample such processes mentioned above as assimilation, convergent reasoning, evaluation, abstraction, appraisal or application, to cite only a few of the higher-level elements? In fact, do such reading tests measure any of the significant long-range goals of the reading program, such as creating and stimulating reading interests, achieving breadth and depth of reading experience, enjoying and using reading for personal growth? In his contrast of British and American uses of reading tests, Morris (17) makes the strong criticism that American schools, by depending so naively on test scores, actually fail to measure their own progress in achieving any of the really significant aims of reading instruction.

Even the test construction experts are confused as to the nature of comprehension and the ways of measuring its development. In a group of reading comprehension tests that was surveyed, there was at least one skill measured in each test that no other of the twenty-five tests measured. Apparently, almost every reading test constructor has unique ideas regarding the components of comprehension. Still other studies show that many test questions depend entirely on the informational background of the reader rather than the thinking required by the selection. And, questions frequently can be answered by the information actually given in surrounding items of the test itself.

Finally, Dorothy Lampard's study (15) found that, independent of intelligence and maturation, reading tests of comprehension have little relationship to such applications as outlining, summarizing, or problem solving of reading materials. Comprehension ability as measured by tests was not highly related to the ability to reorganize or synthesize ideas just read, in this study.

1. Comprehension tests do not measure the mental processes involved in the act of reading, despite their titles. They deal with end results, giving the author's own labels to the types of questions the reader can answer.
2. These tests do not reveal the thinking of the reader because without intensive interviewing we do not know how he obtained the answers to the questions— whether by faulty or sound logic, by intuition or inference, by sheer guess, or by previous knowledge.
3. Comprehension tests are not a complete analysis or record of the reader's comprehension, for he might be able to answer more questions than we ask. All the test score means is that he answered a certain proportion of the questions asked, under the conditions imposed by the nature of the test (cloze, true–false, multiple-choice, time allowed, etc.).
4. Comprehension tests are not a scale of understanding from zero to perfection. Low scores do not necessarily represent no comprehension, for we may not have sampled some of the ideas he gained, as interviewing would probably show. High scores do not mean that the reader has obtained all the facts and interpretations possible, for we probably have not sampled all of them.
5. High scores do not indicate "a good comprehender" or low scores "a poor comprehender" except in reference to the particular selection and content in which the pupil was tested. Comprehension will vary from one kind of reading matter to another, according to the difficulty of the material, which is determined largely by its vocabulary and the reader's informational background in that area of knowledge.

   To illustrate the importance of informational background, how many adults can answer the following question?

"Machiavelli wrote that persons who lived near to Rome were less religious than those who lived far away from Rome. Why did he think so?"*

The question is taken from a mid-sixth-grade social science book and can be answered by most pupils when they have read the preceding portion of the textbook. Does such a question measure a skill such as drawing conclusions, recalling stated facts, generalizing on given information, making inferences, interpreting ideas implied but not stated, perceiving relationships, or what? Or does it depend upon previous information? Is it a measure of comprehension?

Lest the reader think we have chosen an unfair example, let us cite our experiences in constructing a half-dozen commercial reading tests. Like other test authors, we discovered that 30 to 40 percent of the questions could be answered by readers of appropriate ages, without reading the selection, and try as we would, this factor could only be reduced, not entirely eliminated.

Understanding the vocabulary of a reading selection is even a more obvious reflection of background of the reader (as well as his ability to infer meanings from the context). And word meanings, as we have shown, are a primary component of what is called comprehension.

6. Comprehension test questions are not really scaled in difficulty or by grade levels. If a pupil can answer the questions which yield a score of 3.0, it does not necessarily mean that he reads like a beginning third grader. His performance signifies that he understood enough of the words, recognized the relationships among the ideas, and had sufficient previous information about the subject to answer that many questions.

In constructing a comprehension test, the author frames as many questions as he can think of for each reading sample. Then he tries these on a sample of pupils of approximately the grade level for which the test is intended. He scores the answers, separates high scorers from low, and computes the percentage of correct answers for each of these groups. Some questions are answered correctly just as often by high or low scorers, and these are discarded. Those that discriminate better are retained for the final test. But the actual difficulty of these differs from one question to the next irregularly, for if they must parallel the reading selection, they cannot be arranged from easiest to most difficult. Hence the sequence of questions represents only a sampling of all the ideas present, and their order is irregular in difficulty, not a continuous scale.

The grade score obtained from a comprehension test tells us simply that the testee answered about as many questions correctly (no matter which ones or what their relative difficulty) as children of a certain grade level on whom the test was tried out. We are not told anything about the quality or depth of his comprehension, or how it was obtained, or how much more he may have learned from the reading, or how much he knew about the subject before he read our test selection.

We might sum up this discussion of the definition of comprehension by tests as almost a meaningless effort. Reading tests tend to claim to measure skills which experts cannot show to exist. Test scores bear little or no relationship to

* From *The Age of Western Civilization* (Boston: Allyn and Bacon, Inc., 1975), p. 102.

most of the major components of comprehension, if indeed, they actually measure anything more than sophistication in taking tests and the reader's informational background. Reading tests fail to assess the abilities to organize, synthesize, or apply the facts read, or, in other words, any of the really useful aspects or long-range values of reading ability. Certainly reading tests do not help us understand or even define the process of comprehension.

DEFINING CRITICAL READING

As we have seen, the reading behaviors often thought of as critical reading are included in the broad definitions of comprehension, as in the models of Guilford, Cleland, and Robinson discussed earlier. If we summarize their thinking, they and other authors seem to include these elements in their desciption of critical reading:

1. An inquiring attitude toward the material and its author.
2. Sufficient informational background to supply standards for critical evaluation.
3. Skill in suspending judgment and the influence of one's own feelings until the selection is thoroughly understood.
4. Ability to analyze the logic of the material to differentiate fact and opinion, and detect omissions and distortions.
5. Evaluation of the author's background and intentions, his beliefs and implications.

Thus far, it has not been possible for researchers to separate critical reading and comprehension. There is considerable overlap among critical reading tests, reading comprehension, and vocabulary. Some analysts feel that their data indicate that common reading tests are as much a measure of critical reading as the tests so labeled, (5,6). Others insist that critical reading is something different than ordinary comprehension, and continue to construct tests purporting to sample such critical reading skills as literary analysis, comprehension of underlying elements, and logical analysis. But factorial analysis of these tests reveals only that the kinds of questions used tend to form related groups within the test. It does not prove that these questions measure reading skills distinctly separate from ordinary comprehension.

Therefore, we are inclined to consider critical reading as a type of comprehension which involves critical and value judgments based on the attitudes and experience of the reader. To us, critical reading means that the reader approaches the material with an inquiring, analytic attitude. We have learned from those who built tests of critical reading that this attitude is not necessarily present just because the reader usually shows excellent comprehension of other types. Intelligence and maturity play a part in these judgmental reactions of the reader, and yet we know that even young pupils can be taught to exhibit critical thinking. In the later discussion of how to stimulate comprehension, we will treat critical reading as a type of comprehension and suggest its develpment for pupils of all ages and all levels of comprehension ability.

Training in critical reading may be approached among intermediate and upper elementary pupils by helping them to recognize some of the propaganda tricks employed by writers in advertisements, television commercials, and other matter. Among the concepts recommended are (2):

1. Bandwagon—slogans implying that the reader should imitate other people in order to be accepted, as "Everyone likes cereal."
2. Glittering generalities—statements that exaggerate the qualities of a product, such as "super," "wonderful," "fantastic."
3. Testimonials—using prominent persons or impressive professionals to endorse products, as Joe Namath endorsing a certain popcorn maker.
4. Plain folks—attempts of an individual to secure identification with others, as a politician seeking votes—"I'm just a dirt farmer at heart, like you."
5. Pseudo-research—claiming that the great majority of people sampled prefer a certain brand of product when no information is offered regarding how many samples had to be taken to get the claimed result, such as "Six out of eight doctors recommend aspirin."

These are but a few of the many advertising and writing techniques used to impress or convince the reader or listener to which children may be alerted. Their study can become a fascinating subject to be explored, illustrated, and discussed if the teacher wishes to promote critical thinking.

FACTORS INFLUENCING COMPREHENSION AND CRITICAL READING

Before approaching the question of how we might teach comprehension, it would be wise to consider some of the factors that influence or affect successful comprehension. With this background information, the teacher may then attempt to modify her teaching of comprehension in terms of pupil differences, variations in materials, and the purposes for reading.

The factors influencing comprehension may, for convenience, be arranged in three categories: those inherent in the material being read, the characteristics of the reader himself, and the influences dependent upon the manner of reading. These categories overlap, of course, but they permit a more organized review of the extensive literature.

The Material Being Read

A primary influence upon the reader's comprehension is his ability to deal with the vocabulary—the word factor so frequently mentioned in factor analyses of the process. In a sense, the reader's success in recognizing the technical terms and the denotations and connotations of the words the author chooses depends upon his reading and informational backgrounds. But his comprehension also depends upon his skill in word analysis by structural, contextual, and visual clues. Thus, although the vocabulary difficulty is an inherent characteristic of the material, like most reading behaviors, solution of the problem rests upon the reader's abilities. An obvious implication of this factor is, of course, that pupils cannot be expected to show successful comprehension in materials with very unfamiliar vocabulary, presenting concepts beyond their experiential background. Nor can they deal readily with reading materials when they lack word analysis skills.

The difficulty of structure, style, and concept density are other characteristics of the material being read which may affect its comprehension. The presence of visual aids, which for some become visual handicaps, such as maps, graphs, and tables, also affects comprehension. Ruddell (20) has shown that, as we might expect, pupils can read more effectively in materials in which the sentence structure resembles that which they customarily use in oral language than when patterns are unfamiliar to them. Another study found that adult students comprehended best a text accompanied by a graph, more poorly a text with a table, and poorest when reading the text alone. A number of other studies show that many students never develop any great facility with these textual aids, and they prefer to skip them entirely rather than comprehend less by using the graphic aids.

The name or prestige of the author also tends to influence the reader's comprehension or, in other words, his acceptance of the ideas offered. When known or familiar authors are attributed to comparable selections, even college students tend to understand and accept better those selections supposedly by famous authors. Elementary children are, of course, even more susceptible to this prestige element. The implications present in these observations are fairly apparent: children will need help in dealing with complicated sentence patterns which extend beyond their usual auditory and oral experience, and in dealing with the various graphic aids in their textbooks. They must also be guided in judging materials at face value no matter who the author happens to be, even in their textbooks.

The Reader

Because of the strong component of reasoning in comprehension, which is also a recognized component of intelligence, we observe many marked relationships between the intelligence of the reader and his literal comprehension. The abilities to recognize inductive sequences of ideas leading to a conclusion, to apply deductively a principle to new situations, to recognize cause–effect, comparison, contrast, and other idea relationships depend to a marked degree upon the reader's intellectual powers. Pupils of less than average mental ability can be taught to use these types of thinking while reading, but only within the limits of their capacities in most instances.

A number of recent studies by interview techniques have tried to delve into some of the less obvious differences between the good and the poor comprehender. The interviews of elementary children by Piekarz (18) and of college students by Wark (29) while the students were reading indicate that the good comprehender tends to respond to reading in greater quantity of ideas and associations, in longer fragments and sentences. Samuels (21) has demonstrated this influence of associative thinking in a laboratory-type experiment. His results again indicate that when material contains ideas that are readily associated (moon–bright–earth–light–night–plane), the reader responds with faster reading and better comprehension.

Major influences upon comprehension, as shown in many studies, are the beliefs, attitudes, and prejudices of the reader. Readers of all ages comprehend best those ideas that confirm their own opinions and beliefs and tend to forget opposing views and facts, even when the latter are recognized clearly during the reading (18). Even the mistakes in literal comprehension tend to be exaggerations rather than minimizations of the facts. Attitudes or prejudices do not appear to interfere with literal comprehension, but when judgment or evaluation is involved, their influence is manifest. In fact, reading materials such as newspapers, magazines, and even books do not seem to create opinions on important issues so much as to reflect the beliefs of the public they seek to serve (8).

The reader can, upon occasion, be induced to accept certain beliefs temporarily, provided they do not conflict with his previous ideas on the subject. The prestige of the author, the tone of the material, naive acceptance of the printed word, lack of background information, and the writer's skillful use of the propaganda tricks of his trade, as well as lack of training in critical reading or thinking, often lead the reader to blind acceptance of ideas. This uncritical reading is, as we have implied, most common in subjects or areas when the reader does not feel involved or that his beliefs are challenged.

The influence of the reader's beliefs and attitudes upon comprehension and critical reading must be reckoned with when we are attempting to improve these reading behaviors. We must employ such techniques as presenting materials offering opposing views on an issue, intensive group discussion of the factual and opinionative content, free exchange among pupils of arguments for their viewpoints, and opportunity for the group to make evaluations and judgments independently of the teacher's viewpoint. In all seriousness, one study even suggests that we should recognize the facilitating effect of eating while reading upon the reader's acceptance of persuasive materials. Perhaps we should conduct our efforts to improve comprehension and critical reading during lunch period or class parties.

Recent research on the relationship of personality as reflected in thinking habits, or cognitive style, as it is called, to reading has begun to yield interesting insights. For example, Santostefano (22) found differences between good and poor readers on a *Constricted-Flexible* test of thinking. Poor readers seemed less able to limit their attention to the most significant elements of the stimulus field. As better tests and clearer definitions of cognitive style are evolved and validated, we may expect to discover more about this relationship between the reader's cognitive characteristics and his comprehension.

As Shnayer (25) has shown, interest significantly influences comprehension at all levels of reading ability. Using selections two grade levels above their grade level, both boys and girls in the sixth grade comprehended better in those of high interest to them. The effect of interest upon comprehension was less as reading ability increased, but was still manifest.

Pupil difficulties with comprehension may be due to a variety of contributing factors and are not quickly corrected by so-called comprehension workbooks or such materials. Among the causes are*:

1. Too rapid rate for the difficulty of the reading matter, with consequent superficial comprehension.
2. Lack of informational background to deal with the concepts offered.
3. Inadequate reading vocabulary, reflecting perhaps poor breadth of reading experiences or ineffectual word analysis techniques.
4. Weak organizing skills, such as note taking, summarizing, outlining, and underlining, in dealing with textbooks.
5. Anxiety, tension, and emotional problems in dealing with tests, or lack of sophistication in taking tests.
6. Poor reasoning capacities, owing to low verbal intelligence or lack of training.
7. Too slow a rate of reading because of habit or lack of training, resulting in mind wandering while reading.
8. Too much emphasis upon word analysis rather than securing ideas.

The Reading Process

In addition to factors inherent in the material and the reader himself, the manner in which a reading task is approached and executed certainly affects comprehension. The purposes of the reader, as clarified by prereading discussion, teacher's questions, or by the reader himself, determine the type or kind and degree of comprehension that he achieves. If the reader thinks that his purpose is to secure only general ideas, he neglects and fails to retain the details, and vice versa. His rate of reading is influenced by the purposes he sees, and this, in turn, determines the degree of comprehension. Students who can set strong purposes for their reading comprehend significantly better than those who set vague purposes. This relationship is present whether the student or the teacher clarifies the purposes of reading, an obvious implication for instructional efforts to improve comprehension.

One other factor inherent in the reading process which significantly affects comprehension is rate of reading. In turn, rate of reading reflects the reader's purpose for reading, as well as his set or attitude toward acquiring information. Contrary to popular assumption, rapid reading is not always synonymous with good comprehension, nor are good comprehenders necessarily rapid readers. Rapid reading contributes to better comprehension only when the material is easy or familiar, and the rate of reading approximates the reader's speed for associating

*Diagnosis and treatment of these causes of poor comprehension are treated in detail in the senior author's *Diagnosing and Correcting Reading Disabilities* (Boston: Allyn and Bacon, Inc., 1976).

ideas. When the material is difficult for the reader, a fast rate of reading results in lessened comprehension. When the reader attempts to read at a rate faster than he can associate ideas, the end result again is less than normal comprehension. On the other hand, rapid reading of easy material pushes the reader toward better comprehension because it tends to focus his attention on the stream of ideas rather than on the words. In reading in this way, the reader's concentration is increased and the reading act becomes more like the act of thinking.

Conversely, slow reading in easy or average materials allows the reader to depart from the printed ideas in tangential, irrelevant thoughts, since he can usually think faster than he is reading. Slow reading focuses the reader's attention on word recognition, word meanings, and other mechanical aspects of the process, with consequent loss of retention of the ideas being expressed. Ideally then, we should teach each reader to process easy or hard materials about as fast as he can manage them with maintenance of good comprehension. This suggests that pupils should be trained to read different materials at varying rates according to their ability to comprehend each readily and as fully as the task demands.

DEVELOPING COMPREHENSION AND CRITICAL THINKING

As John E. Merritt pointed out in his review of comprehension at the International Congress on Reading in Paris, 1966 (16), there have been two opposed viewpoints on developing comprehension which have both failed to solve the problem. One group emphasizes long lists of comprehension skills and the need to develop these by carefully planned teacher-directed exercises. Apparently this group believes answering a lot of questions, time after time, will enable the student to show whatever type or degree of comprehension later reading tasks demand. Another group of experts believes that the answer to comprehension development is to start with students' experiences and interests and exploit them. Actually both groups borrow ideas and training materials from each other and neither really practices what it preaches.

As a compromise between these viewpoints, this English reading expert suggests that:

1. Competence in comprehension may be developed only when reading materials are within the experience of the student and the reading is significant to the student.
2. Skill in comprehension will appear from the needs of a student engaged in reading to fulfill his own purposes.
3. It is the job of the teacher to arrange sequences of situations in reading which call forth the variety of comprehension behaviors desired.

To implement his suggestions, Merritt suggests early reading experiences must be experience-based—that is, the language experience approach. Using his own and other children's work as models, we can move toward critical evaluations, judgment, and retention of facts and inferences much more readily than when children are asked to react to the writing of an adult. Difficulty levels, Merritt points out, are almost automatically controlled in vocabulary, style, subject matter, concept load, and similar aspects. Gradually other types of reading material from other sources will be introduced, first as reference materials, later as study sources. At the same time, the experiential background of the pupil will be constantly expanded by a variety of audiovisual aids, library and reference materials, and firsthand experience.

Like the writers of this book, Merritt believes that development of comprehension and critical skills commences very early in the reading program. We also share the belief that comprehension and critical reading depend heavily upon the reader's background, with the obvious implication that this must be strengthened by audiovisual aids, resource materials, discussion, informational presentation by the teacher, and vocabulary development.

To these concepts of comprehension development, we would add two more points of emphasis. First, the types and degree of comprehension and critical reading that students will learn to show reflect the direct influence of the teacher's habits of questioning. Second, few of the reading behaviors we expect to see in comprehension or critical reading, except perhaps vague main ideas and retention of scattered details, appear spontaneously among pupils. Even students who are good readers in that they can handle the materials of their grade level do not either feel the need or show facility in reading critically, unless urged or trained to do so. Even high school and college students focus on remembering facts and show little awareness of the need for evaluation, despite the fact that the materials they read may be slanted, distorted, or questionable. Is it feasible, then, from the very beginning stages of reading to direct children toward the patterns of comprehending and critical thinking we feel are essential by the nature of our questioning?

STRATEGIES FOR COGNITIVE GROWTH

Experts from several disciplines such as educational psychology, creativity, and reading are vitally concerned with the problem of teaching students to think. These efforts have necessitated some redefinitions of both teaching and thinking. As Hilda Taba (28) points out, we have been accustomed to the concept of teaching as pouring out information to pupils, and then, by direct, factual questioning, asking pupils to recite this material back to its source. We have conceived of thinking "as a global process which seemingly encompasses anything that goes on in the head, from daydreaming to constructing a concept of relativity" (28, p. 534). Both of these naive definitions are undergoing radical change, as we will illustrate.

The primary point of attack on this problem is the question of whether teachers' questions presently stimulate the various types of thinking we wish children to employ. Secondary questions are the identification of the cognitive processes to be stimulated and the relationship between these processes and teacher questioning.

By taping teachers' questions in classrooms, Guszak (12) tried to categorize their types, the proportions answered correctly by the pupils, and the sequences of questions and responses that were common. He found that recall of memory questions formed 66.5 percent in second grade, 48.4 percent in fourth grade, and 47.6 percent in the sixth grade. Other types of questions, such as translation, explanation, and evaluation, were not used more than about once in every five questions. Moreover, the evaluation questions were quite superficial, for they usually demanded no more than a "yes" or "no" answer.

Pupils' accuracy in answering questions was greatest in the second grade, perhaps because so many demanded only recall of details. In the intermediate grades, teachers often accepted incorrect answers from the children because they themselves could not recall so many details from the selections. The most frequent pattern of question–response was simply a direct, correct answer to the teacher's question, accounting for more than half of the pupil–teacher interactions. Other common interactions were those in which a teacher offered a guiding remark or question and then, without waiting for a response, asked a second direct question. Sometimes teachers asked for verification of an answer from the textbook, or justification of a response by the pupil or by other pupils. Guszak concluded his observations of teacher questioning strategies with the remark, "About the only thing that appears to be programmed into the students is the nearly flawless ability to anticipate the trivial nature of the teachers' literal questions . . . the students have learned well to parrot back an endless recollection of trivia" (12, p. 234).

In her study of children's thinking, Taba (28) carried the study of teacher-pupil interaction somewhat further than Guszak. For example, she studied sequences of questions and their effect upon the level of thought manifested in children's responses. Taba distinguishes three levels of thinking—concept formation (differentiating, grouping, categorizing); generalizations and inferences; explanation or prediction. She strongly urges that teachers should address their questions to the objective they have for the class's thinking, sequencing questions to elicit the types of thinking desired. As types of teachers' questions, she identifies those that focus on a fact; refocus thinking on a different level—for example, from factual to explanatory; extend thought by a question to which a number of children can contribute; and control thought by suggesting a line of thought by the children, as classifying or explaining.

Taba's study of classroom discussions revealed some very interesting facts about teachers' effects upon children's thinking. She found that when teachers attempted to raise the level of thought too early in the discussion, children's ability to maintain thinking at the level was soon exhausted and discussion rapidly deteriorated to a lower level. However, by first focusing thought (on concepts, categories, observed facts), then extending the thinking to a number of children, and later lifting the level to more complex modes of thinking (generalizations, inferences, explanations), the discussion results in a gradual movement of the majority of students toward higher levels of thinking. In any such sequence of questions, the time spent focusing on a certain level of thinking would, of course, depend upon the depth of the material being discussed. Thus, although the general trend of level of questions would gradually move upward, various sequences would differ perhaps in the number of each type of question, as the thinking moved from the concept level to generalizations and inferences to explanations and predictions.

We have provided sufficient background for acceptance of the concept that comprehension and critical reading are, in large measure, the outcome of the teacher's strategy in handling questions on the reading materials. We have also reviewed some of the research on comprehension and noted several significant implications. These indications for classroom practice might be summarized in this fashion.

1. Pupils cannot be expected to show good comprehension or critical reading in unfamiliar materials or those burdened with difficult vocabulary.
2. Pupils will need direct training in handling the graphic and study aids commonly found in textbooks.
3. Comprehension and critical reading abilities might be limited by the child's reasoning capacities.
4. Readers who show good comprehension are characterized by a strong tendency to associative thinking, reacting while reading.
5. Pupils need to be taught how to suspend judgments based on their personal beliefs or prejudices until they have clearly understood the author's presentation, when reading passages that differ from their viewpoints. Growth in this ability may be promoted by providing frequent opportunity to read and discuss contradictory viewpoints.
6. Teachers should make every effort to clarify the purposes for reading all assigned materials. Pupils should be given frequent opportunity to state and discuss their purposes, and the manner in which they adapt their reading to those avowed purposes.
7. Training in reading materials at different rates according to their difficulty and the purposes for reading should be given all children.
8. Training in increasing rate of reading up to that point where comprehension begins to decrease should be offered in simple materials to all children. This is most effective if conducted on an individual basis of each child competing with himself, rather than trying to equal the rates of reading of other pupils.
9. We must constantly be aware that comprehension is based upon the experiential background the reader brings to the printed page. Therefore we must ensure that the reader can relate to the content by providing a variety of prereading activities which help to prepare him for that content.
10. Among younger pupils, we can most readily promote analytic and critical behaviors if we employ reading materials composed by other children. Then as his experiential background grows through the activities and resource materials the teacher provides, the child may gradually approach textbook-like materials, while maintaining his analytic and critical reading abilities.

11. The kinds of comprehension and critical reading behaviors that pupils learn reflect the teacher's habits in probing the outcomes of their reading.
12. Skill in literal comprehension does not ensure ability in analytic or critical thinking in the act of reading.

TEACHERS' QUESTIONS AND CHILDREN'S READING

We have mentioned some of the research on teacher strategies for stimulating children's thinking. Perhaps the most practical next step would be to implement this research by illustrating precisely what kinds of teacher questions might be used in this approach to comprehension. We will follow the categories of questions discussed in the excellent book on this subject by Sanders. His book, *Classroom Questions: What Kinds?* presents its subject in much greater detail than we can here. It will be very profitable reading for any teacher attempting to improve her interaction with pupils, particularly when teaching in the content fields.

1. Memory—recognizing or recalling information as given in the passage. Sanders distinguishes four kinds of ideas on the memory level of thinking:
    (a) Facts—
        Who did _____?
        When did _____?
        How many _____?
        What are _____?
    (b) Definitions of terms used, and perhaps explained, in the text—
        What is meant by _____?
        What does _____ mean?
        What meaning did you understand for _____?
        Define _____ .
        Explain what we mean by _____ .
    (c) Generalizations—recognizing a common characteristic of a group of ideas or things
        What events led to _____?
        In what three ways do _____ resemble _____?
        How did _____ and _____
            effect (cause) _____?
    (d) Values—a judgment of quality
        What is said about _____?
            Do you agree?
        What kind of a boy was _____?
        What did _____ do that you wouldn't?
2. Translations—expressing ideas in different form or language
    (a)   Tell me in your own words how _____?
        What kind of a drawing could you make to illustrate _____?

How could we restate _____?

Could we make up a play to tell this story?

How?

What does the writer mean by the phrase _____?

Write a story pretending you are _____ .

3. Interpretation—trying to see relationships among facts, generalizations, values, etc. Sanders recognizes several types of interpretation

  (a) Comparative—are ideas the same, different, related, or opposed?

    How is _____ like _____?

    Is _____ the same as _____?

      Why not?

    Which three _____ are most alike in _____?

    Compare _____ with _____ in _____ .

    How does _____ today

      resemble _____ in _____?

  (b) Implications—arriving at an idea which depends upon evidence in the reading passage

    What will _____ and _____ lead to?

    What justification for _____ does the author give?

    If _____ continues to _____, what is likely to happen?

    What would happen if _____?

  (c) Inductive thinking—applying a generalization to a group of observed facts

    What facts in the story tend to support the idea that _____?

    What is the author trying to tell you by _____?

    What does the behavior of _____ tell you about him?

    What events led to _____?

    Why?

  (d) Quantitative—using a number of facts to reach a conclusion

    How much has _____ increased?

    What conclusions can you draw from the table (graph) on page _____?

    How many times did _____ do _____? Then what happened?

    How many causes of _____ can you list?

  (e) Cause and effect—recognizing the events leading to a happening

    Why did the boy _____?

    How did the boy make _____ happen?

    What two things led up to _____?

    When the girl _____, what had to happen?

    Why did _____ happen?

4. Application—solving a problem that requires the use of generalizations, facts, values, and other appropriate types of thinking

    How can we show that we need a traffic policeman at the crossing at the south end of our school?

    If we want to raise hamsters in our classroom, what sort of plans will we have to make?

    John has been ill for several days. What could we do to help him during his illness? To show him we think of him?

5. Analysis—recognizing and applying rules of logic to solution of a problem; analyzing an example of reasoning

  Discuss the statement, "All teachers are kind and friendly."

  Some people think that boys can run faster than girls.
   What do you think?

  John was once bitten by a dog. Now John dislikes all dogs. Is he right or wrong in his feelings?
   Why?

6. Synthesis—using original, creative thinking to solve a problem

  What other titles could you think of for this story?

  What other ending can you think of for this story?

  If John had not _____ , what might have happened?

  Pretend you are a manufacturer of pencils who wishes to produce a much better pencil. Tell what you might do.

7. Evaluation—making judgments based on clearly defined standards

  Did you enjoy the story of _____? For what reasons?

  What do you think of _____ in this story?
   Do you approve of his actions?

  In the textbook, the author tells us that _____ felt _____ . Is this a fact or the author's opinion? How do you know?

  This story has a very happy ending. Should all stories end happily? Why not?

  The author of our textbook apparently believes that the American colonists were right in their actions. Do you agree? What do you suppose the British said about the colonists?

  Write a short story about your favorite person in history. Tell why this person is your favorite.

HOW TO USE QUESTIONING AND TO STIMULATE COMPREHENSION

There are a number of facts revealed by the related research which can be used as a guide to effective questioning. They are important enough to be discussed at great length, but we shall try to summarize their implications for the convenience of our readers.

1. Prereading questions tend to direct children toward finding the answers, with little incidental learning and little depth of comprehension (8).
2. Prereading discussion which brings out related terms and ideas, and related activities or experiences of the pupils is preferable to a set of questions (21).
3. Advance organizers, as they are called, should be suggestions on how to recognize the relationships present, how to organize the material, hints about generalizations or principles that might be present and are effective for some pupils (7,8).
4. When material requires recall of many details, help pupils in thinking up of mnemonic memory schemes ("Thirty days has September . . .") or acronyms,

in which each letter stands for a fact to be learned (7,8). Even this rote memory learning must be supported with flexible, meaningful, associated ideas if it is to be retrieved later. There is no such thing as rote memory–rote retrieval or parrotlike recall of a series of related facts (30) without some organizing scheme to link them together.

5. Postreading questions, used at relatively short intervals, as after each paragraph, particularly in the last half of the material, promote depth and breadth of comprehension both literal and critical as well as better understanding of new terms (7).

6. Questions requiring pupil reactions, insights, judgments, or reflection before answering are highly effective.

7. Questioning procedures should give time and encouragement to slow responders, and should follow up inadequate responses by clarifying questions.

8. Relevant comments and questions from the pupils should be encouraged as well as discussion of their answers and using the text to prove answers.

9. Repeating .questions in the same form or repeating pupils' answers is not desirable. Rephrase questions that evoke inadequate or no response; comment on or ask for supporting evidence for pupils' answers (3).

10. In content materials such as science, relatively direct rather than open-ended questions are more effective. Summarizing, with the aid of the pupils, at the end of each lesson is better than reviewing past lessons before beginning a new one (32).

11. Davidson (3) observed that "Both teachers and pupils seemed to believe that there is an answer for *every question!*" Recognize that many questions require viewpoints, all of which may be defensible. Admit when you do not know an absolute answer to a question, perhaps proposed by the children, and take the opportunity to involve them with you in searching for possible, even incomplete answers.

12. Feedback from the teacher should do more than indicate that an answer is correct. Elaboration or explanation clarifying why it is correct or not; help to the student in improving his response by "Can you explain that a bit more?" "Why is that so?" etc.; and more positive response from the teacher than the usual "good," "OK" are very desirable, as "Yes, that's correct because . . ." (24).

David B. Doake of Christchurch Teachers College (4) has contributed additional facts to these suggestions for questioning procedures. He distinguished between factual and reasoning prereading and postreading questions. His results indicate prereading reasoning questions produced the best long-term retention of key ideas and the supporting facts. In contrast, prereading factual questions, as we have noted, result in poor immediate recall of related facts or, in other words, limit total comprehension; and also increase the students' reading time.

Postreading reasoning questions help the student retain the key ideas of a selection, but not necessarily all the facts supporting these ideas. Postreading factual questions helped retention of key ideas and supporting facts, but not any more than prereading factual questions or instructions "to read carefully." To summarize, if we want to stress a few basic ideas, we may use prereading factual questions. If we want broader comprehension, we should use prereading reasoning questions.

Other observations of the effects of teachers' procedures in reading lessons indicate that (1) using the same text for all pupils leads to a lack of pupil–teacher interaction; (2) the more lecturing and criticizing, the greater the loss in comprehension and the more pupil withdrawal from spontaneous interaction with the teacher; (3) vocabulary gains are stimulated when the teacher promotes freedom of pupil oral expression (23). One study indicates that comprehension is helped and vocabulary knowledge increased by simultaneous silent reading by pupils while listening to teacher read. This is superior to having children read orally one after the other or read silently, particularly in dealing with difficult textbooks.

As Nila B. Smith has noted (26), a teacher cannot be expected to remember to try all the types of questions we have listed above (unless perhaps she posts a checklist on her desk). It will be more practical to identify the types of thinking you wish to stimulate in your lesson plan and concentrate on one or two types during each lesson. As your skill in framing the different types becomes greater, you can expand the variety, and learn to move from concrete or literal recall, to interpretation or explanatory types, to analytic and synthetic (creative) and evaluation types during the course of a lesson, as Taba suggests (28).

In this chapter we have tried to provide a depth of background for the teacher who is attempting to improve comprehension. As we have shown again and again, comprehension and critical reading are modes of thinking which are taught to children by the stimulus of the discussion in the classroom. We did not provide examples of "good comprehension exercises" as most reading textbooks do. We believe that such printed exercises or tests have a place in the development of comprehension, but a minor part to be sure. What we have tried to show is that if employed, such exercises must be used selectively, critically in fact, by the teacher. All too often such exercises sample only the simplest types of thinking, memory, or parrotlike recall of details.

Nor can such an approach to teaching comprehension be justified because it appears to enable students to score better on reading tests. The broader concept of comprehension we are suggesting will also accomplish this short-sighted goal, as well as promote the development of comprehension and critical reading in depth.

We intended to present the complete picture of thinking in reading, to encourage teachers to make exercises and tests and ask questions which cover the entire gamut of cognitive processes. Development of any real depth of comprehension or the faculty of intelligent, critical reading is impossible, if we depend upon drill books, workbooks, and other stereotyped, repetitive materials. Our goals will be reached only by diversifying our questioning constantly, and by including on almost every occasion as many as possible of the types of stimuli to thinking we have outlined above.

DISCUSSION QUESTIONS

1. What is your concept of comprehension and of appropriate ways of stimulating it?

2. Would more intelligent children be more likely to develop deeper comprehension and more evidence of critical thinking spontaneously, regardless of the classroom practices?

3. Suggest ways in which a teacher can promote more active reacting and associating while reading among pupils who read with poor comprehension.

4. Which comprehension skills do you think are most important? Why? What evidence can you give that these skills really involve different intellectual or reading behaviors than are supposedly present in other skills?

5. What are your reactions to the definition of comprehension as being simply a few basic types of thinking processes?

6. In your opinion, is critical reading a type of comprehension or a separate group of skills or what?

REFERENCES

1. Cleland, Donald L., "A Construct of Comprehension," *Reading and Inquiry,* Conference Proceedings, International Reading Association, 10, 1965, 59–64.

2. Cook, Jimmie E., "I Can't Believe I Ate the Whole . . .," *Elementary English,* 51 (November–December 1974), 1158–1161.

3. Davidson, Roscoe, "Teacher Influence and Children's Levels of Thinking," *Reading Teacher,* 22 (May 1969), 702–704.

4. Doake, David B., "An Investigation into the Facilitative Effects of Two Kinds of Adjunct Questions on the Learning and Remembering of Teachers College Students During a Reading of Textual Materials with an Associated Study of Student Reading Improvement Incorporating a Survey of Their Textbook Reading Habits, Attitudes and Problems," Master's thesis, University of Canterbury, New Zealand, 1972.

5. Follman, John, Lowe, A. J., and Wiley, Russell, "Correlational and Factor Analysis of Critical Reading and Thinking Test Scores—Twelfth Grade," in *Reading: The Right to Participate,* 20th Yearbook, National Reading Conference, 1971, 128–136.

6. Follman, John, and Lowe, A. J., "Empirical Examination of Critical and Critical Thinking Overview," *Journal of Reading Behavior,* 5 (Summer 1972–1973), 159–168.

7. Frase, Lawrence T., "Learning from Prose Material: Length of Passage, Knowledge of Results and Position of Questions," *Journal of Educational Psychology,* 58 (October 1967), 266–272.

8. Frase, Lawrence T., "Boundary Conditions for Mathemagenic Behaviors," *Review of Educational Research,* 40 (June 1970), 337–348.

9. Gall, Meredith D., "The Use of Questions in Teaching," *Review of Educational Research,* 40 (December 1970), 707–721.

10. Guilford, J. P., "Frontiers in Thinking That Teachers Should Know About," *Reading Teacher,* 13 (February 1960), 176–182.

11. Gustafson, Richard A., "Factor Analyzing the Iowa Tests of Basic Skills," *Psychology in the Schools,* 7 (1970), 226–267.

12. Guszak, Frank J., "Teacher Questioning and Reading," *Reading Teacher,* 21 (December 1967), 227–234.

13. Jenkinson, Marion D., "Information Gaps in Research in Reading Comprehension," in *Reading: Process and Pedagogy,* 19th Yearbook, National Reading Conference, 1971, 179–192.

14. Keislar, Evan R., "Learning Sets in a Stimulus–Response View of Classroom Motivation," paper read at American Educational Research Association meeting, Atlantic City, N.J., February 17, 1960.

15. Lampard, Dorothy M., "Reading and Writing Abilities of High School Students," in *New Frontiers in Reading,* Conference Proceedings International Reading Association, 12, 1967.

16. Merritt, John E., "Developing Competence in Reading Comprehension," in *Reading Instruction: An International Forum,* Proceedings of the First World Congress on Reading. Newark, Del.: International Reading Association, 1967.

17. Morris, Ronald, *Success and Failure in Learning To Read.* London: Oldbourne Book Co., 1973.

18. Piekarz, Josephine, "Getting Meaning from Reading," *Elementary School Journal,* 56 (March 1956), 303–309.

19. Robinson, Helen M., "The Major Aspects of Reading," in *Reading: Seventy-five Years of Progress,* Supplementary Educational Monographs, No. 96. Chicago: University of Chicago Press, 1966.

20. Ruddell, Robert B., "The Effect of Oral and Written Patterns of Language Structure on Reading Comprehension," *Reading Teacher,* 18 (January 1965), 270–275.

21. Samuels, S. Jay, "Effect of Word Associations on Reading Speed and Recall," in *Proceedings,* American Psychological Association, 1966, 255–256.

22. Santostefano, Sebastiano, Rutledge, Louis, and Randall, David, "Cognitive Styles and Reading Disability," *Psychology in the School, 2* (January 1965), 57–62.

23. Schneyer, J. Wesley, "Classroom Verbal Interaction and Pupil Learning," *Reading Teacher,* 23 (January 1970), 369–371.

24. Schwartz, Elaine, and Sheff, Alice, "Student Involvement in Questioning for Comprehension," *Reading Teacher, 29* (November 1975), 150–154.

25. Shnayer, Sidney W., "Relationships Between Reading Interest and Reading Comprehension," in *Reading and Realism,* J. Allen Figurel, ed. International Reading Association Conference Proceedings, 13 (1969), 698–702.

26. Smith, Nila B., "The Many Faces of Reading Comprehension," *Reading Teacher, 23* (December 1969), 249–259.

27. Spache, George D., *Toward Better Reading.* Champaign, Ill.: Garrard Publishing Company, 1963, 66–73.

28. Taba, Hilda, "The Teaching of Thinking," *Elementary English, 42* (May 1965), 534–542.

29. Wark, David M., "Reading Comprehension as Implicit Verbal Behavior," in *Multidisciplinary Aspects of College–Adult Reading,* 17th Yearbook, National Reading Conference, 1968, 192–198.

30. Weaver, Wendell W., Kingston, Albert J., Bickley, A. C., and White, W. F., "Information-Flow Difficulty in Relation to Reading Comprehension," *Journal of Reading Behavior,* 1 (Summer 1969), 41–49.

31. Williams, Gertrude, "Provisions for Critical Reading in Basal Readers," *Elementary English,* 41 (May 1959), 323–330.

32. Wright, Clifford, and Nuthall, Graham, "Relationship Between Teacher Behaviors and Pupil Achievement in Three Experimental Elementary Science Lessons," *American Educational Research Journal,* 7 (November 1970), 477–492.

SUPPLEMENTARY READING

Dawson, Mildred A., compiler, *Developing Comprehension Including Critical Reading.* Newark, Del.: International Reading Association, 1968.

Lee, Doris, Bingham, Alma, and Woelfel, Sue, *Critical Reading Develops Early.* Reading Aids Series. Newark, Del.: International Reading Association, 1968.

Russell, David H., *Children's Thinking.* Boston: Ginn and Co., 1956.

Sanders, Norris M., *Classroom Questions: What Kinds?* New York: Harper & Row, Inc., 1966.

Stauffer, Russell G., ed., *Dimensions of Critical Reading.* Proceedings of the Annual Education and Reading Conferences, Vol. XI. Newark, Del.: University of Delaware, 1964.

Stauffer, Russell G., and Cramer, Ronald, *Teaching Critical Reading at the Primary Level.* Reading Aids Series. Newark, Del.: International Reading Association, 1968.

14
Approaches to Classroom Management

PREVIEW

We have been experimenting with patterns of classroom management ever since the first school was built in America. Even in the past half-century we have had two periods of great interest in grouping schemes, first in the 1920s to 1930s and again in the past two decades. At each peak in this cycle we sought solutions to our educational problems in trying many types of arrangements without, as we shall see, finding all the answers. Currently we are drawing upon some hitherto unused resources of the community in using parents, other adults, and other pupils as tutors, and soliciting the technological know-how of industry, as in performance contracting. Other new developments in the past two decades are team teaching, cluster grouping, the open school, pupil teams, and the like.

There are a number of problems both recognized and hidden in adopting a new grouping scheme for a classroom or a school. While most such changes are justified by the persons involved as attempts to provide differentiated instruction keyed to pupils' needs and abilities, this laudable goal is often lost sight of among the new problems created. New patterns of classroom management often fail because:

1. There is not sufficient or significant information about pupils to warrant a new arrangement. Pupils may be grouped in this or that arrangement on the superficial grounds of the results of a single general reading test, or that plus a mental test. As a result, there are only slight differences between the groups and hence no differential results.
2. The available instructional materials may be inappropriate or inadequate to the new arrangement, as in shifting from basal groups to individualized reading or cluster grouping without changing greatly the variety and quantity of reading materials.
3. Many patterns of grouping make the assumption that the children assigned to a unit are at the same point in reading development, use their reading skills about the same way, have similar interests, need the same kind of instruction, and will progress similarly. And all these assumptions are, again, often based on a test or two of overall reading or mental ability. Categorically speaking, this group of assumptions is almost never true in ordinary school situations.
4. New grouping schemes depend for success on the efforts of the teacher, perhaps more than any other variable, for a competent teacher can make any system look good. Yet teachers are not always consulted about their opinions of the grouping arrangement nor are teacher assignments often related to teacher interest, experience, or even willingness to experiment. Individual teachers may fail in trying a different arrangement because their concept of a teacher's proper role conflicts with the procedures demanded in the new plan. For example, they find they cannot endure the noise, movement, pupil freedom, and constant personal demands of cluster grouping or individualized reading as in the open-school concept.
5. Changes within a school or even within a classroom imply that the teachers involved have administrative support and encouragement, as well as in-service training in the new procedures. Some grouping arrangements depend heavily upon the help of the librarian, special teachers, the reading supervisor, and others of the school staff. Even with the best efforts and intentions, a new plan may well be defeated by the lack of teacher preparation and support.
6. Experiments in classroom management often turn out to be social class stratification because of the relationship between reading success and language and cultural backgrounds. Minority, economically disadvantaged, and bilingual children tend to be channeled into certain groups, with consequent negative attitudes toward the scheme (and the school) of the pupils, their parents, and some of the teachers.

Whether we are considering a new way of grouping within one classroom, or a major change in the school organization, these are a few of the factors which limit its success. We are not negative to changes, for they are excellent experiences in promoting classroom competence, flexibility, and deeper self-insights. But each shift has its own peculiar disadvantages, as well as advantages, as we shall point out.

HOMOGENEOUS VERSUS HETEROGENEOUS GROUPS

Probably the commonest type of grouping in many schemes is the attempt to bring together pupils of similar ability, in other words, a homogeneous population. Pupils of similar reading ability or mental capacity or both seem to be a unit lending itself to maximum effectiveness of teaching and minimum teacher effort. Since the pupils are all starting at about the same level and are supposed to learn at about the same rate, whole group instruction with perhaps only one type of material and one lesson plan preparation appears quite feasible.

But pupils grouped by reading level still vary in reading grades as well as various important reading skills. The range of reading levels is only reduced about 20 percent in homogeneous elementary classes according to one survey (7). In other words, rather than having a range of four to five grade levels in the classroom, a homogeneous fourth grade may now have a three- to four-grade range. And using mental test results also in selecting the pupils would further reduce the range only by about another half-year. In other words, unless the number of pupils at a grade level is very large, and performances in a number of reading skills, plus intelligence, plus interests, plus learning modality, plus academic motivation are the criteria for the formation of the groups, the experimentation with homogeneous grouping is not feasible. Unless these factors are considered, the group formed is not really homogeneous, and one of these factors may be as responsible for the results as the grouping itself.

The Research. A quick review of the voluminous research on the achievement of homogeneous versus heterogeneous classes uncovers just about as many favoring either approach. Most studies reached no definite conclusions because the groups compared differed only in one trait, as high versus low reading or mental ability. There is some indication that homogeneous grouping is inclined to be advantageous for high-ability pupils in increasing their achievement. At the same time, the segregation by mental or reading ability or both reduces the competition present in groups of mixed ability. As a result, the high self-ratings of gifted students drop, self-assessments of slow pupils increase, while average pupils are unaffected. Motivation appears to decrease, particularly for the high and low students in homogeneous grouping. These undesirable side effects should certainly be considered as significant as the unsure effects upon achievement (4,37).

Homogeneous grouping is often attempted in some systems when pupils leave self-contained (mixed) classes to enter a departmentalized arrangement at intermediate or upper elementary school ages. There is very little research exploring the effects of this shift to the pattern in which each subject area is taught by a different teacher and the class usually moves as a body from one room to another. Lamme (21) has shown that teaching reading as a separate subject, in this arrangement, has a distinct effect upon children's reading practices. The influence of the teacher markedly lessened, as shown by the fact that the departmentalized pupils read fewer books, used the classroom library very little, and depended upon self-selection, not the teacher or their peers, for their choices, which were more often paperbacks than books.

Intraclass Patterns

We described and criticized earlier the most common three-reading-group plan observed so often in basal reading instruction. We emphasized its inadequacy in dealing with the actual range of reading levels in using only three or four levels of instructional materials. We stressed particularly its failure to provide for the full capabilities of gifted students. We claimed that teacher-organized reading groups violate all that we know about how natural groups operate, develop leaders and followers, and show cohesiveness in working toward a self-selected goal. Pupil relationships and interests, and the possibilities in self-motivation, group esprit, and growth in independence are all ignored (2,23).

Teachers who utilize this type of intraclass grouping by reading levels with the avowed intention of meeting individual differences were challenged. Rather, it was shown that their selections of children for the groups was based on very weak grounds or no real evidence of diagnosis of pupil strengths or weaknesses. Moreover, the arbitrary nature of these selections is demonstrated in that, after the first few weeks of school, very few changes in placement of the children are made, no matter how the pupils progress. Finally, although the evidence is not strong, there is certainly an effect upon pupil self-concepts when they are segregated and labeled according to their abilities (15,16).

Perhaps we are overconcerned with the stereotyping of pupil self-concepts. But there are other significant effects that are undesirable. When a teacher uses a single textbook for each reading group, as she usually does, she reduces the possibilities of teacher–pupil interaction, reduces pupil spontaneity and mobility. She also makes less provision for individual differences and like the children offers fewer positive verbal remarks than if she were using multilevel texts (25). Moreover, how realistic in terms of the actual reading levels of the children is this use of one reader for each group? The low reading group often actually extends over a two- to three-year range, while the high group has an even greater range of reading levels, in almost any grade from the third grade on. When the instructional procedures are adapted to a recognition of the diversity of abilities in each group by the use of multilevel texts and supplementary reading materials, we find more positive teacher and pupil behavior, fewer negative interactions among pupils, more independent and creative activities initiated by teacher or pupils, and quicker assumption of responsibility and of leadership in the group by the pupils. Does the three-group plan appear to be a defensible practice?

Interest Groups

The learning stations approach that we described elsewhere will tend to function in the development of interest groups. Criscuolo (9) describes several other interesting versions of these, as *Art-Cart*—materials to do illustrations and express feelings; *Help-Self-Shelf*—a collection for independent small-group activities and games; and *Label-Table*—science and nature-study objects for categorizing and classifying. Another pair of authors sampled teachers' techniques for stimulating reading interests. Their responses included an auction of books with paper money; arranging reading to or with a partner; taping portions of interesting books for use in group guessing games; writing one's own book; arranging to share books by posters; bulletin boards; reading selected portions to peers; puppet shows; and role playing (32). Obviously, the conditions must be favorable to permit this development of interest groups. Freedom of choice, time to enjoy, lots of books and related materials, as well as such teacher practices as reading carefully selected, interesting books to children, discussing them in depth rather than in detail, and enthusiasm for reading are all essential (18).

Interest grouping or allowing pupils to form their own reading groups on the basis of friendship, a common reading interest, mutual admiration, age, or whatever would seem a very realistic approach. If the teacher feels this is impractical because she wants to give instruction to pupils in a group with similar needs, she can form such arrangements at other times. But any type of silent reading, assigned or supplementary; project or creative activity; class newspaper, mural, diorama, or other project should be done by a self-selected group. Even study exercises should be similarly arranged, as we will point out later in our discussion of pupil teams, for the learning will be better and the work done more efficiently. Or are we to continue to think that pupils learn best by teacher-directed activities with which the group does not identify and whose goals they never discuss or understand?

INTERCLASS GROUPING

Cross-class or interclass grouping involves parallel scheduling of reading lessons among several sections of one or several grades. The pupils go to different rooms, at the appointed time, according to their general level. Thus teacher A teaches all the fourth graders who read at third-grade level, teacher B instructs the fourth graders of fifth-grade ability, and so on. There is present in this arrangement the assumption that the range of abilities is thus reduced in each classroom, and the teacher's job is made easier. In actuality, these goals are not achieved, for the range of differences in major reading skills is not appreciably lessened since the selection criteria are so superficial.

Some advocates of the Joplin plan, as it was commonly called, seem to find merit in the arrangement in short-term experiments. But, in longer studies, any favorable results in achievement tend to disappear after one semester. Several studies have shown that, in the majority of trials, superior results were obtained in the self-contained classroom (26), particularly for better-than-average readers.

Interclass grouping ignores age and maturity in combining pupils from several grade levels upon many occasions. It also separates reading from all other language activities as though it were a nonlanguage type of learning. The information derived from observation and personal experience with children is often not transmitted from teacher to teacher. The particular problems of the poorest readers may be unknown by the teacher assigned these pupils. Thus reading instruction becomes less efficient and more difficult because of the compartmentalizing of pupils and related facets of language development. As a result, it has been shown that the poor readers developed less favorable attitudes, unhappiness with their placement, and poorer personal relations with the other pupils. Their parents, as we might well expect, were negative to the interclass grouping.

NONGRADED OR UNGRADED PRIMARY

Arrangements of classes with a wider than usual age span and no regard for academic performance, nongraded classes, are in use in elementary and secondary schools. It is claimed that such groups promote interaction of different age levels and are therefore stimulating to achievement.

Ungraded primary programs emphasize informal grading and grouping by achievement levels. Children are regrouped each year by rough reading levels, or even more frequently if multiple levels are recognized. The pupils sometimes may continue with the same teacher for the three and one-half or four years allotted for this program.

The research on nongraded classes is almost nonexistent, but the claim persists that this plan adapts instruction to pupil rate of growth. Such a result could, of course, be obtained in any classroom by individualizing instruction and materials. A recent study indicated unfavorable effects upon the peer status of younger pupils, when mixed ages were combined for instruction (1).

Nongraded classes offering an individualized curriculum are based on the belief that repeating a grade, as often occurs in graded schools, did not improve academic achievement and had poor effects on a pupil's self-concept. In contradiction, some studies show that nonpromotion has a beneficial effect upon immature children's marks, school behavior, and home behavior. But the spread of various versions of a nongraded program has continued and the majority of recent comparative studies support its favorable effects upon achievement and mental health, particularly for poorer achievers (30).

There is a version of nongraded arrangements presently called continuous progress. In this plan there are no formal promotions from grade to grade, and children are encouraged to progress academically at their own rate of learning. McLoughlin's study of the effect of the continuous progress approach indicates that the grouping plan required several consecutive years to make an impact upon pupil achievement (24). One-year trials were inconsistent in their results; changing teachers each year and grouping heterogeneously appeared the most effective procedures, in comparison with the usual graded schools, in producing acceleration in achievement.

The studies regarding ungraded primary groups are much greater in volume since the idea has been in use in schools since the 1940s. Most of the reports show higher reading achievement in instances when the plan extended over several years (19). Parental and pupil attitudes also tend to favor the ungraded scheme. The ungraded primary has the advantage over nongraded classes of avoiding the complications of differing ages and maturity, and of widely varying levels of reading ability. With the groups formed on the criterion of reading progress, the division into ten to fifteen stages during the primary grades does reduce the demands on the teacher for instruction on many levels, does tend to encourage progress at the child's own rate, and approaches individualization of instruction more than ordinary classrooms. Most important, it tends to push teachers toward the recognition of individual differences, a trend reacted to favorably by both parents and pupils.

PUPIL TEAMS AND PUPIL TUTORS

In the early 1960s, several studies by students of Donald D. Durrell (11) described successful experiments with pupil pairs or teams working together in reading. The more competent pupil would help his classroom peer, or three or four would work together as a team. The research confirmed the opinions of many teachers who had used the arrangement, and the idea of using other pupils to assist or tutor poor readers spread widely. We now find dozens of reports of trials with older pupils tutoring younger. Some of these are very simple arrangements, as in Dolores Lawrence's article on sixth graders helping first graders with their language experience stories (22). Typically, the tutors gained in their own writing mechanics as a result of the relationship. Other reports show more carefully planned arrangements, in which the tutors receive some training in how to relate to a younger child, and in how to respond and support (33). Often the tutors are selected because they, too, are poor readers, and, as expected, their skills improve significantly in helping a younger pupil. Sometimes tutors and tutees are carefully matched in race, as black with black, Chicano with Chicano. A few schools have used a reading specialist to diagnose the young child's needs and prescribe the remedial materials. Others keep the relationship more spontaneous and informal and simply provide the tutor with a choice of materials and some ideas on how to chart progress (31). Even teacher-training institutions have recognized that a tutoring experience is a realistic introduction to classroom practices, particularly during a course in reading methods (33), and may even result in some reading improvement for the college student.

TEAM TEACHING, CLUSTER GROUPING, AND THE OPEN CLASSROOM

The arrangements of team teaching and cluster grouping are almost identical in that two or three classes are combined in one oversized area with a staff of several teachers. One teacher may instruct the entire class or a group in an area of her particular competence, while the other teachers work with individuals or other groups. Teachers may alternate as instructor or resource person in various subjects, and relate their areas more closely by mutual planning. The shifting of teacher responsibilities tends to make for flexibility in grouping, for more opportunity for teacher–pupil interaction, and a wider variety of instructional activities, according to its supporters (5).

Most reports on team teaching or cluster grouping are not research evaluations. It has yet to be demonstrated whether the schemes result in better academic progress, or the other advantages in recognition of individual differences that appear to be present. It is apparent, however, that these plans demand more than usual creativity, competence, and compatibility among teachers, as well as motivation, independence in work habits, and adaptability to different teaching styles among pupils.

It may be that longer studies in comparing the self-contained classroom with a team-teaching arrangement are needed to clarify the values of the latter approach for pupil achievement. For example, Lambert (20) found the self-contained classroom better in gains after the first year; the team teaching, better after the second year. The arrangement creates certain problems for teachers, as we have suggested, and also has effects upon pupil peer relationships. Perhaps because of the number of children present, the pupils in one study (8) experienced increased difficulties in finding friends and relating to classmates. Conceivably, this trend could effect the morale and cohesiveness of the class and thus reduce its progress.

The lack of formal research reports on the effects of combining classes and teachers, or simply placing them in a large undivided area, as in the open school, as it is called, has not deterred a current trend in this direction. Many American schools are being designed to operate in this way, in what is intended to be a model of the British open primary school. A physical resemblance is easily constructed, with art, music, work, or study centers, easily accessible libraries, group and individual work areas, and the like. But some observers doubt that some of the more subtle elements of the British open school can be as readily substituted for traditional American school practices.

To illustrate, British children do not all enter school the same day, but rather upon their fifth birthday or four designated admission dates during the year.

As a result, the first-year program is characterized by much greater flexibility than most American primary teachers offer. This flexibility extends to the choice or even creation of instructional materials, which, unlike so many American schools, are the prerogative of the teacher. Freedom of choice of materials, management procedures, and curriculum permeates the elementary grades. Reading tests are not highly valued and their use is infrequent, possibly because of their irrelevance to what are considered the major goals of the reading program. The goals are not development of reading skills for their values per se; indeed, hardly any teacher manuals or workbooks are issued for the readers to guide the teacher in skill development. Rather the emphasis is placed upon development of maturity in the uses and applications of reading, the appreciation of and interest in literature, and permanent reading interests keyed to one's life goals. For example, it is considered much more important to be able to talk and write about what one has read than to report on its details.

Several authors have been very critical of the impetuous rush of American schools to imitate the British open school. They point out that American educators have failed to recognize that the British system is not revolutionary but has evolved slowly over a period of twenty-five to thirty years to serve its own closely knit society and its philosophy of education (10). The British people are characterized by stability, strong family life, lack of mobility, and by courtesy and respect for other people. Its education is child-centered with emphasis upon the here and now of children's abilities and interests (29). The first aim is to produce people who read and want to read; the secondary aim is to help them to read effectively. If the secondary aim is given priority, as it is in American schools, Vera Southgate of Manchester (34) points out that the first goal will probably never be achieved.

John Downing says that the open school has become a fad with open space buildings going up all over to contain the same conventional closed education practiced in the old buildings (10). Perhaps this explains why the few research studies we have on the outcomes of this new mode tend to be negative. After two and one-half years in the open school, the achievement of fifth-grade pupils was inferior to that in traditional schools in all areas and subjects except spelling and language (38). In another study, pupils' attitudes toward school, teachers, reading, and the freedom in the classroom become less and less favorable as their years in the open school increased (3).

It remains to be proved that an educational system so different from our own in rationale, goals, materials, and classroom procedures can be transported in toto to an oversized American classroom and made to function with advantage.

PARENTS AND PARAPROFESSIONALS

We are witnessing a growing practice in the use of parents and other adults as paid or volunteer assistants to the teacher. The programs take many forms: aides or parents working with an individual or small group while the teacher conducts a lesson for the others; tutoring by parents after school hours; aides or parents simply helping with clerical work, marking workbooks, making displays or other audiovisual materials, and performing many of the other tasks inherent in the operation of a school.

Once they have overcome their fears of interference from the nonprofessional adults, or from the demands on their time to train their aides, many teachers have reacted positively to this new source of assistance (6). And a few small studies of the results of tutoring by adults (35) seem to indicate improved academic motivation and achievement for the pupils involved.

When volunteer or paid aides are used to assist in instruction, it has become apparent that they need a modicum of professional training in how to relate to children positively, how to teach a simple skill, and how to judge pupil progress. The length and content of the training program that will help produce effective aides is gradually being evolved (27). Many manuals for paraprofessionals, as they are called, offering various training programs are listed in the bibliography of this chapter.

Another approach to employing adults in reading instruction has developed from the experiments of Ellson in devising a practical, programmed sequence in word recognition. His scheme has changed from using an automatic flash-card machine with verbal reinforcement to a programmed tutor's guide. Using common readers, all the interaction of the pupil and the adult is spelled out step by step. Thus presumably someone untrained in reading methods can work with a beginning reader with profit for the pupil, following training sessions on the guide and in emulating the teacher's role, and after a short period of supervision. Ellson's programmed guide for adults has been tried in many school systems and the initial reports are favorable (36). Some of the results have been a reduction in nonpromotions, and good performances on tests based on the readers used, which are rather dramatic outcomes from daily fifteen-minute tutoring sessions added to the regular basal instruction. Such results might be due to the motivation imparted by the individual attention of the tutor as much as by the exact nature of the programmed guide. We recall that similar outcomes were mentioned above as the result of pupil teams of an older and a primary child, without using such detailed instructions. It will be profitable for us to learn eventually exactly how much direction the adult or pupil tutor needs to conduct profitable sessions. Meanwhile, it would seem desirable to continue using adults as aides or tutors for pupils who need individualized help.

There remain to be answered such questions as the number of aides that proves effective, or whether having several aides in the classroom may prove to be too much of a good thing. Only one study has attempted to attack this problem. One, none, and up to five aides per class were contrasted. Using one aide produced superior readiness scores for kindergarten children to using no aide, but no significant gains above this were noted as more aides were added (13).

Those evaluating the National Head Start program's use of untrained adults as aides concluded that:

1. Learning is an intensely personal thing, depending directly on human interaction. Aides can increase this interaction.

2. Successful aides have an interest in children and a supervising teacher who knows how to utilize her aides well.

3. Learning by doing, at least for young children, is a reality of life supported by firsthand experiences. Aides can help provide this essential variety of experiences.

DISCUSSION QUESTIONS

1. What classroom arrangements have you witnessed or participated in? Share your reactions with the class.

2. Why do you suppose that so many experiments in grouping fail to give very definite results? Is it because of their length, the Hawthorne effect, the lack of differentiation in instruction and materials, the criteria for selecting children for grouping, or what?

3. The variable of teacher competence and enthusiasm seems to be significant in many of our grouping trials. How

could this influence be controlled to give greater significance to the experimental results?

4. Is it conceivable that a trial of a type of grouping will create more problems than it might solve? How might the difficulties in initiating a new type of grouping be overcome?

5. What is the true goal of any organizational pattern, in your opinion? Do some attempts lose sight of this goal? How and why?

REFERENCES

1. Ahlbrand, William P., Jr., and Reynolds, James A., "Some Social Effects of Cross-Grade Grouping," *Elementary School Journal,* 72 (March 1972), 327–332.

2. Alexander, J. Estill, and Filler, Ronald Claude, "Group Cohesiveness and Reading Instruction," *Reading Teacher,* 27 (February 1974), 446–450.

3. Arlin, Marshall, "Open Education and Pupils' Attitudes," *Elementary School Journal,* 76 (January 1976), 219–228.

4. Borg, W. R., "Ability Grouping in the Public Schools: A Field Study," *Journal of Experimental Education,* 34 (1965), 1–97.

5. Brownell, John A., and Taylor, Harris A., "Theoretical Perspectives for Teaching Teams," *Phi Delta Kappan,* 43 (January 1962), 150–156.

6. Chapman, Ruth, "They're a Plus: Volunteers are IN," *Florida Schools,* 34 (November–December 1971), 11–15.

7. Clarke, S. C. T., "The Effect of Grouping on Variability in Achievement at the Grade III Level," *Alberta Journal of Educational Research,* 4 (September 1958), 162–171.

8. Cooper, Dan H., and Sterns, Harvey N., "Team Teaching: Student Adjustment and Achievement," *Jour-*

nal of Educational Research, 66 (March 1973), 323–327.

9. Criscuolo, Nicholas P., "Interchange," *Reading Teacher,* 27 (March 1974), 624–625.

10. Downing, John, "Language Arts in Open Schools," *Elementary English,* 52 (January 1975), 23–29.

11. Durrell, Donald D., "Pupil-Team Learning: Objectives, Principles, Techniques," in *Changing Concepts of Reading Instruction,* Proceedings International Reading Association, 6, 1961, 75–78.

12. Frazer, Stanley, and Stern, Carolyn, "Learning by Teaching," *Reading Teacher,* 23 (February 1970), 403–405, 417.

13. Goralski, Patricia J., and Kerl, Joyce M., "Kindergarten Teacher Aides and Reading Readiness in Minneapolis Public Schools," *Journal of Experimental Education,* 37 (1968), 34–38.

14. Green, Donald Ross, and Riley, Hazel Walker, "Interclass Grouping for Reading Instruction in the Middle Grades," *Journal of Experimental Education,* 31 (March 1963), 273–278.

15. Groff, Patrick J., "A Survey of Basal Reading Grouping Practices," *Reading Teacher,* 15 (January 1962), 232–235.

16. Hawkins, M. L., "Mobility of Students in Reading Groups," *Reading Teacher,* 20 (November 1966), 136–140.

17. Hill, C. H., and Tolman, R., "Tutoring: An Inexpensive Alternative," *Journal of Reading Specialist,* 10 (1970), 19–23.

18. Huck, Charlotte S., "Strategies for Improving Interest and Appreciation in Literature," in *Reaching Children and Young People Through Literature,* Helen W. Painter, ed. Newark, Del.: International Reading Association, 1971, 37–45.

19. Jones, J. Charles, Moore, J. W., and Devender, Frank Van, "A Comparison of Pupil Achievement after One and One-half and Three Years in a Nongraded Program," *Journal of Educational Research,* 61 (October 1967), 75–77.

20. Lambert, Phillip, et al., "A Comparison of Pupil Achievement in Team and Self-Contained Organization," *Journal of Experimental Education,* 33 (Spring 1965), 217–224.

21. Lamme, Linda Leonard, "Self-Contained to Departmentalized: How Reading Habits Changed," *Elementary School Journal,* 76 (January 1976), 208–218.

22. Lawrence, Dolores, "Sparta Revisited," *Reading Teacher,* 28 (February 1975), 464–472.

23. McGinley, Pat, and McGinley, H., "Reading Groups as Psychological Groups," *Journal of Experimental Education,* 39 (1970), 35–42.

24. McLoughlin, William P., "Continuous Pupil Progress in the Non-graded School," *Elementary School Journal,* 71 (November 1970), 90–96.

25. Morrison, Virginia B., "Teacher–Pupil Interaction in Three Types of Elementary Classroom Reading Instruction," *Reading Teacher,* 22 (December 1968), 271–275.

26. Nichols, Nancy J., "Interclass Grouping for Reading Instruction: Who Makes the Decisions and Why?" *Educational Leadership,* 26 (1969), 588–592.

27. Niedermeyer, Fred C., *Parent-Assisted Learning.* Inglewood, Calif.: Southwest Regional Laboratory, 1970.

28. Niedermeyer, Fred C., and Ellis, Patricia, "Remedial Reading Instruction by Trained Pupil Tutors," *Elementary School Journal,* 71 (April 1971), 400–405.

29. O'Brien, Thomas C., "Some Comments on British Education," *Elementary School Journal,* 75 (October 1975), 42–49.

30. Pavan, Barbara Nelson, "Good News: Research on the Non-graded Elementary School," *Elementary School Journal,* 73 (March 1973), 333–342.

31. Richardson, Donald C., and Havlicek, Larry L., "High School Students as Reading Instructors," *Elementary School Journal,* 75 (March 1975), 389–393.

32. Roeder, Harold H., and Lee, Nancy, "Twenty-five Teacher-Tested Ways to Encourage Voluntary Reading," *Reading Teacher,* 27 (October 1973), 48–50.

33. Schoeller, Arthur W., and Pearson, David A., "Better Reading Through Volunteer Reading Tutors," *Reading Teacher,* 23 (April 1970), 625–630, 636.

34. Southgate, Vera, "The Language Arts in Informal British Primary Schools," *Reading Teacher,* 26 (January 1973), 367–373.

35. Vellutino, F. R., and Connolly, C., "The Training of Paraprofessionals as Remedial Reading Assistants in an Inner-City School," *Reading Teacher,* 24 (March 1971), 506–512.

36. White, Jean, "The Programmed Tutor," *American Education,* 7 (December 1971), 18–21.

37. Williams, Mary Heard, "Does Grouping Affect Motivation?" *Elementary School Journal,* 73 (December 1973), 130–137.

38. Wright, Robert J., "The Affective and Cognitive Consequences of an Open Education Elementary School," *American Educational Research Journal,* 12 (Fall 1975), 449–468.

SUPPLEMENTARY READING

Abbott, Jerry L., *The Auxiliary Teacher Program: A Complete Manual and Guide.* West Nyack, N.Y.: Educators Book Club, 1974.

Blackie, John, *Inside the Primary School.* New York: Schocken Books, Inc., 1971.

Danish, Steven J., and Hauser, Allen L., *Helping Skills:* *A Basic Training Program.* New York: Behavioral Publications, 1973.

DeRosier, Cynthia, *You and Your Charge: A Brief Handbook for High School Tutors Working under the Waianae Model Cities Tutorial Plan.* ERIC/CRIER ED 056 011.

Featherstone, John, *An Introduction: Informal Schools in Britain Today*. New York: Citation Press, 1971.

Fry, Edward B., *The Emergency Reading Teacher's Manual*. Highland Park, N.J.: Drier Educational Systems, 1971.

Getz, Howard G., *Paraprofessionals in the English Department*. Urbana, Ill.: NCTE/ERIC, 1972.

Grolier Society, *First Steps in Reading*. New York: Grolier Society, 1962. A programmed primer for parents.

McClellan, Billie Frances, *Student Involvement in the Instructional Process Through Tutoring*. ERIC/CRIER ED 055 046.

McManama, John J., *An Effective Program for Teacher-Aide Training*. West Nyack, N.Y.: Educators Book Club.

Orlick, Gloria, *Reading Helpers*. Brooklyn, N.Y.: Book-Lab, Inc., 1969. Eight-book series for tutors and pupils.

Rauch, Sidney J., compiler, *Handbook for the Volunteer Tutor*. Newark, Del.: International Reading Association, 1969.

Schoeller, Arthur W., ed., *Problems, Pitfalls and Prescriptions for Organizing Volunteer Reading Tutoring Programs*. Milwaukee, Wis.: Reading Clinic, University of Wisconsin–Milwaukee, 1971.

Snow, Lawrence, *Using Teacher Aides*. Highland Park, N.J.: Drier Educational Systems, 1972.

Von Harrison, Grant, *Beginning Reading I: A Professional Guide for the Lay Tutor*. Provo, Utah: Brigham Young University Press, 1972.

Weinstein, Gerald, et al., *Youth Tutoring Youth. A Manual for Trainers. For the Tutor. Tutoring Tricks and Tips. You're the Tutor*. ERIC/CRIER ED 063 543. The first is a supervisor's manual; the second deals with materials; the last three are addressed to the tutor.

Index

Achievement, and economics, 20–22
Additions, reading errors, 347–348
Age, and reading readiness, 148–149
Aides, parents and paraprofessionals as, 471–473
Arithmetic, and reading, 301–303
Articulation:
  and decoding, 163
  and readiness, 219–220
Associational learning, reading as, 30–34
Attention, 249–250
Auditory comprehension, 218–219
  tests of, 177–178
Auditory discrimination:
  basic approaches, 34–35
  exercises, 215–216
  as readiness factor, 161–164
  tests, 176–177
  training in, 211–216
Average pupils, and combined primary program, 258–264

Basal readers:
  content of, 56–61
  criticism of, 52–53
  and grouping, 63–65
  improvement of, 68–70
  limitations of, 55–61
  methods, 46–52, 53–55, 61
  and oral reading, 66

  readiness program, 55–56
  and silent reading, 66, 252–254
  typical lesson, 49–51
  using manuals, 259
  vs. other approaches, 70–73
  vocabulary control, 43–46
  word attack skills, 67–68
  workbooks, 61
Behavior modification, 96–99
Bender Visual-Motor Gestalt Test, 154
Bilingual education, and reading progress, 265–269
Book-sharing activities, 324–325
British primary school, 470–471

Charts:
  experience, 230–234
  and graphs, reading of, 287
Checklists:
  oral reading, 347
  readiness for individualized reading, 347
  reading readiness, 168
Classroom management. *See* Grouping
Cloze procedure, 340, 404, 406
Clymer–Barrett Prereading Battery, 173
Cognitive growth, strategies for, 452–459
Comprehension:
  auditory, 177–178, 218–219
  as decoding process, 440–441

(Comprehension, cont.)
    as defined by tests, 443–446
    development of, 451–452
    factors influencing:
        material read, 447–448
        reader, 448–450
        reading process, 450–451
    models of, 441–444
    as skill development, 440
    as thinking process, 441–443
    training in, 452–459
Computer-assisted instruction, 93–99
Concepts, children's, of reading, 230
Conferences, individual:
    follow-up, 324–325
    and individualized reading, 88–89
    initiating, 319–324
    record keeping, 328–332
    scheduling, 327–328
    taking inventory in, 337–340
    use for diagnosis, 340–350
Content reading:
    basic skills for, 278–307
    in literature, 303–307
    in mathematics, 301–303
    plan for unit, 295–297
    in science, 298–301
    in social science, 298–301
Contextual analysis, 402–406
Critical reading:
    definition, 446–447
    training in, 452–459
Cultural background, and reading, 19–24

Decoding. *See* Phonics
Delacato training program, 191–193
Development:
    physical, and readiness, 150
    skill, reading, 4–7
Dialect:
    and oral reading, 212–213, 350
    and reading progress, 18–19
Dictionary:
    skills, 426–428
    use of, 425–428
Differences, individual, and sight vocabulary, 419–422
Directionality, 194–198

Disadvantaged pupils:
    characteristics of, 21
    and language experience, 132–133
    and primary program, 265–269

Economically disadvantaged:
    characteristics of, 21
    and language experience, 132–133
    and primary program, 265–269
Emotional adjustment, and reading readiness, 105–166
Errors, oral reading, 342–350
Exercises:
    auditory discrimination, 215–216
    directionality, 194–198
    form perception, 201–205
    ocular motility, 198–201
Experience charts and stories, 230–235, 239–242

First-Grade Reading Studies, 71–73, 90–92, 115–116, 135–138, 364
Follow-up activities in individualized reading, 324–325
Form perception, 201–205
Frostig Test of Developmental Perception, 153–155
Frostig training program, 154–155

Gates–Macginitie Readiness Skills Test, 174–175
Gesell Institute Readiness Tests, 173
Gifted pupils, and primary program, 256–258
Globe and map skills, 282–286
Graphic cues in reading, 349
Graphic materials, reading of, 282–287
Graphs, reading of, 287
Group dynamics vs. current practices, 466–467
Grouping:
    and basal readers, 63–65, 262–263
    cluster, 470–471
    homogeneous vs. heterogeneous, 465–466
    interclass, 467–468
    interest, 467

intraclass, 466–467
nongraded, 468–469
pupil teams, 469–470
pupil tutors, 469–470
team teaching, 470–471
ungraded primary, 468–469

Harrison–Stroud Reading Readiness
    Test, 171, 173–174
Head Start program, limitations of,
    147–148

Individual differences, and sight vocabu-
    lary, 419–420
Individualized approach to reading:
    and conferences, 88–89, 332–350
    follow-up activities, 324–325
    method, 79–84
    objectives and assumptions, 78–79
    organizational problems, 86–88,
        316–319
    principles of, 85
    record keeping, 328–332
    research, 90–92
    scheduling, 327–328
    skills practice, 88–90
Information processing, reading as,
    27–30
Intelligence, and readiness, 156–158
Intermediate grades, reading program
    for, 275–312

Kindergarten, and readiness, 147–148

Language development, and reading,
    18–19
Language experience approach:
    current applications of, 131–133,
        231–244
    limitations, 133–135, 243–244
    and manuscript writing, 239
    method and materials, 230–244
    objectives, 125–126
    other concepts of, 129–131, 242–243
    research, 135–138
Language facility, and readiness, 158–
    161

Language training:
    in articulation, 219–220
    in auditory comprehension, 218–219
    in fluency, 216–217
    in sentence structure, 217–218
Learning:
    preschool, and readiness, 144–147
    programmed, and vocabulary, 410
Learning stations, 320–321, 467
Lee–Clark Reading Readiness Test, 174
Letter-naming systems, 363
Letter sounds, and word recognition,
    421–422
Library:
    relations with, 290–291
    skills, 289–290
Linguistic approach to reading:
    limitations, 108–115
    materials, 106–108
    research, 115–116
Literature:
    reading and, 303–307
    what does, does not work, 305–307

Map and globe skills, 282–286
Management systems, 93–99
Manuscript writing, and reading progress,
    239
Mathematics, and reading, 301–303
Meaning vocabulary, 422–426
Memory, visual and auditory, 32–33
Metropolitan Readiness Test, 174
Mills Learning Methods Test, 326, 391,
    419–420
Modality teaching, 326, 419–420
Monroe Reading Aptitude Test, 171, 174
Murphy–Durrell Diagnostic Reading
    Readiness Test, 171, 174

Newspapers, use of, 325–326
Notetaking skills, 291–294

Ocular motility, 198–201
Omissions, definition, 348
Open classroom, 470–471
Operant conditioning:
    advantages of, 96

(Operant conditioning, cont.)
   limitations of, 97–99
   materials and methods, 93–96
Oral reading:
   and basal readers, 66
   behaviors, recording, 346
   checklist, 347
   and dialect, 212–213
   errors, 342
   and primary program, 244–256
   pros and cons, 245–254
   recording, 346–350
   substitutes for the circle, 254–255
Organizing skills, 291–294
Outlining skills, 294–295

Paraprofessionals, as aides, 471–473
Parents, as aides, 471–473
Perception:
   in infancy, 12
   in reading, 12
   visual:
      and readiness, 187–194
      training in, 152–156
      training materials, 189–204, 205–209
Phonics:
   alternatives to, 387–391
   current practices, 366–380
   suggested practices, 380–387
Phonologists' definition of reading, 104–105
Physical development, and readiness, 150
Poetry, teaching of, 303–305
Predictive Index Tests, 155
Preschool learning, and readiness, 144–147
Previewing, 278–280
Primary grades:
   and grouping, 262–263, 323–324
   and oral reading, 244–256
   program for:
      average pupils, 258–264
      disadvantaged pupils, 265–269
      gifted pupils, 256–258
      slow learners, 264–265
   use of basal in, 46–55

Program:
   content reading, 275–312
   for intermediate grades, 275–312
   for primary grades, 227–269
   readiness training, 187–222
Programmed learning, 96
Programmed materials, word recognition, 410
Psycholinguists' definition of reading, 106

Question strategies, examples of, 452–459

Readers, basal. *See* Basal readers
Readiness. *See* Reading readiness
Reading:
   as associational learning, 30–34
   basal reader approach, 46–73
   and behavior modification, 93–99
   computer-assisted approach, 96–98
   concepts of, children's, 230
   content, skills for, 278–307
   critical, 446–459
   and cultural background, 19–24
   defining, 35–36
   definitions of:
      phonologists', 104–105
      psycholinguists', 106
      structuralists', 105–106
   in graphic materials, 287–288
   individualized approach, 85–92
   as information processing, 27–30
   in kindergarten, 147–148
   and language development, 18–19
   language experience approach, 125–138
   letter-naming systems, 363
   linguistic approach, 106–116
   and literature, 303–307
   and mathematics, 301–303
   multimedia approach, 353
   and operant conditioning, 93–99
   oral. *See* Oral reading
   as a perceptual act, 11–18
   in preschool, 144–147
   process, defined, 35–36

as psycholinguistic process, 24–27
as reflection of cultural background, 19–24
research, systems approaches, 93–99
and science, 298–301
silent. *See* Silent reading
as skill development, 4–7
and social science, 298–301
as a visual act, 7–11
Reading readiness:
  basal reader program in, 55–56
  checklist, 168
  current practices, 184–187
  defined, 166
  factors influencing:
    age, school entrance, 148–149
    auditory discrimination, 161–164
    emotional adjustment, 165–166
    intelligence, 156–158
    kindergarten, 147–148, 169
    language facility, 158–161
    physical development, 150
    preschool learning, 164–165
    sex, 149–150
    vision, 150–152
    visual perception, 152–156
  future practices, 228–229
  language training, 216–218
  reading concepts, 220–221
  tests, 171–174
  training, 172–175
    auditory discrimination, 211–216
    visual perception:
      basic approaches, 187–194
      directionality, 194–198
      form perception, 201–205
      materials for, 189–204, 205–209
      ocular motility, 198–201
  values of, 187–188
Record keeping, and individual conferences, 328–332
Repetitions, reading errors, 348
Reporting skills, 291–294
Research:
  grouping, 465–466
  individualized reading, 90–92
  language experience approach, 135–138
  linguistics approach, 115–116

Resources for the teacher:
  content field reading, 309–312
  disadvantaged pupil, 270–271, 273, 311–312
  graphic materials, 310
  individualized reading, 356–358
  language experience approach, 272
  library skills, 310–311
  organizing and reporting skills, 311
  programmed materials, 410
  readiness, 205–209
  vocabulary, 434–436
  word recognition skills, 409–411
Reversals, reading errors, 349

Scanning, 280–282
Scheduling individual conferences, 327–328
Science, reading in, 298–301
Self-concept, 267–269
Sex:
  and reading progress, 263–264
  and reading readiness, 149–150
Sight vocabulary:
  and experience stories, 243–244, 419–420
  and letter sounds, 421–422
  and word form, 422–423
Silent reading, 11, 252–254, 256
Skill development, reading as, 4–7
Skills:
  basic, for content reading, 278–307
  chart and graph, 287
  development, 4–7
  dictionary, 425–428
  in individualized reading, 88–90
  library, 289–290
  map and globe, 282–286
  note taking, 291–294
  organizing, 291–294
  outlining, 294–295
  previewing, 278–280
  reporting, 291–294
  skimming, 280–282
  tables and diagrams, 287
  word recognition, 362–432
Skimming, 280–282

Slow pupils and reading program, 264–265
Snellen Test, 170–171
Social background, and reading, 19–24
Social science, reading in, 298–301
Structural analysis:
   in basal program, 392–396
   meaningful units, 397
   rules for, 392
   visual units, 397
Structuralists' definition of reading, 105–106
Substitutions, reading errors, 348–349
Syllabication:
   criticisms of, 398–401
   rules for, 398–399, 401
Systems approach, 93–99, 352–353

Tables and diagrams, skills, 287
Tests:
   auditory comprehension, 177–178
   auditory discrimination, 176–177
   informal, 340–342, 351–352
   the I.R.I., limitations of, 338–339
   intelligence, 156–158
   reading readiness, 172–175

vision, 170–171
visual perception, 152–156
Training:
   auditory discrimination, 213–216
   language, 216–220
   visual perception, 187–194

Vision, testing, 170–171
Visual act, reading as, 7–11
Visual discrimination, 31–32
   tests of, 171
Visual perception:
   in infancy, 12
   in reading, 11–18
   and readiness, 152–156
   tests, 152–156
   training in, 187–194
   training materials, 189–194, 205–209
Vocabulary:
   and basal readers, 43–46
   building:
      use of context, 428–429
      use of dictionary, 425–428
   growth, influences upon, 415–418
   meaning, 422–426